Regional Development
in
Britain

Regional Development in Britain

Second Edition

GERALD MANNERS

Reader in Geography, University College London

DAVID KEEBLE

Lecturer in Geography, University of Cambridge

BRIAN RODGERS

Professor of Geography, University of Manchester

KENNETH WARREN

Lecturer in Geography, University of Oxford

JOHN WILEY & SONS

Chichester · New York · Brisbane · Toronto

British Library Cataloguing in Publication Data:

Regional development in Britain — 2nd ed.
  1. Regional planning — Great Britain
  2. Great Britain — Economic policy — 1945-
  I. Manners, Gerald
  330.9'41'0857   HT395.G7   79-42901

  ISBN 0 471 27636 7 (cloth)
  ISBN 0 471 27635 9 (paper)

Typesetting by Photo-Graphics, Stockland, Honiton, Devon and printed at the Pitman Press, Bath.

Contents

Preface

Geographical contrasts in the nature and the pace of economic development have captured the public imagination in recent years. At one level, the creation of the regional economic planning councils in the 1960s, the subsequent burst of official surveys, studies and strategies, and then the more recent debate about Scottish and Welsh devolution, have all been of importance in this development. But above all it has been the obstinate persistence of a set of economic and social problems which have a regional rather than a national expression—the unemployment level on Merseyside, migration from North East England, and the weak industrial base of Strathclyde, for example—that have retained the attention of public and political interest. At the same time, but on another scale, there has evolved of late a heightened concern about the physical deterioration, the lack of local employment, and the concentration of acute social problems in the inner areas of the country's largest urban centres. Not only has this concern stimulated a vigorous debate and a political response in its own right, but it has challenged in some measure the traditional priorities of public policies towards the amelioration of geographical variations in economic and social opportunity. This book does not attempt to specify a solution to this and other spatial planning dilemmas. Rather, it seeks to improve and widen an understanding of them. It describes and interprets the trends, the problems and the uncertainties that are associated with the evolving pattern of spatial economic change; it evaluates the political responses to them; and it provides a bench-mark for considering something of the prospective geography of Britain in the 1980s.

The first three chapters offer a necessary international and national perspective on these matters without which the subsequent regional chapters, making up the greater part of the book, would be much less intelligible. The regional division that has been adopted substantially follows the lead set by the government in its delimitation of 'standard economic regions', a map of which appears on the back end-paper. These are regions which have received much official study and interpretation in recent years, and for which a widening range of socio-economic statistics is readily available (especially in the annual *Abstract of Regional Statistics* prepared by the Central Statistical Office). It is judged, however, that many of the problems associated with spatial development can be better understood through a slightly modified regionalization. For example, without denying the historical identity and the political integrity of the Principality of Wales, it is widely accepted that many of the development problems—and certainly the prospective economic opportunities—of the southern industrial counties can best be understood either in their own right or in relationship to Severnside and southern England, rather than in association with the rural counties to the north; moreover, the growing recreational and overspill links between Central Wales and the West Midlands, and the close economic and social associations between the counties of North Wales and the Merseyside conurbation, suggest the advantage of considering these other parts of Wales alongside their neighbouring English regions rather than with each other, at least for the purposes of this book. Likewise, it is evident that the future development of Cumbria is more likely to lie in a strengthening of its socio-economic relationships with Lancashire than with North East England, a region with which it has been officially associated through the former Northern Economic Planning Council and the Regional Planning Board since 1965.

The geographical balance of the book, and especially the heavy emphasis placed upon South East England, demands a word of explanation. In the broad allocation of space to the discussion of different parts of the country, it was decided that population and economic importance rather than area should provide an initial yardstick, and that the complexity of spatial problems would afford a secondary criterion. On this basis, the 17 million people living in the South East more than justify the three chapters devoted to their geography and problems; on these criteria, also, the difficulties facing the sparsely populated Highlands and Islands of Scotland could also be given appropriate examination. The decision to omit Northern Ireland from the book was taken with some regret; however, it was judged that the distinctive economic and political characteristics of the Province demand its exclusion from many generalizations appropriate to the rest of the United Kingdom, and that its development problems justify rather more sensitive and extended treatment than would have been possible in this volume.

Although I have acted as general editor of this volume, *Regional Development in Britain* is the product of four authors, each of whom naturally prefers the maximum freedom from editorial constraints. In consequence, no stamp of uniformity has been imposed upon the regional chapters, and the interpretation of development characteristics and problems in different parts of the country has been approached from a variety of personal standpoints. Such contrasts as may be found in the focus and accent of those chapters reflect their author's intellectual stance as well as the distinctiveness of the regions themselves. Nevertheless, the reader will find that in all cases the emphasis is upon the problems of industrial and urban development, to the relative neglect of rural and agricultural affairs. This is a bias that springs logically from the first of the two yardsticks noted earlier. The reader might also find the book at times unfairly sceptical towards the objectives and achievements of regional planning in Britain. In no way is this meant to understate the considerable successes which might reasonably be claimed or to overlook the admiration for some British policies that is to be found overseas. Rather it stems from a belief that only by approaching the record and problems of regional development and planning in a critical frame of mind can the student—and this book is primarily intended for those in the early stages of higher education—come to a fuller understanding of the issues involved and perhaps in time make some contribution to their solution.

University College London

GERALD MANNERS

List of tables

List of figures

All the figures were drawn by Ken Wass and Christine Hill in the Cartographic Unit of the Department of Geography, University College London.

CHAPTER 1

National and International Perspectives

GERALD MANNERS

1.1 Introduction

At the root of changes in the economic geography of an advanced industrial society lies the evolution of its consumer demands. Motor cars and washing machines, carpets and television sets, lawn mowers and refrigerators have all been purchased in ever-increasing quantities as the people of Britain have increased and redistributed their wealth over the past thirty years. Simultaneously, either directly or through government, families have come to spend an increasing proportion of their income on education and health, travel and entertainment, sport and recreation and a widening range of personal services. As a consequence, the number of jobs available in these growing manufacturing and service activities has steadily increased, and the firms or organizations engaged therein have occasionally been faced with embarrassing shortages of labour. In other sections of the economy, however, the story has been quite different—for the growth of national affluence has by no means affected all industries in the same way. The demand for some manufactures and services is relatively inelastic; thus, a decreasing proportion of the nation's income has been spent on clothing and household goods, on food and tobacco, and upon such services as public transport and cinemas. The market for others—for example, men's hats, steam locomotives, slate tiles and domestic servants—has contracted severely, and as a result jobs in these industries have shrunk both relatively and absolutely.

The changing structure of employment opportunities in an advanced and 'open' economy is influenced, of course, by other factors as well—especially by the shifting nature of the world political economy, by developments in international markets and the domestic entrepreneurial response to them, and by those technological developments which influence the extent to which capital is substituted for labour. Whilst trade between Britain and the rest of Western Europe has increased in both relative and absolute importance over the last quarter-century, transactions between Britain and the countries of the Commonwealth have become relatively less significant. In parallel, overseas sales of cars and lorries, of motor components and aircraft engines, of chemicals and electronic equipment, and of a variety of professional and scientific services have increased persistently and profitably. At the same time many of the more 'traditional' exporting activities of the country, such as cotton textile manufacture, coal mining, shipbuilding and much entrepôt trade, progressively have come to be less profitable and now play a much smaller role in Britain's international trade. Jobs in all these industries as a

1

Table 1.1 Britain: the changing structure of employment by industry, 1961, 1966, 1971 and 1976 ('000s)

	1961	1966	1971	1976
Primary sector	1,547	1,340	1,036	728
Agriculture, forestry, fishing	827	772	643	382
Mining & quarrying	720	568	393	346
Secondary sector	10,306	10,855	10,250	8,710
Food, drink and tobacco	744	790	739	691
Coal & petroleum products	58	52	62	37
Chemicals & allied industries	394	411	469	421
Metal manufacture	624	596	541	469
Engineering	1,967	2,148	2,134	1,796
Shipbuilding & marine engineering	236	181	170	175
Vehicles	827	813	800	733
Metal goods	580	640	599	519
Textiles	789	731	588	480
Leather, leather goods and fur }	605	581	517	403
Clothing and footwear				
Bricks, pottery, glass, cement, etc.	320	333	309	258
Timber and furniture	302	303	303	259
Paper, printing and publishing	601	625	623	536
Other manufacturing	249	333	323	321
Construction	1,592	1,904	1,707	1,269
Gas, electricity and water	374	416	364	343
Tertiary sector	11,318	12,340	12,626	12,601
Transport and communication	1,662	1,629	1,583	1,453
Distributive trades	3,159	3,287	3,080	2,669
Insurance, banking, finance & business				
services	719	851	960	1,087
Private services	2,666	3,078	2,930	2,727
Public services	3,185	3,562	4,073	4,665
Total in employment	23,245	24,651	23,912	22,048
Unemployment rate %	1.4	1.4	3.4	5.5

Source: Department of Employment.

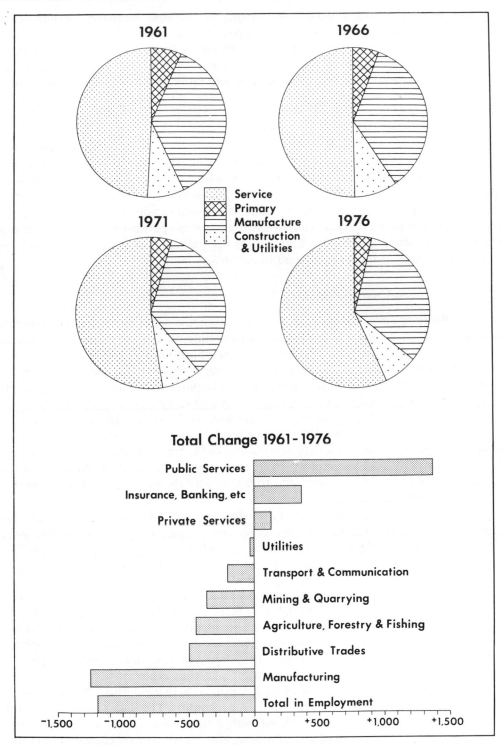

Figure 1.1 Britain: the changing structure of employment by industry,
1961-1976
Source: Department of Employment data ('000s)

consequence have shown a persistent tendency to decline. Moreover, technological developments in which capital has been progressively substituted for labour have simultaneously accelerated the reduction of employment opportunities not only in many of these contracting export-oriented activities, but also in other trades such as metal manufacture and engineering that have experienced a more sustained demand, plus a third group of industries including the railways that serve an essentially domestic market. Without such a contraction, however, it is difficult to see how the growth industries could in fact have been manned in the 1950s and 1960s.

The shifting structure of employment in Britain between 1961 and 1976 is recorded in Table 1.1 and illustrated in Figure 1.1. Most noteworthy amongst the many changes have been the persistent decline of employment in primary production (agriculture, forestry, fishing and mining), the more recent decline in total manufacturing jobs, the growth of employment in private services, and the quite substantial expansion of the public sector services. Whether or not these are entirely desirable trends—particularly the recent growth of public sector services—need be of no concern here, although some commentators have been highly critical of them (Bacon and Eltis, 1976).

1.2 Changing Locational Preferences

Each industry or activity in an economy has a distinctive set of locational requirements and characteristics. Changes in the structure of an economy, therefore, inevitably express themselves in a new geography of employment opportunities. Moreover, industries frequently alter their locational preferences through time, as advancing technology, changing labour requirements or shifting market opportunities alter the economics of enterprise in different places. Sometimes the decline of one industry in a particular town or region is quickly and spontaneously counterbalanced by the expansion of another. It has been a characteristic of British economic growth, however, that most of the newer industries that have expanded particularly vigorously in recent decades—and indeed, ever since the turn of the present century—have instinctively expressed different locational preferences from many of the older industries that were the foundation of the country's economy in the late nineteenth century.

During the late Victorian and Edwardian period of rapid and precocious industrialization, one of the most important influences upon the geography of enterprise and employment was the ready availability of coal, and its particular attraction for manufacturing firms when it was found in association with other industrial raw materials. As a consequence, major manufacturing and urban concentrations emerged in Central Scotland, South Wales, East Lancashire, the East and West Midlands, West Yorkshire and North East England. Their specialisms, besides coal mining, were iron and steel production, shipbuilding, cotton and wool textile manufacture, and heavy engineering. The development of these coal-based regional economies afforded a geographical counterbalance to London, which was not only the traditional seat of Imperial Government and the Court but also a major industrial centre in its own right, the country's largest port and the focus of its commercial activities. They also generated a major redistribution of population within the country. The late-nineteenth-century pattern of urban settlement was filled out with a traditional scatter of market towns related principally to the agricultural economy, and a rash of new coastal resorts that stretched from Brighton to the Clyde coast, and from Skegness to the Isle of Man, and that satisfied the growing holiday demands of the burgeoning industrial population.

Since Edwardian times, the attractions of the coalfields for the establishment and expansion of industrial enterprise have steadily weakened, and other factors have become progressively more important in the location of economic activity. Proximity to large or specialized consumer markets, or to the suppliers of component parts or sub-assemblies, has emerged as one of the most decisive factors for manufacturing industry. That proximity is strongly conditioned by the geography of the country's most modern transport facilities—the major roads, railways and ports. After 1918, these facilities were to be found most readily in southern England generally, and especially in Greater London and the West Midlands. As a consequence it was there that the new industries making vacuum cleaners and electric heaters, cookers and refrigerators, radios and television sets, typewriters and adding machines, cosmetics and pharmaceuticals, computers and data-processing equipment, motor cycles and motor cars, and all the paraphernalia of modern life first came to be located. And it was there too that for several decades they preferred to expand.

This is not to deny the importance of a variety of other influences playing upon the location of twentieth-century industrial enterprise. The availability of appropriately skilled labour, the importance of a variety of natural endowments and the role of innovation and enterprise, for example, are not to be discounted. Nor is it to overlook the importance of changes in transport technology, and the persistent reduction in the real costs of movement: these have eroded the importance of distance, and have simultaneously permitted the utilization of a new and wider range of sites for economic development in the present century. Nevertheless, whereas at one time it was the railway that attracted to its vicinity the greater part of manufacturing and even office activities, in recent years it has been the new arterial road and motorway system, together with the country's major international airports, that have progressively assumed a paramount importance in these matters (Figure 1.2). The geography of these new transport facilities is crucial. In common with the initial phase of liner train developments by British Rail, with the 400 kV grid of the Central Electricity Generating Board, with the first bulk transmission pipelines of both the Gas Council and the petroleum industry, and with the country's major deep-sea container facilities, their concentration within southern England is outstanding. As a result, that nodality and the relative attractiveness of the London-Midlands zone for economic activity has been steadily increased.

The distribution of population within Britain is closely linked to the broad geography of economic opportunity and employment. Apart from minor differences in local demographic characteristics and activity rates, therefore, *inter*-regional shifts in the two have been virtually identical. *Intra*-regional changes in the distribution of population and employment, on the other hand, have begun to exhibit important contrasts—even though they have been moulded by forces for change similar to those at the inter-regional scale. Especially since 1950, the rising level of national wealth has in part been invested in improved housing at lower residential densities. Such an investment could only be made following the simultaneous acceptance of the necessity for and the costs of constructing homes further away from centres of employment, and a lengthening of the daily journey to work. Rising levels of personal wealth have also created demands for a widening range of facilities and services, the more specialized of which can only be provided economically in larger urban centres. Combined, therefore, these changes have led to a growing concentration of people in a handful of larger and ever more sprawling conurbations and city-regions, the evolution of which has rested heavily upon innovations in and the improvement of both public and private transport. The tram and the bus, the tube and the trolley-bus, the electric railway and the urban motorway have each in their time and distinctive fashion permitted a growing separation of work and home, and have powerfully moulded the urban geography of twentieth-century Britain at the intra-regional scale.

1.3 Some Resultant Problems

These spatial tendencies—for both employment opportunities and people to move away from the coalfield industrial areas towards the centre of national economic gravity in southern England, and for urban and suburban development to proceed at relatively low densities (by historical standards), with a lengthening journey to work—represent the two principal features of the changing economic geography of Britain since World War I. They reflect both the individual and the collective decisions of many people concerning the best locations for their business, their work and their homes. However, these decisions, taken in the perceived self-interest of individuals or groups of individuals, have presented the community as a whole with a number of major problems. Four of these stand out above the rest, and are closely inter-related.

First, by creating some regions with relatively rapid and often highly localized economic development, the new inter-regional locational preferences presented some parts of the country with a complex set of 'urban' difficulties, that stemmed from the progressive geographical concentration of both people and traffic, from an intense and increasing competition for the use of land there, and from the necessity for public bodies to resolve the most appropriate size, location and timing of new and frequently very costly intra-structural investments. Whilst these problems had to be faced in many parts of the country, in one way or another, they were posed in their most challenging and urgent form in South East England and the West Midlands. Second, the same inter-regional forces and tendencies simultaneously left certain localities and even larger areas of the country with a generally slow rate of economic growth, with associated and often substantial social problems, and occasionally with the characteristics of stagnation and decay. These less prosperous regions persistently experienced higher than average rates of unemployment, low activity rates and a steady net loss of population through migration; they were left with a considerable proportion of the country's older urban infra-structure, a substantial share of its poorer housing stock and extensive areas of derelict mining and industrial land; and they were located particularly in the north and the west of the country (Table 1.2; Figure 1.3).

Third, at the intra-regional scale, the new locational preferences threatened and occasioned the extensive loss of agricultural and amenity land on the fringe of the country's urban areas. Unrestrained, they could have created a formless sprawl of suburban housing and land uses that would have defied the provision of infrastructure and many public services at a reasonable cost. Certainly during the 1930s it was seen on the periphery of Greater London in particular how an unchecked process of urban sprawl could cause considerable and permanent environmental damage. Fourth, and last, the spatial dynamics of the modern city-region left some localities in the inner areas of the conurbations and larger cities with an apparent inability to adjust adequately their land uses and human activities towards a suitable contemporary role. This final problem was

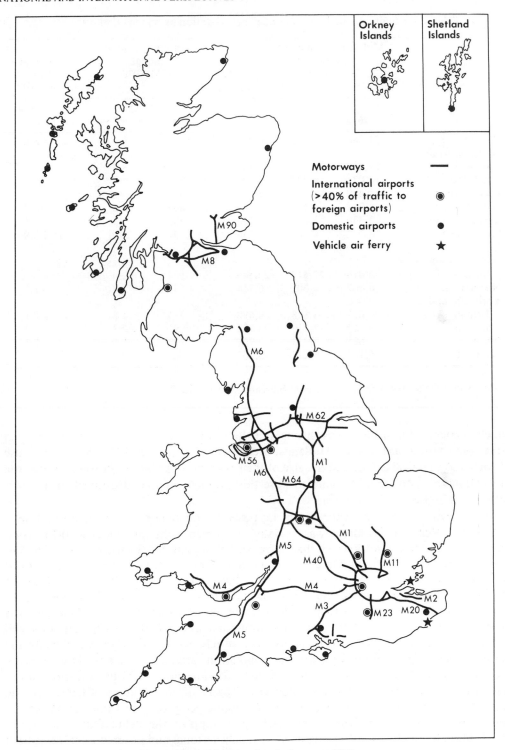

Figure 1.2 Britain: major roads and international airports, 1979

Table 1.2 Britain: population change and net migration by region, 1961-1976

	Mid-year estimated home population '000s			Total population change 1961-1976		Average net annual migration 1961-1971
	1961	1971	1976	'000s	%	Per '000 in 1971
BRITAIN	51,380	54,071	54,389	3,009	5.9	− 0.6
More prosperous regions	29,364	31,524	31,849	2,485	8.5	..
South East	16,071	16,994	16,894	823	5.1	− 0.2
East Anglia	1,489	1,686	1,803	314	21.1	+ 7.2
West Midlands	4,762	5,121	5,165	403	8.5	− 0.3
East Midlands	3,330	3,635	3,733	403	12.1	+ 2.1
South West	3,712	4,088	4,254	542	14.6	+ 5.9
Less prosperous regions	22,016	22,547	22,540	524	2.4	..
North West	6,407	6,602	6,554	147	2.3	− 1.7
Yorkshire and Humberside	4,677	4,868	4,892	215	4.6	− 1.5
Northern	3,113	3,137	3,122	9	0.3	− 3.3
Wales	2,635	2,723	2,767	132	5.0	− 0.1
Scotland	5,184	5,217	5,205	21	0.4	− 6.2

Source: Central Statistical Office, Regional Statistics, No.13, 1977.

widely recognized in urban areas throughout the whole of the country, not least in such large conurbations as the West Midlands, Merseyside, Glasgow and Manchester; because of their geographical extent and the size of their resident population, however, it was the inner areas of London that came to pose this problem of maladjustment in its most substantial and challenging form.

These, then, are the four central problems posed by the dynamics of Britain's economic geography. Regional planning was initially concerned with ameliorating their worst effects. In addition, however, it has increasingly sought to recognize, interpret and selectively use the underlying forces for change in order to create a better economic, social and physical environment. In the process it has tried to reconcile a wide range of frequently conflicting forces relating to the growth of population, the propensity to migrate, industrial and commercial efficiency, alternative urban and sub-regional patterns of settlement, investment in transport and communications, and many matters of social welfare. For example, regional planners have sought to influence inter-regionally the national distribution of employment and population, attempting selectively to increase the rate of growth, to lower the unemployment rates, to check the out-migration and to raise the activity rates of the less prosperous parts of the country. Changes in the functions, the relative importance and the economic geography of these regions are of course inevitable; but evidence is not lacking to support the belief that some public intervention to accelerate their adjustment to a new national and international role is both possible and, moreover, economically and socially advantageous for the country as a

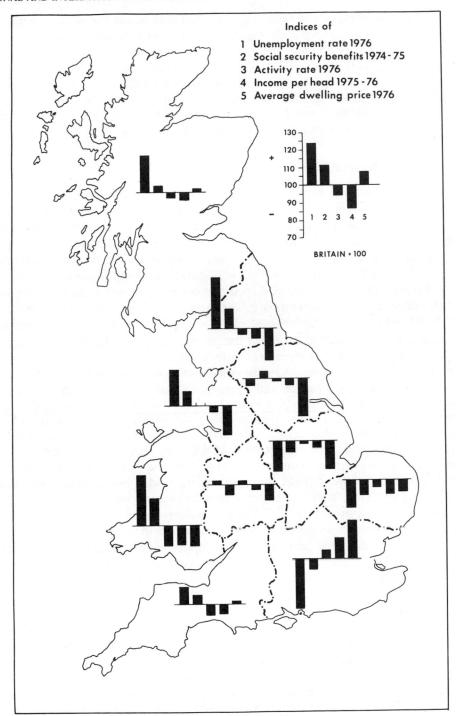

Figure 1.3 Britain: economic and social indicators, by region, mid-1970s

Source: *Abstract of Regional Statistics,* H.M.S.O.

whole in the longer term. At the same time, regional planners at the intra-regional scale have been persistently concerned with shaping and at times containing the spread of urban development, seeking to balance considerations of transport efficiency with criteria reflecting environmental values, weighing the industrial and commercial needs for space against the land requirements of agriculture and recreation, and evaluating the lower costs of greenfield developments against the higher costs and urgency of urban renewal. The intervention of the planners has had its successes—and its failures. It is transparent, however, these matters cannot be left solely to the workings of the market.

1.4 The Case for Regional Planning

The case for regional planning rests partly upon the more general case for government intervention in the workings of the market economy. Even the most extreme defenders of private enterprise accept than an efficient and just allocation of resources and incomes demands a minimum level of public supervision over, and participation in, economic decision making. Consumer sovereignty in itself cannot be relied upon to reflect a society's needs according to its values. People frequently demand goods and services to a degree that is harmful to themselves and society at large (for example, the excessive use of private cars in congested urban centres); by the same token they often underbid for things that are beneficial to them in the longer term (for example, the reservation of public open space for recreation, or the creation and preservation of a good physical environment). In consequence, some degree of government paternalism is necessary. Moreover, whereas 'perfect competition' might optimize the allocation and distribution of resources in theory, it rarely exists in practice and everywhere market imperfections abound. A notable market failure, for example, was the tendency for office activities in Britain to concentrate excessively in central London until the middle of the 1960s (p.76ff.). Imperfections particularly characterize the market for land. Signals of its real worth are often poor as a consequence of the institutional and emotional influences that bear upon its owners; and the problem of monopoly takes on a special meaning with land since it is frequently the case that one piece or tract of it cannot readily be substituted for another (particularly at the urban scale, as in comprehensive redevelopment schemes).

The market mechanism further suffers in spatial development matters from its failure to give sufficient weight to longer-term considerations and to what are known as external costs and benefits. The initial economic and social decline of a locality or a sub-region might be only slightly reflected in the market prices for land, buildings and labour; but it could presage an avoidable disintigration of a community with the loss or gross under-utilization of its valuable social capital. And to the extent that private decisions can impose substantial costs upon the community as a whole, in the form of noise nuisance or air pollution, or through the need for substantial additional investments in infrastructure and social service provision, a case exists for at least some public influence over the spatial aspects of the economic development process.

In any case, the market does not produce particularly efficiently a large number of goods and services that are fundamental to economic development. Road, railways, ports, water supplies and sewerage facilities, for example, often fall into this category, and normally they have to be provided by the state or under close public supervision. Since their location, and the timing of their provision, leave a crucial impress upon the development process, regional planners must seek to ensure that such investments are made in accordance with the broad objectives of spatial policy, to the extent that it can be specified.

The case for regional planning is further strengthened by the fact that, whether or not the workings of the market produce a 'rational' distribution of resources and income, they certainly generate abundant inequalities, both social and spatial. Many governments believe these to be unjust and to require some measure of compensating public intervention. With the exploitation of all natural resources, and particularly in the case of land use change, increases in value arise that cannot be readily related to either the effort of the owner or the real worth of ownership. Public investments in infrastructure, for example, or simply the growth of population plus the development process, often lead to new and higher demands upon particular pieces of land, and thereby create an 'unearned increment' in its value. Rightly or wrongly, land use planning has often been seen as an instrument through which the associated inequities might be redressed.

The case for public intervention in the spatial development process at a variety of scales is therefore clear. It does not follow, however, that intervention is invariably wise or successful, or that particular types of intervention are necessarily correct. Whereas planning might in all logic be able to improve upon the consequences of unrestrained market forces, it is often a matter for debate whether its results in fact are better than those that would have occurred from the operation of (imperfect) market forces alone. Any evaluation of specific instances must rest upon the motives and the objectives of intervention. It is to their variety that attention is now turned.

1.5 The Political Response

For some time there has been a significant political element in the forces moulding the economic geography of Britain. The Royal Commission on the Distribution of Industrial Population (1940) rightly condemned the high levels of long-term unemployment in northern England, Wales and Scotland during the inter-war years, and in its famous report pointed to what were seen as the social, economic and strategic disadvantages of the further growth of the London city region. It therefore endorsed the objectives of the earlier 1934 Special Areas legislation (McCrone, 1969, pp.91 ff.), and accelerated the creation of a Ministry of Town and Country Planning in 1943 which was charged with 'securing consistency and continuity in the framing and the execution of a national policy with respect to the use and development of land'. A few years later in the spate of legislation that followed World War II—in particular, the Distribution of Industry Acts of 1945 and 1949, the New Towns Act of 1946, and the Town and Country Planning Act of 1947 (Self, 1957)—there was secured for Britain one of the most comprehensive bodies of regional and environmental planning legislation in the whole world. Although the Barlow Commission rightly emphasized the many interrelationships that exist between the different scales of spatial planning, the basic notions behind this and subsequent legislation can best be interpreted through an examination of the inter-regional and intra-regional components.

1.5.1 Inter-regional Planning

Government action to secure a better inter-regional distribution of economic activity was inspired initially by the simple humanitarian desire to provide all members of the community with a reasonably equal opportunity to earn a living, and to lessen the hardship, the frustrations and the misery that were particularly prevalent in those parts of Britain suffering from high levels of unemployment. Straightforward programmes of job-creation in those parts of the country experiencing economic decline and an endemic problem of surplus labour, therefore, have been a feature of British inter-regional planning since the middle of the 1930s. Indeed, apart from the strategic arguments of the Barlow Commission, which saw a dispersed pattern of industry advantageous in the context of the military technology of the 1930s, social considerations were the principal motive behind government involvement in regional development until the 1960s. Since then, however, a variety of economic and more overtly political motives have also inspired government policies in this sphere.

Attempts to accelerate economic growth during the early 1960s reasoned that regional policies could help to make fuller use of the country's productive resources. The National Economic Development Council (1963) argued that regional planning—by lowering the rates of localized unemployment, by raising the characteristically low female activity rates, and by helping to shift labour out of less productive and into more productive work in the less prosperous regions—could both increase the quantity and improve the quality of the labour inputs into the national economy. Cameron (1974) subsequently estimated that a reduction of the unemployment rates of the so-called Assisted Areas (see p.37ff.) to the national level, and a 50 per cent reduction in the difference between their activity rates and the national average, could add 1.7 per cent to the national labour force. To make use of this reserve of labour would, of course, cost money. But other observers have sought to demonstrate how government expenditure on such policies can generate a justifiable economic return (Moore and Rhodes, 1973). It has also been argued that the less prosperous parts of the country, in addition to their underutilized manpower, contain considerable resources of social capital in the form of houses, roads, schools, churches, and the like, resources which could be more fully utilized through regional policies. Such arguments demand qualification with the recognition that the built environment of the coalfield industrial areas by the 1960s urgently needed a major overhaul, and that despite their persistent net out-migration the population living there was nevertheless continuing to increase. Moreover, theoretically attractive though the labour reserve argument remained, remedial policies for the less prosperous regions failed to bring about a significant reduction in their absolute levels of unemployment; indeed, both national and regional rates of unemployment increased rather than decreased in the 1960s and 1970s. Partly this was a consequence of quickening international economic change, (until the arrival of North Sea oil) Britain's balance of payments difficulties, and the imperfections of national economic management; partly it was a function of accelerating structural change in the British economy.

One of the persistent macro-economic dilemmas of the British economy in the years since 1945 has been the way in which, at each upswing of the business cycle, inflationary pressures allegedly generated in the more prosperous parts of the country have increased the national propensity to import and thereby demanded measures to dampen down aggregate home demand. It followed that the rate of national economic growth, which was already slow by international standards, was yet further restrained, since the temporary amelioration of balance of payments problems in this way meant that successive governments were denied the opportunity of exploiting the under-utilized resources of labour and capital in the less prosperous regions. A further economic argument for regional planning in consequence came to rest upon the assumption that inflation could be better controlled and national economic growth accelerated by deflecting some resource demands away from southern England and into the less prosperous regions (First Secretary of State, 1965, p.11; Department of Economic Affairs, 1969, pp. 91-94). In some measure, regional policy thus came legitimately to be regarded in part as a new attempt to manage, with rather more discriminating tools than conventional fiscal and monetary policies, the level of aggregate demand in the national economy. To the extent that these policies were able also to reduce inter-regional migration, it was suggested by some observers (Needleman and Scott, 1964) that inflationary pressures in southern England would be further checked, since the investment required by migrants is likely in the short run to increase the income of the more prosperous regions rather faster than their output. The inflationary effects of such population movements, however, remain highly speculative. The argument rests substantially upon the assumption that a reduction in inter-regional migration is likely to reduce the amount of social overhead and productive investment required by the economy in a given period of growth. The poor state of much social capital in the less prosperous regions, and the need to restructure their economies, hints that this might not in fact be the case. Indeed, to the extent that the income generated in the coalfield industrial economies by major infrastructural investments (which are a feature of some regional programmes, as will be noted later) is not in the short run matched by a commensurate increase in output, it can be suggested that regional planning has contributed to, rather than checked, inflationary tendencies in the national economy. Of course, other factors such as money supply policies, energy price increases, substantial wage increases and falling productivity are widely recognized as the major generators of the substantially higher rates of domestic inflation that came to be experienced in the 1970s.

On another level, the economic case for public intervention in the space economy has been endorsed by the realization that market forces are frequently imperfect for determining the best location of at least some economic activities. For example, by comparison with other cost variations in their production function, many industries exhibit such small differences in their locational costs that a low priority is rightly accorded to questions of location in investment decisions. Many managements therefore treat the issue of location superficially, as a result of which 'adequate' or 'convenient' rather than 'the best' places are often selected for their operations. Moreover, even when firms—and it is usually the larger ones—take the trouble to calculate the costs and benefits of alternative locations, they are naturally concerned solely with their own efficiency, and pay no attention to any costs which might be transferred to the community as a whole. By its decision to operate in a particular place, a factory or an office may impose upon a local authority the need to construct a wider road, a larger hospital, or a new school. These are expenses which might be only partly covered by the contribution the firm makes to local public income. This argument has been extended to suggest that, in large metropolitan areas such as Greater London, considerable social costs are generated by the excessive concentration of economic activities, and that these costs are not borne by the industries primarily responsible for them. As a result the expansion of such urban areas continues, in spite of the (alleged) diseconomies involved.

Any interpretation of the motives behind inter-regional planning would be incomplete without some mention of its political content. It is natural for Members of Parliament elected from constituencies in the less prosperous parts of the country to press for and to expect some public assistance for their communities. From the middle of the 1960s, however, a new political development resulting in part from a growing disenchantment with central government gained strength. This was the emergence of a more articulate regional spirit in provinical England, and increasingly vocal nationalistic movements in Scotland and Wales. The development was given initial expression, and possibly was even encouraged, by the creation (in 1964-1965) of the Regional Planning Boards and Economic Planning Councils. The boards comprise senior civil servants who are responsible for the activities of their (central government) departments within a particular region, and they seek to ensure consistent interdepartmental policies at the regional scale. The Economic Planning Councils, on the other hand are appointed by the Secretary of State for the Environment from various sections of the community—especially from business, the trade unions, local government and the universities—and they are asked to advise on the implications and shortcomings of national government policies as they affect their particular regions. The existence of these bodies provided a forum within which central government policies came to be more carefully scrutinized for their spatial implications, and regional dissatisfaction could be given a more formal expression. The subsequent discovery of major oil-bearing structures off the coast of Scotland (p.409ff.), plus the enormous rents that their exploitation makes available for the public purse, gave this movement a new impetus in the 1970s. Whatever reforms eventually result from the Kilbrandon Royal Commission on the Constitution (1973) and the subsequent attempts to provide a measure of legislative and administrative devolution for Scotland and Wales, there can be no doubt that the public awareness of the several regions and nations that comprise Britain is greater today than for many decades past. The changing character of inter-regional planning in the last decade has been related in part to this new political phenomenon, the aspirations it has encouraged, and the perceived need to adjust spatial planning policies accordingly. The creation of a Scottish Development Agency (p.38) is a case in point.

1.5.2 Intra-regional Planning

Because local problems are more readily perceived than those at a broader geographical scale, intra-regional planning has had a somewhat longer history than inter-regional policies in Britain. It evolved from the accumulated experience of town management and planning, plus the inspired thinking of such men as Howard, Unwin, Geddes and Abercrombie (Hall, 1974, ch.3), all of whom were concerned to improve the quality of Britain's urban environment. The motives for public policies at this scale derive primarily from social, economic and environmental considerations. All are rooted in the realization that the real wealth of a society cannot be measured in money terms alone, and that the unbridled pursuit of maximum financial gain by a community can quickly lead to a rapid deterioration in the quality of its urban and rural environment. The relatively untamed search for 'wealth' in the northern industrial centres of Britain during the nineteenth century created many a bleak urban environment with extensive industrial spoil and dereliction. Unrestrained, a similar set of values today would almost certainly lead to the under-provision of parkland and other amenities in towns; it would pollute rivers and the atmosphere beyond their already sadly high levels; it would allow land and air traffic noise to exceed tolerable proportions; and it would probably litter the countryside with advertisements. Whilst it has for many decades been acknowledged that town planning can materially contribute to the well-being and true wealth of the community, it is only more recently that sub-regional and regional planning have begun to be similarly recognized. Spatial planning at these scales undoubtedly and transparently imposes upon both individuals and the community at large certain recognizable costs, especially through the delays imposed upon development and the restraints that surround enterprise, and its reputation frequently suffers from the less tangible nature of some of its benefits and achievements.

Some of the earliest initiatives in intra-regional planning stemmed from the problems of the slums, the overcrowding and the poor health found in the inner areas of the larger cities. Social arguments for government intervention in the process of urban growth have thus centred upon the advantages of small and 'balanced' communities. Ebenezer Howard (1904), for example, founder of the British garden city movement, was amongst the most hostile critics of large cities and conurbations; in his *Garden Cities of Tomorrow* he argued that large cities were impersonal and inimical to the development of a sense of community, while smaller towns of 50,000 or 100,000 afforded a readier environment for the development of community spirit and better social relationships. Such views as these have had a substantial influence upon the evolution of land use planning in Britain, most notably in the programme of new town construction as a means of dispersing population and economic activity away from the largest of the conurbations (p.84ff.). Despite such policies, however, the problems of inadequate housing in those urban concentrations have persisted, and they clearly remain central to the vicious spiral of social deprivation and localized poverty that continues to attract the attention of public and planners alike—more especially now that it has come to be associated in some areas with a concentration of ethnic minority groups.

The second motive for intra-regional planning has been economic, and is related to the debatable economics of large urban areas and their associated suburban growth. Whilst the economics of agglomeration clearly afford considerable benefits to many individual enterprises in cities and conurbations, and those areas simultaneously provide individuals having marketable skills with a wider range of employment choice, it has often been argued that unrestrained market forces can lead to substantial public costs and substantial collective diseconomies in urban areas above a certain size. These high costs are the result of the very much greater difficulties involved in the provision of additional infrastructure and public services such as roads and public housing in large cities, compared with the provision of similar goods and services in smaller towns. For example, the estimated costs of a new motorway in inner London in the late 1960s was £12 million per kilometre (£19 million per mile), of which 30 per cent was the cost of acquiring the necessary land and buildings along its route; by comparison the cost of motorway construction around smaller urban centres at that time was of the order of £1 million per kilometre. Similarly, housing land in London by 1972 had risen to £34,000 per hectare (£84,000 per acre), a figure well over three times the value of housing land in England and Wales as a whole. A further economic argument for intra-regional planning is based upon the recognition that, unless there is some coordination of land use changes at the growing edge of large urban areas, there can develop not only an inconvenient and unattractive juxtaposition of unrelated activities, but also an inadequate provision of basic public infrastructure— water supplies, sewage facilities, roads, public transport, schools, hospitals and the like. And the costs to the community of subsequently providing such necessary facilities and services, after uncoordinated land use changes have taken place, can be very high indeed.

The environmental motives for intra-regional planning focused initially upon the desire to preserve certain rural areas from the spread of housing, factories, shopping facilities and the like. Such areas were frequently and uniquely attractive in their own right; their preservation was therefore justified on conservation grounds alone. In addition, these rural zones were increasingly regarded as a particularly valuable means of meeting the rising recreational needs of the growing urban population. Yet, unrestrained, market forces would in many cases have encouraged a change in their use to aesthetically less attractive purposes. There has also been a desire to prevent the indiscriminate conversion of specifically agricultural land to urban and suburban uses, partly to preserve the rural environment and community, but also to minimise the burden of agricultural imports on the country's balance of payments. Short-term market economics can rarely provide a higher return from agricultural land uses than from most alternative suburban functions on the urban fringe. Physical controls have in consequence been widely accepted.

With rising living standards, there has been a growing number of protracted, vocal and at times fierce debates on the location and even the wisdom of certain categories of land use change. For example, major infrastructural and productive investments such as motorways, airports, nuclear power stations and new coal mines have been increasingly opposed by an active coalition of interests, including local amenity groups, national conservation societies and even international organizations that seriously doubt the conventional assumptions of society about the desirability of economic growth and the historically acceptable routes towards it. Particularly noteworthy was the highly vocal and successful opposition to the plans for a series of urban motorways within Greater London (p.136), the extended and unresolved debate about the expansion of airports within South East England (p.137) and the powerful opposition to the recovery of coal from the Vale of Belvoir (p.186). While the issues at stake were exposed in the many national forums for public debate, and while the final decisions had to be made at a central government or even at a Cabinet level, the conflicts exposed were substantially matters of intra-regional environmental concern and had to be resolved within the framework of planning law and planning institutions.

Conservation movements are not only involved in attempts to preserve the rural environment and the prevention of gross urban intrusions into it. There also exists an equally strong and widespread desire to preserve much that it best in the man-made urban environment. Yet the strength of commercial and business pressures is such that the construction of new offices, shops, hotels, parking facilities, roads and the like could readily justify in economic terms the demolition of many older buildings and even districts within the towns. Generally speaking, this issue of preservation is essentially a matter for town planning. However, it may also be necessary, in order to relieve development pressures from a town or city, to adopt a sub-regional strategy of land use change that ensures the deflection of those pressures elsewhere. The use of green belts around such cities as York and Bath (p.84), for example, has served to restrain the full impact of modern urban life there and to preserve something of their historical beauty.

1.6 Changing Circumstances

At both the inter-regional and intra-regional scales, therefore, social, economic, political and environmental motives have inspired the political response to the problems posed by the nation's changing economic geography. At the inter-regional scale, where government strategy has been largely in the hands of the Department of Industry (and its predecessor, the Board of Trade), and where the problems have centred on the implications of relative or even absolute economic decline, economic and political concerns and motives have been the mainsprings of policy. At the intra-regional scale, on the other hand, where planning has been administered through the Department of the Environment (and its predecessors, the Ministry of Housing and Local Government and the Ministry of Town and Country Planning), and where problems have focused on the challenges presented by urban and suburban growth, social and environmental motives and concerns have been of greater significance. At both scales, however, policies have been formulated, introduced, modified and sometimes abandoned against the background of changing economic, social and political circumstances. The macro-economic context of policy, the rate of growth of the population, the anatomy of the British labour market, and the nature of perceived spatial problems were all very different in the 1940s, 1950s and 1960s from the milieu of policy today. It is worth recalling the principal elements in this changing environment of British regional planning.

1.6.1 *The Changing Macro-economic Environment*

The shifting international context of the British economy is the first element. In the 1940s, 1950s and 1960s regional policies were forged in the twilight of Empire and by a country excluded from the European Economic Community. No longer is this the case. In consequence there has been a need for spatial management in Britain to become increasingly conscious of the growing integration of its economic and social affairs with those on the European mainland. More and more, Britain has come to compete with other Community countries for internationally footloose jobs and investment capital, for enterprise and management skills, and for product and service markets. These changes have come to shape the location of much private industrial and commercial investment. Public infrastructural planning, especially port and road construction, has also responded to the changed circumstances and needs. The implications of Britain's commitment to Europe were faced only slowly in regional development programmes, however, although the Community's investment and social funds (p.57) came increasingly to be seen as a valuable weapon in the armoury of development planning, especially in the less prosperous parts of the country.

The evolving nature of enterprise is a second and related element in Britain's changing macro-economic environment. In common with many other countries, over the past thirty years the British economy has come to be increasingly dominated by larger and larger firms, first national and then international in character and ownership. Compared with the single plant or single office of the relatively small firm that they have replaced, these multi-facility, multi-process, multi-product, multi-service corporations not only have quite different decision-making styles, but also a constrasting set of locational perceptions and options. They can switch their processes between plants; they can import (at transfer prices) components or information from overseas; they can measure the productivity of comparable facilities in different centres; and they can invest and expand accordingly. Less responsive to controls, they more readily react to incentives and political persuasion. The larger national and international corporations have thus played a substantial and innovative role in the restructuring of the manufacturing economies of Scotland, Wales and northern England. At the same time, however, they have shifted many of their control functions into the South East. The instruments of regional policy have not fully reflected the changing origins and character of private and corporate enterprise. In part they have remained inappropriately oriented towards the behaviour of the small firm with its limited locational options. Policy adaptations have occurred, however, to reflect the growing importance of both British and foreign-owned multi-national enterprise in the growth and planning of the space economy, in particular the softening of floorspace controls and the greater use of selective assistance.

Spatial management must also reflect sooner or later yet a third important element in the country's changing macro-economic environment. This is the shifting priorities of government in economic management. For some thirty post-war years, successive British administrations in general pursued policies of full employment through monetary expansion and deficit financing; these policies were constrained by a persistently weak balance of payments (in part related to the maintenance of fixed exchange rates), and pursued against the background of only short-lived public restraints upon the 'free collective bargaining' of wages. By the middle of the 1970s, however, it had become glaringly obvious that a new set of policy priorities was emerging in national economic management and that these changes were beginning to influence the style, if not the objectives, of regional planning. Fixed exchange rates were abandoned. The inflationary consequences of unrestrained 'free collective bargaining' (at least within the existing institutions for labour supply) were widely recognized. Most important, however, was the growing realization that the problem of unemployment, and the associated defects of national, regional and local labour markets, could not be solved by resort to the printing press and deficit public financing. As the problem of national and regional unemployment came to be increasingly interpreted as an expression of rigidities in the labour market, therefore, more emphasis came to be placed upon the encouragement of labour retraining in response to the shifting industrial and occupational structure of the economy, upon achieving a greater geographical mobility of labour in the daily journey to work, and upon the development of more efficient housing markets so that a greater flexibility will emerge in many people's attitudes towards their place of residence. This was a very different policy emphasis from the regional planning reaction to unemployment twenty or even ten years earlier.

1.6.2 *The Rate of Population Growth*

The years after World War II were characterized by three demographic trends. First, birth rates increased markedly in a 'baby boom' of the late 1940s. Second, fertility rates also increased as a consequence of earlier and more universal marriage. And, third, there was a general gain from net international migration. The result was that the population of the United Kingdom grew from 50.3 million in 1951 to 54.7 million twenty years later. Against this background, and the expectation that recent historical trends would continue, it was projected (in 1968 for example) that the country's population would increase to 59.6 million in 1981 and 63.6 million in 1991. The spatial planning implications of such a prospect were substantial, especially the need to accommodate on the map considerable areas of urban and suburban growth. In consequence, both inter-regional planning, notably in the search for suitable sites on the 'growth estuaries' of Severnside, Humberside and Tayside (pp.56-57), and intra-regional planning were cast within an essentially expansionist mould.

By the early 1970s, however, the situation had begun to change. Birth rates had begun to fall. Projections came to be revised. National population dynamics began to move towards a 'no growth' situation. By 1973, the 1981 projection for the population of the United Kingdom was 56.3 million and the 1991 projection 58.0 million—nearly 5 million fewer than had been projected only five years earlier. The implications for spatial planning were immediately apparent. The proposals for major urban expansion on the growth estuaries were set aside. More importantly, however, attitudes towards sub-regional planning took on a new character, with serious objections to further planned decentralization from the conurbations being increasingly raised. In later chapters, contemporary attitudes towards the development of the London city-region especially (p.167ff.), but also the West Midlands (p.242ff.) and the two conurbations of South Lancashire (p.297ff.), are shown to be substantially altered from those that sponsored the new towns of the 1950s and the deliberate public encouragement of urban growth in the Outer Metropolitan Area of the South East and beyond the green belts of the provincial conurbations.

1.6.3 *The Changing Structure of Employment Opportunities*

The initial 'package' of regional policies was conceived at a time when jobs in British manufacturing industry were growing and thought likely to increase yet further. Certainly, throughout the 1950s and the early 1960s this was so. After 1966, however, as was noted earlier (Table 1.1), an actual contraction in manufacturing jobs was experienced—nearly 17 per cent in the ten years to 1976. The share of manufacturing jobs in total employment fell from 36 per cent to 32 per cent between 1961 and 1976. In contrast, the major growth

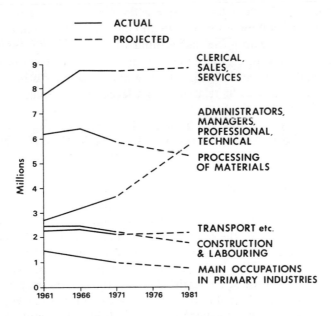

Figure 1.4 Britain: the changing structure of
employment by occupation, 1961-1981
Source: Woodward (1975)

of jobs in the late 1960s and the 1970s was in the fields of education, health and public administration (with far-reaching implications for public expenditure) and in insurance, banking and private services (see Figure 1.1). Slower rates of growth were recorded in construction, transport and distribution. In occupational terms this meant an expansion of higher-level jobs in office-type activities, alongside a decline of blue-collar employments in factories, with the prospect of this continuing (Figure 1.4).

Another major element in the altered environment for regional planning, therefore, has been this changing anatomy of the labour market. Whilst the first public policies designed to shape the inter-regional pattern of employment opportunities concentrated heavily upon the relocation of manufacturing jobs, by the 1970s this had very little logic when all regions were experiencing difficulties in adjusting to a decline in the labour requirements of this sector of the economy. Meanwhile, the fastest growing industries—education and health—were totally outside the established regional planning controls of central government. Indeed, those spatial policies that were directed towards a sector of employment growth—services in general and offices in particular—were in fact developed somewhat tangentially to the mainstream of inter-regional development initiatives. The initial decentralization of the civil service and the creation of the Location of Offices Bureau, for example, were both the result of official perceptions of 'the congestion' of central London in the early 1960s. Only subsequently was it accepted that office policy needed to be moved nearer to the centre of inter-regional policy, and that a new set of attitudes and programmes was required that recognized the distinctive nature and behaviour of the office sector in its locational requirements.

1.6.3 *The Changing Nature of Perceived Spatial Problems*

Regional planning in the immediate post-war decades was pursued in the context of continuing and substantial population growth and the expectation that it would continue. Policy was also framed against the background of the country's population moving towards the largest urban centres, especially the conurbations of Greater London and the West Midlands; and this migration stemmed substantially from a distinctive geography of unemployment which persisted at relatively high levels in such places as South Wales, North East England and Scotland.

By the mid-1970s, however, the country not only found itself in a period of economic uncertainty in which the actual and the opportunity costs of all public policies were more carefully counted, but a revised set of population, migration and unemployment prospects could not be avoided. Population growth slowed, as has been seen, and forecasts were revised substantially downwards. The historical patterns of inter-regional migration shifted to the extent that the South East and the West Midlands began to record a net out-migration of population; indeed, Greater London experienced a particularly rapid fall in its population. And the spatial expression of unemployment began to change, with the West Midlands for the first time exhibiting signs of structural economic weakness, and the inner areas of Greater London recording localized rates of unemployment as high as those in the Assisted Areas. Indeed, the map of unemployment (Figure 1.5) threw substantial doubts on the wisdom of persisting with a set of inter-regional policies that had been forged against a quite different magnitude and geography of labour surplus. By the mid-1970s there were as many unemployed in Greater London as there were in the whole of Scotland, and twice as many as in the Principality of Wales.

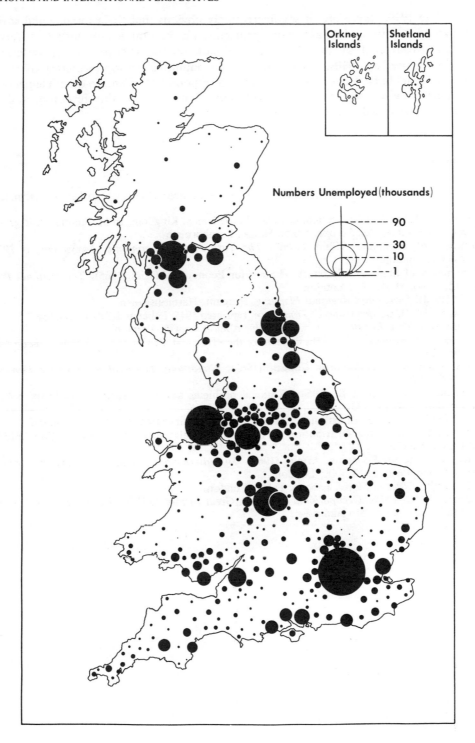

Figure 1.5 Britain: unemployment, 1978

By the late 1970s, therefore, it was increasingly obvious that the economic and social geography of Britain, and its associated problems, was becoming substantially different from that investigated by the Royal Commission on the Distribution of Industrial Population in the late 1930s, or even the Hunt Committee's study (Secretary of State, 1969) thirty years later. Policy had, therefore, to respond to this and to other elements in the changing environment of regional planning. Something of this response, and its adequacy, are analysed in the chapters that follow.

REFERENCES

Bacon, R., and Eltis, W. (1976), *Britain's Economic Problems: Too Few Producers,* Macmillan, London.

Cameron, G. (1974), Regional economic policy in the United Kingdom, In M. Sant (ed.), *Regional Policy and Planning for Europe,* Saxon House, Farnborough.

Department of Economic Affairs (1969), *The Task Ahead. Economic Assessment to 1972,* H.M.S.O., London.

First Secretary of State and Secretary of State for Economic Affairs (1965), *The National Plan* (Cmnd. 2764), H.M.S.O., London.

Hall, P. (1974), *Urban and Regional Planning,* Penguin, Harmonsworth.

Howard, E. (1904), *Garden Cities of Tomorrow,* reprinted 1945, Faber and Faber, London.

McCrone, G. (1969), *Regional Policy in Britain,* Allen & Unwin, London.

Moore, B., and Rhodes, J. (1973), Evaluating the effects of British regional policy, *Economic Journal,* **83,** 87-110.

National Economic Development Council (1963), *Conditions Favourable to Faster Growth,* H.M.S.O., London.

Needleman, L., and Scott, B. (1964), Regional problems and the location of industry policy, *Urban Studies,* **1,** 153-173.

Royal Commission on the Constitution (1973), *Report* (Cmnd. 5460), H.M.S.O., London.

Royal Commission on the Distribution of Industrial Population (1940), *Report,* (Cmnd.6153), H.M.S.O., London.

Secretary of State for Economic Affairs (1969). *The Intermediate Areas* (Chairman: Sir Joseph Hunt) (Cmnd.3998), H.M.S.O., London.

Self, P. (1957), *Cities in Flood,* Faber & Faber, London.

Woodward, V.N. (1975), *Occupational Trends in Great Britain 1961-81,* Department of Applied Economics, University of Cambridge.

CHAPTER 2

Inter-regional Development and Planning

GERALD MANNERS

2.1 Introduction

Between 1951 and 1971, the British population increased by about 10 per cent, or some 4.9 million. Of this increase, 3.9 million were to be found in the five more prosperous regions in the South and Midlands of England. The South East alone increased by 1.9 million people, of which more than 0.5 million was the result of net inter-regional and international migration; at an even faster rate, the population of the West and East Midlands increased by 1.1 million. The growing concentration of the British people in the southern parts of the country, and more particularly in the London and Birmingham city-regions, slowed somewhat in the 1970s. Nevertheless, the longer-term trend undoubtedly reflected the perceived private advantages of locating economic developments there. It also drew attention to the problems of the northern and western parts of Britain, which, for over fifty years now, have suffered from comparative decline. Since the end of World War I, slow population growth, relatively high levels of unemployment, low activity rates and a steady net out-migration of people have characterized much of industrial North East England, North West England, West Yorkshire, the central valley of Scotland, and the industrial areas of Wales (Tables 1.2 and 2.1). All of these areas have suffered from the same basic inability to provide enough jobs for the people living there. And with these essentially coalfield industrial zones can be associated the rural parts of northern England, Scotland, Wales, and the South West of England, which have also experienced a steady depopulation as a consequence of the changing structure and the contracting labour inputs of agriculture.

The relatively high levels of local unemployment in these less prosperous and, in relation to the centre of the national market, peripheral regions, has naturally varied through time. Their worst experience of unemployment was during the inter-war years, and more particularly during the years of the depression. It was then that Wales had over 36 per cent of its insured labour force unemployed, whilst the other peripheral industrial areas all had unemployment levels of more than 27 per cent; the national figure in 1932 was 22 per cent. After 1945, the national rate of unemployment was lower, although from the middle of the 1970s there was a persistent tendency for it to move upwards to higher levels. For twenty-five years it ranged between 1.5 and 2.5 per cent, but by 1977 adjusted monthly figures of over 6 per cent were being regularly recorded. Nevertheless, the differential between the national percentage and those of the less prosperous regions—albeit narrowing (Figure 2.1)—has remained. In the Northern region, for example,

23

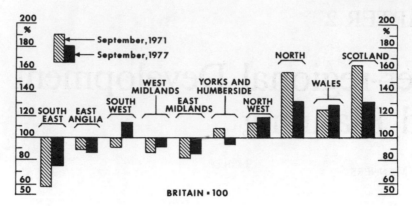

Figure 2.1 Britain: unemployment rates, by region, 1971 and 1977
Source: Department of Employment data

unemployment has varied between 2.4 and 7.5 per cent—levels that would have been greater but for the steady movement of people out of the region.

Out-migration has characterized all the less prosperous regions for many years. During the period 1923-1931, the annual average migration of people from Scotland, for example, was between 35,000 and 40,000. In the middle of the 1960s, the annual net loss once again rose briefly to about 40,000, but more recently the figure has fallen to much lower levels, partly as a result of government policies, partly as a consequence of the beneficial employment effects of North Sea oil (p.409ff.). More persistently, the proportion of the potential labour force in the less prosperous regions that is actually in employment—the activity rate—has remained substantially lower than in South East England and the West Midlands. In 1976, the activity rates of those two regions were 73.4 and 71.1 per cent respectively; the figures for Wales, the Northern region and Scotland, in contrast, were 61.6, 67.3 and 67.8 per cent (Table 2.1). The resultant inability of these areas to hold on to all of the natural increase in their population and their continuing experience of net out-migration is illustrated in Table 1.2. These features, then, are the principal symptoms of an enduring malaise in the north and west of the country. They demand explanation.

2.2 Underlying Forces for Change

Throughout the present century the British economy has been subject to persistent and fundamental structural and geographical changes. Resources of capital and labour have been withdrawn from those manufacturing industries which changing technology and comparative economic advantage have left as misfits in the contemporary world. These industries, characterized especially by their production of specialized, high-quality, almost craft products in limited quantities, have been replaced by modern industries which have been subject to contrasting locational forces. Based upon rapidly advancing technologies and concerned especially with the mass production of standardized goods, these new industries appeared, succeeded and subsequently expanded in southern England. The two largest city-regions there thus came to have a wide diversity of industrial and commercial activities, amongst which ranked a large percentage of growth

Table 2.1 Britain: selected economic indicators, by regions, 1970-1976

	Employment (civilian)			Activity rates	Unemployment rates	Total personal income			Average weekly expenditure per person
	1970 ('000s)	1976 ('000s)	Change 1970-1976 (%)	1976 (%)	1976 (%)	(£ m.)	1975 (%)	Per head (%)	1975-1976 (£)
BRITAIN	23,825	23,865*	+0.2	69.7	5.8	94,987	100.0	100.0*	20.91*
More prosperous regions:									
South East	7,920	7,860	−0.8	73.4	4.2	33,063	34.8	112.6	23.72
East Anglia	694	746	+7.5	66.7	4.9	2,858	3.0	92.6	19.48
West Midlands	2,400	2,342	−2.7	71.1	5.9	8,697	9.2	96.8	19.92
East Midlands	1,567	1,615	+3.1	68.7	4.8	6,248	6.6	96.6	20.23
South West	1,626	1,700	+4.6	65.1	6.4	6,961	7.3	94.8	20.54
Less prosperous regions:									
North West	2,919	2,845	−2.3	69.5	7.0	10,986	11.6	96.3	19.59
Yorkshire & Humberside	2,115	2,123	+0.4	69.3	5.6	8,172	8.6	96.3	19.52
Northern	1,311	1,330	+1.4	67.3	7.5	5,110	5.4	94.2	20.11
Wales	1,076	1,099	+2.1	61.6	7.4	4,223	4.4	88.1	19.49
Scotland	2,196	2,205	+0.4	67.8	7.0	8,669	9.1	96.0	19.73

+ Excludes 8,700 U.K. employees whose regional location unascertained. *U.K. average.
Sources: Central Statistical Office, *Regional Statistics*, annually.

industries satisfying the rapidly expanding sectors of both the national and international markets. In contrast, the coalfield economies of the North and the West were left with the greater part of the country's old, stagnant and contracting sources of employment. Considerable resources of capital and labour in these peripheral economies—capital assets which had for the most part been invested in the hey-day of Victorian expansion—came thereby to be underemployed. Even when some of the older and traditional industries of the less prosperous regions were able to retain a substantial market for their products, changing economics often demanded the substitution of capital for labour. As a result, a divergence between the trends in their output and the employment opportunities they provided was frequently recorded. During the last decade, for example, the iron and steel industry has been in a position whereby only through planning or a severe reduction in its labour force—a reduction of perhaps one-third, or some 100,000 men—could it realistically envisage competitive success and an expansion of its markets and output (p.387ff.; Manners, 1968b). Historical, economic and social forces were at work to produce these regions of relative, and in some localities absolute, decline.

2.2.1 The Legacies of History

One of the historical reasons why a new economic base failed to emerge in the less prosperous economies was the fact that many of the country's new and expanding industries grew out of the existing lighter engineering trades which had never been well represented in the coalfields. It was especially important that the *quality of the labour force* of these trades—their diverse skills, their distinctive tradtions, and their apprenticeship and supplementary training schemes, for instance—provided a natural springboard from which new enterprises could readily develop in southern England. The carriage trade of London, for example, was not only a forerunner of the modern motor industry in a technological sense; it had also nurtured over the years a labour force with skills that could easily be adapted to the new industry's requirements. However, these were skills which unemployed coalminers, shipbuilders, the operatives in heavy engineering industries, tinplate workers and the like in the northern industrial areas could not immediately offer prospective employers.

The very *size of the labour markets* in London and the West Midlands was also important. It meant that the possibility of attracting the right sort of skills when and where they were wanted was much greater there than anywhere else in the country. In the service sector, of course, the position was even more extreme. Central London by the middle of the 1960s had some 16.6 million square metres (179 million square feet) of office space, and the rest of the South East region a further 22.0 million square metres (237 million square feet); together these represented about half of the total office space in England and Wales. As a consequence the South East Economic Planning Region provided employment for about half of the 4.6 million office workers in England and Wales, and some 0.8 million were employed in central London alone. It was naturally very difficult for any other part of the country to compete with such a remarkable concentration of skills.

The less prosperous regions did have, of course, the compensating advantage of a large number of unemployed men and women readily available for new industries. These workers could have been cheaply trained and utilized by new manufacturers. But in the formative inter-war years, when aggregated demand in the British economy was low, adequate supplies of labour were always available in southern England either indigenously or through migration; there was in consequence no incentive for the growth industries to move north in search of it. Moreover, when labour demand in the country as a whole was subsequently much higher, inter-regional differentials in the cost of labour came to be substantially reduced by the growing tendency for wages to be bargained and agreed at a national level. Of course, labour costs in southern England have long been relatively high. For many firms, however, and especially for the smaller entrepreneur, the greater diversity, flexibility and size of the labour markets there permit efficiencies in operation and the possibilities of growth which more than justify the marginally higher costs that have to be paid for employees.

A second historical factor explaining the plight of the peripheral regions was their lack of *indigenous enterprise*. Few observers would doubt that, with a little local initiative, many new factories could have been established in these areas and a large number would have succeeded. The profitability and success of the many enterprises induced by the government into the peripheral economies since 1936 is evidence enough. But enterprise was not forthcoming. One of the reasons for this lay in the industrial history of the less prosperous regions, and the nature of the economy and society that had been powerfully shaped by events in the nineteenth century. With the industrial revolution, these regions attracted and prospered with a group of industries which by and large were oligopolistic in structure, and in which entrepreneurial decisions were concentrated in relatively few hands. Their societies, as a consequence, were denied a widespread tradition of enterprise, and contrasted vividly with the type of highly entrepreneurial society which was to be found especially in London and Birmingham. Stemming also from their tradition economic structures was the relative *scarcity of entrepreneurial capital*, for the older industrial regions did not nurture institutions and traditions which made capital readily available to the small man anxious to pioneer a new enterprise. Unlike London and Birmingham, therefore, where a long tradition of highly competitive, small-scale industries spawned both formal and informal means of making relatively small amounts of risk captial available to the entrepreneur, the peripheral economies inherited yet another factor deficiency which hindered their industrial adjustment and revival.

2.2.2 *Economic Factors*

These historical forces shaping Britain's changing industrial geography were endorsed by a second group of powerful forces that were economic in nature. The most important of these was the *geography and influence of the home market*. Whereas in the nineteenth century Britain in her industrial precocity had been able to open up huge export markets with little difficulty, after 1918 industry had to face increasingly severe overseas competition. To this was added during the inter-war years economic nationalism, currency chaos and a world economic depression. In consequence, the growth industries of this period were established primarily to serve the home market. Characterized by their low inputs of raw materials and by their assembly of components and high-value sub-assemblies, they were unlikely to be attracted to locate on or near to the country's coalfields which were generally eccentric to the hub of the national market; the latter centred upon the Greater London-West Midlands zone in general, and on London in particular.

Table 2.1 shows that nearly 35 per cent of Britain's net personal income in 1975 was to be found in the South East region, and a further 16 per cent was in the West and East Midlands — over 50 per cent in all. As an alternative measure of market opportunities throughout Britain, Clark (1966) produced an index of 'economic potential'. This index measures the relative proximity of a place to total purchasing power as it is distributed geographically throughout the country. Purchasing power is broadly defined as the net earned income of the resident population, although account is taken of the advantage of accessibility to export outlets by allotting a notional overseas income to the country's main ports. Proximity is measured not in terms of geographical distance, but of tapered freight transport rates. Clark's calculations (Figure 2.2) revealed that the place with greatest 'economic potential' in Britain, measured in this way, is in fact London. From the metropolis, economic potential values, and hence relative accessibility to the markets for goods and services, fall in all directions. Birmingham has a value 7 per cent below that of London, Leeds 15 per cent below and Glasgow 30 per cent below. An advantage of this sort, translated into increased sales through lower transport costs and closer contact with customers, helps considerably to explain the remarkable growth of London and the West Midlands in the present century, and the disadvantages of the less prosperous regions. Prospectively, as illustrated by Figure 2.3, it suggests the continuing relative disadvantage of peripheral Britain within the European Economic Community (Clark, Wilson and Bradley, 1969).

Although it is rooted in the distribution of the British population and income, this pattern of market accessiblity is also a function of the country's *transport facilities and costs*. As has been seen, the geography of road and rail transport in Britain affords a unique and advantageous nodality to both London and Birmingham. In terms of frequency of rail service to the rest of the country, London is without equal. A measurement of travel times on the British Rail passenger network, however, reveals Birmingham as having the most accessible point of interchange (Figure 2.4). Moreover, measures of nodality on the motorway and major road system reveal the M1/M6 interchange and Birmingham, once again, as the most accessible nodes (using different system definitions) and other Midlands cities as having a singularly advantageous centrality (Williams, 1977).

London fares relatively poorly on simple travel-distance and travel-time criteria alone. However, other transport investments work in its favour, especially the size and the role of its ports. Historically the most important single geographical advantage promoting the development of the capital was its position at the head of ocean navigation on the most important estuary in the country. Today, the focus of Western European trade is increasingly coming to be concentrated upon the large and small ports of the 'Narrows'— principally London, Southampton, Le Havre, Antwerp and Rotterdam, Felixstowe, Harwich, Seaford, Dunkirk and Ostend. Their industrial hinterlands, which extend from Birmingham in the north to Paris in the south, and from the Ruhr in the east to South Wales in the west, form the economic heart of contemporary North West Europe. The industries of southern England, therefore, especially through the use they make of the seaports of London (which include Felixstowe, Harwich, the Medway, Dover, Folkestone and in certain respects even Southampton), need to be considered in some senses as an integral part of a greater European economic complex; the same claim cannot be made with the same force for the industries of peripheral Britain, important though their international role has become. In addition to their seaports, London and the South East also have the advantage of the major international airports at Heathrow and Gatwick.

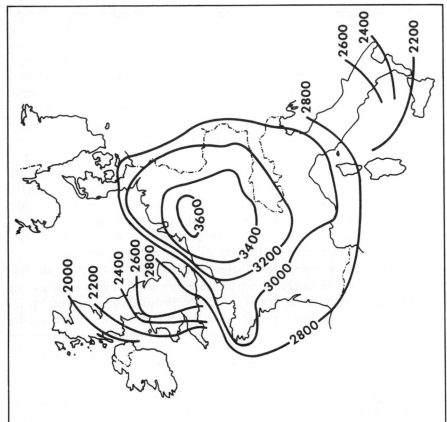

Figure 2.3 North West Europe: economic potential, *circa* 1965
Source: Clark, Wilson and Bradley (1969)
Note: Economic potential is an abstract index of the relative proximity of a place to total purchasing power as it is distributed spatially throughout a country or a region; see p.28

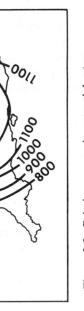

Figure 2.2 Britain: economic potential, *circa* 1965
Source: Clark (1966)

Not only has the former become the most important port in the country, in terms of the value of goods handled, but it has also been a major stimulus to sub-regional economic development which is not shared by the other regions of the country.

Many manufacturers—particularly in their early innovatory years, if not subsequently —elect to serve the whole of the national market from a single place of production. Because most firms absorb the costs of distributing their final products to the consumer through selling at a (nationally) uniform delivered price, it is clearly advantageous for them to be located where these transport costs are at a minimum. The long-standing concentration of the British population in southern England, therefore, placed manufacturing industries there at considerable advantage. Distribution costs are at their lowest and convenient access to consumers is most likely to be assured. More especially in the case of a wide range of service activities, there can be very little doubt as to the centrality of London in the national market. Since the cost of transporting most manufactured goods from factory to the domestic wholesaler, retailer or consumer normally represents only about 2 to 4 per cent of total production and marketing costs— even in the case of Scottish manufacturers (Report of a Committee, 1961, p. 73)—this point needs to be kept in perspective. Nevertheless, the fact that industry in the less prosperous regions (particularly before the construction of the motorway network and the introduction of freightliner and other improved services by British Rail) was relatively ill-served with transport and communication facilities to the rest of the British market did impose an additional inconvenience and higher costs upon its operations. Moreover, as exports increasingly became important after 1945, the relative inaccessibility of the coalfield industrial areas (South Lancashire apart) to the country's major ports stood further to their disadvantage.

Manufacturing, of course provides less than one half of the total number of jobs in Britain, and as the economy has matured so have service activities become relatively more important. Some services are clearly related to local needs, and their distribution has tended to parallel inter-regional shifts in manufacturing employment and population. There are in addition, however, a large number of service activities which serve both regional and national markets. Once again they have been attracted to the more prosperous regions. Table 2.2 illustrates this point in the case of office employment. All service jobs have a tendency to gravitate towards a central place in the market that they serve. With improvements in communications, service activities tend to increase the spatial extent of their market areas and thereby cause a centralization of related employments. During the last fifty years, as a result, with Greater London standing as the focal point in the domestic and international transport network, the relative role of the less prosperous regions in matters of trade, commerce, banking, finance, government and law has tended to decline. The Bank of England no longer operates branches in Swansea and Norwich, for example. The provincial commodity markets have virtually disappeared. With this relative decline of employment opportunities in the service trades there developed a scarcity of readily available and appropriately skilled white-collar labour in the less prosperous regions upon which any reversal of past trends could be based. These transport and labour supply situations were just two aspects of the relative absence of external economies which faced manufacturers in the peripheral regions of Britain.

Economic development in southern England has been powerfully aided over the years by advantages that might be loosely grouped under the heading of 'external economies'. A

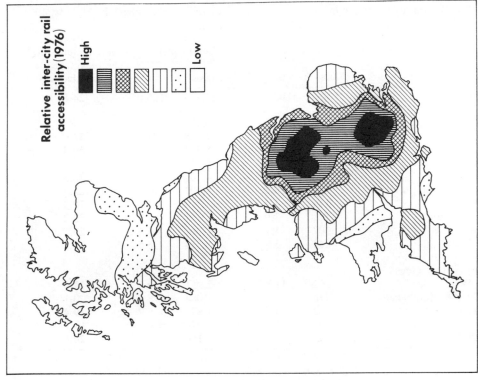

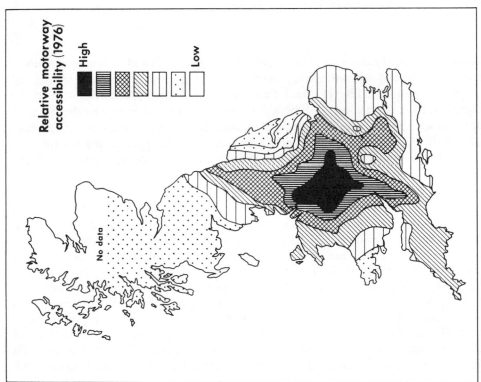

Figure 2.4 Britain: relative motorway and inter-city rail accessibility, 1976
Source: Williams (1977)

Table 2.2 Britain: office employment as a proportion of total employment, by regions, 1971

	Office Employment		Total Employment		Office employment/total employment (%) (rounded up)
	('000s)	%	('000s)	%	
BRITAIN	5,886	100.0	23,733	100.0	24.8
More prosperous regions:					
South East	2,552	43.4	7,988	33.7	32.0
Central London	756	12.8	1,253	5.3	60.4
Greater London area (total)	1,565	26.6	4,086	17.2	38.3
Rest of the South East	988	16.8	3,902	16.4	25.3
East Anglia	144	2.4	714	3.0	20.2
West Midlands	523	8.9	2,351	9.9	22.2
East Midlands	307	5.2	1,494	6.3	20.6
South West	340	5.8	1,553	6.5	21.9
Less prosperous regions:					
North West	692	11.8	2,951	10.9	23.4
Yorkshire & Humberside	418	7.1	2,084	8.8	20.1
Northern	262	4.5	1,354	5.7	19.4
Wales	201	3.4	1,079	4.5	18.7
Scotland*	446	7.6	2,164	9.1	20.6

*Scotland figure produced residually from Great Britain and England and Wales totals.
Source: 1971 Census, Occupation by Workplace Tables.

large number of firms regularly purchase from other firms goods and such supplementary services as transport and subcontracting, advertising and market consultancy, specialized broking and computing skills. The fact that Greater London especially, but also the West Midlands, offer these goods and services locally in greater variety than other parts of the country is an important asset in their economic development. New firms can take advantage of them. And the arrival of these new firms both enlarges the market for such purchases and also signals the possibility of yet further external economies by permitting the emergence of even more specialized facilities, manufactures and services. The type of firm said to benefit most from such externalities is the relatively small business producing goods or services for a new and uncertain, or a fluctuating, market; in a large metropolitan economy it is in a position to share with other firms in the industry, or with the regional economy in general, activities and costs which it might elsewhere be required to internalize. However, there are no theoretical reasons why comparable benefits should not be exploited by firms of different sizes, organization and technology. Thus, for any firm, the hire of additional lorries to meet a temporary upsurge of demand can normally be more readily arranged in London than in Grimsby, and the stocks or inventories carried by a Birmingham motor component manufacturer need to be very much smaller than those of a similar enterprise in the Central Valley of Scotland. The traditions of vigorous entrepreneurship and innovation that have characterized the two main conurbations of southern England for many generations have relied upon such externalities. They have also relied upon the impressively wide range of social, cultural, and educational facilities that are associated with London in particular, and have played a significant role in regional economic development. There can also be little doubt that the location of the central government in London, plus the fact that the greater number of its research establishments are within easy reach of the capital, have given the South East a substantial economic advantage. These and other considerations are discussed further in Chapters 4 and 5.

2.2.3 *Social Considerations*

The historical and economic forces shaping Britain's economic geography in recent decades have been reinforced by a number of social factors. In the matter of amenities, for example, the less prosperous regions were in no position to offer an employer or an employee an urban environment and social capital equal to that of southern England. With relatively little new investment after 1914, even by the early 1960s these older industrial areas were characterized by an essentially Victorian urban inheritance. All the relevant indices of social progress—the age and condition of housing (Table 2.3), the quality of the schools, the area of derelict land (Table 2.4), the availability of recreational facilities, and the like—recorded and perpetuated the disadvantages of the coalfield economies. In terms of cultural facilities, too, such as concert halls and theatres, or art collections and museums, the assets of the less prosperous regions were scattered and relatively poor. Undoubtedly, these deficiencies contributed to their failure to attract sufficient alternative employments. The ease of access which the peripheral regions afforded to natural environments of high quality—the Brecon Beacons in South Wales and the Cheviots in North East England, for example—was too small a compensating factor. This is not to deny, of course, the importance of these natural amenities as assets likely to prove attractive to some types of entrepreneur in the long run.

In considering the complex of forces shaping inter-regional change over the last thirty years and more, it is important to acknowledge explicitly that the many advantages of southern England in general, and of the London and Birmingham city-regions in particular, have been and remain relative rather than absolute in nature. Nevertheless, they have been decisive in creating there a distinctive set of development characteristics which are shared in smaller measure with the country's other more prosperous regions, but which have been persistently elusive in the rest of the country. Since nothing breeds success like success, they would undoubtedly have been even more influential but for the intervention of public policies that sought to shift some of Britain's economic growth— but not, of course, the population—from southern England towards the less prosperous parts of the country. These policies were designed to bring about a 'proper' distribution of industry and a better 'balance' between regions—without exactly specifying the meaning of either 'proper' or 'better'. The next section of this chapter examines these policies.

2.3 Public Policy Responses

The nature and the magnitude of the difficulties experienced by the less prosperous regions has varied through space and altered with time. Their problems were, and remain, relative and not absolute. Some have argued that they exhibit nothing more than an acute case of a disease that afflicts the whole of the British economy (Chisholm, 1974). Moreover, it must be remembered that these are all regions of increasing population, despite their characteristic of net out-migration. In a very real sense, therefore, they are also areas of growth. Nevertheless, the difficulties of the less prosperous regions are real and they will undoubtedly persist well into the 1980s, despite several decades of government policies which have sought to ameliorate the problems of the coalfield industrial areas in particular.

Several major components can be recognized in the programmes of public assistance devised to assist the less prosperous regions directly. Underlying and supporting them have been a continuing series of macro-economic policies designed to ensure a relatively high level of aggregate demand in the economy as a whole. Any amelioration of the problems of the peripheral economies, therefore, undoubtedly owes a considerable debt to Keynesian economics and policy achievements. This might prove to have been only a temporary palliative for, even with a Keynesian stability superimposed upon an advanced economy, it could well be that in future the problem of structural unemployment will increase as a direct consequence of major changes in international trade and competition, accelerating technological change, and the institutional inflexibilities of an older industrial society. Macro-economic demand management, therefore, could well become relatively less important in reducing the problems of the less prosperous regional economies in the future than it has been in the past.

2.3.1 *Assistance to the Traditional Industries*

One important component of public policy towards regional problems has been the various measures designed to assist the traditional industries of the coalfields—the coal, steel, textile and shipbuilding industries especially—in order to slow down their rate of decline, or to restructure these traditional activities into a more appropriate contemporary form. Subsequent to its (post-war) production peak in 1955, the coal industry has been a major beneficiary of such policies. For example, various *ad hoc* measures have been employed to protect the markets for coal, particularly in the period up to the energy crisis if 1973 and the dramatic increase in world oil prices. These measures have included a tax on fuel oil, and periodic government pressures upon the Central Electricity Generating Board to burn coal rather than oil or natural gas. Following the publication of the 1967 White Paper on a national fuel policy (Minister of Power, 1967), considerable sums of public money were made available to the National Coal Board (N.C.B.) to allow it a dignified retreat from many of the country's energy markets. By writing off the Board's debts, by decelerating the rate of mine closures, by financing surplus stocks, by offering money to assist the movement of miners to the lower-cost mines and coalfields, and by providing special assistance to attract alternative employments onto the coalfields in the so-called Special Development Areas, the government cushioned the adverse social effects of employment decline. Simultaneously, public capital helped to reorganize the industry and to permit the concentration of its remaining production upon its most efficient units, especially the mines of the East Midlands and South Yorkshire. In the wake of the 1973 energy crisis, plans were made to expand the industry once again, to modernize some existing mines and to open up new coalfields such as that at Selby (p.315). Successive Acts of Parliament provided the necessary finance. But, in fact, additional production, and enlarged markets, proved to be unexpectedly elusive and by 1978 the industry was still

Table 2.3 England and Wales: housing conditions, by regions, 1967-1968 (estimated percentage of an area's housing stock)

Regions	Date of estimate	Dwellings statutorily unfit %	% Dwellings lacking exclusive use of: an internal w.c.	a fixed bath
TOTAL ENGLAND AND WALES	Feb. 1967	12	19	13
South East	Feb. 1967	6	11	9
Northern, Yorkshire & Humberside & North West	Feb. 1967	15	25	17
Rest of England & Wales	Feb. 1967	14	20	14
Conurbations				
English conurbations	Feb. 1967	11	18	14
West Midlands	Dec. 1967	10	23	12
South East Lancashire	Dec. 1967	15	28	18
Merseyside	June 1968	9	20	14
(Liverpool)	June 1968	(12)	(28)	(22)
Tyneside	June 1968	8	24	16

Source: Secretary of State for Economic Affairs (1969), p.29.

Table 2.4 Britain: estimates of derelict land, by regions, *circa* 1965

	Hectares	(Acres)	%
BRITAIN	34,041	(84,113)	100.0
More prosperous regions:	9,960	(24,726)	29.3
South East	1,527	(3,772)	4.5
East Anglia	694	(1,714)	2.0
West Midlands	4,032	(9,964)	11.8
East Midlands	2,172	(5,367)	6.4
South West	1,582	(3,909)	4.6
Less prosperous regions:	24,034	(59,387)	70.6
North West	3,961	(9,788)	11.6
Yorkshire & Humberside	2,926	(7,253)	8.7
Northern	6,100	(15,074)	17.9
Wales	5,371	(13,272)	15.7
Scotland	5,666	(14,000)	16.6

Source: Secretary of State for Economic Affairs (1969), p.29.

only producing 124 million tons of coal, some 6 million tons less than three years earlier (Manners, 1976a, 1978). Without continuing public support, the N.C.B. would undoubtedly have to espouse a quite different scale, mode and geography of operations— to the detriment of employment prospects in the less prosperous regions.

In the case of the steel industry, until 1967 largely in private ownership, the government again intervened to influence its investment programmes, the magnitude of its employments and its geography (Manners, 1971, pp. 95-98; Warren, 1970). After World War II, the government retained the right to supervise all the major investment decisions in the industry. This allowed public intervention in the actual siting of some works—for instance, the decision in the late 1940s to locate two major tinplate plants in Swansea and Llanelli rather than a single larger plant adjacent to the new integrated strip mill at Port Talbot—and in the regional allocation of major investments. In 1959, for example, the Cabinet insisted that the industry's new strip mill capacity should be shared between Llanwern in Wales and Ravenscraig in Scotland. Following the nationalization of the greater part of the industry in 1967, investments under the initial corporate plan of the new British Steel Corporation (B.S.C.) were broadly formulated in the light of the best economic and commercial evidence available. However, it was widely accepted that any attempt to establish integrated steel-making capacity on a large scale in southern England (locations on Thames-side and Southampton Water might have been considered) would have faced substantial political obstacles. It also quickly emerged that any attempt to rationalize the corporation's productive capacity through the closure of older plants was likely to meet strong political obstacles in areas of relatively high unemployment. The result was persistent delays in the implementation of plans to concentrate production on a limited number of high-volume sites (p.367ff.), the perpetuation of an historical and unsatisfactory geography of steel making, and an additional reason for the low (even negative) rate of return upon capital.

The cotton textile industry has also received substantial public assistance. Under a 1960 Act of Parliament, government money was made available to encourage the reorganization of the industry into fewer but individually larger units, in the expectation that it would then be better able to face the increasing severity of international competition. In the case of the shipbuilding industry, successive government measures — initially to help the industry in general to survive, subsequently to assist only where the industry was prepared to rationalize its structure, and most recently to bring the greater part of the industry into public ownership — were also fundamental to the industry's changing geography (p.369ff.).

No aggregate figure is available which quantifies the scale of public financial assistance over the last thirty years to the older staple industries that at one time flourished in the coalfields, that once dominated their economies, and that still remain major sources of especially male employment there. It is, moreover, impossible to estimate the size and the geography of these trades today had there not been substantial public intervention in their affairs. These uncertainties, however, must not blind us to the enormous cost and the outstanding significance of the assistance provided by the government to these industries in the overall strategy of regional development. It has preserved tens of thousands of jobs; it has modernized production facilities; and it has bought time for the less prosperous regions to adjust to new circumstances, even if it has not produced a final solution to the problems of some of their staple trades.

2.3.2 *Assisted Area Policies*

In addition to assisting directly their older industries, public money has also been used to diversify and restructure employment in the peripheral economies. It was as early as 1934, following the Special Areas (Development and Improvement) Act, that the British government embarked upon an enduring, though not always consistent, attempt to lessen the dependence of the less prosperous regions upon their older and declining industries, which had been the success stories of Victorian times. The policies of the 1930s created a number of non-profit-making industrial estates, and also financed the construction of standard factories by government agencies in advance of demand. These policies amounted to a set of primitive inducements designed to attract manufacturers away from the locations of their first choice in southern England. This was probably the most that could be achieved in the political climate of the time.

With the outbreak of World War II, however, the government was able quickly to acquire rather greater powers. In particular, it was able to direct industry away from southern England for strategic and defence purposes, and thus came to possess a much more powerful weapon for the manipulation of the country's industrial geography. The 'war' industries that arrived in South Wales, North East England, North West England and Scotland between 1939 and 1945—aluminium and aircraft production, ordnance and vital engineering activities, for example—were an important foundation stone for the subsequent diversification of those regional economies.

After 1945, the government sought a middle course. It rejected the geographical direction of industry. Instead, a stronger and more varied set of weapons were developed to influence the location of manufacturing enterprise. Under the Distribution of Industry Act of 1945, the Town and Country Planning Act of 1947 and the Local Employment Act of 1960, the government was given wide powers to attract industry to the peripheral economies. It extended the system of industrial estates; it built more factories ahead of demand; and it subsidized their rents. In addition, the government was able to offer grants and loans to industrialists locating or expanding in the less prosperous economies, and (later) made certain tax concessions to new enterprises there. The magnitude and nature of these inducements varied through time. By 1964, for example, they represented grants of 10 per cent on the cost of buildings and 25 per cent on the cost of machinery; in addition, the government allowed free depreciation, which meant that the whole of an industrial investment could be written off immediately against tax. They were substantially increased with the 1966 Industrial Development Act when the keystone of assistance to manufacturing industry in the less prosperous regions became a 40 per cent investment grant, which was 20 per cent higher than that available in southern England. In addition the government was prepared occasionally to give a 35 per cent grant for the purchase of land by a manufacturer. Construction grants of 25 per cent were also available and could be increased to 35 per cent if the firm was likely to employ a high proportion of male labour. Advance factories, made available at rents below those charged on the open market, were also constructed in greater numbers by the Industrial Estates Corporations of England, Scotland and Wales, and in the Special Development Areas they were made available rent-free for five years. Money was also set aside to assist the cash-flow of firms moving into the Assisted Areas. Criticism that this 'package' of government assistance was too heavily biased towards subsidizing the capital expenditure of firms in, or moving to, the less prosperous areas, whereas the regions concerned had more than anything else a problem of labour surplus, were met through the 1966 Selective Employment Payments Act. This gave all manufacturers in the peripheral economies a Regional Employment Premium (R.E.P.), a labour cost subsidy that was eventually valued in 1977 at £3 per week per man employed, and a rather smaller sum for other employees. In addition, special financial assistance was made available through the Department of Employment to train employees in skills required by new industries. This scheme was designed to supplement the labour retraining facilities provided in the government centres that were established under the 1964 Industrial Training Act. Yet two further items of public assistance to the less prosperous regions were the provision of housing for those 'key' workers who were required to transfer to the regions with their firms, and the marginal preference given by both government departments and the nationalized industries to firms located in Development Areas when contracts were being placed. As a consequence of all these measures, government expenditure designed to attract new manufacturing employments into the less prosperous regions rose from approximately £51 million in 1960/1961 to £270 million in 1970/1971 (Table 2.5).

It has been estimated that during the 1940s and 1950s the government spent approximately £1,000 per job directly created by its distribution of industry policies in the less prosperous regions, a figure which almost certainly was less than the alternative costs of unemployment benefits and public assistance that would otherwise have had to be paid. This figure, of course, does not take into account the costs of the large infrastructural investments in those regions which undoubtedly attracted investment and aided in their recovery. At the same time, however, it neglects the additional employment gains in those areas associated with the local and regional multiplier effects of the new industries. It could well be that £1,000 per job overestimates the costs of the policies at that time. As the level of public expenditure in the less prosperous regions rose in the late 1960s, however, the costs per job clearly rose in parallel. Estimates vary, but at one extreme was an observation that in the Northern Development Area public assistance at a large capital-intensive plant represented over £20,000 per additional job. Although this was clearly well above the average cost of creating employment in the peripheral regions, it raised serious questions about the cost-effectiveness of the government's programme.

Expenditure nevertheless continued to rise—although the precise nature of government incentives to industrial expansion in the older industrial areas was subject to fairly regular changes. Under the Finance Acts of 1970 and 1972, tax allowances on capital expenditure by manufacturing industry in the Development Areas were first reintroduced and then increased. The Industry Act of 1972 gave the Secretary of State for Industry new discretionary powers to vary the rates of grants and the qualifying activities. To advise on this selective financial assistance, an Industrial Development Advisory Board was established. The Act also created a national Industrial Development Executive—which included a special unit recruited from the civil service, the City of London and industry to assist with the appraisal, negotiation and monitoring of major projects in the Assisted Areas—plus six regional Industrial Development Boards in the less prosperous regions that were encouraged to adopt a more entrepreneurial style in the matter of regional development. This notion was carried a stage further in 1975 and 1976 when Scotland and Wales were given separately financed Industrial Development Agencies with the ability to take more aggressive development initiatives and, indeed, a central role in the restructuring of those regions. The 1975 Industry Act, in the meantime, had created the National Enterprise Board for the whole of Britain with wide powers to offer selective

Table 2.5 Britain: level of differential government expenditure on Assisted Areas, 1947-1971
(£ million)

	1947/1948	1954/1955	1960/1961	1965/1966	1970/1971
Recoverable or mainly recoverable aid					
Government factory building	12.5	4.5	21.0	12.4	7.9
Loans	0.3	1.7	23.5	9.6	28.0
Total recoverable aid	12.8	6.2	44.5	22.0	35.9
Non-recoverable aid					
Under Local Employment Acts:					
building grants	—	—	3.3	13.8	30.1
plant & machinery grants	—	—	—	6.1	0.2
other grants	—	—	2.7	0.5	4.0
Investment grants	—	—	—	—	90.0
Free depreciation	—	—	—	45.0	—
Regional Employment Premium	—	—	—	—	110.0
Regional development grants	—	—	—	—	—
Selective regional assistance (loans and grants)	—	—	—	—	—
Total non-recoverable aid	—	—	6.0	65.4	234.3
Grand total, all aid	12.8	6.2	50.5	87.4	270.2

Source: Keeble (1976), p.231.

financial aid to industry and a commitment to the objectives of regional development; the Act also introduced the notion of planning agreements between the Department of Industry and private companies under which an investment programme would be agreed and regional assistance guaranteed for a number of years.

The idea of selective intervention was not, of course, new. In addition to the general policies aimed at regional employment diversification, some industries were subject to more direct political pressures in their investment and locational decisions. One such industry was motor car manufacture, which in the period 1958-1960 was about to embark upon a major expansion programme. After lengthy negotiations with the then Board of Trade, often at very high levels of government, each of the major assembly firms was persuaded to put a significant part of its new capacity in the Development Areas—in return for which they were granted industrial development certificates (i.d.c.s.) for some expansion of their existing major facilities in the West Midlands and Greater London (p.224ff.). Again in 1966-69, the aluminium smelting industry for the first time indicated an interest in major British investments, and after a great deal of political manoeuvring agreement was reached to construct three relatively small plants in North Wales, North East England and Scotland; the public and private costs of these investments both in the long as well as the short term, were widely criticized (p.406ff.; Manners, 1968a).

Until 1973, financial incentives to expand the employment opportunities of the older industrial regions were largely confined to the manufacturing sector of the economy. Only gradually was it recognized that the service industries might play an important role in the

Table 2.6 Britain: summary of incentives for industry in the Assisted Areas, 1978

Sector	Incentive	
Manufacturing	Regional development grants for: (a) New machinery and plant 22% (b) Buildings and works 22% in Special Development Areas 20% / 20% in Development Areas Nil / 20% in Intermediate Areas	
	Selective assistance loans	On favourable terms for general capital purposes for projects which provide additional employment;* on non-preferential terms for other projects that maintain or safeguard employment if the finance required cannot reasonably be obtained from commercial sources.
	Interest relief grants*	As an alternative to loans on favourable terms, grants towards the interest costs of finance provided from non-public sources for projects which provide additional employment.
	Removal grants*	Grants of up to 80% of certain costs incurred in moving an undertaking into a Special Development or Intermediate Area.
	Government factories	Two-year rent-free period,* or for sale
	Tax allowances: (a) Machinery and plant	100% first-year allowance on capital expenditure incurred on machinery and plant (other than private passenger cars).
	(b) Industrial buildings	44% of the construction costs can be written off in the first year and subsequently 4% per year. Note: these tax allowances apply to the country as a whole.
	Finance from European Community funds	Loans may be available on favourable terms from the European Investment Bank (E.I.B.) and the Europen Coal and Steel Community (E.C.S.C.).
	Training assistance	Special courses.
	Help for transferred workers	Free fares, lodging allowances and help with removal expenses.
	Contracts preference schemes	Benefits from contracts placed by government departments and nationalized industries (not Intermediate Areas)

Sector		Incentive
Service	Service industry removal assistance	For offices, research and development units, and other service industry undertakings moving into the Assisted Areas, a fixed grant of £1,500 for each employee moving with his work, up to a 50% of jobs being created. A removal grant of up to 80% of the reasonable costs of removal of office equipment, etc., and the employer's net statutory redundancy payments at the old location, when an undertaking is moved from any part of Britain outside the Assisted Areas.
	Free offices	A grant to cover the whole of the approved rent of the premises for a period of up to seven years in locations in the Special Development Areas, up to five years in the Development Areas, and up to three years in the Intermediate Areas. Equivalent grants are given where premises are purchased or purpose-built.
	Employment grants	A grant of £1,500 in the Special Development Areas and £1,000 in the Development Areas for each job created in these areas.
	Selective assistance	Help towards capital expenditure other than on accommodation by way of loans at concessionary rates of interest, or interest relief grants towards the cost of finance raised by the employer.

Note: Incentives marked* are subject to the provision of sufficient additional employment to justify the assistance sought.

Source: Department of Industry.

solution of the problems of the less prosperous regions. For some years, of course, the government had been involved in transferring many of its own activities from central London (p.76ff.), and had steadily increased the number of civil service posts in the Assisted Areas. The hotel trade had been offered some assistance in the Development Areas, and the universities there were occasionally excluded from the general restraints imposed upon public expenditure that followed the country's periodic balance of payments crises. But it was only in 1973 that the service industries in general were brought formally into the policy of offering financial incentives to firms able and willing to move into the peripheral regions. Funds were made available to subsidize the costs of transferring office workers with their jobs into the Assisted Areas, and grants towards the costs of office accommodation there were made available; in the Development Areas, five years rent-free accommodation could be negotiated through the Department of Industry by the incoming firm.

All these changes—and the 1978 range of incentives available in the Assisted Areas is shown in Table 2.6—were reflected in the rising level of public expenditure on regional policy (Table 2.7). By 1975-1976 direct subventions to manufacturing and service industries for regional development purposes were costing the taxpayer some £584 million each year. They were complemented by policies pursued in the more prosperous parts of the country that sought to restrain major developments by means of industrial and office floorspace controls. The Departments of Industry and Environment were able to withhold industrial development certificates (i.d.c.s) and office development permits (o.d.p.s) from certain proposed developments in southern England (p.74ff.). By this means, 'push' as well as 'pull' elements characterized the inter-regional development programmes. By this means, also, a hidden and unquantifiable cost was added to regional policy, for there were not a few developments that were denied to the country altogether as a result of the unwillingness of investors to accept a location in the less prosperous regions.

The rationale underlying all these policies aimed at the diversification of the economic structure and the employment opportunities in northern England, Wales and Scotland had five principal components. First, it was recognised that within a mixed economy, government influence could be brought to bear most effectively upon the expanding and

Table 2.7 Britain: the cost of regional support and regeneration, 1970/1971 and 1975/76 (£ million at 1975 prices)

	1970/1971	1975/1976
Regional Development Grants	—	248.0
Provision of land and buildings	22.1	25.7
Selective Financial assistance to industry	—	76.0
Other regional support	6.6	11.6
Regional Employment Premium	212.4	215.0
Expenditure under Local Employment Act, 1972	53.0	− 4.9
Scottish & Welsh Development Agencies	—	12.7
Total	294.1	584.1

Source: Chancellor of the Exchequer (1976), pp.32, 33.

mobile (national or international) firm, responding to its need for additional floorspace or labour. Second, it was believed that the private costs of the industries steered into the less prosperous regions would, after a short initial settling-in period, be no higher than in southern England. Location theory suggested, and various empirical studies such as those conducted by Luttrell (1962), Tothill (Report of a Committee, 1961), and Cameron and Clark (1966) demonstrated, that a wide range of manufacturing enterprise was in this category and could generically be termed 'footloose'. Third, in so far as locational questions ranked relatively low in the investment considerations of many firms expanding within Britain (if they ranked at all), the possibility existed that some entrepreneurs might be encouraged by these policies to discover a location in the Assisted Areas which offered them a (private) cost advantage. Fourth, there was a significant social gain to be obtained from the policy for reasons already discussed, and yet it was possible to argue that the net cost of these policies to the public purse (when full account had been taken of savings in social security payments, the taxes paid by those employed through the policies, and the higher national levels of economic activity that the geographical diversion of resource demands to the north and west implied) could under certain assumptions be quite small (Moore and Rhodes, 1973). And, finally, the policies could be adapted and used in part to attract international investment to Britain.

With the Department of Industry (and before it the Board of Trade) considering each application for an i.d.c. 'on its merits', it was hoped that those expanding firms whose costs were relatively insensitive to different locations could be persuaded to acquire a site in an Assisted Area and take advantage of the incentives available; other firms with strong economic reasons for remaining in southern England could be, and were often, allowed to do so. Even by the late 1970s, however, research was not available to demonstrate just how much of manufacturing and service industry is relatively insensitive to locational costs, and what proportion could advantageously be steered by public policies away from metropolitan centres to the less prosperous regions and the new towns. The distribution of employment policy, as a result, had to proceed on the somewhat unsatisfactory assumption that there would be 'enough' mobile enterprise to achieve its objectives. As jobs in the manufacturing sector of the economy began to decline from the mid-1960s onwards, this assumption became increasingly untenable.

2.3.3 Variations Through Time

All these policies of regional 'protection' were subject to important historical and geographical variations. It is possible to identify several distinct phases during which the government's distribution of industry policies have been forcefully pursued. The years before 1939 were comparatively unimportant. Small inducements (in the north) without controls (in the south) brought only limited results. In any case the economy as a whole was not growing at a particularly fast rate, and there were only a few entrepreneurs who were looking for sites and whose locational decisions could in fact be influenced. The early war years, however, were quite different. The dispersal of strategic industries away from southern England was achieved speedily and on a considerable scale. This movement was to be of fundamental importance later, for with it the less prosperous regions acquired not only substantial investments in capital plant and a labour force with new skills; but they also gained the invaluable evidence that many manufacturing activities other than those of Victorian origin could be successfully pursued there.

Table 2.8 United Kingdom: employment resulting from principal movements of manufacturing industry, by regions, 1945-1965

('000s)

Origin	Destination				
	South East and East Anglia	West Midlands	Rest of England	Peripheral areas	United Kingdom
(A) Moves taking place in 1945-1951 (lower limit for inclusion: emp. of 8,000)					
Greater London	53	—	—	65	124
Rest of South East region	—	—	8	19	34
East Anglia	—	—	—	—	8
West Midlands conurbation	—	13	—	17	36
Rest of West Midlands	—	—	—	18	22
East Midlands	—	—	9	14	23
North West ex Merseyside	—	—	—	18	22
Yorkshire & Humberside	—	—	11	24	36
Abroad	—	—	—	41	45
All origins (inc. others not detailed above)	67	16	53	237	373
(B) Moves taking place in 1952-1959 (lower limit for inclusion: emp. of 6,000)					
Greater London	92	—	7	15	115
Rest of South East region	11	—	9	6	27
West Midlands conurbation	—	8	—	7	17
Rest of West Midlands	—	—	—	—	11
East Midlands	—	—	6	—	10
North West ex Merseyside	—	—	—	6	13
South West ex Devon & Cornwall	—	—	—	9	12
Yorkshire & Humberside	—	—	7	—	11
Abroad	12	—	10	18	41
All origins (inc. others not detailed above)	123	16	56	79	274

Immediately after 1945 there was a notable burst of government (Board of Trade) activity to steer industry into the peripheral economies. A high level of aggregate demand in the national economy, and a large number of firms wishing to reestablish themselves after the war, meant that factory space, industrial sites and permission to build new plants were all at a premium. The result was that the government was able easily to persuade industrialists to move away from southern England and the economies of the less prosperous regions were injected with much new life. By 1948, however, macro-economic policies demanded a reduction in the rate of capital investment in the economy, and the

Table 2.8 continued

Origin	Destination				
	South East and East Anglia	West Midlands	Rest of England	Peripheral areas	United Kingdom
(C) Moves taking place in 1960-1965 (lower limit for inclusion: emp. of 4,000)					
Greater London	49	—	5	35	89
Rest of South East region	7	—	4	26	37
West Midlands conurbation	—	4	—	15	24
Rest of West Midlands	—	—	—	8	13
East Midlands	—	—	—	—	6
North West ex Merseyside	—	—	—	5	8
Yorkshire & Humberside	—	—	—	5	8
Abroad	4	—	—	17	23
All origins (inc. others not detailed above)	65	6	30	122	223

Source: Howard (1968), p.19.

amount of new factory construction fell abruptly. At the same time, with a fairly high level of employment persisting throughout the country, the government began to show progressively less interest in the location of industry policies and devoted its energies to other things. This tendency continued into the late 1950s, by which time the use of the i.d.c. to influence the location of manufacturing industry had been all but abandoned. It was possible to build a factory almost anywhere in the country provided local planning permission could be obtained.

By 1960, therefore, any success which the government might have claimed for having helped to rehabilitate the peripheral economies owed much to three factors in particular. First, the country had a substantial amount of experience in matters concerning the relocation of industry dating back to the inter-war years, but more especially from the war years. Second, the Barlow and other government war-time reports ensured that a body of legislation was on the statute book and able to influence industrial location very shortly after 1945. Third, immediately after the war there was elected into office a government which firmly believed in exerting an influence over the distribution of employment.

After a lapse of a decade, however, industrial location policies were revived once again. With the 1958-1959 recession, the level of unemployment in the peripheral economies rose sharply. As a result the government instructed the Board of Trade to issue i.d.c. approvals in southern England with some reluctance once again, and to start building more factories in the less prosperous regions (either for lease to specific firms planning expansion there or ahead of actual demand). This policy was endorsed in 1963 with the White Papers on North East England and Central Scotland. It was yet further strengthened in the middle and late 1960s as unemployment levels rose nationally, as a further set of major structural adjustments were required of the British economy, as a new attempt at economic management was made through the short-lived Department of Economic Affairs, and as successive governments were persuaded of the desirability of maintaining and strengthening inter-regional policy.

The work of Howard (1968) indicates something of these historical variations in location policies (see Table 2.8). His evidence shows how the total volume of inter-regional industrial movement involved about 53,000 jobs per year in the period 1945-1951, 35,000 per year in the period 1952-1959 and 37,000 per year in the period 1960-1965. It further demonstrates how the less prosperous regions received some two-thirds of all manufacturing movement (in terms of employment) in the first period, but how during the following eight years the main flow of jobs was from Greater London to the rest of South East England. Between 1960 and 1965, however, the peripheral areas were once again the principal destination of firms on the move. Howard's research also underlines the regional importance of the Development Area policies by showing that nearly 30 per cent of all employment in manufacturing industry in Wales in 1965 was attributable to moves into the Principality during the previous twenty-one years; the corresponding proportion of the Northern region's jobs was about one-fifth, and of Scotland's one-eighth.

Following the oil crisis and the international recession of the middle of the 1970s, there were signs of changing governmental priorities once again. Under the Labour government, the R.E.P. was withdrawn in 1978 as part of a major and sustained programme of public expenditure economies. The magnitude of unemployment nationally—it rose to more than 1.6 million, over 6 per cent, in 1977—justified a variety of measures for its amelioration that were made available to the whole of the country. Amongst these was the Temporary Employment Subsidy, the job creation programme, and the Youth Employment Subsidy. The policy of the Department of Industry towards the withholding of i.d.c.s in southern England was substantially relaxed. Quite clearly, investment and job-creation anywhere in Britain came to be regarded at least as urgent as the objectives of regional policy, a view that was even more strongly held by the new Conservative government elected in 1979. As part of its programme to restrain the growth of public expenditure, the regional development grant in the Development Areas was reduced to 15 per cent, whilst that for buildings in the Intermediate Areas was abolished. (The 22 per cent grant in the Special Development Areas remained unchanged). Together with a more selective use of discretionary aid funds, and changes in the map of regional assistance (see below), it was hoped these changes would reduce regional incentives expenditure by more than one-third. In addition, the i.d.c. exemption limit was raised to 4,625 square metres (50,000 sq. ft.) throughout all the control areas, including the South East, to confirm a new preference for national rather than specifically regional investment. Given the macro-economic prospects before all older industrial economies, this shift of priorities could last well into the 1980s.

2.3.4 *The Changing Geography of Assistance*

Programmes to assist the less prosperous parts of the country have to be applied to clearly defined geographical areas. These too have changed with time. With the 1934 legislation, four 'Special Areas' were designated (see Figure 2.5). These were South Wales, North East England, Cumberland and Central Scotland. Their extent was determined by local levels of unemployment. Because the major towns there—Cardiff and Swansea in South Wales, Newcastle in North East England, etc.—recorded lower rates of unemployment than their hinterlands, however, these regional capitals were excluded from the benefits of the Special Areas legislation. After 1945, this geography of protection was changed. The Special Areas became 'Development Areas' (see Figure 2.5). More regions were included, such as Merseyside and the North Wales coalfield. The delimitation of these areas was again determined by their (inter-war and immediate post-war) record of unemployment, but by this date the problem was interpreted as regional rather than local in nature; hence the regional capitals were included in the areas made eligible for government help. By 1958, however, it was realized that other parts of the country were also suffering persistently from unemployment but, because they were outside the Development Areas, they were not eligible for public assistance. In response, the Distribution of Industry (Industrial Finance) Act was passed to make help available to any such areas through the Development Areas Treasury Advisory Committee (D.A.T.A.C.). Their problems tended to be either seasonal unemployment, or labour market responses to changes in agriculture and rural depopulation. The greater geographical and functional flexibility of this programme was initially seen to be so advantageous that in 1960 all the previous distribution of industry legislation was replaced by a new Local Employment Act. Under its provisions, any locality (that is, any Department of Employment labour exchange area) in which unemployment existed, or appeared likely to exist, became eligible for help as a Development District (see Figure 2.5). However, once the level of unemployment fell below about 4 per cent, the locality was expeditiously removed from the list of districts and assistance was withdrawn. The flexibility offered by this legislation certainly had administrative advantages. Soon, however, it was to create grave problems for the less prosperous regions. Government assistance became increasingly variable through time and space, and the problems of structural economic change came to be interpreted in a local, rather than in the more appropriate regional, context once again.

In handling the location of industry policy in the years immediately after 1945, the Board of Trade attempted to strike a geographical balance between the two possible extremes within the coalfield industrial economies. On the one hand, it could have sought to steer new jobs as near as possible to the sources of surplus labour there—that is to the colliery villages and the cotton mill towns—and to what were often amongst the least attractive localities from the viewpoint of a modern manufacturer. On the other hand, the Board could have insisted that the labour should move, either daily or permanently, towards new sources of employment sited at the best locations within the less prosperous regions. There are always some localities where the relative disadvantages of these regions are at a minimum—sites in or near the regional capitals, for example, tend to be particularly attractive. Yet invariably these were not the worst areas affected by unemployment and out-migration. The middle course steered by the Board of Trade was inherently quite flexible in its spatial emphasis. Where possible the Board encouraged the construction of factories, and the location of new industry, in places which for a modern manufacturing concern were certainly not the best within the peripheral economies; but they were by no means the worst locations, and they often committed the indigenous labour force to a certain amount of daily commuting. Thus, in South Wales, an emphasis was placed upon steering industry to the mouths of the coal mining valleys, rather than allowing all new industry to agglomerate in and around the relatively attractive Cardiff-Newport area, or forcing the newcomers to site themselves in the narrow, constricted and isolated valleys themselves (see p.357ff.). However, the 1960 Local Employment Act required the Board to provide assistance only to firms who were prepared to locate in (what were in effect) the least attractive parts of the less prosperous regions. These were localities which persistently had the highest rates of unemployment and were classified as Development Districts. Meanwhile, good industrial sites only a few kilometres away were ineligible for the government help that might have attracted firms and jobs there with relative ease. The inherent weaknesses of this approach were soon exposed. Its validity was quickly challenged in the press and in Parliament, and within three years it was virtually abandoned. From 1963, government attitudes towards spatial planning and the redevelopment of the peripheral economies, as a consequence, took on another new look.

At about this time, not only did inter-regional planning suddenly assume a new public respectability—it was given the blessing of the National Economic Development Council and the (then) Federation of British Industries; and the President of the Board of Trade assumed the additional title of Minister for Regional Development—but with the publication of White Papers on North East England and Central Scotland a new emphasis was given to the rehabilitation of the problem economies in the north and the west. The 1960 Act remained on the Statute Book. Funds continued to be available to assist the less attractive parts of the less prosperous regions. But the decision was taken to channel the greater part of the public effort and expenditure into the most attractive—and what were regarded as potentially the most economically and socially rewarding—places in the peripheral economies from the viewpoint of contemporary development. These were invariably adjacent to the larger and more accessible communities within the regions. They were the towns and cities which had access to the largest labour force and the widest range of labour skills. They were places which afforded the greatest opportunities to exploit the (limited) external economies and social amenities of these problem regions. In some instances new towns, such as Livingston near Edinburgh or Washington near Newcastle, were designated where it was judged a new urban environment would help to attract contemporary enterprise. 'Growth points' were defined in Central Scotland, and a 'growth zone' was delimited in North East England. In these areas funds were allocated to improve the infrastructure, to provide additional trading estates, to build new transport facilities, and to modernize the environment. By taking advantage of the best-endowed localities within the peripheral economies, government policies thus took on what many regarded as a more realistic and more forward-looking character. And it was clearly the intention of the government to extend this philosophy of planning to South Wales, North West England and other problem regions.

In 1964, however, there was a change of government. As a result, both the strategy and the style of regional planning in Britain was subjected to yet a further major reappraisal. The planning machine was reorganized once again. Whilst the Board of Trade retained its role in regard to the inter-regional distribution of industry, and the Ministry of Housing and Local Government remained responsible for the preparation of land use plans, the coordination of government action with reference to regional development passed into the hands of the newly created Department of Economic Affairs. For the first time Britain was divided into ten planning regions, with the intention that each would prepare studies and (subsequently) plans that would be integrated within a national plan. It was hoped that the new arrangements would permit a reconciliation of competing regional ambitions, and encourage much more coordination of policy in the regions between different government departments and between those departments and the local authorities than had been common in the past. Simultaneously, the government extended the areas eligible for assistance under the Local Employment Acts, especially in Wales and in North West England. It was significant, however, that only the relatively less attractive parts of these regions were included, and it became increasingly clear that the growth point philosophy of 1963 was meeting strong political opposition.

Under the subsequent 1966 Industrial Development Act, the Development Districts were in fact abandoned in favour of a new set of Development Areas. These were defined to include the whole of Scotland (except a small area around Edinburgh), the whole of the Northern region, Merseyside, the whole of Wales (except the north eastern and south eastern parts of the Principality), and a large area in the remoter part of South West England. A year later, and following the publication of the White Paper on fuel policy, additional assistance was made available to a number of Special Development Areas on the coalfields, where the problems of mine closures and unemployment were particularly acute. Later still, Millom was added, and then in the spring of 1971 much of West Central Scotland (including Glasgow), Tyneside and Wearside, Peterlee, Hartlepool and additional parts of South Wales were made Special Development Areas (Fig. 2.4). For these localities, there were normal Development Area aids plus a subsidy of 30 per cent on wage and salary costs during the first three years of a plant's operation and a rent-free period of five years in government factories. Nevertheless, the essential characteristic of Development Area policy from the mid-1960s became the extensive availability of assistance throughout the less prosperous regions. This approach was based upon the argument that, above all else, geographical flexibility was required within the regions for the administration of development policies. In particular, it permitted the relevant regional authorities to elect their own spatial priorities if they so desired. In the Northern region, for example, opinion generally continued to favour the concentration of new development in the growth zone of 1963, and more especially in its Tyneside and Teesside components—and the North East Development Council adopted a policy of welcoming new firms to the region regardless of their sub-regional preferences. In South Wales, on the other hand, the opportunities for development on Severnside were foregone in favour of a policy which continued to steer industrial development and employment opportunities to the west of Cardiff, and hence nearer to those communities experiencing high levels of local unemployment.

As the level of public assistance for the Development Areas rose during the years 1965 to 1967, another set of problems began to appear on the map. These were the difficulties that were being encountered by the so-called 'grey-areas'. Some of these areas were quite small in extent. Located adjacent to the existing Development Areas, they were clearly and painfully losing new investment and potential sources of employment to nearby communities which were able to offer considerable sums of public money and other incentives to development. The estuarine strip in the south east of South Wales was one case in point (see Chapter 12). Such places as Cardiff, Newport and Cwmbran began to experience considerable difficulties in their search for new industry largely because they were outside the Welsh Development Area, and could not match the substantial financial assistance that was available to manufacturers only a few kilometres away. Indeed, not a few firms in this estuarine zone elected to move into the Development Area in order to take advantage of the subsidies available there (p.357). More important, however, were the problems posed by those more extensive areas in the north of England such as the West Riding of Yorkshire or East Lancastria that were excluded from the Development Areas, and yet that for some time had experienced serious economic problems. Their difficulties were spelled out most fully by the Hunt Committee which reported in 1969 on what it called the Intermediate Areas. Hunt pointed to ten 'causes for concern' there (Secretary of State for Economic Affairs, 1969, pp. 10 ff.). These were the sluggish or falling levels of employment experienced in many parts of these regions; a slow growth in personal incomes; the slow appearance of new industrial enterprise; above average levels of unemployment; low or declining proportions of women at work; low average earnings per head by national standards; a heavy reliance upon industries whose demand for labour was growing slowly or even falling; relatively poor communications; a decayed or inadequate environment; and a substantial net outward migration of population. The Intermediate Areas, then, were those regions and localities in which unemployment was below a level that would justify their inclusion in a Development Area, yet whose recent experience of, and prospects for, growth were singularly gloomy. They exhibited many of the fundamental problems of the Development Areas, such as inappropriate labour skills for growth industries, relatively inconvenient access to the national market, and a largely Victorian and Edwardian legacy of a comparatively unattractive urban environment. They may have had within their factor endowments and economic structures a potential for recovery—perhaps more than the designated Development Areas—but this potential was more than offset by the local absence of government assistance, plus its availability elsewhere. Few disagreed with the contemporary observation that the 'distinction between black and grey Britain is too sharply drawn at present, and Development Area policy is much too blunt an instrument to ensure a rational and fair distribution of new industrial investment' (Rodgers, 1969, p.8).

Although its report was far from unanimous, the Hunt Committee advocated a measure of public assistance to the Intermediate Areas. It urged, however, that south east South Wales and the Plymouth area should be excluded from such benefits on the grounds that, provided appropriate transport and communication improvements were forthcoming, their inherent growth potential would in time overcome their existing difficulties. For the more extensive 'grey areas' in northern England, the committee proposed the introduction of government aid in the form of industrial building grants, financial assistance for industrial training and education, and a determined effort to improve the quality of the environment through the reclamation of derelict land. The committee also advocated that the Economic Planning Councils of the North West and of Yorkshire and Humberside should identify potential growth zones within their regions, and that priority should be given to the provision of any necessary new infrastructure for their accelerated development. In this, the committee leaned heavily upon the philosophy of the 1963 White Papers on North East England and Central Scotland.

On the same day in 1969 that the Hunt Committee's Report was released, the government announced its plans. Contrary to the advice of the committee and under the 1970 Local Employment Act, assistance was in fact offered to those problem localities bordering on the Development Areas in south east South Wales, the South West (Plymouth) and Scotland (Leith). The subsidies that were offered included factory building grants of 25 per cent, government-built factories financed on the same basis as in the Development Areas, and the full range of Development Area training grants and other training assistance for new industries. The same package of assistance was also offered to substantially larger zones outside the Development Areas in northern England (see Figure 2.4). However, the government refused to endorse the growth zone idea, and decided to allocate its assistance geographically by criteria of 'need'—defined by the character and level of local unemployment and the rate of outward migration—rather than any criterion of 'opportunity'. Thus, the Yorkshire coalfield, the Erewash valley of Derbyshire, parts of Humberside and the main industrial areas of North East Lancashire (to the east of the proposed new city of Leyland-Chorely were made eligible for assistance. Later, with the Industry Act of 1972, the whole of Yorkshire and Humberside and the North West region (outside Merseyside), plus North East Wales, were given Intermediate Area status, with a 20 per cent development grant for buildings and works there (Figure 2.5). In 1974, Merseyside and parts of North East Wales were made Special Development Areas; Cardiff and Edinburgh were given Development Area status; and Intermediate Area assistance was extended to Chesterfield in the East Midlands and Oswestry in the West Midlands. Further adjustments, such as the granting of Development Area status to parts of Humberside, came in 1976 and 1977 to produce the 1978 map of the Assisted Areas (Figure 2.6).

By 1978, some 45 per cent of the country's population resided within the Assisted Areas. And voices in some of the non-Assisted Areas, such as the West Midlands suffering from an historically uncharacteristic bout of high unemployment, were calling for their inclusion too. It was not surprising, therefore, that many observers of inter-regional planning should feel a growing disquiet about the geography of assistance. Still elusive was a formula which would appropriately combine a due recognition of development opportunities with a realistic specification of social need; which would serve equally well for both the service industries—especially offices—and manufacturing enterprise; which would be readily understood by businessmen making locational decisions but not so extensive as to reduce its policy impact; and which would be politically acceptable.

With reductions in public expenditure their principal aim, the new Conservative government in 1979 grasped the nettle and rolled back the areas of assistance to cover around 25 per cent of the employed population. The three-tier structure of assistance was retained (Figure 2.7). But the relevance of the new map to the geography of opportunity remained unclear. Once again, local levels of unemployment provided the delimiting criterion.

2.3.5 *Public Policy Responses: Further Components*

A review of the public policy responses to the dilemmas of the less prosperous regions would not be complete without a recognition of several other components in the government's strategy. The first concerns the *retraining of labour,* on which very little public money was spent for many years—except perhaps through the N.C.B. whose schemes tended to benefit other industries in the Development Areas as much as the coal industry itself, since many of the board's electricians, fitters and the like moved out of mining once they had acquired a marketable skill. Since the early 1960s, however, a growing volume of resources has been spent on facilities for the retraining of labour. The impact of the 1964 Industrial Training Act was outstanding in this respect, as to a lesser extent was the Coal Industry Act of 1967 which made special provisions for the retraining

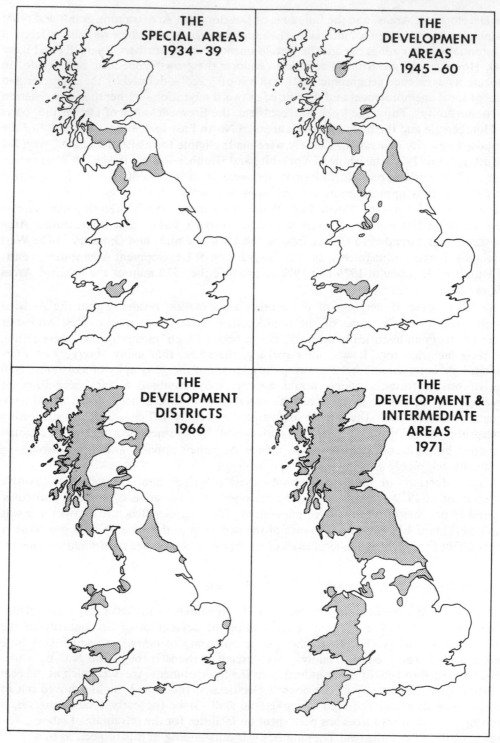

Figure 2.5 Britain: the changing geography of regional assistance, 1934-1971

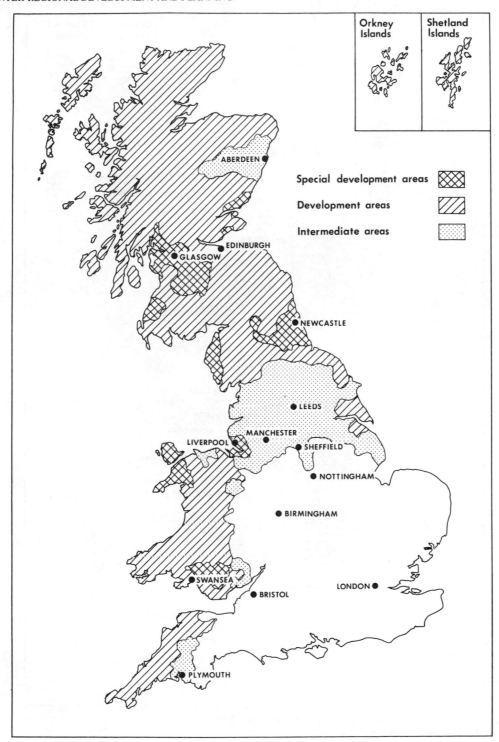

Figure 2.6 Britain: the Assisted Areas, 1978
Source: Department of Industry

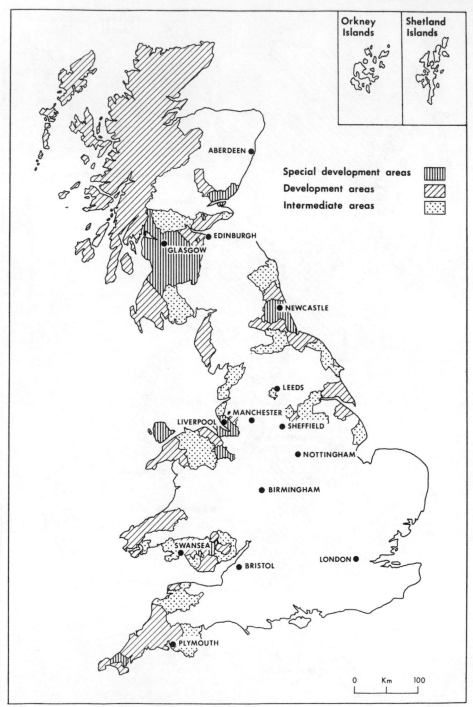

Figure 2.7 Britain: the Assisted Areas, late 1979*
Source: Department of Industry

*Note: this geography of assistance will be phased in over a three year period up
to 1982, and is subject to changes in detail.

of redundant miners. In addition, under the Employment and Training Act of 1973, the responsibility for running the necessary services was handed over to the Manpower Services Commission (M.S.C.). The national programme of labour training and retraining—both in industry and at government Skill Centres—was reorganized and steadily expanded. It took particular note of the needs of the Assisted Areas, as did some of the special job-creation programmes of the mid-1970s which sought to provide short-term employment in labour-intensive projects of social value in areas of high unemployment.

Another component of public policy towards the Assisted Areas was the expenditure of funds to improve their *infrastructure*, and especially their roads. Throughout the post-war period, the necessity of such investments was widely recognized, but it was judged to be of particular importance in the early 1960s when the White Papers on Central Scotland and North East England committed the government to substantial investments in roads, airport facilities, new towns and the like in those regions. The relative importance of such infrastructural investments as compared with measures to subsidize the capital costs or labour expenses of firms in the less prosperous regions remains a matter of dispute (Secretary of State for Economic Affairs, 1969, p.155ff.). But there was little doubt by the mid-1970s that the economic performance and future prospects of the Assisted Areas rested considerably upon the new and under-utilized investments in infrastructure that had been made there. Of equal importance, of course, were the much improved inter-regional communication facilities—the national motorway network and dramatically improved trunk road system (Figure 1.2), the inter-city passenger services and the freight-liner facilities of British Rail, the expanded telecommunication services of the Post Office, and (in a few instances) the improved facilities for internal air transport.

Yet another feature of inter-regional policy was the effort made, especially from the mid-1960s onwards, to improve the *amenities and the built environment* of the less prosperous regions. To this end, the redevelopment, refurbishment and cleaning of provincial city centres, the increased activities of the regional arts associations, and the clearing and planting of derelict land, for example, all served to enhance the attractions of these regions from a developmental point of view. The New Towns Acts of 1946 and 1965 were also used to considerable effect in this context. Fourteen new communities were designated in the Assisted Areas—Runcorn, Skelmersdale, Warrington, the Central Lancashire New Town in the North West; Peterlee, Aycliffe and Washington in the North East; Newtown and Cwmbran in Wales; and Glenrothes, East Kilbride, Cumbernauld, Irvine and Livingston in Central Scotland. Offering a new urban infrastructure as well as an alternative urban environment in the Assisted Areas, these towns have played a notable role in the attraction of footloose manufacturing investments into regions of high unemployment (Table 3.4).

Within the more prosperous, as well as the less prosperous, regions of Britain there are extensive *rural areas*. As a consequence both of improving communications and of higher living standards, the country's increasingly mobile population has placed many of them under growing development and especially recreational pressures. Simultaneously, the changing structure and characteristics of agriculture, with its burgeoning inputs of capital and its declining job opportunities, have posed major problems for large areas of the countryside. In the South West, East Anglia, mid-Wales, the Cheviots, and in large tracts of northern Scotland, the story is the same: the declining manpower requirements of agriculture have generated a steady rural depopulation. Especially in the more remote parts where an offsetting countermovement of middle-class commuters is not to be found, this has posed considerable problems for those running public and social services. In particular, the provision of public transport, hospitals, utilities and education is increasingly expensive by comparison with costs in the more urbanized parts of the country. A further element in inter-regional policy, therefore, has followed from the general acceptance of a need to subsidize these and other rural services, and embraces specific policies that have sought to ameliorate the problems of such rural areas. These have had two aims. First, they have sought to assist the spatial concentration of many services and amenities in fewer villages and towns, to make their provision more economic. Second, they have attempted to create alternative sources of non-agricultural employment. The Mid-Wales Industrial Development Association, for example, has encouraged many lighter manufacturing industries to move into the towns of mid-Wales and so to provide a wider economic base for the population there. Of more general importance is the work supported by the Development Commissioners, appointed originally under the Development and Road Improvement Fund Acts of 1909 and 1910, who have sponsored the practical role of C.O.S.I.R.A. (the Council for Small Industries in Rural Areas), and liaised with the Industrial Estates Corporations of England, Scotland and Wales which have powers to build factories in rural areas. Deliberate attempts have also been made to widen and encourage the recreational role of many rural communities and to make further provision for tourism. Both national bodies, such as the Countryside Commission, and local associations have played an important role in these matters.

One final, and largely abortive, element in inter-regional policy stemmed from a set of planning studies conducted within the Ministry of Housing and Local Government in the middle of the 1960s at a time when the projections of the Registrar General indicated that the population of Britain would increase by some 20 million people by the year 2000. In response to this somewhat alarming prospect, the government set up an interdepartmental special committee, the Central Unit for Environmental Planning, to investigate the land use and regional planning implications of such an eventuality. Out of their deliberations came a decision to examine the possibility of creating several large, new urban complexes in parts of the country that were relatively lacking in development, but that appeared at first sight to be capable of supporting a major expansion of population. The three areas that came under government scrutiny were Humberside, Severnside and Tayside, and economic, land use and traffic studies were initiated in relation to their development potential. The Humberside study was published in 1969. Demonstrating the existing and potential attractions of that section of eastern England, it predictably indicated the feasibility of large-scale urban development there provided the appropriate infrastructural investments were made. Although the government was not immediately willing to commit itself totally to these investments, it did decide to construct a new road bridge across the river Humber, plus several associated motorways, one of the keystones in any large-scale development of the sub-region (see Chapter 10). The Severnside and Tayside studies were subsequently published (see Chapters 12 and 14), indicating the broad possibility of substantial urban growth there, the alternative sites available and the investment that would be required. By the time these studies were made public, however, some of the urgency of such new estuarine developments had been dissipated by the downward revision of the Registrar General's population forecasts, and with the emergence of national economic circumstances in which the possibility of committing the large sums of infrastructure capital needed for such schemes became increasingly remote. The *growth estuary studies* nevetheless remain an interesting example of inter-regional planning responding to the criteria of opportunity, rather than the more common yardsticks of need.

2.4 Membership of the European Economic Community

Following Britain's accession to the Treaty of Rome in 1973, a new set of influences began to shape the style and the nature of inter-regional policy. Membership of the European Economic Community clearly began to mould the political and economic environment within which British industry and commerce increasingly came to operate, and regional policy had to respond. The Community, moreover, began to impose certain constraints upon the types of instruments and policies that could be used to serve inter-regional policy objectives. At the same time a cluster of Common Market initiatives, aimed at ameliorating the problems of the less prosperous parts of the Community, were made available to the Assisted Areas of Britain.

Membership of the Community, *inter alia,* meant that the British economy was more formally seen as part of a larger Western European whole. This was by no means a new situation, for the previous quarter-century had seen British trade increasingly oriented towards Western Europe and away from the Commonwealth. However, the political affirmation of the accession both represented an endorsement of an historical trend and presaged an acceleration of commercial exchange across the North Sea and Channel. In consequence, international and inter-regional competition with other countries and regions of the Community began to increase as the barriers to trade were lowered—and but for the oil crisis and the world recession, the effects of this trend might have been more noticeable by the late 1970s. A particularly important implication of Community membership was the fact that increasingly industrial and commercial investment in Britain, to be fully justified, needed to afford the prospect of a better, or at least a comparable, rate of return compared with investment in other parts of the Community. With timing an important element in investment decisions, planning procedures thus had to recognize the costs of administrative delays and, compared with the past, to become less bureaucratic, in style and effect. In addition, to the extent that some investments in manufacturing plant or administrative offices were designed to serve either the whole of the Common Market or substantial parts of it, the locational advantages of southern and eastern England with their easy market access were enhanced to a significant, albeit unquantifiable, degree (Figure 2.3). Ease of access to sea and air transport facilities with good European connections, in other words, took on a new importance. The meaning of British geographical space was in consequence modified.

'Entry in Europe' also began to change attitudes towards the meaning of relative prosperity. Whereas the South East of England, as has been noted, for long has stood as the wealthiest region in Britain, set in an E.E.C. context it ranked only seventeenth in income per head in 1970, with a Gross Domestic Product per capita only 40 per cent of the richest E.E.C. region (Table 2.9). Such comparisons raise all manner of questions about the validity of the exchange rate conversions, about the role of different regions in the various national economies of Western Europe, and about the implications to be drawn for inter-regional policies. Nevertheless, the low rankings of all the British regions, and the relatively poor status of its most successful, at the very least challenge traditional notions about the ways to restrain development in southern England — and raise some doubts about the wisdom of restraint at all.

Table 2.9 European Economic Community: regional indices, *circa* 1970

Rank	Region	G.D.P. per capita £ 1970	Rank	Region	G.D.P. per capita £ 1970
1	Hamburg	2278	26	Mediteranee	772
2	Bremen	1681	27	Est-France	771
3	Brussels	1399	28	Paris Basin	763
4	West Berlin	1380	29 {	Emilia Romagna	757
5	Hessen	1357		Nord-France	757
6	Nordrhein-Westfallen	1325	31	*East Midlands*	746
7	Baden-Wurtemburg	1275	32	*East Anglia*	743
8	Brabant	1217	33	*North West*	731
9	Bayern	1193	34	*Yorkshire & Humberside*	729
10	Paris Region	1147	35	Sud-Ouest	726
11	Rheinland-Pfalz	1114	36	*South West*	723
12	Saarland	1102	37	*Scotland*	705
13	Niedersachsen	1090	38	Ouest-France	695
14	Schleswig-Holstein	1058	39	Lazio	681
15	West Holland	984	40	*Wales*	666
16	Flemish Region	918	41	*North*	656
17	*South East*	894	42	Nord Est	639
18	Lombardia	866	43	Centro	620
19	South Holland	860	44	Northern Ireland	531
20	Wallon Region	850	45	Sardinia	476
21	Nord Ouest	831	46	Sicily	440
22	Oost Holland	825	47	Azruzzi-Molise	434
23	West Midlands	807	48	Campania	427
24 {	Centre Est	804	49	Sud-Italy	401
	Noord Holland	804			

Membership of the E.E.C. imposes a number of constraints upon the actions of member governments in the implementation of their regional policies, and Britain is no exception. The goal of the Community is to create a market within which there exists an equality of competition between all productive enterprise, whatever its national or regional location. Under the Treaty of Rome, in consequence, the Commission has the power to examine all state aids to industry, and to rule whether or not they are likely to distort competition. The Commission have published guidelines for national governments concerning the nature and the level of incentives, and in particular they have set upper limits to state aids for the purposes of encouraging or relocating private investment. The aids must be no more than 20 per cent of the cost of an investment in the Community's central areas (such as the South East, or the Paris basin), no more than 25 per cent in the 'semi-central' areas (mainly Denmark), and no more than 30 per cent in the peripheral regions (including the British Assisted Areas). The Commission has also imposed a freeze on the level of aids currently available in the very poorest regions of the E.E.C. (such as the Highlands and Islands of Scotland). In addition, the Commission has insisted that all state aids should be clearly measurable in order that international comparisons might readily be made, and to prevent member states from overbidding against each other for

Table 2.9 continued

Rank	Region	Growth in G.D.P. per capita £ 1966-1970		Rank	Region	Growth in G.D.P. per capita £ 1966-1970
1	Sardinia	53		26 {	Est-France	34
2	Abruzzi-Molise	51			Centre-Est	34
3	Sicily	50			Mediteranee	33
4	West Berlin	45		28 {	Nord-France	33
5 {	Hamburg	44			Rheinland-Pfalz	33
	Nord Est	44		31 {	Niedersachsen	32
7	Nord Ouest	43			Brabant	32
	Bremen	42		33 {	*Scotland*	31
	Emilia Romagna	42			Brussels	31
8	Centro	42		35	Baden-Wurtemburg	
	Sud-Italy	42			*Wales*	29
12	Lombardia	41		36	*South East*	29
	Lazio	40			North	29
13	Saarland	40			Wallon Region	29
	Northern Ireland	40		40 {	*South West*	28
	Hessen	40			*East Anglia*	28
17 {	Campania	39		42	*North West*	26
	Schleswig-Holstein	39		43 {	Yorkshire & Humberside	25
19	Nordrhein-Westfallen	37			*East Midlands*	25
20	Sud-Ouest	36		45	*West Midlands*	23
	Paris	35				
	Paris Basin	35				
21	Ouest	35				
	Bayern	35				
	Flemish Region	35				

Table continued next page

footloose international investments. The Commission is trying, in other words, to make sure that similar regions with similar problems get similar assistance, and espouses the hope that regional aids will be used to create new and profitable industry, and not to prop up enterprises of an old, inefficient and outdated kind. As part of this strategy, the Commission seeks to deny any regional measures that smack of permanent subsidies to industry in the assisted regions. For this reason it was critical of the Regional Employment Premium; and undoubtedly one of the reasons for the removal of that aid in 1978 from the package of British regional incentives was the opposition to it that had been voiced by the Commission in Brussels.

The European Commission assists, as well as constrains, regional development policies, and Britain's Assisted Areas are eligible for a variety of financial aids administered from Brussels. The oldest instrument is the European Investment Bank, which will lend up to 40 per cent of the fixed capital costs of projects that can be shown to be generally advantageous for the development of a less prosperous region; the bank also lends funds for the modernization of undertakings, or for the development of fresh economic activities, that are necessitated by the progressive establishment of the Common Market. The interest rates of E.I.B. loans are commercially attractive—for industrial projects the

Table 2.9 continued

Rank	Region	Average unemployment 1970-1973 %	Rank	Region	Average unemployment 1970-1973 %
1	Baden-Wurtemburg	0.6	25	*East Anglia*	2.7
2	Hamburg	0.8	26	Sud-Ouest	2.8
3	Est-France	1.0	27	Oost-Holland	3.1
4	Hessen	1.1		*South West*	3.3
5 {	Nordrhein-Westfallen	1.3	28 {	*Yorkshire & Humberside*	3.3
	West Berlin	1.3		Nord-Est	3.3
7 {	Rheinland-Pfalz	1.6		*North West*	3.5
	Paris Basin	1.6		Emilia Romagna	3.5
9 {	Bremen	1.7	31 {	Centro	3.5
	Centre-Est	1.7		Zuid Holland	3.5
	Bayern	1.8		Flemish Region	3.5
11 {	Saarland	1.8	36	Lazio	4.1
	South East	1.8	37	Mediteranee	4.2
14 {	Niedersachsen	1.9	38	*Wales*	4.3
	Lombardia	1.9	39	*Scotland*	5.1
16 {	Schleswig-Holstein	2.0	40	*North*	5.2
	West Holland	2.0	41	Wallon Region	5.8
18 {	Paris Region	2.1	42	North Holland	5.9
	Nord Ouest	2.1	43	Abruzzi-Molise	6.4
20	Nord-France	2.3	44	Northern Ireland	7.2
21 {	Ouest-France	2.5	45	Sardinia	7.9
	Brabant	2.5	46	Sud-Italy	9.4
23 {	*West Midlands*	2.6	47	Sicily	10.4
	East Midlands	2.6	48	Campania	10.8

loans extend for seven to twelve years— but they are usually made available only for large projects of not less than £¼ million. In 1977 the E.I.B. lent £940 million which, it is claimed, helped in the creation of 20,000 permanent jobs and 100,000 temporary construction jobs lasting between two and six years. The European Council of Ministers in 1978 agreed to increase the size of the bank's capital assets; together with other E.E.C. loan facilities, therefore, investment funds available for regional development will shortly be running at between £2 billion and £2.5 billion each year.

In addition to the E.I.B., development loans are available in the E.E.C.'s less prosperous regions from the funds of the European Coal and Steel Community. The latter provides soft loans for investment projects in the coal and steel sectors of the Community's economy, particularly where there is a prospect of minimizing redundancies or, through improvements in productivity, strengthening the competitive stance of European producers. The E.C.S.C. is also in a position to finance projects outside these sectors where there is a reasonable probability that a proportion of the new jobs so created would be available to redundant coal miners or steel workers. The social fund of the E.C.S.C. in addition provides money for the resettlement and retraining of workers leaving those two industries as a result of plant closures and rationalization.

A further, and prospectively more important, instrument in E.E.C. regional policy is the Regional Fund. Now running at £410 million each year, it is designed to support projects in the less prosperous regions of the Community in the context of coherent regional development programmes. It is allocated substantially on a quota basis, with Britain currently qualifying for 28 per cent of the total. In the period 1975-1977, some 1,450 projects in Britain were approved by the fund; these represented 44 per cent of the total number approved in that period. Although the fund is available for funding infrastructural investments in the Community, the preference of the Commission is for the attraction of labour-intensive growth industries to the less prosperous regions; and the use of the fund differs from that of the E.I.B. to the extent that it is accepted that short-term subsidies may be necessary in order to achieve certain regional development objectives. Although in the British case funds from the Community currently play a relatively small part in the inter-regional planning effort, the role and the magnitude of both the bank and the Fund seem likely to increase, particularly if progress is made towards the stabilization of European currencies and in time the establishment of a common currency.

2.5 Changing Circumstances

Before evaluating public policies towards the problems posed by inter-regional imbalance, it is important to recognize that the context in which they have been pursued has been subject to significant and persistent changes. It is possible that the forces generating these changes have been more influential in reshaping the inter-regional geography of Britain than has public policy itself. Some of them have been touched upon already; others require brief specification. Some have worked in the same direction as public policy; others have worked against it.

Of the changing circumstances that have undoubtedly assisted regional policy, none has been more important than the reevaluation of the meaning of distance and space during the past thirty years. The coming of the motorways — leading to the full exploitation of the potentialities of road transport, plus the consequent reduction in the real costs of travel and haulage — together with the relentless advance in the efficiency of rail and air transport and telecommunications, have caused a substantial shift in the attitudes of the population in general and the management of industry in particular towards the different parts, the geography, of Britain. Plymouth and Preston, Swansea and Sunderland, Grimsby and Glasgow, for example, are no longer perceived to be distant from the largest urban centres of the South East and the Midlands. Their chances of attracting productive investment, in consequence, have been significantly increased. By the same token, London and Birmingham are no longer seen in spatial terms as *the* outstanding centres of manufacturing and service enterprise. Their relative attractiveness to footloose activities, therefore, has been substantially reduced. Moreover, with transport advances a permissive rather than a dynamic element in regional development, these improvements in communications and the erosion of the effective distance between the Assisted Areas and southern England have made it much easier for government to steer industry and employment into the former in order to serve the perceived public interest. Given the existence of a national distribution of employment policy, transport improvements must be regarded as one of the principal catalysts in any revival of the less prosperous regional economies.

A second and related element in the changing environment of spatial planning, and one that has also assisted policy, is the shifting preferences and attitudes of entrepreneurs towards different locations. As will be seen in Chapter 3, the geography of both manufacturing and service industries during the last thirty years has been subject to a powerful set of centrifugal market forces that have encouraged the outward movement of employment within and from the major conurbations. Quite independent of government policies, therefore, these forces have encouraged firms in the manufacturing sector of the economy especially to forego the close physical linkages with other firms in the conurbations which previously they had valued highly, and to accept a pattern of material and information exchanges over a much larger geographical area. Although in the case of office activities there has been a time lag of perhaps fifteen to twenty years in these matters, the same tendencies towards dispersal—particularly the dispersal of the more routine forms of office work—cannot be escaped. Given such a spatial tendency, it has been that much easier for government policies to influence the scale and the distance of dispersal in order to serve the objectives of regional policy.

Moreover, the growth of larger firms, and the increasing importance of national and international corporations—a third force in the changing environment of spatial policy —have endorsed this situation. Such larger firms tend to internalize activities which in the case of smaller enterprises are external to the firm—transport services and component manufacture, accountancy and market research, for example—and as a consequence they have a greater degree of geographical flexibility. Much evidence exists to support the 'dual population hypothesis' of Keeble (1976, p. 135), which describes the tendency of smaller firms to move their plant and activities over relatively short distances within a metropolitan region, in contrast to larger firms that have had a tendency to migrate over longer distances, more especially to move from southern England to the less prosperous regions. Such a contrast in the migration behaviour of firms simply reflects the differential abilities of the large and small organizations to manage their affairs over different geographical scales. The growing importance of the larger firm in the total population of British enterprise has in consequence assisted the cause of regional policy.

New natural resource considerations have further altered the balance of geographical advantage in favour of the Assisted Areas. Apart from the fact that, because of their natural harbours, the less prosperous regions have come to have a substantial share of the country's oil-refining capacity (at Swansea, Milford Haven, Stanlow, Grangemouth, Teesside and Humberside), the discovery of major hydrocarbon reserves under the North Sea has been of enormous inter-regional significance. The exploitation of, first, natural gas in the relatively shallow waters off the costs of East Anglia and Lincolnshire, and, subsequently, the major oil province off the east coast of Scotland, has had outstanding implications for the British economy as a whole. Not least has been the medium-term transformation of the country's balance of payments circumstances and outlook, and the removal of a major historical constraint upon the growth of the national economy. More directly within Scotland, as is discussed in Chapter 14, the discovery and production of oil has generated substantial local and regional benefits in the form of employment and wealth, both within the oil industry itself and in many associated manufacturing and service activities. There can be little doubt that the relative improvement in the unemployment rates of Scotland by comparison with those of, say, the Northern region or the North West is in considerable measure a result of the exploitation of off-shore oil.

At the same time as these changes in the environment of regional policy have helped to reduce spatial imbalance, there have been other developments that have worked in the opposite direction. As noted earlier, one of these has been the growing importance of the

Western European market for British manufacturing and service activities, and the advantages afforded by locations within easy reach of appropriate communication links —the short-distance sea ports, and the largest international airports at Heathrow and Gatwick. Few would doubt that British membership of the European Economic Community has served to the particular advantage of the South East region and East Anglia; and, although hard evidence is elusive, inter-regional policy has been faced with an increased challenge as a result of the new political context of the British economy.

Another change that has constrained the recent effectiveness of regional policies has been the low level of national growth since the energy crisis of 1973. With the national and international recession, the number of firms in both manufacturing and service industry that have sought to expand or even reinvest has contracted severely. Since it is expanding firms that are the most mobile, the greater part of the middle and late 1970s have witnessed low levels of industrial movement by comparison with the levels attained in the previous decade. For the same reasons, had the British economy in the post-war years in general achieved levels of growth equivalent to those of its continental neighbours, then the regional issue might have been more persuasively tackled. The prospects of the less prosperous regions in the 1980s will be substantially influenced by the macro-economic performance of the national economy.

Quite apart from the effects of the global recession, a further challenge presented to inter-regional policy has been the marked tendency for the number of jobs in the manufacturing sector of the economy to decline after the mid-1960s. Since it was the growth in manufacturing jobs which provided the springboard for regional policy in the preceding twenty years, a substantial component in the apparatus for shaping regional development appears to be decreasingly cost-effective. There exist, of course, government policies that seek to support and strengthen the manufacturing sector of the British economy—the so-called Industrial Strategy was launched in 1975 with this objective in view—but there are legitimate doubts as to whether these efforts will do more than restrain the decline in manufacturing employment, given the productivity gains that might be grasped in most manufacturing sectors of the economy. In consequence, inter-regional policy has come to rely increasingly upon shifting the geography of service, and especially office, activities. Yet this is an area, as has been noted, in which policy formulation and experience is relatively limited.

A final new factor in the environment of inter-regional development—and one which has, if anything, made government's policy objectives more elusive—has been the growing importance of residential space preferences in the location decisions of manufacturing enterprise. This change reflects the growing desire and ability of entrepreneurs increasingly to locate their activities in places that afford them, their families, and their employees the fullest possible range of perceived personal benefits. Increasing affluence, shorter working hours and increased leisure time have together placed a considerable premium upon appealing urban and suburban environments, attractive local scenery, recreation amentities and the like. The coastal location, the historic town, and a range of psychological and social factors have thus entered more fully into the locational debate. In his major investigation of the changing patterns of manufacturing activity, Keeble (1976, pp. 114) was able to demonstrate for the first time the considerable importance of residential environments and general sub-regional 'images' in locational choice. Whilst such a development undoubtedly encouraged the dispersal of employment away from the large conurbations, it simultaneously did relatively little to help the less prosperous regions, particularly those with a substantial legacy of Victorian housing and all the environmental attributes of older coal mining and heavy industrial enterprise. The growing importance of the service sector in the economy further underlines this point. It is not without significance that the first long-distance moves of major office employers from London were to such Baedeker cities as Norwich, Exeter and Cheltenham, rather than older industrial centres at no greater distance from London and perhaps with a better long-term supply of appropriate labour.

It was in this shifting context of counteracting geographical forces that regional policy was pursued and developed. The next section evaluates its effects.

2.6 An Evaluation of Public Policies

The sum of all the policies aimed at ameliorating the problems of the less prosperous regions eludes total quantification. Demonstrably, their higher than average levels of structural unemployment remain, net out-migration continues, a considerable reliance upon the country's declining industries persists, and a political reluctance to forego further assistance is all too obvious. Since it is impossible to judge what would have happened in these areas without government assistance, however, it is equally impossible to spell out with clarity the full implications and achievements of public intervention in their development.

The persistence of the problems of the less prosperous regions might initially be interpreted as a measure of policy failure. Certainly, the fact cannot be escaped that in a number of important respects government policies in the less prosperous regions—policies that were frequently designed primarily to cure the principal symptom of their economic distress, unemployment—left some of the fundamental causes of their long-standing problems relatively untouched. (This is not to imply that the difficulties could necessarily have been completely overcome with alternative policies.) In regard to the problem of labour quality in the Assisted Areas, for example, whilst government initiatives have increased the variety and the size of the skilled labour force available to incoming industry and employers, and considerably improved the quality of the training and educational facilities available there, the reality remains that the range of skills in none of these areas can compare with that available to businessmen in (say) the East or West Midlands; their relative disadvantage consequently persists. Again, in regard to the problems posed by the relative absence of enterprise and entrepreneurial capital in the Assisted Areas, the characteristic firm arriving and succeeding there has tended to be large —a branch plant of a London or a Midlands firm—but it has elected to retain its head office and key decision-making functions in southern England. The capital requirements of such firms have tended to be satisfied either from their own resources or on the London capital market. Manufacturers such as these, therefore, can make only a limited contribution to the solution of a region's lack of entrepreneurial skills and capital. Similarly, as far as the external economies and amenities in the peripheral regional economies are concerned, the fundamental inter-regional contrasts—although lessened in some regards—remain.

Nevertheless, by the late 1970s a considerable body of evidence has emerged to indicate that government policy in fact has had an undoubted impact upon inter-regional disparities of wealth and job opportunities in Britain. From the mid-1960s especially, a striking convergence can be traced in most of the regional indices of economic performance, blurring the historical contrasts in this matter betweeen the different parts of the country. Between 1965 and 1975, for example, the assisted regions increased their share of national manufacturing employment, whilst the South East and the West Midlands experienced a decline. Throughout that same period, a narrowing of regional unemployment rates has been sustained; and, although the South East remains the most favoured region by this criterion, the relative improvement in the performance of Wales and Scotland contrasts with the relative deterioration of the West Midlands. Falling net inter-regional migration figures further indicate a relative improvement in the employment prospects of the Assisted Areas, whilst average regional earnings data confirm a narrowing of inter-regional personal prosperity. Of course, aggregate regional data need to be handled with caution. Much of the employment and population decline of the South East is nothing more than the continuing outward spread of the functional region centred upon the capital—now expressed in part as natural and planned overspill into the neighbouring regions of East Anglia (Peterborough, for example), the East Midlands (Northampton) and the South West (Swindon, Poole). The convergence of regional earnings could well be primarily the result of national incomes policies, rather than the result of regional policy initiatives. Beyond these points, however, there remains substantial evidence that one of the principal factors affecting the inter-regional balance of economic activities in Britain has been regional policy—working especially through shifts in the location of manufacturing industry and the manipulation by government of the geography of industrial movement.

The scale of these shifts, and their relationship to regional policy, is clearly brought out in a series of independent analyses using data on employment, the movement of firms and individual company surveys (Department of Trade and Industry, 1973; Keeble, 1976; MacKay, 1976, 1978; Moore and Rhodes, 1973, 1976a, 1976b). In particular these analyses yield evidence concerning the effects of variations in the intensity of regional policy during the last thirty years; and they have been able to demonstrate the much greater movement of firms into the Assisted Areas, the much higher levels of factory building there, and differential shift in regional employment performance (by comparison with the national economy, and given the existing economic base of the less prosperous regions) during the periods 1945 to 1950 and especially 1963 to the early 1970s—when policies were being pursued vigorously—by comparison with the intervening years (see Figure 2.8). Despite the difficulties of data evaluation, the overall picture remains unquestionably clear. There was a recognizable and important industrial response to the intensification of regional policies in the 1960s, and without the incentives and controls of regional policy the level of employment in the Assisted Areas would be considerably lower today. Moreover, it can be argued with Moore and Rhodes (1973) that the resource costs of these policies have been close to zero. Provided it is accepted that the jobs created in the Assisted Areas through regional policy were a *net* addition to total national employment (a matter, of course, of some dispute), then the net cost to the public purse as a result of associated national insurance contributions, company corporation tax, income tax, indirect taxes and lower unemployment benefits—the so-called 'Exchequer clawback'— was of much the same order of magnitude as direct public expenditure on the regional policy.

At the same time, not a little disquiet legitimately remains about the cost-effectiveness of particular components of regional policy. The Regional Employment Premium may have been withdrawn in 1978, for example, but it remains unclear whether investment

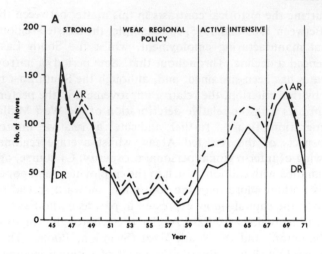

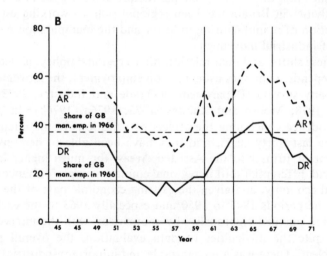

grants rather than some form of labour subsidy are the most appropriate means of reshaping the geography of manufacturing industry, especially manufacturing of a capital-intensive nature. Further, in the restructuring of the older regional economies, questions about objectives remain, not only about the geography of assistance discussed earlier (p.51), but also about the most appropriate degree of specialization or diversification of the new activities being encouraged there. It has been argued that, since the historical strength of the coalfield economies derived from their highly-specialized Victorian industrial structures, it is unwise to diversify those economies indescriminately and thereby to deny them the external economies of a more specialized mode of redevelopment. Again, it is by no means clear what the socially 'optimum' speed of workforce contraction for a declining industry might be. In the case of the coal industry, Lord Robens argued that the rate of run-down of manpower should not exceed 10 per cent each year; it was a view, however, that was unsubstantiated by any clear evidence. The

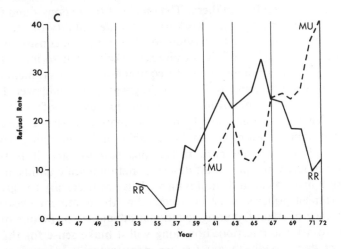

Figure 2.8 Britain: measures of policy intensity and
their effects, 1945-1972
A. Movement of firms into 'development
regions' (DR) of the North, Scotland,
Wales and Ulster and 'assisted
regions' (AR) of the North West and
South West.
B. Share of employment expected from
manufacturing building approvals in
the 'development regions' (DR) and
'assisted regions' (AR).
C. Refusal rate of industrial development certificates in the South East,
West Midlands and East Midlands
(RR), expressed as a percentage of
employment expected from all
applications; and male unemployment
in those same regions (MU).

Source: MacKay and Thomson (1979)

social as well as economic worth of preserving old communities is another unknown in the
matter of regional policy. Obviously some balance has to be struck between the movement
of people and the movement of jobs, both inter-regionally and intra-regionally; but
evidence on the best mix has still to be produced. It was partly because of the persistence
of these uncertainties, and the *ad hoc* quality of much regional policy, that the House of
Commons Expenditure Committee (1973) memorably recorded its opinion that policy in
this area was 'empericism run mad, a game of hit-and-miss, played with more enthusiasm
than success'.

Two points can be made in conclusion. First, and only too obviously, regional policies
have had a significant and discernible influence upon the inter-regional geography of
economic activity in Britain. Over the years, government actions have removed some of
the more fundamental constraints upon the economic growth of the Assisted Areas. The
factor endowments of those regions have been much improved. New and vigorous

economies are slowly being forged there. The image of the regions—and this is important in convincing management and key workers of the desirability of moving to them—is steadily being enhanced. Indeed, in view of the rather inconsistent application of government policies through time, it is quite remarkable that so much has in fact been achieved. Second, and more challenging, the combination of government regional policies with the other forces reshaping the country's geography could well have turned the locational balance of manufacturing advantage in favour of the more peripheral economies. As Keeble (1976) has noted, this combination of spatial forces has rendered invalid the traditional notion of an inexorable and continuing concentration of manufacturing industry in the more prosperous regions, and it is the (centrifugal) periphery-centre model which now best describes national-scale trends in the distribution of manufacturing investment and employment. It is not necessary to agree with Keeble's view that government policies 'must be accepted as the dominant reason for the recent shift in the balance of manufacturing locational advantage in favour of the periphery' (1976, p. 288), to ask the question: how long will it make sense for the government to continue policies that broadly favour further manufacturing investment in the Assisted Areas? Particularly in the light of the growing importance of residential space preferences in the locational behaviour of firms, the fact cannot be escaped that the historical bias of policies towards the location of enterprise pays insufficient regard to the problems of the larger conurbations, both within and outside the Assisted Areas. With their rising levels of unemployment (Figure 1.5), their transport problems substantially unresolved, and their inner areas exhibiting environmental and social signs of distress, it was natural that some commentators should begin to call for an alternative spatial framework within which the elegibility of different places for development assistance might be more properly judged (Keeble, 1977; Manners, 1976b). The next chapter looks at the evolution of planning problems and attitudes at this intra-regional scale.

REFERENCES

Brown, A.J. (1972). *The Framework of Regional Economics in the United Kingdom,* Cambridge University Press.
Caesar, A.A.L. (1964). Planning and the geography of Great Britain. *Advancement of Science,* **21,** 230-240.
Cameron, G.C. (1974). Regional economic policy in the United Kingdom. In Sant (1974b).
Cameron, G., and Clark, D.B. (1966). *Industrial Movement and the Regional Problem,* Oliver & Boyd, Glasgow.
Central Office of Information, (1977). *Government Employment and Training Services,* H.M.S.O., London.
Central Statistical Office (annually). *Regional Statistics,* H.M.S.O., London.
Chancellor of the Exchequer, (1976). *Public Expenditure to 1979-80.* (Cmnd.6393), H.M.S.O., London.
Chisholm, M. (1974). Regional policies for the 1970s. *Geographical Journal,* **140,** 215-231.
Chisholm, M. (1976). Regional policies in an era of slow population growth and higher unemployment. *Regional Studies,* **10,** 201-214.
Clark, C. (1966). Industrial location and economic potential. *Lloyds Bank Review,* **82,** 1-17.
Clark, C., Wilson, F., and Bradley, J. (1969). Industrial location and economic potential in Western Europe. *Regional Studies,* **3,** 197-212.

Coates, B.E., and Rawstron, E.W. (1971). *Regional Variations in Britain,* Batsford, London.
Daniels, P.W. (1969). Office decentralisation from London—policy and practice. *Regional Studies,* **3,** 171-178.
Daniels, P.W. (1975). *Office Location,* Dent, London.
Department of the Environment (1971). *Long Term Population Distribution in Great Britain—A Study,* H.M.S.O., London.
Department of the Environment (1976). *The Office Location Review,* D.O.E., London.
Department of Trade and Industry (1973). Memorandum on the inquiry into location attitudes and experience. *Minutes of Evidence,* Trade and Industry Subcommittee of the House of Commons Expenditure Committee, Wednesday, 4 July, Session 1972/1973, H.M.S.O., London.
First Secretary of State and Secretary of State for Economic Affairs, (1967), *The Development Areas—Regional Employment Premium* (Cmnd.3310), H.M.S.O., London.
Hall, P. (1974). *Urban and Regional Planning,* Penguin, Harmondsworth.
House, J.W. (ed.) (1973). *The U.K. Space,* Weidenfeld & Nicolson, London.
House of Commons Expenditure Committee (1973). *Regional Development Incentives,* Second Report, Session 1973/1974, H.M.S.O., London.
Howard, E. (1904). *Garden Cities of Tomorrow,* reprinted 1945, Faber & Faber, London.
Howard, R.S. (1968). *The Movement of Manufacturing Industry in the United Kingdom, 1945-65,* H.M.S.O., for Board of Trade, London.
Keeble, D. (1976). *Industrial Location and Planning in the United Kingdom,* Methuen, London.
Keeble, D. (1977). Spatial Policy in Britain: Regional or Urban? *Area,* **9,** 3-8.
Location of Offices Bureau (1964 onwards). *Annual Report,* L.O.B., London.
Location of Offices Bureau (1975). *Statistical Handbook,* L.O.B., London.
Luttrell, W.F. (1962). *Factory Location and Industrial Movement,* N.I.E.S.R., London.
McCrone, G. (1969). *Regional Policy in Britain,* Allen & Unwin, London.
MacKay, R.R. (1976). The impact of the Regional Employment Premium. In Whiting (1976).
MacKay, R.R. (1978). The death of regional policy, Discussion Paper 10, Centre for Urban and Regional Development Studies, University of Newcastle upon Tyne.
MacKay, R.R., and Thomson, L. (1979). Important trends in regional policy and regional employment: a modified reinterpretation. *Scottish Journal of Political Economy,* November.
Manners, G. (1968a). Misplacing the smelters. *New Society,* 16 May, 712-713.
Manners, G. (1968b). Reshaping steel. *New Society,* 19 December, 907-908.
Manners, G. (1971). *The Changing World Market for Iron Ore, 1950-1980,* Johns Hopkins, Baltimore.
Manners, G. (1976a). The changing energy situation in Britain. *Geography,* **61,** 221-231.
Manners, G. (1976b). Reinterpreting the regional problem, *Three Banks Review,* September, 33-55.
Manners, G. (1978). Alternative strategies for the British coal industry, *Geographical Journal,* **144,** 224-234.
Minister of Power (1967). *Fuel Policy,* (Cmnd.3438), H.M.S.O., London.
Moore, B.C., and Rhodes, J. (1973). Evaluating the effects of British regional economic policy. *Economic Journal,* **33,** 87-110.
Moore, B.C., and Rhodes, J. (1976a). Regional economic policy and the movement of manufacturing firms to Development Areas. *Economica,* **43,** 17-31.
Moore, B.C., and Rhodes, J. (1976b). A quantitative analysis of the effects of the Regional Employment Premium and other regional policy instruments, in Whiting, (1976).
National Economic Development Council (1963a). *Growth in the United Kingdom Economy to 1966,* H.M.S.O., London.
National Economic Development Council (1963b). *Conditions Favourable to Faster Growth,* H.M.S.O., London.
Needleman, L. (1965). What are we to do about the regional problem? *Lloyds Bank Review,* January, 45-58.
Needleman, L., and Scott, B. (1964). Regional problems and location of industry policy *Urban Studies,* **1,** 153-173.
Nevin, E. (1966). The case for regional policy. *Three Banks Review,* **72,** 30-46.
Packman, J. (1968). *Child Care: Needs and Numbers,* Allen & Unwin, London.

Report of a Committee (1961). *Inquiry into the Scottish Economy, 1960-1961.* (Chairman: J.N. Tothill), Scottish Council, Edinburgh.

Rhodes, J., and Kan, A. (1971). *Office Dispersal and Regional Policy,* Cambridge University Press.

Rodgers, H.B. (1969). The Hunt Report: prospects for Pennine England. *Area, 3,* 1-9.

Royal Commission on Local Government in England (1969). *Report.* (Chairman: Lord Redcliffe-Maud) (Cmnd.4040), H.M.S.O., London.

Royal Commission on Local Government in Greater London (1960). *Report* (Chairman: Sir Edwin Herbert) (Cmnd.1164), H.M.S.O., London.

Royal Commission on the Constitution, 1969-1973 (1973). *Report* (Chairman: Lord Kilbrandon) (Cmnd.5460), H.M.S.O., London.

Royal Commission on the Distribution of Industrial Population (1940). *Report* (Chairman: Sir M. Barlow) (Cmnd.6153), H.M.S.O., London.

Sant, M.E.C. (1974a). *Regional Disparities,* Macmillan, London.

Sant, M.E.C. (ed.) (1974b). *Regional Planning and Policy for Europe,* Saxon House, Farnborough.

Secretary of State for Economic Affairs (1969). *The Intermediate Areas* (Chairman: Sir Joseph Hunt) (Cmnd.3998), H.M.S.O., London.

Secretary of State for Industry, Trade and Regional Development (1963). *The North East,* H.M.S.O., London.

Secretary of State for Scotland (1973). *Central Scotland,* H.M.S.O., Edinburgh.

Warren, K. (1970). *The British Iron and Steel Industry since 1840,* Bell, London.

Whiting, A. (ed.) (1976). *The Economics of Industrial Subsidies,* H.M.S.O., London.

Williams, A.F. (1977). Crossroads: the new accessibility of the West Midlands, In F. Joyce (ed.), *Metropolitan Development and Change in the West Midlands: A Policy Review,* University of Aston, Birmingham.

CHAPTER 3

Intra-regional Development and Planning

GERALD MANNERS

3.1 Introduction

For more than fifty years, a persistent feature of the changing map of Britain has been the attraction of population towards, and the decentralization of people within, the country's larger urban areas. The city-regions of London, Birmingham, Liverpool and Bristol, for example, have thus come to house, through natural increase and migration, more and more people within and on the edge of their existing built-up areas. Simultaneously, an increasing preference for residential and working conditions at lower than previous densities has encouraged a movement of people and activities away from the urban cores, into the surrounding suburban rings, and even further afield into peripheral zones of smaller and loosely associated settlements on the edge of the city-region. The rates and the magnitude of these changes have varied from urban area to urban area. But the consistency of the generalization is impressive throughout the country as a whole. Examining the shifting geography of population within a framework of Metropolitan Economic Labour Areas—regions that are basically major employment centres plus their associated commuting hinterlands—researchers at the London School of Economics (Drewett et al., 1975, 1976) have shown how population growth in both the urban cores and their surrounding metropolitan rings characterized the 1950s especially; in the subsequent decade, however, growth took place further away from the centre (in the metropolitan rings and outer metropolitan rings), whilst the urban cores experienced a notable population decline (see Table 3.1). Together with the associated but contrasting changes in the geography of employment within the city-region, these trends and their associated problems have posed the principal challenges to intra-regional planning in Britain since World War II.

Table 3.1 Britain: population 1971, and changes by urban zones, 1951-1961 and 1961-1971

	1971		Change 1951-1961		Change 1961-1971	
	'000s	%	'000s	%	'000s	%
Urban cores	25,524	47.4	486	1.9	− 729	− 2.8
Metropolitan rings	17,147	31.9	1,721	13.3	2,512	17.2
Outer metropolitan rings	8,838	16.4	245	3.1	786	9.8
Unclassified areas	2,312	4.3	− 21	− 0.9	− 32	− 1.4

Source: Drewett et al. (1976), p.11.

71

3.2 Shifting Perceptions of Urban Problems

The attraction of urban areas, and especially the larger urban agglomerations, to more and more people reflects the wider range of employment opportunities that exist there, and the growing social preference for the services and the amenities that are more readily provided in larger concentrations of population. The outward expansion of urban areas similarly reflects both economic and social forces that have encouraged substantial changes in the geography of residence, of job opportunities, of journeys to and from work, and of social provision. It is not a new process. For centuries, cities have grown outwards. As their populations have increased and their wealthier inhabitants reached out for more residential space, so have a variety of economic and social activities found advantage in functioning from locations further and further away from their historical cores. Shops and schools, doctors and dentists, solicitors and accountants, amongst other services, have dispersed from the centre to serve the growing communities on the urban fringe, and they have been joined there by many other economic and social activities— repair shops and garages, manufacturing activities and printing, local government services and hospitals, research establishments and commercial offices. Some of these activities have been born on the urban periphery or in the outer metropolitan zone. Others have been moved physically from sites nearer to the centre, and so have left room there for the remaining activities to expand or new activities to be born. With each innovation of transport technology—the train and the tram, the underground and the bus, the trolley-bus and the car—the pace of this process has quickened and the advantages of decentralization have been confirmed.

In the past, the central and inner areas of cities have adapted their functions and land uses to the changing opportunities of the day. In London, for example, the earlier coffee house and trading functions of Fleet Street long ago gave way to the newspaper industry, just as the initial residential function of Harley Street was usurped by a more profitable medical role. The logic of the transfer of London's main airport from the cramped suburban field near Croydon to the more open spaces of Heathrow is readily understood, just as the downstream movement of London's seaport functions from the Pool of London to the up-river docks, and then more recently to the more modern facilities at Tilbury, Dover, Felixstowe and Southampton, has an obvious geographical rationale. In the 1930s, many of London's manufacturers found that their locational requirements were best satisfied on the new suburban industrial estates—estates such as Park Royal, adjacent to the main road leading west towards Bristol; more recently, however, manufacturing firms have found their interests better served and their productivity higher when they have located within the outer metropolitan area and within easy reach of the national motorway network.

Such changes in the pattern of urban activities need give little cause for concern provided that the processes of land use and employment change occur smoothly, that the peripheral urban expansion takes an acceptable form, and that the inner urban areas experiencing a population and employment change are able to find new and successful roles within the metropolitan economy. In Britain, however, these prerequisites have not been fully met by the operation of market forces alone. Consequently, a place has been found, and mechanisms have been devised, for the intervention of spatial planners both to influence the form and the scale of metropolitan expansion, and to modify the processes of urban change. The foci of planning concern have changed somewhat through time.

The rapid growth of the country's largest cities and conurbations initially led to fears that, unchecked and unshaped, such a process would not only cause the permanent loss of valuable and irreplaceable agricultural land and amenity countryside on the urban fringe, but would also spawn in all probability an unsatisfactory spread of suburban housing and associated land uses without an adequate provision of appropriate public services. Planning procedures were therefore established after World War II to deny the type of formless urban sprawl that had characterized much of Britain's inter-war urban growth, and to ensure that new suburban developments took proper account of public as well as private costs—including the environmental costs and benefits of different patterns of land use change.

Concerns about the form of conurbation growth were paralleled at an early date by worries about the very speed and scale of urban development in some parts of the country, most notably in Greater London and the West Midlands. The (1940) Royal Commission on the Distribution of Industrial Population (Barlow Commission), for example, was of the opinion that the continuing growth of London in particular presented the country with strategic as well as economic and social problems. Yet military strategists rarely argue against further urban growth in southern England today. Similarly, whilst there was once some evidence to suggest that the populations of large conurbations generally had a rather poorer record of physical health than those of other urban areas, this is certainly no longer the case—although it has been suggested that the social and psychological stresses of living in large urban communities are not without their costs. The Barlow Commission also asserted that the London area faced a major problem of 'congestion', a pejorative indictment which has subsequently appeared regularly both in government reports and private writings, yet one which invariably has lacked a precise meaning. In so far as the concentration of people and their work in urban areas is likely to afford considerable benefits of agglomeration, it is obviously confusing to regard all centres of concentrated activity as inevitably 'congested'. The word is better reserved either for those situations in which high densities make it impossible to achieve certain minimum environmental standards of housing, employment or noise, or for those instances in which the costs resulting from further agglomeration demonstrably exceed the simultaneously generated benefits. In this context, such sweeping phrases as 'congested and insanitary urban areas', and 'sprawling agglomerations of humanity', read less impressively and relevantly today than they did in the Barlow Report forty years ago. Nevertheless, two complex sets of problems stemming from rapid and concentrated urban growth have persisted as both practical and intellectual challenges to the intra-regional planner.

The first challenge relates to the movement of both people and goods within the larger urban areas. With the increasing ownership and use of road vehicles, the internal transport problems of any city or metropolitan area pose highly complex problems relating to such issues as the most appropriate forms of traffic management, and the most desirable levels and types of new transport infrastructure investment. These difficulties are at their most acute, however, in the largest urban areas, where the techniques used in their analysis are highly sophisticated, the alternative lines of action very costly, and the proposed solutions to a degree inconclusive. Such controversial matters as the amount and the nature of public transport subsidies required in a given conurbation, or the relative advantages of rail or road improvements in a particular urban situation, remain essentially unresolved, as the discussion of the London transport situation in Chapter 5 (p.136ff.) makes all too clear. The second challenge is the task of seeking to ensure a minimum set of acceptable environmental conditions for the whole of the urban population. With rising national living standards, of course, the definition of an acceptable minimum in matters of urban amenity has inevitably tended to rise. Perennially, the resources of both private investors and the public purse available for the improvement of living conditions in the poorest urban districts are invariably too limited. In consequence, the need to clear slums, to lower residential densities, to improve depressed neighbourhoods, to replace older factories and offices, to modernize such social investments as schools and health centres, to extend urban recreational space, and the like, are just as much a task for the 1980s as they were of the 1940s. And once again, the problems appear to be the largest, and the least tractable, in the largest urban areas.

It was particularly the reaction of the planning profession to the form, the speed and the scale of urban growth in the country's largest conurbation—Greater London—that substantially informed the initial style of intra-regional planning in post war Britain. As is elaborated below, measures were adopted to restrain the speed of growth of its employment opportunities and the extent of its expansion; simultaneously, policies were launched to disperse some of its population growth away from the urban core and into new and separate communities some distance away. In different degrees, planners in other conurbations followed suit. Broadly in line with—though naturally accelerating—natural spatial tendencies, such policies of decentralization were not without success. In time, however, a quickening rate of population and employment dispersal away from the largest urban centres began to generate mounting concern for the future of the conurbation cores. In itself, the net loss of population was acceptable. It could even be seen as beneficial to the extent that it offered the opportunity of redevelopment at lower residential and working densities. However, the failure of many inner urban areas to find newer and viable roles, the appearance of ever larger areas of derelict land and the evidence of exceptionally high levels of unemployment, together suggested the need for some form of remedial policy, possibly to slow down the rate of their population and economic decline, and certainly to encourage their adjustment to the economic and social opportunities of the day. The inner area dimension of spatial policy only came into serious consideration from the mid-1970s, and is still in an essentially formative mould. Quite properly, it raises questions about the continuing validity of earlier policies concerned with the encouragement of urban dispersal; it also challenges some traditional attitudes towards inter-regional planning priorities and methods.

3.3 Policy Responses

3.3.1 Restraining Employment Growth

Partly in response to the problems of environment and mobility in the London and Birmingham city-regions (particularly in their conurbation cores), and partly as a result of perceived but not necessarily proven disadvantages of continued employment expansion there, public policy after 1945 sought to steer the physical development and restrain the economic growth of the country's most dynamic city and economic regions. In the process the policy not only sought to prevent the merging of the two into a single English megalopolis, but it also helped to alleviate the problems of the less prosperous parts of the country.

Although the Barlow Commission had advocated a ban upon further industrial developments in London, after 1945 the post-war Labour government embraced a policy which sought merely to restrain the pace of economic development there and in the West Midlands. Under the 1947 Town and Country Planning Act, local planning authorities (then the counties and county boroughs) whose policies were subject to loose Whitehall control, were given the power to prohibit or approve changes in the use of land from one activity to another. Rural or residential land, therefore, could not be converted to industrial purposes without their permission. Theoretically, an even more important means of control over industrial development, however, was the industrial development certificate (i.d.c.) which was a natural successor to various wartime and immediate post-war government controls. From 1947 this had to be issued by the Board of Trade for any industrial building over 465 square metres (5,000 square feet) or representing a 10 per cent addition to existing industrial premises. By withholding certificates in South East England and the West Midlands, the Board thus came to exert a powerful influence over manufacturing movement within, and the economic geography of, the country. In addition, as was seen earlier (p.37ff.), various financial and other incentives were made available to manufacturers moving to or located in the less prosperous regions. There was no blanket refusal of i.d.c. applications in southern England. Each application was 'viewed on its merits', and priority after the Assisted Areas was given to new and expanded towns in accordance with decentralization and overspill objectives. Applications were also viewed in the light of shifting planning doctrines and development priorities. The Board (subsequently the Department of Industry) was much more reluctant to grant certificates in the period to 1949, and from about 1960 to 1970, than it was during the intervening or subsequent periods when successive governments tended to discount the value of regional planning, or were desperate for new manufacturing investment wherever it might be encouraged. In the early and mid-1970s nearly 90 per cent of all i.d.c. applications in the South East region received approval. Howard (1968) has fully demonstrated the much slower pace of industrial movement away from the South East and West Midlands during the 1950s (see Table 2.8; Figure 2.8).

Not only changing political attitudes limited the effectiveness of i.d.c. policies. The certificates relate to factory floorspace. But a large proportion of manufacturing enterprises took up less than 465 square metres, and hence lay outside the instrument's control. New, pioneering and rapidly growing firms especially were found in this category. And many other firms, which might well have taken up more space, deliberately kept their size below 465 square metres simply in order to avoid the inconvenience of moving away from southern England. It is quite possible that the efficiency of some firms suffered as a result. In 1966 the government responded to this situation by reducing the size of plant needing an i.d.c. first to 280 square metres (3,000 square feet) and then to 93 square metres (1,000 square feet). Such was the administrative and economic burden of these fine-grained controls, however, that in 1971 the limit was raised to 465 square metres again, and by 1978 to 1,162 square metres (12,500 square feet) in the South East and 1,395 metres (15,000 square feet) elsewhere outside the Assisted Areas. More fundamentally, however, it is clear that an administrative tool regulating industrial floorspace is bound to be a somewhat insensitive device for the control of employment opportunities, which was the fundamental objective of policy. Further, when a firm elected to move out of London or Birmingham its premises were invariably taken over by another manufacturing enterprise. The policy thus had little chance of stabilizing the number of jobs available in manufacturing industry either regionally or sub-regionally in southern England in the 1950s and early 1960s. Only if public authorities had bought up vacated industrial sites at market prices could this have been achieved—but that cost was too high, and it is not clear it was required.

Some expansion of manufacturing activities and jobs in the London and Birmingham city regions was in any case both necessary and unavoidable. Quite apart from the employment needs of the new and expanding communities in the Outer Metropolitan Area (O.M.A.) of the South East and on the periphery of the West Midlands conurbation, the population of both regions was growing as a result of natural increase as well as immigration—and it needed an expanding economic base. Moreover, there are some firms which primarily serve markets in Greater London or the West Midlands; others are highly dependent upon a site near to an international airport or seaport for their efficiency; a third group are closely tied to other firms in southern England. All of these industries could produce powerful and acceptable economic arguments for their location or expansion in the south. There was also a need to renew and redevelop industrial premises and zones within the conurbations if working conditions there were not to remain or fall below acceptable standards.

As time went on, however, misgivings were increasingly expressed concerning the wisdom of these industrial restraint policies. In particular it was felt that they were having a debilitating effect upon the long-term prospects of the manufacturing sector in southern England, and especially within the conurbations there. To the protesting voices of many West Midlands industrialists and the reservations expressed by the Confederation of British Industries (which nevertheless applauded the broad objectives of government inter-regional policies), there was added in 1969 the disquiet of the Greater London Council (G.L.C.). In common with the authorities in many other large metropolitan areas in the world, it had come to be alarmed by the steady decentralization of its manufacturing activities (Chapters 4 and 5). Sooner or later, it was feared, this was bound to present the central city and its inner suburbs with a long-term threat to their economic and employment base. The plea in the G.L.C.'s *Development Plan* (1969a, pp. 78 ff.), therefore, was for a new approach by central government towards i.d.c. applications, and preferably for the control to be handed over to the strategic planning authority (the G.L.C. in the London case) which would accept only those industries with a record of relatively high productivity in conurbation locations. It was a plea which represented a major challenge to a fundamental element in the regional planning procedures of post-war Britain and which, although it was rejected, presaged a shift of attitude by the Department of Industry in the late 1970s. With the growing concern for the future of the inner areas in all cities and conurbations, the government substantially modified its attitudes towards i.d.c. procedures in parts of inner London and inner Birmingham. It began to allow some speculative industrial building there, and in 1978 it placed the needs of these areas second only to the Assisted Areas (and before the new towns) when adjudicating specific applications.

Throughout the 1940s and 1950s, measures to curb the rate of economic growth in southern England were related entirely to the manufacturing sector of the economy. Yet the fastest growing employments were services. In the late 1950s, jobs in Greater London were estimated to be growing at 45,000 per year, and those in central London at 20,000; of the latter, 15,000 were in offices. In response, a policy was initiated in 1963 designed to persuade office employers to move out of central London, and in that year the Location of Offices Bureau (L.O.B.) was established 'to encourage the decentralization of office employment from congested [sic] central London to suitable centres elsewhere'. In particular, it sought to publicize the relatively high cost of office floorspace in London (Table 3.2), and the Bureau offered free and well-researched advice to management on the advantages of alternative locations. Through advertising and publicity, it was L.O.B.'s task to alter the climate of opinion concerning the advantages of different locations for the conduct of office activities, and to rectify a market failure that was imposing unnecessary economic and social costs upon the community. Simultaneously, the government began to disperse some of its own activities from the capital. Parts of Customs and Excise were moved to Southend; much of the routine tax work for the London area was transferred to provincial centres; and the Post Office Savings Bank was moved to Glasgow. *The Economist* (8 December 1962, p. 989) even advocated the creation of an entirely new national capital—Elizabetha—somewhere in the Vale of York.

Controls were soon added to persuasion in the private sector. Following the 1965 Control of Offices and Industrial Development Act, an office development permit (o.d.p.) had to be granted by a central government department—initially the Board of Trade, subsequently the Department of the Environment—before any new office building or conversion exceeding 280 square metres (3,000 square feet) could be undertaken. The control initially applied only to the London Metropolitan Region and to the West Midlands conurbation; it was soon extended (in 1966) to the whole of the South East and to both the East and West Midlands. However, from 1967 the exemption limits were gradually raised and then abandoned outside South East England, and by 1978 the control applied only to quite substantial office development of more than 3,530 square metres (30,000 square feet). Nevertheless, throughout this period, o.d.p.s were used to serve intra-regional and, at times, local planning ends, with the Department viewing most favourably applications for development in the new and expanded towns and in the growth areas of the Strategic Plan for the South East (p.166ff.), and applications for sites where a broader planning gain such as the associated redevelopment of a public transport facility could be achieved. Meanwhile, the decentralization of central government offices—as well as the devolution of some administrative responsibilities to the Regional Planning Boards and the newly-created Welsh Office (p.354)—was pursued with increasing vigour at both the inter-regional and the intra-regional scales (Daniels, 1975; Goddard, 1974).

The transitional costs of moving an office job from the largest single concentration of office activities in Britain, central London, are perhaps higher than generally realized— £2,000 per transferred employee, perhaps, at 1978 prices. On the other hand, despite higher communications costs, the operating expenses of a decentralized office can be as much as 20 per cent below its central London counterpart as a result of lower rents, lower salaries and a lower rate of staff turnover. However, there is no continuous cost gradient with increasing distance from London, and the savings in operating expenses do not generally increase beyond the O.M.A.; indeed the cost of office space in some provincial centres is relatively high by O.M.A. standards (Table 3.2). It was not unnatural, therefore, for office developers and decentralizing employers initially to show a particular interest in such places as Basingstoke, Brighton, Bletchley, Chichester, Croydon, Guildford, Horley, Reading, Reigate, Southend, Worthing and the London new towns— rather than places further from London. The number of jobs moved out of central London each year under the auspices of L.O.B. (and these probably represent about one

Table 3.2 Britain: variations in the rents of new offices, by regions and towns, 1978

		Rent per square metre (£)	Rent per square foot (£)
SOUTH EAST			
Central London:	City	72.77-189.24	6.76-17.58
	West End	120.67-176.21	11.21-16.37
London, inner areas:	Brixton	45.53	4.23
	Hammersmith	69.97-85.58	6.50-7.95
	Lewisham	58.67	5.45
	Wood Green	53.82-69.97	5.00-6.50
London, outer areas:	Bromley	56.51-63.72	5.25-5.92
	Croydon	64.59-88.91	6.00-8.26
	Kingston	63.94	5.94
	Wembley	66.30	6.16
Rest of South East:	Ashford	16.15-34.98	1.50-3.25
	Basingstoke	45.75-59.20	4.25-5.50
	Brighton	37.67-48.33	3.50-4.49
	Luton	50.70	4.71
	Milton Keynes	37.67	3.50
	Southampton	28.31-40.37	2.63-3.75
SOUTH WEST:	Bristol	18.84-34.98	1.75-3.25
	Gloucester	18.84-31.00	1.75-2.88
	Poole	37.67-42.52	3.50-3.95
	Swindon	35.31-42.84	2.28-3.98
EAST ANGLIA & EAST MIDLANDS:	Derby	18.84-21.53	1.75-2.00
	Ipswich	34.98	3.25
	Norwich	10.76-21.53	1.00-2.00
	Leicester	6.46-17.76	0.60-1.65
WEST MIDLANDS:	Birmingham	13.46-34.98	1.25-3.25
	Coventry	16.15-24.22	1.50-2.25
YORKSHIRE & HUMBERSIDE:	Leeds	51.13	4.75
	Sheffield	48.44	4.50
NORTH WEST:	Liverpool	40.37-43.06	3.75-4.00
	Manchester	5.38-40.90	0.50-3.80
NORTHERN:	Darlington	27.23	2.53
	Newcastle	24.22-32.29	2.25-3.00
WALES:	Cardiff	31.75	2.95
	Newtown	10.76	1.00
SCOTLAND:	Dundee	37.67	3.50
	Glagow	34.98-45.75	3.25-4.25

Source: Location of Offices Bureau.

half of the total private and government moves, since not all decentralizers contacted the Bureau) rose to a peak of 14,700 in 1973/1974. But despite the office controls the greater number of the office employers—representing 90 per cent of the jobs associated with L.O.B. between 1963 and 1976—were reluctant to move their activities more than about 130 kilometres (80 miles) from London; only 6 per cent of the firms (with 10 per cent of the jobs) were willing to move into the Assisted Areas where financial incentives were available from 1973 (p.39ff.; see Figure 3.1).

The rate of private office decentralization from central London varied, of course, from year to year (Table 3.3). After a peak of office movement in 1967-1968, the amount of vacant office space both in London and the country as a whole contracted severely, and the cost of office accommodation in the centre of the capital rose quite dramatically. The dilemma facing the government became clear. Whilst its policies were restricting the short distance movement of offices out of central London through the imposition of floorspace controls in the South East and the Midlands, there remained insufficient encouragement for office employers to move longer distances into the provinces and Assisted Areas. Meanwhile, of course, the population of Greater London continued to disperse outwards in search of homes and amenity. Without a parallel movement of jobs in the longer run, such a trend implied an overall lengthening of the journey to work, a prospect which the creation of L.O.B. had sought to counter and which received planning doctrine abhorred. Some relaxation of floorspace controls, by both central and local government, therefore, was introduced. Stimulated by high central London rents and business expansion, a further surge of movement away from the City and the West End ensued, and peaked with the buoyant economic conditions of 1973-1974. After that date, in contrast, economic recession caused many office firms to reduce their staffs; in consequence one of the two principal reasons given by firms for office relocation—expansion—ceased for the time being to be a force in office geography. With the recession also, office demand in central London slackened, surplus space appeared, rental levels fell in real terms, and the difference between the costs of offices in central London and other places narrowed to the point where the other major reason for movement—economy—was less persuasive than in the past.

By the mid-1970s, however, although the rate of office decentralization had slowed, it was clear that the strength of market forces in periods of economic growth had become such as to throw substantial doubt about the wisdom of leaving L.O.B. with its original remit. By this time, also, the plight of inner urban areas was being more openly recognized. A review of office policy was therefore undertaken by government, and in 1977 the role of the Bureau was adjusted to match the shifting goals of urban planning. The Bureau was charged with continuing the strategic role it had earlier espoused in office policy—that is, serving as a centre of information for both the office employer and public authorities, making 'the market' more transparent so that locational decisions could be taken in the light of the best available evidence, and pursuing research into the many questions surrounding the location of office activities— but it was also asked to embrace two new tactics to serve spatial planning ends (Manners, 1977a, 1977b). First, it was asked explicitly to promote the advantages of office employment in the country's Assisted Areas. Second, and in the light of the new inner areas initiative, it was asked to promote office activities in the inner areas of the large conurbations. The new policy assumed, therefore, that central London would continue to be the major source of office movement, but that the Bureau, rather than encouraging this movement and being

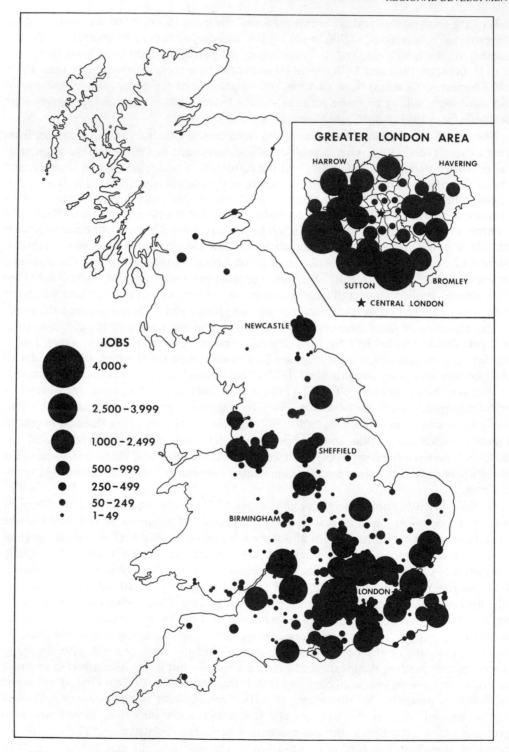

Figure 3.1   Britain: office movement out of central London,
                 1963-1977
Source: Location of Offices Bureau

Table 3.3 Britain: office decentralization from central London, 1963-1977

Years	Inquiries	Jobs to be moved as represented by inquiries	Firms moved	Jobs moved
(A) *Moves assisted by the Location of Offices Bureau*				
1963/1964	346	30,972	5	185
1964/1965	510	32,823	99	6,665
1965/1966	385	30,845	154	10,601
1966/1967	300	23,927	145	11,437
1967/1968	245	19,301	198	13,978
1968/1969	200	12,920	145	11,220
1969/1970	168	15,835	130	8,288
1970/1971	252	26,220	111	8,632
1971/1972	284	23,616	169	12,845
1972/1973	398	39,445	182	10,002
1973/1974	421	38,244	216	14,700
1974/1975	290	23,931	161	13,087
1975/1976	245	17,703	175	12,623
1976/1977	185	14,096	136	10,896
TOTAL (1963/1977)	4,229	349,878	2,026	145,159
(B) *Estimated independent private moves*				
1963/1977	—	—	—	c. 116,000
(C) *Government departments*				
1963/1977	—	—	—	c. 29,000
GRAND TOTAL	—	—	—	c. 290,000

Sources: L.O.B.; author's estimates.

indifferent to the destinations of its clients, should accept and exploit it in order to encourage appropriate types of office activities to consider locating in those places needing additional employment. (In addition, the Bureau was charged with promoting Britain as a location for internationally footloose office firms and activities.)

After thirty years of policies seeking to restrain the expansion of manufacturing and service employments in the larger conurbations, therefore, the mid-1970s saw the deliberate encouragement of decentralization by government first questioned and then substantially abandoned. As will be noted later, such was the intrinsic strength by that time of market forces encouraging the movement of economic activities away from certain parts of the inner urban areas, that political energies were adjusted to a new set of planning priorities. Before examining the new policies, however, other aspects of the earlier phase of intra-regional planning demand attention.

3.3.2 *Constraining Physical Expansion*

Paralleling the attempt to control employment growth in the largest city-regions of southern England was the decision, made possible by the immediate post-war land use planning legislation, to control the physical expansion of Greater London and the West Midlands, and indeed the other conurbations and large cities as well. The idea of constraining the growth of London by physical controls was by no means new (Thomas,

1970). The Elizabethan 'Cordon Sanitaire' and the ideas of Pepler were the natural forerunners of the green belt proposed in Abercrombie's plan for Greater London in 1944. The intention was that within this 'sterilized' zone—which could continue in a primarily agricultural role, but at the same time offer recreational opportunities for Londoners—only developments which conformed to the existing pattern of essentially rural land uses were to be allowed. As a result the continuing outwards sprawl of the conurbation, which had been a persistent feature of the inter-war years, could be checked. To a large extent the policy succeeded. A variety of associated problems nevertheless gradually emerged. Since land uses within the green belt were from the outset mixed in character—there were villages and towns, quarries and sand-pits, airfields and hospitals, industry and (often in old country houses) offices, as well as parks and farmland—the notion of 'conforming uses' proved far from easy to define in the day-to-day administration of the policy. The initial pressures for urban and suburban developments there were considerable. They increased as the population of Greater London grew, as the land designated for housing was gradually used up, and as regional planning decisions were avoided during the 1950s. Local planning authorities and central government nevertheless defended the policy well into the next decade. By that time, however, the doctrine of the green belt was the subject of increasing scepticism and criticism.

It came to be recognized that with sustained population growth, with the 'fission' of households and with the redevelopment of central residential areas at lower densities, there had been a considerable underestimation in the immediate post-war years of the need for housing land within the conurbation. Abercrombie, for example, had mistakenly assumed a static London population in his plan. It was argued by some, therefore, that more land should be released for housing, and that at least some of this should come from the green belt, especially those parts which demonstrably had little recreational value. At the same time questions arose as to whether the green belt was in fact being used for those recreational purposes that were in part its justification. Certainly, the number of formal recreational facilities was limited, whilst informal recreation there remained of interest to only a small section of the urban community. A more positive approach towards the use of green belt land was obviously required. Above all, there developed a sense that urban areas are dynamic phenomena and need to change and 'grow', and that without conclusive evidence on the optimum size of cities at various levels of the urban hierarchy this requirement should not be frustrated.

A new school of planning thought thus began to emerge. It stressed the advantages of allowing the physical expansion of large urban areas along their major radial lines of communication, saw green wedges between those growth sectors as an alternative to the green belt, and advocated the deliberate creation of country parks within the green wedges to serve metropolitan recreational needs. The wisdom of the green belt policy was first questioned in an official publication, *The South East Study* (Ministry of Housing and Local Government, 1964b); its long-term value was further challenged in *A Strategy for the South East* (South East Economic Planning Council, 1967) in which 'country zones', wedged between radial sectors of urban expansion, were given the role of shaping metropolitan growth and affording recreational opportunities. Neither publication, however, had an operational status. With the subsequent approval of the 1970 *Strategic Plan for the South East* (South East Joint Planning Team, 1970), traditional attitudes and vested interests substantially prevailed, and an extended metropolitan green belt was confirmed on the map of the region. At the same time, bolder notions of countryside preservation over much larger tracts of the South East were espoused in the interests of agriculture, recreation and the shaping of urban growth (see Chapter 6).

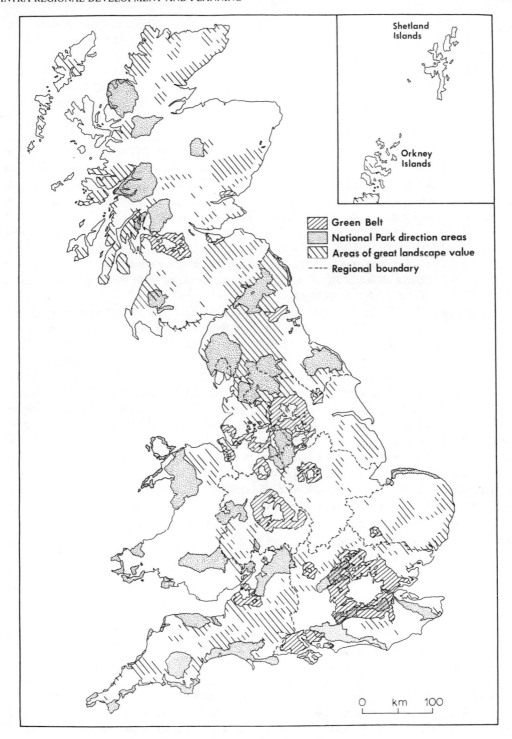

Figure 3.2 Britain: principal physical land use constraints upon
development, mid-1970s

Source: Department of the Environment and Scottish Office
sources

The physical containment of urban growth in the West Midlands had a somewhat different history. There, it was rivalries and disagreements between the several local authorities responsible for the physical planning of the Birmingham city-region which more than anything else prevented the transfer of land to urban uses and restrained the outward spread of the conurbation for the first two post-war decades. By 1965, however, a ministerially approved green belt had been agreed and drawn upon the map. It was shaped not only to restrain the outward growth of the main built-up areas within an essentially polynuclear urban complex, but also to keep them apart. Thus, besides helping to maintain the identity of such places as Nuneaton and Bedworth, it also served to separate towns like Redditch, Bromsgrove, Kidderminster and Stafford from the mass of the West Midlands conurbation. Curiously, therefore, whilst the usefulness of a green belt for the London city-region was being challenged in the mid-1960s, the idea was being more firmly embraced in the West Midlands. It was nevertheless made clear in the 1965 West Midlands *Regional Study* by the Department of Economic Affairs that the precise boundaries of the green belt might have to be adjusted in the light of further transport and land use studies. It is also noteworthy that the concept of sectoral growth is not absent from the subsequent strategic thinking of planners concerned with shaping urban growth in the West Midlands (see Chapter 8).

Elsewhere in Britain, green belts were employed to check the sprawl of built-up areas, to prevent the merging and retain the physical integrity of formerly separate towns, and (in such cases as York and Bath) to preserve the unique character of particular urban centres (Figure 3.2). Whilst their designation came to be an essential tool of regional strategic planning and of sub-regional physical planning, many unresolved dilemmas concerning green belt administration remain. In the absence of adequate public funds, positive approaches to land use change in a green belt are severely constrained. With developments in the technology, management and economics of agriculture, the response of green belt farmers can be expensively constrained by planning priorities. And, most important of all, the behaviour of land owners in the green belt—affected as they are by the 'hope values' residing in their property, and recognizing the possibility that a change in its use could eventually be allowed—frequently militates against both the wisest husbandry and public recreational objectives.

3.3.3 *The Overspill Arrangements*

Intimately related to the policies designed to restrain the employment and physical growth of the London, Birmingham and other large city-regions were the arrangements made to provide the opportunity, and indeed deliberately to foster, the growth of population at specific places beyond their green belts. This was the policy of overspill. Even on Abercrombie's assumption of a static London population, it was recognized that the redevelopment of the inner areas of the conurbation would necessitate the designation of an area of land for housing which was simply not available within the London contained by the green belt. Naturally some new, and quite major, housing estates or 'satellites' could be (and were) built within what is now Greater London—Roehampton and St Mary Cray are two examples—but additional accommodation was also clearly required. This need was wedded to the ideas of Ebenezer Howard and the new towns movement, which deplored many aspects of Victorian and Edwardian urbanization, and sought to create new, medium-sized, self-contained and balanced communities for working and living.

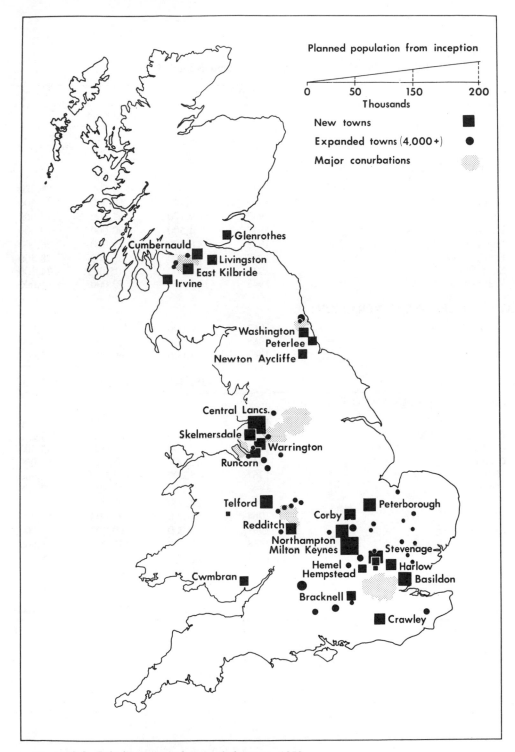

Figure 3.3 Britain: new and expanded towns, 1979
Source: Town and Country Planning Association

Table 3.4 Britain: progress in the new and expanded towns, 1978

		Population		
A: NEW TOWNS				
	Date of designation	Original	Proposed	31st Dec. 1977 (est.)
LONDON, FIRST GENERATION				
Basildon	1949	25,000	130,000	91,420
Bracknell	1949	5,140	60,000	47,500
Crawley	1947	9,100	85,000	75,500
Harlow	1947	4,500	90,000*	79,500
Hatfield	1948	8,500	29,000	26,000
Hemel Hempstead	1947	21,000	85,000	78,500
Stevenage	1946	6,700	105,000*	74,500
Welwyn Garden City	1948	18,500	50,000	41,000
LONDON, SECOND GENERATION				
Milton Keynes	1967	40,000	200,000	80,000
Northampton	1968	133,000	180,000	147,000
Peterborough	1967	81,000	160,000	112,000
LONDON, TOTAL		352,440	1,174,000	852,920
OTHERS IN ENGLAND AND WALES				
Aycliffe	1947	60	45,000	27,500
Central Lancashire	1970	234,500	285,000	248,200
Corby	1950	15,700	70,000	53,500
Cwmbran	1949	12,000	55,000	45,000
Newtown	1967	5,000	13,000	7,900
Peterlee	1948	200	30,000	27,500
Redditch	1964	32,000	90,000	56,000
Runcorn	1964	28,500	95,000	57,900
Skelmersdale	1961	10,000	60,000	40,000
Telford	1968	70,000	150,000	98,500
Warrington	1968	122,300	170,000	135,400
Washington	1964	20,000	80,000	48,000
OTHERS IN ENGLAND AND WALES, TOTAL		550,260	1,143,000	845,400

Table 3.4 continued

A: NEW TOWNS continued				
		Population		
	Date of designation	Original	Proposed	31st Dec. 1977 (est.)
SCOTLAND				
Cumberland	1955	3,000	70,000	45,600
East Kilbride	1947	2,400	90,000	76,300
Glenrothes	1948	1,100	70,000	35,000
Irvine	1966	34,600	120,000	57,300
Livingston	1962	2,100	100,000	33,340
SCOTLAND, TOTAL		43,200	450,000	247,540
BRITAIN, GRAND TOTAL		945,900	2,767,000	1,945,860

B: EXPANDED TOWNS (Summary)			
		Dwellings	
Dispersing area	Number of schemes agreed	To be built	Completed
Greater London	28	86,407	54,774
Birmingham	12	18,259	11,822
Bristol	4	2,278	2,278
Liverpool	4	13,085	5,959
Manchester	4	5,828	1,378
Newcastle-upon-Tyne	2	10,517	3,018
Salford	1	4,518	4,518
Walsall	2	444	444
Wolverhampton	4	4,527	4,527
Glasgow and others	42	18,705	12,728
BRITAIN, GRAND TOTAL	103	164,568	101,446

*Under review.
Source: Town and Country Planning, February 1978.

With prototypes already built and financed by private capital at Letchworth (1903) and Welwyn Garden City (1920), the government designated between 1946 and 1949 eight new towns in South East England under the 1946 New Towns Act (Figure 3.3). For each, a Development Corporation was appointed and charged with the responsibility of acquiring land, preparing plans, and administering the overspill of industry and population from the inner parts of London. Only three of the ten sites preferred by Abercrombie were in fact selected, and alternative locations were chosen that were either more accessible to London, or better able to serve a variety of other physical planning objectives as well as overspill. After a somewhat slow start, which was inevitable for such a pioneering programme within a mixed economy, by the early 1960s the new towns were becoming significant centres of economic and population growth (Thomas, 1969). They developed an expanding and frequently high-wage industrial base; in time they came to be attractive to decentralizing offices and other services; the quality of their social amenities was outstanding in relation to their size; and they proved to be a financial success. By early 1978 they had a total population of 514,000, of which some 416,000 represented the overspill component (Table 3.4), and their revised target population was some 650,000.

Although the new towns idea was simultaneously taken up boldly in the planning of the Glasgow city-region, and adapted to serve the needs of several of the Development Areas, during the late 1940s and 1950s none was designated for the West Midlands conurbation. Throughout that period local pressure groups such as the Midlands New Towns Society urged upon both central and local government, and upon the public in general, the necessity for providing adequate overspill facilities beyond the (as yet undesignated) green belt. However, the same lack of cooperation between the local planning authorities which had plagued the region's green belt policy prevented any agreement until 1963. In that year Dawley was selected as the first new town for the city-region. Subsequently Redditch was also designated and the scale of the Dawley proposals enlarged to make the new planned city of Telford (p.236ff.). Local authority antagonisms were also substantially responsible for the delays in new town designation and construction in North West England; Skelmersdale (1961), Runcorn (1964) and Warrington (1968) have made only belated contributions to the overspill needs of Liverpool and Manchester.

Throughout the 1950s, in fact, successive government ministers were also reluctant to approve further new town schemes, partly on the grounds of their initially high capital cost, partly following a belief that existing towns could also make a substantial and less expensive contribution to the process of metropolitan overspill. Financial assistance was first made available for expanded towns under the 1952 Town Development Act. The London County Council, in particular, made numerous arrangements with such places as Thetford and Haverhill, Ashford and Andover, Aylesbury and Banbury (see Figure 3.3). Similarly, the Birmingham authorities agreed to encourage the movement of industry and population to several Staffordshire towns, to Shrewsbury and even to some Welsh communities. Although these and similar arrangements in Scotland facilitated the decentralization of some conurbation activities and people, the Town Development Act in retrospect has left only a relatively small imprint upon the urban geography of Britain (see Table 3.4). Only in the case of Swindon, where the urgent need to restructure the local economy (following the contraction of jobs in the town's principal source of employment, the railway workshops) was fortuitously combined with rare local authority initiatives, and at a later state at Basingstoke, did the Act serve as a mechanism for large-scale overspill.

By the early 1960s, therefore, a crisis in the land use and regional planning of the

London and Birmingham city-regions especially was becoming all too apparent. Earlier miscalculations concerning the growth of population and housing needs of the conurbations, the continuing net immigration which could not be checked, and the powerful natural forces encouraging the decentralization of employment and population, together rendered the existing overspill arrangements grossly inadequate. The scale of the problem in the London case was such that it was decided to experiment not only with the creation of several very large new towns (each with a planned population of about ¼ million) but also—and once again using the Development Corporation mechanism— with the expansion of some existing and substantial towns by 100 per cent or more. Although the designated area of Milton Keynes included several small communities, one of which (Bletchley) already had an overspill agreement with the G.L.C. under the 1952 Act, this scale of urban development represented a major innovation in British planning. Similarly, the decision rapidly to double the size of Peterborough and Northampton made entirely new use of the new towns idea.

Ideas about planned overspill have changed in several respects since 1945. Quite apart from the need to revise notions concerning the layout of new communities, and especially the need for architects and urban planners to come to better terms with the motor car, three changes are particularly outstanding. The first concerns the size of community considered to be both desirable and feasible for an overspill population. Whereas the pre-war, private enterprise new towns were designed to become communities of about 30,000 people, the first generation of new towns under the 1946 Act were planned to be significantly larger and in the 55,000 to 80,000 range. The largest, Basildon, was initially intended for a population of rather more than 100,000. Subsequently the population targets of several of these towns were revised upwards. Stevenage, for example, where the original design was for 60,000 people, revised its plans to cater for 135,000; Crawley's plan was altered to house 120,000 rather than 56,000. (Both of these were, however, subsequently revised downwards again; see Table 3.4.) The new cities designated in the mid-1960s marked yet a further increase in the scale of the planned components in metropolitan overspill, and, with the *Strategic Plan for the South East,* the new towns came to be associated with major and medium growth areas in the outer metropolitan area (O.M.A.) and outer south east (O.S.E.); the indicative population of these areas by the year 2001 was in some cases over 1 million. The growing size of individual overspill plans was partly a matter of economics, for it can be shown that the unit (public and private) costs of developing a community of 150,000 are lower than those of a smaller community of 100,000. It was also related to the fact that the increasingly specialized demands of a progressively more affluent society required larger communities to provide a satisfactory range of services and amenities. In addition, the more recently designated overspill communities were further away from major metropolitan centres than their earlier counterparts. Hence they are in locations which central place theory suggests are spatially suited to larger urban centres.

A second change which can be noted in overspill arrangements is the transformation of ideas concerning the economic base of the planned communities. Immediately after 1945, the new towns were considered primarily a place for manufacturing industry, plus those services which were required by the local community. With time, however, research establishments connected either with local industry or with the associated metropolitan economy came to be established. They were followed by service industries and offices which had a regional or even a national market. With the movement of the Meteorological

Office to Bracknell, British Petroleum to Harlow and Kodak to Hemel Hempstead, for example, not only was the economic base, but also the social structure, of the new towns gradually changed. Later, when the prospective employment and social structure of Milton Keynes came to be analysed, it was accepted from the outset that offices and service jobs would in all probability provide a major driving force in expansion there.

A third major change in ideas on metropolitan overspill relates to the spatial role of the new communities. The thinking of Abercrombie, like that of Howard before him, envisaged the creation of towns which in large measure would be self-contained in employment and services. The new towns have gone some considerable way to achieve this objective. Most of the people living in these communities also work there. However, the continuing erosion-of the costs, and hence the importance, of distance has led to a greater movement of people in and out of the towns for work and for the provision of services. Whilst new town houses are generally made available to the workers of an incoming factory or office, should they be requested, there is nothing to stop a tenant subsequently looking for and taking work in a nearby town or even in the conurbation centre. The rest of his household are in the same position. Hence, the vastly improved commuter services between the London new towns and central London, and the accessibility of many of the new communities to the radial motorways, have not only enormously enhanced the attractiveness of these places for industrial and commercial development, but also more firmly embraced them in the metropolitan labour market. There is no inherent virtue in increasing the distance travelled to work or recreation. Yet it is often the price that has to be paid for choice, opportunity and specialization in matters of employment and leisure. It is a development which is likely to increase rather than diminish. This feature, and also the recognition of the strong industrial and commercial linkages which exist between the new towns and other communities (particularly in their parent conurbation), emphasize the need to reinterpret metropolitan green belt and overspill policies primarily in terms of a means of shaping urban growth—rather than a devise for stopping it in order to create separate and smaller urban communities.

Such changing ideas on the most appropriate scale, the potential economic base and the ultimate spatial role of overspill communities have been paralleled by a growing recognition of the advantages of the Development Corporation as a mechanism for their creation and growth. These statutory bodies, now appointed by the Secretary of State for the Environment, benefit from their predictable access to government funds and hence to the large sums of capital which are required for initiating and completing large-scale urban development of this sort. They are geographically flexible, and thus are able to handle developments which cut across established local authority boundaries. They can reflect a regional or national interest, where it is judged this needs to overrule local preferences. They are one of the few positive instruments of spatial planning in a mixed economy, and they can also advantageously combine within the same organization research, decision-making and executive functions. The Regional Development Agencies, proposed (but never accepted) in the steering group's report in *Traffic in Towns* (Ministry of Transport, 1963) as a means of adjusting the existing urban fabric to widespread motor car ownership and use, were consciously based upon the new town Development Corporations and their success. By comparison—and this was the main weakness of the Town Development Act—existing local authorities and more especially the smaller ones generally neither have, nor can afford, the expertise required to combine research and executive skills, and to initiate major development schemes. Development Corporations naturally have to work alongside existing local authorities, a requirement which is not without friction at times, and they have been criticized for their non-elected nature. Their past achievements, and hence their credibility as development agencies, however, ensure them an important place in not only the history but also the future of British regional planning.

The precise nature of that future role is open to some debate, however. With the mounting public concern for the future of the inner urban areas and with the downward revision of population forecasts in the mid-1970s, it was decided by the Secretary of State for the Environment to slow down the rate of planned overspill from the conurbations. Clearly the case for exploiting existing infrastructure in new and expanding towns was powerful. Such were the perceived needs of the older parts of the city-regions, however, that the formal programmes for new town expansion were extended over a longer period, the planned size of some of the new communities was substantially reduced (Milton Keynes, for example, was asked to scale down its ultimate size from 250,000 to 200,000) and the priority of the new communities for footloose industry and office investment as expressed through the administration of i.d.c. and o.d.p. policies was lowered. Henceforth, it was judged, public development money would be more properly spent in the inner urban areas. It is to these that we next turn.

3.3.4 Urban Renewal and Inner Area Concerns

Metropolitan planning for long has had to respond to another set of dilemmas, this time in the central and inner areas of conurbations and cities where there often exists a huge task of renewing an old and substantially worn-out built environment. Quite apart from the extensive areas of central London in particular that needed to be rebuilt after the bombing of World War II, economic and social blight has for long afflicted considerable tracts of older properties adjacent to the central business districts in all major cities. Both public and private initiatives are required for their reconstruction. Simultaneously the transport needs of these same areas change with time, and it is frequently possible to combine urban renewal with modified and redesigned circulation systems within the city. All this—the speed at which, and the way in which, blighted areas at and near the centre of cities are renewed—has a considerable bearing upon the rate of population overspill and the pattern of metropolitan geography as a whole.

Since 1945, public policy has sought to give urban renewal a reasonably high priority in conurbation and city affairs. Aided by substantial rate support grants, a subsidy on high-rise accommodation and other housing subsidies, the inner London boroughs and Birmingham authorities especially have been able to retain a much larger population than might otherwise have been the case. Legislation has also allowed the compulsory purchase by local authorities of extensive tracts of urban land for comprehensive redevelopment. Not only has this substantially assisted in the redevelopment process and permitted a higher standard of urban design, but it has also allowed major (if local) improvements in traffic flows.

By the mid-1970s, however, the problems posed within the central and inner areas of the conurbations began to mount, for the general world recession in economic activity coincided with the effects of substantial structural changes in the country's labour markets. An absolute decline in manufacturing employment naturally hit most severely those inner urban area localities that not only specialized in declining trades but also had traditionally been exporters of jobs through the process of decentralization. Simultaneously, the number of service sector employments within the inner areas of cities —particularly in transport and distribution functions—contracted severely as the full decentralization impact of the inter-urban motorway system and the rationalization of the railways combined with such special local circumstances as the downstream shift of activities in the Port of London. Serious concern thus came to be expressed at both the speed and the nature of these changes which threatened the economic base and exacerbated the social problems of the inner areas. The Greater London Development Plan of 1969, anticipating what was to become a more general plea by conurbation authorities, appealed for radical changes in spatial policies that would assist them in seeking to ameliorate the problems of their inner areas. Piecemeal and tentative gestures by government in response came to be consolidated into a broad set of initiatives in the White Paper on *Policy for the Inner Cities* (Cmnd. 6845) in 1977, and the Inner Urban Areas Act of 1978.

Under this initiative, government offered assistance to (specified) local authorities in the inner urban areas so that they might help to regenerate their economic base, refurbish their built environment and ameliorate their social ills. Singled out initially for particular attention and combined central government-local government planning measures were the so-called Partnership Areas of Lambeth, Islington-Hackney and Docklands in London, Birmingham, Manchester-Salford, Liverpool and Newcastle-Gateshead. Beyond these, the Secretary of State for the Environment also named 'designated districts' that could take advantage of central government finance to assist with their industrial regeneration. These districts included additional inner London boroughs and Leicester, as well as many smaller towns in the Assisted Areas (see front end-paper). At the same time changes were made in the criteria applied by government departments in the adjudication of i.d.c. and o.d.p. applications, giving the Partnership Areas a priority second only to the Assisted Areas, and before the new towns and non-Assisted Areas. And from mid-1977, the Location of Offices Bureau was asked, as had been noted, to assist in attracting office employment into the inner areas (Damesick, 1979).

Although the latter proposal had considerable merit—already national and international firms were located in such inner London centres as Hammersmith, Lewisham and Stratford and were making a significant contribution to local employment and income there—it was inevitable that the greatest initial concern in the inner areas focused upon manufacturing industry. This, after all, had been the largest source of traditional employment for the inner area workforce. Department of Industry research (Dennis, 1978) quickly established that the largest single component of manufacturing employment decline in Greater London—nearly 50 per cent—was the complete closure of existing factories; and the proportion was even higher, 80 per cent, in the case of Glasgow (Firn, 1976). To this extent the problem could be regarded as structural rather than locational, reflecting in some measure the uncompetitive nature and unprofitability of many of the traditional firms and industries concentrated in the inner areas. However, Keeble (1978) has drawn attention to two geographical features of manufacturing decline in the inner areas that could be equally or more important. One is the fact that industrial migration from the inner areas of conurbations and cities is normally prompted by the growth of individual firms. This process is bound to be selective of the more dynamic firms and industries, and in time likely to have a debilitating effect upon the residual industrial environment. Since mobile firms have been characterized by a high level of inter-firm linkage, the loss of their activities from the inner areas has removed an important local market for many of the firms remaining there. The other locational aspect of the inner area manufacturing problem follows from the growing importance of multi-plant firms in the overall structure of British industry. Evidence indicates that many of the factory closures in the inner urban areas are a response to a growing preference of these firms for a less urbanized environment and their ability to make a deliberate locational choice between different plants and sites when making investment decisions.

The fact cannot be escaped that there are today significant disadvantages in attempting to conduct manufacturing activities in many of the inner areas of cities and conurbations. Industrial sites and premises are expensive, and the latter are very frequently old and of exceedingly poor quality. Road communications are difficult. The local urban residential environment is shabby and tending to get worse. And both central and local government policies have in the past been at best indifferent to the needs of manufacturing enterprise: the reluctance of central government to give floorspace permissions, the incentives available in the Assisted Areas, the delays in local authority planning permissions and disruptive redevelopment schemes, all have hindered inner area enterprise. In recognizing these features, it becomes evident that a reversal of the decline of manufacturing jobs in the inner areas is most unlikely. The policies of government, therefore, must concentrate their attention upon providing assistance to existing firms in the inner areas and, through the provision of modern and reasonably priced industrial premises, seeking to encourage the birth of new ones and to keep them there. In addition, the need to improve the quality of the inner area residential environment to retain management, skilled and semi-skilled workers is obvious, and the transfer of public funds through a readjustment of the rate-support grant to the conurbation authorities has a valid logic.

Three more general points need, however, to be noted in connection with the inner urban areas policies of the late 1970s. The first is that the London case stands in bold contrast to that of other conurbations in towns in Britain — a contrast based essentially upon the extent of the inner urban areas, and the size of the population living there. The second is that a distinction needs to be drawn between the central city, with its inherent and considerable economic strengths in such matters as retail trade, entertainments, tourism, office activities and the like, and the surrounding collar of the inner suburb in which the processes of land use and functional change have proceeded less speedily and less effectively in recent years; nowhere is this distinction more acute than in the case of London. The third is that the processes generally at work in the inner areas are far from new, since land use change, and the decentralization of economic activities, have characterized the inner areas of cities for centuries. The new elements in the situation of the 1970s were both the speed and scale of employment decline, and the apparent failure of market forces and local institutions, especially public authorities, to respond effectively to the situation and its problems with speed.

Implicit in the new inner urban areas policy of the 1970s, of course, was a challenge to the spirit of earlier conurbation-planning policies that had centred upon the notion that the processes of decentralization needed a measure of public support and encouragement. Indeed, in 1977, as has been seen, the scale and speed of the existing new town programme was reduced, and the role of L.O.B. was amended. However, the conflict was more apparent than real for at least some of the loss of manufacturing jobs in the inner city was the result of the death of firms rather than decentralization. Other firms needed to leave in order to remain competitive and survive. The loss of employments in the service sector, especially in distribution and transport, was unlikely to be reversed for equally good economic and geographical reasons. And some of the problems of the inner cities, and in particular the concentration there of underprivileged social groups, could partly be ameliorated by helping some of these people to move into new and expanded towns where a better environment, job training, employment opportunities and the like were immediately available. There exists in fact a fundamental complementarity in government overspill and inner area policies which demands a more widespread appreciation.

3.3.5 *Further Components of Public Policy*

There were two further components in the public policy response to the problems posed by conurbation and city-region growth. One was a changing set of policies relating to urban transport. Initially *transport policy* was not considered as an intimate part of the metropolitan growth dilemma, and attitudes towards the improvement of roads and public transport services were discussed and then adopted substantially outside of a spatial planning context. But with the growing ownership and use of cars, plus all the problems of road congestion that follows, increasingly was it realized that decisions affecting transport facilities and costs have fundamental implications for the geography of urban growth. To put it at its simplest, the further urban circulation shifts away from public and towards private transport, the greater will be the tendency towards a geographical dispersion of metropolitan functions and development. By the mid-1960s, therefore, there had been initiated in Greater London, in the West Midlands and indeed in all large conurbations and cities, major traffic and land use surveys which sought to relate the two sides of the urban development coin. Although *The South East Study* of 1964, and *A Strategy for the South East* of 1967, for example, had both to be formulated without any clear assurances from the then Ministry of Transport and other transport authorities concerning prospective road and public transport improvement schemes, the Greater London Development Plan of 1969 did have the benefit of the London Traffic Survey behind it. Similarly the 1970 *Strategic Plan* was evaluated against a set of specified transport objectives and constraints. Earlier, in 1968, the two Whitehall ministries primarily concerned with regional and transport planning were brought together for the first time under a single department (Local Government and Regional Planning), which was subsequently restyled the Department of the Environment. (The two were separated once again in 1976 for essentially administrative reasons.)

Meanwhile, the G.L.C. was in the process of assuming overall responsibility for London (passenger) Transport, and arrangements for closer cooperation with British Rail concerning the planning of commuter services were being put in hand. The crucial importance of welding traffic and land use proposals together, and in particular the advantages of blending public transport policy with regional and sub-regional plans, caused the government to create (under the 1969 Transport Act) Passenger Transport Authorities in all the provincial conurbations and major city-regions. These bodies, responsible to the local authorities in their respective areas, are charged with the task of framing policy and supervising finance. By settling the broad lines of metropolitan transport strategy—including such matters as fare structures, subsidies and the quality of service—these transport authorities are in a powerful position to assist in the realization of the broad land use objectives set by local and regional planning bodies. In this respect Greater London came to be less well served than other large urban areas, for it proved impossible to find the administrative means and the political will to create a single passenger transport authority which would absorb the commuter services of British Rail into an executive planning agency.

The geographical *framework and organization of planning* is the second and final component in public policy demanding attention at this point. The Development Corporations of the new towns apart, the spatial structure of intra-regional planning was for long shaped out of local government areas dating from the late nineteenth century. With the changing nature of economic life, and particularly with the changing technology of transport, however, the arrangement under the 1948 Town and Country Planning Act whereby counties and county boroughs were primarily responsible for making land use plans became increasingly obsolete. Until 1964 the traditional structure had to serve. In that year, however, the major reorganization of London's local government, proposed by the Herbert Commission in 1960, was put into effect with the creation of the G.L.C. which was given responsibility for the overall structure plan of its area. This represented a considerable advance on the previous situation — although there were many who argued that such a responsibility should have been commissioned on an even larger scale in order to embrace the whole of the city-region. Meanwhile, county councils had begun to cooperate in their regional planning research and decisions. In 1959, the County Planning Officers' Conference was founded under the general guidance of the Ministry of Housing and Local Government to provide an official channel of communication in sub-regional planning matters. Then in 1962 the Standing Conference on London and South East Regional Planning was created; serving twenty-one local planning authorities it supports joint research and examines mutual problems. Similar cooperative moves were slower to develop elsewhere, but by 1970 several liaison bodies bridging the gap between the geography of local government and the scale of economic and social life relevant for decision making in intra-regional planning had come into existence. From 1965, in addition, the Regional Economic Councils and Planning Boards provided an intermediate level of advice and (in the case of the boards) executive authority between central government and the local authorities. The outmoded geography of the latter, however, remained. It was left to the Royal Commission on Local Government in England in 1969 to point to the need for, and the possibilities of, a major reorganization in the 1970s. The government, however, elected to pursue a less radical reform in which 1,210 local authorities were replaced in 1974 by rather fewer than 400, comprising (shire and metropolitan) counties and districts (in the London case called boroughs), each with major planning functions (Secretary of State for the Environment, 1971).

With the new local government arrangements (Figure 3.4), and following the 1968 Town and Country Planning Act, spatial planning in England thus became a three-tier affair. (Slightly different situations prevail in Wales and, particularly, Scotland.) At the top there are produced the regional strategies, formulated by joint teams representing the Regional Economic Planning Councils, the Department of the Environment and the standing conferences of local authorities; next, constrained by the strategy, the counties prepare broad-brush structure plans for their areas; and at the local level the (county and metropolitan) districts prepare the detailed land use plans. Such a framework powerfully shapes the nature and content of the public response to intra-regional planning problems.

Figure 3.4 Britain: local government divisions, 1979

3.4 Interim Evaluation

Throughout the last thirty years intra-regional planning in Britain has been dominated by a single spatial philosophy concerning the preferred geography of larger urban areas. Drawing heavily upon the thinking and ideals of Ebenezer Howard, planners have sought to restrain the further physical extension of the major conurbations, and simultaneously to promote the construction of smaller and physically separate daughter settlements that are protected by firm land use controls. In certain very fundamental respects the planners have succeeded in their objectives. The physical spread of British urbanization has been contained, most notably in the case of Greater London where the metropolitan green belt has been held and had a major influence upon the emerging urban form in South East England, but also in the case of the provincial cities and conurbations where a relatively clean edge to the urban fringe has been imposed upon the geography of land use. At the same time, urban land has been used intensively and (by the standards of most technologically advanced societies elsewhere in the world) with relatively little waste. Public services in consequence have been provided at relatively low unit costs. Meanwhile, less agricultural land has been lost than might otherwise have been the case, and extensive areas of the British countryside have been left remarkably unspoilt.

Clawson and Hall (1973), in comparing British and American urban planning experiences, have underlined these achievements. At the same time, they have recorded a number of disadvantages or costs that have followed in the wake of British intra-regional planning. The suburbanization of people within and beyond the green belt rings has resulted in journeys to work that are much longer than might have followed from less formal urbanization schemes. Housing densities have been kept relatively high, partly because the planners have so specified in local plans, but also as a consequence of the rapid rise in land values that inevitably accompanied plan-created scarcities of housing land. And it cannot be denied that the considerable gains in countryside planning—many of them gains of an essentially aesthetic nature—have given utility to only a minority of the population and, indeed, to an already privileged section of the community.

Since the middle of the 1970s, however, this planning philosophy has come under increasing criticism and scrutiny. Several developments in particular have been responsible for the change. First, the falling birth rate and the revised forecasts of population growth have generated uncertainties about the need for deliberate public policies that encourage urban dispersal. Second, the natural decentralization of manufacturing industry in particular, and a wider spectrum of economic and social activities in general, from the city and the conurbation core has further questioned the historical role of policy in yet further encouraging what has come to be a natural tendency, especially as the problems of the inner areas have grown in scale and attracted mounting public attention. Third, the national economic performance and the need to reduce the level of public expenditure have led to a questioning of the country's ability to pay for many of the less urgent, long-term investments that were once more readily accepted. And, fourth, the vision and self-confidence of the intra-regional planners have begun to fade as all these changes have interacted with, for example, the major new uncertainties that stem from the energy price rise and its possible implications for the medium-term transport objectives in urban planning, the mounting criticism of the high costs of physical planning procedures and decisions, and a growing concern for the social consequences of much town and country planning (Simmie, 1974). The result of all this has been above all a shift towards incrementalism in planning—the end of bold spatial designs and a search by planners for means whereby the immediate land use needs of communities can be broadly satisfied whilst the maximum number of longer-term spatial development options are kept open—plus a growing desire to specify economic and social objectives in the intra-regional planning process, each with a less articulate spatial dimension. The late 1970s, therefore, saw intra-regional planning in a state of both change and some intellectual uncertainty. Together with public expenditure concerns, this persuaded the government to abolish the Economic Planning Councils in 1979, and at the same time to dispense with the services of the Location of Offices Bureau.

Simultaneously, there was a growing desire of central government, in response to national economic difficulties and forecasts, to encourage economic development and especially employment growth almost wherever such opportunities were forthcoming; and there was a partial shift in the interests and priorities of policy away from the long-standing concern with inter-regional disparities in economic performance and welfare towards a new awareness of intra-urban and particularly inner area problems. In consequence, the intra-regional planning system came to be characterized not only by change but also by variety. Although in theory all land use planning in Britain is ultimately subject to the approval of the Secretary of State for the Environment, in reality a highly decentralized system encourages a considerable and, arguably, a healthy diversity in the ways in which local planning authorities react to their specific planning problems and opportunities. Within the somewhat loose strategic overviews provided by the Economic Planning Councils, standing conferences and central government, the precise response of the county and district planning authorities to very similar problems, therefore, varied from conurbation to conurbation, and from city-region to city-region. To appreciate the many dimensions and the variety of the intra-regional planning response to the changing situation and perceived needs of the different parts of Britain, therefore, it is necessary to examine the specific circumstances and the shifting policy objectives in the various regional components of the national economy. The following chapters do just this.

REFERENCES

Clawson, M., and Hall, P. (1973). *Planning and Urban Growth,* Johns Hopkins Press, Baltimore.
Damesick, P. (1979). Offices and Inner-urban regeneration, *Area,* 11, 41-47.
Daniels, P. (1975). *Office Location,* Bell, London.
Dennis, R. (1978). The decline of manufacturing industry in Greater London: 1966-74. *Urban Studies,* **15,** 63-74.
Department of the Environment (1976). *Office Location Review,* D.O.E., London.
Department of the Environment (1977). *Inner Area Studies: Liverpool, Birmingham and Lambeth,* H.M.S.O., London.
Department of the Environment (1978). *Strategic Plan for the South East: Review, Government Statement,* H.M.S.O., London.
Drewett, R., Goddard, J., and Spence, N. (1975). What's happening to British cities? *Town and Country Planning,* **43,** December, 523-530.
Drewett, R., Goddard, J., and Spence, N. (1976). What's happening to British cities? *Town and Country Planning,* **44,** January, 14-24.

Firn, J.R. (1976). Economic micro-data analysis and urban-regional change: the experience of G.U.R.I.E., in establishment-based research: conference proceedings. Urban and Regional Studies Discussion Paper No.22, University of Glasgow.

Goddard, J.B. (1974). *Office Location in Urban and Regional Planning,* Oxford University Press.

Greater London Council (1966). *London Traffic Survey,* 2 vols, G.L.C., London.

Greater London Council (1969a). *Development Plan: Report of Studies,* G.L.C., London.

Greater London Council (1969b). *London Transportation Study—Movement in London.* G.L.C., London.

Hall, P. (1974). *Urban and Regional Planning,* Penguin, Harmondsworth.

Hall, P. with Drewett, R., Gracey, H., and Thomas, R. (1973). *The Containment of Urban England,* 2 vols, Allen & Unwin, London.

Howard, R.S. (1968). *The Movement of Manufacturing Industry in the United Kingdom 1945-1965,* H.M.S.O., London.

Keeble, D. (1976). *Industrial Location and Planning in the United Kingdom,* Methuen, London.

Keeble, D. (1978). Industrial decline in the inner city and conurbation. *Transactions of the Institute of British Geographers,* **3,** 101-114.

Location of Offices Bureau (annually). *Annual Report,* L.O.B., London.

Manners, G. (1977a). New tactics for LOB. *Town and Country Planning,* **45,** October, 444-446.

Manners, G. (1977b). The strategic role of LOB. *Town and Country Planning,* **45,** January, 25-30.

Ministry of Housing and Local Government (1964a). *The Green Belts,* H.M.S.O., London.

Ministry of Housing and Local Government (1964b). *The South East Study 1961-81,* H.M.S.O., London.

Ministry of Transport (1963). *Traffic in Towns,* H.M.S.O., London.

Royal Commission on the Distribution of Industrial Population (Barlow Commission) (1940). *Report,* H.M.S.O., London.

Secretary of State for Scotland (1971). *Reform of Local Government in Scotland* (Cmnd.4583), H.M.S.O., Edinburgh.

Secretary of State for the Environment (1971). *Local Government in England: Government Proposals for Reorganisation* (Cmnd.4584), H.M.S.O., London.

Secretary of State for the Environment (1977). *Policy for the Inner Cities* (Cmnd.6845), H.M.S.O., London.

Secretary of State for Wales (1971). *The Reform of Local Government in Wales: The Consultative Document,* H.M.S.O., Cardiff.

Self, P. (1957). *Cities in Flood.* Faber & Faber, London.

Simmie, J. (1974). *Citizens in Conflict,* Hutchinson, London.

South East Economic Planning Council (1967). *A Strategy for the South East,* H.M.S.O., London.

South East Joint Planning Team (1970). *Strategic Plan for the South East,* H.M.S.O., London.

South East Joint Planning Team (1976). *Strategy for the South East: 1976 Review,* H.M.S.O. London.

Thomas, D. (1970). *London's Green Belt,* Faber & Faber, London.

Thomas, R. (1969). *London's New Towns,* P.E.P., London.

CHAPTER 4

The South East: I Regional Dominance, Growth and Decline

DAVID KEEBLE

4.1 Regional Dominance

South East England, however defined, is the single most populated, economically important and prosperous region of Britain. Within the 27,000 square kilometres of the South East Standard Region, comprising only 12 per cent of the country's land area, are crowded no fewer than 16.9 million people, or 31 per cent of Britain's total population. No other region, with the exception of the North West, contains even as much as 10 per cent.

Not surprisingly, given this huge concentration of people, the South East also represents by far the country's single largest cluster of economic activity and jobs. In 1976, for example, the region's manufacturing firms employed 1.9 million workers, or 26 per cent of Britain's total manufacturing workforce. In a host of major industries, such as food and drink, chemicals, electrical, mechanical and instrument engineering, clothing, and paper, printing and publishing (Figure 4.2), South East factories employ more workers and produce more goods than those in any other region. Particular industries which traditionally are highly concentrated in this region include pharmaceutical and toilet preparations (49 per cent of national employment), office machinery (59 per cent), instrument engineering (50 per cent), television and broadcasting equipment (59 per cent), electronic computers (50 per cent), electronic capital goods (71 per cent), and newspaper and periodical printing and publishing (56 per cent). Many of the South East's manufacturing industries are also very important exporters. Whereas nineteenth-century Britain relied for exports and prosperity upon the coal, steel, ships and textiles of such regions as the North East and South Wales, the twentieth century has witnessed the growth of the South East as the greatest single export manufacturing region of the country, providing some 30 per cent by value of national visible exports. Many of these are shipped through the Port of London and London (Heathrow) Airport, which are now the country's two leading export outlets, measured by value of goods handled.

Yet the importance of the South East's manufacturing industries relative to those of other regions is in many ways surpassed by that of its so-called service trades (Figure 4.2). In 1976, the South East's service industries, excluding construction, employed 4.9 million people or 38 per cent of the British total. So the South East's economy is unusually biased towards service industry—68 per cent of the region's employed workforce—compared with Britain as a whole (only 59 per cent). Of course, many of the South East's services, such as primary and secondary education, local government and health services, and retailing, are largely concerned with meeting the needs of the region's own very large population. But a significant number, most of which are clustered in London, fulfil national and international roles of great importance to Britain's economy.

The chief example here is the interrelated group of insurance, banking and finance trades. In 1976, South East firms in this service industry employed 587,000 workers or 54 per cent of the national total: and at least a third of these worked in the City of London, one of the world's two greatest financial centres (the other being Wall Street, New York). The importance to Britain's economic prosperity of the City's financial activities, centred on institutions such as the Bank of England and the Stock Exchange, is illustrated by their net contribution to Britain's foreign exchange earnings from 'invisible exports', estimated at a record £2,307 million in 1978 (compared with a total net national surplus from all invisibles of £2,210 million). Another example of a 'national' service industry in the South East is central government administration. In 1976, national government departments employed some 281,000 workers in the region, or 45 per cent of the national total; and half of these work in the huge government offices which cluster around the Houses of Parliament, in the West End of London. Greater London and the South East also, respectively, account for 26 per cent and 41 per cent of national wholesaling employment, another service industry traditionally concentrated here. By contrast, retailing is much more widely spread in relation to population, although London's larger share of national retailing employment (17 per cent) than of population (13 per cent) does illustrate the capital's role as a national—and international—retailing centre, with such world-famous shopping districts as Oxford and Regent Streets, Savile Row and Carnaby Street.

Less easy to categorize, but of major and growing importance in the South East, are a whole host of service activities loosely classified as 'professional and scientific' and 'miscellaneous'. Regional employment in these two industries totalled 1.27 million and 801,000 workers, respectively, in 1976. Many of these activities—ranging from theatre, cinema and hotel companies to advertising agencies, consulting engineers, and medical, legal, architectural and other professional bodies of many different kinds—fulfil important national needs. Those especially concentrated in South East England include legal services (42 per cent of national employment), accountancy (45 per cent), research and development services (57 per cent), and the television, broadcasting, theatre and cinema industry (58 per cent). As one would expect, London alone accounts for a remarkable share—44 per cent—of national employment in the last category.

The South East's dominance of national and international communications—the seaports of London, Southampton and Dover, and the airports at Heathrow, Gatwick and Luton, for example—explains the region's above-average share (42 per cent) of employment in the transport and communication industries. London alone accounts for 27 per cent of the national total. In air transport, remarkably concentrated in the South East, the region's and capital's shares are no less than 83 per cent and 68 per cent, respectively.

4.2 Twentieth-century Prosperity and Growth

The remarkable concentration of people and economic activity in England's south eastern corner is traditionally associated with above-average prosperity and growth. In

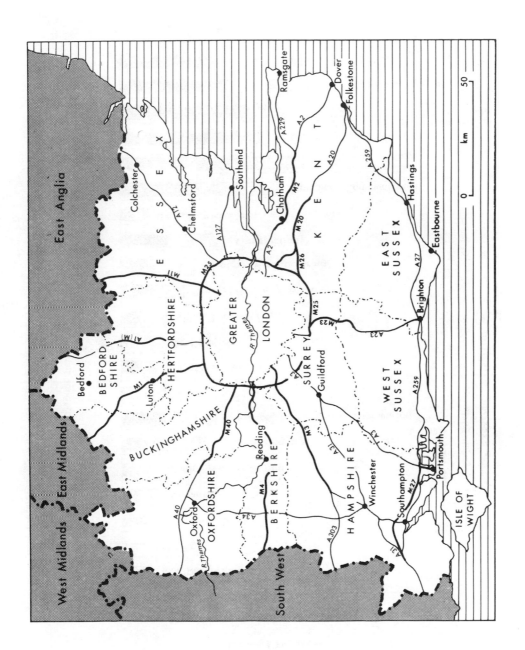

Figure 4.1 South East England

Note: the M25 motorway is still under construction, and to be completed during the 1980s

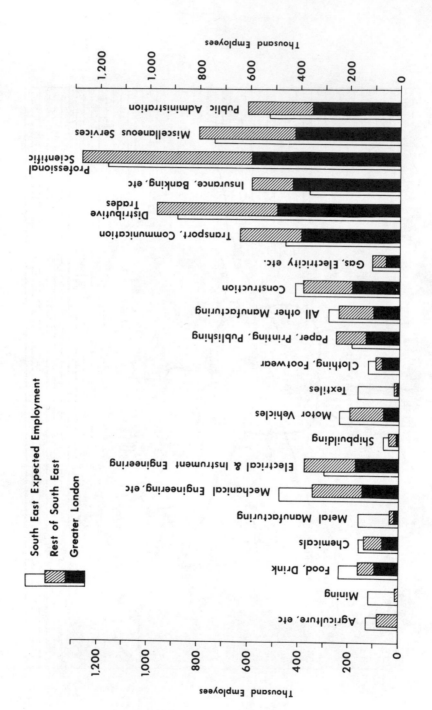

Figure 4.2 South East England: employment structure, 1976
Note: 'expected employment' is calculated assuming a 32.9 per cent South East share
(this being the region's share of total national employment in all industries) of
national employment in each particular industry

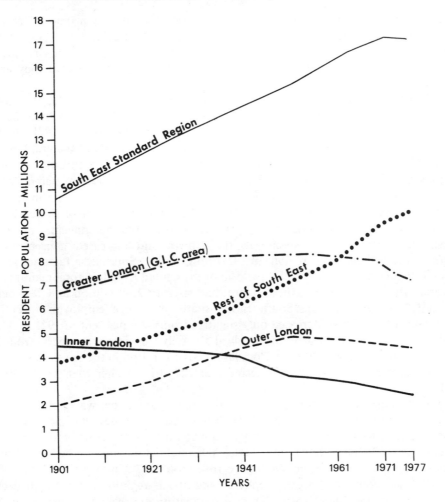

Figure 4.3   South East England: population trends, 1901-1977

1975/1976, for example, weekly household income in the South East averaged £86.40—11.3 per cent above the United Kingdom average of £77.60. In 1976, weekly earnings for South East full-time male employees alone were 7.2 per cent above the British average of £71.80, while male employees working in Greater London received on average £82.20—14 per cent more than the national figure. These differences would, of course, be even greater if comparison were with the rest of Britain, rather than a national average itself boosted as it is by high South East incomes.

The explanation for this apparent above-average prosperity is undoubtedly complex. One important factor is the region's industrial and occupational structure, with a low percentage of workers in such traditionally poorly-paid industries as agriculture, and an unusually high proportion of well-paid professional and managerial jobs. The region also enjoys the lowest unemployment rate and highest female activity rate in the country, both of which must boost average household income, relative to other regions. Yet another important factor is the traditional general shortage of labour in the South East, which has forced up wages and earnings relative to other areas. Last but by no means least, high wages undoubtedly reflect in part the higher cost of living in the South East, especially the expense of housing. In consequence, regional differences in disposable income after allowing for basic living costs are less than the above figures suggest; they are still considerable, nevertheless.

The contemporary wealth and prosperity of South East England reflects, of course, the twentieth-century tendency for British population and industry to become more concentrated in this region. Figure 4.3 indicates that between 1901 and 1971, the South East's population grew from only 10.5 million to 17.0 million. What the graph does not show, however, is that during nearly the whole of this period the South East's population grew consistently faster than that of Britain as a whole. So the region's share of national population steadily increased, from 27.5 per cent in 1901, to 29.7 per cent in 1931, 30.5 per cent in 1951 and 31.3 per cent in 1961. The South East's peak share—31.5 per cent—was reached in 1966. Interestingly, this relative population concentration appears primarily to have been a response to the growth and increased concentration of *manufacturing* activity in the region. In 1921, for example, South East factories provided jobs for 1.46 million workers or 21.4 per cent of the United Kingdom total manufacturing workforce. By 1961, however, these figures had risen to 2.42 million and 28.4 per cent respectively. In contrast, the South East's share of service employment, excluding domestic service workers, increased only slightly, from 37.0 per cent in 1921 to 37.5 per cent in 1961, although of course this involved a massive growth in numbers, from 2.9 to 4.5 million (Lee, 1971, pp.230-237). Population concentration in the South East up to the 1960s thus seems chiefly to have reflected manufacturing rather than service industry growth.

Perhaps because manufacturing workers are usually paid higher wages on average than service employees (Keeble, 1976, p.204), South East incomes also appear to have increased relative to the rest of the country. Data do not exist for years before about 1950, but Lee (1971, p.247) has shown that average personal net incomes in the South East as a percentage of the United Kingdom figure rose from 107.3 in 1954/1955 to 108.7 in 1964/1965. In contrast, most peripheral industrial regions recorded a declining percentage. Until the 1960s, then, dynamic population and economic growth in South East England seems to have gone hand in hand with an increasing localization there of national prosperity and wealth.

4.3 The Reasons for Regional Growth

The reasons for above-average twentieth-century growth in the South East and the Midlands have been examined from a national perspective in Chapters 1 and 2. But in the specific South East context, the variety of factors that have played some part in this expansion deserve reemphasis.

One of these, sometimes singled out as of crucial importance, is the inheritance of a very favourable industrial structure. Unlike other regions with a residual specialization on industries such as shipbuilding, textiles and coal mining which have declined during the twentieth century, the South East in 1900 possessed a wide and diversified array of economic activities with a bias towards those—motor vehicles, electrical engineering, for example (Figure 4.2)—already expanding at an above-average rate. Most of the latter were in fact located in London. The extent of this highly favourable industrial structure has recently been measured by Brown (1972, p.134) for the 1921-1961 period, using a statistical technique which splits regional employment growth into two main components. One of these—the composition component—is the amount of growth which may be ascribed simply to a regional specialization on industries which happen to have been growing unusually rapidly nationally (a *negative* value for this component indicates specialization on industries which have been declining or growing less rapidly than average). The other component—Brown calls it the 'growth' component—measures extra growth (or decline) over and above what might be expected simply on the basis of industrial structure. This sort of statistical technique is often termed 'shift-and-share analysis' (Keeble, 1976, ch. 3). Brown's study, which used a complex version of the technique, found not only that employment growth in the South East between 1921 and 1961 was greater and faster than in any other region of the United Kingdom, but also that approximately three-quarters of the extra growth which took place, over and above the South East's 'fair share' based on the national average growth rate, was due to a uniquely favourable industrial structure. The remaining quarter reflected some sort of extra locational advantage.

This said, however, explaining the growth of employment, and hence population, in terms of a favourable industrial structure is in one sense most unsatisfactory. It begs the further vital question: why does the South East possess such a structure in the first place? Put another way, why did the region attract so many of Britain's twentieth-century growth industries—aircraft, motor vehicles, electronics, pharmaceuticals, broadcasting and television services, financial and business consultancy and so on—in the first place? The explanation for this seems to lie in a variety of other, inter-linked, factors.

Possibly the most important of these is exceptional market accessibility. Much evidence suggests (Keeble, 1976, pp.46-51) that close and rapid access to customers is rated very highly by many modern manufacturing and service firms in Britain. For example, the 1966/1967 London Employment Survey conducted by the Greater London Council found that, on the basis of replies from no fewer than 30,000 manufacturing and service firms, the most frequently cited location factor, given by 80 per cent of the firms as an important reason for operating in London, was 'access to customers'. The only other factors recorded as important by 50 per cent of firms or more were labour considerations and access to suppliers (Hoare, 1973, p.304). The importance of market access today of course reflects the expansion of light manufacturing industry which is untrammelled by the traditional ties of transport costs to fuel, raw material, or break-of-bulk locations, and the growth of many service industries whose *raison d'être* is close and efficient customer contact.

The unrivalled market accessibility of the South East, and especially London, stems partly from the region's concentration of population, economic activity and wealth. This concentration is longstanding. The region's population in 1901, for example, was already double that of any other region. Its present-day inhabitants, representing 31 per cent of the national population, command 35 per cent of national purchasing power measured by personal incomes. Location here thus permits many firms producing consumer goods to achieve scale economies that are greater than those possible in smaller regions; thereby the firms increase their profits and market strength. The South East's capital goods firms, too, benefit from rapid access to the region's 32,000 manufacturing firms, and from proximity to the unique concentration of headquarters offices in central London, where numerous purchasing decisions are taken concerning both government and private spending on equipment of all kinds. And well over half of the region's service industry is engaged simply in meeting the needs of the South East's own population and industry.

The exceptional nodality of the South East and London in terms of the national pattern of road, rail and air communications also increases their market accessibility. Access to the national market, 80 per cent of which is in any case within 300 kilometres (190 miles) of London, is easier from the capital via the motorways, trunk roads and express rail services which lead directly to Bristol, Birmingham, Liverpool, Sheffield, Newcastle and Edinburgh, than from almost any other British city, with the possible exception of Birmingham. Lastly, export markets are also more accessible from the South East than from any other region. The geographical range and frequency of cross-channel and deep-sea sailings from London, Southampton, Dover and the Haven ports (Felixstowe, Harwich, Ipswich) are far greater, taken together, than those available within a similar-sized area elsewhere. And London's airports—Heathrow, Gatwick, Stansted and Luton—totally dominate the pattern of international flights to and from Britain, with 84 per cent of all United Kingdom international terminal passengers in 1976.

Closely associated with market accessibility is a second key factor explaining above-average economic growth in the South East—London's innovation leadership. Recent geographical research on the spatial spread of new ideas, techniques and activities within countries suggests that many innovations affecting new types of manufacturing and service activity are first adopted and tested in the largest urban centre (Robson, 1973, p.137). They then spread to other cities and towns according to the twin principles of 'hierarchical' and 'neighbourhood' diffusion. The former means that they then appear at the next level of urban centre in the hierarchy (Birmingham, Manchester, Liverpool in the British case), then at the level after that, and so on. The latter implies the local, distance-constrained, spread of innovation around the original urban centre.

The explanation for this innovation leadership lies in the crucial advantages enjoyed by entrepreneurs in a country's dominant urban centre in terms of information-maximization and risk-minimization. There is no doubt that the availability of information of all kinds even in developed countries such as Britain is spatially biased towards the largest centre, which acts as a nodal point in national and international information networks. Moreover, the concentration of people there permits intensity of interaction between individuals and hence the local transmission of new ideas. This encourages above-average invention and innovation rates. Usually, the leading urban centre is also the least-risk location for testing and promoting an innovation aimed at the population at large, because of its sheer size, above-average wealth, and more cosmopolitan character and attitudes. The largest urban centre is therefore the safest market for innovation testing. Only later, when and if the innovation has proved successful, is diffusion to smaller surrounding settlements and other urban centres feasible.

This simple theory of the origin and diffusion of innovation may account for much of London's twentieth-century industrial and employment growth. In a modern competitive world, the firm or area which first succeeds in launching a new product or service, or utilizing a new technology, tends to cream the profits: subsequent imitators are generally forced to accept much lower rates of return. As Berry has noted, 'biggest means first, earliest means most'. Thus the high profits and growth rates characteristic of the successful industrial pioneer may in part explain London's traditional industrial vitality.

Specific evidence concerning this hypothesis of innovation leadership is available for both indigenous and 'imported' innovations. That London and the South East have led the way in the creation or adoption of 'British-made' innovations of all kinds is strongly suggested both by the concentration of research activity there and by many individual cases. The remarkable twentieth-century concentration of industrial and scientific research in and around the capital is well documented. In 1955, for example (Department of Scientific and Industrial Research, 1958, p.19), no less than 45 per cent of the United Kingdom's total research workforce in private industrial and scientific research establishments were employed in the South East and East Anglia. More recently, Buswell and Lewis (1970) have estimated that the South East contains 49 per cent of all research establishments in the United Kingdom. The reasons for this striking geographical concentration of research activity include the attractiveness of residence in South East England for highly-qualified research personnel, the existing concentration of modern technology-oriented industry there, the unrivalled role of London as the country's leading university city and scientific centre, and its unparalleled international communications nodality. Its effect is to encourage a greater volume of industrial and technological innovations in the region, and particularly in London, than in other regions or centres.

Individual examples which appear to fit the hypothesis are numerous, especially in the service industries. Often, however, service innovations have a direct impact upon allied manufacturing trades, so that London-based innovation has occurred in both sectors. One of the most obvious cases is broadcasting. Radio broadcasting began in London in 1922, programmes only becoming available in other regions after 1925 and the inauguration of the Daventry transmitter. Television broadcasts from Alexandra Palace in north London began in 1936: a second, Birmingham, transmitter was not inaugurated until thirteen years later. In other words, the London area led the way in radio and television transmission and reception. The same pattern of initial innovation adoption by London is evident in such contrasting spheres as civil aviation and the opening of clothing 'boutiques'. The first-ever scheduled civil aviation service in Britain began operation in 1919 between London and Paris, symbolizing the dominance which London has exerted over commercial and private flying in Britain from the earliest days of powered flight. More recently, the 'boutique' phenomenon of the 1960s began entirely in London, giving wordwide fame to Carnaby Street and King's Road, Chelsea, and dictating changes in teenage clothing fashions throughout the country.

London's innovating role in each case reflects its position as the country's largest, most affluent and hence lowest-risk market. At the same time these successful service innovations have not only generated a remarkable twentieth-century growth of service employment in the capital, but also spawned associated manufacturing innovation and industry. Thus, London's dominance over early broadcasting, at a period when equipment was bulky, fragile and undergoing rapid technological change, resulted in a remarkable concentration of radio manufacturing in London. By 1939, 80 per cent of British employment in the radio and television manufacturing industry was provided by factories in the capital. Again, the concentration, from their very beginning, of civil aviation services in London inevitably encouraged the growth of aircraft manufacturing in and around the metropolis. Such famous names as De Havilland, Handley Page, Napier, Sopwith and Hawker all first appeared in London, which was the country's leading aircraft manufacturing centre up to the early 1920s. Lastly, London's innovating role in the boutique phenomenon greatly benefited the capital's clothing industry during the 1960s, both by the reflected prestige of a 'Made in London' label, and because of the speed with which it could detect and respond to fasion changes dictated by Carnaby Street.

Imported innovations have also played a part in London's leadership. The capital's unrivalled international nodality, coupled with its geographical proximity to Europe, has meant that many innovations originating abroad have reached Britain through its firms. A good example is motor vehicle manufacturing. Early car making in Britain was greatly influenced by technological developments in France and Germany. These developments, together with imported components such as the famous French De Dion engine, reached Britain through London. Not surprisingly, London's vehicle firms were thus able to lead the way in adopting and adapting foreign innovations, while several French firms such as Darraq, Citroen and Aster established or licensed London factories to manufacture their products for the first time in Britain. Another example is the early motion-picture manufacturing industry. In this instance it was American technological innovations which reached Britain through London, and the resultant leadership in their adoption, particularly by the London scientific instrument maker Robert Paul, helped the capital to become the unrivalled centre for motion-picture and camera manufacture in the country.

Further factors which help to explain the South East's remarkable twentieth-century growth include the quality of its labour-force, the availability of so-called agglomeration economies, and various entrepreneurial and institutional considerations. The above average quality of the labour force of the region is evident in various ways. In addition to the fact that its population is unusually biased towards the 15-44 working age group (40.4 per cent of the total, compared with only 37.8 per cent and 38.7 per cent in the South West and Wales, respectively, in 1976), official statistics reveal that rates of absenteeism from work are lower, and levels of educational attainment higher, than in most other regions (Keeble, 1976, 65). So firms in the South East can draw on a labour force which is likely to be more productive than is the case elsewhere. These characteristics probably reflect a traditional bias in migration to the South East towards younger, more enterprising and qualified individuals—as indicated by Brown's finding that 'the South East is a great magnet for the young ..., with those aged 15 to 24 about 20 per cent more numerous among its incomers than they are among interregional movers generally' (Brown, 1972, p.259).

Not surprisingly, a further advantage enjoyed by firms in those growth industries which have become specially concentrated in the South East during the twentieth century is a parallel concentration of appropriately trained labour. Such a concentration can be measured by its location quotient. The latter is obtained by calculating the percentage of the national total of a particular group of workers which are found in a given area, and the percentage of the national total of all workers which are found there. The former is then divided by the latter. A location quotient greater than 1.00 means that the area's labour force is unusually biased towards that particular group. In the South East case, examples of above-average concentrations include electronic engineering workers (1.64 in 1976), instrument engineering workers (1.51), insurance workers (1.49), workers in advertising and market research (2.21), and research and development service workers (1.76). In terms of occupational qualifications, one of the most significant concentrations is of administrators and managers, with a South East quotient of 1.27 in 1971 (Keeble, 1976, 69).

Industrial expansion in the South East has been aided further by agglomeration economies. Such economies are cost savings accruing to firms because of the concentration of a large volume of economic activity within a relatively small area, enabling firms in effect to share some of their (external) expenses with others. Traditionally, such economies have most commonly been associated with industry in London; but increasing ease of movement of lorries and goods has undoubtedly widened the availability of such economies to include today locations in the rest of the South East, too. Examples of agglomeration economies are a readier availability of factories or offices for firms seeking larger premises than in smaller centres or regions, and the existence of specialist firms providing all kinds of ancillary services to other manufacturing and service establishments. These specialist firms include stockholders of raw material, firms engaged in packaging and despatching manufactured exports, road haulage specialists, machinery service firms, business management, market research and advertising consultants, insurance, banking and finance firms, and so on. A form of agglomeration economy which has attracted much attention is local industrial linkage. Manufacturing plants are said to be industrially linked when flows of goods—usually semi-finished parts or components—take place between them. In other words, one manufacturing firm acts as a market for another. Smaller firms in the South East, especially in London's clothing and mechanical engineering industries, are quite often dependent on linkages of this kind within the metropolis or region. At the same time, through specialization, they may be able to achieve production economies which are then passed on through lower charges to their customers. Basically similar functional interrelationships also characterize many central London office firms. But in this office linkage case, the flows are of information and involve abstract transactions, not goods. The benefits of specialization associated with intense office linkages are a major factor in the efficiency and growth of the financial industries of the City of London.

A final factor helping to explain growth in the South East concerns the region's entrepreneurial and institutional advantages. Much evidence suggest that the South East's residential environment is attractive to entrepreneurs—individuals willing to bear the responsibility and financial risks of establishing and directing new firms. A concentration of potential entrepreneurs is certainly suggested by the South East's high location quotient for managers, noted above, by its high proportion of younger, possibly more progressive, immigrants and by the above-average educational level of its inhabitants. An interesting special case here is the concentration in Greater London (1966 location quotient: 2.21) of migrants, often refugees, from Central and Western Europe—German and Polish Jews, Czechs, Hungarians and others. Unusually biased towards professional and managerial workers, this migrant group has produced a surprising number of entrepreneurs, to the considerable benefit of metropolitan economic growth. The region's general residential attractiveness—for reasons, no doubt, of climate, scenery, history and cultural heritage, plus the advantages conferred by London's unique role and facilities—is illustrated by such studies as that of Gould and White (1968). This found that school-leavers throughout Britain generally ranked the South East more highly on residential environment grounds, assuming freedom to live anywhere, than any other region, with the exception of the South West and, possibly, East Anglia.

Institutional advantages refer to the existence of supporting institutions in the South East, oriented towards promotion and reinforcing economic growth. An illustration of this is the readier availability and lower cost of private finance capital. In a recent survey of electronic manufacturing firms in London, the Outer Metropolitan Area of the South East, and Scotland (McDermott, 1977), it was found that a significantly higher proportion of firms in the former two areas were able to obtain the bulk of their finance for capital investment privately, from commercial banks, than was the case with the Scottish firms investigated. The latter, therefore, had to rely more heavily on government aid. Similarly, a 1972 *Times* survey noted that the commercial interest rate on loan finance for industrial development in South East England was only 7¾ per cent, compared with over 9 per cent for what were presumably regarded as higher-risk projects in regions such as the North and Wales (Keeble, 1976, 71). Thus institutional and entrepreneurial factors also help to explain the traditionally more rapid industrial, and hence population, growth in the South East region.

4.4 Relative Regional Decline

The traditional twentieth-century image of the South East is thus one of a dynamic, prosperous region enjoying cumulative economic and population growth at the expense of other parts of Britain. However, this traditional picture is no longer completely valid. For since the mid-1960s, there has occurred what is in many ways a dramatic reversal of previous trends: relative growth has been replaced by relative decline. Thus the South East's share of national population, employment and earnings has been falling, not rising, since about 1966. The region has also experienced an absolute decline in employment, especially in manufacturing, and since 1972 in population. Thus Table 4.1 shows that the South East's population share was by 1977 back to a percentage lower than that of 1961; and that the average net population migration gains of the early 1960s had been replaced, by 1973-1977, with the largest net migration *losses* of any region of the country. Since 1972, the peak year for South East population (17.02 million), the actual number of people living in the region has also been falling. On the employment side, manufacturing jobs have declined at a remarkable rate, both absolutely and relatively, although total employment losses have been smaller because of the continuing expansion of service jobs. A slight relative decline in manual earnings has also occurred. By examining the changing geography of three major industries in a national context, the processes at work can be in part exposed.

4.4.1 *The Clothing Industry in a National Context*

The clothing industry is perhaps the classic case of a 'small-firm' industry. In 1968, average employment per clothing factory in Britain was only fifty-two workers: and most factories undoubtedly employed fewer than this, given the inflation of the national mean by the unusually large men's tailoring firms found only in West Yorkshire. In women's clothing, the average was only thirty-nine workers. This characteristic reflects two things. One is the ease of entry to the industry by potential entrepreneurs. All that is needed to set up a clothing firm is a few employees, some sewing machines, and a room in which to operate. The clothing industry has thus long been characterized by a high birth rate of new firms—offsett, of course, by an equally high, if not higher, death rate. The other factor is the industry's dependence on the vagaries of fashion. This is admittedly more true of some branches—women's clothing most notably—than others. But in these branches, the flexibility of operations and speed of response to the changes in fashion that characterize small firms appears to give them competitive advantages over larger, perhaps more cumbersome, concerns.

Employment in the British clothing industry has been contracting ever since 1900. By

1976, it had fallen to 291,000, with a decline of 26 per cent since 1965 alone. In part, this reflects increasing competition in the British market from imports of cheap clothing originating in Third World countries. The largest clothing trade, by employment, is women's dresses, lingerie, etc. (90,000), with men's tailoring close behind (74,000). An important characteristic of the industry is its unusual dependence upon female labour. In 1976, 81 per cent of its workers were women, compared with only 29 per cent for all manufacturing industry, and only 9 per cent for such heavy industries as iron and steel. The industry is also exceptionally labour-intensive, in that labour costs as a proportion of total costs are higher than in almost any other manufacturing industry, with the exception of textiles and footwear (Keeble, 1976, pp.172-181).

Throughout the twentieth century, the geography of the clothing industry in Britain has been dominated by the three conurbations of London, Manchester and Leeds. In 1959, for example, these three centres alone accounted for over half the national total of clothing workers, with London, by far the largest centre, employing approximately 117,000. Elsewhere, the industry was fairly widely scattered, in rough proportion to the distribution of urban population—though the West Midlands was an anomaly in this respect, with a much smaller clothing industry than its urban population might suggest.

This simple aggregate picture conceals important variations in the location of the different clothing trades within the industry. Greater London, for example, specializes on the manufacture of women's clothing, both dresses and lingerie, and women's tailored outerwear. Both of these are of course characterized by very small plants: indeed, in the remarkable East End clothing 'quarter' studied by Martin (1964, p.129) the average clothing establishment employed only nineteen workers in 1955, with 900 tiny factories employing 17,000 workers crammed into only one square mile around Whitechapel. The London clothing industry, in fact, developed in response to the great demand for clothing from the capital's wealthy population: and its specialization on fashionable women's wear reflects the great advantage of close contact with West End clothing designers, fashion experts, and national retail stores. Being small, inner London clothing firms have also long exhibited a remarkable degree of inter-firm industrial linkage, with semi-finished clothing being transferred between different firms specializing in different processes. Such linkage has traditionally afforded the whole industry external economies of scale, despite the smallness of its individual firms.

Clothing manufacturing in Manchester and Leeds has slightly different origins, developing as it did out of the local cotton and wool textile industries. In Manchester, the industry specializes to some extent in the production of weatherproof outerwear—a reflection of the region's climate?—together with women's clothing. The availability of a large supply of industrially trained female labour is a further traditional reason for the industry's development here, as it is also in West Yorkshire. In the latter conurbation, however, the industry came to specialize in the different trade of men's outerwear (70 per cent of West Yorkshire clothing employment), and has seen the development of unusually large clothing factories, specializing in the 'mass production' of suits, jackets and trousers for the national market. West Yorkshire firms have been badly hit in recent years by foreign competition and shifts in demand.

Since 1945, the geography of the clothing industry in Britain has changed considerably. The three great traditional centres have all lost very large numbers of clothing firms and jobs. By 1976, clothing employment in Greater London had fallen to only 49,000, involving the staggering loss since 1959 of nearly 70,000 jobs, or 58 per cent of the 1959 total. In striking contrast, clothing employment in many traditionally non-industrial parts of Britain has grown. This is particularly true of the assisted regions of Wales, northern England and Scotland (up by 12,000, or 20 per cent, 1965-1976) and of rural areas such as East Anglia and north Yorkshire. As a result, clothing production is now more geographically dispersed than probably any other British manufacturing industry. This dispersion partly reflects a particularly high post-war migration rate of firms, usually from the conurbations to other areas (Keeble, 1975).

The reasons for this shift are clear (Keeble, 1976, pp.179-181). One is the acute shortage in the conurbations of relatively cheap female labour, a serious problem for an industry which is highly conscious of the cost of labour. Moves by clothing firms between 1964 and 1967 were thus more frequently prompted by a search for cheap labour than was the case with any other manufacturing industry (Department of Trade and Industry, 1973). A second factor is government incentives to locate in the assisted regions. Again, the 1964-1967 survey revealed that these incentives had been a major locational influence on more clothing firms (45 per cent) than was the case with all but two other industries. With continuing conurbation population and hence workforce decline, further losses of this classic inner city industry by its traditional centres seem inevitable, whatever government inner city policy tries to do to halt it.

4.4.2 *The Electrical Engineering Industry in a National Context*

Electrical engineering is Britain's second most important manufacturing industry, measured by employment (730,000 in 1976). Yet the industry scarcely existed at all in 1900, while even as recently as the 1960s, two types of electrical manufacturing—telecommunications and electronic engineering—were still amongst the eight (out of 108) fastest-growing individual manufacturing categories, with respect to jobs, in the country (Chisholm and Oeppen, 1973). The twentieth-century history of electrical engineering is one of constant growth and technological change, with the development of an enormous variety of products, ranging from domestic goods such as light bulbs, irons, washing machines and television sets, to hospital x-ray and kidney machines, electrical equipment for cars and aircraft, telephones, electricity generators, and electronic computers. Indeed, electronic control components are now being incorporated in so many engineering products that it is becoming very difficult to distinguish 'electrical' from 'mechanical' engineering. This 'electronic revolution' does not, however, mean that employment in the industry is still growing rapidly—quite the reverse. Technological changes mean that electronic equipment may soon require less than one-tenth of the production workforce needed only ten years ago! So a considerable decline in employment in this industry is possible, though the importance and output of electronic devices of all kinds is bound to grow.

The early development of electrical engineering in Britain was heavily concentrated in London. By 1939, for example (section 4.3), Greater London's radio and television equipment firms employed no less than 80 per cent of all British workers in this branch of the industry. Even by 1976, after considerable dispersal of firms to other areas, Greater London was still by far the leading electrical engineering centre of Britain with 128,000 workers or 18 per cent of the British total. The South East as a whole accounted for 290,000 workers, or 39 per cent, representing a slight decline from its 1965 share of 42 per cent. Throughout the twentieth century, London and the South East have been especially attractive locations for those branches of electrical engineering undergoing the fastest technological change, and where research and innovation have been progressing most rapidly. The electronics industry is a classic example. By 1959, the South East accounted for no less than 63 per cent of national employment in this brand-new activity, with over two-fifths in London alone (Keeble, 1976, p.193). The country's leading computer firms—I.B.M., I.C.L., Honeywell—are still almost entirely concentrated in or run from the South East.

The reasons for this remarkable concentration centre on three things—the industry's need, all else being equal, for maximum accessibility to the customers; for the minimization of risk in an innovatory, technologically dynamic, industry; and for access to human resources, especially highly-skilled research engineers and scientists. These are all discussed in general terms in section 4.3. But it is worth stressing that, in their early stages of development, the London area afforded most branches of electrical engineering—telephone equipment, radio and television, electronic computers—a combination of advantages unrivalled anywhere else. Here were to be found the country's largest, most cosmopolitan and wealthiest market, the greatest concentration of skilled workers and research engineers, the biggest pool of trained female production workers, maximum access to information from abroad on the latest technological developments, and a remarkable number of potential entrepreneurs willing to take risks and experiment with new products and processes. These advantages made the concentration in London of most branches of electrical engineering in their early stages more or less inevitable.

Since 1945, however, the electrical engineering industry has become more geographically dispersed throughout Britain. This reflects a higher rate of migration by existing firms (including both complete transfers and branch factories) than by all but two other industries (out of eighteen) prompted by above-average growth (Keeble, 1976, 127-131). Dispersal has occurred both *within* the South East, from London to the outer parts of the region, and *between* the South East and other regions, notably the peripheral Assisted Areas of Scotland, Wales and northern England. The share of national employment in those three regions has therefore risen (from 14 to 17 per cent, 1965-1976), while that of the South East, and especially London, has fallen. London alone has probably lost no fewer than 80,000 or so electrical engineering jobs since 1959. Why has this happened?

Part of the answer is what has been called 'decentralization with maturity' (Keeble, 1968, p.16). As different branches of electrical manufacturing have matured, rapid early technological change has often given way to mass production of standardized goods. Such mass production is 'labour-intensive', in that labour costs make up a high proportion of total production costs. The industry thus becomes very sensitive to geographical variations in the availability and hence cost of production workers, especially women. The result has been the establishment, often by London firms, of large electrical engineering branch factories in the assisted regions, where there is greater labour availability. The huge Hoover washing machine plant at Merthyr Tydfil is a good example.

This trend has also been powerfully aided by government regional policy. Thus a 1964-1967 government survey of over 600 mobile factories found that more electrical engineering firms claimed to have been significantly influenced in their choice of a new location by regional policy than was the case with all but two or three other industries. This was in fact the second most important locational influence for them, after labour availability (Department of Trade and Industry, 1973).

On the other hand, the shift of electrical manufacturing *within* the South East appears especially to involve research-oriented firms. It reflects such influences as the increasing age and obsolescence of factory premises in London, and the residential attractiveness of the South East outside London to essential research staff. The establishment by I.B.M. of major units at Hursley, Hampshire (research and development), and Havant, Portsmouth (computer manufacturing), epitomizes this type of development in or near residentially attractive areas (Keeble, 1976, p.198).

4.4.3 *Finance, Banking and Insurance in a National Context*

The phenomenal post-war growth of service industry and employment in Britain is nowhere better illustrated than by Order XXIV of the official Standard Industrial Classification, covering insurance, banking, finance and business services. In 1965, for example, this group of service activities still employed fewer workers—792,000—than the country's two biggest manufacturing industries, mechanical and electrical engineering. By 1976, however, employment in finance, banking and insurance had grown to no fewer than 1,087,000, an increase of nearly 300,000 workers or 37 per cent in only ten years: and it was by then substantially bigger than any individual manufacturing industry.

In a sense, of course, this group of service trades does not constitute as clearly defined an industry as, say, shipbuilding or clothing manufacturing. Included in it is a rich variety of service organizations, such as insurance firms and banks, stockbrokers and building societies, property companies and estate agents, advertising, market research, computer and employment agencies, and certain headquarter offices. Nevertheless, it clearly embraces the financial sector of the country's economy and, as such, is of great importance to both national economic development and the balance of payments. Moreover most firms within the order provide so-called 'higher-order' services, utilized principally by other firms and only occasionally by individual customers. Their geographical distribution is thus much less a simple reflection of the location of population than is the case, say, with retailing, or primary and secondary education.

This lack of direct relationship to population distribution is one factor behind the extraordinary concentration of this service industry in South East England, and most notably London. In 1976, no less than 54 per cent of national employment in finance, banking, insurance and business services (587,000 jobs) was to be found in South East England (compared with the region's 33 per cent share of *all* employment); and the bulk of this (426,000 jobs, or 39 per cent) was in Greater London. The tiny area of central London alone contained organizations in this industry employing no fewer than 250,000 workers. Outside the London city-region, the two biggest centres of the industry were the Manchester and Birmingham conurbations, each with about 50,000 workers.

Why has this concentration developed? The heart of the explanation, in more senses than one, lies of course in the City of London, the dominant focus of financial activity in Britain and, indeed, Europe (section 5.5). Historically, the financial organizations which cluster in the so-called 'Square Mile' grew out of the shipping and trading activity of the Port of London, itself reflecting Britain's historical role as a great trading nation. Twentieth-century expansion has followed, in a process of 'cumulative causation'. Because the City of London already contained the greatest concentration of national and international banks and insurance firms, enjoyed the closest links with government and the Treasury, and was the hub of an international financial communications network, new financial activities naturally developed there rather than elsewhere in Britain. In turn, this encouraged still further improvement of the City's financial facilities and enhanced its attractiveness to new organizations. The influx to the City in the 1960s of American banks—Chase Manhattan, Citicorp International, etc.—is a classic example of this cumulative causation process. Interestingly, within the City, different financial activities tend to cluster in different areas (Goddard, 1968): finance and banking firms are grouped closely around the Bank of England and Stock Exchange, but trading activities, including risk insurance, are further east around Lloyds, the centre of the international risk insurance business. In all this, the pressing need by many firms for close daily, or even hourly, contact with the City's money markets and other firms—summed up in the phrase 'knowledge in a hurry'—provides a very powerful bond tying them to this small area.

This said, it is also true that the last decade has witnessed some decentralization of firms in this service industry from central London to other areas—though to a far smaller degree than with other London industries, especially manufacturing ones. This is probably the main reason for the decline in the shares of national employment in the industry recorded by both Greater London and the South East in the 1970s—from 42 to 39 per cent (Greater London), and from 59 to 54 per cent (South East), 1971-1976. The absolute numbers of workers in the industry in London and South East have however increased slightly. Most of the decentralizing London firms have moved only short distances into the rest of the South East or adjacent regions—to towns such as Reading, Bristol and Ipswich; and decentralization has usually involved only relatively routine activities, such as the accounts and records departments. The reasons for such movement are the very high cost of clerical staff and office space in central London, the latter substantially the result of planning policies (section 5.5). Indeed, Rhodes and Kan (1971) estimated that in 1969 total annual operating costs (salaries, rent, rates, telephones, etc.) per employee in a central London office were approximately one-third greater (£2,202) than those incurred in other parts of Britain (£1,657). Criticism of government policy for significantly increasing the costs of City financial services which cannot move yet are vital to the balance of payments, and concern over inner city unemployment, have however produced a recent easing of government office building controls in London.

4.4.4 *Some Causes of Relative Decline*

In one sense, of course, a reversal into relative population and employment decline was only to be expected at some stage or other in the South East's development. It would seem inevitable that sooner or later forces would come into play to halt the process of cumulative growth, given the intrinsic absurdity of the only logical alternative outcome, 100 per cent concentration of British population and economic activity in the region! However, the nature of the forces that have occasioned the reversal demands attention. These forces can be considered under the two headings of agglomeration diseconomies, and government regional policy.

The impact on the South East in general and London in particular of substantial agglomeration diseconomies, offsetting to a considerable degree the agglomeration economies and other advantages enjoyed by the region, seems to have intensified in recent years. This intensification probably reflects both the diseconomies themselves and, more significantly, a growing unwillingness by the South East's population and industry to tolerate them. The unwillingness in turn is related to rising living and space standards, and

Table 4.1 South East England: changes in population, employment and earnings, 1966-1977

	Population		Employment		Manufacturing employment	
	'000s	% Britain	'000s	% Britain	'000s	% Britain
1966	16,719	31.5	7,522	33.0	2,363	28.1
1977	16,834	31.0	7,279	32.8	1,878	26.1
	Average annual net migration per 1,000 base year population					
1962-1967			+0.64			
1973-1977			−2.82			
	Average weekly earnings, male manual workers, as a percentage of U.K.					
1967-1968			104.1			
1976-1977			102.4			

growing expectations, linked to rising real incomes. From the viewpoint of population, the chief agglomeration diseconomies are probably housing costs and shortages, journey-to-work times and costs, and a residential environment which in places is no longer as attractive as it once was to many families. All these diseconomies reach a peak in London.

The cost of housing in the South East, reflecting very high land and building costs and above-average demand, has for years been much greater than the national average. In 1973, for example, the average prices of houses mortgaged by members of the Building Societies Association in Greater London (£14,447) and the rest of the South East (£13,164) were 44 per cent and 31 per cent respectively above the national average (£10,020). And the differential with prices in the United Kingdom excluding the South East was, of course, substantially greater than this, given the inflation of the national average itself by the size of the South East housing stock and its very high values. Interestingly, the United Kingdom/South East differential has declined since 1973, although it was still a considerable 22 per cent in 1978. A further point is that, especially in London, the quality of available housing is frequently poorer than in parts of other regions where the housing stock is newer.

Average journeys to work are longer and hence more costly in the South East than elsewhere. In 1973, 37 per cent of work journeys in the region took thirty minutes or more, compared with a national average of only 28 per cent and values for adjacent East Anglia and the South West of only 19 and 16 per cent respectively.

The problems of the region's residential environment are confined almost entirely to London. A major factor here is that increasing incomes seem to be associated with an increasing unwillingness by many families to accept the high residential densities and lack of living space which traditionally and inevitably characterize the capital. In addition, the growth of traffic congestion and noise problems, increasing crime and, possibly, declining standards of some local services such as public transport have caused a real deterioration in London's residential environment. The overall result is clearly illustrated by surveys such as Gould and White's (1968) which yielded a London residential preference score some 30 per cent below that of the nearby south coast, South West England and East Anglia.

Regional industrial decline is probably less directly influenced than is population change by agglomeration diseconomies. However, the residential preferences of industrialists undoubtedly influence industrial location decisions to some extent (Keeble, 1976, 83-85), while the problems posed by factory obsolescence and cost, plus the very high rents and rates of offices, in London are powerful restraints upon further investment. These diseconomies have undoubtedly encouraged an increasing migration of metropolitan manufacturing and office firms to neighbouring South West England, East Anglia and the East Midlands, where modern premises can be obtained more readily and cheaply. This movement is, of course, paralleled by that of population, these three regions accounting for the great bulk of the South East's substantial net population losses through migration. Thus a net population migration loss by the South East between 1974 and 1976 of 79,300 compares quite closely with a net migration gain to the South West of 58,900, to East Anglia of 37,100 and to the East Midlands of 9,700. Significantly, these were the only British regions, other than Wales, to record any net migration gain at all during those years, all other regions recording losses.

The effect of agglomeration diseconomies in the South East, then, is now encouraging some dispersal of the region's population and industry to neighbouring areas and regions. In a sense, therefore, it could be argued that the region's statistical boundary no longer adequately contains the functional London-focused South East, since with continuing communication improvements, people and firms can move into adjacent regions but still enjoy the advantages of relative proximity to London. This is certainly argued by the 1976 review of the Strategic Plan for the South East when it notes that a 1971-1975 population decline in the region of 60,000 could well be 'an accident of boundary definition since the ring of 22 districts immediately beyond the regional boundary increased by a quarter of a million' over this period. Thus 'the population of the "South East region" is static or declining but that of the wider "South East" may be expanding' (South East Joint Planning Team, 1976, p.12). In this context, it should be noted that dispersal to these adjacent areas has been accelerated somewhat by planning policy in the South East, and the designation of two new towns—Peterborough and Northampton —and fourteen expanded towns in these adjacent regions, taking population and industry from London and its surrounding towns. The willingness of population and firms to move to such places, however, reflects of course the underlying agglomeration diseconomies within the South East noted above; 'planned overspill' is in any case only a minor component—30 per cent of total net migration to East Anglia in 1971-1974, for example—in dispersal across the regional boundary.

The impact of government regional policy on decline in the South East is more controversial. The South East review, for example, claims that its 'adverse effects . . . on the South East are often exaggerated. Most applications for industrial development certificates in the South East are in fact granted . . . . Industrial location policy has only a limited impact on growth in the region and only very few moves to the Assisted Areas result from refusal of an IDC' (South East Joint Planning Team, 1976, p.11). However, other evidence does point to the intensification of regional policy since 1966 as a prime cause of the region's remarkable *manufacturing* employment decline. The loss of 485,000 jobs (Table 4.1), or 21 per cent of the total, between 1966 and 1977 has been greater *and* faster than that of any other region. In turn, this manufacturing decline must have had some effect on the population and earnings trends noted in Table 4.1. As was seen in Chapter 2, the evidence indicating a substantial 'policy effect' on regional manufacturing employment, both through diverting existing South East firms to the Assisted Areas and through holding back manufacturing investment in the region, is varied. Thus, for example, Moore and Rhodes's (1976) statistical analyses imply quite clearly a diversion by regional policy incentives and controls of approximately 100,000 manufacturing jobs from the South East to the Assisted Areas in 1960-1971; two-thirds of these were accounted for by the physical movement of firms, while the remaining third may be thought of as entirely new developments which, in the absence of regional policy, would have been located in the South East. The dominant role of regional policy since 1966 with respect to migrant manufacturing firms is also clearly attested by the statistical analyses of Sant (1975, pp.148-159) and Keeble (1976, pp.142-145). Indeed, in the latter case Assisted Area status was identified as the single most important influence upon sub-regional net migration rates, as measured by employment changes between 1966 and 1971.

That regional policy has also held back manufacturing investment in the South East by firms which have not moved production is suggested by Clark's work (1976: quoted in Keeble, 1976, pp.24-25) on regional manufacturing investment rates in 1966-1969. Thus, official Department of Industry statistics show that over this period manufacturing investment per employee in the South East was lower, at £428, not just than the national average (£576), but than any other British region. The comparison with the North (£1,101), Wales (£1,019) and Scotland (£770), the highest-scoring regions, is particularly striking. While different industrial structures obviously play an important part in this differential—Wales is noted, for example, for the capital-intensive steel and oil-refining industries—the position of the South East, the region with the most favourable overall manufacturing structure in 1965, would seem difficult to explain without some reference to regional policy, its constraints and incentives.

The intensified and adverse impact of regional policy on manufacturing in the South East since about 1966 has, of course, coincided with a substantial and very serious decline in the level of national manufacturing employment and industrial competitiveness (Chapter 1). Britain's manufacturing workforce fell by 1.20 million or 14 per cent between 1966 and 1977; and, as noted above, no fewer than 485,000 or 40 per cent of these lost jobs were shed by firms in the South East. National manufacturing decline has in consequence been singled out by the government since 1975 as the principal long-term economic problem facing Britain, a problem which it is trying to tackle by means of its so-called 'industrial strategy'. It seems clear, however, that in theory, at least, there is some degree of conflict between a policy of national manufacturing regeneration and one of constraining industrial growth in Britain's most important manufacturing region, the South East. The latter, after all, contains the country's biggest single concentration of exporting firms, many of which, as McDermott (1978) has shown for the electronics industry, are characterized by above-average growth of productivity and turnover, implying greater efficiency and faster technological change than firms elsewhere. This is especially true for firms in South East England outside London. Such firms need surely to be encouraged, not constrained, to expand still further their production and employment: and if, as various writers have suggested (e.g. Keeble, 1976, pp.46-71; Manners, 1977), South East England still affords a particularly favourable environment for company growth and development in most modern industries, should this not be regarded by the government as a major asset in its campaign for national manufacturing regeneration? In the changed national and international economic conditions of the 1970s and 1980s, a restrictive regional policy towards manufacturing industry in South East England would seem at best inappropriate, and at worst a possible subsidiary cause of national industrial decline.

REFERENCES

Brown, A.J. (1972). *The Framework of Regional Economics in the United Kingdom,* Cambridge University Press.
Buswell, R.J., and Lewis, E.W. (1970). The geographical distribution of industrial research activity in the United Kingdom. *Regional Studies,* **4,** 297-306.
Chisholm, M., and Oeppen, J. (1973). *The Changing Pattern of Employment: Regional Specialisation and Industrial Localisation in Britain.* Croom Helm, London.
Clark, A. (1976). Government policy and the spatial distribution of investment in Great Britain, 1964-1969. Unpublished Ph.D. thesis, University of Cambridge.
Department of Scientific and Industrial Research (1958). *Estimates of Resources Devoted to Scientific and Engineering Research and Development in British Manufacturing Industry, 1955,* H.M.S.O., London.
Department of Trade and Industry (1973). Memorandum on the inquiry into location attitudes and experience. *Minutes of Evidence.* Trade and Industry Sub-Committee of the House of Commons Expenditure Committee. Wednesday, July 4th, Session 1972-73. H.M.S.O., London, pp.525-668.
Goddard, J.B. (1968). Multivariate analysis of office location patterns in the city centre: a London example. *Regional Studies,* **2,** 64-85.
Gould, P.R., and White, R.R. (1968). The mental maps of British school leavers. *Regional Studies,* **2,** 161-182.
Hoare, A.G. (1973). The spheres of influence of industrial location factors. *Regional Studies,* **7,** 301-313.
Keeble, D. (1968). Industrial decentralisation and the metropolis: the North-West London case. *Transactions of the Institute of British Geographers,* **44,** 1-54.
Keeble, D. (1975). Industrial mobility: in which industries has plant location changed most? *Regional Studies,* **9,** 297-99.
Keeble, D. (1976). *Industrial Location and Planning in the United Kingdom,* Methuen, London.
Lee, C.H. (1971). *Regional Economic Growth in the United Kingdom Since the 1880s,* McGraw-Hill, London.
McDermott, P.J. (1977). Regional variations in enterprise: electronics firms in Scotland, London and the Outer Metropolitan Area. Unpublished Ph.D. thesis, University of Cambridge.
McDermott, P.J. (1978). Changing manufacturing enterprise in the metropolitan environment: the case of electronics firms in London. *Regional Studies,* **12,** 541-50.
Manners, G. (1977). The 1976 Review of the Strategic Plan for the South-East—some outstanding economic issues. *Planning Outlook,* **20,** 2-8.
Martin, J.E. (1964). The industrial geography of Greater London, in Clayton, R. (ed.), *The Geography of Greater London,* George Philip, London.
Moore, B.C., and Rhodes, J. (1976). A quantitative analysis of the effects of the Regional Employment Premium and other regional policy instruments. In A. Whiting (ed.), *The Economics of Industrial Subsidies,* H.M.S.O. for the Department of Industry, London.
Rhodes, J., and Kan, A. (1971). *Office Dispersal and Regional Policy,* Cambridge University Press, London.
Robson, B.T. (1973). *Urban Growth: An Approach,* Methuen, London.
Sant, M.E.C. (1975). *Industrial Movement and Regional Development: The British Case,* Pergamon, Oxford.
South East Joint Planning Team (1976). *Strategy for the South East: 1976 Review,* H.M.S.O., London.

CHAPTER 5

The South East: II Greater London

DAVID KEEBLE

5.1 Introduction

Greater London is the functional heart of the South East. As this description suggests, London, though physically fairly distinct in terms of bricks and mortar, can be thought of as extending functionally over a much wider area than the 1,580 square kilometres (616 square miles) governed by the Greater London Council. Indeed, the 'London city-region', defined in journey-to-work terms, now extends to up to 95 kilometres (60 miles) from Charing Cross (Figure 5.4). Within this region many people look to London for specialized shopping, entertainment and culture. They watch regional television programmes produced in London. They work in factories, offices or shops which are often controlled from, or linked by daily contact with, the capital. In this sense, London's citizens and industries are today as much to be found in Brighton and Basingstoke as in Holborn and Hounslow. Such has been the effect of the twentieth-century spread of London's influence, population and industry, through steadily improving communications, upon the formerly more isolated towns and villages of the outer South East and adjacent East Anglia.

But this said, 'London' as a densely built-up area administered by a single strategic local authority—the G.L.C.— is not only viewed as a distinctive place by most of the region's population, it also undoubtedly possesses its own characteristics and problems, which are now in considerable contrast to those in the rest of the South East (or the R.O.S.E., as it is often termed for convenience). So separate evaluation of these characteristics is necessary, with reference where appropriate to the interrelationships that link the metropolis with its surrounding region.

5.2 London's Population

Greater London contains the largest single concentration of people in Britain. In 1978, the G.L.C. area housed a resident population of 6.92 million (Figure 4.3), at an average density of 4,380 people per square kilometre (11,230 per square mile). This is much the highest average density of all Britain's major conurbations, although of course averages can be misleading with respect to inner city densities. Three aspects of London's demography are especially worth noting. These are the age structure of the population, the concentration here of immigrants from other countries, and London's recent population decline.

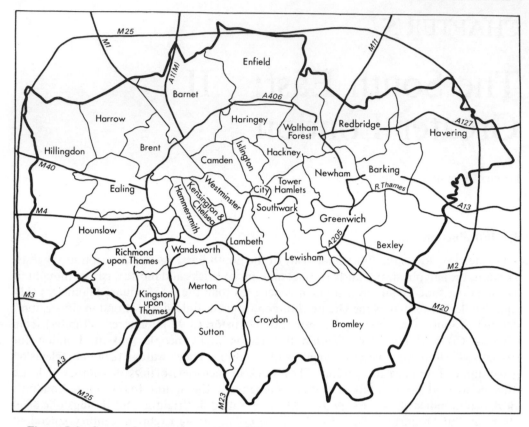

Figure 5.1 Greater London: boroughs, 1979

As Figure 5.2 shows, the age structure of London's resident population differs significantly from that of the rest of England and Wales. Children and teenagers (ages 0-19) are considerably under represented, whereas young adults (ages 20-29) are considerably over represented. There is also a relative concentration of older people (ages 50-64) in the metropolis, although the 80+ age group is proportionately less common. These differences strongly suggest that London is peculiarly attractive to young, childless adults, single and married, in the early stages of their working lives; but that with the birth of children, families move out of the capital (Stone, 1978, p.98). The low proportion of children may also indicate a smaller average family size in London, for those families with children who do remain in the metropolis. The most important planning implication of this pattern is the unusually high demand for housing in London from households of only one or two persons. Not only do such households often prefer particular types of accommodation—furnished flats, for example—but they also need more dwellings per thousand people than other sections of the population. So housing demand in London is greater than its overall population alone might suggest.

London also differs from elsewhere demographically in containing by far the largest single concentration of foreign-born immigrants in Britain. The 1971 Census showed that 1.07 million Londoners, or 14 per cent of the capital's population, had been born outside

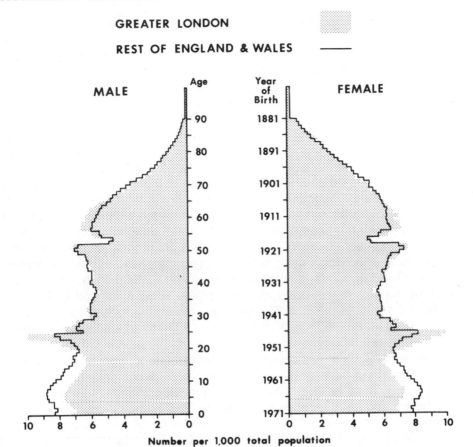

Figure 5.2   Greater London: population by age and sex, 1971
Source: Greater London Council

the United Kingdom. The largest immigrant groups were from India/Pakistan/ Bangladesh (137,000), the West Indies (169,000) and the Irish Republic (241,000), although there were also substantial numbers from European and African countries. Their marked relative concentration is indicated by the fact that the metropolis, with 14 per cent of Britain's population, contained 30 per cent of the country's immigrants from India/Pakistan/Bangladesh, 34 per cent of those from Eire, and no less than 56 per cent of those from the West Indies. The 352,000 immigrants from 'old' Commonwealth countries—Canada, Australia and New Zealand—and all other non-Commonwealth countries represented 31 per cent of the British total. It should be noted that these figures undoubtedly understate the actual numbers in certain categories, perhaps by 15 to 30 per cent. Further, in the case of West Indians and Asians, the relationship between country of birth and colour is by no means exact. For example, one-third of British immigrants from India are thought to be white, while the figures above by definition exclude the children of coloured parents born in Britain (Peach *et al.*, 1975, p.397).

Within London, different immigrant groups are concentrated in particular areas. The Irish have traditionally clustered to the north, north west and west of inner London, in Camden, Islington, Paddington, Hammersmith and Willesden. West Indians are especially concentrated in three areas, Willesden, Hackney-Haringey, and inner London south of the river (Wandsworth-Lambeth-Lewisham). Southall and Hounslow in outer west London, and the inner East End (Spitalfields), contain the most notable clusters of Asians (Shepherd *et al.*, 1974, pp.50-54). As these patterns indicate, these three immigrant groups are most commonly found in localities of older, dilapidated housing within inner London, just outside the central core. Their relative concentration here is thus associated with very poor housing conditions and considerable overcrowding. At the same time, their relatively low levels of skill contribute to the markedly high immigrant unemployment rates in some of the areas, especially amongst the Irish and West Indians (Lomas, 1974, p.16). Thus, inner city problems have come to be most acutely expressed and felt by these immigrant groups. At the same time, it must be noted that far from becoming more concentrated in incipient inner city ghettos, the three immigrant groups are modifying their geographical distribution quite rapidly. In particular, each group of immigrants recorded faster emigration rates from the inner city in 1961-1971 than did the 'indigenous' population of this area (Shepherd *et al.*, 1974, p.56). In the Asian and Irish cases, this largely reflected a shift of the main immigrant concentrations to locations further away from central London. But with the West Indians it also involved a substantial dispersal of their communities throughout London (Peach *et al.*, 1975, pp.409-410).

That Greater London's population is today declining both more rapidly and substantially than that of any other British city may seem surprising, given the traditional image of the capital as an irresistible magnet for population and industry. In fact, however, the largest population of what is now the G.L.C. area, 8.6 million, was recorded as long ago as 1939 (Figure 4.3). Since then, population numbers have been falling, and falling at an increasing rate. Thus the annual population loss in 1971-1978 was 74,000, compared with only 56,000 in 1961-1971 and 23,000 in 1951-1961. The geography of this decline within London, its components and its causes, all demand attention.

As Figure 5.3 shows, recent population decline has been heavily concentrated in inner London. Thus between 1961 and 1975, the group of fourteen inner London boroughs shown there recorded a loss of no fewer than 681,000 people, or 19.5 per cent, compared with a loss of only 199,000 or 4.4 per cent for the group of nineteen outer boroughs. Inner London is here defined in terms of boroughs largely built up before 1914. The highest individual rates of loss have been suffered by Islington (– 33 per cent), Tower Hamlets (– 27 per cent), Kensington and Chelsea (– 26 per cent) and Southwark (– 25 per cent). In contrast, the three outer London boroughs of Bexley (+ 3 per cent), Bromley (+ 1 per cent) and Croydon (+ 0.1 per cent) actually recorded very slight population growth.

The components of population change in London indicate very clearly, as might be expected, that decline is basically due to a very high volume and rate of out-migration. True, the dramatic fall in the national birth rate in recent years—from 18.5 per thousand population (England and Wales) in 1964 to a mere 11.5 per thousand in 1977—has had its impact on London as elsewhere; in particular, it is one reason for the increasing annual rate of population decline noted above. Morover, simple net out-migration figures mask the very substantial gross flows of population in *and* out. Thus a net migration loss in 1970-1971 of 110,000 conceals an influx of 245,000 (104,000 of whom came from outside Britain), but a loss of 355,000 (108,000 of these going abroad). None the less, it is net out-

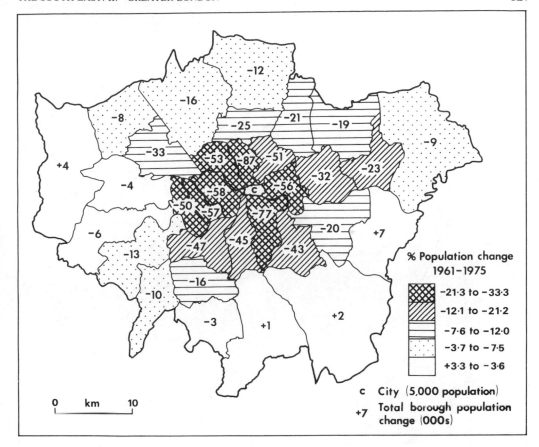

Figure 5.3   Greater London: population decline, 1961-1975

migration, continuing at a high level since 1971, which is basically responsible for London's now rapid population decline.

The causes of decline, and its concentration in inner London, are naturally less easy to identify, or indeed quantify. One major factor, undoubtedly, is the traditionally very high cost of private housing in the metropolis, noted in section 4.4.4 earlier. Hall (1975), in discussing London's recent migration losses, with their bias towards young married couples, has suggested that 'these people are being driven out of London by housing problems—above all, high prices'. And the problem of high house prices has been exacerbated by high local rates, London's average domestic rate per ratepayer in 1977/1978 being £162 compared with only £108 in the rest of England and Wales.

Continuing population losses would seem likely, all else being equal, eventually to reduce demand to a point where house prices will fall, at least in relation to the rest of the region. Strikingly, recent Building Society Association figures indicate that this is precisely what happened, with a decline from a peak 1972 differential of 12 per cent between Greater London and ROSE house prices to one of less than 2 per cent in 1978. *If* the house price differential was historically a significant cause of London's population decline, this substantial change may result in at least a slowing down in population loss;

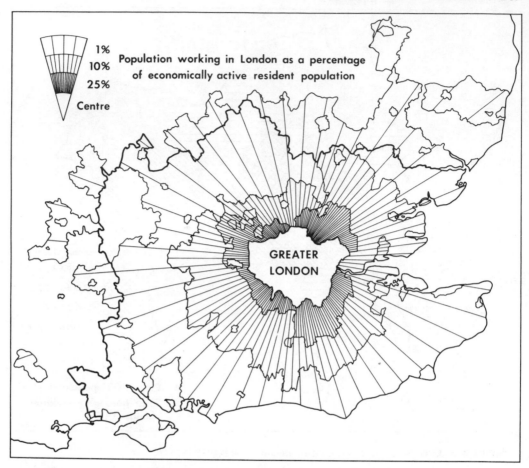

Figure 5.4 South East England: commuting into Greater London, 1971

indeed a somewhat lower annual average decline was recorded in 1974-1978 (60,000) than in 1971-1974 (93,000). On the other hand, the other important factors behind population decline discussed in section 4.4.4, notably the increasing antipathy to congested urban living conditions and a deteriorating residential environment, seem bound to sustain a fairly high level of metropolitan losses, whatever happens to house prices. Certainly the G.L.C.'s own projections suggest that by 1981, population will have fallen to only 6.4-6.7 million, with a possibility of a 1991 total of only 5.5 million (Stone, 1978, p.100).

5.3 London's Workforce and Commuting

Until the 1970s, the population loss of London was not matched by a proportionate fall in the size of the capital's workforce, for decline in London's resident workforce was partly offset by increased commuting to London by workers living outside the metropolis. London's total workforce thus fell in 1961-1971 by 304,000 workers (to 4,079 thousand); but the number and proportion of these workers who were commuters from outside

London increased, from 410,000 to 539,000—and from 9.4 per cent to 13.2 per cent respectively.

A large number of these commuters were workers travelling short distances from just across the G.L.C. boundary to work in London's outer boroughs. These short-distance journeys to work are a major factor in the belt of high (above 25 per cent) London commuting rates surrounding the G.L.C. area mapped in Figure 5.4. The most interesting feature of this map, however, is the geographical extent of dependence upon London for employment. Thus the 10 per cent commuting zone extends outwards from the G.L.C. boundary for 50 kilometres to the south, west and north east; and the 1 per cent zone encompasses virtually the whole of the South East region, with the exception of South Hampshire and part of Oxfordshire, but spilling over into adjacent East Anglia and, to a lesser extent, South West England. These two zones covered in 1971 significantly wider areas than they had in 1961, especially to the north and west. Indeed, by 1971, 88,000 (16 per cent) of total inward commuters lived beyond the O.M.A.

As might be expected, the majority of these longer-distance commuters worked in the very heart of Greater London, the conurbation centre. This centre was the destination for some 261,000 (48 per cent) of Greater London's total 1971 inward commuters, and for 53,000 (60 per cent) of all those from beyond the O.M.A. The dependence of the conurbation centre upon long-distance commuters has increased substantially in recent decades (Greater London Council, 1969a, pp.161-163). By 1971, centres such as Bedford, Colchester, Herne Bay, Hastings and Worthing were sending over 500 workers a day to central London; while the traditional massive flow from Brighton and Hove involved no fewer than 3,700 commuters to central London. For journeys into Greater London as a whole, Brighton and Hove's contribution was 5,400, while daily flows of more than 300 workers travelled from as far away as Cambridge, Ipswich, Bournemouth, Southampton and even Bristol. These commuting figures reflected, of course, both recent transport improvements in the South East (see section 6.4.2) and the search of London's employed population for cheaper homes and more pleasant residential environments. Since 1971, however, rapidly rising rail fares and continuing job losses in London could well have reversed this trend. Figure 5.4 possibly maps, therefore, the maximum-ever extent of London's commuting hinterland, while declining commuting helps to explain London's even faster rate of workforce contraction (5.9 per cent, 1971-1976) than of population loss (5.6 per cent) in the 1970s.

5.4 Manufacturing Industry

5.4.1 Structure and Pattern

London is Britain's greatest single cluster of economic activity. The capital's share of manufacturing industry, measured either by employment (794,000 workers; 11 per cent of the United Kingdom total in 1976) or net output (14 per cent in 1968), has for years been greater than that of any other conurbation. Its first notable characteristic is its remarkable diversity, and bias towards new, innovative and nationally-growing industries. This diversity is strikingly illustrated by Chisholm and Oeppen's calculation (1973) of an index of the diversity or specialization of manufacturing employment in each of sixty-one British sub-regions, for both 1959 and 1968. The index, known as the Tress score, was based on a division of manufacturing into 108 different, detailed industries. For this number of industries, the index's maximum possible range was between 5,450, signifying maximum diversification (with all 108 industries possessing exactly the same 0.93 per cent share of the sub-region's total manufacturing employment), and 10,800, signifying maximum specialization (one industry accounts for 100 per cent of sub-regional employment, with zero employment in all other manufacturing industries). The resultant 1959 Tress score for Greater London was 8,505, the smallest value—indicating the greatest diversity—of all British sub-regions. Though this had increased slightly by 1968, to 9,017, London still possessed one of the four more diversified manufacturing structures in the country.

London's bias towards new, potential growth industries may also be illustrated from Chisholm's data. These reveal that between 1959 and 1968, thirty-five of the 108 industries expanded their employment nationally by 10 per cent or more, whereas thirty-one recorded a national employment decline of 10 per cent or greater. In 1959, some 56.4 per cent of London's manufacturing employment was in the former growth industries, and only 12.6 per cent in the declining industries. Subtraction of the latter from the former percentage gives a simple structural index which measures the degree to which London's manufacturing activity was dominated by nationally-growing industries, and this index (+43.8) was higher in 1959 than that of all but four of the United Kingdom's sixty other sub-regions (Keeble, 1976, p.100).

The spatial pattern of manufacturing within London is traditionally focused on what Hall (1962, p.32) has termed the 'Victorian Manufacturing Belt', which encircles the commercial centre north of the Thames. In 1966, inner London firms employed 48 per cent of London's manufacturing workforce, although their share is probably nearer a third today. Traditionally, inner London manufacturing differs from its suburban counterpart. Firms are smaller. They occupy older, multi-storeyed premises. And the characteristic industries—clothing, furniture, printing and specialized engineering—are different. These inner London industries, a legacy from the nineteenth century, are still found clustered in 'industrial quarters', small districts with a marked though now declining concentration of particular industries. Traditional examples are the East and West End clothing quarters, the Fleet Street and Shoreditch printing quarters, and the Clerkenwell precision engineering and printing quarters.

The most important traditional reason for the existence of these quarters is local industrial linkage, coupled with suitable premises. Small firms in these industries can, by specialization and linkage with other local concerns, compete efficiently with firms elsewhere, especially where demand for their products changes rapidly, as in fashion clothing. The quarters also benefit from access to the central London market and, traditionally, available skilled workers. However, the decline of these quarters over the last decade suggests that these advantages have been diminishing, possibly as a result of technological and structural changes in these industries.

Outer London industry is the product of the capital's twentieth-century industrial growth, centred on activities such as electrical, mechanical and instrument engineering, motor vehicles and pharmaceuticals. Factories are larger and more often single-storeyed than in the inner areas. And the spatial pattern of industry is different, with clusters of factories radiating outwards like beads on a string, following radial roads and railways, especially to the west and north west. This clustering does not really reflect local linkage. Rather, it is a product of industrial estate development by building companies during the 1920s and 1930s, with sites selected to provide easy access for lorries and workers.

Especially good access to the national market beyond London helps to explain the concentration of this outer London industry to the north west; over half of all American-owned factories set up in Britain in the 1930s, for example, were located here or in Slough, probably for this reason.

A third distinctive though declining component of London's industrial geography is Thames-side. Traditionally, industry along the Thames has made substantial use of water-borne materials, as with grain and saw milling, sugar refining and boat repairing. The drastic recent decline of such industries in London's eastern docklands has, however, created a major planning problem (see pp.148-50).

5.4.2 Manufacturing Decline

As hinted at earlier, the contraction of manufacturing employment in the South East is entirely due to massive losses in London. The peak year for manufacturing employment in the capital was 1961, when Greater London factories employed about 1,400,000 workers. By 1971 this had fallen to 1,050,000 and by 1976 to only 790,000. This colossal reduction of 600,000 jobs or more than 40 per cent over only fifteen years renders London by far the greatest centre of industrial decline in Britain's twentieth-century history. It raises at least three major questions: namely what are the components of, and reasons for, decline, and what are its planning implications? The last of these is discussed in section 5.8.5.

Recent Department of Industry research (Dennis, 1978) reveals that over the period 1966-1974, the greatest single component in manufacturing decline was the complete closure of existing factories (Table 5.1). Losses through the movement of existing London firms to other areas—movement being defined to include both complete transfers and the establishment of branch factories with the parent plants remaining in London—were a second major component. Between them, these two components accounted for about three-quarters of total job losses over the period. The rest was largely a reflection of declining employment in firms which continued operating in London.

While complete closures were the biggest component in losses over the eight-year period to 1974, it can be argued that migration is probably the more significant long-term factor in London's industrial decline. Between 1945 and 1965, for example, migrant London firms established no fewer than 1,300 new factories, employing 330,000 workers (by

Table 5.1 Greater London: the components of manufacturing employment change, 1966-1974

	Manufacturing employment change	
Losses through migration of firms	− 105,000	
of which, migration to Assisted Areas		− 36,000
migration to new and expanded towns		− 26,000
migration elsewhere		− 43,000
Losses through complete closures	− 183,000	
Losses in small firms (less than 20 workers)	− 26,000	
Gains (new firms, new branch factories)	+ 13,000	
Residual shrinkage	− 89,000	
Total change	− 390,000	

Source: Dennis (1978).

1966), elsewhere in the United Kingdom (Howard, 1968, p.15). And this earlier migration, as with its continuation since 1965, was highly selective of *growing* firms and industries of a type which, had they stayed in London, could have offset employment losses from closures (Keeble, 1976, pp.127-129). However, growth is in many cases the basic reason for leaving London, given the constraints on expansion imposed by conditions in the capital. The most important of these constraints is the shortage (at least until the 1970s), the nature and the cost of factory premises. A century of industrial growth has bequeathed a legacy of cramped factory sites, and of old, badly designed and dilapidated buildings. Competition for factories and land had raised industrial land prices in London by the late 1960s to values over twice those in the rest of the South East, and four times greater than the all-England average (Keeble, 1978). For some industries, labour shortages and high wage costs have been a secondary consideration (Keeble, 1968), while a third factor has been government regional and new town policies, encouraging migration to the Assisted Areas by incentives and to the new towns by availability of housing for workers. Until recently, Department of Industry (i.d.c.) controls have also restricted the building of modern premises or the redevelopment of old. Lastly, though very difficult to quantify, the residential preferences of industrialists and skilled workers have led many smaller London firms, and especially those employing skilled staff, to relocate in more attractive areas outside the metropolis.

The factors prompting migration also explain in part the massive employment losses through plant closures. This is because many such losses are in larger, multi-plant firms, which can compare operating conditions and costs in London and in other locations. No doubt the age and the inefficiency of the factory buildings they occupy, plus the incentives available for expansion in the Assisted Areas, are especially important influences on such firms in closing London plants. The closure of many small firms could reflect both the loss of markets through closure or migration of bigger local firms, and the emigration of entrepreneurs to more attractive residential areas outside London. Given the evidence of Chisholm's data and various shift-and-share analyses (Weatheritt and Lovett, 1975: Gripaios, 1977), it is certainly clear that closures are not due to London's industry being biased towards nationally declining activities.

5.5 London's Service and Office Industries

In contrast to manufacturing, London's service industries have continued to expand their employment. By 1976, services provided 2.73 million jobs in the capital, or 74 per cent of total employment. This reflected a growth of some 43,000 jobs since 1971 because of the expansion of 'basic' services (+121,000 or 9 per cent). The latter represent industries such as insurance and banking, professional and scientific services, and public administration, which serve largely national or international demands. Employment in so-called 'non-basic' services—those mainly geared to the needs of the local population such as retailing, education and health—simultaneously fell (−78,000, or −6 per cent), as is only to be expected given London's population decline (Keeble, 1978).

The continuing growth, until the mid-1970s at least, of its higher-order 'basic' services reflects London's dominant role as the greatest 'central place' in the United Kingdom. London's financial institutions dominate and regulate the economic life of Britain. It is the seat of national government, and contains the headquarters of the majority of the country's biggest industrial and commercial companies—60 per cent of the top 500 in

1971 (Evans, 1973). It is by far the greatest cultural, educational, medical, and retailing centre of Britain, the country's leading communications focus, and the operating base for national newspapers, radio and television broadcasting.

London's unrivalled dominance in service activities quite naturally arouses frequent regional resentment. Regional critics argue, for example, that its share of the nation's cultural cake is out of all proportion, given the needs of other areas. Why should London possess four national orchestras, when some large British cities have none? Similarly, national government is frequently regarded as being too London-oriented, a viewpoint which has encouraged growing demands in recent years for greater administrative autonomy, if not independence, for Scotland, Wales and the English regions. Anti-London criticism was also stimulated by the continuing concentration until the 1960s of many new national service facilities and activities in the London area—facilities such as the huge South Bank complex including the National Theatre, and the headquarters of new public bodies such as the National Coal Board, the British Gas Corporation and the British Steel Corporation. Increased regional hostility to London's service preeminence is thus a factor both in the growth of separatist movements in other parts of Britain, and in the recent attempts by government to disperse service activities to other regions.

Perhaps the most important aspect of London's preeminence in service industry is its unique central office complex. This complex, divided into the two sub-centres of the City of London and the West End (including Westminster) is remarkable for its size and economic importance. Office firms and organizations in the central area employ 700,000 workers, while commercial offices alone occupy 9.7 million square metres (104 million square feet) of office space. The former represents 14 per cent of office employment in England and Wales, the latter 24 per cent of commercial floorspace. Within the centre, however, there is a very important difference between the West End and the City. The former has developed during the twentieth century largely as a diversified 'prestige' office district, catering for a wide variety of office functions. Especially important are government offices, clustering around the Houses of Parliament, and also a remarkable concentration of the headquarter offices of national and international industrial concerns. In addition, the West End houses many learned societies, publishing firms and such relatively new activities as television and cinema organizations, air transport and advertising companies. The district thus contains a heterogeneous mixture of office activities which, though of importance to the functioning of the South East and national economies, are not especially tied to one another. Most have probably located there for general reasons of access to customers and staff, as well as the prestige of a West End address.

The City sub-centre, on the other hand, presents a different picture. Although it boasts only about half of the West End's office space, and three-quarters of the latter's office workers, the financial activities of the 'Square Mile' are of exceptional importance to Britain's economy and its balance of payments (Greater London Council, 1969a, pp. 70-73). Moreover, its characteristic office functions are bound to each other by very strong ties (Dunning, 1969, pp.208-212). For centuries, the City has performed a dual role as a centre for commodity trading and shipping activity on the one hand, and for finance, insurance and banking on the other. Its shipping and trading interests cluster around the commodity markets of Mincing Lane, whilst its function as one of the world's greatest financial centres is symbolized by the presence at its heart of such institutions as the Bank of England, the Stock Exchange and Lloyds. The distinctive localization of these activities in the City partly reflects historical connections with the Port of London, and an easy availability of office workers from throughout London and its city-region. But the main justification for its present-day existence is the vital need on the part of its constituent firms for frequent, rapid and 'face-to-face' contact with other firms and institutions within the Square Mile. A very high intensity of local contacts, necessitated by rapid, almost hour-by-hour, changes in international financial affairs, represents a vital functional bond tying many financial firms to a City location.

During the early 1960s, many observers expressed great concern over the apparent rapid growth of office employment in central London, claiming that resultant peak-hour commuting increases were putting intolerable pressures on the capital's public transport system and road network. As a result, the government established in 1963 the Location of Offices Bureau with the task of stimulating office decentralization from central London; this was followed by the imposition in 1964 of wholly new government controls on office building in the London Metropolitan Region, with o.d.p.s being required for all new buildings of over 350 square metres (3,000 square feet). Administered first by the Board of Trade, but then by the Department of the Environment, o.d.p. policy was initiated partly with a view to encouraging inter-regional office decentralization (p.77ff.).

In fact, however, the statistical basis of the arguments which led to the institution of this policy was inaccurate. Later figures revealed that office employment in central London had ceased to grow by the early 1960s; and since 1971 it has probably declined slightly despite a 27 per cent increase in office floorspace between 1967 and 1976 (Department of the Environment, Urban Affairs and Commercial Property Directorate, 1976). Moreover, total employment in the central area, including non-office occupations, has been falling ever since 1961 (from 1.40 million to 1.16 million, 1961-1975), resulting in a steady decline in commuting into the centre from 1.26 million to 1.08 million in 1961-1975 (Standing Conference on London and South East Regional Planning, 1977). So before o.d.p. policy began, the trends it was designed to combat appear to have been halted if not reversed.

Since 1964, government office decentralization policy has had two chief effects. The first has been a reduction in the amount of office construction in central London, leading to a massive rise in office rents. Between 1964 and 1974, for example, rents for prime City office blocks soared from £32 to no less than £205 per square metre (£3 to £19 per square foot), largely because of a shortage of new office space as a result of planning controls. These controls were relaxed in 1970, then tightened substantially again in 1973. In 1977, however, o.d.p. limits were raised from 1,400 to 2,800 square metres (15,000 to 30,000 square feet), while the government announced its intention to approve permits for some speculative office projects in inner London outside the central area. This change reflected a growing government concern with inner city employment problems. Variations in borough planning policies and conflicting attitudes towards office development have, however, in the past restricted office development to particular inner areas, such as Southwark and Hammersmith, rather than Islington or Wandsworth (see section 5.9). The power possessed by London local authorities to refuse or grant planning permission for new offices is indeed one very important determinant both of the scale and geography of office development within the capital, and has been as influential as central government o.d.p. controls (Damesick, 1979). Indeed, the latter were abolished in 1979.

The second main effect of government policy has been to accelerate the natural trend towards office decentralization. Very high rents and L.O.B. publicity have been major factors behind decentralization since the mid-1960s. So too, however, have been non-policy considerations, notably the relatively high staff costs in central London and, more recently, substantial rate increases following the 1973 revaluation. By 1977, the cost of accommodating a clerk in a City office involved a rate burden of no less than £1,054 per annum, or 39 per cent of the total cost of rent and rates (Blake, 1977). Outside central London, costs are considerably lower. The Department of the Environment, Urban Affairs and Commercial Property Directorate, estimated that, in 1975, the total annual cost of employing a City secretary in an office which was not air-conditioned (£3,235) was over 70 per cent greater than that incurred by office firms in Bristol or Manchester. It should be noted, however, that within London the dynamics of the property market and office demand have resulted in recent years in the development of two distinct sub-markets for office premises, with very different levels of rents and rates. Thus older and relatively austere office premises which are not air-conditioned are more readily available and much cheaper in central London than new air-conditioned premises. Buoyant demand, illustrated by the influx of foreign banks and the oil industry to the City of London and the West End respectively in the 1960s and 1970s, has meant that new, air-conditioned offices are in relatively short supply despite the office boom of the early 1970s, when finance capital was poured into new office development in expectation of high returns on investment. The central London/rest of England office rent differential is correspondingly greater for new offices than for older premises.

The scale of office decentralization from central London can only be estimated. The Location of Offices Bureau (1977) calculates that between 1963 and 1976 its clients moved nearly 150,000 office jobs out of central London. To this total must be added moves by office firms which did not contact L.O.B., involving perhaps another 150,000 (Department of the Environment, Urban Affairs and Commercial Property Directorate, 1976), together with the decentralization of government offices (Table 3.3; Figure 3.1). The latter, largely for reasons of regional policy, has already resulted in some 20,000 to 30,000 government jobs being transferred to the Assisted Areas. Following the 1973 Hardman report on government office decentralization, plans exist to move another 31,000 central London jobs, all but 3,000 of them to the Assisted Areas. There also appears to have been some increase in long-distance private office moves, following the 1973 introduction of financial incentives in the Assisted Areas for mobile service industry. The great majority of private moves have, however, been over relatively short distances, since most firms or decentralized departments retain important links with other central London offices and are therefore reluctant to move far away.

The most striking result of office decentralization has been the rise of important suburban office centres at Croydon and in west London. Croydon's central office district now employs over 25,000 workers, while numerous office blocks have been constructed in Hounslow, Ealing and Richmond. Office floorspace in outer London as a whole expanded by 1.7 million square metres (18 million square feet) or 94 per cent in 1967-1976, compared with only 27 per cent in central London. The particular success of Croydon and west London in attracting office development is partly due to deliberate local authority planning action, and partly to speculative office developers choosing locations thought to be attractive to prospective clients. Their locational attractions include excellent rail links with central London; a large local pool of office labour; nearness to London Airport (Heathrow); and relative proximity to desirable residential areas for managers and executives. In the 1960s, rents were relatively low outside central London. Beyond Greater

London, towns such as Reading, Southend, Maidenhead and Basingstoke have also attracted mobile office firms. There seems little doubt that with a continuing fall in London's population, and continuing high rents and rates in the central area, office decentralization to the rest of Greater London, to the rest of the South East and, indeed, beyond will continue. At the same time, changes in planning attitudes are making central and inner London office development easier than in the recent past. So it is unlikely that London's office and 'basic' service industries will undergo anything like the dramatic decline of the capital's manufacturing sector.

5.6 London's Communications

The 1960s and early 1970s witnessed intense controversy over planning proposals for new communications—notably roads and airports—in or near London, primarily because of their environmental implications. Communication improvements are, however, judged by many observers to be essential both for the efficient functioning of London's economy, and for any slowing down of London's economic and especially manufacturing decline. The nature and development of London's communications are therefore discussed here, although the problems facing the transport organizations which utilize these communications, notably London Transport, are examined later (section 5.7.2).

London's road network has grown up haphazardly over the centuries and is now poorly designed for modern levels and speeds of vehicle movement. Recent improvements, such as the elevated M4 motorway at Brentford, the A40 Westway dual carriageway, and the Brent Cross multi-level flyover on the North Circular Road, have been restricted to particularly serious bottlenecks, generally in outer rather than inner London. The abandonment in 1973 of the G.L.C.'s 1967 Ringway plan—the only attempt at comprehensive highway planning for London since 1945—indicates, however, the strength of environmental opposition within London to more wide-ranging schemes. This plan, estimated to require an investment of £1,700 million (at 1970 prices), proposed the construction of three orbital urban motorways, Ringways 1, 2 and 3, together with many improved secondary roads. Ringway 1, the so-called inner London Motorway Box, would have been the terminal point for such incoming radial motorways as M1, M4 and M23. At £30 per year for each London car owner, the cost of this plan, though considerable in total, was not excessive in relation to car usage and schemes elsewhere. Morover the validity of the case for Ringway 1 was accepted by the independent 1970-1972 Layfield Committee of inquiry into the 1969 Greater London Development Plan, which embodied the Ringway proposals, even though the committee rejected Ringways 2 and 3 in favour of an upgraded North Circular Road and priority for the M25 orbital motorway, the latter outside London altogether.

On the other hand, fierce opposition to the Ringway plan was stimulated by its proposed destruction of 20,000 dwellings and the disruptive environmental implications for many parts of the capital, especially inner London. Inevitably, too, political considerations entered into the argument; the return of the Labour party to power following the 1973 G.L.C. elections on a manifesto opposing the Ringway plan marked the end of the scheme. Subsequent road improvements were therefore very limited, with the (Labour-controlled) council channelling funds to public transport rather than road construction. G.L.C. road investment averaged only £13 million a year between 1973 and 1978. The latter year, however, saw the announcement by a new (Conservative-controlled)

G.L.C. of its intention to allocate £855 million for strategic road improvements in London over the fifteen-year period to 1993, on the grounds that improved roads are essential if London's manufacturing decline is to be stemmed. Attention will be focused on areas such as inner west London, the A23 corridor, the docklands southern relief route and new east London river crossing (Thamesmead), the A2 corridor, and the south circular route. The council hopes that new tunnelling and cut-and-fill construction techniques may get round some of the intractable environmental problems which have aroused such fierce public opposition in the past. In addition, the Department of Transport plans to upgrade the A406 North Circular Road for which it is responsible to dual carriageway standard, and to extend it east to the A13 by the later 1980s, at a cost (1976 prices) of £175 million. If they are actually carried out, these plans could result in a signficant improvement in London's internal strategic road network over the next fifteen or so years.

As noted in section 4.1, London is the focus of national and international air routes. London Airport (Heathrow) is far and away Britain's leading airport, handling in 1978 some 26.5 million passengers (compared with only 5 million in 1960), or 57 per cent of all those arriving at or departing from British airports. For international air passengers alone, its share was even higher, at 64 per cent, as was its share of air cargo shipments to and from Britain (over 70 per cent by value); indeed, in value terms, Heathrow handled 12 per cent of the country's total exports and 10 per cent of its imports. Not surprisingly, Heathrow now directly employs over 50,000 workers, with many more indirectly dependent for their livelihood upon the airport, its activity and workforce. The other London area airports are Gatwick (5.7 million passengers in 1978), Luton (1.8 million) and Stansted (0.3 million). Thus four airports together handle two-thirds of all passengers through British airports (34 million out of 46.2 million in 1978).

As with London's roads, official proposals for airport development to cope with the expected growth in air passenger movements through London's airports, especially Heathrow, have been the object of fierce controversy. The concentration of international flights through Heathrow is a direct result of its excellent position at the centre of the South East, past massive investment in runways, terminals and other facilities, and the remarkable volume of demand for flights by South East businessmen, residents and tourists. Thus, surveys show that no less than 80 per cent of all passengers arriving by air at Heathrow are bound for destinations within South East England. However, growth forecasts during the 1960s suggested that Heathrow and Gatwick would not be able to cope with the flood of air passengers anticipated for the 1980s and 1990s; hence the 1964 government and British Airports Authority proposals for a new international airport at Stansted, Essex, which already possessed a first-class runway. Fierce local opposition to this proposal resulted in the appointment of the Roskill Commission to investigate in depth alternative sites for a third London airport, excluding Stansted. The commission's recommendation, Cublington in Buckinghamshire, was however in turn rejected—in 1971—by the then Conservative government, on environmental and planning grounds, in favour of Maplin (originally called Foulness) on the Essex coast. The Maplin scheme was then itself abandoned, after the return to power in 1974 of a Labour government, on the grounds that London's existing airports could with more modest investment in fact handle expected increases in passenger volume, given the introduction of wide-bodied aircraft and downward-revised passenger forecasts.

The latest stage in this saga of indecision took the form of the 1978 Airports Policy

White Paper, following earlier consultation documents. This announced (subject to a public enquiry) the probable expansion of capacity at Heathrow with a fourth terminal to 38 million passengers a year, together with the construction of a second terminal at Gatwick. The latter would boost capacity there from 16 million to 25 million passengers a year, the former figure itself reflecting the 1978 completion of a £100 million redevelopment programme. Capacity at Luton and Stansted would also be increased, to 5 and 4 million passengers respectively. These developments should, the White Paper argued, provide for growth up to 1990. Beyond that, however, further expansion might necessitate reopening the question of constructing a wholly new international airport somewhere in the region.

Some commentators have argued that all this extraordinary shilly-shallying over airport development in the South East has, fortuitously, been beneficial, in that recent reductions in forecasts and technological changes in aircraft capacity and noise levels indicate that the earlier third airport proposals were unnecessary. This is very much a moot point, however, as the 400,000 or so Londoners living within Heathrow's current 45 N.N.I. (Noise and Number Index) contour, indicating moderate or greater noise disturbance levels, would no doubt point out. Many observers, especially those representing the air transport industry, seem convinced that a new international airport will be needed in due course anyway, whatever short-term solutions are adopted.

In striking contrast to London Airport (Heathrow), the recent history of London's seaport—the Port of London—is one of decline. Thus the Port of London's share of United Kingdom exports by volume fell dramatically between 1967 and 1977 from 29 to only 11 per cent, while its share of imports declined from 27 to only 15 per cent. The total volume of traffic has also fallen, from a 1968 peak of 60 million tonnes, to only 43 million by 1977. Decline in the port's workforce—from 26,000 in 1967 to only 9,000 in 1978—has been equally dramatic, reflecting in part increased labour productivity through containerization. The latter, and the scale economies associated with large, purpose-built container vessels and berths, explain both the closure of up-river docks (see section 5.8.5) and the expansion of container facilities down-river at Tilbury. Tilbury now posesses, for example, the world's largest terminal for refrigerated containers, with the completion in 1978 of a £16 million scheme on a 26 hectare (64 acre) site. Despite decline—due in part to fierce competition from other smaller ports in the South East and East Anglia (Southampton, Dover, Harwich, Felixstowe)—the Port of London is still Britain's largest single port with regard to non-fuel trade (17 million tonnes, or 14 per cent of the national total in 1977), and planned improvement of its landward communications, notably by the building of the M25 (and M11), should help it to maintain this position in the 1980s. Its share of national trade seems unlikely to increase, however, given the relative manufacturing decline of London and the South East, its dominant hinterland.

5.7 Metropolitan Planning: Traditional Problems

5.7.1 Housing and Land

As noted in section 5.1, London's population density is greater than that of any other British conurbation. This concentration of people and buildings illustrates clearly the traditional pressure on, and competition for, land in London. This in turn reflects the traditional economic advantages of location in London for economic activity of all kinds, and the resultant pressure for housing by the capital's workforce. Up to a point, such competition may have beneficial effects, in that it provides a mechanism for the allocation of particular plots of land to those functions which can make the best use of them, as measured by profits. Thus department stores, for example, are able to pay higher prices than most other users for highly accessible and hence desirable sites at the centres of cities, such as Oxford and Regent Streets in London, because of the higher income they are able to generate there. Manufacturing firms, on the other hand, tend to locate further out, for instance in Wembley, Enfield or Croydon, where land and building costs tend to be lower, since their income does not depend nearly as much on accessibility to urban customers or suppliers. Thus, competition for urban land between different economic activities such as these tends to result in a reasonably appropriate arrangement of land use within the city. Unfortunately, however, this is not nearly so true when housing, the provision and arrangement of which needs to be assessed in social as well as economic terms, is considered. For example, poorer families generally cannot afford to live very far from the workplace of the head of the family, because of commuting costs. Yet many jobs in a great city like London are in or near the centre, where land values and housing costs are highest. It is thus very difficult to provide adequate, reasonably priced housing for such families without some sort of public subsidy.

In London, pressure on land for housing finds expression not just in exceptionally high housing costs (section 4.4.4) but in a longstanding and serious housing shortage, estimated by the G.L.C.'s Development Plan (Greater London Council, 1969a, p.19) as involving a shortfall of no less than 270,000 homes in 1967. This represented an infinitely greater housing shortage both absolutely and relative to population than that facing any other conurbation in England and Wales. Not surprisingly, the number of homeless people rose substantially in London in the 1960s, while inner London today contains the greatest number of homeless people in the country (Department of the Environment, 1977, p.121). However, rapid population decline since 1967 coupled with a steady increase in London's total dwelling stock had by 1976 brought the number of dwellings (2.65 million) and households in London into a rough balance (South East Joint Planning Team, 1976, p.33). Moreover, the Strategic Plan review suggests that the total number of households in London could fall substantially, by 190,000 in 1976-1991; this latter figure is based on a somewhat optimistic 1973-based Office of Population Censuses and Surveys (O.P.C.S.) population projection, and may therefore underestimate the possible decline in housing demand (South East Joint Planning Team, 1976, p. 18).

Such broad statistics might suggest that housing problems in London are now of limited scale and significance. Such a conclusion would, however, almost certainly be wrong, for various reasons. First, acute shortages of housing undoubtedly still exist in certain areas and in respect of certain types of accommodation. Shortages are especially common in the inner London boroughs, such as Lambeth, and with regard to privately rented and local authority housing. Thus in 1971, inner London accounted for no less than 22 per cent (Coffield, 1975) of the most severely overcrowded 5 per cent of British enumeration districts, measured by persons per dwelling, a share second only to Clydeside amongst British conurbations. Privately rented accommodation is declining rapidly, despite a projected substantial *increase* in the number of one-person households, one of the main sources of demand for such housing, of 125,000 by 1991 (South East Joint Planning Team, 1976, p. 18). Overcrowding in this type of accommodation in London is therefore serious, with 31 per cent of tenants renting privately living at densities of more than one person per room in 1971. In addition, the shrinking availability of privately-rented accommodation is throwing more people onto local authority housing waiting lists, which expanded by 50 per cent in 1965-1973 (South East Joint Planning Team, 1976, p.34).

A second major point is that London's housing problems are of *quality* as well as numbers and location. In inner London, for example, much of the housing stock was built before 1918 and many properties are dilapidated and in need of considerable rehabilitation or replacement. The 1971 Census once again showed that, of the worst 5 per cent of enumeration districts in the whole of Britain lacking in 'basic amenities' such as lavatories, bathrooms and hot water, inner London contained over one-fifth (22 per cent). No other inner city accounted for so large a share of these 'bad-housing' districts. And as incomes and living standards rise, people's housing expectations naturally rise too, so that estimates of the number of 'substandard' inner London homes have risen steadily over the years.

A third major housing problem is lack of choice. For many households, this is of course a reflection of the exceptionally high cost of housing, a result of competition for land and very high building costs. As the 1976 Strategic Plan review points out, in London 'the declining number of private rented dwellings, rising house prices, mounting costs of housing finance and lengthening local authority waiting lists have all narrowed the choice open to different groups' (South East Joint Planning Team, 1976, p.19). Thus, in some boroughs, virtually only one type of housing is available—public rented accommodation in such inner boroughs as Tower Hamlets and Southwark (75 per cent and 60 per cent of their total housing stock, respectively), owner-occupied in outer boroughs such as Harrow and Richmond (90 per cent and 86 per cent of housing stock, respectively). Low-income families thus find accommodation extremely difficult to obtain in some outer suburbs: conversely, inner London households wishing and able to purchase their own homes frequently find it impossible to buy suitable dwellings locally. An important subsidiary aspect of this housing problem, occasioned directly by pressure on available land, is the fact that even newly constructed London housing may well be of a type which is by no means in greatest demand today, namely multi-storey flats. Thus in inner London between 1970 and 1973, only 8 per cent (3,800 dwellings) of completed new dwellings were two- or three-storeyed family houses. The rest were flats, with no less than 56 per cent (26,200 dwellings) in blocks of more than five storeys (Whittick, 1976). There has been a swing away from the erection of high-rise blocks since 1973. But even so, inner London contains very few modern family houses of the type which so many households today seem to prefer.

Land shortages and costs also, of course, affect industrial and office firms, and the provision of public facilities—roads, railways, schools and hospitals. The very high cost of the inner circular urban motorway (Ringway 1) proposed by the G.L.C. in 1967—£12 million per kilometre, or £19 million per mile, at 1971 prices—was one factor behind the abandonment of this scheme in 1973. The perceived environmental consequences, including the necessary demolition of some 20,00 existing dwellings lying in the proposed path of the motorway, were however even more important reasons for this reversal, which resulted from the shift of G.L.C. control from Conservative to Labour.

In addition to the measurable consequences of land shortage and congestion, London's very high density creates several less tangible but no less important difficulties for its citizens. The shortage of open spaces and parkland, and distance from attractive countryside, undoubtedly rank high as drawbacks to residence in London for many of its inhabitants. Despite slum area redevelopment and the existence of such famous central area amenities as the royal parks, parts of inner London such as Islington, Shoreditch and Southwark still have little or no public open space. Traffic congestion aggravates the problem of sheer distance from the countryside, enforcing laborious journeys of an hour or more's driving upon inner London residents spending a day in the country. More controversial than these amenity matters is the question of urban living and mental health. Various studies (for example, Faris and Dunham, 1965) have revealed that residence in the inner built-up areas of large cities is commonly associated with unusually high rates of certain types of mental illness. In the case of London, a 1966 survey revealed that East End districts such as Stepney then possessed an incidence of schizophrenia two and a half times the national average, and one of depressive illness nearly twice as great. While the reasons for this pattern are undoubtedly complex, it does seem at least possible that the physical character of the inner areas of conurbations, with their cramped and often dilapidated buildings, plays some part.

5.7.2 Transport Problems

The provision of adequate transport facilities, both public and private, is another traditional London planning problem. London's public transport system, comprising the London Transport Executive's underground and bus services, and British Rail's suburban lines, has been faced with major problems in recent years. Use of London's buses, for example, fell from 2,004 million journeys in 1964 to 1,374 million in 1977, a decline of 31 per cent—although this does conceal a slight increase in 1972-1974. London Transport underground rail journeys simultaneously fell by 6 per cent, from 674 to 636 million. In an attempt to cover sharply rising costs—from 1.8 pence per bus passenger mile in 1967 to 7.0 pence in 1976, for example—fares have had to be increased steeply—from 1.6 pence to 4.3 pence per bus passenger mile in 1967-1976 (Hall, 1977b)—which in turn has encouraged increased use of private cars in a vicious spiral. Even rapidly rising fares have failed to prevent the development since 1973 of a massive gap between London Transport's income and expenditure, on bus and underground journeys, totalling £125 million in 1975 and £114 million in 1976. This deficit, representing almost one-third of London Transport's expenses, has in turn had to be met by London's ratepayers in the shape of the G.L.C., the body to whom the London Transport Executive has been responsible since 1970. Thus, a major problem of public transport finance exacerbates further the apparently separate problem, noted in section 5.2, of high domestic rate charges on London citizens. An exactly similar financial problem faces British Rail's London commuter services, which were subsidized in 1975 by over £80 million of government money. The problem is especially acute on suburban services which, as the 1976 transport policy consultative document acknowledges, 'have no prospect of viability, as far as can be seen' (Department of the Environment, 1976, p.57).

The reasons for British Rail and London Transport's longstanding financial difficulties centre on the problems of 'peaking' in time and space. Many of the passenger flows handled are concentrated in the peak 'rush-hour' morning and evening periods, while flows are also heavily focused on central London. Peaking in time necessitates expensive provision of vehicles, rolling stock, equipment and staff which are fully used only during rush-hour periods. Peaking in space creates great difficulties of access and capacity at the centre, as with London's main line railway stations. A more equitable distribution of travel demand through the day and throughout Greater London—provided journeys are still focused on major employment or shopping centres—could help to improve the efficiency and economics of London's public transport system. As it is, however, no easy solutions appear to exist to the growing financial problems of public transport in London.

Problems of planning for private transport centre on the exceptionally high cost of road improvements, already mentioned, and traffic congestion. Up till the mid-1960s, substantial growth in the ownership and use of cars in London resulted in growing traffic congestion, falls in average speeds, more accidents, and so on. By 1966, traffic congestion throughout the conurbation was probably costing Londoners and London firms as much as £150 million per annum (Greater London Council, 1969a, p.172), a sum which subsequently must have increased substantially. Since 1966, vehicle ownership in London has continued to grow, from 2,022,000 to 2,224,000 by 1978 (an increase of 10 per cent). However, this conceals some decline since 1976, especially of private cars, and an actual improvement in both peak and off-peak average traffic speeds in central London since 1968. The latter reflects numerous traffic management schemes including computer operated traffic lighting and control systems. It could also be that with falling population the number of cars, if not other vehicles, in London may begin to fall rapidly. None the less, exceptional road congestion in London remains a major planning problem, limiting efficient movement of goods and people and encouraging the emigration of families and firms.

5.8 Metropolitan Planning: New Problems

The planning response to the traditional problems outlined in section 5.7 has of course been to encourage the movement of people and industry from London to its surrounding region. This decentralization policy is described in detail in Chapter 6, and is one factor in metropolitan population and industrial decline. However, the rate and scale of decline has aroused increasing concern amongst commentators, planners and politicians since the later 1960s. They argue that decline is occasioning new and major problems for London and its remaining inhabitants, and possibly the country as a whole.

5.8.1 *The Economic Efficiency Argument*

One of the earliest arguments advanced by critics of traditional decentralization policy, notably the G.L.C., was that rapid decline was threatening the efficiency of London's economic activity, and could thus damage the national economy. In its draft 1969 Development Plan, the G.L.C. emphasized the national economic importance of London's industry and commerce, its high productivity and its outstanding contributions to the national balance of payments through both visible and invisible exports. It thus concluded that for national as well as local reasons, policy must 'foster the commercial and industrial prosperity of London', a viewpoint on which it offered 'no compromise' (Greater London Council, 1969b, p.10).

The G.L.C.'s argument involved two separate strands. One concerned the needs of central London office activities, notably in the City, for modern buildings and an adequate workforce. In the council's view, the o.d.p. and other government policies should be operated much more selectively, lest 'shortage of space for legitimate expansion' impair the efficiency of London's unique office complex. This argument certainly seems to have impressed the 1970-1974 Conservative government; the o.d.p.s granted annually in London increased from 121,000 to 1,100,000 square metres (1.3 million to 12.3 million square feet) between 1966 and 1972. More recently, the Standing Conference of South East planning authorities (Standing Conference on London and South East Regional Planning, 1977, p.9) opposed government proposals for big fare increases for South East rail commuters, arguing that such increases would intensify still further the staff recruitment difficulties of central London employers, 'with serious implications for London's economic base and for the special functions of central London in the national economy'.

On the other hand, the G.L.C.'s second 1969 argument, that labour productivity and hence efficiency in most of London's manufacturing industries was higher than in the rest of the South East, was more debatable. True, census of production data do indicate that in 1958 at least ten London manufacturing industries, including vehicles, clothing, printing, timber and furniture, and other metal goods, achieved a significantly higher labour productivity than their counterparts in the nearest comparable area, the rest of the South East (plus East Anglia). London's overall value of net output per employee in manufacturing was therefore greater than in any other region except Wales (Greater London Council, 1969a, pp. 73-75). The more recent 1968 census placed London top of the league in this respect, with the R.O.S.E. second and Wales third (Keeble, 1976, p.218).

This very interesting labour productivity argument can, however, as the Greater London Development Plan itself carefully acknowledges, be challenged on various grounds (Manners, 1970). For one thing, the exclusion of capital stock values, for which regional data are not available, renders the G.L.D.P.'s analysis partial rather than complete as an authoritative study of regional variations in returns to all the factors of production. For another, the analysis perforce deals only with average productivities, whereas locational policy ought to be based on a knowledge of marginal productivities and returns to marginal production increments in different places. The most important criticism, however, is that net output per head is in many ways an arguable index of relative regional efficiency in manufacturing, because of the impact upon it of varying regional labour costs, in turn reflecting variations in the cost of living. Thus high net output values in London may partly or wholly reflect the need for firms in the capital to pay high wages to attract workers, the cost of these high wages then being passed on to customers in the form of higher prices and value of output. Put another way, high manufacturing net output values in London may be 'a matter more of necessity than of virtue' (Brown, 1972, p.158).

The conclusions of the G.L.C.'s analysis are therefore open to debate, especially as a guide to the policy merits of industrial expansion in London as compared with the R.O.S.E. While the scale of the productivity difference between the South East as a whole and most other regions is sufficiently great to suggest some validity for the argument at that geographical level (Keeble, 1976, p.219), slight within-region differences are another matter. Most independent observers would thus probably agree with the Economy Group of the South East Joint Planning Team (1976, p.20) that in terms of industrial efficiency at least, 'it is difficult to see any reason why growth within the region should not be allowed to occur where it appears to prefer'. This, of course, generally means outside London.

5.8.2 *The Local Authority Income Argument*

A more recent and perhaps more powerful argument against traditional decentralization policy, with its corollary of a declining population and economic base in London, concerns local government costs and incomes. Put simply, protagonists of this view, such as Eversley (1972) and perhaps Kirwan (1973), argue that population and industrial decline do not reduce proportionately the local authority costs of providing essential services and social infrastructure. Indeed, these costs may even rise, partly because the remaining population is biased towards people and households in social need, partly because of London's increasing role as an international and tourist centre. The decline may well, however, reduce local authority income, through declining rate yield, and/or necessitate an increased rate burden on those families and firms which do remain in the capital. In Eversley's words (1972, p.63),

> London's burdens are not reduced because population and employment decline. Given its growing international, national and regional role, the need to maintain the social infrastructure continues. Tourism adds to the load. The remaining population includes a higher proportion of people needing subsidized housing, special educational facilities, welfare services and public service provision of all kinds. The continuous rising requirement of services has to be supported by investment which is becoming disporportionately more costly per unit of building.

Various evidence supports the argument that London's local authorities incur unusually high and rising costs of service provision. The classic illustration is council housing. In 1974, the average cost of constructing a council dwelling in England and Wales was £9,520. The equivalent cost in outer London, however, was £14,720, and in inner London no less than £18,580 (*New Society*, 1977). This massive cost differential meant that inner London authorities received over one-fifth of all council housing investment in England and Wales, but constructed less than one-eighth of the council dwellings completed in that year (South East Joint Planning Team, 1976, p.38). The enormously high council dwelling costs incurred in inner London are only partly due to very high land costs (£6,875 per dwelling in 1974, as compared with £2,485 in England and Wales as a whole). Very high building costs are also involved (£11,705, compared with £7,035 nationally). Not surprisingly, a much higher proportion of London's council housing costs have to be subsidized by central government and the rates than elsewhere. In 1976, actual rents (before rebates) met only 40 per cent of expenditure on council housing in London, compared with over 64 per cent elsewhere.

Very high costs also characterize the maintenance of transport facilities (section 5.7.2), and the provision of local authority social services. A 1976 G.L.C. study revealed that in 1973-1974 London boroughs on average spent no less than 68 per cent more per head of population on providing personal social services—child and family care, and care of the elderly and mentally ill—than the average for all authorities in England and Wales. And inner London boroughs spent on average twice as much as the outer London boroughs. It is not therefore surprising that London domestic and commercial ratepayers tend to have been paying relatively high rates in recent years. The G.L.C. pointed out in evidence to the Layfield Committee on Local Government Finance that, in 1974/1975, average domestic rates per head in London were £32 compared with £23 in the rest of England and Wales. Even allowing for higher London household incomes, domestic rates as a percentage of annual income were still 29 per cent higher than elsewhere. Commercial rates—for example, on offices—are also very high (section 5.5). These facts seem to provide some support for the G.L.C.'s 1975 assertion that there exists 'an increasing gap between needs and resources and an unbearable strain on London rate-payers both in terms of the rate burden and the quality of services available'.

However, there is another side to this argument; and opponents of the G.L.C. view stress at least three qualifications. The first concerns the quality and range of local government services. High expenditure may reflect high costs. But it may also reflect a deliberate decision by London authorities to provide better-quality and more varied services than elsewhere—more leisure and recreational facilities, higher-quality social services, or cheaper public transport with concessionary fares for particular groups such as the elderly. If this is the case in some London boroughs—and measuring the quality of local authority services is very difficult indeed—it can be argued that in a period of acute national financial stringency, London authorities cannot expect to be subsidized by central government to provide better services than are available elsewhere.

A second qualification concerns resources. Despite the G.L.C.'s warnings about rising rate burdens, it is still true that in terms of the rateable value of buildings, London is better off than any other part of the country. In recent years, central government financial support through the Rate Support Grant (R.S.G.) to local authorities has been divided into four components; these are specific grants for police and transport, relief for domestic ratepayers, the 'needs' element, and the 'resources' element. The third of these is based on an estimate of an authority's needs, its particular problems and population structure. The fourth reflects an estimate of local revenue-raising resources in the shape of the rateable value of buildings. In 1976-1977, and ignoring specific grants, the total R.S.G. in England and Wales comprised 11 per cent for domestic relief, 60 per cent on the needs element, and 29 per cent to offset limited resources. In that year, incidentally, R.S.G. was expected to provide for 65.5 per cent of total local government expenditure in England and Wales. The point here, however, is that only twenty-eight boroughs in the whole of the country enjoyed rateable values per head of their population great enough to warrant them receiving no resources element grant at all, and no fewer than twenty of these were London boroughs. Three-fifths of all thirty-three London boroughs are to be found in the top 7 per cent of local authorities in England and Wales measured by local revenue-raising resources.

The last qualification is the most important of all. By 1973, and before the G.L.C.'s 1975 statement on needs and resources, central government had already recognized and accepted the case for additional financial help to London authorities. Thus between 1970/1971 and 1973/1974, London's share of total South East authority revenue expenditure went up from 48 to 57 per cent (South East Joint Planning Team, 1976, p.38); and since 1973, there has been a dramatic further increase in London's share of the national (England and Wales) needs element of the R.S.G. from 16.5 per cent in 1974/1975 to no less than 21.6 per cent in 1978/1979 (Jackman and Sellars, 1977). This substantial increase has been at the expense of the non-conurbation, or 'shire', authorities, whose share dropped steeply from 58.2 per cent to only 51.9 per cent. As a result, London local authorities received an additional £410 million between 1975/1976 and 1978/1979, compared with the grant they would have received on the basis of their already increased 1974/1975 share; meanwhile, the shire counties 'lost' £550 million. So a major shift in central government resource allocation to London has taken place, along the lines argued by the G.L.C., but to the direct detriment of local authorities elsewhere (see section 7.1.4).

5.8.3 *The Personal Income Argument*

A somewhat parallel argument against decentralization policy concerns personal and household incomes in London. Again, commentators such as Eversley (1972) and the G.L.C. have argued that incomes in London are falling, especially for certain groups, relative to those elsewhere. The key mechanisms which might explain such a trend are the rapid loss of manufacturing jobs, which are generally better paid than service employment (Keeble, 1976, p.204), and a selective emigration from London of higher income workers and households at a more rapid rate than low-income workers. Manufacturing decline might explain the fact that, as the G.L.C. (1973) has pointed out, the real income (i.e. after allowing for rises in national average costs of living) of the poorest 25 per cent of households in Greater London actually fell between 1965 and 1971 by 1.7 per cent, whereas the real incomes of similar households elsewhere grew (by 22.6 per cent in the R.O.S.E. for example). These statistics lead Eversley (1973, p.31) to assert 'the existence of a large, and very likely increasing, mass of people with incomes which are increasingly insufficient in comparison with the average for London, let alone the rest of the region'. Eversley also stresses that the existence of this group of low-paid workers is obscured by average earnings figures boosted by the unusually high salaries paid to skilled and professional workers. In other words, the range of incomes in London is greater than elsewhere. More recent data from *Social Trends,* a government statistical publication, suggest that in terms of household incomes, even average London values have declined slightly relative to the country as a whole, given that between 1971/1972 and 1975/1976 London's average weekly household incomes grew less fast (86 per cent) than in the United Kingdom as a whole (91 per cent). The London/United Kingdom differential thus narrowed from 16.3 to 12.9 per cent.

Evidence on relative incomes in London is, however, by no means clear-cut. Indeed, in some ways there are too many statistics, suggesting contrary conclusions. Thus Foster and Richardson (1973) present evidence that the real household incomes of each of four income groups, including the lowest, increased faster in London in the late 1960s than in the rest of Britain (excluding the R.O.S.E.). Similarly, the South East Joint Planning Team (1976, p.35) concluded that despite a complex picture, 'it is difficult to see how earning levels overall have been adversely affected by the decline in manufacturing'. Most recently of all, Simon (1977), after detailed examination of trends in earnings, not incomes, argues that 'there are no signs of a relative deterioration' in London's position, at least up to 1974/1975. In his view, 'the evidence is overwhelming that as far as London as a whole is concerned, average earnings are well above the national average and any of the regions; and there are signs that the gap is widening, certainly as far as women are concerned' (Simon, 1977, p.91). Even the relative position of the lowest-earning group of workers (the bottom 25 per cent) did not, he maintains, alter significantly between 1970 and 1975. Simon also presents evidence that the earnings of workers in some inner London boroughs, singled out on other criteria as economic problem areas, are by no means low. Male manual workers employed (though not necessarily resident) in Newham,

Tower Hamlets, Lambeth and Southwark in 1975 received on average weekly earnings some 8, 8, 12, and 13 per cent, respectively, above the British average. London as a whole was 7.5 per cent above. Conflicting evidence thus makes it difficult to establish whether or not a significant decline of relative personal incomes is occurring in London in the 1970s, or whether particular groups or areas are experiencing real hardship because of especially low incomes. The latter is, however, more of a possibility than the former.

5.8.4 *The Unemployment Argument*

The massive loss of manufacturing jobs sustained by London in recent years has naturally prompted expectation in certain quarters of a parallel rise in unemployment within the capital. After all, industrial decline in the present Development Areas during the 1920s and 1930s was the direct cause of massive unemployment there: is this not to be expected in London, too?

Perhaps surprisingly, the evidence clearly suggests that in general decline has not created worsening unemployment in London, over and above that due to national trends. The topic is examined in detail in Foster and Richardson (1973) and Lomas (1974). The former, after looking at male and female unemployment and job vacancy figures for Greater London, the R.O.S.E. and rest of Britain during the 1960s, conclude that they do not indicate any relative deterioration in London's overall unemployment position over the period. Nor can they find any evidence for a relative worsening with regard to particular zones of London, or particular London industries. Lomas, focusing especially on manufacturing decline, by far the largest component in London's job losses, comes to a similar conclusion: 'over much of Greater London, the rundown of manufacturing seems to have left remarkably little trace in the unemployment register'. More recent unemployment figures also tend to support this view. London's 1978 unemployment rate, at 63 per cent of the average for Great Britain, was not significantly different in relative terms (though much greater absolutely) from values recorded in the 1960s, such as 73 per cent in 1967 and 69 per cent in 1961.

The main reasons for this lack of impact are probably two. First, resident manufacturing workers may have left London for homes elsewhere at a rate equal to or faster than the decline in factory job opportunities in the capital. Second, erstwhile manufacturing employees may have found alternative jobs in service industries, some of which are still expanding in London. Londoners may also have taken over some jobs formerly held by commuters from outside the metropolis.

On the other hand, even if London's decline in manufacturing jobs does not appear to have aggravated unemployment significantly, the debate on the issue has drawn attention to the existence of serious longstanding unemployment problems in the capital which have hitherto attracted much less concern than they deserve. These problems centre on the high rates of unemployment in certain localities and amongst certain groups of workers, the latter reflecting in part a lack of skills. London's unemployed workforce, which incidentally comprises nearly double the number of unemployed workers in the whole of Wales, is especially concentrated in inner London, in a broad belt encircling the conurbation centre. The 1971 Census, one of the few reliable sources of data at this scale, revealed that Tower Hamlets, for example, had a male unemployment rate of 9.7 per cent, Camden 7.3 per cent and Hackney 7.0 per cent; Southwark's rate was 8.2 per cent, whilst that of Kensington and Chelsea was 7.3 per cent. These compared with values in the

Development Areas of between 4 and 11 per cent, the latter being for Clydeside as a whole (G.L.C., 1973). The spatial pattern of high unemployment in London, as Shepherd *et al.* (1974, p.88) point out, is closely related to a concentration in these boroughs of manual workers, and particularly workers formerly employed in semi-skilled and unskilled jobs. Perhaps even more worrying is the fact that the pattern also reflects the geography of a high proportion of London's West Indian and Irish population (section 5.2). As the 1971 Census showed (Lomas, 1974), these two groups experience much higher levels of unemployment in London than does the rest of the population. Moreover, amongst the West Indians at least, the problem focuses especially upon young people, aged between 15 and 20, whose unemployment rates are more than double those of others in that age group. Unemployment amongst young West Indians seems to have been growing in the 1970s, especially in inner London south of the river, and is almost certainly linked to their lack of skills. Indeed, as Lomas (1974, p.20) stresses, in inner London 'relatively few of the total unemployed are out of work because of an overall lack of job opportunities'; the situation is 'rather that a high proportion are on the margins of employability'. Finding a solution to this significant and, possibly, growing problem is therefore unlikely to be easy, although Lomas suggests a mixture of tactics, including job creation (in east London), communication improvements, the development of service industries, and migration assistance (away from inner south London).

5.8.5 *The Future of Docklands*

Inner London decline has probably been at its most dramatic in London's dockland, along the Thames eastwards from Tower Bridge. Since the mid-1960s, the Port of London Authority has gradually closed the oldest up-river docks, such as the East India Dock (closed 1967), the London Docks and St Katharine (1968), and the Surrey Commercial Docks (1970), because of lack of demand. The container revolution has shifted trade away from these small, old and cramped facilities, with their congested access roads, to down-river container terminals as at Tilbury, where larger ships can handle ten times the tonnage in the same turn-round time and with the same workforce. The P.L.A., beset by financial losses on its port operations (£2.4 million in 1977), now wishes to close most of the Royal and West India Docks, too. In addition, various traditional water-orientated industries have been closed down or reduced their activities; ship repairing, sugar refining and the milling of animal feedstuffs are in this category. Employment in docklands has thus shrunk dramatically, with the Port of London's workforce alone falling from 26,000 in 1967 to only 9,500 in 1978. The P.L.A. wants to cut this still further, to only about 5,000, by the 1980s. Manufacturing jobs in Canning Town, just north of the Royal Victoria Docks, declined by nearly 40 per cent in 1966-1972. In addition, the changes have left vacant large areas of derelict industrial land, totalling about 1,300 hectares (3,200 acres), between Tower Bridge and Barking Creek. Most of this is owned by public or semi-public organizations (Hall, 1976, p.39). So the docklands' decline represents both a major challenge for economic planning, and a major opportunity for physical reconstruction.

Recognition of the special status and problems of docklands resulted in a government decision in 1971 to commission, jointly with the G.L.C., a special study of the area. This study, prepared by Travers Morgan, consultants, was published in 1973, and suggested five alternative development options, aimed at tackling the key problems diagnosed by the consultants. These problems were the housing shortage, the narrow range of available jobs and housing types, and the very poor physical environment. Each of the options was, however, rejected (after public participation in the debate) by the then newly-elected Labour G.L.C., and further planning was made the responsibility of a new Docklands Joint Committee, comprising representatives of the G.L.C., the five docklands boroughs, and the Department of the Environment. The result of this committee's work was the *London Docklands Strategic Plan,* published in 1976. This envisaged a pattern of new roads and district shopping centres, the development of four major industrial estates, and the creation of considerable open space, including Thames-side walks. Some 76,000 new jobs would be needed in docklands over the next twenty years. Of key importance to the plan was the proposed construction of a new underground railway, the River Line, crossing the Thames five times to link Thamesmead in the east with the City in the west: this would alleviate one of the key problems diagnosed by the planners, namely, the isolation and lack of access to much of docklands imposed by the winding barrier of the Thames.

The full implementation of this strategy, however, is at risk. True, the government agreed in 1976 to support the plan in principle. Docklands was also one of five areas in Britain to be offered a special partnership arrangement with central government for urban renewal in the spring of 1977 (see p.91ff.). Special funds for dockland redevelopment will include a £17 million allocation (out of the £100 million promised for inner city construction projects during 1977-1979), and no doubt some share of the increased spending (£125 million a year by 1979/1980) under the government's Urban Programme. The G.L.C. has also allocated £8 million to docklands renewal.

However, these sums pale into insignificance when compared with the Docklands Plan's own estimate of the investments required for its full implementation—£2,000 million by 1997. In the public expenditure climate of the late 1970s, a sum of this magnitude is just not available from government sources. Morover, and unlike the G.L.C., the government has firmly rejected one of the plan's central features, the underground railway, despite its new and evocative title of the Jubilee line. The reasons are largely financial, given a capital cost of £250 million and a government estimate of annual operating deficits of £23 million. Instead, the government currently favours investment in roads as a more direct means of attracting new industry to docklands. Of particular importance here would be completion of the so-called east cross route, linking the London end of the new M11 via the Blackwall tunnel with the A2/M2 Dover road. The government has also proposed another Thames crossing slightly further to the east to extend the north circular road from Dagenham to Thamesmead. Such roads, the government appears to be saying, are more likely to make docklands attractive for industrial investment and new jobs than the very expensive construction of an underground line (Hall, 1977a).

A further major problem centres on the administration of docklands redevelopment. The G.L.C. and dockland boroughs, jealous of their democratic rights, have so far insisted on strong local authority representation on the existing policy-making and executive body, the Docklands Joint Committee. However, the South East Economic Planning Council, amongst others, argued that the effective implementation of any redevelopment plan demanded the establishment of a more independent, new town-style docklands development corporation. This view was implicitly endorsed by the refusal of the committee's first two choices for full-time manager—both of them existing new town managers—to take on the job without an assurance of greater executive independence and hence long-term continuity of planning and decision making. With the implementation of the Docklands Plan thus likely to be delayed if not jeopardized by conflict between democratic principles and the practical realities of redevelopment, the government in 1979 decided to create for the first time an urban development corporation in the expectation that it would provide a realistic administrative basis for the area's rehabilitation.

Nevertheless, in the foreseeable future docklands redevelopment appears likely to be on a more local, limited and piecemeal basis than envisaged by the docklands strategic plan. Such redevelopment has already begun, but only on the most favoured and accessible western edges of docklands, close to the City of London. In the St Katharine's development by Tower Bridge on a 10 hectare (25 acre) site, there has already been completed the 826-bedroom Tower Hotel, the restoration of old warehouses as a trade centre, apartments, restaurant and boutiques. The old dock is now a yacht marina. The scheme also envisages construction of 700 dwellings (Hall, 1976, p.42). Elsewhere, planning permission has been granted for office and warehousing projects, such as the World Trade Mart in Southwark's former Surrey Commercial Docks, and offices in the Riverside London scheme on the London Docks site in Tower Hamlets. Industrial sites have been prepared and buildings erected in Beckton. The obvious danger overall, however, is that office construction will initially dominate redevelopment, preempting the most favoured dockland sites close to the City, but leaving untouched large areas of derelict land in the more isolated dockland communities further east.

5.9 Relative Metropolitan Decline: Interim Conclusions

The arguments against traditional decentralization policy and for a measure of government assistance to metropolitan industry and local authority finance, especially in inner London, have had considerable impact in recent years. Admittedly, the 1976 review of the Strategic Plan (see section 6.3.5) was by no means entirely convinced by these arguments, concluding that 'the extent to which the decline or rate of decline in population or employment poses threats to London's future is debatable. In some ways the trends can be regarded as a desirable process of adjustment to changing circumstances' (South East Joint Planning Team, 1976, p.36). This judgement is, of course, supported by much of the evidence discussed in earlier sections. It also reflects additional considerations, such as the much lower cost of development in the R.O.S.E. than in London. As the team pointed out (p.9), land costs double as one moves from the periphery of the south East to inner London, while new housing costs increase by a factor of 1.9. In addition, the redevelopment of sites occupied by existing buildings, as in much of inner London, is usually 50 to 100 per cent more costly than construction on a green-field site. So provision of new housing, both to replace substandard dwellings and to provide for the projected increase in households, is likely to be cheaper outside London, quite apart from consideration of the current residential preferences of South East families, which seem heavily to favour the R.O.S.E.

On the other hand, the 1976 review team did accept the existence of certain more specific problems in London—such as bad housing, homelessness, and pockets of high unemployment and low incomes—and suggested the need 'to try to slow things down in order to ease problems which arise through an excessive rate of change', and to 'ease the adjustment process and minimize adverse effects on individuals whilst London adapts to the changing situation' (South East Joint Planning Team, 1976, p.36). They therefore urged a concentration of effort upon improving London's environment, especially housing, with particular regard to specific areas where the rates of decline were greatest. Housing policy in inner London should make more provision for home ownership; and some new roads would be essential if industry was to be preserved or attracted. Central and local government policies towards economic activity should aim at encouraging, not curtailing, employment creation—for example, the case for retaining i.d.c.s and o.d.p.s was limited. At some stage, the financial resources at London's disposal should be increased.

The review's cautious approach to this major planning controversy has, however, been overtaken by events. Shortly after it was published, the government announced a major reevaluation of urban and new town policy, prompted by inner city decline (see Chapter 3). The conclusions of this reevaluation, embodied in the 1977 White Paper *Policy for the Inner Cities* (Secretary of State for the Environment, 1977) and the 1978 Inner Urban Areas Act, in many ways have gone further, and certainly faster, than the Strategic Plan review envisaged. As far as London is concerned, important subsequent changes have included further considerable shifts in both the 1977/1978 and 1978/1979 Rate Support Grant allocations to London authorities at the expense of other areas, the establishment —with full effect from 1 April 1979—of special partnership schemes for inner area regeneration between central and local government in three inner London areas, Lambeth, Docklands, and Hackney/Islington, and increasing aid under the D.O.E.'s expanded Urban Programme to support inner London social, industrial, environmental and recreational projects. Though not accorded full partnership status, Hammersmith has also been singled out for special assistance. As a start, the docklands boroughs were allocated £17 million and each of the other two partnership schemes £5 million for construction projects in 1978/1979. London as a whole was granted an allocation of £824 million for capital expenditure on housing in 1978/1979, or 34 per cent of the total for England; its population share was only 15 per cent.

On the economic front, the inner London partnerships now receive priority in allocation of i.d.c.s to mobile industry second only to the Assisted Areas and in front of new and expanded towns, while the residual i.d.c. controls (p.46) are being operated flexibly over the whole of inner London. O.d.p.s and L.O.B. publicity, before they were withdrawn, were used to steer office firms to inner areas outside central London. The 1978 Inner Urban Areas Act permits specified inner London local authorities—initially Brent, Ealing, Hammersmith, Haringey and Wandsworth—to assist local industry in various ways, including the provision of loans and factories, and the designation of industrial improvement areas. Small firms—up to 200 employees—in the London partnership scheme areas also benefited from a short-term Small Firms Employment Subsidy for taking on extra workers in 1978/1979.

The reasons for this very rapid shift of government policy lie, of course, partly in a much increased public awareness of the planning problems facing inner London and other conurbations, as a result of increasing publicity and lobbying by their local authorities and other commentators. But politics is also undeniably involved. The Secretary of State for the Environment from 1976 to 1979, Peter Shore, is a Member of Parliament for an inner London constituency, Stepney and Poplar; one of his junior ministers at the time was M.P. for Greenwich; and the Minister for Housing and Construction was Mr Reginald Freeson, M.P. for the west London constituency of Brent, East. More important, nearly all inner city constituencies, in London as elsewhere, are traditionally safe Labour seats. Inner London's thirty-eight constituencies (including Newham) returned thirty-two Labour M.P.s in the 1974 election. So economic and population decline in London and other inner city areas is naturally of considerable concern to a Labour government especially, over and above the non-political planning issues involved.

The new inner city policy, as set out in the 1977 White Paper and 1978 Act, still leaves unanswered many questions, not least those regarding the precise roles and relationships of central and local government in tackling the problems of inner London. An important point here is the markedly contrasting attitudes of different inner London boroughs towards economic development initiatives, of the sort perhaps envisaged by central government. Tower Hamlets, for example, has adopted a positive policy for encouraging private sector investment, notably in offices (section 5.8.5), as one way of replacing jobs lost through manufacturing and port decline. So, too, has Hammersmith, where office development, much of it geared to demand from international firms seeking premises on the route linking central London with Heathrow Airport, has also proceeded fairly rapidly. In contrast, Islington and Wandsworth appear to be opposed to private investment in office construction, preferring instead policies geared to manufacturing and public expenditure. These differences are, at the least, important determinants of recent trends in office development within inner London; while they may also indicate differences in attitudes to local economic development generally which could have a significant long-term influence on the geography of inner city employment and population change, in addition to any differences stemming from the limitation of central government partnership schemes to particular inner boroughs as noted above (Damesick, 1979).

Probably the most important question mark over the new inner city policy, however, concerns its likely effect. It undoubtedly represents a major shift in traditional regional planning policy for London and the South East. However, it comes at a time when government policy initiatives of all kinds are severely constrained on financial grounds by Britain's international economic position. And in complete contrast to Abercrombie-based decentralization policy (see section 6.2), it represents an attempt to halt, rather than swim with, the tide of population and economic change. Such attempts can, as regional policy has shown, be reasonably successful given substantial finance. Without this, however, it would seem unlikely that the new policy will be able to do more than slow somewhat the rate of population and employment decline in London, or cushion particular needy groups or areas from the worst effects of high unemployment, low incomes or declining services.

REFERENCES

Blake, J. (1977). Backhand LOB. *Town and Country Planning,* **45,** 344-347.
Brown, A.J. (1972). *The Framework of Regional Economics in the United Kingdom,* Methuen, London.
Chisholm, M., and Oeppen, J. (1973). *The Changing Pattern of Employment: Regional Speciali-sation and Industrial Localisation in Britain,* Croom Helm, London.
Coffield, F. (1975). Deprivation in detail. *New Society,* 24 April, 206.
Damesick, P. (1979). Offices and inner-urban regeneration, *Area,* 11, 41-47.
Dennis, R. (1978). The decline of manufacturing employment in Greater London: 1966-74. *Urban Studies,* **15,** 63-73.
Department of the Environment (1976b). *Transport Policy: A Consultation Document,* H.M.S.O., London.

Department of the Environment (1977). *Housing Policy: A Consultation Document,* H.M.S.O., London.

Department of the Environment (1978). *Strategic Plan for the South East: Review, Government Statement,* H.M.S.O., London.

Department of the Environment, Urban Affairs and Commercial Property Directorate (1976a). *The Office Location Review,* D.O.E., London.

Dunning, J.H. (1969). The City of London: A case study in urban economics. *Town Planning Review,* **40**, 207-232.

Economy Group, South East Joint Planning Team (1976). *Report,* Department of the Environment, London.

Evans, A.W. (1973). The location of the headquarters of industrial companies. *Urban Studies,* **10**, 387-395.

Eversley, D.E.C. (1972). Rising costs and static incomes: some economic consequences of regional planning in London. *Urban Studies,* **9**, 347-368.

Eversley, D.E.C. (1973). Problems of social planning in inner London. In D. Donnison and D. Eversley (eds.), *London: Urban Patterns, Problems and Policies,* Heinemann, London, 1-50.

Faris, R.E.L., and Dunham, H.W. (1965). *Mental Disorders in Urban Areas,* University of Chicago Press.

Foster, C.D., and Richardson, R. (1973). Employment trends in London in the 1960s and their relevance for the future. In D. Donnison and D.E.C. Eversley (eds), *London: Urban Patterns, Problems and Policies,* Heinemann, London, 86-118.

Goddard, J. (1968). Multivariate analysis of office location patterns in the city centre: A London example. *Regional Studies,* **2**, 69-85.

Greater London Council (1969a). *Greater London Development Plan: Report of Studies,* G.L.C., London.

Greater London Council (1969b). *Greater London Development Plan: Statement,* G.L.C., London.

Greater London Council (1973). *Population and Employment,* G.L.C., London.

Gripaios, P. (1977). Industrial decline in London: an examination of its causes. *Urban Studies,* **14**, 181-189.

Hall, J.M. (1976). *London: Metropolis and Region,* Oxford University Press.

Hall, P.G. (1962). *The Industries of London Since 1861,* Hutchinson, London.

Hall, P. (1975). Migration. *New Society,* 6 February.

Hall, P. (1977a). Dockland tube. *New Society,* 4 August, 231.

Hall, P. (1977b). On Tory lines. *New Society,* 12 May, 284-285.

Howard, R.S. (1968). *The Movement of Manufacturing Industry in the United Kingdom 1945-1965.* H.M.S.O. for the Board of Trade, London.

Jackman, R., and Sellars, M. (1977). The distribution of RSG: The hows and whys of the new needs formula. *CES Review,* **1**, 19-30.

Keeble, D.E. (1968). Industrial decentralization and the metropolis: The North-West London case. *Transactions of the Institute of British Geographers,* **44**, 1-54.

Keeble, D. (1975). Industrial mobility: In which industries has plant location changed most? — a comment. *Regional Studies,* **9**, 297-299.

Keeble, D. (1976). *Industrial Location and Planning in the United Kingdom,* Methuen, London.

Keeble, D. (1978). Industrial decline in the inner city and conurbation. *Transactions of the Institute of British Geographers, N.S.,* **3**, 101-113.

Kirwan, R. (1973). The contribution of public expenditure and finance to the problems of inner London. In D. Donnison and D. Eversley (eds.), *London: Urban Patterns, Problems and Policies,* Heinemann, London, 119-155.

Location of Offices Bureau (1977). *Annual Report,* L.O.B., London.

Lomas, G. (1974). *The Inner City,* London Council of Social Service, London.

Manners, G. (1970). Greater London Development Plan: location policy for manufacturing industry. *Area,* **3**, 54-56.

Martin, J.E. (1964). The industrial geography of Greater London. In R. Clayton (ed.), *The Geography of Greater London,* George Philip, London, 111-142.

New Society, (1977). Council housing. *New Society,* 8 September, 493.

Peach, C., Winchester, S. and Woods R. (1975). The distribution of coloured immigrants in Britain. In G. Gappert and H.M. Rose (eds), *The Social Economy of Cities,* Sage, Beverly Hills.

Rhodes, J., and Kan, A. (1971). Office dispersal and regional policy. *University of Cambridge, Department of Applied Economics Occasional papers,* No.30.

Secretary of State for the Environment (1977). *Policy for the Inner Cities,* (Cmnd.6845), H.M.S.O., London.

Shepherd, J., Westaway, J., and Lee, T. (1974). *A Social Atlas of London,* Clarendon Press, Oxford.

Simon, N.W.H. (1977). The relative level and changes in earnings in London and Great Britain. *Regional Studies,* **11,** 87-98.

South East Joint Planning Team (1976). *Strategy for the South East: 1976 Review,* H.M.S.O., London.

Standing Conference on London and South East Regional Planning (1977). *Rail Commuting to Central London,* Report by the Technical Panel, SC 784 R.

Stone, P.A. (1978). The implications for the conurbations of population changes (with particular reference to London). *Regional Studies,* **12,** 95-123.

Weatheritt, L., and Lovett, A.F. (1975). Manufacturing industry in Greater London. *G.L.C. Research Memorandum* 498, G.L.C., London.

Whittick, A. (1976). We are only half way there. *Town and Country Planning,* **44,** 65-68.

CHAPTER 6

The South East: III Outside London

DAVID KEEBLE

6.1 Introduction

The recent relative decline of the South East is almost entirely due to the massive loss of population and manufacturing employment from London. In the rest of the South East (R.O.S.E.), population, employment and even manufacturing industry, have all grown substantially over the last two or three decades. Thus the population of R.O.S.E. grew from 7,008,000 in 1951 to an estimated 9,914,000 in 1978, an increase of 2,906,000 or 41 per cent. Employment in the area expanded by 31 per cent in 1960-1976, with a growth from 2.7 to 3.5 million (figures adjusted to the post-1971 Census of Employment basis). Manufacturing activity in the R.O.S.E. also grew rapidly in the 1950s and early 1960s, with an increase of 180,000 jobs or 20 per cent in 1959-1971. Since 1971, however, manufacturing employment in the area has declined. At least until the late 1960s, then, there is no doubt that the R.O.S.E. was Britain's leading growth region on all three counts.

6.2 Decentralization Policy: Abercrombie

The R.O.S.E.'s remarkable post-war growth has in the past been ascribed by some observers to successful regional planning policies, following the proposals put forward for the South East by Sir Patrick Abercrombie in his *Greater London Plan* (1945). This classic regional plan recommended the reordering of population and industry in the South East, with planned decline in London and growth in the R.O.S.E., so as to achieve a better spatial arrangement of dwellings, workplaces and land use. It thus reflected at regional level the same concern over urban congestion and decentralization that had preoccupied the 1940 Barlow Commission on national spatial policy, a commission of which, incidentally, Abercrombie had been a member.

Abercrombie's thinking was dominated by essentially metropolitan planning problems. His central recommendation was a substantial dispersal of people and industry from Greater London to surrounding settlements. The transfer of over 1 million Londoners was to be effected chiefly through government action, in the form of the planned expansion of existing towns (525,000 migrants) and the creation of several wholly new towns (380,000 migrants) along lines successfully pioneered by Ebenezer Howard and the 'garden cities' of Letchworth and Welwyn. Migration on this scale, Abercrombie claimed, would reduce the conurbation's population to little more than 7 million, and permit the redevelopment

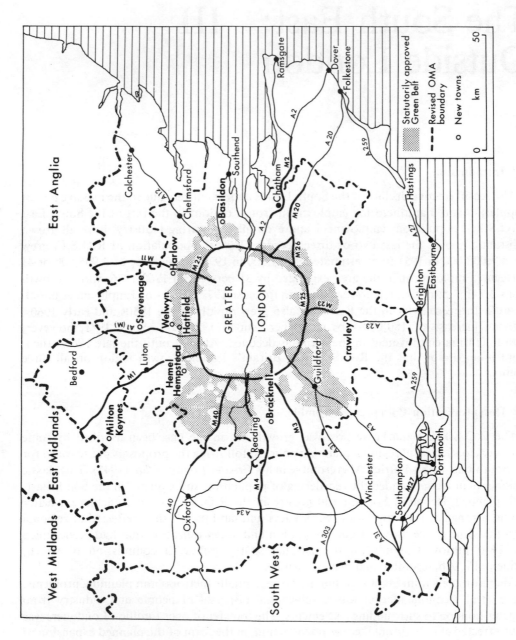

Figure 6.1 South East England: the Abercrombie legacy

of inner congested housing areas at lower net residential densities. Existing R.O.S.E. towns proposed for expansion included Slough, High Wycombe, and St Albans, while examples of the new towns envisaged were Chipping Ongar (Essex) and Crowhurst (Surrey). Most of these were thus within 65 kilometres (40 miles) of central London.

At least four considerations were fundamental to Abercrombie's proposals. The first was that the government would take powers to prevent any further outward extension of the built-up area of London. To this end, the conurbation would be encircled by a green belt, about 8 kilometres (5 miles) wide, within which new urban development would be very strictly controlled (although the green belt was to be punctuated by certain gaps containing new towns or towns suggested for expansion). The second was the assumption that further growth of the South East's population would not take place. In 1944, official demographers forecast a balancing-out of births and deaths, with a falling birth rate as in the 1930s, and Abercrombie assumed that net immigration to the South East would cease as a result of the government's regional development policies. The third consideration was the considerable emphasis placed on the movement of employment, interpreted almost wholly as manufacturing industry, to outlying parts of the South East. This was regarded as an essential corollary of population migration. As Abercrombie rightly stressed, the decanting of people but not employment from London would simply result in increased long-distance commuting to the metropolis, and would intensify rather than ameliorate existing journey-to-work problems. The last point was that development in the R.O.S.E. must be restricted spatially to a limited number of new and expanded settlements. Wholesale development of housing and industry throughout the South East outside London would defeat the basic aims of the plan: 'if industry . . . is allowed to settle in almost any village or town of the Region. . . then the whole fabric of the industrial proposals for the positive building-up of selected towns will fall to the ground' (Abercrombie, 1945, p.58).

Abercrombie's proposals were accepted, in principle, by the post-war Labour government, and constituted the framework for South East regional planning until the mid-1960s. The most striking and tangible results by that time were the creation of eight new towns and nearly thirty 'expanded' towns in the R.O.S.E. and adjacent regions, plus the existence of the London green belt. These warrant detailed consideration before any general evaluation of the impact of Abercrombie's decentralization policy.

6.2.1 *The New and Expanded Towns*

The passing of the 1946 New Towns Act provided the necessary powers and mechanisms for the designation by 1949 of eight, so-called Mark I, South East new towns. Although only Stevenage and Harlow were actually on sites recommended by the *Greater London Plan* itself, all of the towns—the two above, plus Basildon, Bracknell, Crawley, Hatfield, Hemel Hempstead and Welwyn Garden City—were located in accordance with Abercrombie principles. They were all no more than about 50 kilometres (30 miles) from central London, possessed good communications with the metropolis, and were physically well separated from other existing settlements. Each town was the responsibility of a separate Development Corporation, whose master plans none the less followed somewhat similar lines, based on the division of the town into distinct areas—pedestrianized central shopping districts, one or two large industrial estates, and discrete housing zones termed 'neighbourhood units'. Original target town populations ranged from 25,000 (Hatfield,

Bracknell) to 80,000 (Basildon). All were to be developed as 'balanced and self-contained' communities. Growth was to be by the simultaneous movement of London families and firms, daily commuting out of the towns to London was to be discouraged, and each town was to have adequate local services and facilities for the needs of its inhabitants.

In many ways, these early South East new towns have been very successful. By 1978, they provided homes for some 514,000 people, the great majority of them originally from London. Their present population—91,000 at Basildon, 48,000 at Bracknell, for example—in many cases reflects an upward revision of their original target populations, following 1960s forecasts of a substantial growth in the South East's population and their proven attractiveness to London industry and families. Industrial development has involved the construction of some 900 factories, and the creation of over 100,000 manufacturing jobs. At least three-quarters of their industrial firms are migrants from Greater London. And the industries represented tend to be heavily oriented towards the modern, science-based growth sectors of the economy, employing above-average proportions of skilled and highly-paid workers. Good examples are electrical (including electronic), instrument and mechanical engineering, and vehicles; the first three of these account for over one-third of manufacturing employment in virtually all the South East's new towns (Keeble, 1976, p.253).

Admittedly, the towns have so far been less active in attracting service industries, such as mobile offices, although several are developing as important sub-regional shopping centres. Despite early fears, commuting back to London has also been kept to a minimum, with fewer daily journeys than for many other towns of a similar size and distance. In 1971, for example, Hemel Hempstead had a commuting rate to Greater London of only 1.9 per cent, compared with 3.1 per cent for nearby St Albans. The towns have also attracted a reasonable social balance, with proportions of residents in professional, managerial and skilled occupations being close to the national average. An important, though very subjective, qualification to their achievements, however, concerns their residential environments and doubts as to whether they are as attractive as they might be, or will need to be in the future, particularly in those neighbourhoods with high housing densities enforced on the Development Corporations by government policy during the 1960s. Apart from this, there are good grounds for concluding that in general they have been very successful.

Development of so-called 'expanded towns' has been much slower and involved less growth. Because of acute housing shortages in many existing South East towns, Abercrombie's recommendations for a planned expansion of particular R.O.S.E. communities were shelved until after 1952 and the passing of the Town Development Act. The latter was designed to encourage voluntary agreements between large conurbations and smaller surrounding settlements for the transfer of population and industry, by providing financial grants from the Treasury for necessary housing and infrastructure. Slow negotiations, limitations of staff and expertise, and the small size of most of the towns seeking agreements with London, explain the slow population growth—140,000 or so by 1977—of the twenty-eight expanded towns in the R.O.S.E. and adjacent regions. The 'towns' include such centres as Luton and Plymouth, where large existing towns have agreed to very small expansions, as well as such tiny settlements as Witham (Essex), Sandy (Bedfordshire) and Mildenhall (Suffolk) with expansions of fewer than 5,000 newcomers. The biggest individual expansions have been at Basingstoke (20,000), Swindon and Bletchley (14,000 each). These examples also indicate that the

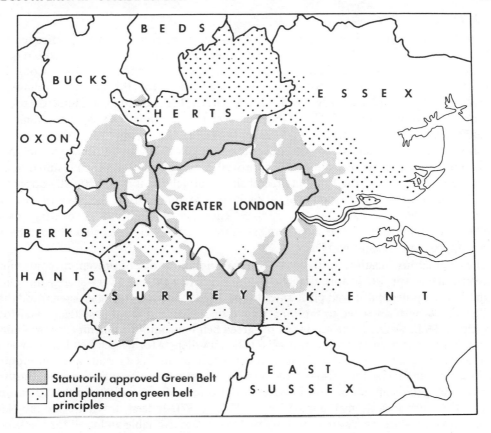

Figure 6.2 The London green belt, 1979
Source: Department of the Environment

expanded towns are located further away from London than are the early new towns. Indeed, thirteen of them are outside the South East altogether, eight being in East Anglia, three in the South West and two in the East Midlands. Greater distance, and poor communications in certain cases (e.g. Haverhill in Suffolk), may be additional reasons for the slow development of the expanded town programme. They have none the less attracted a large number of smaller industrial firms from London; Swindon, with 140 firms occupying 840,000 square metres (9 million square feet) of factory space, has been the most successful in this respect. Like the new towns, the expanded towns possess employment structures biased towards manufacturing activity rather than services. Surveys suggest that most incoming families appreciate the modern housing and general environment of the towns, but miss the benefits of scale—local hospitals, higher-order shops and entertainment facilities—which they enjoyed in London. This point underlies much of the recent thinking on an optimum planning strategy for the R.O.S.E., as noted later.

6.2.2 *The Green Belt*

Abercrombie's green belt proposals have also been of considerable significance for post-war R.O.S.E. planning. These proposals built onto earlier attempts to preserve the countryside immediately around London, such as the London County Council's programme of financial aid to surrounding authorities for the actual purchase of agricultural land. This was made possible by the Green Belt (London and Home Counties) Act of 1938. By 1963, the L.C.C. had helped in the preservation of 113 square kilometres (28,000 acres) by this means (Thomas, 1964). However, it was Abercrombie's recommendations, accepted by the government in 1946 and enshrined in the local development plans that were statutorily approved during the 1950s, which resulted in the formal establishment of the London green belt. Although the initial, officially approved belt extends only for approximately 14 kilometres (8 miles) from the edge of Greater London, a wider area, extending for up to 50 kilometres (30 miles) and covering nearly 5,000 square kilometres (2,000 square miles), is today effectively protected through being either approved or proposed (Figure 6.2).

The original justification for the green belt was the simple one of preventing continuing outward urban sprawl. In this aim, the belt appears to have been very successful. Only limited development has taken place since the early 1950s within green belt areas, and that has generally been restricted to 'infilling' in and on the edge of existing settlements. More questionable, however, is the success of the green belt in promoting amenity, by providing opportunities for countryside recreation by urban dwellers. Much green belt land is owned and used for agriculture, and is not available for recreation. As a result, a recent inquiry concluded that despite the existence of the belt, 'there is a critical deficiency in outdoor recreational provision not only in London but also immediately to the north and east of London' (South East Joint Planning Team, 1970, p.37). Indeed, leaving aside the New Forest in Hampshire, there are only 120 open space sites available and used for non-local informal recreation in the whole of the R.O.S.E., and only thirteen of these are bigger than 400 hectares (1,000 acres). So while successful in certain important respects, the London green belt has not fulfilled the recreational role that some early protagonists of the concept had hoped it might.

6.2.3 *Abercrombie: Policy Impact*

At first sight, the implementation of Abercrombie's Greater London Plan proposals appears to have met with considerable success. Most important, of course, is the massive shift in the location of population and industry, from London to the R.O.S.E., documented earlier. Abercrombie's target for population decentralization from London, of 1.03 million, has been exceeded with the decline in London's population in 1951-1978 of 1.3 million people, as also has his target for the dispersal of 260,000 manufacturing jobs. And a majority of migrant Londoners and London firms have landed up in the R.O.S.E. and adjacent regions, as Abercrombie proposed. The new and expanded towns have played an important part in this, of course, while the green belt has rigorously constrained any significant further outward expansion of London's built-up area. And, within London, redevelopment of inner city slums has been carried out, notably in the East End districts of Stepney and Poplar.

These successful aspects of Abercrombie-based policy must, however, be heavily qualified, in at least two ways. First, his basic assumption of static regional population proved to be wildly inaccurate. The key reason for this was the substantial post-war rates of natural increase. Although falling until 1955, the birth rate in the country as a whole and the South East in particular rose rapidly and unexpectedly until 1964. As a result, the region's population grew through natural increase by nearly 1.2 million people between 1951 and 1966. This was augmented, despite the government's efforts to stem the drift of population from regions of higher unemployment, by the net immigration of over half a million new residents. The effects of this unexpected surge of population growth upon the implementation of Abercrombie's proposals was to slow down, until the mid-1960s, the rate of population decline in London, at the same time as speeding up population growth in the R.O.S.E. Until the late 1960s, the planners thus found it more difficult than expected to redevelop inner London at lower population densities, while an insatiable demand for new houses in such counties as Hertfordshire, Essex and Berkshire forced them to permit building development there on a larger scale than Abercrombie had envisaged. Only in the 1970s, with a steeply falling birth rate and greater success for regional policy (Keeble, 1977), has the kind of demographic situation envisaged by Abercrombie actually materialized.

The second major qualification is that decentralization within the South East has in many ways been even more the product of powerful natural forces than of government action. This judgement is supported by considerable evidence. For example, only about 440,000 people, or 30 per cent of total 1951-1971 population growth outside London (1.46 million), were actually housed in government-sponsored South East new or expanded towns. In 1971, the great majority of new residents in the outer parts of the South East lived outside these planned reception areas, which Abercrombie had proposed should take four-fifths of future population growth. Indeed, during the 1960s, only one in eight actual migrants from London to the R.O.S.E. settled in these official overspill centres, the remainder moving entirely of their own volition to other towns and villages. The wide spatial spread of this voluntary movement was in direct conflict with Abercrombie's aim of geographical selectivity.

A similar judgement applies to industrial decentralization. Not only did manufacturing industry expand during the 1960s in almost every town, large and small, of the R.O.S.E. (Keeble and Hauser, 1971), but most migrant London firms settling in the rest of the region chose locations other than the new and expanded towns. The latter attracted only some 40 per cent of moves by 1971. Moreover, the principal reasons for outward movement revealed by surveys of firms appear to be such factors as building congestion and expansion problems, rather than the impact of local planning policies or displacement by comprehensive redevelopment schemes. Underlying industrial movement, as well as population migration, for example, is the influence of changing residential preferences, a 'natural' agglomeration diseconomy discussed in section 4.4.4.

In sum the tidal wave of post-1945 decentralization from London seems to reflect not only the operation of regional planning policy but also, and to a greater extent, the impact of natural centrifugal forces, aided no doubt by communication improvements which have effectively shrunk the distances separating the R.O.S.E. from its metropolitan hub. Planning policies have been successful in certain ways, notably in channelling some decentralized population and industry to the new and expanded towns. But there can be no doubt but that, even without Abercrombie, there would still have been a substantial shift in the geographical balance between London and its surrounding region over the last thirty or so years.

6.3 Decentralization Policy Since 1964

6.3.1 *The South East Study*

By the early 1960s, it was becoming obvious that the continually rising birth rate was playing havoc with the mathematics of Abercrombie's decentralization plan for the South East. Moreover, development of the second 'wave' of planned overspill settlements—the expanded towns—was proceeding far too slowly to offer hope of coping with then current and projected growth of the R.O.S.E. So a major review of regional planning problems and policy in the South East was put in hand by government, culminating in the publication in 1964 of the Ministry of Housing and Local Government's *South East Study 1961-1981*. The study's main conclusion was that, despite massive post-war decentralization from London, the rapid natural increase in the region's population would necessitate the transfer from the capital of a further 1 million Londoners between 1961 and 1981. Homes would also be needed outside London for a further 2.5 million people, comprising immigrants from other regions and the natural increase of the rest of the South East. The problem was, 'Where?'

The study's answer was in some respects vague—even confused—in that it claimed that the local planning authorities in the Outer Metropolitan Area (O.M.A.) could cater for most of this growth (Figure 6.1). Yet it failed to suggest any guiding strategy for spatial arrangements within this zone. The study was clear, on the other hand, in calling urgently for a second generation of much bigger London overspill towns, to be located in or beyond the Outer South East (O.S.E.), as potential counter-magnets to the capital. Compared with the first-generation new towns, these large centres would be cheaper to build (in terms of cost per household); they would provide a much wider range of facilities, services and jobs; and, in the case of the expansion of existing large towns, they would be able to attract London population and industry from the outset by providing good shops, schools and services. By locating them beyond the O.M.A., undue pressure on this already rapidly expanding zone could be avoided. The study thus suggested the creation of three new cities, one in the Bletchley area (for 150,000 overspill immigrants), one at Newbury (150,000), and one (250,000) between Southampton and Portsmouth; two large new towns (100,000 each) were proposed for Ashford and Stansted; and major expansions, involving from 50,000 to 100,000 migrants each, were suggested for Peterborough, Ipswich, Northampton and Swindon. The last four are of course outside the South East region, Peterborough and Ipswich being in East Anglia, Northampton in the East Midlands, and Swindon in the South West. These schemes, greater than almost anything previously envisaged or attempted anywhere in the world, implied a rate of planned industrial movement over twice as fast as that achieved with the earlier new towns.

In effect, the study's proposals aimed at the creation of a polynuclear city region in the South East, with the continued expansion of towns in the O.M.A., and with the creation of major new outlying cities, one or two of which would be big enough to act as counter-magnets to London. However, despite the massive proposed decentralization, the study anticipated no significant decline of population or employment in London. Natural increase and economic buoyancy would continue; London's 'population at the end of the period is expected to be close to its present level of 8 million', whilst 'the number of jobs—particularly office jobs—in London is likely to go on rising for some time' (Ministry of Housing and Local Government, 1964, p.98). The hazards of regional and urban forecasting are, of course, well illustrated by the striking difference between these expectations and what has actually happened (sections 5.2 and 5.3) long before the end of the period with which the South East Study was concerned.

6.3.2 The Counter-magnet New Towns

The South East Study's great achievement, however, was the government's acceptance of the need for some large-scale urban development at or beyond the edge of the South East region. Its proposal for major new cities at Newbury and in South Hampshire, and for substantial expansions at Ashford, Stansted and Ipswich, were eventually rejected, in part because of fierce local opposition to such schemes. Additional factors, however, were enforced cuts in public expenditure in the later 1960s, and the downward revision of estimates of the scale of decentralization needed following the fall in the national birth rate after its post-war peak in 1964 (ironically the very year of the South East Study itself). In South Hampshire, a special local planning unit was none the less established to cope with the area's anticipated considerable natural growth.

The study's proposals were accepted with respect to the creation of a large new city in the Bletchley area, and substantial expansions at Swindon, Northampton and Peterborough. With the exception of Swindon (discussed earlier in section 6.2.1), all these places were officially designated as new towns under the New Towns Act of 1965. The boldest decision was the 1967 designation of a huge, largely rural, site—9,000 hectares (22,000 acres) at Milton Keynes in Buckinghamshire (see Figure 6.3), for a wholly new city of 250,000 people. The design team's 1970 master plan anticipated that three-fifths of these would come from London, as would much manufacturing and office employment. In that year, the site housed only 40,000 people, notably in the settlements of Bletchley, Stony Stratford and Wolverton. It also contained the headquarters of the Open University. The plan has attracted considerable attention, not only because the scale and rate of growth originally envisaged—an additional 210,000 residents by the early 1990s— was greater than for any other British new town, but also because of the originality of the proposed layout. The latter is based on a grid road plan, moulded to fit the local topography, with low housing densities and a primary road network of more than 132 kilometres (82 miles). Milton Keynes is thus a city designed for living space and the private car. Despite the massive economic recession of the mid-1970s, its population had doubled (to 85,000) by 1978, with an employment expansion of 20,000 jobs. Interestingly, less than 3,000 of these jobs were actually transferred from London, although 60 per cent of Milton Keynes's immigrant population came from London. The first phase of central Milton Keynes, a large and totally new 1 million square foot regional shopping centre in the middle of the designated area, was opened in 1979. It will eventually provide jobs for 29,000 workers, in offices, shops and other services.

The two other counter-magnet new towns, Peterborough (designated 1967) and Northampton (designated 1968) have also expanded considerably since 1970. Peterborough, with an original population of 81,000, had grown to over 112,000 by 1978: Northampton had expanded from 133,000 to 147,000. It is interesting that job growth, as in Milton Keynes, has been somewhat less dominated by manufacturing than was the case with the first-generation London new towns, partly because of a substantial national decline in manufacturing employment in recent years, and hence the dearth of mobile industry, but also because of the greater attractiveness of these larger centres to service trades, including office activities and warehousing. A key factor in the success of these counter-magnet new towns in attracting firms in very difficult economic circumstances has been their excellent road and rail communications with London and the rest of Britain. This is particularly true of Milton Keynes, sited beside the M1 and electrified London-Birmingham rail link, and Peterborough, served by the highspeed Newcastle-London rail service and close to the A1.

Future development of these three new towns will not, however, be as substantial as was originally envisaged. Following the government's 1976/1977 review of new town policy, prompted by its concern over inner city problems (see sections 3.3.4 and 5.8), the target population for each of the towns has been reduced. Milton Keynes will now plan for only 110,000 immigrants (and hence a total population of 150,000, given the existing inhabitants) by the mid-1980s, with possible further natural growth to 200,000. Northampton and Peterborough's targets have been cut from 230,000 to 180,000, and from 180,000 to 160,000, respectively. The total for the three thus comes down by at least 120,000 residents, or about one-fifth. The reason for the cut is partly resources. Increased Department of the Environment grants to the inner cities have to come from somewhere, and the new town budget is an obvious source, in the long if not the short term. But the changes also reflect the dramatic fall in the birth rate since 1964, and the expectation of a static population in the South East over the next twenty years. In many ways, the counter-magnet new towns are fortunate to have escaped as lightly as they have from the review. This reflects their success in arguing that a gross under-utilization of already installed infrastructure and capital investment would be a very wasteful use of economic resources, and that they are making an important contribution to housing lower-income, unskilled and semi-skilled, London households. Thus 37 per cent of all London migrants in 1971-1974 to the three towns were in this category, compared with a proportion of only 13 per cent for London migrant households to all communities.

6.3.3 *A Strategy for the South East*

As noted above, one important deficiency in the 1964 South East Study was its failure to spell out a coherent spatial strategy for natural growth in the O.M.A. This gap prompted—through the Standing Conference on London and South East Regional Planning—both the local authority proposal that O.M.A. growth should be concentrated in certain limited areas of relatively poor land in terms of agriculture and scenery, and the sharply contrasting 'growth-sector' recommendations of the 1967 *Strategy for the South East*. The latter document, produced by the newly-established South East Economic Planning Council, argued that the spatial pattern of future South East growth should be closely related to that of the region's main road and rail communications, and that development should be channelled into sectors, radiating outwards along major lines of communication from London (see Figure 6.3b).

Such a strategy certainly conformed in part to post-war trends in O.M.A. growth (see section 6.4.3). Moreover, it was supported by at least two theoretical arguments. On the one hand, the very high cost of public investment in modern communications is warranted only if they are heavily used. Location of new housing and industrial areas close to new motorways and electrified rail routes would help to ensure that these expensive communications were used intensively. On the other hand, the South East's increasingly affluent population is becoming increasingly mobile, and demanding rapid access to jobs,

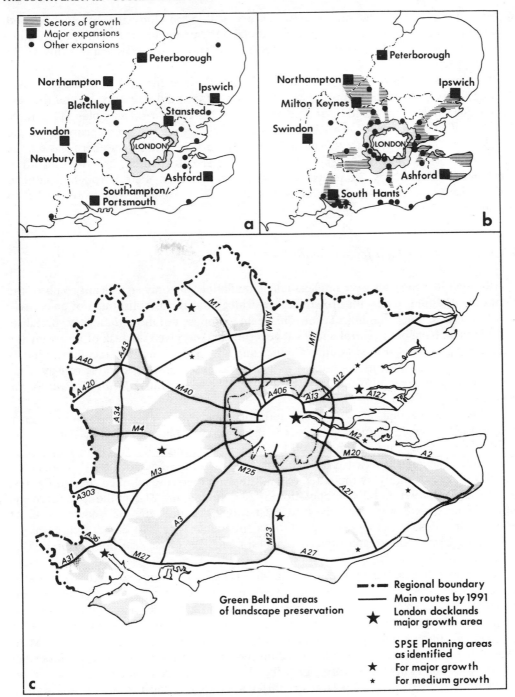

Figure 6.3   South East England: planning proposals
    (a) in *The South East Study*, 1964
    (b) in the *Strategy for the South East*, 1967
    (c) in the *Strategic Plan for the South East (SPSE)*,
       1970—as revised in 1978

shops and leisure facilities—many of which are in London. Industry, too, needs good communications with the capital, and a wide labour catchment area. Thus, by locating housing and industry close to major radial communications both people and firms would be able to benefit.

Other arguments in favour of the Planning Council's growth-sector proposals included the possibility of more easily preserving wide tracts of unspoilt countryside, and the ease with which this strategy could be grafted onto the earlier counter-magnet plan. Thus three of the council's four major growth sectors led to counter-magnet cities proposed in the *South East Study*. One ran south west to Southampton-Portsmouth, another followed the M1 north west to Milton Keynes, a third led north east to Ipswich, and the fourth ran south east to Canterbury. Minor growth sectors—to Swindon, Peterborough, Southend and Ashford—paralleled each major sector and a fifth, isolated, minor sector led to Brighton.

6.3.4 *The Strategic Plan for the South East*

Although its proposals were intellectually stimulating, the only significant result of the Economic Planning Council's growth-sector strategy was the establishment of an entirely new South East Joint Planning Team. This team, composed of more than fifty specialists and planners from both central and local government, was given the task of reviewing the alternative proposals of the Planning Council and local authorities, and recommending its own preferred and definitive strategy. Its work was based on considerable research, far more than for any previous study. The results were the authoritative *Strategic Plan for the South East*, published in 1970.

Rightly arguing that existing local authority plans and new and expanded town commitments would largely determine the regional pattern of population and employment change up to about 1981, the team confined its recommendations to 1981-2001. The latest forecasts then available suggested that the South East's population could grow considerably by the latter years. The team therefore adopted 'design figures' for the region's 1991 and 2001 population of 20.0 million and 21.5 million, respectively. These figures were not themselves forecasts, but did indicate the general level of population which the plan was designed to accommodate. The 2001 design figure was 4.2 million, or 24 per cent greater than the then estimated 1969 base year population of 17.3 million.

The approach adopted by the team was to evaluate in detail two alternative spatial strategies to cope with this growth. One—the 1991A strategy—was based on the Economic Planning Council's sector ideas, together with an accent on counter-magnets on the edge of the region. The other—1991B—envisaged a lower eventual population for London (7 million instead of 7.3 million) with more growth concentrated in the O.M.A. Evaluation of these alternatives was based on certain criteria. One of the most important was the desirability of concentrating growth, whether located in counter-magnets or close to London, into a relatively few large urbanized areas. Such concentration, it was argued, results in the development of a large labour market which offers firms access to a wide range of skills, and workers access to varied job opportunities. Possibilities for industrial linkage are enhanced. Socially, large centres can offer a much wider range of services to their inhabitants (see section 6.2.1). Public transport is also more efficient and economic in larger centres. Lastly, concentrated development is the best approach for preserving extensive areas of open countryside.

Another important criterion for evaluating the two alternative strategies was feasibility, notably in terms of the ease of attracting manufacturing and office employment from London, at the required rate of perhaps 15,000 to 20,000 jobs per year in both categories. Local economic buoyancy, generating indigenous employment growth by existing firms, was also important here. A third key criterion was the particular need to improve job opportunities, housing and social facilities for lower-income families, especially those at present living in inner London. The team's recommended strategy is shown diagrammatically in Figure 6.3c.

As is immediately clear, this strategy was a blend of the two alternatives considered. Of the five major growth centres proposed, two—Milton Keynes-Northampton, and South Hampshire (with eventual populations of 0.8 million and 1.4 million, respectively)—were 'traditional' counter-magnets, located in the O.S.E., while the others—Reading/Basingstoke, South Essex, and the Crawley area (with eventual populations of 1.2 million, 1.0 million and 0.5 million, respectively)—were in the O.M.A. and close to London. Of the less important medium growth areas, three—Ashford, Eastbourne-Hastings and Bournemouth-Poole—were in the O.S.E., while four—Maidstone-Medway, Aylesbury, Bishop's Stortford-Harlow and Chelmsford—were in the O.M.A. Growth areas were thus located in all sectors of the South East, and at a variety of distances from London. However, in terms of their overall spatial balance and compared with those of the *South East Study* and *Strategy*, these proposals implied a significant shift away from a policy of long-distance transfers of London population and industry to the periphery of the region, in favour of a more flexible plan catering for considerable but still nucleated growth closer to the metropolis. This shift stemmed in many ways from an awareness of the strength of natural trends, of the limited distances over which many London manufacturing and office firms are prepared to move, and of the social and economic advantages, especially for lower-income families, of planned growth close to the capital. The urgent need for rehabilitation if not redevelopment in inner London, and population trends during the 1960s, also led the team to anticipate an eventual metropolitan population of about 7 million.

The *Strategic Plan for the South East* thus eschewed the drama of counter-magnets and growth sectors in favour of a more varied, pragmatic and apparently realistic approach than earlier planning studies. Involvement of both local and central government in its preparation also minimized subsequent controversy. Despite certain criticisms (Keeble, 1971), therefore, it was, not surprisingly, approved by the government in 1971 with only minor modifications (notably the abandonment of the Bishop's Stortford-Harlow medium growth area), as the official framework for future South East regional planning.

6.3.5 *The 1976 Review*

The *Strategic Plan*'s great predecessor, Abercrombie's *Greater London Plan 1944*, remained unchallenged for nearly twenty years. Such was the pace of change in the 1970s that a major review of the *Strategic Plan* was launched a mere four years after its publication! The results of this exercise, again conducted by a joint team of central and local government planners, were published as the *Strategy for the South East: 1976 Review*. Why was a review needed, and what were its findings?

The review was not intended to challenge the fundamental framework of the 1970 *Strategic Plan*. The latter remains the accepted basis for the planning of the South East, and the review was conceived as a 'development and updating' exercise, rather than a total rethink. However, at least four major changes or considerations necessitated some such reevaluation. One of these is the dramatic reduction in population forecasts consequent upon the falling birth rate. Thus instead of growing by nearly 3 million in 1969-1991, as conceived likely by the 1970 plan, the South East's population is now expected to remain virtually static (1976 actual, 16.89 million; 1991 forecast, 17.11 million). Another is the effect of the 1973 world oil price rise on energy costs, with the resultant national economic recession and high unemployment. A third is the need for much greater restraint than formerly in future public expenditure, because of the national economic situation. The last is increased concern over the decline of London, as documented in chapter 5; London's population in 1976 (7.03 million) had already reached the lowest eventual figure anticipated by the 1970 *Strategic Plan*. Changes in the structure of local government in the South East in 1974 were also a minor factor in the reevaluation.

By and large, the review accepted that the 1970 framework still made considerable sense. Although the regional population might not increase, there was every likelihood of a continuing and substantial shift of population out of London to the R.O.S.E. Together with natural increase, this could lead to a growth of 1.0 million to 1.5. million in the R.O.S.E. by 1991, and a roughly similar decline in London. Moreover, this shift would be compounded by changes in household structure, with a big increase in small households (of one or two persons). The R.O.S.E. could thus gain an additional 950,000 households, with London losing 200,000. In consequence there would still be a need for very considerable housing development in the 1970 plan's growth areas. And concentrating development geographically still makes sense in cost-efficiency terms, especially with regard to the lower costs of public investment (see section 5.8).

On other issues, however, the 1976 review is more equivocal, reflecting perhaps the 'political' problems raised by conflicts of view between different interested bodies—the different local authorities and central government, in particular. For example, the review's attitude to London and its problems is not entirely clear-cut, although in general it argues that London's difficulties stem chiefly from too rapid a rate, rather than the fact, of decline. The latter is seen as inevitable (see section 5.8). In this respect, it tends to support the 'shire' counties outside London, against the currently prevailing G.L.C. and central government viewpoint. It is perhaps even weaker when it raises, but shies away from, the implications for regional and national economic policy of the fact that the South East is traditionally Britain's most successful economic region—yet is subject to more official restraints on industrial and office growth than any other area (Manners, 1977). The review thus came under fire from very different interests, while central government policy on London in any case was moving further to assist the inner areas than it seemed to favour (see section 5.8).

The government response to the review was published in 1978 and took the form of a 'free-standing' document that set out the position of the Secretary of State in relation to strategic planning in the South East; the *Strategic Plan for the South East* (Department of the Environment, 1978) thus became the new formal basis of government policy. With this plan, the balance of government priorities and goals within the region shifted further in favour of London, with docklands being given as much prominence on the summary map as the major growth areas, and the latter being designated as areas where growth *could* occur (rather than places where growth *should* occur, as in the 1970 strategy). The need for an early completion of the M25 orbital motorway was stressed, but at the same time it was recognized that in its immediate vicinity policies of development restraint would need to be reinforced in order to preserve the inner part of the green belt and support the London economy. Other restraint policies, however, were substantially unchanged save to insist that the green belt was most properly conceived as a discrete zone some 18-24 kilometres wide and should not be extended further into the O.M.A. as a part of general development restraint policies. The latter are more properly left for definition within the structure plans of the county authorities.

6.3.6 *County Structure Plans*

The 1970 and 1978 strategic plans were of course conceived in order to provide a regional framework within which local authority plans dealing with smaller areas could be fitted, in an integrated manner. However, it must be recognized that local authority planning has, especially since 1974, assumed considerable importance in its own right, as a factor likely to influence the changing and future geography of population and economic development in the South East outside London. The reason for this is that the 1972 Local Government Act, in creating a two-tiered system of local government based on counties and districts, accorded considerable strategic planning powers to the higher, county-level, authorities. These authorities, which came into existence in April 1974, are legally responsible for the production of the 'structure plans' required by the 1968 Town and Country Planning Act. Structure plans are broad statements of local authority policy towards land use development, traffic management and the improvement of the physical environment (Cullingworth, 1974, pp.99-101); and while they must take full account of any approved regional plan covering the area concerned, the size and importance of the counties, and the uncertainties over the 1970 *Strategic Plan*, have undoubtedly afforded some scope for the adoption of distinctive structure plan policies by different South East county councils.

In particular, counties immediately around London in the Outer Metropolitan Area—Surrey, Berkshire, Hertfordshire, etc.—seem to have opted for more restrictive local planning policies than those either in force previously or envisaged by counties further out in the Outer South East. An excellent example of a restrictive structure plan is that of Hertfordshire (1976), which proposes a 'low-growth strategy' designed 'to restrain development pressures associated with the growth spiral, and to divert these pressures to growth areas elsewhere in the region, or to development areas elsewhere in the country'. Its basic theme is thus one 'of consolidation following two decades of rapid change', with strict development control policies with regard to the granting of planning permission for housing, factories and offices designed to achieve 'lower employment, housing and population growth. Development pressures are to be restrained and redirected'. In detail, the Hertfordshire planners will seek to restrict housing development and hence population growth to only 90,000 to 131,000 people in 1971-1991—a growth rate of only 10 to 14 per cent—as compared with an actual growth in 1951-1971 of 364,000 or 65 per cent, and a feasible high-growth strategy for 1971-1991 of 250,000 people, or 27 per cent. Industrial and office development will also be tightly controlled, with a ban on factory and office building for incoming firms and permission for only limited expansion by local companies. Development in the metropolitan green belt and rural Hertfordshire will not be allowed.

Similar restrictive policies have been adopted by counties covering other parts of the O.M.A., such as Buckinghamshire and Essex. The former's 1976 structure plan proposes stringent controls on development throughout southern Buckinghamshire, with an extended green belt and strict maintenance of the officially designated Chilterns Area of Outstanding Natural Beauty. New development is to be channelled further out, notably to Milton Keynes and, to a lesser extent, centres such as Aylesbury. In the Essex case (1978), the structure plan adopts an especially unequivocal local and restrictive viewpoint: 'further growth (of population) is undesirable. The strategy must, therefore, seek to slow down previous rates of population growth and concentrate on meeting the housing needs of the County rather than those of the South East'. Strikingly, the plan thus rejects the idea both of substantial population growth close to London in South Essex, and medium growth around Chelmsford, both of which were envisaged by the 1970 regional *Strategic Plan*. In contrast to Hertfordshire, however, Essex is nevertheless also anxious to encourage new—i.e. incoming—industry and offices in order 'to increase local job opportunities and reduce the dependence on London', notably in urban centres such as Basildon, Chelmsford, Colchester, Southend and Thurrock. This difference clearly reflects *inter alia* the greater rate of commuting to jobs in London from Essex than from Hertfordshire revealed by the 1971 Census (see Figure 5.4).

The accent in structure plans for counties covering areas of the Outer South East is, however, less dominantly one of restriction, and there is a greater acceptance in several of the need to accommodate a certain amount of growth. This is evident from the North Buckinghamshire case cited above. An even better example, however, is given by the South Hampshire structure plan, where provision is made for considerable future expansion of population and employment, first in established urban areas and then, from the early 1980s, in five principal growth sectors, as at Eastleigh and Totton: a sixth, at Waterlooville, was rejected by the Secretary of State for the Environment when approving the plan in 1978. The Bedfordshire structure plan (1977) also, while aiming 'to achieve a slowing down of previous rates of population growth' by a planning policy designed 'to resist housing demands originating from areas outside the County', in fact envisages a rate (23 per cent) of population growth in 1971-1991 which is considerably greater than that proposed by such O.M.A. counties as Hertfordshire; its policy towards the expansion of industrial employment is also much more positive. In the Oxfordshire case, the draft plan again aims at a policy which in fact permits more rapid population expansion than in most O.M.A. areas, with a preferred 'medium growth' strategy designed to cope with an increase of 21 per cent in 1971-1991. As with Bedfordshire, this is only half the population growth rate for the previous twenty years, but is none the less significantly faster than that envisaged by areas nearer London.

Of course, structure plans are long-term statements of intent rather than tightly controlled programmes of actual development: the degree to which different counties will in practice be able to manipulate or restrict development is open to question. The difference in emphasis between counties close to and further from London is noteworthy, however, and could have an influence on the future geography of population and employment change in the region, over and above the impact of the approved regional strategy.

6.4 The R.O.S.E.: Growth and Structure

6.4.1 *The Reasons for Growth*

The remarkable post-war growth of the South East outside London can only partly be explained by a successful policy of decentralization. In particular, the R.O.S.E. still enjoys many of the regional advantages for economic and population growth (discussed in section 4.3) without suffering from most of the considerable disadvantages which underlie the rapid recent decline of London (section 4.4). Indeed, as might be expected, most of the R.O.S.E.'s growth reflects the movement of population, industry and other economic activity *from* London; and it is only to be expected that the forces behind growth in the area are in many ways the obverse of those occasioning decline in London.

Another factor is the R.O.S.E.'s very favourable industrial structure, and its concentration on industries whose products have enjoyed growing demand nationally since 1945. Thus in 1959, both the O.M.A. and Sussex coast possessed manufacturing employment structures in the top eleven sub-regions (out of sixty-one in the whole country) as measured by the structural growth index described in section 5.4.1; and two of the other four R.O.S.E. sub-regions (Bedfordshire-Oxfordshire, and Essex) were in the top twenty (Keeble, 1976, p.100). Only the Solent sub-region, with traditional but declining shipbuilding and ship repairing industries, recorded an unfavourable structural index— and this area probably enjoyed a better *service* employment mix than any other R.O.S.E. sub-region. A favourable industrial structure, admittedly related in many areas to an earlier immigration of growth industries from London, is thus an important factor in R.O.S.E. expansion.

The forces behind the considerable migration of people and employment to R.O.S.E. from London may be grouped under four headings. Three of these are referred to briefly under the discussion of agglomeration diseconomies in section 4.4. The first is increasing space needs, for London households and industry, linked to rising real incomes and technological change. Many families nowadays can afford and demand more spacious housing—extra rooms, garages, garden space—than was the case thirty years ago. For industry, changes in production technology are leading to steadily increasing requirements for ground-floor factory space. Indeed, the area of new factory floorspace actually constructed per employee in South East England trebled—from 46 to 140 square metres (498 to 1,511 square feet)—between 1960 and 1969, a rate of growth faster than that in any other region of Britain (Keeble, 1976, p.75). The R.O.S.E.'s ability to provide more living and working space than London for homes and factories is a major reason for its growth. This is, of course, linked to a second factor, the traditional differential in house, factory and land prices between London and the R.O.S.E. (see section 5.1). In the period 1964-1969, for example, industrial land prices in the R.O.S.E. (at £49,000 per hectare— £20,000 per acre) were only 40 per cent of those for sites in Greater London (£124,000 per hectare, £50,000 per acre; Vallis, 1972).

A third compelling force behind population migration to the R.O.S.E. is the increasing importance of residential amenity considerations in household location decisions, given rising real incomes and the ability of many workers to commute considerable distances to their jobs. The pull of the R.O.S.E. in this respect, with its many historic towns and attractive villages, and its outstanding rural and coastal scenery in the Chilterns, North and South Downs, Kent, Sussex and on the Solent coast, for example, is clearly illustrated by residential preference surveys (section 4.4). It is also strikingly borne out by the actual migration patterns of that one class of migrants whose decisions are totally unconstrained by employment location considerations—retirement migrants. As Law and Warnes (1976) have shown, by far the largest flow of such migrants in Britain is from London and its surrounding towns to the southern half of the Outer South East from Kent to Hampshire. The next largest flows are from the London area to South West England and East Anglia. Law and Warnes argue that the basic reason for these flows is the perceived residential attractiveness of these areas. It should also be noted that there is growing evidence that residential amenity factors also influence many industrialists in their location decisions, again to the benefit of areas such as the R.O.S.E. (Keeble, 1976, pp. 83-85).

6.4.2 Communication Improvement

The last factor behind R.O.S.E. growth is the improvement in communications. Since the late 1950s, substantial improvements have taken place in the radial communication links between London and the R.O.S.E. The most important have been new motorways, radiating outwards from London. Britain's first full-scale motorway, the M1, the M40 section of the London-Oxford road, the M4 from inner London towards South Wales, the M3 to Basingstoke, the M23 to Gatwick and Crawley, the M2 and M20 stretches on the Dover and Folkestone roads, respectively, the M11 towards Cambridge, and the A1(M) north of Stevenage, have all greatly increased the speed and ease of road access from the capital to outlying South East towns and villages. In aggregate, no less than 515 kilometres (320 miles) of motorway have already (1978) been built in South East England: and all but 50 kilometres (30 miles) of this total are radial links, radically improving access to the R.O.S.E. from London. Future motorway building, with the exception of the M11 extension up to and around Cambridge, is, however, likely to focus on the orbital M25 route (Figure 6.3c), singled out by government in 1977 as deserving of the highest national priority. By the mid-1980s, this will encircle Greater London, providing essential transfer links between all the existing radial motorways focusing on London. The only other non-radial motorway in the South East is the M27, linking and bypassing Southampton and Portsmouth.

Recent improvements in rail communications are also almost wholly radial in nature. Most striking has been the expensive electrification of the Waterloo-Bournemouth and Euston-Lancashire main lines. The total cost of the latter, over one-quarter of which traverses the South East, was £160 million. The former, with all its 160 kilometres (100 miles) of track in the South East, cost £15 million. The justification for electrification was, of course, the heavy traffic already carried by these lines. In turn, the much-shortened journey times made possible by track realignment and electrification have attracted even greater flows of passengers, if not freight. Southampton and Bournemouth are now only 70 and 100 minutes respectively from London, while the fastest non-stop services to Bletchley take only 37 minutes to cover the 73 or so kilometres (45 miles) from Euston. Areas on the very periphery of the South East have thus been brought considerably closer to London in terms of journey time. The same has happened with the 1978 opening of the 65 kilometre (40 mile) King's Cross-Royston electrification scheme, constructed at a cost of £66 million. Electrification of the St Pancras-Bedford line, due for completion by 1982 at a cost of £80 million, will cut 15 minutes off the current fastest time (50 minutes) for the 80 kilometre (50 mile) journey. Further radial electrification schemes—Bishop's Stortford-Cambridge, and London-Ipswich, for example—are quite likely. Such schemes, and radial motorway construction, have undoubtedly greatly stimulated R.O.S.E. growth, by permitting if not encouraging the movement to the area of London commuters (see section 5.3) and London manufacturing and office firms requiring continuing close contact with the metropolis.

6.4.3 *The Pattern of Growth*

The forces encouraging growth in the R.O.S.E. have not operated uniformly, either spatially or structurally. Certain types of growth, and certain areas of the R.O.S.E., have been favoured more than others. In structural terms, population growth in the O.M.A. and in the O.S.E. to the north and west of London has tended to be heavily biased towards younger workers and their families, moving out to new towns or in search of cheaper homes and more attractive residential areas. In 1965/1966 for example (South East Joint Planning Team, 1971, p.26), 65 per cent of all net migrants from London to the O.M.A. were younger adults (ages 25-44) or children (ages 1-14). Population growth in the O.S.E., especially along the South Coast, has in contrast been biased more towards retired individuals (53 per cent of net migrants from London to the O.S.E. in 1965-1966 were over 45 years of age). Again, growth in economic activity has tended to be biased towards space-extensive or rapidly-expanding industries, forced out of London by land costs or expansion constraints.

The selective impact of the forces for growth helps to explain the different employment structure of the R.O.S.E., as compared with London. In 1976, total employment in the two areas was roughly equal—London 3,710,000, the R.O.S.E. 3,540,000. However, no less than 74 per cent of London's employment was in services, with only 21 per cent in manufacturing; whereas in the R.O.S.E., manufacturing provided some 30 per cent of employment, with only 62 per cent in services. This difference reflects the attractiveness of the R.O.S.E. since 1945 to expanding London manufacturing firms, together with the powerful constraints which still bind most London service firms to a metropolitan location.

Within the R.O.S.E., the O.M.A. is especially dependent on manufacturing, with no less than 35 per cent of total employment in 1973 in this category. The Outer South East— 28 per cent manufacturing in 1973—is more similar to London in this respect. Conversely, the O.S.E. depends on service industry (63 per cent of total 1973 employment) to a greater extent than does the O.M.A. (only 58 per cent in 1973). These differences within the R.O.S.E. reflect the fact that until recently, most migrant London manufacturing firms choosing new locations in the region moved only as far as the O.M.A., often, of course, to one of its first-generation new towns. At the same time, the bigger towns and cities which exist in the Outer South East—Brighton, Portsmouth, Southampton, Oxford, Bedford—have always specialized in, and attracted growth in, higher order services of different kinds—three of the above are university towns, for example! More mobile manufacturing firms from London are, however, now moving further out within the region than was the case in the 1950s and earlier 1960s, while there is also a growing movement from the O.M.A. itself to the O.S.E. (Keeble, 1976, p.272). As a result, the O.S.E. gained a larger share—56 per cent—of the manufacturing jobs created by the movement of firms within the South East in 1966-1974 than did the O.M.A. (42 per cent). So the employment structures of the two zones may become more similar in the future.

The geography of population and employment change within the R.O.S.E. has obviously altered over time. In the 1950s, the O.M.A. was by far the greatest zone of population growth in Britain, with a ring of settlements in a belt 30 kilometres (18 miles) wide around London all growing at decennial rates of 20 per cent or more. Radial sectors of growth also followed certain corridors out from London, notably to Brighton, to Newbury, and to Southend. The principal factors behind this pattern were the new towns, the outward movement of London commuters in search of cheaper housing, and the reluctance of mobile firms to move too far from the capital. Since the mid-1960s, however, rapid communication improvements, together with increasing planning constraints and rising land and house prices in the O.M.A., have pushed growth further out, into the O.S.E. and beyond. The pattern of this growth is much more fragmented, with many traditionally rural areas and smaller settlements being involved. Significantly, the London zone of population decline has now crept outwards, to envelope by the mid-1970s quite a large number of encircling O.M.A. towns, especially in inner Surrey and Hertfordshire. Population decline also characterizes several larger O.S.E. towns— Brighton, Southampton and Portsmouth, for example—although the population in the rural areas around them is still expanding to some extent. These trends support the contention that many households today prefer the residential environment provided by smaller towns and villages, although planning controls may also be involved.

Recent trends in the location of manufacturing within the R.O.S.E. can be summed up in one word—*dispersion*. Dispersion involves shifts of manufacturing activity , like shifts of population, both from the O.M.A. outwards to the edges of the region, and from large to small centres. Thus in the later 1960s (and very probably since), nearly two-thirds of the R.O.S.E.'s nineteen largest manufacturing centres recorded manufacturing employment decline, whereas nine-tenths of the R.O.S.E.'s forty-four least industrialized local labour market areas experienced manufacturing growth. This striking trend may relate both to residential preferences on the part of industrialists and entrepreneurs, and to the effects of agglomeration diseconomies and planning controls in the bigger centres. In contrast, however, service employment growth, some of it the result of office migration from London, does seem to have been concentrated in the larger outlying towns. The latter, therefore, seem to be increasing their functional importance within the region, as centres for employment, shopping, entertainment and higher-order services generally. With the decline of London, the South East's space economy is thus developing a polynuclear structure, with increasingly complex journey-to-work patterns focused both on the metropolis and the region's other larger towns, and an urbanized life-style even in traditionally rural areas.

REFERENCES

Abercrombie, P. (1945). *Greater London Plan 1944,* H.M.S.O., London.
Cullingworth, J.B. (1974). *Town and Country Planning in Britain,* Allen & Unwin, London.
Department of the Environment (1978). *Strategic Plan for the South East,* H.M.S.O., London.
Keeble, D. (1971). Planning and South East England. *Area, 3,* 69-74.
Keeble, D. (1976). *Industrial Location and Planning in the United Kingdom,* Methuen, London.
Keeble, D. (1977). Spatial policy in Britain: regional or urban? *Area, 9,* 3-8.

Keeble, D.E., and Hauser, D.P. (1971). Spatial analysis of manufacturing growth in outer South East England 1960-1967. I. Hypotheses and variables. *Regional Studies,* **5,** 229-262.

Law, C.M., and Warnes, A.M. (1976). The changing geography of the elderly in England and Wales. *Transactions of the Institute of British Geographers,* N.S., **1,** 453-471.

Manners, G. (1977). The 1976 review of the Strategic Plan for the South East: some outstanding economic issues. *Planning Outlook,* **20,** 2-8.

Ministry of Housing and Local Government (1964). *The South East Study 1961-1981,* H.M.S.O., London.

South East Economic Planning Council (1967). *A Strategy for the South East,* H.M.S.O., London.

South East Joint Planning Team (1970). *Strategic Plan for the South East,* H.M.S.O., London.

South East Joint Planning Team (1971). *Strategic Plan for the South East, Studies Volume 1, Population and Employment,* H.M.S.O., London.

South East Joint Planning Team (1976). *Strategy for the South East: 1976 Review,* H.M.S.O., London.

Thomas, D. (1964). The green belt. In J.T. Coppock and H.C. Prince (eds), *Greater London,* Faber, London, 292-312.

Vallis, E.A. (1972). Urban land and building prices 1892-1969. *Estates Gazette,* **222,** 1406-1407.

CHAPTER 7

East Anglia and the East Midlands

DAVID KEEBLE

7.1 East Anglia

East Anglia, the economic planning region comprising the three counties of Norfolk, Suffolk and Cambridgeshire, is Britain's fastest growing region, in terms both of population and manufacturing industry. This growth, remarkable both for its rate and volume, is fundamentally a reflection of pressures propelling families and firms out of London and the South East (see section 4.4), coupled with the locational and environmental attractions of East Anglia itself. It is logical, therefore, to move on from the South East of England to consider one of the key reception areas for migrants from that region.

7.1.1 *Regional Growth*

Since the early 1960s, the population of East Anglia has been growing at a faster rate than that of any of the other nine British planning regions. Between 1961 and 1971, for example, it increased by nearly 200,000, or 13.2 per cent; while between 1971 and 1978, population growth, at 160,000 or 9.5 per cent, was both faster than in any other region, and greater in volume than in all but the South West—despite the fact that East Anglia is by far the smallest of all Britain's regions (1978 population; only 1,843,000). Although East Anglia's natural increase of population was quite high in the 1960s (8,400 per annum), the key reason for expansion is, of course, a very high rate of net immigration, averaging well over 15,000 people a year in 1971-1978. This flow has sustained the region's population growth at a high level despite a sharp fall in natural increase (down to 1,500 only in 1977-1978), the latter due to the nationally declining birth rate. The great majority of the region's immigrants—77 per cent in 1966-1971—are from South East England, including of course London. And they differ from the existing population in being biased simultaneously towards two contrasting groups—retired people aged 60-70 (18 per cent in 1966-1971), and young couples aged 20 to 35 with children (46 per cent in 1966-1971). The picture is thus one of a tidal wave of migrants, moving on retirement or as young families in search of new homes into East Anglia from the more congested South East.

This population growth and migration has proceeded hand in hand with a rapid growth and migration of manufacturing firms. The expansion of manufacturing industry in East Anglia since the mid-1960s has been quite remarkable. Between 1965 and 1976, East

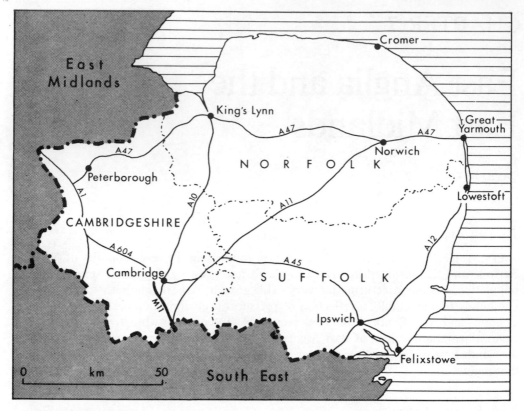

Figure 7.1 East Anglia

Anglia was the only region in Britain to record any net growth of manufacturing employment, the rest suffering losses, in several cases substantial losses. And East Anglia's growth, of 29,000 jobs or 17 per cent, was substantial by any standards, in terms of both volume and rate. As with the R.O.S.E. (section 6.4.1), this manufacturing growth partly reflects a favourable manufacturing structure. In 1959, the Cambridge sub-region was in the top eleven of U.K. sub-regions in terms of a favourable structural index, while two of the other three East Anglian sub-regions were in the top twenty. Only the Norwich sub-region, with declining traditional footwear industries, was below the national median value (Keeble, 1976, p.100).

However, recent manufacturing growth in East Anglia has primarily reflected the migration of firms from London and the South East. Between 1966 and 1970, for example, migration accounted directly for 40 per cent (9,000 jobs, 147 immigrant firms) of the region's manufacturing employment growth, quite apart from the indirect effect of the continuing expansion of firms which had moved in before 1966. More recently (1971-1974), new jobs provided by immigrant firms have accounted for 66 per cent (5,100 jobs, 111 firms) of regional manufacturing employment growth. And nearly 90 per cent of these jobs were in firms which moved in from the South East (London alone provided 53 per cent). Most of the factories established involved complete transfers, the firm moving lock, stock and barrel to East Anglia rather than just setting up a branch factory in the region. These firms have been predominantly mechanical and electrical engineering firms, so that the region's manufacturing structure is becoming increasingly biased towards this type of industry.

Not surprisingly in view of the rapid population growth, service industry has also expanded quickly in East Anglia over the last decade (26 per cent), although the region is not outstanding in this respect compared with other areas. By 1976, services provided 58 per cent of East Anglia's total employment, manufacturing some 29 per cent (cf. the figures for the R.O.S.E. in section 6.4.3). The decline of agricultural employment (by 24,000 workers, or 36 per cent, in 1965-1976) because of increasing mechanization, farm amalgamation, and competition for workers from better-paid manufacturing jobs, had reduced agriculture's share of East Anglia's workforce to only 6 per cent by 1976. The region's agriculture remains, however, amongst the most efficient and productive in Britain.

Despite the steep fall in the birth rate in 1964-1977, current forecasts of population growth in East Anglia indicate the likelihood of substantial future expansion. One estimate (Rees, 1977) suggests a growth of 460,000 people or 26 per cent in 1976-2001, even allowing for eventual declining migration from the South East because of the latter's own projected decline in population, and for a relatively low future birth rate.

7.1.2 Why Growth?

The reasons for population and manufacturing growth in East Anglia are more or less the same as those accounting for expansion in the R.O.S.E. discussed in section 6.4.1, and need not therefore be repeated in detail here. However, it is worth stressing certain points specific to East Anglia. Land and building prices, for example, have been markedly lower in the region than in either London or the R.O.S.E. In 1973, the average price of East Anglian houses mortgaged by members of the Building Societies Association was only £9,849, or 2 per cent *below* the national average; whereas the London and R.O.S.E. values were 44 per cent and 31 per cent, respectively, *above*. Moreover, the differential between R.O.S.E. and East Anglian prices has persisted since that date, the 1978 prices being £18,915 and £13,968 respectively. So substantially cheaper houses in East Anglia remain an important attraction to migrants from the South East.

Another reason is the region's environmental attractiveness. East Anglia is noted for its attractive villages, such as the famous 'wool villages' of Lavenham, Long Melford and Kersey in Suffolk, and for its historic towns, notably Cambridge and Norwich. It also possesses a lengthy coastline, while its rural nature is indicated by the lowest crude population density of any English region. Not surprisingly, therefore, perception surveys such as that by Gould and White (1968) rate East Anglia more highly in terms of residential attractiveness than any other area north of London. This factor has also apparently influenced many of the migrant firms—most of them small, single-plant businesses—which have settled in the region. Thus a Department of Industry survey of firms moving into the region between 1964 and 1967 found that environmental attractiveness was reported as a factor in locational choice more frequently (81 per cent of firms) than were any other factors except labour availability (93 per cent) and encouragement by local authorities, including the G.L.C. and expanded town authorities (also 81 per cent).

Some migrant firms have been influenced in choosing East Anglia by the region's proximity to, and excellent communications with, mainland Europe. The latter is strikingly illustrated by the remarkable three-fold growth in tonnage of trade shipped through East Anglia's ports, notably Felixstowe, Ipswich and Great Yarmouth, over the last decade (1966-1976). This growth, faster than that of ports in any other region, reflects the rapid growth of national trade with the rest of Europe, and East Anglia's favoured position for handling such trade (East Anglia Economic Planning Council, 1977). This locational advantage, and the acknowledged efficiency of East Anglia's ports, explain why the Department of Industry survey mentioned above found that more firms (24 per cent) that had settled in East Anglia reported 'proximity to ports' as a major reason for doing so than was the case with firms locating in any other region of Britain.

The last point worth noting is that unlike growth in the R.O.S.E., East Anglian expansion preceded, rather than followed or even accompanied, improvements in communications with the South East. Indeed, communications with the South East and East Midlands, the two regions adjacent to East Anglia, have traditionally been very poor. The first-ever motorway to impinge on the region, the M11 to Cambridge, was not fully opened until 1979; while other slightly earlier trunk road improvements have been east-west, not north-south, notably along the A45 Felixstowe-Midlands lorry route. Future improvements in links with the South East, which may include rail electrification to Cambridge and Ipswich, seem likely to strengthen the forces behind decentralization from the South East to East Anglia, and the region's growth.

7.1.3 *The Geography of Growth*

Within East Anglia, the pressure for development exerted by migrants from the South East has naturally had its greatest effect on the south and south-west of the region, rather than the north and north-east. Cambridge and Ipswich, after all, are only 80 kilometres (50 miles) and 115 kilometres (72 miles), respectively, from London. And much of southern East Anglia was by 1971 incorporated within the London commuting zone (section 5.3). Over the 1961-1975 period, therefore, the fastest-growing areas of East Anglia in population terms were the Bury St Edmunds-Thetford district (an increase of 60,000, or 46 per cent) and the Ouse Valley centred on Huntingdon and St Neots (an increase of 45,000, or 64 per cent). Elsewhere, growth has tended to focus on villages around major centres, notably Cambridge, Norwich and Ipswich. In the 1970s, growth has quickened in the Peterborough area, and in rural mid-Norfolk. The north Norfolk coast was the only part of East Anglia to record population decline in the 1960s: in the 1970s, this was replaced by slight growth.

These population trends have on the whole been mirrored by trends in the location of manufacturing industry, with the Bury St Edmunds-Thetford and Ouse valley areas recording by far the greatest manufacturing job growth in 1971-1975 (3,900 and 2,600 extra jobs, respectively). However, service employment growth has been heavily concentrated in the bigger towns, notably Norwich (14,200 extra jobs in 1971-1975) and Ipswich (10,700 jobs). Manufacturing and services thus reveal different locational trends, the former tending towards a more dispersed locational pattern (three of the four areas recording manufacturing decline in 1971-1975 were three of the region's four major towns), the latter towards a more concentrated spatial pattern. The sub-regions containing the four largest towns (Cambridge, Ipswich, Norwich and Peterborough) none the less still accounted in 1975 for 53 per cent of the region's manufacturing employment, and 58 per cent of jobs in services, indicating the importance of these centres to the economic life of the region.

The geography of growth within East Anglia, of course, owes much to the existence of eight 'expanded towns', which received a considerable number of migrant Londoners and small London manufacturing firms from the late 1960s (see section 6.2.1). Indeed, the concentration of these towns in the Bury-Thetford and Ouse valley areas is the principal factor behind their substantial population growth. More recently, the expansion of Peterborough, as a designated new town (see section 6.3.2), has substantially boosted growth there. However, the importance of these planned developments must not be overstated. Planned migration to the expanded towns and Peterborough between 1961 and 1975 accounted for only 16 per cent (47,000 immigrants) of the region's population growth, and the largest single impact—140,000 or 48 per cent—came from voluntary migration to other settlements. The remaining 36 per cent was natural increase. Perhaps the chief significance of the planned centres is their role in strengthening the 'urban fabric' of the region—in making possible the provision of urban facilities, services and jobs in parts of the region somewhat removed from the larger towns. Of particular importance in this respect has been the development of Bury St Edmunds, Thetford, King's Lynn and, to a lesser extent, Huntingdon.

7.1.4 *Local and Regional Planning*

Until the mid-1960s, East Anglia was regarded, if at all, by regional planners as an appendage or periphery to the South East. The *South East Study*, for example, treated the whole of the South East and East Anglia as a single unit; the effect of the Abercrombie-based London expanded towns programme has been noted earlier. In 1966, however, the distinctiveness of East Anglia, as at present defined, was recognized both for statistical and economic planning purposes by the establishment of the East Anglia Economic Planning Council. The distinctiveness focuses, of course, on the rural nature, low population density, and consequent peculiar planning problems of the region, together with its more recent exceptional population growth. These problems have been the concern of both local and regional planning strategies.

The chief local planning problems in East Anglia are the widespread occurrence of relatively isolated villages and small market towns, often with declining or stagnant services, limited job opportunities and declining agricultural employment, and inadequate or non-existent public transport links with larger centres. The lack of urban facilities, and the employment problems faced by young people growing up in these areas, account for the loss of such individuals and hence the ageing population structure of many villages and small towns—particularly in the 1950s and 1960s, and especially in the rural north and east of the region. Along the north and east coasts of East Anglia, this problem has been exacerbated by an influx of many retired people, attracted by the local environment. Rural depopulation was widespread in many areas until the later 1960s; the degree to which this phenomenon has been masked more recently by retirement migration and, possibly, increasing second-home ownership is not clear.

The chief response by East Anglian county planners to this set of problems has been the adoption of a 'growth village' or 'growth centre' strategy. An early example was the approach proposed in the Cambridgeshire County Council's 1965 development plan review, which proposed a development strategy based on the selection of eight outlying and well-dispersed Cambridgeshire villages. All were fairly large, with some local industry, secondary schools and shops. All but one were at that time surrounded by areas experiencing rural depopulation. The strategy envisaged the channelling of what local population growth did occur, as well as expanding industry from Cambridge itself, into these growth villages. Increasing size, it was hoped, would in turn attract or justify shops, services or firms which require a larger local market or labour supply, and which had not existed in these areas before. In this way, a wider range of services and job opportunities would have been made available to rural dwellers within about 16 kilometres (10 miles) of these selected villages than would otherwise have been possible. This sort of strategy is both realistic and plausible in the context of a rural area such as East Anglia. A *de facto* if not ministerially approved policy along these lines has been successful in Cambridgeshire where, for example, the population of Melbourn, one of the villages designated as a growth centre, more than doubled between 1956 and 1976, to 3,200 inhabitants, with an associated growth of local shops, schools and light industry. The county planners anticipate the eventual stabilization of Melbourn's population at about 4,000, after 1981.

More recent planning documents recommend or adopt market-town 'growth centres', for similar reasons. A key report here was the 1972 *Small Towns Study,* prepared by a joint team under the auspices of both the Economic Planning Council and local authorities, which recommended the establishment of several such centres in each East Anglian county. The towns actually investigated were Diss-Eye, Fakenham, East Dereham and Wisbech. The report stressed the need to attract mobile industry to such centres as the only feasible basis for employment and population growth.

This report clearly underlies the thinking of the subsequent *Norfolk* (1976) and *Cambridgeshire* (1977) *Draft Structure Plans,* especially the former's proposed 'rural area employment growth centres'. Comprising Fakenham, North Walsham, Swaffham, Diss, Downham Market and East Dereham, these six small market towns are explicitly defined as rural centres in need of, and with potential for, employment growth. Need was estimated on the basis of such factors as scale and rate of male unemployment, local job dependency on agriculture, and losses of young people during the 1960s, while potential related to rail and road accessibility, the capacity of local infrastructure, local availability of skilled labour, existing industry and so on. The centres are well dispersed throughout the rural areas of the county. Industrial and commercial development in these centres will be promoted by the County Council through a variety of policies, including promotional campaigns and priority in the provision of local authority infrastructure. The Cambridgeshire Draft Structure Plan adopts a similar, though perhaps less selective, approach in proposing that new development in the rural areas of the county should be concentrated primarily in eight market towns (Huntingdon, St Neots, St Ives, Ely, March, Wisbech, Ramsey and Whittlesey). In addition, certain 'key rural centres', such as Chatteris, Somersham, Littleport and Sawston, have been selected explicitly for 'the maintenance and improvement of community facilities and services for the surrounding areas and villages'; some development will thus be permitted in them, in contrast to the tight planning controls envisaged elsewhere in rural Cambridgeshire.

The first attempt at broader regional planning solely for East Anglia was the Economic Planning Council's *East Anglia: A Study,* published in 1968. This document emphasized the spatial and functional organization of the area into four main 'city-regions', focused upon Cambridge, Ipswich, Norwich and Peterborough, together with three smaller 'town-regions' around King's Lynn, Great Yarmouth-Lowestoft, and Bury St Edmunds.

Although inadequately spelt out in terms of its practical implications, the council's thinking seemed to be that the provision of the necessary facilities needed by a growing regional population and industrial base would be easier and more economic if growth were channelled to or around these cities and towns. By virtue of their organizing role, growth in these centres would in turn benefit the whole city-region or town-region around them. The council's thinking at that time thus seems close to that of the 1970 *Strategic Plan for the South East*, with its emphasis on growth-area concentration.

As with its South East counterpart, the Planning Council's proposals were not formally accepted by government as a long-term framework. Instead, another joint team of local and central government planners was established to produce a mutually acceptable regional plan for East Anglia, along the lines of the successful South East exercise. The team's report, *Strategic Choice for East Anglia,* was published in 1974. While breaking new ground in devoting greater attention than most previous regional planning documents to non-spatial issues, such as local and central government capital investment, financing and the provision of health, education and other services to the region's inhabitants, the report none the less recommended a specific locational strategy to cope with the anticipated population and industrial growth. Broadly, this involved a shift in emphasis in the location of growth away from the south and west, to the more central, northern and eastern areas of East Anglia. This would necessitate stricter planning controls on future expansion in the southern and western parts of Suffolk and Cambridgeshire, with the acceptance if not promotion of growth in much of Norfolk. The logic behind this proposed shift was a desire to limit development in some areas—such as Cambridge itself —which had already experienced the impact of significant growth in the 1960s. This was coupled with the need to ameliorate the economic and social problems of the rural north and east of the region, where better urban facilities and a more secure and varied economic base were required. An important subsidiary aspect of these proposals was thus the recommended development of a set of 'secondary centres' outside the four main city-regions, notably King's Lynn, Thetford, Bury St Edmunds and (possibly) Diss-Eye, to strengthen the region's urban fabric. This report was strongly endorsed by the Economic Planning Council.

Unfortunately, however, the reorganization of local government which coincided with the report's publication disrupted the consensus which the exercise had attempted to create. And in the face of considerable opposition to the report from certain local authorities in the region, notably Norfolk, central government's response largely rejected as an official framework the team's suggested strategy. Instead, the response implied that future population growth, which it accepted was likely to be considerable, could quite adequately be catered for by county-level planning, and that questions of restraint, conservation and rural economic need were a matter for decision at that level. It is thus not too harsh a judgement on the government's response to conclude that at present no officially approved integrated planning strategy exists for East Anglia.

Perhaps not surprisingly, recent developments at the county structure plan level bear out the view that in a region as small as East Anglia, the absence of a regional plan raises serious problems. On the one hand, both the Suffolk and Cambridgeshire draft plans follow closely the spirit and indeed letter of the 1974 *Strategic Choice* report, in explicitly recommending a shift of emphasis within each county in the longer term towards encouraging growth in rural problem areas, in northern Suffolk and north-eastern Cambridgeshire. The Cambridgeshire 'Fenland strategy' thus involves, for example, a shift in road investment within the county to upgrade the A141 and A142 routes which link the Fen towns of March and Chatteris to the outside world. This strategy is also being supported by the Development Commission, an agency financed by central government, which with the Council for Small Industries in Rural Areas (C.O.S.I.R.A.) in 1977 designated the Cambridgeshire Fens generally and the towns of March and Wisbech in particular as priority areas within East Anglia for small factory development. This follows the earlier designation by the Development Commission of North Norfolk as another such area in need of assistance to small industrial firms.

On the other hand, the draft Norfolk structure plan proposals appear to be somewhat opposed to the recommendations of the *Strategic Choice* report—as they are entitled to be, given the government response to the latter. Far from welcoming or even permitting increased future employment and population growth in the county, the plan assumes, contrary to most forecasts, that growth in Norfolk will be substantially less in future than in the past; and even this growth is not exactly welcomed, with proposals for deliberate planning restraint in much of rural Norfolk, on the grounds of the limited availability to local government of investment resources. The latter is certainly a major problem facing planning authorities in East Anglia in the early 1980s, with the considerable shift since 1974 in central government grants to local authorities, via the Rate Support Grant, from rural 'shire' counties to London and other conurbations. This shift has hit East Anglia very badly. Indeed, one recent study (Jackman and Sellars, 1977) estimates that Suffolk, the worst-affected East Anglian county, was by 1977/1978 receiving *no* extra government grant over and above its 1974/1975 allocation to allow for subsequent inflation— although the national allocation to all local authorities had increased by 95 per cent! Cambridgeshire and Norfolk were receiving only about 15 per cent and 35 per cent, respectively, of the extra which might have been expected on the basis of growth in the national total. So the financing of facilities needed by the growing population of East Anglia has become a very serious problem, although the extent to which it will be possible actually to restrain growth on grounds of local authority financial stringency, as proposed by Norfolk, is highly uncertain.

7.2 The East Midlands

In physical and economic terms, the East Midlands is one of the least clearly defined economic planning regions established by the 1965 Labour government. Indeed, the absence of obvious boundaries at many points is clearly illustrated by the aerial enlargement of the region in 1974, following local government reorganization, to take in most of Lindsey to the north east, and all of the High Peak district of Derbyshire. A further problem with regard to a distinctive regional identity is the existence of several, rather than one, major urban centres, in particular Leicester (278,000 population in 1978), Nottingham (281,000) and Derby (215,000), Northampton (151,000 population) in the south of the region also acts as a major focus for its surrounding area. In functional terms, therefore, the region is fragmented into several and sometimes overlapping major labour market and shopping catchment areas, while centres outside the region—notably Sheffield, only a few miles to the north of the East Midlands boundary, but also to some extent Birmingham, Manchester and Peterborough—also attract East Midland workers and/or shoppers. There are also major sub-regional variations in economic structure and recent demographic history, with contrasts in particular between Northamptonshire

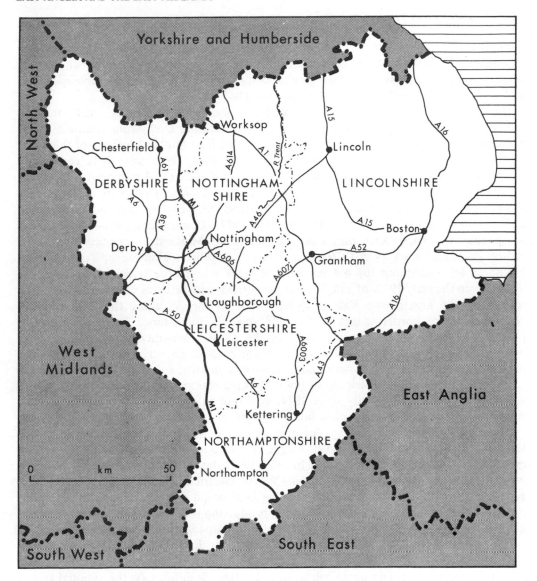

Figure 7.2 The East Midlands

(expanding especially through population and industrial immigration from the South East into an official London new town), Lincolnshire (a rural area suffering until recently from localized depopulation), and the three major urbanized counties in the centre and north west of the region, with their post-war economic prosperity and stability. These internal differences must be borne in mind as consideration turns to region-wide indicators, the latter being dominated by conditions and trends in Nottinghamshire, Derbyshire and Leicestershire.

7.2.1 *Economy and Demography: Characteristics and Trends*

The East Midlands, with 3.7 million inhabitants in 1978, is Britain's fourth smallest region, with a lower absolute population and population density than any of its neighbouring regions excepting East Anglia. None the less, it is of considerable economic and demographic significance, on various grounds.

One major factor here is the importance of the region's coal resources, chiefly those in the southern half of the great Yorkshire-Nottinghamshire-Derbyshire coalfield which stretches along the eastern flanks of the Pennines. The East Midlands section of this field, together with the much smaller Leicestershire and South Derbyshire field centred on Coalville, produce more coal than any other part of Britain (35.5 million tons in 1976/1977, or 30 per cent of Britain's total output). And productivity in its large modern pits is also way ahead of that in any other coalfield (56.1 cwt per man-shift, compared with the national average of only 43.6 in 1976/1977.) Coal-mining jobs—and earnings —are thus an important component in the East Midlands' economy, with the industry's 66,000 workers in 1976 (more than in any other region except Yorkshire and Humberside) accounting for 4.4 per cent of total jobs in the region. Moreover, the discovery in the early 1970s of a massive new coalfield, with reserves of at least 450 million tonnes, in the area of the Vale of Belvoir west of the A1 along the Leicestershire-Nottinghamshire border, suggests that the region's importance in national energy production could increase still further in the future. Whether or not fierce local opposition to the development of this field, on grounds of countryside conservation and preservation of a hitherto unspoilt and attractive rural area, will prevent its exploitation remains to be seen. While helping to boost average regional earnings through the high wages they provide, especially since 1974, coal-mining jobs have, of course, declined substantially in recent years, with a fall of 35,000, or one-third, since 1965.

The region's coal resources have led directly to a second major economic role for the East Midlands, that of being a major source of the country's thermally-generated—and especially coal-generated—electricity. In 1976-1977, the East Midlands' large coal-fired power stations produced 48,000 million kWh of electricity, or 26 per cent of all that generated in England and Wales by burning coal or oil (23 per cent of all electricity produced, including nuclear). East Midlands production is dominated by a string of eight giant stations which line the valley of the river Trent; together, five of them—Cottam (1,950 megawatts), West Burton (1,900), High Marnham (1,000), Ratcliffe-on-Soar (2,000) and Drakelow (1,900)—have a capacity of nearly 9,000 megawatts. Their sites reflect the need for cooling water, while their electricity is shipped via the national grid to the markets of the West Midlands, the North West and South East England. The East Midlands' central position within Britain has thus been one further important reason for their development. Since the stations employ only a small workforce, their main significance for the region's economy is in providing the most important market for locally-produced coal, and hence guaranteeing a considerable future demand for and production of coal in the East Midlands.

A third important regional attribute is the relative and unusual specialization of the East Midlands economy upon manufacturing industry. In 1976, the region, with 6.6 per cent of total United Kingdom employment of all kinds, accounted for 8.1 per cent of workers in manufacturing industry. Put another way, the percentage of manufacturing workers in the East Midlands workforce—39.2 per cent—was greater than that in any other region of the country, except the West Midlands; the national average was only 32.2 per cent. Moreover, until the 1960s the East Midlands was one of the most buoyant industrial regions of Britain, with a much faster rate of growth in its manufacturing workforce in 1921-1961 than that for the United Kingdom as a whole (+ 40 per cent, compared with + 26 per cent). This East Midlands growth rate was exceeded by only two other regions, the South East and West Midlands (Lee, 1971). Even recently, when manufacturing employment decline has affected all regions except East Anglia, the East Midlands losses (33,000 jobs, or 5.3 per cent, in 1965-1976) have been smaller than those of all but three other regions.

Twentieth-century manufacturing growth in the East Midlands, at least until the 1960s, is particularly noteworthy in that the region has tended to specialize within manufacturing on industries which have been declining nationally. This specialization is clearly illustrated by the structural index described in section 5.4.1. In 1959, two of the East Midlands' four sub-regions, Nottingham/Derby and Northamptonshire, were in the bottom third of United Kingdom sub-regions, and Leicestershire in the bottom half, with regard to this structural index, indicating a relatively unfavourable manufacturing structure. Indeed, on this basis, the East Midlands exhibited a worse manufacturing structure than, for example, Wales, a classic 'problem' industrial region (Keeble, 1976, p.100). The key to this situation is the region's historic specialization in textiles, especially hosiery, in clothing and footwear, and to a much lesser extent, in iron and steel. Even by 1976, after years of relative and absolute decline, these three industries still accounted for 18 per cent, 10 per cent and 7 per cent, respectively, of regional manufacturing employment. Their continuing national importance is indicated by the region's possession in that year of 62 per cent of employment in hosiery manufacturing in the United Kingdom, and 41 per cent of workers in the footwear industry in the United Kingdom.

If the East Midlands has historically been characterized by a relatively adverse manufacturing structure, how has growth been achieved? One factor here is the presence within the region of a wide variety of other industries which, though not strictly fast-growing, have in aggregate expanded considerably during the twentieth century. Examples are pharmaceuticals, for which industry the East Midlands is the country's third most important location after the South East and North West, the manufacture of construction and earth-moving equipment (where the East Midlands is the leading region) and aerospace equipment (East Midlands employment in this industry is the fourth largest amongst United Kingdom regions). Another factor is the success of the region's firms, even in declining industries, in countering or at least performing better than, the national trend in that industry. Thus, for example, hosiery firms in the East Midlands reduced their labour force by only 4.8 per cent in 1971-1976, despite a national rate of decline in this industry of no less than 11.9 per cent. Again, iron and steel employment losses in 1971-1976 were 11.6 per cent, compared with a national decline of 15.5 per cent.

The surprisingly good industrial performance of the East Midlands, given its inherited industrial structure, may also reflect a vitality and quality of entrepreneurship which finds expression in the creation of an above-average number of new firms. Gudgin (1978) has shown how, over the period 1948-1967, manufacturing employment (excluding that in the steelworks at Corby) in the East Midlands expanded by some 96,000 jobs, or just over 20 per cent (Table 7.1). However, this masked a much greater gross increase in new jobs (i.e. jobs which had not existed in the region at all in 1947) of no less than 231,000, this total being offset by losses from the closure of existing factories of about 135,000 jobs. The

Table 7.1 East Midlands: manufacturing employment accounts, 1948-1967

1.	Employment in factory closures	134,800
2.	Net increase in manufacturing employment	96,200
3.	New manufacturing jobs (row 1 plus row 2)	231,000
4.	Manufacturing employment as % of row 3	
	in new firms	28%
	in permanent establishments	46%
	in new branches of local firms	11%
	in immigrant establishments	15%

Source: Gudgin (1978), p.62.

interesting and, in Gudgin's view, surprising finding is that nearly 30 per cent of the gross job increase was due to the birth and subsequent expansion of a large number—nearly 3,000—of entirely new firms, nearly all of which reflected the enterprise of local individuals. To this was added a considerable expansion by firms already in existence in the region in 1947 (46 per cent), together with employment in new branches of local firms and some immigrant plants. While many entered the region's traditional trades, the entirely new firms were also a key factor in spearheading the shift in the region's industrial structure over this period away from the declining textiles, clothing and footwear industries. A good example is the development of plastics manufacturing, which by 1976 was employing 10,000 East Midlands workers, the fourth largest total for this industry amongst Britain's regions; most of these jobs were in entirely new firms, as in the Leicester area, where sixty new plastics firms were employing over 3,000 workers by 1971 (Gudgin, 1978, p.299).

Of course, unusually vigorous entrepreneurship, as indicated by the above figures for the successful creation of new firms, itself demands an explanation. Gudgin (1978, p.301) speculates that such an explanation might be found in the region's history of greater economic security than in other areas. In other words, the East Midlands' steady economic growth, and continuing above-average economic prosperity, over the last hundred years have encouraged entrepreneurs to set up new firms and experiment with new products, by reducing the apparent risks inherent in such enterprise. This hypothesis is clearly a variant of the 'nothing succeeds like success' concept, which in turn forms part of the notion of 'cumulative causation' in regional industrial growth put forward by Myrdal (1957; see also Keeble, 1967). Another factor may be a bias in the region's industrial structure towards 'small-plant' industries, which by their nature permit easy entry by new entrepreneurs and hence high rates of formation of new firms. Certainly average factory size in the East Midlands in 1972 (118 workers), for plants employing more than ten workers, was smaller than both the national average (124 workers) and the average in a number of more peripheral regions.

However, broader environmental factors may also be involved in high rates of formation of new firms, at least in the long term. One obvious possibility is excellent *national market access*. Although the East Midlands market is not itself large, the region lies close to the geometric centre of gravity of the national market for manufactured goods, measured by population or industry. Within only 160 kilometres (100 miles) of

Leicester, for example, is to be found a consumer market of no less than 33 million people, or over 60 per cent of Britain's total population. And proximity to the national industrial market, measured by the geographic distribution of manufacturing industry, is even greater, with nearly 70 per cent of Britain's manufacturing employment located within this radius. Moreover, the region is linked to this national market by excellent communications, notably the M1 London-Leeds motorway, the M6 to Birmingham and the North West, the A1 London-Newcastle, and two high-speed inter-city rail services, London (St Pancras) to Leicester and Sheffield, and London (King's Cross) to Grantham and Newark. The short M69 Leicester-Coventry motorway was opened in 1977. The M1 also acts as the major internal north-south corridor of movement within the region, linking as it does Nottingham, Leicester and Northampton. Altogether the region possesses no less than 350 kilometres (220 miles) of motorway or dual-carriageway trunk road, and excellent access to adjacent regions (with the possible exception of links north west to Manchester from Derby and Nottingham). In view of the advantages, real and perceived, conferred on modern industry by good access to customers (Keeble, 1976, pp. 45-51), the East Midlands' advantages in this respect may well be a factor in above-average rates of development of new firms in the twentieth century.

Industrial growth in the East Midlands has, then, been largely a self-generated process. Indeed, Gudgin points out that although the region did experience some immigration of factories from other regions between 1948 and 1967 (Table 7.1), this was in a way offset by 'losses' through the establishment by East Midlands parent firms of branch factories in other, usually assisted, regions. Thus the 1968 Howard Report revealed that between 1945 and 1965, East Midlands firms established 130 or so factories elsewhere in the United Kingdom, and that the latter were, by 1966, employing some 31,000 workers. About 60 per cent of these were in the Development Areas, with a further 24 per cent in adjacent Yorkshire and Humberside. Gains from immigration to the East Midlands, largely from the South East, totalled 27,000 jobs in just over 100 factories. More recently, however, with the designation and growth of Northampton as a London new town, industrial immigration may have become more important, at least in reducing the net losses of manufacturing employment suffered by the East Midlands, along with almost all other regions, since 1971.

The traditional vitality of East Midlands manufacturing industry, and the wealth generated in the region during the twentieth century, in turn help to account for the above-average economic prosperity, as measured by the high incomes and low unemployment, of its inhabitants. True, weekly earnings from employment are, somewhat surprisingly, below those in most other areas. In April 1976, for example, full-time male workers in the East Midlands received an average wage of £67.30, or 6.3 per cent below the British average of £71.80, the region being third from bottom of the regional league table in this respect. This is surprising, given the region's bias towards manufacturing industry, in which wages are usually above those in other sectors (Keeble, 1976, p.204), and the greater significance of coal-mining employment, with its high earnings. However, in terms of household incomes, the East Midlands' above-average prosperity is clear. In the two years 1975-1976, the average weekly household income in the East Midlands, at £75.30, was greater than in all other regions of Britain except the South East and West Midlands. The difference between this position and that for male earnings from employment probably reflects a greater component of self-employed workers (individual entrepreneurs and small business men?), above-average female activity rates, and possibly greater investment income derived from past prosperity, in the East Midlands compared with other regions.

Traditional prosperity and economic buoyancy is linked with relatively low levels of unemployment. In July 1977, the East Midlands unemployment rate, at 5.8 per cent, was not only below the national rate, but lower than that in all other regions except the South East (4.9 per cent) and East Anglia (also 5.8 per cent). The contrast with the West Midlands (6.7 per cent), where traditional economic vitality has given way since the 1960s to major structural problems and relative economic decline, is particularly striking. However, there are those who suggest that the East Midlands could follow in the wake of the West Midlands in this respect, bearing in mind the exceptional dependence of both on manufacturing activity, the uncertain future of such key East Midlands industries as textiles, clothing and footwear in the face of acute low-cost foreign competition, and a possible continuing decline in coal-mining employment. The serious problems facing the above three East Midlands manufacturing industries are clearly indicated by national figures on Temporary Employment Subsidy grants, paid by government between 1975 and 1978 to manufacturing firms which would otherwise be forced to sack employees because of lack of work. By 1978, no fewer than 105,000, or 58 per cent, of the 180,000 workers whose jobs were being preserved by this subsidy were in the textile, clothing and footwear industries; the East Midlands was one of the three regions (the others being Yorkshire and Humberside, and the North West) most affected, with 41,000 manufacturing jobs of all kinds supported (East Midlands Economic Planning Council, 1978). Many regional commentators thus regard the continuation of traditional government *constraints* on industrial expansion in the East Midlands, through i.d.c. controls in the major industrial centres, as most undesirable, especially if the East Midlands is to play its full part in any national industrial revival. The very close integration of the region's industry with the wider national economy, and its dependence on manufacturing, certainly mean that the success or failure of government attempts at national revival in the 1980s could be of the greatest importance for the future economic prosperity of the East Midlands.

The last regional characteristic which demands attention is recent population growth. Throughout the twentieth century, the East Midlands has been one of the fastest-growing regions of Britain in terms of population. Between 1921 and 1961, for example, population in the pre-1974 East Midlands (see section 7.2) grew by 883,000, or 31 per cent; this rate of growth was faster than in all but two other regions of the United Kingdom, the West Midlands and South East. Rapid growth has continued since, with an increase of 420,000, or 12.6 per cent, between 1961 and 1978—again faster than in all but two other regions, this time East Anglia and the South West. Indeed, for the period 1975-1977, the East Midlands was one of only four British regions (the others being East Anglia, the South West and Wales) to record any population growth at all, all others exhibiting decline. This recent East Midlands growth is noteworthy because, unlike the situation in the other regions which are still growing, the increase was due almost as much to natural change—an excess of births over deaths—as to net immigration. The former contributed just under, the latter just over, half of the 1975-1977 East Midlands growth of 13,600 people. Some continuing natural increase of population—which by 1977 was occurring in only four regions of Britain—reflected both a relatively high birth rate and a relatively low death rate. Net immigration, on the other hand, almost certainly reflects the impact of movement of households from the South East, especially to Northamptonshire and its

London new town, and possibly adjacent Leicestershire. Whether recent official projections of continuing future regional growth in population—by 174,000 to 3,921,000 in 1991, according to 1977-based projections—are realistic, however, is more debatable, given the uncertainties facing the region's economy, the downward revision in the target for Northampton (6.3.2), and the competition offered, as it were, to potential migrants from the South East by such alternative destinations as the South West and East Anglia. In the latter connection, it is important to stress that South East migration to the East Midlands, which has in any case been on a much smaller scale than that to the other two adjacent regions, does not seem to be underpinned to the same degree by the force of residential preference on environmental and amenity grounds. Thus surveys such as that by Gould and White (1968) suggest that the East Midlands, with the exception perhaps of Lincolnshire, form part of what those authors term the 'Midlands mental cirque' of relatively low residential preference, with values below 50 per cent of the maxima attained along England's south coast. The relatively limited net movement into the region from the South East may well thus chiefly reflect planning policy, rather than the operation of powerful natural forces as with East Anglia or the South West.

7.2.2 Regional Planning

Unlike the South East and East Anglia, the East Midlands has not been the object of any joint local/central government regional planning study, a fact which perhaps again reflects the nature of the region as a group of separated and distinctive city-regions, each of which is now the object of a different county structure plan. The only available regional framework for these plans is the 1966 East Midlands Study, prepared somewhat hurriedly by the East Midlands Economic Planning Council as its first task after being established in 1965. Moreover, the authors of this study were at pains to disclaim any pretension that it was a 'regional plan', viewing it instead as an account of the region and the way it was then changing, with some reference to planning problems and opportunities. However, the study did emphasize the probability of substantial future population growth, at a rate above the national average; the expectation at that time was for an increase of 730,000 over the period 1965-1981. This compares with an actual growth in 1966-1977 of only 244,000, and a 1977-based projected increase of only 33,000 in 1977-1981.

The study also suggested that the fastest-growing area of the region would be Northamptonshire, although the greatest volume of additional population would accrue to Nottinghamshire-Derbyshire. It expressed concern that growth in the latter area could lead to the development of a congested Birmingham-type conurbation by the end of the century unless great care was taken by local planning authorities to concentrate development into suitable existing urban nodes, separated by open countryside. More detailed comments included the suggestion that Corby was likely to continue as an area of rapid employment growth, with no appreciable decline in steel employment (see section 7.2.5), that substantial expansion of population and industry in the eastern lowlands of Lincolnshire was undesirable, and that Leicester's planning problems were chiefly of local rather than regional significance—traffic congestion, for example. The study thus raised one or two important general issues, notably the question of the best form of development in Nottinghamshire-Derbyshire. But its judgements, even though updated briefly in 1969 (East Midlands Economic Planning Council), have been somewhat overtaken by events;

they have provided only the broadest of regional frameworks for more local planning. The council's most recent publications (East Midlands Economic Planning Council, 1976, 1978) are not concerned with regional land use planning or population distribution, but with aspects of the development of the East Midlands economy in the context of current national industrial and employment policies. The onus is now very clearly on county structure plans to cope as each county thinks fit with any local housing problems or population growth. In the context of the much-reduced population projections of the late 1970s, there seems to be little pressure for the development of any new and integrated regional planning strategy for the East Midlands. The remainder of this chapter thus now turns to consider separately each of the East Midlands' distinctive sub-regions.

7.2.3 *Nottingham/Derby and the Intermediate Coalfield Area*

The adjacent counties of Nottinghamshire and Derbyshire are the industrial and urban core of the East Midlands, containing in 1978 some 1.87 million people, or exactly half the region's population, and firms employing 300,000 manufacturing workers, or 51 per cent of the manufacturing workforce. Of the two cities, Nottingham is the more important on almost all criteria, especially in terms of its function as the highest-order regional service centre and, in a sense, administrative capital of the East Midlands. This role is symbolized by the presence of institutions such as the University of Nottingham and the regional offices of the various departments of central government, including the Department of the Environment and the East Midlands Economic Planning Board. Traditionally, the manufacturing sector of the economy of Nottingham and its surrounding settlements depended heavily on the hosiery and related—clothing and lace-making—industries. In 1971, Nottingham hosiery firms still employed some 9,000 workers, providing over 5 per cent of total local employment; the hosiery workforce had not declined greatly since 1945 (Rake, 1974). The East Midlands hosiery industry—which incidentally is concentrated even more in the Leicester area (section 7.2.4)—comprises several distinct trades, which have the knitting process in common. Typical products are knitwear, including knitted outerwear, underwear, and hose (stockings, tights, socks). Most workers in the industry are women, and the firms traditionally are small. Vertical integration by such big firms as Courtauld Ltd, the synthetic fibre producer, has, however, resulted in considerable concentration of ownership, though not location, in recent years. By 1971, for example, Courtaulds owned and operated no fewer than fourteen hosiery factories in the Nottingham area alone, and a total of forty-one in the whole East Midlands region; with additional factories in some other regions, it thus controlled no less than one-quarter of United Kingdom hosiery production capacity (Rake, 1974).

However, as elsewhere in the East Midlands, the manufacturing base of Nottingham has for many years been even more dependent upon a variety of engineering firms, including electrical and heavy engineering, machine tools and vehicle components. Nottingham is also the headquarters of Raleigh Ltd, now part of the Tube Investments group, and is thus the largest cycle-manufacturing centre in Britain. Electrical engineering—telecommunications—is important at Beeston and Long Eaton, just outside Nottingham. Other major industries in the city are pharmaceuticals—Nottingham is the origin, headquarters, and chief production centre of Boots the Chemists—and the manufacture of tobacco—the firm of John Player, now part of Imperial Tobacco, originated here, and the production of cigarettes, cigars and pipe tobacco is still of great importance.

In general, though, employment in Nottingham is more heavily biased to service industry, of many different kinds, than is the case with almost any other part of the East Midlands. In 1966, for example, some 53 per cent (93,000 jobs) of total employment in the Nottingham employment exchange area was in service trades, with only 44 per cent (77,000 jobs) in manufacturing (*Nottinghamshire and Derbyshire Sub-regional Study,* 1969). Employment change since then has undoubtedly boosted significantly the former percentage relative to the latter, following the marked concentration of the East Midlands' considerable service employment growth (25 per cent, or 146,000 extra jobs in 1965-1976) in Nottingham and, to a lesser extent, the other three major towns. The population of Nottingham itself is fairly static, although surrounding settlements and villages have grown rapidly over the last twenty years.

In contrast to Nottingham, Derby, its local but somewhat smaller rival, is traditionally more dependent upon manufacturing than services for employment and incomes. In 1966, manufacturing firms in the Derby employment exchange area provided some 65,000 jobs, or 52 per cent of local employment; services accounted for only 47 per cent (58,000 jobs). Derby's manufacturing sector is dominated by Rolls Royce Ltd, the major international aero-engine firm. Despite recent reductions in its workforce, the firm, both directly and through a large number of local linkages with smaller component suppliers, is still of great importance for prosperity and jobs in Derby and surrounding settlements. Its orientation to research and development—40 per cent of the workforce—is a major factor in high average local earnings. Other important local industries include heavy engineering, metal castings for the motor industry, and railway workshops. Interestingly, Derby has been the destination of the largest single cluster of private office moves from central London to the East Midlands, according to Location of Offices Bureau records, with nearly 2,000 jobs in decentralized offices by 1977. The relative availability of female labour in a town dominated by male-employing industries may perhaps have been a factor in attracting these offices.

Northwards from Nottingham, and straddling the border with Derbyshire, is the East Midlands section of the National Coal Board's 'central' coalfield, the production of which was discussed in section 7.2.1. The population of this area lives in a wide scatter of settlements, including mining villages and a variety of small and medium-sized towns. The largest are Chesterfield and Mansfield, with 1976 district populations of 94,000 and 97,000 respectively (Mansfield itself is smaller than Chesterfield, but the district boundary encloses more surrounding settlements). The whole coalfield area has a population of about 700,000, although the great majority of these people depend upon jobs which are not related to coal mining. Mansfield and Sutton-in-Ashfield, for example, are important hosiery centres. In many ways, the area is one of the chief problem zones, from a planning viewpoint, in the East Midlands. The problems are at least four-fold, including industrial dereliction, pollution, old and not very attractive housing, and declining local job opportunities, especially for men.

The problem of industrial dereliction is a major one. In 1967, a county survey revealed (*Nottinghamshire and Derbyshire Sub-regional Study,* 1969) that the coalfield zone contained at least 140 sites in need of major or intermediate reclamation, while actual derelict land, of one sort or another, amounted to 3,160 hectares (7,800 acres). Not surprisingly, 90 per cent of this was land associated with collieries and colliery tips, derelict mineral workings, and waste disposal. The scale of this problem was recognized by central government in 1970, when virtually the whole of Nottinghamshire and Derbyshire was designated the North Midlands Derelict Land Clearance Area. Such status enables local authorities to claim special 75 per cent government grants for land reclamation and, for 1972-1974, it included the availability of 20 per cent regional development grants to private manufacturing firms for constructing new factories in the area. Despite considerable progress since then, a great deal of work still remains to be done to improve the landscape and bring derelict land into some form of productive use. Air pollution has also been a major problem in most of the coalfield area, with especially bad conditions—winter mean smoke concentration of over 180 microgrammes per cubic metre—in a zone from north of Nottingham and Derby up to Chesterfield. The high pollution rate in this area reflects both domestic and industrial pollution, and compares with rates of only 40 to 60 microgrammes per cubic metre in the rural parts of the region. Slow progress is being made in the designation of smoke control zones by local authorities.

Housing problems centre on the large number of small, old and often terraced houses dating from between 1875 and 1940, which are scattered throughout the coalfield area. While most are structurally sound, many have minor defects or are lacking in space, sanitary facilities, room for vehicles, and surrounding grass, gardens or children's play areas. Programmes of renewal or even replacement of many of these houses will be necessary for a long time to come.

The economic problems of this northern area centre on the long decline of coal mining, agriculture, and some previously associated industries (e.g. metal fabricating, tubes and pipes, and mining machinery), with a particular effect on job availability for unskilled and semi-skilled men. Despite some compensating manufacturing growth in the early 1960s, attracted by the availability of labour, the persistence of relatively high local unemployment led to the designation by central government in 1969 of Alfreton, Heanor, Sutton-in-Ashfield and Worksop as the North Midlands Intermediate Area. This was extended to include the Chesterfield, Clay Cross, Eckington and Stavely areas in 1974. This zone has thus benefited from the availability of 20 per cent regional development grants for the construction of new factories, and from the building of Department of Industry advance factories—five, totalling 7,400 square metres (80,000 square feet), were occupied or under construction by 1978. Fully-serviced industrial sites have also been provided by the County Councils, notably Derbyshire, which has built over 9,300 square metres (100,000 square feet) of factory premises, mainly in Alfreton and Chesterfield. The area also, of course, benefits from the presence of the M1 motorway, which runs north-south through Ashfield and Bolsover. These attractions have brought in a relatively large number of new jobs, generally from firms already operating elsewhere in the East Midlands, as at Alfreton. Indeed, by 1976, most parts of the North Midlands Intermediate Area were recording unemployment rates below the national average, directly as a result, according to the East Midlands Economic Planning Council (1976), of central government assistance.

The remaining part of the Nottinghamshire-Derbyshire sub-region, the east and north east, contains both small industrial towns—Belper, with its hosiery industry, for example—and the High Peak district of Derbyshire. The latter thus includes the bulk of the Peak District National Park, established in 1951 to conserve and enhance the natural beauty of an area whose scenery renders it of national as well as regional significance. The chief planning problem here, apart from coping with massive pressures for informal recreation from the urban inhabitants of nearby Manchester, Sheffield and Nottingham, is the conflict between landscape preservation and mining. The area contains valuable deposits of limestone, fluorspar and other minerals. Quarrying of these minerals, and the granting by the Peak Park Joint Planning Board of permits for quarry extension, have been and remain a cause of considerable controversy.

7.2.4 *Leicestershire*

Leicester, with a population of 278,000 in 1976, is the East Midland's second biggest city, at least as defined by district council boundaries. Moreover, unlike Nottinghamshire or Derbyshire, its chief rivals in terms of population size, the county of Leicestershire has been growing quite quickly in recent years, with an expansion in 1974-1978 of over 12,000 people, or 1.4 per cent. Its economy is also even more specialized upon manufacturing than the region as a whole, with a county share of 45.9 per cent in 1975, as compared with 38.1 per cent for the rest of the East Midlands. Unemployment is slightly lower and earnings are slightly higher, than the regional average. So in many ways, Leicester and its surrounding region epitomize the traditional picture of a prosperous, growing, manufacturing-based East Midlands.

The twentieth-century prosperity and growth of Leicester were founded upon the three great manufacturing industries of the city, namely hosiery, footwear and engineering. In 1970, these three provided two-fifths of the 200,000 jobs existing in the Leicester employment exchange area (Pye, 1972). Leicester is by far the greatest single centre of hosiery manufacturing in the East Midlands, with 25,000 workers in 1971, nearly three times the total in Nottingham, the region's second largest centre. Nearby Hinckley, with 8,500 workers, was third, while firms in Loughborough to the north provided nearly 5,000 jobs (Rake, 1974). Most firms in the industry are relatively small, while hosiery employment in Leicester has declined somewhat in recent years. The latter is even more true of footwear manufacturing, East Midlands employment in which fell between 1951 and 1971 by nearly 40 per cent, from 64,000 to ony 40,000 workers. Employment in Leicester, still the region's leading single footwear centre, has fallen faster than in the region as a whole, to only 10,000 workers by 1971. A higher proportion of the industry's jobs are held by men (45 per cent), however, than is the case with hosiery employment. Traditionally, Leicester has specialized in the production of women's and children's shoes; smaller surrounding centres, such as Hinckley and Loughborough, also produce men's shoes. A notable feature of post-war change in the industry has been the development of large multi-plant firms operating both factories and retail shops, the latter throughout Britain. The chief example here is the British Shoe Corporation, formed by mergers and takeovers during the 1950s, and by the later 1960s operating eight main factories, several of them in Leicestershire, together with 1,750 shops throughout Britain. The corporation's headquarters are at Braunstone, in Leicestershire. Increasing low-cost foreign competition has, however, seriously affected the industry in recent years, with a decline in regional employment of over 9,000 jobs, or nearly one-quarter, in 1971-1976, despite government help through the Temporary Employment Subsidy.

Declining hosiery and footwear employment in Leicestershire has been more than offset by the growth of a wide range of engineering industries. By 1976, engineering firms in the county employed some 62,000 workers, with probably about two-thirds of these in or adjacent to Leicester itself. Very diverse production includes the manufacture of hosiery machinery, machine tools, electrical and electronic equipment, and motor vehicle and aircraft components. Loughborough is especially dependent upon local engineering employment. The vitality of Leicester's manufacturing sector, including engineering, is indicated by Gudgin's estimate (1978) that 44 per cent of all new manufacturing jobs created in the city and adjacent settlements between 1947 and 1967 were in entirely new firms, with a further 46 per cent in existing firms. An excellent example of the creation of new enterprise in Leicester, already noted, has been the growth of a large number of plastics manufacturing firms.

Of course, Leicester itself is also a major regional centre, with a national university, major shopping facilities, and offices of national service industry firms. Indeed, the growth of offiee space in Leicester during the 1970s has been considerable, prompted perhaps by the absence of the office development controls which have been in force to the south, across the boundary of the South East region. But the economy of the city, as of the East Midlands as a whole, remains solidly based upon its manufacturing sector. Post-war labour shortages and relative prosperity help to explain the large number of Asian immigrants—notably Punjabis and Ugandan Asians—now resident in the city, and comprising one-sixth (46,000) of its inhabitants.

7.2.5 Northamptonshire and Lincolnshire

Northamptonshire is the area of the East Midlands most influenced by the outwards surge of migrants from the South East which is so important in adjacent East Anglia and the South West. Indeed, recent population growth in the county—by 15,000, or 3.0 per cent, in 1974-1978—has been closely related to the progress of official London overspill schemes, notably those for Northampton itself (see section 6.3.2) and the expanded town of Wellingborough. By 1977, the latter had received an influx of some 9,000 Londoners and more than forty manufacturing firms. In addition, Northamptonshire also contains the first-generation new town of Corby, and the Birmingham-linked expanded town of Daventry. Designation of the former in 1950 reflected the need for local housing for workers in Corby's steelworks, together with a desire to diversify its industrial base by attracting light industry from London. Overspill population growth by migration from the capital was a secondary consideration. The town has none the less expanded by some 38,000 inhabitants since designation, to a total of 54,000. Since about 1960, Corby has also attracted some fifty manufacturing firms to factories on its industrial estates. Daventry, Birmingham's second largest expanded town, had by 1977 received approximately 7,000 newcomers and seventy immigrant manufacturing firms, occupying in fact more than double the factory space built at Wellingborough.

Industrially, Northamptonshire was traditionally noted for its footwear industry, concentrated in the four towns of Kettering, Rushden, Wellingborough and Northampton itself. Between them, these centres accounted in 1971 for nearly 60 per cent—23,000 jobs—of employment in the East Midlands in this industry, with Northampton, the largest of them, providing some 6,500 jobs (Rake, 1975). Unlike Leicester, these Northamptonshire centres have traditionally specialized in the manufacture of men's shoes, Northampton itself being noted for high-quality production. As in Leicestershire, many formerly independent shoe firms have become part of larger corporations by merger and takeover since 1950, and national companies such as the British Shoe Corporation,

Norvic, Ward White, and the Wearra Group all now operate factories in Northamptonshire. The reputation of the area for high-quality production has helped local firms to expand export production in recent years. But foreign competition has had its effect on jobs, as noted in section 7.2.1.

Like Leicestershire, the economy of Northamptonshire owes much to the growth of the engineering and electrical goods industry over the last twenty years, with a great variety of firms and products. Indeed, the percentage of the county's workforce in this industry— 18.6 per cent in 1975—is greater than in any other East Midlands county except Derbyshire. Machine tools, for example, are manufactured at Daventry, Kettering and Wellingborough, with electrical engineering at Northampton, Wellingborough and Towcester. Many small electronic engineering firms have developed in the Northampton area, as also has the manufacture of motor vehicle components for West Midlands assembly plants. The latter is also important at Corby, Wellingborough and Kettering. While many of these varied engineering firms are entirely new, indigenous, concerns, the county has also attracted a larger share of immigrant factories than any other part of the East Midlands. Excluding the steelworks at Corby, Gudgin's figures (1978) suggest that 30 per cent of net manufacturing job growth in the county in 1948-1967, was in immigrant plants, compared with an East Midlands-wide figure of only 15 per cent. This difference no doubt reflects Northamptonshire's location adjacent to the South East, and the role of official new and expanded towns. The same factors also help to explain Northampton's role as the second most important destination within the region for mobile office firms from central London. LOB records indicate that by 1977 the new town had received nearly 1,000 jobs from the immigration of such firms.

As noted above, the establishment of a first-generation new town at Corby is explicable only in terms of the existence there since 1936 of a major—1.2 million ton capacity, 1977 —integrated iron and steel plant, built originally by Stewarts & Lloyds of Scotland, but now operated by the British Steel Corporation. Iron making has long been an important industry in Northamptonshire, with blast furnaces until the 1960s at both Kettering and Wellingborough. Now only Corby remains. Its inter-war establishment reflected the existence of Britain's largest Jurassic iron ore field, which runs in a northward inclining arc from Northampton through Corby to Grantham. Though substantial, the iron ore deposits are low-grade—28 to 34 per cent fe content only—and hence cannot bear the cost of transport over any distance. Corby specializes in the manufacture of steel tubes, and its future as a steel finishing unit in this respect is assured. However, the availability of cheaper, imported, high-grade ore at coastal steel plants meant that in 1979 the B.S.C. decided to close basic iron and steel-making there. The continuing over-dependence of the town upon the steel plant is indicated by the fact that in 1979 it provided jobs for about three-fifths of all male workers resident in Corby. Earlier redundancies in the steel industry, and the closure of newer factories—e.g. in electrical engineering—attracted since the war by the availability of female workers, explain Corby's very high unemployment rate in recent years (8.5 per cent in July 1976 compared with a regional average of only 5.4 per cent). Despite its new town status, Corby thus faces very considerable local economic problems. The view of the Planning Council that the locality needs active government assistance to create new jobs was accepted in 1979 when Corby was designated a Development Area. (East Midlands Economic Planning Council, 1978).

Trends and planning problems in Lincolnshire are in many ways more akin to those in neighbouring East Anglia than in the rest of the East Midlands. Topographically the

Fenlands of southern Lincolnshire and of Cambridgeshire comprise a uniform region of flat, low-lying and fertile land, and the planning region boundary which cuts through them has no physical validity. Like East Anglia, Lincolnshire is much more dependent economically on agriculture than other areas, with no less than 11.2 per cent of total employment in agriculture (plus forestry and fishing) in 1975 compared with a regional average for the East Midlands of only 2.5 per cent. Conversely, manufacturing provides only 27.4 per cent of jobs, compared with the regional figure of 39.9 per cent. This economic structure is also clearly related to the county's exceptionally high unemployment rate—7.1 per cent in July 1977, compared with the regional average of 5.8 per cent. Yet Lincolnshire is attracting population by net migration, with an expansion of over 8,000 residents in 1974-1978. The problem is that many of these are probably retired or semi-retired individuals, moving, for example, to the coastal resorts of Skegness and Mablethorpe or to inland villages, attracted by cheap housing and rural surroundings. Losses of younger people from the county have in the past been considerable. The problem of access to jobs is aggravated by the low population density, by relatively poor road communications, especially in the Fens, and by the special economic situation of the coastal strip north of Skegness. The latter's holiday industry provides much seasonal summer employment in services, but closes down almost completely in winter. From an employer's point of view, the attraction of new manufacturing firms to diversify Lincolnshire's employment base is rendered the more difficult by the small *size* of the available labour pool—despite high unemployment *rates*—in many areas, because of the dispersed rural population pattern.

This said, Lincolnshire has attracted some immigrant industry since 1945, often in the form of small, female-employing branch plants of firms in such cost-conscious industries as footwear and hosiery. Most of it has gone to the larger centres, such as Grantham, Sleaford and Stamford, or to the North Lincolnshire Intermediate Area. The latter, designated in 1972, comprises Gainsborough, Horncastle, Louth, Mablethorpe and Skegness employment exchange areas, and reflects the high unemployment rates which still (1979) characterize the area. Gainsborough has also been helped to some extent by its status as a London expanded town, as also has Grantham, more strategically located on the A1 further south. Development in these two small centres has, however, been much less than in the other overspill towns of the East Midlands, such as Wellingborough and Daventry. By 1977, Gainsborough had received only about 400 Londoners and twenty migrant factories, whilst Grantham's totals were 1,300 and only two, respectively. In Gainsborough, as in many of Lincolnshire's small towns, employment is still over-dependent on a single major firm (in Gainsborough's case, it is the engineering concern of Marshall-Fowler, now part of British Leyland's Special Products Division). Other smaller settlements are being helped by the Development Commission. Working closely both with local planning authorities and its own advisory service to industry, C.O.S.I.R.A. (see p.184), the commission has been active in rural Lincolnshire for some time. In particular, funds have been provided for small advance factories in seven different rural centres— Spilsby, Horncastle, Alford, Louth, Kirton, Donington and Billingborough. The problems of rural Lincolnshire, as in the more isolated parts of East Anglia, are, however, deep-rooted in a sparse population, with declining local services and public transport provision. Car ownership in these rural areas is thus a necessity, not a luxury, explaining Lincolnshire's much higher than average car and van licence rate, of 295 per 1,000 of the population in 1976, compared with the regional average of only 258. East Anglia was even higher, at 305—and this despite lower (in Lincolnshire's case, much lower) than average earnings per worker in both areas. However, unlike much of East Anglia, Lincolnshire probably does not enjoy significant advantages in attracting industry and population with respect to the quality of its residential environment, in the form of attractive villages or coastal scenery. While Lincoln itself, with a 1976 population of 74,000, is a fairly thriving city based on engineering and service industry, the provision of adequate jobs and public facilities for the population of the rest of the county seems likely to pose significant problems to local planners for many years to come.

REFERENCES

East Anglia Economic Planning Council (1968). *East Anglia: A Study,* H.M.S.O., London.
East Anglia Economic Planning Council (1977). *Seaports in East Anglia,* D.O.E., London.
East Anglia Regional Strategy Team (1974). *Strategic Choice for East Anglia,* H.M.S.O., London.
East Midlands Economic Planning Council (1966). *The East Midlands Study,* H.M.S.O., London.
East Midlands Economic Planning Council (1969). *Opportunity in the East Midlands,* H.M.S.O., London.
East Midlands Economic Planning Council (1976). *East Midlands — A Forward Economic Look,* D.O.E., Nottingham.
East Midlands Economic Planning Council (1978). *East Midlands — A Forward Economic Look,* 2nd ed., D.O.E., Nottingham.
Gould, P.R., and White, R.R. (1968). The mental maps of British school leavers. *Regional Studies,* **2,** 161-182.
Gudgin, G. (1978). *Industrial Location Processes and Regional Employment Growth,* Saxon House, Farnborough.
Howard, R.S. (1968). *The Movement of Manufacturing Industry in the United Kingdom 1945-65,* H.M.S.O. for the Board of Trade, London.
Jackman, R., and Sellars, M. (1977). The distribution of RSG: The hows and whys of the new needs formula. *CES Review,* **1,** 19-30.
Keeble, D.E. (1967). Models of economic development. In R.J. Chorley and P. Haggett (eds), *Models in Geography,* Methuen, London, ch.8.
Keeble, D. (1976). *Industrial Location and Planning in the United Kingdom,* Methuen, London.
Lee, C.H. (1971). *Regional Economic Growth in the United Kingdom Since the 1880s,* McGraw-Hill, London.
Myrdal, G. (1957). *Economic Theory and Under-developed Regions,* Duckworth, London.
Nottinghamshire and Derbyshire Sub-regional Study (1969). Notts/Derby Sub-regional Planning Unit, Alfreton.
Pye, N. (1972). *Leicester and Its Region,* Leicester University Press for the Local Committee of the British Association, Leicester.
Rake, D.J. (1974). Spatial changes in industrial activity in the East Midlands since 1945, II, The hosiery industry. *The East Midlands Geographer,* **6,** 51-65.
Rake, D.J. (1975). Spatial changes in industrial activity in the East Midlands since 1945, III, The footwear industry. *The East Midlands Geographer,* **6,** 173-184.
Rees, P.H. (1977). *The Future Population of East Anglia and its Constituent Counties (Cambridgeshire, Norfolk and Suffolk),* East Anglia Economic Planning Council, London.
Small Towns Study (1972), East Anglia Economic Planning Council and East Anglia Consultative Committee.

CHAPTER 8

The West Midlands and Central Wales

BRIAN RODGERS

8.1 A Profile of the West Midlands

It is very difficult, with any confidence, to sketch a profile of the West Midland region, from the perspective of the late 1970s. Taking an historical view, this has been a region of sustained growth and almost uninterrupted prosperity for the last two centuries. Shortening the time scale somewhat, the West Midlands suffered less from the economic vicissitudes of the half-century 1920 to 1970 than almost any other British industrial region. A successful, expanding, adaptable manufacturing base, aligned towards the growth industries of the period, underpinned the rapid and persistent growth of employment and population at a high general level of personal prosperity. In consequence, the shock of the general recession of the 1970s was a sharp one, and was exaggerated by the peculiar difficulties of the motor car industry. Unemployment doubled between 1967 and 1971; total employment fell by 2.7 per cent between 1970 and 1976; and population growth had virtually ceased by 1973/1974. Yet, by 1976, unemployment had eased and some growth of the volume of work had recommenced. Are these trends of the 1970s the end of an era, or a short-term fluctuation of a kind that the region has encountered before, and surmounted? It is much too early to read a trend from the data, and the uncertainties of the position are stressed in the account that follows.

Until the general recession of the early 1970s, no other major industrial region of Britain had enjoyed such sustained economic progress, over so long a period and with so little interruption, as the West Midlands. It is almost true to say that the last general brake on the region's growth and prosperity was the charcoal famine of the early eighteenth century. This was ended by the coke-iron revolution that led to the massive concentration of iron smelting and metal working on the South Staffordshire coalfield, which was producing a quarter of the nation's pig iron by the early decades of the nineteenth century (Johnson, 1951). Certainly, parts of the region have had their problems, from time to time. Coventry was a troubled city after the French commercial treaty of 1860 removed the protection on which the silk industry relied. Some of the heavy metal working towns of the central and south east Black Country were as depressed, briefly but acutely, during the early 1930s, as were many parts of less prosperous Britain. And today Kidderminster depends somewhat on a carpet industry that has falling labour requirements. Yet so great has been the versatility and adaptability of West Midland industry that these problems of readjustment have been local and temporary. The occupation of Coventry's empty silk workshops by a bicycle trade, from which the modern vehicle industry is a lineal

201

descendant, is an oft-told tale; but it is typical of the enterprise of the region and the resilience of its economy. The graphs of population growth, both for the region as a whole and for the Birmingham-Black Country conurbation that is its industrial core, show smoothly rising curves from 1801 to 1971. They are unbroken by decline and, until World War I, very closely mirrored the national trend; but after the 1920s the regional growth-graph steepened in relation to the national trend. From 1951 to 1976 the population of the West Midlands grew at an average rate of 0.9 per cent per annum, compared with a value for England and Wales of 0.49 per cent, and the region steadily increased its share of the national population—from 7.9 per cent in 1921 to 10.5 per cent in 1976. This is the crux of the region's problems. Like the North West, West Yorkshire and the North East, it is an area in which quick nineteenth-century growth preempted considerable tracts of land in and near to the congested industrial core; unlike them it is an area of (until recently) unabated expansion. Indeed, to a greater degree than in any other British industrial region, the conurbation at its centre long continued to grow both in population and employment, and resisted the dispersal both of people and of work. The 1971 Census, however, reveals that the growth of the conurbation has been checked at a population of 2.37 million, a figure similar to that of 1961. Centralizing forces have remained strong enough to frustrate an admittedly feeble public policy for the dispersal of work and people to distant sites.

In summarizing the general character of the West Midlands in a national context, a profile of one of the country's 'fortunate' regions of rapid urban and economic progress, peopled by a segment of the affluent society, clearly emerges. Yet the region has not shown quite such feverish growth as the greater part of metropolitan England; nor is there a level of personal prosperity to match south eastern standards quite so widespread, either in social or spatial terms. There are pockets of industrial difficulty associated with environmental decay. The Potteries conurbation in North Staffordshire, for example, with a population of half a million, is quite atypical; it is an area still heavily dependent on stagnant or declining industries (ceramics and coal mining), an area with a long history of population loss by migration and a low rate of population growth, an area struggling with the problems of a Victorian urban environment and disfigured by two centuries of vigorous economic growth based on extractive industries (Beaver, 1964). The Cannock Chase and East Warwickshire coalfields, despite the relatively high productivity of their mining industries, have been caught up in the rationalization of the coal-mining industry, and so face problems of redundancy and pit closures; indeed, East Warwickshire (like North Staffordshire) was included in the Hunt Committee's study of the 'grey areas'. The rural western fringes of the West Midlands, in Shropshire and Herefordshire, lie far enough outside the boundaries of the English megalopolis to be suffering from rural depopulation of a classic type, uncorrected by suburban dispersal or the social transformation of the rural community by an 'intrusive' element of urban origin. Even here, however, the larger towns have shown a capacity to grow by attracting mobile industry, and the rather isolated industrial area based on the East Shropshire coalfield has shown a surprising level of industrial vitality and population increase.

Two of these outlying sub-regions (North Staffordshire and East Shropshire) are sufficiently significant and distinctive to merit separate treatment as case studies (pp.230-236, and 236-242). The 'rural west' and North Staffordshire are areas of relatively slow population growth—6.1 per cent and 2.2 per cent, respectively, compared with a West Midlands increase of 7.3 per cent between 1961 and 1971. Thus, the industrial

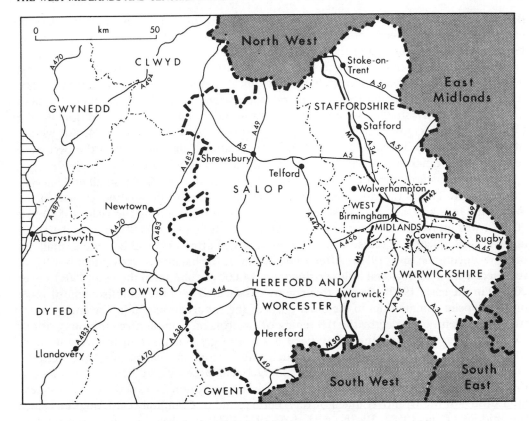

Figure 8.1 The West Midlands and Central Wales

heartland of the West Midlands (the three 'traditional' counties of Worcester, Warwick and Stafford, less the north) not only contains the great bulk of the region's population, but it also generates an even higher share of its growth and, so far, has absorbed its population increase without any significant long-range dispersal. In this 'heartland' population grew by almost 18 per cent—an increment of nearly 640,000—during the period 1951-1971, but with a distinct slackening since.

8.1.1 *Population and Migration*

Given these sub-regional inequalities in growth, it is perhaps surprising that the West Midlands as a whole proved itself a region of such vitality during the three decades after 1945. Yet its population increase of 22.6 per cent over the period 1951-1976 was amongst the highest regional rates in the country, even higher than that of the South East (see Table 1.2). Given the degree of immobility that seems to characterize industry in and near the West Midland conurbation (and which restrains dispersal planning), the regional growth rate was accelerating in a fashion that was positively alarming. From an annual rate of about 0.51 per cent in the early 1950s it had more than doubled to well over 1.00 per cent per annum by the early 1960s, although it fell later. The conurbation itself was not only still growing substantially until very recently (which alone makes it unique among

British conurbations as officially defined), but its rate of increase actually quickened, from about 0.26 per cent per annum in the early 1950s, to 0.66 per cent per annum by 1961; there was, however, a distinct slackening of the growth rate after that date, and the present evidence is that it has passed its population peak. Short-term, inter-censal population trends may not be entirely reliable, but if they are, then there has been a sharp reversal in the trend of the region's central population cluster. The new West Midland County (a slightly smaller version of the conurbation but with the addition of the Coventry complex) lost 32,000 people by migration between 1971 and 1974, not wholly offset by a natural increase of 22,000. Decentralization from the core to the periphery seems to have quickened as the regional growth rate has slackened.

To the longer-term increase in population, in-migration made only a small and varying contribution. This is the chief contrast between the nature of population growth in the West Midlands and the South East. Heavy net out-migration during the 1920s (of almost 70,000) was more than balanced by a net inflow of a little over 100,000 during the 1930s and the subsequent war years. In-migration slackened after 1945 and became a small net outflow during the early 1950s. After 1956, however, the balance of movement was again reversed, with a net regional inflow rising from 14,000 per annum in the late 1950s to over 20,000 in the early 1960s. Part of this rise was associated with the establishment of large non-European communities in the older parts of the conurbation and in Coventry; and it was subsequently reduced by the tightening of controls on Commonwealth immigration. In short, over the years there has been a surprisingly small net inflow to the West Midlands from other parts of Britain, though a huge actual movement of people from the northern regions, Wales and Scotland was largely balanced by an outflow of families to the South East; the rest of the movement into the region is explained by overseas migration—of the Irish over much of this century, and of Commonwealth migrants since the middle of the 1950s. By the period of 1971-1974, however, net in-movement had stopped, and indeed had become a marginal outflow, another indicator of the sudden change in the region's fortunes.

Overall, less than one-fifth of the region's population increase since 1945 can be explained by net in-migration. The rest arises from a relatively high rate of natural increase; at 9 per cent over the period 1951-1964, this was much higher than either the national rate (6.8 per cent) or the rate in the South East (6.6 per cent). This characteristic reflects, of course, the influence of in-migration during and since the 1930s, giving the region a favourable age structure and a high level of fertility during the early post-war years. Clearly, the fact that population growth in the West Midlands owes little to migration and much to high fertility means that in comparison with the South East it is relatively uncontrollable. The national distribution of industry policies sought to damp-down inter-regional migration southwards by limiting employment growth in the more prosperous parts of England; and they have had considerable success in reducing the inflow into the South East, as has been seen (Chapters 2 and 4). But these policies came at least a decade too late to have any great influence, at any rate in the short term, on the course of population growth in the West Midlands.

High—but dwindling—rates of natural increase continued into the difficult years of the early 1970s, declining from about 0.5 to 0.3 per cent per annum between 1971 and 1974, and reflecting a national trend. Yet the regional rate of increase is second only to that of Northern Ireland. Within the conurbation the immigrant community (fertile because it is young) contributes substantially to this increase. There are now 120,000 people of New

Commonwealth birth in the conurbation alone: adding their locally-born children, the total size of the community may be approaching a quarter of a million. If the economy of the Birmingham-based travel-to-work area remains as stagnant as it has been recently, selective unemployment of the immigrant worker is a social problem of potentially appalling size.

8.1.2 *Employment and Income*

Until about 1966, the West Midland region had not the slightest difficulty in generating new employment to absorb both the whole of this great natural increase in its population and the smaller migratory additions. Despite the 'steering' of tens of thousands of West Midlands jobs to the Assisted Areas, the total volume of work available not only grew (by about 1.2 per cent per annum between 1953 and 1963, compared with a national rate of 0.9 per cent), but it accelerated to an annual growth rate of 1.5 per cent during the early 1960s. But as national economic impetus was lost the West Midlands suffered disproportionately; from 1966 to 1970 it lost 3.7 per cent of its total employment compared with a national rate of 2.6 per cent. Since then the regional trend has been no better than the national one. There are continuing weaknesses in the structure of employment in the region. It depends too heavily on the manufacturing sector. This provides 48 per cent of the region's work, but only 35 per cent in the country as a whole; and jobs in manufacturing are declining. Within the manufacturing sector there is intense specialization on a narrow range of metal working, engineering and vehicle manufacture. Some of these are growing far more slowly in the region than nationally; the vehicle industry increased its employment in the West Midlands by only 1.7 per cent during the decade 1953-1963, while nationally its growth was by over 11 per cent, and this adverse trend has continued (p.224). This was a direct consequence of government control over the geography of industrial expansion, and the steering of new projects to the Assisted Areas. Moreover, a number of the region's major industries are sensitive to demand cycles (for example, the manufacture of power station equipment and heavy electrical machinery), or to the Treasury's use of economic regulators to reduce national consumption (for example, firms making domestic equipment and cars). Thus, short periods of localized unemployment have interrupted the general condition of labour scarcity that has been the norm in the region since the 1930s, at least until 1971.

Whether the outbreak of serious unemployment since 1971 is simply such an episode, or a more sinister phenomenon, cannot yet be judged. After a long period of very low unemployment—often scarcely half the national average—Birmingham, Walsall, Coventry and Wolverhampton all experienced rates above the national average (in Coventry's case 50 per cent above) during parts of the period 1967 to 1972. By 1974, however, all were again below a now much higher national average rate. Certainly these problems, widely publicized and indeed dramatized as they were, must have been major factors in turning the net migration balance into an outflow.

In fact, a major change is slowly occurring to the employment structure of the West Midlands, as manufacturing is replaced by service activities. The latter are of somewhat stunted development—in 1961, they provided only 48 per cent of the work available, compared with 61 per cent nationally and almost 70 per cent in the South East—but they are growing quickly in the West Midlands. The industrial vitality and the high level of personal prosperity in the region are the chief driving forces of this growth in service activity. The symptoms are diverse and impressive. The huge investment represented by the almost total remodelling of the Birmingham city centre; the fact that shop and restaurant floorspace is growing six times as fast in the West Midland conurbation as in the Manchester conurbation, and office floorspace more than twice as quickly; the very high rates of increase in financial and professional employment; these are all evidence of a major economic, and indeed social, transformation. Its latest expression, a latter-day symbol of the traditional enterprise of the region, is the building of the large new National Exhibition Centre between Birmingham and Coventry, on a site near the airport and with its own station on the electrified London railway: the site was chosen after a vigorous contest with south eastern alternatives. But a continued complaint within the region is that it receives no encouragement to diversify its employment structure away from the manufacturing base. For example, of 26,000 civil service jobs relocated from London since 1963, the West Midlands got 0.1 per cent, while 25 per cent were moved to new locations within the South East.

Perhaps the best-known expression of the economic vitality of the West Midland region is the very high level of income enjoyed by the mass of the population. Although the region is not free from environmental poverty, it is almost without personal poverty. The terraced street along which the cars are packed as tightly as the houses is not an untypical regional image. Indeed, the Coventry car workers for a time became almost a new social archetype, a community of manual workers with an average income level that permitted them to develop their own variant of a middle-class life-style. But Midland prosperity is easily exaggerated. Average male earnings are second only to those in the South East, and yet they are below the national average. On the other hand, the West Midlands has a higher proportion of earners in the upper-middle bracket than even the South East; in 1973, 35 per cent of regional earnings were in the range £2,000 to £5,000. Moreover, high activity rates among both men and women push up household income levels: thus 35 per cent of families in the region had weekly incomes between £60 and £80 in 1973, also the highest proportion among all the regions. In brief, the real measure of the region's prosperity is the high proportion of households in the upper-middle income ranges, far above a subsistence level; and these are almost as likely to be 'blue-collar' as 'white'. But these measures are somewhat meaningless in a region that includes both a Stoke-on-Trent and a Coventry.

8.1.3 *Traditional Economic Strengths*

There are many reasons, all interacting and complex, for the vigorous economic development of the West Midlands during the present century and particularly between 1945 and the late 1960s. A relative absence of stagnant or declining industries, and the dominance of what are, in a national context, the growth sectors in the manufacturing economy, are the two chief background causes. In short, there is a structural explanation for the prosperity of the regional economy; but such an explanation is not in itself fully adequate. Except for those industries that have been most effectively retarded in their regional development by government intervention (particularly vehicles and electrical goods), the growth industries have expanded even more quickly in the West Midlands than in the country as a whole (especially mechanical engineering and the miscellaneous metal trades); and some of those trades which are declining nationally (such as railway engineering, clothing and textiles) have contracted much more slowly in the region. Clearly there is evidence of powerful non-structural factors at work.

Some of these geographical factors are discussed at greater length later. They include the extraordinary versatility of so many West Midland metal-working firms producing components, semi-products, and the like; such producers are not tied to specific market outlets, but rather adapt their products and processes to take advantage of new market opportunities, and so gear themselves to what are, for the time being, growth sectors. There is little of the monolithic specialization that has been so serious a problem elsewhere, though the ultimate dependence of so much of the region's employment on the vehicle industry has its obvious dangers.

Similarly, the West Midlands has always enjoyed a high birth rate of new industrial enterprises, a process which is facilitated by the important—indeed, the dominant—role of the small firm in the complex of metal-processing trades. Entrepreneurial vigour and enterprise have never been lacking in the region, which probably gives the 'small man' a better chance of developing a new business than any other part of Britain. This is one of the primary reasons why government action to guide industrial development out of the region has been rather ineffectual in halting the growth of manufacturing employment, and it is certainly a powerful balance to the dispersal of industry from the conurbation to fringe locations. As fast as employment is decanted, either from the conurbation or the region, new and growing enterprises occupy the vacant floorspace in a game of musical chairs. In any case, while i.d.c. approval was necessary only for projects of over 464 square metres (5,000 square feet), a good deal of new floorspace was bound to be created without licensing in a region of relatively small industrial units. Certainly throughout the 1960s the region's industrial impetus showed no signs of slackening: in the two years 1967 and 1968, almost 1.8 million square metres (19 million square feet) of manufacturing space was approved in the region, a greater two-year total than for any pair of consecutive years in the previous decade.

There has in fact been a progressive relaxation in the application of i.d.c. controls to the region. Approvals between 1967 and 1970 represented a total of about 18,900 jobs, of which 3,400 were sited within the conurbation. For the period 1971 to 1974 these values rose to 27,300 and 10,400 respectively. The data give some indication of the level of job creation in the manufacturing sector in the region. Though none of these estimates can be trusted implicitly, it appears that 46,000 jobs were made available by i.d.c. approvals for sites within the region over the period 1967 to 1974; in contrast, between 1960 and 1971 59,000 jobs were lost by the West Midlands to other regions by i.d.c. refusals. Perhaps about half the increment in employment growth created by significant developments in the manufacturing sector was allowed to remain within the region. But this ignores the considerable quantities of employment generated by developments that could pass through the loopholes in the system of control by i.d.c., outlined below.

Almost from the beginnings of significant industrial growth on the South Staffordshire plateau, two spatial factors have been a continuing stimulus to economic advance: the centrality of the region within Britain, and the progressive development of an infrastructure of communications which has quickly responded to each new revolution in transport technology, thereby translating centrality into real nodality. The location of the Birmingham-Black Country metal-working complex, straddling the central English watershed, inevitably made it the focus of the evolving canal system. As early as 1790, Birmingham lay at the focus of a system of slow but cheap transport for bulk commodities that extended from Bristol to York and from London to Lancashire. No other part of Britain has since rivalled the West Midlands in terms of inter-regional accessibility. Railway development quickly confirmed the focal role of Birmingham. A two-hour service between London and Birmingham was an early achievement of the Victorian railway companies, so that for more than a century a Midland businessman has been able to spend a working day in London and return to dine in his Edgbaston villa. Indeed, Birmingham's passenger communications with the rest of the country in the late nineteenth century were so good that they have been capable of only marginal improvement since. Isochrones drawn from Birmingham as centre, for the fastest available means of land transport, would show little radical difference if the 1870 pattern were compared with that for 1970. Inter-city air transport has done less for Birmingham than any other major provincial centre, while a century of railway improvement, culminating in electrification, had reduced the Birmingham-London journey time by only twenty minutes. Although railway electrification has transformed inter-city accessibility within the English megalopolis, its relative effect has been least within the West Midlands. Certainly, freight movement has accelerated almost to passenger speeds, but the short range of so much commodity movement within the West Midland region limits the effect of railway improvements. It is significant, for example, that the Midlands' car firms use rail transport much less than their south eastern and South Lancashire rivals.

Motorway development has brought a far greater acceleration of commodity flow than of passenger movement, over short ranges as well as long. It therefore has a more vital significance for the region than railway improvements. There will clearly be a period, probably lasting several decades, during which the West Midlands will dominate the developing British motorway system, as it did the early expansion of the canal and railway nets. The M1 London-Yorkshire motorway skirts the region on the east, and the short M45 spur runs from the M1 westwards towards Coventry. From the north the M6, from Carlisle, deeply penetrates not merely the region but also the conurbation; similarly the M5 Birmingham-Bristol-South Wales motorway enters and crosses the conurbation to join the M6 south of Walsall in the very heart of the Black Country. An east-west route from this junction across north east Birmingham skirts Coventry on the north, to link up with the M1 near Rugby. These Midland motorways are not only key links in the national system, joining the M5-M6 and M1-A1 routes running independently north-south through western and eastern England respectively; they have also become the chief arteries of intra-regional traffic flow. Slicing through the densely built-up urban area and some of the most congested industrial zones, they give this conurbation a distinction, long likely to remain unique, of being intersected by 'main line' motorways. The effect on the speed and cost of commodity flow is dramatic. South Lancashire is within two hours of Birmingham for a typical heavy delivery vehicle, and so are Severnside and South Wales. Neither London nor industrial Yorkshire lies much beyond the two-hour isochrone. The whole of the industrial heart of the region once again enjoys that immense relative advantage over the rest of the country that it possessed most strongly during the early phases of both canal and railway development. In brief, with the completion of the motorway links, some 68 per cent of the nation's population, almost 75 per cent of its manufacturing employment, and an even higher share of its purchasing power, are within the three-hour isochrone. Can it be hoped that industry will voluntarily leave the conurbation for the fringes of the region—as it is asked to do in order to implement overspill policies—in the face of accessibility advantages of this magnitude?

8.2 The Spatial Framework of the West Midlands

The urban and industrial heart of the West Midlands has formed upon and about a coal-rich plateau, although the coalfield and the industrial region are by no means coextensive and mining has been largely abandoned. At the core lies the Birmingham-Black Country conurbation of some 2.4 million people (Figure 8.2). This itself is divided between what may be described as Greater Birmingham (the city, together with its suburban extensions chiefly into Solihull and Sutton Coldfield) in the east and south east, and the Black Country towns perched on the coalfield plateau to the west. A surprisingly tenuous ribbon of dense urbanization pinched between semi-rural salients joins Birmingham to the Black Country; and the two halves of the conurbation—in fact they have roughly equal shares of the total population—are complexly contrasted, though less sharply today than a half-century ago (Rosing and Wood, 1971).

Industry in Birmingham is varied. The emphasis lies, of course, on the light metal trades and the assembly industries, but there is diversity outside the metal-working group and service employment considerably exceeds manufacturing. Service activities, in contrast, are only weakly developed in the Black Country; there the bulk of work is provided not only by the manufacturing sector, but dominantly by metal working, and with a strong accent on semi-finished materials and components. The urban landscape of the Black Country is that of a confused patchwork. Old housing and industry—clustered about the town and village nuclei, and ribboned along a chaotic road system—alternate irregularly with areas of modern public and private housing that have been forced into the interstices of the Victorian urban framework. Similarly, both large and small modern factories rise everywhere from the obsolescent remains of the old industrial zones that are aligned along canals and railways or embedded in the urban cores. Birmingham displays a much simpler dichotomy between a collar of nineteenth-century development (an amalgam of both industrial and residential slums, now well advanced towards renewal) and the suburban spread to the south and east, with its dispersed and chiefly large-scale industrial development. The problem of substandard housing is roughly equally shared between the Black Country and the city; however, the problem is much more localized in the latter. The Black Country has the bulk of the derelict land problem—still about 1,600 hectares (4,000 acres) after twenty-five years of active reclamation and continuing to spread to new localities. This, then, is a bipartite conurbation, structurally unusual in that the dominant city is eccentrically placed towards the south east margin, whilst powerful sub-centres on which the strong sub-regional consciousness of the Black Country is focused, play a distinctive role in the west.

Beyond the margin of the conurbation, and separated from it by a planned green belt that is in fact very grey and scarred, lies a ring of free-standing industrial towns. Most of them are situated beyond mass-commuting range of Birmingham, but they are bound closely enough by ties of industrial linkage and social affiliation to be, in a real sense, part of the West Midland city-region. Kidderminster and Worcester to the south west; Stratford, Warwick and Leamington to the south east; the towns of east Warwickshire, namely Tamworth, Nuneaton, Rugby and Coventry itself; and Lichfield, Rugeley, Cannock and Stafford to the north are all firmly tied to the conurbation and its dominant city, though in quite diverse ways. The small towns of East Shropshire are as yet more isolated—yet they are quickly becoming more directly bound to the conurbation with their development as the new city of Telford, expanding partly to receive Birmingham overspill. Burton-upon-Trent in the far north east is anomalously placed in the West

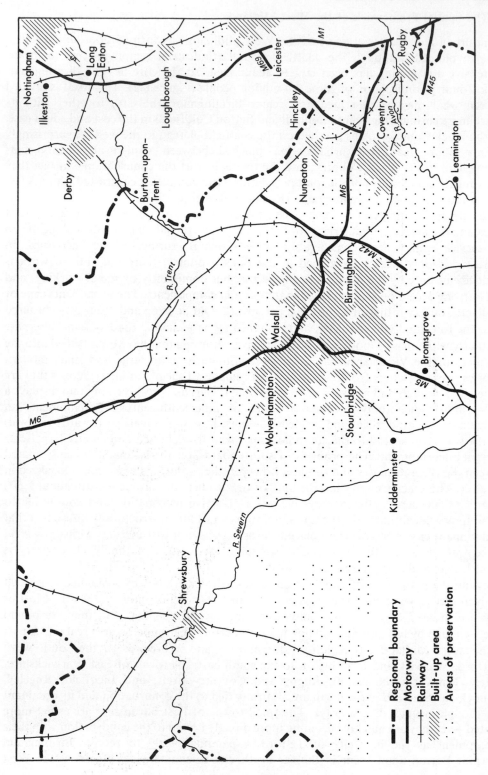

Figure 8.2 The West Midlands: the economic core

Midlands, with which it has little in common industrially; in all roles except administration, it is more commonly associated with the urban complex of the middle Trent valley. The conurbation of North Staffordshire, too, has only rather tenuous links with the core of the West Midlands; it lies astride the watershed of regional affiliation between the West Midlands and the North West.

The nature of the links between these towns of the outer girdle of the urban region and its core, and their relationships with each other, are most simply demonstrated through an examination of commuting patterns. There is a hierarchy of journey-to-work systems, and so of labour market areas, in the urban West Midlands. Clearly the Birmingham-oriented commuter flow dominates the hierarchy. Most of the in-movement to the city is from the adjacent suburban districts of Sutton Coldfield and Solihull, and from those parts of the Black Country that immediately border Birmingham. Feebler flows are generated by areas far beyond the conurbation margin—as far as Tamworth on the east, Stratford on the south, and Worcester on the south west—but there is little commuting to Birmingham from areas beyond the northern and western margins of the conurbation. The Black Country to the west has always deflected the city's suburban outgrowth towards an arc from the north east through to the south west and, except for the Telford project, most of the planned dispersal of population of the conurbation is to sites within the same arc.

A second, lower 'order' of journey-to-work systems in part overlaps the Birmingham commuter zone. Each of the major free-standing towns of the city-region margin (especially Stafford, Coventry, Rugby and Worcester) and the major employment foci of the Black Country (particularly Wolverhampton) is a major net importer of labour. Their industrial growth has been rapid but few have attracted any considerable addition to their dormitory population. Much the greatest of these second-order labour market areas is that based on Coventry. Indeed, here a semi-independent sub-conurbation is evolving: this includes the semicircle of smaller towns that surrounds the city (from Nuneaton to the north, through Hinckley, Rugby and Daventry to the east, and to Warwick-Leamington on the south), where the growth of employment, population and the built-up area has been at rates far above the regional average. A complex pattern of daily labour interchanges binds the 'Coventry belt' together into an integrated urban-industrial unit, with a population of over 600,000. Its rate of growth is so rapid that it is the principal pressure point in the region. Worcester, to the south west, has emerged as a somewhat similar dominant focus of a semi-independent journey-to-work system. It draws labour from an area that extends to Malvern and Evesham, and that on the north overlaps the conurbation margin at Bromsgrove and Redditch. Another focus within a 'second order' of labour market areas, Stafford, has even more complex spatial relationships in that it is the only point of contact between the labour market of the West Midland conurbation and that of North Staffordshire. A feature of recent development in the Stafford journey-to-work system has been its strong extension beyond Stone to the Potteries. At the same time, a longstanding out-movement from Stafford to Wolverhampton continues: in short Stafford imports part of its labour supply from the north but exports to the south. To a degree, therefore, it links an area of labour scarcity (the conurbation) with an area of incipient labour surplus (North Staffordshire). Wolverhampton has the most distinctive journey-to-work pattern among the Black Country towns. It imports from a curiously elongated zone, bordering the conurbation from Bridgnorth on the south west to Cannock and Stafford, and a considerable extension of its commuting hinterland westwards reaches to the towns of East Shropshire.

Apart from this in-movement of labour to important industrial towns, most of them beyond the conurbation edge, a third 'order' in the hierarchy of journey-to-work systems may be discerned. This takes the form of a set of complex patterns of interchange between the smaller towns. Many of these third order systems straddle the conurbation boundary and are a factor linking it with the periphery of the city-region. For example, a Walsall-Cannock-Aldridge-Rugeley sub-system straddles the margins of Wolverhampton, Stafford and Birmingham journey-to-work areas. These third order commuter sub-systems on the conurbation margin have developed strongly since 1951. They represent some degree of both industrial and population dipsersal, and they reflect the new mobility associated with very high levels of car ownership in a prosperous region.

Thus, the urban framework of the region may be discerned. At its heart is the compact Birmingham-Black Country conurbation, itself divided into two contrasting halves, of which the western is relatively self-contained in journey-to-work terms. Beyond the conurbation lies a ring of free-standing cities, each one of which is the focus of a lesser sub-system capable of definition in terms of daily labour flows. Between the conurbation and the ring of peripheral towns, increasingly complex affiliations are being shaped in the form of the third order journey-to-work systems described above. This is, of course, very much the model to which the London city-region has developed during the last quarter-century, and in many respects the Birmingham city-region repeats the trends that have shaped urban growth in metropolitan England, but on a lesser scale. There are, however, some profound and significant differences. The London conurbation, the continuously urbanized area within the green belt, has been losing population for several decades, while that of the West Midland conurbation continued to grow until about 1971. This contrast is not the consequence of a mere trick of definition; the Birmingham conurbation was not delimited more generously than others by the inclusion of large semi-rural fringe areas. It is, however, a conurbation of relatively open texture, broken by many pockets of open (though often derelict or damaged) land in the Black Country, and penetrated by deep semi-rural salients. Its mean population density in 1971 was only 33.6 persons per hectare (13.6 per acre) compared with London's 43.7 (17.7). Thus it has been able to absorb much of its own growth both of population and employment and this, together with the immobility of conurbation industry, for long worked against any marked decentralization from the conurbation. The impression is left, therefore, that the West Midlands houses a quickly growing urban population that clings tenaciously to the conurbation and its immediate margin—for the primary reasons that manufacturing industry holds on to its conurbation or fringe sites with equal stubbornness, whilst service employments grow briskly at the centre. The very limited population dispersal that has taken place has been balanced by a high rate of natural increase and by limited in-migration (from other parts of Britain, Ireland and the Commonwealth).

Despite the uniquely vigorous growth of population within the West Midlands conurbation and on its immediate fringe, the performance of the outlying towns of the city-region has been even more impressive. The Coventry labour market area, for example, increased its population by a quarter between 1951 and 1964 to a total of 612,000. About half of the growth was by in-migration, but the rate of natural increase was almost twice the national average. Without a significant slum clearance problem, almost all housing development here represents net growth. Yet there are some signs that growth in the Coventry belt has come up against problems of land availability. Between 1961 and 1971, the population increase of Coventry itself was slow by West Midlands' standards—5.6 per cent. This suggests that growth is now being deflected within the labour market area to smaller towns like Kenilworth (with a population increase of 39 per cent between 1961 and 1971) and Rugby (13.9 per cent). There is a clear need for a sub-regional plan (see p.250) to give a rational framework within which these pressures can best express themselves.

During the inter-war and early post-war periods, Coventry and its neighbours were the region's outstanding growth point. More recently, however, rates of population expansion have been higher in the towns of mid-Staffordshire, within or beyond the conurbation green belt on the north, particularly within the Stafford-based journey-to-work system. Growth here has been stimulated by a number of small-scale dispersal schemes to which not only Birmingham families but also, to a limited degree, conurbation industries have moved. Stafford itself (with a 1971 population of 55,000) grew by 14 per cent during the 1960s; Cannock (56,000) grew by 18.5 per cent, and Rugeley and Lichfield by 71 per cent and 61 per cent, respectively. Served by the M6 motorway and a generally improved trunk road system, with an expanding indigenous industrial base (especially Stafford's electrical engineering complex), and already demonstrated to be an alternative location that some conurbation firms are prepared to accept, mid-Staffordshire has an obvious growth potential. It already contains a population of about 320,000, and it has the incalculable advantage of being a single area in terms of planning responsibility, under the Staffordshire County Council. On the other hand, a substantial mining industry still exists there in the Cannock coalfield, and with it a potential problem of labour redundancy. The evolving strategy of West Midland planning assigns a substantial role to mid-Staffordshire in the housing of the region's population growth. The largest project here is a scheme developed on county initiatives to expand Tamworth to a total population of at least 70,000.

The last of the major peripheral areas within the Birmingham city-region to merit brief discussion is that based upon Worcester. A significant journey-to-work system is orientated towards this old county town which has a population of about 340,000. Close to the conurbation, it is growing fairly quickly—by 21 per cent at Bromsgrove, and by 20 per cent at Redditch, between 1961 and 1971. But Worcester's own growth (10.9 per cent) has been more modest. As the build-up of population at the Redditch new town progresses, and as both 'voluntary' and planned overspill beyond the conurbation fringe continues especially into north Worcestershire, growth will certainly quicken within this sector; however, it will have to accelerate considerably to match the rates of the northern and eastern sectors of the city-region. Apart from Redditch, there is an agreed overspill scheme for Droitwich, and a longer-term project for a massive expansion of Worcester's population. Thus, an increase in the area's population to over half a million is envisaged, though the reduction in regional rates of growth will at least postpone its realization.

8.3 The Economic Base of the West Midlands

8.3.1 *The Evolution of the Industrial Structure*

As it had developed in its classical form by the middle decades of the nineteenth century, the West Midland industrial region (then still largely confined to the Black Country coalfield and its margin) had developed a complex of metal-working manufactures which were characterized by a high degree of self-sufficiency, almost perfect vertical integration and close linkages between their several branches. The pits working the thick coal, the limestone quarries of the Dudley ridge, and the many shallow ironstone workings fed coking coal, flux and ore into a multitude of small blast-furnaces, of which there were 172 in 1865. Much of the pig iron output went to puddling furnaces (there were 2,100 of them in 1865) and so into wrought iron products. As mild steel replaced wrought iron in many markets, the Black Country turned to steel conversion, but relatively late in the century and never on a massive scale. Alongside the iron trades grew a complex of non-ferrous metal industries, refining and alloying lead, zinc, copper brass, pewter and the precious metals, especially in Birmingham. These primary branches fed an immense variety of metal processing and shaping trades, which cast, rolled, forged, slit, stamped, pierced and machined the metal, to make both finished and intermediate products. At the 'market' end of this linked chain of metal industries were those concerned with finished, and often complex, manufactures: guns and locks, bolts and buttons, chains and anchors, steam machinery (though never locomotives except on a small scale), tools and many engineering products. It is an oversimplification to describe Birmingham as the great focus of the finished-metal trades and the Black Country as its primary supplier, but this was, in a general sense, the relationship of the city with its evolving conurbation (British Association, 1950).

This classical industrial structure reached its zenith in the 1860s, and has now been modified by a century of progressive change. Coal output declined after 1865, through exhaustion and drainage problems, and shifted northwards to Cannock Chase. By 1913 the Black Country coalfield had entered a relic stage in working; output had declined to an annual 3 million tons, and was to shrink to 1 million tons by 1945. Ironstone production declined even more quickly from levels of about 1 million tons each year in the late 1850s. Partly because its local resource base was disappearing, partly because cheap steel (based on imported or Cumberland ores) was rapidly eroding the traditional wrought iron trade, iron smelting passed quickly into decline. Until 1979 the primary branch of iron working was represented by specialized steel production on a relatively small scale; now only scrap remelting and alloying survive. Thus the primary base of the integrated structure of the Victorian West Midlands has been removed.

The fate of the secondary stages in the working of iron and steel has varied considerably. Some of the trades have prospered; others have declined. During the inter-war depression some of the heavier branches of metal shaping became seriously depressed in the Black Country—for example, heavy rolled and forged products and tubes—and these have subsequently tended to disperse from the West Midlands to the major steel-producing districts. Other lighter branches—light pressings and sheet-metal work, for example—have grown strongly. The key to this success is versatility in relation to the market. In parts of the Black Country, and especially in the south-west, the metal-shaping industries are highly specialized in equipment and skill and so serve a single market; they have had their difficulties. In the north west Black Country and Birmingham, on the other hand, these trades are less tied to traditional market outlets in this way. More adaptable, they serve a complex of sub-assembly industries, and so can easily respond to the changing needs of the region's growth industries. Metal press-work firms may serve the car, central heating, and office furniture industries as opportunity offers; a maker of anchors can serve only a single 'assembly' industry. But overlying these structural contrasts is a general tendency towards rationalization and technical innovation in metal processing.

The casting trade, for example, is passing through a somewhat belated change in its technology, in which the many small foundries of the past are being replaced by larger automated units.

It is chiefly on the manufacture of 'finished-metal' products—and in particular the assembly industries making a wide range of both capital and consumer goods—that the present prosperity of the region depends. Few of these are of long standing in the area. Some have a nineteenth-century origin—for example, machine tools—and have subsequently developed in a much more sophisticated modern form, but most are products of the present century, like the motor vehicle industry, electrical engineering, the aircraft industry, and the radio-electronic group. Most of these newer trades are much better developed in Birmingham than the Black Country, but they are even stronger, relatively, in the towns of the outer girdle of the city-region than they are in the central city. Nevertheless, they are closely dependent on the secondary metal-processing trades of the Black Country, and the sub-assembly industries of the conurbation as a whole. Thus the metal working and engineering complex is still highly integrated vertically; it has lost its primary branch, but has enormously strengthened its assembly stages. The inter-linkages are as close as ever, though differently structured and now much more strongly market-orientated. The car assembly plants alone draw body pressings, forged suspension parts, tubes, zinc fittings, engine castings, machined cylinder blocks, pistons and many hundreds of other components from the metal-working complex. Indeed subcontracting is a much more important activity in the vehicle industry of this region than elsewhere.

This is one obvious reason for the immobility of so much conurbation industry in the West Midlands. Each part of the complex clings tenaciously to the main mass, and so to the conurbation, for to move would mean some sacrifice of access both to customers and suppliers. More than in any other British industrial region there is here close integration in

Table 8.1 The West Midlands: employment trends, 1961-1975
('000s)

	1961	1966	1969	1975	% total (1966)	Location quotient (1966)
Metal manufacture	146	152	144	126	6·4	2·5
Metal goods	213	223	209	185	9·2	3·6
Mechanical engineering	168	184	180	132	7·9	1·3
Electrical engineering	128	127	129	112	5·6	1·4
Motor vehicles	148	169	164	160	7·2	3·2
Aircraft	40	29	22	20	1·0	0·8
All vehicles	221	218	204	203	9·0	2·5
Transport	104	112	102	—	4·5	0·7
Distribution	211	223	206	236	9·1	0·8
Finance	32	38	40	—	1·7	0·6
Professional & scientific	168	214	237	276	10·5	0·9
Miscellaneous services	133	157	151	—	6·7	0·7

Source: Department of Employment.

the locational sense accompanied by disaggregation in the organizational sense. Processes performed by the same firm and in the same factory elsewhere are here performed in separate factories by different firms. The complex as a whole, it may be argued, is indivisible. No longer rooted in local mineral resources, its association with the Black Country coalfield is now incidental and historic. It has been said that the complex could be located anywhere in central England without disadvantage—but only if the system moved as a whole. It cannot be dismantled and dispersed without loss of efficiency. This is the rationale of a continuing concentration of development upon the conurbation and the counter-argument to the attractions of decentralization.

8.3.2 *Intra-regional Contrasts in the Structure of Industry*

There are three different and complementary approaches to the study of the modern industrial structure of the West Midlands and its pattern of sub-regional contrast. Firstly, it is possible to make a traditional structural analysis, using data keyed to the Standard Industrial Classification. This is rather ill-suited to this region, in which the dominant characteristic is the complexity of cross-group linkages—for example, of engineering with vehicles. The S.I.C., in consequence, does not describe the structure of manufacturing in the West Midlands in appropriate terms. Secondly, it is possible to categorize industry in the region into the four successive stages by which materials pass through the dominant metal-working complex, from primary metal production to the final assembly of finished articles; and so to restate the structure of industry in these terms. Thirdly, it is possible to examine the industrial problems of the region from the perspective of the present trends and changes in the major assembly industry to which so much of the rest of the economic structure is keyed, motor vehicle manufacture. Each of these three contrasted approaches has something to contribute to an overview of the industrial position of the region, and each is taken up, briefly, in turn. (A much fuller account of the traditional pattern of sub-regional specialization in the West Midlands, the contrasts between the Black Country, Birmingham and Coventry, can be found in the first edition of this book.)

Only a handful of manufacturing sectors dominate the region, and especially its economic heart, the new West Midland County. In 1971 the vehicle industry alone provided 18 per cent of all employment here, the metal goods group 12 per cent, engineering and electrical work 10 per cent and the miscellaneous metal trades 17.5 per cent—nearly 58 per cent in all. Other industries unrelated to the dominant metal-working complex are quite minor employers: chemicals and the timber-furniture group, for example, each provided only 2 per cent of employment. Clearly the regional dominants are those industries that have generated the highest levels of employment growth in manufacturing, nationally, in the post-war period. But in this region their performance in recent years has been indifferent: none is now a growth industry. Taking 1965 employment as 100, the index values for 1971 were 88 for the metal group, 92 for engineering and 95 for vehicles. The chemical industry held its own with an index of 100, while only the miscellaneous metal group and a few minor manufactures generated any employment growth. Only in the service sector was there significant expansion in the volume of work: professional/scientific and public service grew to index values of 123 and 102 respectively; distribution and transport declined to values of 88 and 97, very much in harmony with national trends. This is scarcely a profile of a dynamic economy, led towards expansion by growth in the manufacturing sector.

The metal-processing complex of linked industries provides an enormous proportion of the county's employment about 58 per cent in 1971. Four major stages can be identified in the metal-working complex: metal production, refining and alloying (now chiefly confined to the non-ferrous group); secondary metal processing and shaping; components and sub-assembly work; and, lastly, assembly industries marketing a final product. Taking the region as a whole (and so including North Staffordshire and East Shropshire), about 1.1 million people are employed in manufacturing, three-quarters of them in the metal-working and engineering groups. Primary iron and steel production accounts for only 2 per cent of the total, and this lies largely outside the Birmingham city-region. Metal-fabricating industries producing components and intermediate products employ about 300,000 workers (about 25 per cent of the total in manufacturing), while the assembly and sub-assembly industries employ at least 420,000 workers (35 per cent of the total). Among the last group, the most important individual trades are motor vehicles (160,000), aircraft (20,000), tool making (65,000), mechanical engineering (132,000), and electrical and electronic manufactures (112,000). Outside the metal-working groups are other industries directly related to the assembly stages within them—for example, the production of tyres and plastics. Indeed there are few major manufactures in the region that are totally unconnected with the dominant metal-fabricating complex, and most of these—such as brewing at Burton, carpets at Kidderminster, shoes at Stafford and Stone, knitwear in East Warwickshire, and the pottery group in North Staffordshire—lie either on or beyond the margins of the Birmingham city-region.

These four stages have a varying distribution across the constituent parts of the urban core of the West Midlands. Traditionally the *Black Country towns* were concerned primarily with the early stages of metal production, processing and fabrication. They retain these, in a modified survival of an old-established system of local specialisms: castings from the Tipton-Bilston area, tubes from West Bromwich, forgings and wrought iron work from the southern Black Country are examples. But to a locally varying degree firms producing complex components and sub-assemblies have also grown up in the Black Country, partly by industrial overspill from Birmingham to available sites near the conurbation core, partly by indigenous growth. For example, Wolverhampton—like Birmingham—had metal-fabricating trades that were not strongly specialized as to process, plant and skill. They thereby had a strong versatility of product. Wolverhampton firms were able to serve new component and sub-assembly industries that looked to the major producers in the vehicle and engineering groups for a market. In this situation, the birth and survival rates of new enterprises were high, and there was both a quick growth of employment and strong progress towards industrial diversity. With its important sub-assembly industries, and its interest in the vehicle trade (once cars, now heavy vehicles), Wolverhampton is the closest to Birmingham, among Black Country towns, in its industrial structure. In the south west of the Black Country, in contrast, the metal-fabricating trades were more specialized in their plant, skills, processes and markets. Less flexible, they were not easily able to diversify their products to serve new outlets. Sub-assembly and component enterprises grew less quickly here, the overall birth rate of new firms and units was lower, and employment growth less strong. In the Dudley district, therefore, a more strongly traditional structure of industry survives. Within Birmingham the inner city is dominated by a very large number of tiny firms largely concerned with rather traditional products and processes, whilst the outer, radial industrial zones are dominated by large units of modern assembly activities. The inner city in its old form was (and in part remains) a zone of almost unparalleled industrial congestion. The typical unit is virtually of workshop size. In part of the old gun and jewellery quarters close to the city centre, there were 923 works in a single kilometre square in 1948. This inner factory zone is today a formless confusion of obsolescent industrial premises aligned along abandoned lines of communication, in an advanced stage of total redevelopment. Already the blade of the bulldozer has sliced away huge areas of the industrial collar. But the tiny firms typical of the zone need—or believe they need—a near-central location and immediate contact with their suppliers, customers and rivals. They are in general reluctant to accept (and possibly cannot afford) a peripheral trading estate type of site. Although the city has built a number of 'flatted factories' to house them close to the centre, many of the small firms compelled to relocate by clearance have seeped away into the surviving factory slums or they have moved a short distance to the very similar urban environment on the nearer fringe of the Black Country. This clustering of so many small firms, providing collectively so large a share of industrial employment in the city and conurbation, is part of the cause of the immobility of employment in the region. It presents also an intractable planning problem.

From the nucleus of the old industrial collar drawn so tightly round the city centre, manufacturing zones radiate outwards along the major lines of communication, becoming fragmentary in the modern suburban fringe. Industry in these radial zones has its own distinctive characteristics. The size of the average unit is much larger; virtually all the city's factories employing over 2,500 workers, and almost all the conurbation's factories employing over 5,000 workers, are to be found in the radial ribbons or their broken suburban extensions. Most of the key assembly and component industries, especially the car plants, and most of the major units outside the metals group, are sited in these zones. The first of them to form—and one quite untypical in its industrial mix—was the belt of chiefly heavy, metal-working industry which follows the Birmingham-Wolverhampton railway and canal across the central Black Country. More modern radial extensions follow the Tame valley northwards to Perry Bar, and eastwards to Castle Bromwich. There, large sites available on low-lying land have attracted a number of very large employers, including the Dunlop Rubber Company. To the south east from central Birmingham along the Warwick canal and the former Great Western main railway, a ribbon of factories extends continuously to Tyseley; it is dominated by heavy metal-working firms and electrical engineering. Further out, this zone extends brokenly into Solihull, where the Rover car plant is the major unit. South from the city, beyond the break in factory development interposed by the Edgbaston-Moseley areas of high-income housing, another radial ribbon extends along the Bristol railway. This has more than its fair share of factories outside the metal group—for example, the Cadbury works at Bournville—but it also has the conurbation's most important single industrial employment complex. This is the British Leyland (B.L.) Motors plant at Longbridge, which is important not only for its sheer size, but also because it is the focus of so many complex chains of subcontracting and component supply.

Put into its regional context, the industrial structure of the *Coventry district* takes the contrasts between Birmingham and the Black Country a stage further in the direction of an increasing emphasis on the assembly stages of the metal-vehicle-engineering complex. In Coventry these stages are completely dominant. In the 1950s, for example, the earlier stages in ferrous and non-ferrous metal working accounted for about 10 per cent of factory employment in the conurbation as a whole, but only about 2 per cent in Coventry;

similarly, miscellaneous metal goods, which provided almost a quarter of the conurbation's factory employment, occupied only 5 per cent of Coventry's industrial labour force. On the other hand, motor vehicle manufacture provided jobs for 43 per cent of Coventry's operatives, but only 15 per cent of the conurbation's, while machine tools (9 per cent), radio and electronic engineering (10 per cent), and aircraft manufacture (10 per cent) were the other distinctive manufactures of the Coventry district.

This appears to be an industrial structure ideally geared to derive maximum advantage from the direction of national growth over the last three decades. But, in fact, the growth of factory employment in Coventry itself has been relatively slow, though some of its near neighbours (such as Leamington, Warwick, Daventry and Nuneaton) have added one-third or more to their total volume of manufacturing jobs since 1945. This is in part a natural enough decentralization within the Coventry sub-system but it also reflects more general restraints upon growth. The car industry has not been a strong growth sector (in employment terms) in the West Midlands for twenty years (see below, p.224). Moreover, Coventry felt the full shock of the crisis in the industry during the period 1973-1975. Both major firms in the area, Chrysler and British Leyland, tottered on the brink of failure: both have reduced their employment there, Chrysler most dramatically by transferring much work to Scotland. At the same time the major machine tool firm, Alfred Herbert, fell into equal difficulty. Like the car firms it was rescued only by massive Treasury support. It is possible that this town, which was for so long a symbol of industrial success, has absorbed more government support over the last few years than any comparable community in the Assisted Areas. These events underline a risk inherent in Coventry's economic character, the dominant position of a few very large employers in highly-competitive industries. The aircraft industry, too, has had some grave problems. In general the smaller towns of the Coventry cluster have had fewer of these difficulties to face. Not only their vehicle industries, but also other branches of manufacturing, are concerned more with components than with final assembly—components firms supply 90 per cent of manufacturing employment in Leamington, and 58 per cent in Warwick—and so they are more flexible in relation to the market, and less prone to its vagaries. On the other hand, so close are the journey-to-work links within the Coventry belt that these town by town contrasts are not very meaningful. Taking the sub-system as a whole, there is considerable diversity outside the dominant industries. Coventry itself manufactures artificial fibres, and the East Midland knitwear zone (see p.192ff.) overlaps into east Warwickshire generally. Rugby is essentially an electrical engineering town, though the merger of the two chief companies there (Associated Electrical Industries and English Electric) with the General Electric Company caused some anxiety as rationalization proceeded.

The *other free-standing communities of the Birmingham city-region* are mostly county and smaller country towns that remained essentially unindustrialized until the 1930s. Partly for this reason, and also because of their strong recent population growth, the service sector is relatively more important to them than it is in the conurbation as a whole. But two active coalfields are included within this outer zone of the city-region—the Cannock and East Warwickshire fields. Extractive employment, therefore, still provides high proportions of male employment in the Cannock-Rugeley-Brownhills and the Nuneaton-Tamworth areas. In the Cannock coalfield the regrouping of the mining industry upon a relatively few units (by 1977 there were only three pits, employing a total of 5,100 men) continues, with a slow run down in labour demands; mining redundancy there, however, generally seems to have been absorbed by the vigorous general industrial growth of the area. This has not been the recent experience of the Warwickshire coalfield, however. Since 1959, the total number of active collieries has declined from twelve to five, over 10,000 jobs in mining have been lost and by 1977 the field employed scarcely more than 4,800 men. A local pocket of quite serious unemployment has been created as a result in the Nuneaton area.

In the outer zone, manufacturing employment (which provides 44 per cent of all the jobs there) is both distinctly less important than in the conurbation (where it provides 65 per cent) and very much more diverse. Locally, there are important food and drink industries (brewing, milling, baking) that derive ultimately from the rural past of such country towns as Uttoxeter and Evesham. Other manufactures that are anomalous to the region are also traditional. Stone and Stafford in the north and Daventry to the south east have important footwear manufactures. Kidderminster has its carpet industry. In general (but with notable exceptions) there has been a relatively feeble development of conurbation types of industry in these towns of the outer ring. Taking the zone as a whole, iron founding accounts for only 6 per cent of the total job supply, miscellaneous metal goods only 10 per cent and vehicles (chiefly their components) 6 per cent. In contrast electrical engineering (dominant at Stafford and Rugby) is the strongest single manufacture with 17 per cent of total employment, and hosiery, carpets, footwear and mechanical engineering each account for some 5 per cent to 7 per cent of employment. These general figures naturally conceal strong local contrasts. Some of the outer towns, for example, are very strongly specialized, often in vulnerable industries. Both Stafford and Rugby are uneasily dependent on decisions made in the General Electric Company-English Electric board room. Other towns, in contrast, have great industrial diversity. Worcester, for example, combines employment in machine tools, foundry work, non-ferrous metals, mining machinery, metal cans, and car components with a range of county town trades and a strong service sector. Lichfield and Stratford have almost equal variety on a smaller scale.

There is another approach to the classification of these towns on the fringe, based less on product than on 'stage'. Some towns show a strong emphasis (within their metal working-engineering-vehicle complex of industries) on the 'early' metal processing or shaping trades, or alternatively on the production of capital goods like engineers' tools. Others have strong component and sub-assembly industries, and a third group is dominated by final assembly. This last group of assembly towns (chiefly Stafford and Rugby, Rugeley and Uttoxeter) assembles equipment, such as heavy electrical machinery and earth-moving vehicles, not strongly represented in the conurbation. Although some of their components are drawn from the conurbation, they also come from dispersed national suppliers and the firms' markets are national or international. Industrial linkages with the conurbation are therefore weak. Other towns have a far stronger development of 'early' process work of a conurbation type. A zone to the north and north east of the conurbation, and relatively close to it, produces forgings, castings, bearings, tools and aluminium shapes. This is essentially industry of the conurbation type. Indeed, much of it has moved out in recent years, to Cannock and Aldridge-Brownhills, and also over the greater distance to Lichfield and Tamworth. Significantly, most of these towns are also receiving population overspill from Birmingham. As a result, genuine dispersal and decentralization of people and work is taking place to areas close enough to the core so that the close links with the total industrial complex that are needed by process firms can be maintained. Similarly, in the south west, metal shaping and machine tool work has dispersed strongly to the Worcester-Bromsgrove-Redditch area, another district taking overspill. The group of towns in the outer zone which have a strong component specialization include Warwick, Leamington and Nuneaton as the clearest cases—although both Bromsgrove and Redditch have also attracted a components industry on a large scale. Where the component stage is dominant, linkages both with the conurbation and especially with Coventry are likely to be close. Indeed, many components firms are of conurbation origin (Wood, 1966).

These contrasts have a clear relevance to the problem of industrial dispersal from the conurbation, the key to a regional-planning strategy. Process firms need immediate contact with the industrial complex. They have grown up in, or moved to, areas on the northern and south western fringes, generally within 19 to 32 kilometres (12 to 20 miles) of Birmingham. But they have shown no taste for more distant sites. Component firms, too, have grown far more strongly within 32 kilometres (20 miles) of Birmingham (or 16 kilometres of Coventry) than outside these ranges. Are these the limits to which conurbation industry is prepared to move? Outside these distance limits, most industry—as much as 90 per cent of employment in Stafford and Rugby—comprises assembly firms not closely associated with the Midland complex.

8.3.3 *Intra-regional Mobility: The Decentralization of Employment*

The dominant feature of the industrial geography of the West Midlands is the extreme cohesiveness and therefore spatial immobility of the metal-based complex of manufactures. Any shift of site that would mean extending a firm's component-supply or market linkages by more than a few miles has been resisted stubbornly, and there seem to be strict distance limits within which most mobile firms are prepared to consider alternative sites. Perhaps this almost exaggerated insistence on remaining part of the industrial concentration is beginning to weaken a little, and there are signs of a quicker decentralization of employment—but still dominantly from the conurbation core to its margins. Table 8.2 summarizes employment shifts within the West Midland County from 1959 to 1973. The main trends are obvious: factory employment has fallen substantially in Birmingham after some growth to 1966, and the fall is accelerating. In Coventry, there was strong growth to 1966 followed by steepening decline; the net effect was a small growth in factory employment over the whole period. The inner Black Country has followed precisely the same trend, though with a small overall loss, while the outer ring of Black Country towns—from Walsall through Wolverhampton to Stourbridge—recorded a small overall increase after very rapid increase in factory work to 1966: they, too, are now losing jobs in this sector. The data suggest some dispersal from the centre to periphery. The overall effect has been to accentuate the weakness of the manufacturing sector in the central city, while producing only marginal gains in the towns of the periphery. This is decentralization by decline at the core rather than by growth at the margins. Yet the out-movement is more impressive judged in terms of the floorspace involved. Up to 1965 about 1.2 million square metres (13 million square feet) had been 'exported' from Birmingham to all destinations. Scarcely a tenth represented a shift from the city to the region beyond the conurbation; about half the remainder sought Assisted Area sites; and the rest was short-range intra-conurbation shifts to Black Country sites. Even this large figure considerably understates the real size of the shift from city to sites

Table 8.2 West Midlands metropolitan county: industrial trends, 1959-1973
('000s employees)

Zone	1959 Factory	1959 Service	1973 Factory	1973 Service	Total change 1959-1973 (1959 = 100)
Birmingham	380	227	309	258	96
Inner Black Country	182	43	178	52	102
Outer Black Country	156	93	157	120	110
Coventry	122	43	126	60	102
County	843	409	770	489	102

Source: West Midlands County Council.

elsewhere in the conurbation, for a large amount of older Black Country floorspace has been converted and extended to receive city firms without passing through the planning machine as a change of use. Many small industrial estates have been created on derelict land, by the development of half-abandoned sites, and on land formerly in transport uses; at least 100 developments of this kind have been completed, and together they represent a substantial loophole in the i.d.c. controls. Yet all this has scarcely done more than hold stable the volume of factory employment available in Black Country towns. The chief growth sector here—especially in the larger towns of the outer ring—has been the strong growth of the service trades. Comprehensive redevelopment projects of some size, like the Mander centre in Wolverhampton, have appeared on such a scale that there must be some question that their success has been at the expense of the service complex of central Birmingham.

It would be wrong to give the impression that the growth of the towns on the periphery of the conurbation (Coventry as well as the Black Country) must inevitably depend on the outwards shift of employment from inner Birmingham. In almost all the larger towns of the outer zone, nine-tenths of the 1963 factory employment was in concerns established before 1947. Intra-regional mobility of employment, therefore, has been marginal in their development. Only in some of the smaller towns has new industry (by no means all from the conurbation) made a real contribution to job growth. For example, new enterprises provide almost half of Cannock's factory employment and four-fifths of that in Aldridge—although the latter is a special case, almost the only really successful example of industrial overspill from the core of the conurbation. Industrial decentralization over greater distances has been much more sluggish, and has made an even more limited contribution to the economic growth of towns beyond the margins of the conurbation. Up to the late 1960s Staffordshire attracted about 12,000 new jobs to planned estates, but almost 8,000 of these went to Aldridge-Brownhills on the conurbation's northern margin, and another 3,000 to Cannock, not far beyond. Lichfield, Stafford, Rugeley, Tamworth and a few smaller places shared less than 2,000 jobs between them, and in these areas most of the new firms were not of conurbation origin.

The more recent growth of the major 'dispersal' developments, Telford and Redditch new towns and the Tamworth expansion project, has certainly involved some movement of firms from the conurbation. But Redditch, which has always been relatively successful in attracting enterprises from the inner areas, is virtually a peripheral enlargement of the conurbation. Telford, in contrast, for long found it difficult to attract mobile firms: its growth closely coincided with the general weakening of the regional economy after 1966. Today, however, many of its major employers are companies with conurbation links or origins—G.K.N.-Sankey and Lucas, for example—but some of these must see Telford as an alternative to an Assisted Area site for their expansion. The new town has a special status in relation to regional policy: it has been the practice of the Department of Industry not to refuse i.d.c. approval, at least for firms prepared to move to the area from sites in the conurbation.

Two general points follow from this brief discussion of industrial mobility in the region. First, firms still cling to the conurbation that is the physical embodiment of the industrial linkage system upon which their life depends; and they need particular inducements to move beyond its margins. Second, the quite serious downturn in the volume of work available both in the inner areas and in the West Midland County as a whole suggests that this is not an economic system of such strength that it can afford to lose employment either by short-range dispersal or though inter-regional transfer to the Assisted Areas. Nor has the growth of service work entirely balanced the decline in manufacturing. Taking 1959 total employment as 100, in Birmingham there was a growth to 110 by 1966 and then a decline to 1973: in the county, a growth to 110 in 1966 was followed by a decline to 102. There is, in other words, some substance in the fears now being expressed in the region concerning traditional inter-regional and intra-regional policies.

The course, causes and some of the social consequences of the decentralization of manufacturing employment from the inner areas of the West Midland conurbation have been the subjects of detailed case studies (Smith *et al.*, 1974; Smith, 1976). In a sample of 180 firms that relocated, the great majority (82 per cent) were in the traditional and dominant metal-working and engineering groups, and three-quarters were small, with less than 100 employees. These enterprises showed a very marked reluctance to move over anything except very short ranges: 35 per cent moved less than a mile and only 18 per cent of moves were of four miles or over. Thus the run-down in inner area manufacturing noted in Table 8.2 in no sense reflects a desire of firms to escape from near-central locations. Most moved because they had no choice: half lost their old premises by redevelopment or compulsory purchase, another 38 per cent found expansion impossible or space too limited. The planning process is clearly a major cause of industrial disturbance. At a local level the fall in the number of inner area enterprises is very serious indeed. In a sample area of inner south east Birmingham, the number of employing units fell by 19 per cent between 1960 and 1974 (but in a redeveloped area the fall was by 41 per cent). In this area 2,400 jobs were lost by death or closure and 410 by movement out. Only 80 jobs were replaced by the birth of new enterprises, though 300 were created by in-movement of firms. More than two-thirds of the industrial work in the area was lost over the period. This is perhaps an extreme case of contraction in a congested Victorian urban environment, but the trend is general throughout the older industrial districts of Birmingham. A city-wide study showed that a total 'stock' of about 2,000 metal-working firms in 1956 had been reduced by 32 per cent by 1967. Net deaths accounted for 23 per cent of the loss, and the remainder reflected transfer to the city fringe or beyond. Persistent and prolonged closure and migration among the mass of relatively small enterprises in the inner city has produced serious overall job losses and unemployment. There is now a steep inner city to suburban fringe unemployment gradient in Birmingham:

male unemployment in 1975 stood at 13.5 per cent in Handsworth and 10 per cent in Small Heath (both areas of ethnic mixture) while in most Black Country manufacturing communities and in the greater part of the suburban zone, rates were in the 3 per cent to 6 per cent range. Persistent unemployment (of over twelve months) was largely localized to the old, declining inner industrial areas.

8.3.4 *The Motor Vehicle Industry of the West Midlands, in its National Setting*

The substantial growth of the British motor vehicle industry, especially after 1945, was for long a symbol of the adaptability of the British manufacturing economy in re-aligning its structure to meet the changed demands of the modern world. It has become, more recently, rather a symbol of the country's economic weakness, an industry in which over-manning, combined with under-investment, have resulted in productivity far below that of its rivals, and in which profitability was so reduced that by 1975 two of the four major firms (British Leyland and Chrysler) were saved from bankruptcy only by massive government help. Certainly motor car manufacture was the corner-stone of the great prosperity of the West Midland region during the post-war quarter-century. About 16 per cent of all employment in the region, and in the conurbation at least a quarter, depends directly or indirectly on this single industry. Perhaps this is the most extreme case of regional industrial specialization in modern Britain. Thus the present crisis in the industry is at the heart of a wave of doubt and anxiety that has broken over the region in the last five years. That the foundations of the region's prosperity were somewhat insecure was demonstrated with quite remarkable clarity by the crises at British Leyland and Chrysler, the two major car assemblers in the region, responsible ultimately for an enormous volume of employment.

Vehicle manufacture was one of the great post-war growth industries, not only prosperous and expanding itself but also capable of generating great volumes of new employment through its multiplier effect upon the subcontracting industry. By 1971 there were, nationally, about 300,000 car workers, and some 500,000 if the industry is defined in a broader sense to include heavy vehicles; there were perhaps 1.3 millions if all employment in components, materials and distribution is added. By British standards it was an efficient industry with a net output per employee distinctly (about 8 per cent) above the national average and an index of labour costs marginally below. National employment increased by 34 per cent between 1959 and 1971. It is, of course, possible to interpret this growth as evidence of weakness, for certainly the industry became more labour-intensive than its foreign rivals. Two recent analyses (Central Policy Review Staff, 1975; West Midlands Metropolitan Council, 1974) quantify some of the industry's failings. Specific labour productivity for many operations is half or less than that of European and Japanese rivals. An index of fixed capital formation shows the car industry to compare poorly with many other manufacturing industries. After higher levels of investment in the late 1960s, the index dropped by 1972 to barely above the 1962 figure. Profitability followed much the same trend.

The industry blames part of its problems on government intervention. As a major consumer goods producer, and one with extensive and intricate linkages, it became a victim of successive applications of the economic regulator, changes in purchase tax and credit restrictions aimed at cooling an 'overheated' national economy. The effect, it is argued, was to cream off profits at their trade cycle peaks and hence the funds needed for investment. It became, too, a prime target for regional policy, which sought to disperse the industry's expansion from its traditional regions of concentration to peripheral sites in the Assisted Areas, so extending its complex web of production linkages and adding to its costs. The extraordinary vulnerability of this intricately structured industry to disruption through industrial unrest is common knowledge. So complex are the production flows, so dependent on continuity in output in both the parent plants and the suppliers, that a stoppage by a few workers can cause progressive plant closures throughout the whole system. Whatever the cause of its recent difficulties, there is no doubt about their scale, or about the competitive weakness of the industry. Car exports fell (in value, at 1970 prices) by 36 per cent between 1970 and 1974; imports rose by 123 per cent to claim 40 per cent of the British market in some months, and have risen since to take 45 per cent of the market in 1977. Car-kit exports held up better, and components exports materially increased in value. Thus the overall trade balance in cars and parts deteriorated (by 22 per cent) yet remained in surplus, overall. At 1974 prices the industry retained a net positive trade balance of £700 million; but components, rather than cars, have made an increasing contribution, despite the world recession in car output. The components industry is virtually as large as the assembly branch. Their net values added in 1974 were £745 million and £635 million, respectively. Together with heavy vehicles, the 'parts' industry is now the strongest sector of the entire manufacturing complex, in the international context.

Broadly speaking, the locational history of the motor vehicle industry has been one of progressive concentration into two dominant regions (the South East and West Midlands) followed by a forced decentralization to Assisted Area sites. Spatial concentration went hand in hand with a progressive dominance of the industry by a few (now only four) very large companies and the emergence of a limited number of plants, and plant complexes, of a very great size. The average plant size is three times that for manufacturing industry as a whole. The infant car industry was regionally scattered, in the form of many small firms producing craftsmen-built cars. Glasgow, West Yorkshire, Manchester, shared this early growth with the West Midlands and London. From the time of World War I, volume production began, internal scale economies increased and a few large firms replaced the many small producers. Even at this early stage, the West Midlands had 53 per cent of car output; but over a quarter of national output came from the first Ford plant (1911) in Manchester's then new Trafford Park industrial estate. Between 1918 and 1939 the industry shifted southwards, to become concentrated in a few successful firms located

Table 8.3 Britain: the balance of trade in cars, 1970 and 1974
(£ million, 1970 prices)

	1970	1974	Change 1970-1974
Car exports	228	145	(−36%)
Car exports C.K.D.*	100	95	(−5%)
Car imports	85	190	(+123%)
Component exports	327	395	(+21%)
Overall trade balance	570	445	(−22%)

*Kits needing final overseas assembly.
Source: Central Policy Review Staff (1975).

entirely in the West Midlands and South East; by 1938 the output shares of these two regions were 60 per cent and 39 per cent respectively. Elsewhere the industry had become vestigial. Many small firms in peripheral locations, struggling on at uneconomic levels of output, were eliminated by bankruptcy during the inter-war depression. Overseas investment became a major force in the industry's growth, and foreign firms invariably chose sites on the London fringe. Ford transferred their plant from Manchester to Dagenham in 1931: General Motors chose Luton and Dunstable for their Vauxhall subsidiary, Citroen and Renault for a time assembled cars in outer London. The pull of the market (centred on the prosperous South East and Midlands) and the prestige of the capital were clearly powerful factors, together with London's innovatory role in new industrial development.

The West Midlands—the major—concentration was somewhat differently based, though it shares access to the major market with London. The growth of the industry in its mass production phase here rested firmly on the foundation of the innumerable component and materials suppliers of the Birmingham-Black Country metal-working complex. Most primary components of the motor car were already in production, or could be easily adapted, by the region's metal trades. Tubes and girders for the chassis, engine castings, crankshaft forgings, body pressings, non-ferrous mouldings were all available: springs, axles, gears, lights and electrical systems were all developed by specialist firms who re-aligned their production towards the needs of the new industry. Oddly enough, what is now the major material by value (about 20-25 per cent), strip-steel, is not a local product. But there was little in the early wood or canvas body, and for today's unitary form of construction the strip-steel comes in from South Wales. The rather different origins of the South Eastern and West Midland car industries express themselves in somewhat different structures. The dominant firms in the former area, especially Ford, sought to be fairly self-contained and integrated (though even Ford now 'buy in' at least a third of the car in component form). In contrast, the West Midland Assemblers have traditionally relied to a much higher degree on the purchase of components and sub-assemblies from the myriad specialist producers of the region. To a degree this system still survives, though B.L. have tended to absorb many of their main suppliers: thus the four main assembly complexes (Longbridge, Solihull and both the Jaguar and Triumph plants in Coventry) are backed by about a dozen components plants within the company. Many hundreds of independent firms contribute their specialist products. So complex a system of materials flows is obviously a hostage to wage-bargaining. Moreover, in this initially craft-based structure of employment, piece-rates were the traditional system of payment. Every change of model or of production techniques caused its crop of disputes as new rates were negotiated.

The motor vehicle industry is obviously complex in its structure and difficult to define and delimit. Broadly, it has three parts: car assembly, components supply, and heavy vehicle (chiefly bus and truck) production. The official definition is that of the Minimum List Heading 381 in the Standard Industrial Classification (a heading which includes 'fringe' products like tractors and caravans, but excludes non-metal components). Both the components and heavy vehicle branches show significant locational differences from the car assembly side. The components industry is itself complex in structure. Some firms in it are subsidiaries of assemblers (S.U. and A.C. Delco, for example). Some of these supply only their parents, but some trade with rivals, too. For example Pressed Steel, the major body producer, built plants to serve many assembly factories (Linwood, for example) in its independent phase: now it continues to supply some rival assemblers, as a B.L. subsidiary. Of some components suppliers it is possible to say that they are positively part of the vehicle industry, in that all their output is absorbed by it. But to other companies the vehicle trade is simply a major—even dominant—but not exclusive customer, as it is for G.K.N.-Sankey (wheels), Pilkington-Triplex (glass), Dunlop (tyres) or Rubery-Owen (general metal work). Some component firms, such as Automotive Products, are industrial conglomerates of great size, owning many subsidiaries. Lucas, for example, employed 57,000 workers as early as 1960 and had seventeen factories in the Birmingham area. They are about as large as Ford. Locationally, the components branch has always been more dispersed than assembly. Certainly, the major concentration has always been—and remains—in the West Midlands. But here it is less confined than assembly to the Birmingham-Coventry zone. Towns on the periphery of the region—Worcester, Warwick-Leamington, Newcastle, Telford and Redditch new towns—have their share of its employment.

Components manufacture has proved to be geographically less stable than assembly. Many firms have responded to the lure of the incentives offered by regional policy and have been attracted to Assisted Area sites, in South Wales and on Merseyside especially: less notably in the North East and Scotland. In short, the multiplier effect of car assembly has not been locationally constrained or confined to the dominant regions; and a significant part of the outflow of mobile jobs from the West Midlands since 1945 has been of car components firms. Thus, the growth of the vehicle industry was in part deflected to the Assisted Areas some time before the more dramatic shift of assembly units in the 1960s. What makes this especially significant is that, in general, the components industry has been more successful commercially and less sensitive to recession than the assembly side. It has become a major exporter in its own right, and suffers a negligible erosion of its home market by imports. Naturally enough there is a feeling in the West Midlands that it has been milked too much and too often of new enterprises in what has become the major growth point in the vehicle industry.

There is another branch of the motor vehicle industry with a somewhat distinct commercial and locational history, the building of commercial vehicles. This has never been to any dominant extent concentrated into the South East and West Midlands, except for light vans and trucks that share components with cars. Historically, many of the major heavy vehicle producers are an outgrowth from steam engineering. Firms like Foden and Leyland began as steam-waggon enterprises, and their sites in South Cheshire and Central Lancashire are in areas with a tradition of steam engineering (which was oddly absent from the West Midlands, though present in London). Certainly heavy vehicle production has had, traditionally, a much wider national distribution than car assembly. Clydeside, Manchester, Bristol, London and some of the towns of the outer metropolitan region have all had a share in it: so have a few West Midland towns (for example Wolverhampton), but on a relatively small scale. Specialist vehicle producers, too, have a nationally dispersed rather than a strongly concentrated pattern of distribution. Tractors and earth-moving and construction machinery are built in Central Scotland, in Manchester and the West Riding, in the East Midlands as well as in the West Midlands and South East.

In all of these sectors of the vehicle industry the West Midlands has a much smaller share than it has of car assembly. This, too, has some significance for the prosperity of the region. Heavy and specialized vehicles have had a history of greater and more consistent commercial success, both in home and export markets, than the car industry has been able to claim. There is little import penetration of the British market in these sectors, and they have a much better record of profitability. The West Midlands' limited (and somewhat dwindling) share in this side of the vehicle industry is a distinct weakness in its industrial balance.

The distribution of vehicle manufacture so far described is that which pre-dated the enforced dispersal of the industry in the mid-1960s. In 1959 the South East and West Midlands (including the Oxford outlier) had 72 per cent of the industry's employment. The pattern of location had remained unchanged for at least a quarter-century. No major new investment had sought a location outside this dominant region, except for some early dispersal of the components industry. All four of the industry's giants (British Leyland, Ford, Vauxhall, Rootes/Chrysler) were almost wholly confined to sites within this zone. All four wished to increase plant capacity on the tide of prosperity of the early 1960s. All four were forced to consider Assisted Area locations after it become clear that i.d.c.s would be refused for their parent locations. Three of the four (all except Chrysler) chose to base major expansion on sites in Merseyside, which thus became within a very few years a major focus of the car assembly industry. The detail of this is reviewed elsewhere (p.281). Expansion into other Assisted Areas was on a smaller scale, more half-hearted, and has generally proved less successful. A new plant was built by Rootes/Chrysler at Linwood, near Glasgow, to employ 7,000. British Leyland built a truck-tractor plant at Bathgate, near Edinburgh. Neither of these has operated consistently at capacity since its completion, and both have had troubled histories of non-profitability, and Linwood has been threatened by closure. Both Ford and British Leyland established plants near Swansea and at Cardiff. This period of de-concentration in the industry dramatically reduced the share of total employment within the traditional regions of dominance: by 1971 the West Midlands and South East had only 58 per cent. But this did not mean any actual reduction in employment there: in the West Midlands there was limited growth; and in the London region an actual decline in the inner zone was counterbalanced by growth in the Outer Metropolitan Area. A significant point for the West Midlands was that the dominant firm, British Leyland, was proportionately the least affected of all the four major companies. Expansion equivalent to about 10,000 jobs was deflected to the Assisted Areas (about 7 per cent of total employment), but almost three-quarters of the company's workforce remained in the West Midlands. Rootes/Chrysler (and therefore Coventry) suffered a greater disturbance: Linwood employs more workers than the major (Stoke) plant in Coventry and represents over a quarter of total company employment.

There has been considerable debate on the question of the effect of these enforced locational changes on the general structure of costs in the industry, and on its overall efficiency and competitiveness. Broadly speaking, relatively short-range shifts to sites within or close to the main mass of the British economic heartland have been accommodated successfully enough: longer-range movement (especially to Central Scotland) has been less successful. There is no doubt that the incentives offered as part of regional policy would not have been sufficient, alone, to persuade the industry to move its growth out of its dominant regions. The full rigour of i.d.c. controls was required. While 58 per cent of mobile vehicle firms reported, in response to an official inquiry, that financial inducements were a major reason for their moves, this compared with two-thirds who reported that i.d.c. controls were causes of their shift in location. Diseconomies of congestion in the areas of origin were also powerful forces in encouraging movement;

limited sites for expansion and high land and floorspace costs were considerations in the location decisions of 56 per cent of the mobile firms in the industry. The period of maximum mobility was also one of intense labour competition and chronic scarcity, especially of skilled labour. Easier labour recruitment in the Assisted Area was a factor in the location decision of three-quarters of the firms that moved.

Offsetting these benefits of a shift in location, away from the traditional regions of concentration, are very substantial transport costs reflecting the enormous extensions of the between-plant linkages. None of the dispersed plants was self-contained. Internal scale economies of mass production worked against the establishment of integrated, self-sufficient units. Thus Ford's Dagenham and Halewood plants exchange engines (from Dagenham) for transmissions, and both rely on Swansea for axles. Speke supplied trimmed bodies for British Leyland plants in Coventry, and received engines. Linwood drew all engines and some gearboxes from Coventry and supplied pressings, axles and suspensions in return. In the restructured Chrysler company, it draws many components from Coventry, but supplies little in return. Linwood's extremely peripheral position relative to the main mass of the industry is emphasized by the fact that it draws 78 per cent of its components from distances greater than 400 kilometres (250 miles). The Scottish plants suffer even more significantly from remoteness in relation to the market, since the great bulk of Linwood's output is sold south of the Border. To market the 75 per cent of Bathgate's output of trucks sold in the southern half of England adds a £40 penalty to delivery charges, in addition to an £18 penalty on sending components from the Midland B.L. plants northwards (pp.390-393).

Ford and Chrysler make great use of British Rail high-speed services (now electrified to Glasgow) in the form of shuttle container-trains acting virtually as extensions of the assembly lines. Cheap and quick though these regular, contract services are, they leave great cost penalties, much heavier on final delivery of vehicles southwards than on components exchanges. How these penalties balance agains the sum of cost savings and government assistance associated with Assisted Area sites it is impossible to deduce. But in Chrysler's case the existence of Linwood was obviously a major cause of its failure (though this arose as much from Linwood's concentration on unsuccessful models as from the facts of site and distance). Ford and Vauxhall have fewer longer-term worries about their investments on Merseyside, and so has B.L. now that its loss-making assembly plant at Speke has closed, leaving only a components plant. The problems on Merseyside (the difficulty of training inexperienced labour and the delicate state of industrial relations) have not been site-specific. In the market context, Merseyside has some advantage. The social penetration of car ownership down the income scale means that the regions of high personal prosperity south of the Trent no longer dominate the market, as they did for so long. Ford's expansion to Halewood reduced overall delivery costs to the total national market.

To examine the vehicle industry of the West Midlands only in the British national context is no longer adequate. Since the entry of the U.K. into the European Economic Community the smallest realistic context is the European one. Clearly the British car industry in general is not strongly competitive in international terms: the 45 per cent penetration of the home market by imports is proof of that. But there is a widening gap between relatively successful firms based outside the West Midlands (Ford particularly, but also Vauxhall) and relatively unsuccessful firms strongly associated with the West Midlands (B.L. and Chrysler). Ford has consistently increased its market share (to about

30 per cent) while Vauxhall has made progress on a smaller scale. Both Ford and Vauxhall have integrated their British output closely with that of their continental plants; they operate truly internationally. B.L. has set itself a target of 27 per cent of the British market (much reduced from past performance), but in 1978 was struggling to retain more than a 20 per cent share. Chrysler was the weak British presence of a stronger European company (but itself the child of an ailing American parent). In late 1978 Chrysler decided to withdraw entirely from Europe and to sell its entire interest (including the British plants) to Peugeot, who later revived the name Talbot for its U.K. operations. This now becomes the largest and one of the strongest European car groups, with plants from Spain to Scotland. In this context the fate of Linwood must be at best uncertain if it continues as a loss maker: its lines of intra-firm linkage have been enormously extended. Thus B.L. is left as the only independent British vehicle firm, isolated from the bulk of the European industry. A rather decrepit bride, it has looked for a bridegroom. Renault, in some ways a natural partner, has shown little interest; but a Honda model is soon to be assembled by B.L.

Whatever the outcome of the many uncertainties that face the vehicle industry in the West Midlands, a number of points are clear. It is too weak within the British context—and too isolated within Europe—for hopes of further growth to be realistic. It will do well to retain present capacity and performance. But this conclusion applies essentially to the assemblers. The components industry is much stronger and more competitive, and is already re-aligning itself towards the broader European industry. The more it does so, the more secure the insurance against a disaster to the assembly firms creating a crisis of unemployment within this most dangerously over-specialized regional industrial structure.

8.4 The Potteries Conurbation

North Staffordshire contains a small industrial conurbation, compact to the point of congestion, with a 1976 population of about 510,000. It is centred on Stoke-on-Trent, prior to the reorganization of 1974 a county borough and itself an amalgam of six formerly separate towns of fierce local loyalty merged in 1907. The conurbation includes the strong, growing and now (since 1974) enlarged borough of Newcastle-under-Lyme, together with the urban areas of Kidsgrove, Biddulph and Alsager now merged into the Newcastle and Stoke county districts. Dormitory growth reaches out strongly from this compact urban mass into the surrounding rural fringe, so that the small country town of Stone to the south, the former mining district of Cheadle to the east and the villages to the west and north all show pronounced signs of suburbanization. Decentralization reflects not only a land shortage in the conurbation made worse by a gross problem of dereliction, but also the environmental unattractiveness of its core.

Thus defined, the conurbation and its suburban outposts constitute a sharply defined labour market area. There is a complex system of labour interchanges between the constituent parts, but only slight movements of workers across its boundaries, the main ones being the journey-to-work links with Stafford and the towns of South Cheshire. Beyond this well-integrated urban complex lies a broader region with a total population of about 750,000. It is linked more tenuously with the Potteries. The local evening paper circulates westwards to Crewe, southwards to Stafford, northwards to Congleton and eastwards to Leek and Uttoxeter. This is also the service area of Hanley as a high-rank central place, and of Radio Stoke.

Whether defined in the narrow context of the conurbation, or the wider context of the city-region, this is an urban complex that straddles both county and regional boundaries. It lies not only on the divide between the Trent and Mersey drainage systems but also on a watershed in terms of social and industrial affiliations. Both Birmingham and Manchester (neither more than an hour's journey away) attract the occasional shopping of Potteries people. The textile tradition of Pennine England reaches strongly to Leek and Congleton—even Newcastle had a cotton mill until the late 1960s—but the chief growth industries of the conurbation have stronger links with the West Midland vehicle and engineering groups. Newcastle is typical of the Midland industrialized market town in its structure of employment, its vigorous growth, its great prosperity and its urban form. The former country borough of Stoke, on the other hand, shows distinctly 'northern' features. It has to face the problems of its Victorian urban landscape, large areas of substandard housing, an overdependence upon a low-wage industry with declining demands for labour, and a failure to attract new sources of employment in the growth sectors of the economy. The boundary between Newcastle and Stoke is a margin of 'grey' Britain.

In its economic fortunes North Staffordshire is anomalous within the West Midlands, the region of which it officially forms a part. Between 1961 and 1971, while the population of the region grew by 7.3 per cent that of the conurbation grew by only 2.2 per cent. While the region attracted a net inward balance of migration, North Staffordshire suffered a net outflow but, while the West Midlands as a whole had a high but declining rate of natural increase, the age-selective migration of young adults from North Staffordshire altered the balance of births and deaths sufficiently to bring the sub-regional rate of natural increase down to little more than a replacement level by the early 1970s. The causes of this unfavourable comparison lie in North Staffordshire's poor economic performance since 1945. During a decade of quite vigorous national economic growth, 1953 to 1963, the sub-region had an increase in employment of only 5.8 per cent compared with a regional rate of 13 per cent; but during the years of depression from 1967 to 1975, the gap narrowed and both experienced stagnation in employment growth. Here, then, is a distinctive industrial sub-region, burdened by an archaic economy, and failing to secure a fair share in the national growth of population, industry and personal prosperity. Yet it has never suffered industrial distress sharply enough to develop a serious problem of unemployment and so to benefit from Assisted Area status. In this respect, too, it is typical of Pennine England. Indeed, part of the growth of North Staffordshire's most dynamic industries has been deflected elsewhere by the operation of the government's location of industry policies.

8.4.1 *The Urban Structure*

The urban structure of the conurbation reflects the underlying regional geology and its associated landscape features with remarkable clarity. The Potteries coalfield fills the trough of a south-pitching syncline, one of the several steep folds in the Carboniferous strata of the south west Pennines. Thus the field is triangular, with an apex to the north and a broad base to the south, the latter defined by a bold scarp in Bunter pebble beds. In the centre of the syncline, the productive measures are concealed beneath marls and sandstones of Upper Coal Measure age. On the east and west, bounding ridges of millstone grit enclose the field, and converge northwards to the fine prow of The Cloud. A system of four parallel valleys is incised across the landscape, following the structures, from N.N.W. to S.S.E., with windswept ridges between them. One such ridge, of the Blackband outcrop, located the early pottery industry and so gave a spine to the evolving urban structure. Along its scarp, there grew the line of the Pottery towns—from Tunstall in the north, through Burslem and Hanley, to Fenton and Longton in the south. They had the Trent and Mersey Canal and main north-south railway to their west, as well as a clay supply in the Etruria Marls. Beneath their foundation, and to the east, were rich resources of longflame coals, coarse clays and iron in the Blackband series. On this scarp, the pottery industry rooted itself permanently, showing little inclination to move downhill to the railway and canal.

Thus there is a marked linearity in the urban framework of the conurbation, and a quite remarkable site stability on the part of its staple manufacture. The Blackband ridge provided the basic raw materials. The bottle-ovens of the potbanks sprouted along its entire length. Pit-heads in their scores threw their spoil banks across it. Row after row of terraced houses climbed across the ridge, competing for space with the marl holes and the shraff-heaps of pottery waste. The evolving town centres fought for space—and against each other for trade and influence—as each of them developed the simple urban equipment of small Victorian industrial communities. Here was the disorder of *laissez-faire* industrialism at its very worst; and most of it survived to the mid-twentieth century to present the planner with almost insoluble problems of urban redesign (Moisley, 1951; Beaver, 1964).

Except for scattered iron working and coal mining, there was little spread of industry either east or west from the line of towns smoking furiously on the ridge. Larger areas of open land survived close to the old towns; the ridge accommodated their inter-war and post-war expansion into both publicly owned and speculatively built housing estates, under the shadow of the general smoke pall that was dissipated only during the 1950s. The most favoured direction of suburban expansion was westwards, both uphill and upwind, to the old market town of Newcastle. Between it and the line of pottery towns the Fowlea valley lies largely open, if semi-derelict, despite the presence of major rail and canal communications. Only small clusters of pottery works sought canalside sites. Yet the largest industrial unit in the Fowlea valley was until 1978 the Shelton steelworks, the last major survivor of the once widespread iron industry. On a 100 hectare (250 acre) site, this plant drew coking coal by conveyor from a nearby colliery, was rebuilt to produce an annual 0.4 million tons of steel by the Kaldo process, but closed in 1978.

Beyond the Fowlea valley and on the higher ground of the Upper Coal Measures, Newcastle stands apart from the pottery towns. Nevertheless, it has not wholly escaped their destiny. There are several working collieries on its outskirts, and a line of brick and tile works follows the Etruria Marl outcrop. Since the 1930s, however, Newcastle has developed its own distinctive manufacturing base, with an accent on industries with some growth potential; car wiring systems, electrical and electronic engineering and bakery products are three examples.

It is a general characteristic of the newer manufactures of North Staffordshire that they have taken up a peripheral location, away from the urban tangle of the six towns. Many are aligned along the much improved north-south A34 trunk road (with motorway access). The Michelin factory in Stoke is not far from the southern margin of the urban mass, while the English Electric and I.C.L. complex at Kidsgrove is at the northern limit. Thus, industrial employment is declining quickly in the core of the conurbation—but it is growing quite strongly on its margins. Population too, is decentralizing but it is doing so less quickly than employment; Stoke lost only 5.3 per cent of its inhabitants between 1951 and 1971 but about 10 per cent of its employment. In this faster dispersal of jobs than people North Staffordshire is unusual among British conurbations.

Until the 1960s, little radical change came to the urban texture of the core of the conurbation, though it was by then enveloped in its suburban spread. However, the changes which are now coming to this well-preserved Victorian townscape, though belated, are sweeping. One of the weaknesses of the former county borough as a regional city has been the rivalry of the five town centres as retail foci, which has long hindered the growth of a totally dominant central business area adequate in stature to perform a major sub-regional role. Hanley has long been the chief retail centre, but as first among near-equals. Happily, policy is triumphing over parochialism, and Hanley is emerging as the dominant focus, with a growing range of multiple businesses and office developments. Commercial expansion is creating strong pressures for physical renewal and the improvement of traffic flows, so that the developer and the bulldozer are at last erasing the confused landscape of tiny houses and workshop industry. Thus this conurbation without a centre is at last acquiring one. A second and even more powerful force in the reshaping of the urban structure is the D-shaped loop road from the M6 to the west and through the heart of the conurbation. Completed in 1977, it gives the Potteries the almost unique distinction of being bisected by a road of almost motorway quality and its influence will clearly be profound.

8.4.2 *The Industrial Structure*

'Pits and pots' have for long been the chief supports of this narrowly based economy, and this simple structure of employment has survived with only slow change. As late as 1966, pottery firms provided one-third of total employment in Stoke-on-Trent and a quarter in the sub-region as a whole; while mining gave work to 15 per cent of the men in the sub-region. Even today (1978) these two traditional industries employ about one-fifth of North Staffordshire's working population, but with a much sharper decline in mining than ceramics. The slow run-down of the old industries has caused little persistent unemployment. Even in the depressed conditions of 1973 the rate was only 4.3 per cent, and by 1976 it had fallen far below the national average to only 2 per cent. The weaknesses in this economy of slow change are covert rather than obvious: it depends too heavily on the manufacturing and primary sectors (together providing some 60 per cent of all employment). The feebly developed service sector is actually declining in employment: it shed 7.2 per cent of its labour force in Stoke-on-Trent (the main concentration) between 1966 and 1973.

The Potteries' coalfield is almost a model of a modern mining industry: this is a rich and profitable field with exemplary man-shift productivity (about 50 cwt compared with a national average of 43). There are some 43 metres (140 feet) of coal in thirty seams, worked to a depth approaching 1,220 metres (4,000 feet). Mining has become concentrated upon the deeper resources of the centre and south of the the syncline, and has retreated from the margins. Of the eight pits at work, one is a post-1945 sinking and several others have been largely reconstructed; some stow waste underground and so are better neighbours within the urban mass than any pits elsewhere. Despite the closure of uneconomic pits, output has been well maintained with a slow decline from 6 million tons in 1945 to 5 million in 1978. Rising productivity has reduced labour demand progressively and quickly from 24,000 in 1957 to 8,000 in 1978. The chief market has shifted from the local pottery and steel industries to power generation in the line of generating stations along the upper Trent. Given the greater national stability of the coal-mining industry over the last decade, the future of this efficient field seems secure, but clearly levels of employment will depend largely on the place of coal in the future national energy budget.

Although it is convenient to refer to the 'pottery' manufacture, in fact this is not one industry but several, with varying records and prospects. Firms in the tableware section tend to specialize either upon earthenware or china, the latter being concentrated in the south, especially at Longton. The electrical ceramics and the sanitary ware industries are separate branches, and there is also a once large but now declining brick and tile industry. Ancillary trades include the milling of clay, flints and bones, and the prepartion of glazing materials, dyes and transfers. The common characteristic of all these branches is their declining demand for labour, though at varying rates; the tile industry, for example, has shrunk quickly following the development of other and cheaper roofing and flooring materials. This is one of the common problems of this group of industries, that their products are open to competition from other types of material (especially plastics) that lend themselves better to cheaper mass production.

Perhaps the most distinctive feature of the pottery industries is their small average unit-size. The typical potbank is small and compact; about one-third employ fewer than 100 operatives, and almost 90 per cent have fewer than 500. Until recently, most firms were in family management, and their return on capital employed was low—one reason for their locational immobility. Like the Lancashire cotton firms of a generation ago, the potbanks recruit a highly-skilled workforce from their immediate locality, and there is often a strong family connection with a particular firm. Labour supply, too, is a constraint on movement. The few firms that have moved away from the line of towns along the Blackband ridge are mostly large units in the tile and sanitary ware sections. Wedgwoods are the exception among the producers of fine pottery, having moved to a rural site; its Barlaston factory to the south of the conurbation is, however, linked to the core by rail and has its own station.

Two great changes, neither locational, have come to the industry in recent years. It has almost entirely abandoned both coal firing, and the bottle kiln, in favour of continuous firing using gas, oil or electricity. As part of this change many potbanks have been rebuilt but almost always on their old sites. If the industry were ever going to shift from its traditional pattern of sites, it would have done so during the last twenty years. Yet its general location in 1978 is much the same as it was in 1878, or even, indeed, in 1778. Secondly, the old pattern of small, independent firms in family ownership has broken down quickly as a number of large firms have secured control of a large part of the industry. The process is closely akin to the reconstruction of the Lancashire textile industry. By the 1960s twenty substantial firms had absorbed 80 per cent of the tableware production: merger among these has continued so that by 1976 two dominant companies, Wedgwood and Doulton, account for 70 per cent of tableware output. Their components continue to trade under their old names and the average size of plant remains small. In a trade so dependent on craft skill and creativity, there is no necessary virtue in great unit size, except in the contexts of finance and marketing.

Rationalization has come slowly but remarkably successfully to the pottery industries. Despite their somewhat Victorian image, perhaps they have something to teach more modern manufactures. The labour force has shrunk gradually, but both output and exports have expanded vigorously. Overseas sales are running at about £120 million annually, and imports are negligible. The index of output by volume rose from 100 in 1951 to 160 by 1973: over broadly the same period employment fell by about 35 per cent. In 1976 the ceramics and brick and tile group gave work to almost 50,000 people, and it remains the largest single employer. Most of the loss has been in female employment: in the 1950s women outnumbered men in the industry by two to one, but by 1975 the ratio had fallen to parity. There is little alternative work for women outside the shrinking service sector, and in a low-wage sub-regional economy the income of wives is important not only to the family, but also in terms of its influence upon the sub-region's purchasing power.

There is nothing very surprising in the slow decline of the labour force in a technically conservative craft industry of Victorian growth. A more serious cause for concern is the inadequate development of replacement employment, which has expanded far more slowly in Stoke than the region as a whole. The growth industries in the national context are also the growth sector of North Staffordshire's economy, but their progress in the region has been uneven and uncertain. The electrical and engineering group grew faster in the sub-region between 1953 and the late 1960s than in the West Midlands or the nation—but from a trivial size. Paper and printing and miscellaneous manufacturing also have a good employment growth record, but the vehicle industry actually declined in the sub-region. Perhaps the weakest aspect of the recent economic performance of the Potteries has been the feeble growth of its service industries. Here is the clearest possible demonstration of the lack of a truly dominant focus, able to attract massive retail investment and capable of challenging the distant influence of Manchester and Birmingham. In sum, the growth of 'replacement' employment has scarcely balanced the decline in the older staples, so that the total volume of work available in the sub-region has become stagnant: indeed between 1962 and 1966 it declined by about 1,200 jobs. This is an East Lancashire type of situation in which slow structural change, associated with the replacement of old industries by new, takes place in the context of an overall loss in the total of work available, but it occurs without serious unemployment and is corrected by out-migration and falling activity rates.

The influence of the distribution of industry legislation upon North Staffordshire has been entirely negative. World War II brought the first major progress towards a more diversified economy in the region. Potteries were closed to free labour and new factories were built, later to be converted to more peaceful purposes. Established industries outside the traditional groups—for example, tyre manufacture, which dates from 1926—grew strongly during the war and immediate post-war periods. Some of these growth units are very large, and in trades with a great potential: Michelin employs 9,000, and the Rist car-wiring plant in Newcastle some 4,000. But the impetus towards diversification seems to have been lost. Within the area this is blamed on the effect of regional policies and especially the government's reluctance to approve i.d.c. applications by mobile industry for sites in North Staffordshire. There is some evidence that the vehicle industry has been actively discouraged from considering expansion in the area, and certainly the great bulk of certificates actually approved have been from firms in the traditional pottery and metal trades. On the other hand, the real effect of policy has undoubtedly been indirect rather than overt. Whilst few mobile firms have actually been prevented from entering the region by a direct refusal of an i.d.c., many have been deflected elsewhere by the Assisted Area 'package' of incentives and the known reluctance of the government to grant certificates in the sub-region.

Certainly North Staffordshire has lost part of the growth of its established 'alternative' manufactures to sites elsewhere. Michelin's recent growth has been largely in Lancashire and Ulster. The making of an advanced range of computers was transferred from Kidsgrove to a new factory at Winsford, the nearest point to the parent plant at which Assisted Area incentives were available. For all these reasons, Stoke made a powerfully argued plea to the Hunt Committee to be considered one of the Intermediate Areas, entitled to some Treasury support in modernizing both its economic structure and its urban environment. Except for greater financial help in dealing with its derelict land, the plea went unheard, even with the extension of Intermediate Areas in 1972.

What, then, are the prospects of the sub-region? In one sense they are superb. There is no locality in Britain of greater centrality or developing accessibility. London is less than two hours from Stoke by electric train, Manchester and Birmingham one. The M6 now joins the M1 via the Midland link and both the M62 and M56 motorways; this brings the whole of England from London to Carlisle and from Bristol to Leeds and Tyneside within an easy day's return journey by delivery truck from Stoke. Why then does mobile industry show so little interest in the sub-region? There are, of course, enormous local problems of environmental rehabilitation. Stoke has a greater area of derelict land than any other area of similar size in the country—almost 700 hectares (1,700 acres) or 8 per cent of the city's area. There is as a result a shortage of industrial sites, at least for large units and in the core of the conurbation. There are the accompanying problems of substandard housing and the total 'environmental image' of a Victorian industrial city in which so much of the social capital is decayed and depreciated. About 40 per cent of all the houses in the city date from before 1914. The greater part of the conurbation is liable to mining subsidence—although this is limited by underground waste stowage. But perhaps the greatest obstacle to progress is the absence of any major development proposals in the sub-region.

On many occasions since 1945 a site at Swynnerton, south of the conurbation, has been proposed for new town growth. This is an area of wooded Bunter scarps of high amenity value surrounded by good farmland. There was also a wartime ordnance factory close by, and an M6 interchange is only two miles away. The site has been rejected—doubtless correctly—but the sub-region needs some such project to spearhead its economic growth. Stone has been proposed as a new town site. Stoke itself offered to absorb an overspill population of 50,000; it is not clear, however, where the land could be found. Yet there remain no firm plans for any major growth in or near the conurbation. In the regional planning context, the Potteries conurbation occupies a vacuum, too far from both Manchester or Birmingham to attract growth from either. There are few areas in Britain where such a great development potential is so neglected.

8.5 Industrial East Shropshire and the Telford Growth Point

Set within one of the last of the predominantly rural English counties, 48 kilometres (30 miles) north west of Birmingham, lies the tiny Coalbrookdale coalfield, the focus of a compact industrial region that has many of the characteristics of a Black Country in miniature. It suffers all the latter's environmental problems of surface devastation, but it also shares its industrial vitality and adaptability. Even before its designation as a new town, over the period 1953 to 1964 employment in the area grew by 24 per cent, more than twice the national rate of increase. This outlier of industrial development has often had, in the past, a significance far beyond its modest size. Here, in 1709, the first coke-iron was successfully smelted and by 1780 the area was producing no less than 40 per cent of the entire national output of pig iron. Like East Lancashire, it was a district of remarkable fertility in technical innovation in the eighteenth century: the first cast-iron bridge spanned the Severn by 1779, and what was probably the first successful locomotive came from the Darby works in 1802. The region paid the inevitable price for such vigorous industrial development in the palaeotechnic phase. Coal, clay, ganister, ironstone and road metal were won from it by shallow shaft and open pit workings. Spoil and slag heaps were littered over its surface, and abandoned mines and ironworks were scattered along the ruins of a complex canal system. It was, in part, the extent of this industrial devastation that led to the suggestion that East Shropshire might absorb some of Birmingham's overspill.

Here was a district beyond the West Midlands green belt in which a new town could be built with the minimum loss of farmland of any quality, and with the added advantage that its development would restore a tortured landscape. Thus Dawley new town was designated in 1963. Forty-one per cent of its area of 3,700 hectares (9,168 acres) was affected by past or present mineral working. In its first conception Dawley was to be a middle-sized new town, initially to absorb some 55,000 newcomers, and so reach a population of 90,000 by the mid-1980s, but in 1968 this development programme was augmented to one of new city scale. The designated area was more than doubled to include the towns of Wellington and Oakengates. Dawley as a result became Telford; its initial population was 78,000 and to this about 145,000 overspill migrants will be added to produce a total community, with natural increase, of the order of 250,000. Telford was thus the first of the new city projects to make physical progress. It also represents the first time that an entire industrial region has been scheduled for comprehensive redevelopment under a single authority. In the development of the new town the industrial past is well respected. Close to the wooded slopes of the Severn valley an outdoor industrial museum has been created to preserve a permanent record of the importance of East Shropshire in British industrial history.

The industrial structure of East Shropshire was always directly based on the local mineral resources. The coalfield itself is at the end-stage of exploitation. The shallower seams of the dissected west and south have long been abandoned for large-scale working, as have the bedded ironstones that once supplied the local blast-furnaces. But a considerable volume of open cast working, for both coal and the associated fireclays, survives in the shallow part of the field towards the slopes of the Wrekin. As urban development progresses, surface mineral working has declined, but it remains a problem. At present (1978) a 53 hectare (130 acre) site is being worked for 400,000 tons of coal, but its subsequent restoration will be planned for a major housing development. Underground mining sets fewer constraints on development. The location of collieries is at the last stage in a 'down-the-dip' eastward progression, and large modern pits have penetrated the upper coal measures to reach undisturbed seams below. There were two such pits at work until 1967; the single survivor, Granville colliery, is thought to have an assured future and a development potential of 1 million tons per year at competitive costs. Thus, there remain possible problems of conflict between active (and especially surface) mineral working and the progress of the new city, quite apart from the costs and technical difficulties of handling urban and industrial development in an abandoned mining landscape.

Metal working in East Shropshire has gone through much the same process of evolution as in the Black Country. Smelting has been dead here since the 1930s, and some of the heavier traditional branches, such as constructional steelwork and heavy castings, have tended to decline. The main growth sector within the metal-working group is the production of light, specialized forge and foundry components for the vehicle industry and the domestic equipment market. The influence of the West Midland car assembly industry is seen most clearly in a large plant near Wellington—the sub-region's biggest unit, employing over 6,000 workers—which produces car wheels and other steel pressings. The largest of the ironfounding firms in the area now slants its production towards domestic heating and plumbing equipment, and so is geared to the fluctuating demands of the national housebuilding industry. Through these changes in product emphasis the metal-working trades of East Shropshire are quickly increasing their labour demands, and their growth since 1952 has been at much above the West Midland regional rate. The other major growth industry in the sub-regional economy is the engineering and electrical group. This was feebly developed until 1939, but has subsequently made rapid progress. Indeed, or.e of the strengths of the area's economy since 1945 has been the high birth rate of young engineering firms, supplemented by some movement from the West Midland conurbation; most of these firms have prospered. There is a great variety of product in this sector, but the strongest single element is clearly the production of both mechanical and electrical components for the West Midland assembly industries, and especially for vehicle manufacture, a link strengthened by the movement of firms from the conurbation. At the time of its designation as a major growth point the East Shropshire economy had a strength that belied its then drab, semi-derelict appearance. Excluding the service sector (the area's chief weakness), employment had grown by 38 per cent between 1952 and 1966, compared with a West Midland regional increase of only 8.5 per cent. All the major metal-based manufacturing groups were expanding quickly, metal manufacture by 46 per cent, vehicles by 75 per cent and engineering by 68 per cent over the period. Most of the firms in these sectors are concerned with components and sub-assembly, and have shown adaptability and flexibility in relation to their markets.

There are, however, weaknesses that may perhaps pose serious problems as the new city grows. The service sector is very feebly developed as one would expect in a coalfield without a high-ranking town but under the commercial shadow of both a strong county town, Shrewsbury, and the more distant cities of the conurbation. Though the new city centre has begun to grow, it is still skeletal, and has done little to create new service employment. Scarcely 30 per cent of total employment is provided by service activities and their growth since 1945 has been slow compared with the vigorous expansion of the key manufactures. An associated weakness is the lack of adequate employment opportunities for women. The female activity rate has always been far below the national and regional averages, not only because of the limited number of service jobs but also because there was little use of female labour in the traditional metal-working and metal-using industries. The presence of this pool of unused female labour, only 32 kilometres (20 miles) from the conurbation became a factor in the growth of industry in the sub-region during the period of general labour scarcity in the 1960s. Both clothing firms and new units in the electrical and engineering trades came into the area partly as a response to labour availability, and female employment in manufacturing rose rapidly in consequence. A last problem that faced the East Shropshire economy as it was on the eve of major urban development lay in its undue dependence on a few very large employers. The largest unit employed 6,000 (a third of the total industrial labour force in the late 1960s) and a major defence establishment was almost as large. In an age of industrial rationalization there are risks in an economy dominated by a few giants.

In brief, therefore, the industrial base from which a very large new urban development was to grow was a successful one, which had been able to expand both by indigenous growth and some in-movement of firms. The task of expanding the employment base in phase with the build-up of population was a formidable one—there was a need for 15,000 new factory jobs to be created between 1969 and the early 1980s—but by no means unattainable set against the trends of the recent past. Yet the new city made a most disappointing start in its planned industrial expansion. By 1969 it had succeeded in attracting only 477 jobs in twenty-eight new factories: in contrast, Skelmersdale new town in Lancashire (roughly a contemporary) had secured 4,700 jobs in forty factories. The reasons for Telford's early failure are clear enough. As a major development project it was almost uniquely disadvantaged in that it has neither the attractions of a location firmly within the English megalopolis nor the stimulus of Assisted Area status. On the former count it competed unsuccessfully against the London new towns and the new city projects in the South East. On the latter count Telford was at a great disadvantage in attracting mobile industry compared with North Western development schemes near the M6 motorway and with 'assisted' status, like Runcorn, Skelmersdale and Winsford. More locally, Redditch new town was growing on the outskirts of the West Midland conurbation, within the range of movement that was acceptable to decentralizing industry. All the primary factors were loaded against Telford: its industrial growth began at a time when the Assisted Area 'package' of incentives was very powerful, when i.d.c. control was being applied rigorously and on the eve of the general world recession which so reduced industrial investment and the mobility of firms.

Paradoxically, Telford has had far greater success in attracting new factory development during the depressed years of the 1970s than during the earlier period of its growth. Population growth was not seriously reduced by the early difficulty in expanding the employment base. By 1975, 6,600 new houses had been built and between 1971 and 1976 population grew by about 12,000 to a 'designated area' total of 97,000. The housing programme out-ran industrial expansion, and there was both unemployment and long-distance commuting to the towns of the conurbation. But by the mid-1970s employment growth was much quicker. In 1976 there were about 260 new factories in operation (and another sixty units completed in advance of need) providing some 5,000 new jobs. With a population increasing by 4 per cent per annum this new momentum in employment growth must be sustained. The reasons for quicker industrial expansion are elusive. Increasing disturbance by redevelopment (pp.223-224) has brought some firms in from the inner conurbation; some progress with the M54 motorway to the M6 has begun to reduce the problem of access and remoteness from the conurbation; i.d.c. policy for Telford has been much less restrictive. Foundry firms have come to Telford from the Black Country, a Kidderminster carpet firm has expanded to the town, and national firms with strong West Midland interests (Ever Ready, Lucas) have established plants. Some of the growth has had an indigenous origin: G.K.N.-Sankey have expanded, and their latest major development is an aluminium refinery.

Telford's future remains one of the enigmas in West Midland regional planning strategy. Seen simple as a reception area for the housing of Birmingham-Black Country overspill, it would be difficult, now, to justify a project of such size. The overspill need has been much reduced by recent population trends (p.224): indeed neither Telford's in-coming population nor its new industry have been recruited entirely from West Midland sources. Placed in a broader context, as a major growth point able to absorb part of the general increase of both regional and national population, Telford remains a relatively remote site competing against more accessible rivals for a diminishing increment in population growth. Of course, for a decade, at least, new family formation will be little affected by declining natural increase and housing demand will remain substantial. The longer-term future is much more doubtful. Already there has been a revision and rephasing of Telford's planned growth, but without change in the ultimate target. Looking towards the end of the century, Telford must be seen less as an overspill appendage of the West Midland conurbation, or as an outlier of its closely integrated industrial system, than as an autonomous development able to expand from its own varied and successful economic base. Increasingly, the Telford project is an exercise in sub-regional development, in which a devastated landscape is repaired, restored and redesigned to accommodate a growing population on an interesting site, within a superb setting that has much to offer in terms of the general quality of life.

8.6 Central Wales

Central Wales (broadly the two new counties of Powys and Dyfed) has strengthening associations with the West Midlands, partly as a supplier of water (from the Elan valley reservoirs to Birmingham), but also, increasingly, as the nearest and most accessible upland recreational region to a city-dwelling population of over 4 million. But in moving from a study of the West Midlands to a brief and selective appraisal of some of the problems of mid-Wales we are turning to an area virtually unique in Britain, in that the shaping of regional policy must be related to a distinctive cultural and even political background. The cultural heartland of Wales extends from Snowdonia to the Brecon Beacons and from the upper Severn to the sea. Within these limits a Welsh-speaking society—still sustained largely by a simple pastoral agriculture but increasingly reinforced by tourism—struggles for survival not only against the slow erosion of its linguistic identity, but also against the handicap of an insecure economic base. In general, the proportion of the population that can (and habitually does) speak Welsh rises from east to west, from about 10 per cent in parts of eastern Powys to over 90 per cent in a considerable area of northern Dyfed. The coastal slope, west of the unsettled summit plateaux of the Cambrian mountains, has become the chief redoubt of a living Welsh culture. Unhappily there is a fairly strong correlation between the proportion of Welsh speakers and the rate of rural population decline by migration. The areas that are linguistically the most Welsh are also among the districts of steepest rural population decrease; but these are merely the most critical local examples of a more general problem. For generations population has streamed from Central Wales and the social consequences of migration—the loss of the young, the able and the best qualified—are sharpened by the emotional issues involved (Jones, 1976). Since 1901 the three old counties of Cardigan, Radnor and Montgomery have been losing population at a rate of roughly 4,000 per decade (about 0.5 per cent yearly); but there is some evidence that the rate of loss is slowing for the three counties together recorded a 1.7 per cent increase from 1961 to 1971. Cardiganshire, indeed, has recorded consistent growth since the middle of the 1950s, although this is largely confined to the resort and university town of Aberystwyth and its locality. In the old Radnor population decline has slowed but Montgomery continues to lose by migration at undiminished speed. In these latter two areas population growth is largely confined to small towns in the east, that is, in the least Welsh parts.

Few regional economies in Britain still depend so largely upon farming as this one. Over most of Powys about a third of the working population gets a living directly from agriculture, and chiefly from farms that combine small average size with unintensive types of enterprises, such as extensive sheep and cattle rearing on land of low carrying capacity. Average farm incomes are very low: many farmers take less than a rural labourer's wage from their holdings. Underemployment is common, for over large parts of the area 60 per cent of farms require fewer than 275 man-days of labour annually. Amalgamation of these small holdings continues rapidly: about 20 per cent of Radnorshire farms of less than 40 hectares (100 acres) disappeared between 1957 and 1967. On the coastal slope south of Aberystwyth, and in the Severn valley of Powys more intensive dairying has provided a greater security to farmers, but has not arrested population decline. On the higher ground encircling the upland core of the Cambrian mountains—especially above 260 metres (800 feet)—forestry has partly replaced farming. About 46,000 hectares (114,000 acres) of forest land now exist, not only under Forestry Commission control but also in the hands of private groups who have shown a growing interest in commercial forestry here. However, about 24,000 hectares (60,000 acres) of bleak moorland are too high (over 500 metres) ever to be planted successfully.

In essence, policies to arrest the flow of Welsh speakers from the region take three forms: the attraction of industry to the small towns, the development of recreation and tourism, and planned urban growth on a small scale. A Mid-Wales Industrial Development Association was formed in 1957. Though it has had modest success in attracting twenty-three new enterprises to the area, the most industrialized of the three old counties (Montgomery) had only 10 per cent of its total employment in manufacturing. The Welsh Tourist Board has analysed the character of tourism throughout the area with results that are not altogether encouraging. The Dyfed coast dominates the holiday industry of the region and here (despite the presence of the 'classical' resort of Aberystwyth) half the accommodation is in the form of holiday caravans. This is the type of tourism that generates the lowest cash input into the local economy, while causing serious planning and amenity problems along a fine stretch of coast. Powys's tourist industries are of trivial size, and indeed are seriously underdeveloped in relation to their considerable recreational resources, especially for open-country pursuits. It is perhaps the inevitable destiny of the greater part of mid-Wales to attract relatively low-spending types of visitor (the day tripper, the camper, the climber, the caravaner) rather than the high-spending, long-staying residential visitor who generates much greater levels of service employment and injects a far greater cash flow into the economy. Pressure to create a national park in the Cambrian mountains is unlikely to result in a greater inflow of high-spending tourists.

The most imaginative and radical proposal to arrest population decline in Central Wales is that for the creation of a new town in the upper Severn valley. In its earliest form, this would have taken the shape of a linear new town, centred on Caersws and extending down-valley to Newtown and up-valley to Llanidloes. The principle was to attract both population and industrial overspill from the West Midlands: an ultimate population of 70,000 was envisaged. This was a controversial proposal of doubtful viability: to import Midland overspill seemed a curious way to prop up Welsh culture, while a ribbon town threading its way along a valley of great beauty is not the most obvious stimulus to tourism. In fact the original proposals were replaced by a much more modest scheme to expand Newtown, the most accessible of the three towns, from its 1971 population of 5,500 to 11,000. Even this modest growth has the benefit of new town status, under the Mid Wales Development Corporation.

Given that the project was launched, in 1969, into the chill winds of national depression, progress has been encouraging. Population grew by 30 per cent over the seven years from 1970 and stood at 7,300 by 1977; about 750 new houses were occupied by 1977. Almost a quarter of the new families are from mid-Wales, and half are Welsh. Since 37 per cent of the new population is under 15 years of age the demographic momentum is likely to be sustained into the 1980s, by household formation among the newcomers. But the natural increase will stay only if jobs can be created to absorb them into employment. After a slow start, industrial development has made quick progess in three small factory estates. By 1976, thirty-two units were occupied by a wide variety of firms making records, gears, aircraft components and steel products. Many of the firms have West Midland connections, and clearly the Assisted Area status has helped to bring them in. The success of the project, at a difficult time, is undeniable. Whether it will secure its ultimate objectives—to stabilize population and reverse migration, and so to underpin a living Welsh culture—cannot be predicted.

8.7 The West Midlands: A Strategy for Regional Development

The nub of the regional planning problem in the West Midlands is very simply stated (though difficult almost to the point of impossibility to solve) and can be put in two questions. First, is it correct to assume that the employment, migration, population, natural increase and new family formation trends of the 1970s—all of which show very marked decreases from the 1960s—will be prolonged into the 1980s and beyond, so that they form a reasonably firm basis for the extrapolation of housing demand to the end of the century? On the solution to this puzzle depends any attempt to estimate the need for housing site supply in the region as a whole and, most critically, in its central conurbation. Second, how far can, or should, the Birmingham-Black Country conurbation contain its own growth of population by supplying sites to meet its own future housing demand? Ought it to be permitted to enlarge itself peripherally into its own green belt (see Figure 8.2), and if so where and to what extent? Is it good planning policy to scrape together scattered sites for housing and industrial growth, in a piecemeal fashion, within this rather open textured conurbation, thus reducing the overspill need at the cost of accepting a denser, more compact urban structure? This is an old controversy, in which the problems and the costs of 'congestion' must be balanced against the benefits and economies of concentration, and the environmental attractions of decentralization set against the industrial, infrastructural and social costs involved in dispersal. Together, these issues raise the fundamental but unanswerable question: is this conurbation of about 2.5 million people already too large for its own efficiency and for the quality of life of its inhabitants? There is in the West Midlands a stronger case to be made than in most other instances for accepting some further areal extension, coupled with interior infilling, of the conurbation, and so for a substantial increase in its population. Certainly the case for dispersal cannot rest on the assertion that the need to contain the conurbation within its present physical limits is a self-evident truth.

The case for permitting some further growth of the conurbation can be briefly stated. Through an accident of its nineteenth-century industrial history, much of the conurbation is a mosaic of dense urban development encircling the town and the village centres of the Black Country, interrupted by considerable areas of open but industrially damaged land. The urban fringe is jagged, an alternation of urban and rural salients. The strong suburban development of Birmingham in the two great extensions towards Sutton Coldfield and Solihull has left semi-rural wedges to either side, which bring a quasi-countryside, pock-marked by suburban development, to within 11 kilometres (7 miles) of central Birmingham. The eccentric location of the central city also means that large areas of open land lie within 16 kilometres (10 miles) of the commercial core. Within this indistinctly defined urban mass, there still remains a huge area of derelict land awaiting treatment and some form of use. In 1945 there were 3,660 hectares (9,044 acres) within the conurbation and other large areas on its margin; over half has been reclaimed, but over 1,660 hectares (4,100 acres) survive.

There is constant addition to the total of derelict land (recently at a rate exceeding the progress of restoration) so that during the mid-1970s some 5 square kilometres of 'new' derelict land was being created annually within the West Midlands, most of it in or near the major conurbation. Here is a land bank, still with a substantial balance, which in the last twenty years has materially improved the site supply both for housing and industry. Most of the 120 small industrial estates that exist within the conurbation have been developed on derelict or abandoned sites. In sum, the conurbation is not yet at the end of its land supply, and there seems no overriding reason to fossilize its present somewhat chaotic urban structure by imposing rigorous constraints on some further physical growth. To these factors must be added the reluctance of industry to decentralize—the risk that firms may be steered into a Development Area if they become mobile by expansion or a change in site—and the quick build-up of service employment dominantly in central Birmingham. Employment, therefore, is immobile in location, but not, in the manufacturing sector, strongly centralized. The fragmented pattern of Black Country industrial location and the growth of the radial ribbons in Birmingham bring homes and work places close together, so that journey-to-work distances are low, at least by the standards of Greater London and the South East. Since 1974 the entire conurbation (generously defined and including the Coventry area) has been put under unitary control for purposes of large-scale planning as the West Midland County of 2,780,000 people. An early task of the new county has been to examine housing needs against site supply, and all the present signs suggest that it will be found possible to accommodate a much higher proportion of a slackening growth in housing demand within the new county boundary than was thought possible within the conurbation under divided administration.

8.7.1 *Housing Needs*

Although the need to impose strong and close restraints on the further spatial growth of the Birmingham-Black Country urban mass is, to say the least, much less obvious than it is in the London case, there can be no doubt that a measure of dispersal is inevitable. This has gone through a radical (but as yet incomplete) process of reappraisal over the last five years. In the mid-1960s some very large estimates of the growth of regional population were being calculated and translated into terms of future housing demand. Given a neutral migration factor the region's population was expected to rise by 778,000 over the 1964-1981 period, and net migration inwards might increase this to about 880,000. Over the longer term a growth of population of about 1.5 million was postulated for the period 1981 to 2001. Very approximately, therefore, the forward estimate of total regional population was in the range 5.6 million to 5.7 million in 1981 and 7.2 million by 2001. It was against these projections of probable population increase (now seen to be gross exaggerations) that a broad regional planning strategy began to be worked out early in the 1970s. Almost at once all these projections of future population growth and housing need were overtaken by major demographic changes. Birth rate fell from 19/000 in the mid-1960s to 13/000 in the mid-1970s: by 1976 the annual rate of natural increase was down to a little over 2/000 and falling quickly. There had been a net migratory loss (of about 8,000 per annum) during the late 1960s. Even the new family formation rate had fallen from a peak 17/000 in 1972 to about 15/000 in 1975. Revised population projections now suggest a regional total of only 5.15 million in 1981 and 5.25 million in 1991. The enormous population surge for which planning provision was being discussed in the early 1970s now seems most unlikely to occur.

While these large population increases were being envisaged it was anticipated that about half the total increment would be generated by the conurbation. Clearly it could scarcely contain the whole of the projected increase even to 1981 (which might have added 400,000 to its population), still less the later growth to the end of the century. There was thus a lively debate in the 1960s, backed by much elaborate analysis, on the questions whether the conurbation could absorb any substantial part of its own population increase, and if so how much; and whether any necessary dispersal should be over short ranges or long. With the wisdom of hindsight, much of this discussion has proved somewhat abortive, but it remains relevant as a background to the planning strategy that evolved and has now begun to take a physical shape in the process of urban development in the region. Indeed some of the terms in the housing-demand equation retain a real relevance, especially the extent of housing substandardness and the likely rate of new household formation.

Housing need, as it was estimated in the mid-1960s, is quickly summarized. There was a regional shortfall of 75,000 houses below immediate demand, a need for 275,000 houses between 1963 and 1981 to meet new family formation, and an estimated demand for net in-migration of 30,000. The last of these elements was based on what has proved to be a mis-reading of migration trend, but the family formation estimate is broadly in line with both marriage rates and the growth of separate households over the period since 1963. Slum clearance and the replacement housing need was estimated at 250,000 units in the region by 1981, but this would leave 120,000 houses in use in 1981 that would then be a century old, and over 500,000 that would be more than 65 years old. The estimates are broadly confirmed by the position in the mid-1970s: the region then had 250,000 houses over 80 years old and 480,000 over 65 years old. A very large replacement demand remains. The West Midland Study of 1964 translated these estimates into a total housing demand by 1981 of 630,000 homes (of which 355,000 would be generated by the conurbation). This called for an annual completion rate in the public and private sectors of about 37,000 houses: this was almost exactly the rate achieved until 1971, though since then the depression and financial restraints have reduced the total to about 20,000 to 25,000 annually. Clearly the 1964 to 1981 estimates were realistic measures both of need and of capacity to build. But, almost certainly, longer-term estimates are much less realistic. The report *A Developing Strategy for the West Midlands* (West Midland

Regional Study, 1971) calculated a total need for 894,500 new homes between 1966 and 2001, but on the basis of an end-of-century population of 6.4 million. Unhappily, this major survey of regional strategic development was made on the basis of 1966 data, before the 1971 Census became available, and its statistical basis has been overturned by more recent demographic changes.

There was also much uncertainty as to the availability site supply. The official view of the mid-1960s was that redevelopment sites could accommodate 75,000 new dwellings within the conurbation (chiefly in the high-rise units now becoming the dominant feature of the inner Birmingham townscape), and that the use of 'virgin' sites involving an infilling of the interstices in the urban framework might yield between 65,000 and 95,000 sites. In total about 150,000 to 170,000 sites could be found within the conurbation or at its margin. This would scarcely meet even the existing shortage and the renewal need, and would make no contribution to the demands arising from population growth. It seemed that at least 185,000 houses must be built outside the existing limit of the conurbation during the period 1964 to 1981. This now appears to be a substantial overestimate. Birmingham's own overspill was recalculated at only 48,000 houses in the 1973 Structure Plan, while the actual construction of new houses in the major overspill sites to 1975 was only about 40,000. An 'export' of 185,000 households from the conurbation by 1981 now seems neither necessary nor feasible in terms of construction capacity. Whatever the size of the shift of population from the conurbation, three possibilities existed to accommodate it: substantial peripheral expansion, short-range movement to satellites within commuter range, or long-range dispersal to sites beyond commuting distance involving a major redistribution of employment. These alternatives are bedevilled by the paradox that marginal expansion and short-range dispersal are likely to carry industry with them (as they have in the last decade), while long-range dispersal meets the problem of industrial immobility. In the empirical development of overspill to date there has been a little of all three solutions.

During the decades since 1945 the Birmingham conurbation has been conspicuously successful in accommodating its own population growth. From 1951 to 1963 its population grew by 154,000, so that it retained much the greater part of its natural increase of 178,000. Only in the mid-1960s did the conurbation's population increase cease, and it was then that planned overspill began, on a small scale. The movement has not been enormous: by 1974 about 9,000 households had been transferred to the six major schemes. This represents a small part of the total housing growth in the overspill districts, which have expanded more to absorb the general population increase in the region than specifically to accommodate a Birmingham surplus. But this figure greatly understates the general dispersal of population from the major urban mass. Progressive transfer from the public to the private sectors, in a prosperous population, has meant a progressive, half-controlled seepage of population outwards from the conurbation to villages and small towns in its green belt. These have absorbed a shift of population at least five times greater than the planned overspill in the public sector.

The first of the three alternative strategies listed above, further infilling and peripheral expansion, would merely legitimize present trends. Some of the major recent housing projects are in fact a peripheral enlargement of the conurbation, and can be described as overspill only in the technical sense that they involve the accommodation of Birmingham population in new homes beyond the city boundary. For example, the movement of Birmingham families to Aldridge, on the north eastern edge of the Black Country, over the last decade has been associated with the development of about 70 hectares (170 acres) of new industrial sites, partly on derelict land; yet 80 per cent of the overspill men work outside the district, and about 50 per cent of them in the city of Birmingham. In a mobile society, even vigorous local industrial development is no guarantee against commuting. The new factories of Aldridge merely become part of the general pool of employment available within the labour market of the north of the conurbation. Both the rate and size of 1961-1971 population growth at Aldridge (by 43,000) were far greater than in distant overspill schemes that represented a true dispersal.

Having come within sight of the exhaustion of its own land supply, Birmingham has looked for sites for out-of-town estates. One such project is at Chelmsley Wood (in the former Meriden urban district) just to the east of the city boundary; it is well within 16 kilometres (10 miles) of the central area, and scarcely 8 kilometres (5 miles) from the Tame valley industrial zone. Although there was opposition to this piece of marginal expansion, in fact the site is encircled by patchy suburban growth, and its development is merely a consolidation of the conurbation margin. Houses for 16,000 families (and a population likely to be about 60,000) are being completed and this had made a larger immediate contribution to the solution of Birmingham's public housing problem than any other single project. Even more controversial is a proposal for a scheme of similar size (about 15,000 houses) to be built close to the south western margin of the conurbation in North Worcestershire. Like Chelmsley Wood, this was seen as a 'crash' programme to relieve the city's housing emergency, to commence early in the 1970s and to be completed within five years. In fact a start was made only in 1975. Here too, the development is seen in commuter terms, with little if any movement of industry. The development lies on the northern margin of Bromsgrove, 19 kilometres (12 miles) from Birmingham but scarcely 8 kilometres (5 miles) from the B.L. Longbridge plant. Thus, an existing but skeletal salient of suburban development south westwards from Birmingham to Bromsgrove will be strengthened. These two large public schemes together may house perhaps 120,000 people in conurbation fringe sites, a far greater total than that likely to be removed in the near future to more distant schemes by true dispersal, and the tremendous pressures on rural areas within 24 kilometres (15 miles) of Birmingham for private house building have not been wholly frustrated. Thus the development of the West Midland conurbation in the 1970s has been dominated by its peripheral expansion rather than decentralization from it.

8.7.2 *Planning for Dispersal*

Planning for dipersal has been at two scales, a middle-distance movement to sites within possible commuter range, and a longer-range outflow to projects beyond easy daily travelling radius from Birmingham (though not necessarily from the conurbation margins). In both cases three alternative development procedures have been used: new town designation, town development schemes, and *ad hoc* overspill agreements. Middle-distance dispersal has been to a substantial new town at Redditch to the south, and to a group of industrial towns in mid-Staffordshire, chiefly Tamworth, Lichfield, Stafford, Cannock and Rugeley. The decision to develop Redditch has been criticized as a misuse of the new town concept, to create an essentially dormitory community in a suburban setting close to the margin of the existing urban mass. This is an old metal-working town, almost a Black Country outlier, once dominated by needle manufacture, and later by spring making. It is proposed to increase its population from 29,000 to 90,000 within a designated area of nearly 3,000 hectares (7,200 acres) by absorbing an intake population of about 35,000 from Birmingham. Only 23 kilometres (14 miles) from the city, and 8 kilometres (5 miles) from the conurbation margin—from which it is separated by a mere token of a green ribbon—there is an obvious danger that the town will become a dormitory community. Indeed, it was estimated that 40 per cent of the overspill wage earners would have to commute out daily. Predictably, Redditch has been an industrial success: it has attracted mobile firms both from the conurbation and in a more general national context. By 1976, 242 firms of very diverse types (but with a general West Midland 'flavour') provided 6,600 jobs. Indeed, jobs were being created rather more quickly than the demand for them by population increase: 4,100 houses had been built by 1976 and the 1971-1975 population increment was 8,000.

The industrial and mining towns of mid-Staffordshire have also attracted a growing overspill flow from Birmingham. No fewer than eleven overspill agreements have been concluded between Birmingham or Wolverhampton and various Staffordshire county districts, so that Stafford, Cannock, Lichfield and Tamworth will together absorb a population of 50,000 from the conurbation. The most ambitious project is that for Tamworth, a town of 34,000 that is prepared at least to double its present population, and for which there is a firm development plan. Only 21 kilometres (13 miles) from central Birmingham, Tamworth has grown vigorously in terms of industrial employment, and it has attracted mobile industry not only from the conurbation but also from elsewhere. In fact, overspill to Tamworth will build on proved industrial success. Population growth here has been rapid (by 19 per cent between 1971 and 1975) and is well balanced by the expansion of a diverse industrial base. Lichfield and Cannock-Rugeley, too, have grown quickly (by 8 per cent and 6 per cent, respectively, between 1971 and 1975), partly by dispersal from the conurbation, so that a Trent valley axis of population increase is well established.

Dispersal to ranges beyond easy commuter travel from the conurbation has so far been very limited, despite the fact that this category includes what is by far the largest of the West Midland development projects, the Telford new city. The problems of Telford are reviewed above (pp.236-240). It is necessary here only to recall that its growth was at first slow, largely because the rate of new job formation was at first very sluggish. By 1969 only 2,000 new houses had been built, though construction then quickened, to 5,800 by 1975. But the Birmingham-Telford link has become less relevant to both partners: the former no longer needs to plan for overspill transfers on the scale envisaged in the 1960s, while the latter has been able to generate its own autonomous growth, both of population and industry. The reduction in Telford's growth targets (from 220,000 by 1991 to about 150,000 by 1986) reflects its much slighter relevance for middle-term dispersal planning in the West Midland region.

Two other, much smaller, long-distance dispersal schemes are also in operation, to Daventry and Droitwich, the former almost 48 kilometres (30 miles) south east of Birmingham and the latter about 32 kilometres (20 miles) to the south west. Daventry was, in 1965, a small country town of 5,800, with a traditional boot and shoe manufacture and a new bearings industry. Closely linked to Rugby by journey-to-work ties, Daventry is thus the extreme south eastern outlier of the Coventry-based urban system. Near to the M1, it has obvious attractions as a site for industrial growth yet very little industrial overspill has taken place from the conurbation to the town.

New firms have come in, but chiefly from elsewhere. Nor have Birmingham families flocked to Daventry in great numbers. Almost three-quarters of the 1,000 new houses built in the late 1960s were taken by city families, but by 1970 the link with Birmingham had been weakened to permit Daventry to allocate houses intended for overspill migrants to workers coming with firms from elsewhere. In 1976 the Birmingham-Daventry link was ended. As (and if) Daventry's planned growth to 40,000 proceeds it will be by absorbing some part of the dwindling regional increase of population. But expansion has been slow (by 5,000 people between 1971 and 1975). Here is another piece of evidence that planning both for conurbation overspill and general regional growth has been over-generous; and that projects at any considerable distance from the conurbation suffer from the reluctance of both people and industry to decentralize.

Droitwich is a small and somewhat faded spa, only 10 kilometres (6 miles) north east of Worcester, and partly suburban to it. A rather limited town expansion scheme was agreed in 1963, to take about 13,000 overspill migrants in the course of a planned growth from 8,000 to about 30,000. By 1978, industrial estates and two overspill housing areas were growing, together with a small new town centre scheme. Even within the new and much enlarged county district of Wychavon there was only a 3,000 population increase between 1971 and 1975. A rate of growth of 1 per cent per annum is scarcely dynamic. Although the scheme is a small one, it may have a certain spatial significance in that it strengthens the south west salient of development from the conurbation; it may become in time part of a much larger expansion in this direction.

Excluding Telford and Redditch, this catalogue of small dispersal schemes, some of them indifferently successful, clearly does not amount to a regional strategy. The schemes embody the results of Birmingham's tactical opportunism in securing overspill agreements wherever there seemed some possibility of success. The city is said to have had talks with over a hundred other authorities and has entered into more than thirty agreements, some as far away as Central and South West Wales; but only about a dozen of these ever produced significant transfers of population. Now, however, the responsibility for framing an overspill policy that will become the chief instrument in developing a regional strategy has passed to the Economic Planning Council and the Regional Planning Board. Nevertheless, a local authority consortium has taken the initiative and put forward a set of strategic planning proposals (West Midland Regional Study, 1971).

8.7.3 *Corridors of Growth*

Although a regional strategy is still in the melting pot of debate, a few general principles have emerged. The council is adamant that in principle the growth of the conurbation must be contained (though it is still expanding in fact), and that a true dispersal of people and work must be achieved. To secure this, a strategy of 'corridors of growth' has been proposed. These would permit some short-range dispersal, while encouraging movement to greater distances far outside commuting radii. Such axes of development need not be radial to the conurbation. Indeed, the corridor of improved communication from Daventry-Rugby to Stafford, along the electrified Trent valley railway, and within the V formed by the M1 and Midland link motorways, is an attractive tangential corridor already defined by a number of active or potential growth points. It probably has a much greater capacity for development than so far has been assigned to it. The chief corridors of expansion, however, are likely to be defined in radial terms, extending outwards as a number of sectors from the conurbation. Thus, the future development of the region would be to a stellar model, in which broad but broken urban salients would extend starwise from the outer margin of the green belt; and these would be separated by rural wedges in which growth would be limited to scattered housing development in the private sector. The rural salients would have almost as great a significance in the total design as the urban corridors, for they would contain the short-range outdoor recreational resources for the urban society. This model, in its entirety, was based on assumptions of continuing and rapid regional growth. If the West Midlands persists in its present trend towards a zero-growth state it clearly has a diminished relevance. But there are still substantial middle-term housing demands to be met, for renewal and for net new-household formation: the latter should not slacken significantly for at least twelve to fifteen years.

The axes of growth are becoming clear, at least in general terms. Broadly, they follow the major corridors of communications out from the conurbation. Thus, a south western salient is already evolving along the approach of the M5/M50 motorway to the threshold of the conurbation. The North Worcestershire overspill proposal and Redditch new town will form the base of this development against the green belt; the growth of Droitwich, and a proposed expansion of Worcester by 50,000 overspill migrants (this is likely to be long deferred, however) will extend it. If all the projects under discussion within this south western sector were to fructify, a new population of about 150,000 would be added to the M5 axis and the total population within the corridor would exceed 400,000. This zone has an obvious potential for industrial growth. Motorways link Birmingham with its nearest port at Bristol and with the growing industrial region of Severnside and coastal South Wales. The West Midlands and South Wales are already closely linked industrially, partly through their complementary roles in the metal industries, and partly through the large number of transfers (often of branch plants) from the former to the latter under government direction. Thus the M5 is already a real corridor of commodity flow. Sites close to it are likely to be attractive to conurbation industry, and there is as a result a better hope for a massive dispersal of employment in this direction than in some others. In addition, Worcester provides not only the retail, commercial and social facilities of a high-ranking county town, but also a large and growing pool of service employment. With all these advantages it is a pity that expansion towards the south west has begun so slowly, and that the full capacity may never be needed.

The north western growth corridor consists of the single, massive but rather slowly developing Telford project, although it has also been suggested that Shrewsbury might be considered for planned expansion later in the century. The objections to the latter are the same as those levelled at the Worcester proposal—namely that a county town and historic city of attractive character might be ravaged by the traffic flows and land use pressures that any substantial growth would generate. But the danger to Shrewsbury is remote, for the contrast between the north western and south western axes in the matter of development potential is plain. The former lacks direct motorway access and its railway provision has deteriorated quickly. Most seriously, there is beyond Shrewsbury no major industrial complex in a relationship of interdependence with the West Midlands. Thus the M5 zone is truly a corridor: urban Shropshire more strictly a salient. In any case, the prospect that regional growth pressures will ever be so great as to intrude deeply in Shropshire is now remote: the main problem, rather, is to maintain Telford's momentum.

In contrast with East Shropshire, there is a northern axis of possible development that offers a very great potential, but so far has attracted only limited dispersal. No part of Britain has seen so radical an improvement in communications as the Birmingham-Stoke-on-Trent axis. Along the corridor are aligned not only the M6 with its spurs to Stafford and the Potteries, but also the much improved A34 trunk road, together with the duplicate main lines of the London-Midland electrification. These routes, moreover, link the two largest of the English provincial manufacturing regions, the West Midlands and South Lancashire. This is one of the main streets of industrial Britain. Yet only piecemeal development is proposed, in the regional strategy as presently revealed, for this area. There may perhaps be a limited expansion of Stafford; certainly growth is likely to continue at the northern margin of the conurbation. But the key to a policy for this northern sector lies in the future of North Staffordshire. The problems of this region have already been reviewed (pp.230-236): in essence, any major development is frustrated by the area's gross environmental problems, its massive renewal needs and the weakness of its economic base. Possible new town sites at Swynnerton and Stone have been canvassed fruitlessly. In fact, the city of Stoke-on-Trent was both willing and anxious to accept overspill to balance its own population decline. A much greater potential for growth lies not within the Potteries conurbation, but to its west, in the Crewe area of South Cheshire. This is too remote within North West England to be regarded as a candidate for growth in the near future, and since it lies beyond the boundaries of their region, it has not been seriously considered by the West Midland planners. The whole northern axis of possible development from the West Midland conurbation is, therefore, one of great potential, but of wasted opportunities. But its capacity may never be needed.

These principal growth corridors to the south west, the north west and the north have the greatest capacity for absorbing population increase. Development in other directions offers slighter prospects. A possible north eastern corridor has been identified, extending beyond Lichfield and Tamworth to Burton. Certainly Tamworth is committed to substantial growth by overspill, but any major enlargement of Lichfield would conflict with farmland of high quality and the character of a small and well-preserved cathedral city. Burton is seen as a possible reception site for an overspill population of 50,000; in real terms this would be a transfer from the West Midlands to the margins of the Derby-Nottingham urban complex and its virtues must be considered in the context of an East Midland strategy. Population dispersal to the south east from the conurbation is seriously limited by the indigenous pressures of population growth and land supply within the Coventry belt. In fact, a growth corridor has long been developing here, through the Coventry complex to Rugby and Daventry. Its 1971 population of about 695,000 is bound to rise to over 720,000 by the early 1980s through natural growth alone, and there is almost bound to be some in-migration, both intra-regional and inter-regional. The problem here is to develop a sub-regional plan that will accommodate these increases without a total elimination of the diminishing green ribbons that divide Coventry both from its smaller neighbours and from the conurbation. Except for Birmingham's former interest in Daventry, the south eastern sector cannot absorb significant overspill transfers from the conurbation.

Between these corridors of urban growth, however, lie broad rural wedges within which a triangular conflict of interest is already evolving. This is between the need to protect good farmland, the pressures for high-income dormitory development, and the role of the countryside as a recreational resource. The rural area south of the conurbation, straddling the Warwickshire and Worcestershire boundary, illustrates this problem. One of the most concentrated districts of intensive fruit and vegetable cultivation in Britain occupies the Avon terrace lands, centred on Evesham but extending more patchily to Warwick and across South Worcestershire. To the north are areas of intensive livestock rearing, with a varying local emphasis on milk or beef. These are not types of farming that coexist easily with mass penetration by the urban visitor, but the Avon valley, and the river itself, are recreational amenities of great value, invaded from the conurbations each weekend, even though there is little open-access land. The southern sector is also one of the most favoured by the Birmingham long-range commuter, so that many of the villages and small towns, for example Henley-in-Arden and Alcester, are pressure points for dispersed suburban growth. The planning problems of the rural wedges, therefore, are no less complex than those of the proposed growth corridors. Rather different conflicts and opportunities are evident in the rural areas immediately to the north of the conurbation. Here the forested Bunter plateau of Cannock Chase is largely open to the visitor and has been carefully developed by the county with the help of the Countryside Commission as a major recreation area: it is now designated as the U.K.'s largest country park. But the active Cannock coalfield reaches the borders of the Chase— and indeed penetrates the south—so that commanding prospects of spoil banks and pit villages alternate with views of the fine Bunter scarps. Beyond Cannock lies the Trent, a river punctuated by power stations of great size, for it offers cooling water in a relatively cheap coal area. The terraces contain huge gravel resources of great commercial value. As these are worked, the pits flood, and offer opportunities for the development of water recreation areas in the wake of gravel working. Clearly the most careful local planning is required to reconcile the conflicting interests of electricity generation, gravel working and recreational uses.

Beyond the Severn on the west—another river coming under increasing recreational pressures—lies a more distant hinterland of the West Midlands. This includes the border counties and the upland mass of East and Central Wales, an area of immense but underdeveloped recreational and tourist potential (see pp.240-242). The central Welsh upland offers not only general resources for mountain and moorland recreation, but also developed facilities for the visitor by car, for example at the Vyrnwy and Elan valley reservoirs of Liverpool and Birmingham respectively. Outliers of the Welsh uplands thrust eastwards almost to the Severn, in Wenlock Edge, the Clee Hills and the Longmynd. A single main axis of communication crosses this thinly settled region from north to south, the parallel Shrewsbury-Hereford trunk road and railway, the latter with a somewhat suspect future. Spaced along this are small market towns of historic character and tourist potential like Leominster and Ludlow. Apart from small-scale overspill to Hereford, and the problematical future growth of Shrewsbury, only a trivial growth of population (and substantial rural decline) is to be expected in this remote region of pastoral farming. Oddly, the only substantial proposal for urban industrial development lies yet further west, and even more remotely located, in the upper Severn Valley at and above Newtown (see pp.241-242).

The regional strategy being shaped to guide any substantial future growth of the West Midlands must be seen in broader than regional terms. It is also a plan for the development of the core of the English megalopolis. There is clearly in the process of formation, on the axis joining metropolitan England to South Lancashire and West Yorkshire, a system of city-regions that is already as coherent and as firmly integrated as its counterpart on the eastern seaboard of the United States of America—both in the complex linkage system between the constituent units, and in their progressive penetration of the remaining rural interstices. The elongated motorway triangle of the M1, M6 and M62 defines the axes about which this megalopolis is developing. It already contains an urban population of about 32 millions; and four zones within it—the London city-region, the urban West Midlands, the East Midland city complex and southern Lancastria—will between them generate and absorb the great bulk of the nation's housing demand over the next few decades. The West Midland city-region is clearly the hinge of this urban complex. Planning for decentralization from the West Midlands, is, in effect therefore, planning for a consolidation of England's megalopolis. Most of the growth corridors of greatest potential in the West Midlands are aligned along the interior communications of this system of city-regions. The continuing growth of the Coventry complex, the potential for expansion across Staffordshire to the Potteries, and the development of the towns of the Trent valley all represent an infilling within the existing urban mass. Only the Telford project can be seen to represent an advance of the urban frontier away from the core of the megalopolis. Thus the development of a regional plan involves the taking of decisions that have as great a national importance as they have a regional significance. The most southerly of the Midland dispersal locations, Daventry, is less than fifteen minutes away from one of the more northerly of the major South East projects at Northampton. Any major growth in the Stoke city-region straddles a provincial boundary and must be reconciled with two regional strategies. So must any significant development of Burton. This, of course, is simply a restatement of the centrality and nodality of the West Midlands within urban industrial Britain. If an inadequate regional strategy for the West Midlands were adopted as a blueprint for growth, it would confuse and frustrate national planning for the most efficient distribution of population and economic activity. In this sense, the key to national planning lies in the future shaping of the West Midland region.

But the converse is also true. Whether or not the strategic framework sketched out in the West Midlands to accommodate growth on the scale envisaged during the 1960s is ever called upon to absorb population increase and urban expansion of so massive a size depends primarily on national trends. If Britain's population has reached virtual stability, or does so by the 1980s, then the West Midlands can expect little further urban growth once new family formation has worked its way through the demographic system. In this case the development projects active during the 1970s may well be the high-water marks of that great tide of urbanization that began 200 years ago and reached full flood late in the twentieth century.

REFERENCES

Beaver, S.H. (1964). *The Potteries, A Study in the Evolution of a Cultural Landscape,* Institute of British Geographers, London.
British Association (1950). *Birmingham and its Regional Setting,* B.A., London.
Central Policy Review Staff (1975). *The Future of the British Car Industry,* Cabinet Office, H.M.S.O., London.
Department of Economic Affairs (1965). *The West Midlands: A Regional Study,* H.M.S.O., London.

Eversley, D.E.C., Jackson, V.J., and Lomas, G.N. (1965). *Population Growth and Planning Policy,* University of Birmingham.

Johnson, B.L.C. (1951). The charcoal iron industry in the early eighteenth century, *Geographical Journal,* **117,** 167-177.

Johnson, B.C.L. (1958). The distribution of the factory population in the West Midland Conurbation, *Transactions and Papers, Institute of British Geographers,* **25,** 209-223.

Jones, H.R. (1965). A study of rural migration in Central Wales, *Transactions and Papers, Institute of British Geographers,* **37,** 31-45.

Jones, H.R. (1976). The structure of the migration process: findings from a growth point in Mid-Wales, *Transactions and Papers, Institute of British Geographers,* N.S., **1,** 421-433.

Jones, P.N. (1970). Some aspects of the changing distribution of coloured immigrants in Birmingham, *Transactions and Papers, Institute of British Geographers,* **50,** 199-201.

Ministry of Housing and Local Government (1966). *Dawley, Wellington and Oakengates* (study by John Madin & partners), H.M.S.O., London.

Moisley, H.A. (1951). The industrial and urban development of the North Staffordshire conurbation, *Transactions and Papers, Institute of British Geographers,* **17,** 151-165.

Moyes, A. (1976). The Potteries. In P.A. Wood, *Industrial Britain: The West Midlands,* David & Charles, Newton Abbot.

Raybould, T.J. (1973). *The Economic Emergence of the Black Country,* David & Charles, Newton Abbot.

Rosing, K.E., and Wood, P.A. (1971). *The Character of a Conurbation,* University of London Press, London.

Smith, B.D.M. (1970). Industrial overspill, theory and practice, *Urban Studies,* **7,** 189-204.

Smith, B.D.M. (1976). *The Inner City Economic Problem,* Centre for Urban and Regional Studies, University of Birmingham.

Smith, B.D.M., Ruddy, S.A., and Black, J. (1974). *Industrial Relocation in Birmingham,* Centre for Urban and Regional Studies, University of Birmingham.

Staffordshire County Council (1973). *Structure Plan: Report of Survey,* S.C.C., Stafford.

Stoke-on-Trent County Borough Council (1973). *Structure Plan: Report of Survey,* Stoke-on-Trent C.B.C.

Taylor, M.J., and Wood, P.A. (1973). Industrial linkages and local agglomeration in the West Midland metal industries, *Transactions and Papers, Institute of British Geographers,* **59,** 127-154.

Tolley, R. (1973). Telford new town: Conception and reality in West Midlands industrial overspill, *Town Planning Review,* **43,** 343-360.

Welsh Council (1970). *Land Use Strategy: A Pilot Report for Cardiganshire, Montgomeryshire and Radnorshire,* H.M.S.O., Cardiff.

Welsh Office (1964). *Depopulation in Mid-Wales* (Beacham Report), H.M.S.O., London.

Welsh Office (1966). *A New Town in Mid-Wales* (Economic Associates), H.M.S.O., London.

West Midlands Metropolitan County Council (1975). *A Time for Action: Economic and Social Trends in the West Midlands,* W.M.C.C., Birmingham.

West Midlands Metropolitan County Council (1974).

West Midlands Economic Planning Council (1967). *The West Midlands: Patterns of Growth,* H.M.S.O., London.

West Midlands Economic Planning Council (1971). *The West Midlands: An Economic Appraisal,* W.M.E.P.C., Birmingham.

West Midlands Joint Monitoring Steering Group (1977). *Development in Regional Strategic Locations, 1971-1975,* W.M.J.M.S.G., Birmingham.

West Midlands Regional Study (1971). *A Development Strategy for the West Midlands,* W.M.R.S., Birmingham.

West Midlands Shopping Study (1966). *Journal of the Town Planning Institute,* **52,** 146-149.

Wood, P.A. (1966). Regional planning strategies and manufacturing industry: Some lessons from the West Midlands, *Journal of the Town Planning Institute,* **52,** 323-327.

Wood, P.A. (1976). *Industrial Britain: The West Midlands,* David & Charles, Newton Abbot.

CHAPTER 9

The North West and North Wales

Brian Rodgers

9.1 Regional Contrast in North West England

Taken as a whole and placed in a national perspective, the North West must be recognized as one of those less prosperous regions that have failed to secure their fair share of the national growth in population, employment and personal prosperity. Indicators of its general economic debility are so easy to assemble that there is risk of tedious repetition. Its population growth rate was only 0.19 per cent per annum between 1951 and 1961 and 0.24 per cent from 1961 to 1971, compared with national values of 0.53 per cent and 0.64 per cent, respectively. Losses by out-migration each year were removing 0.19 per cent of the region's population during the 1950s and, although the rate fell to about 0.05 per cent during the period 1961-1966, it had risen by the early 1970s to 0.25 per cent per annum. Indeed by the period 1967-1971 the population of the region had reached stability, at just under 6.75 million. The trend since has been downwards, reflecting the continued decline in birth rate, to 6,557,000 in 1975. The selective migration of young adults has changed the age structure and depressed fertility so that the rate of natural increase has fallen to 0.18 per cent per annum, distinctly below the national rate of almost 0.2 per cent (1971-1974). Between 1952 and 1971 total employment in the region fell by 3.5 per cent while the national trend was a growth of 7.5 per cent. Regional unemployment rates ranged between 2 and 3 per cent until the recession of the mid-1970s, when the value rose to 6 per cent in 1976. They have been consistently 20 to 30 per cent higher than national rates, but the difference has worsened relatively during periods of general economic difficulty. One of the benefits of the decline of the region's weak, and traditionally low-wage, industries is that the average-income gap between the North West and more prosperous regions has been closing, but male earnings were still 2 per cent below national average in 1976.

These are broad socio-economic indicators: they sketch a profile of decline and disadvantage. What is perhaps more serious, in essentially human terms, is the body of varied evidence that the quality of life in the North West is poor even by the standards of the older industrial regions of Britain. In the *Strategic Plan for the North West* (Department of the Environment, 1974) twenty-six indices of the quality of life and the environment were compiled. On eight of these measures the North West is the worst of all the regions of Britain, and on another five it is so close to the worst that the difference is insignificant. It is Britain's most air-polluted region: it has both the worst general smoke and SO_2 levels—in a black belt straddling the two conurbations—and almost the highest proportion of polluted areas awaiting smoke control orders. The dark air shrouds a landscape ravaged by two centuries of industrial activity with the highest proportion of the surface lying derelict among all the regions. Life, it would seem, is nasty, brutal and (relatively) short: both the general and infant mortality levels are the worst in Britain, and the average list-size of doctors the largest. Sickness benefit paid and prescriptions issued, per capita, are among the highest in the country. The region's schools have the worst pupil-teacher ratio in Britain, and they are almost the least successful in retaining pupils after 16 and in sending them into further education. Such a profile is, perhaps, rather a caricature: there is something to be put on the other side—for example, the region has the best community library and theatre facilities, and the lowest level of house prices. But the point of sketching this melancholy portrait is two-fold. Simple economic indices give no real measure of a region's problems; and regional policy, in its classic sense, may be at best an incomplete and indirect attack on these problems. Secondly, regional planning and development must be as much concerned with the quality of life, of environment, of opportunity and of the social services, as it is with the traditional fields of economic and physical planning.

All these values have one characteristic in common. They are meaningless if they are thought to apply to any specific part of the region. They are merely averages for an area whose dominant feature is its dualism, a sharp intra-regional distinction between zones of exceptionally rapid growth in industry and population, and others of equally dramatic decline. In the North West, areas that belong to 'fortunate' and 'unfortunate' Britain are brought into close juxtaposition; indeed the prosperity watershed between the 'two nations' crosses the region, dividing it with remarkable clarity (see Figure 9.1). A line drawn on a map southwards from Lancaster via Preston to Wigan and St Helens, looping eastwards to bisect the Manchester city-region from north west to south east, and finally running southwards along the Pennine flanks, broadly defines these contrasts and divides the region. This is a familiar enough line. Much of its course lies along the western and southern borders of the coalfield, so that all areas to the east and north of it have a textile and mining tradition and a history of precocious nineteenth-century economic growth. In contrast, the areas to the south and west attracted little industrial and urban development in Victorian times, except locally on Merseyside and on the Cheshire Saltfield; they have as a result largely escaped the complex of economic and environmental problems that the older towns of eastern Lancastria face.

Almost every economic and demographic indicator adds strength to this intra-regional contrast. Population trends since 1951 show consistent and heavy losses over the whole of eastern Lancastria, particularly during the period of the long agony of the cotton industry. During the phase of most critical contraction, from 1951 to 1964, North East Lancashire and Rossendale suffered a population loss of 5.3 per cent. There was some later recovery, partly linked to diffused suburbanization, so that the censal period 1961-1971 saw a loss of only 1 per cent overall in 'textile' Lancashire. These trends contrast with population growth rates that—in some cases—exceed not just the regional but also the national average in the sub-regions of the south and west. The Fylde grew by 7 per cent, the Macclesfield sub-region by over 16 per cent; the Liverpool city-region was stable, during the decade 1961-1971. Metropolitan Manchester straddles this intra-regional boundary between areas of growth and decline, but its population trend has conformed progressively more closely to that of the textile areas: between 1961 and 1971 the Metropolitan Labour Area (see p.71) lost 1.2 per cent of its population. The chief

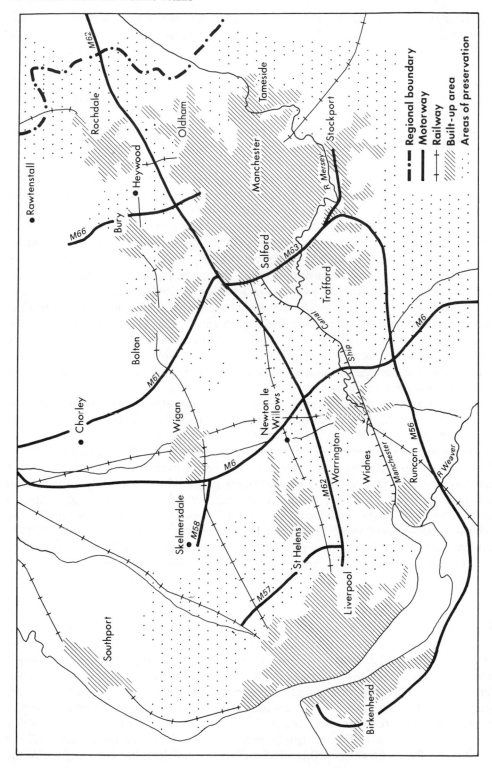

Figure 9.1 North West England: the economic core

immediate cause of this contrast is differences in migration, both from the North West and within it, balanced against a sharply varied pattern of natural increase. On a sub-regional basis (and so discounting local population shifts to suburban areas or overspill sites) migrational losses in the textile areas were as high as 6.2 per cent in Rossendale, while the Manchester city-region lost over 4 per cent. Though the contrast is blunted by the high rate of migration from Merseyside (a consequence of its former very high rate of natural increase) the whole of South Cheshire and West Lancashire gained substantially by a net inward flow of migrants; in the Fylde, however, this is largely a movement of the retired and so of limited economic significance.

The influence of prolonged migratory movement on population structure and fertility is as clear as it ·is difficult to correct. Some of the textile towns of the east are now experiencing a natural decrease of their elderly populations, and they are among the very few towns in Britain (outside the retirement resorts) to do so. The Blackburn, Burnley and Rossendale districts, a contiguous area with a total population of over half a million, all suffered an overall natural decrease during the 1950s, and though there was a dramatic and unaccountable increase in birth rate between 1961 and 1971, the trend is now downwards again towards a low natural increase. But a much more dramatic change is the radical decline in natural increase on Merseyside: this contributed a growth increment of about 10 per cent to the area's population during the decade 1951-1961, but by 1974 the surplus of births over deaths had dwindled almost to nil. This is a major change in the sub-regional demography of the North West of enormous implications for broad planning strategy. Though it is difficult to interpret the evidence, the trend in the region as a whole is for the marked differences in natural increase between its parts to diminish, in a general drift towards low birth rates, scarcely at replacement levels.

The old contrasts will nevertheless continue to have their effect for some time to come on future projections of the size of the labour force available in the sub-regions and on the demand for employment. In every textile town the labour force has been not only reduced but seriously aged by the migration of its younger members. A higher proportion of the workers left are approaching retirement age, and recruitment into the labour force is reduced both by low birth rates and by continuing migration. Increasingly, in-migration of Indians and Pakistanis offsets this migratory loss from the textile towns. Recruited to the mills, they have settled stably and in substantial numbers in the larger towns like Blackburn, Oldham and Bolton. Their presence complicates calculations of the size of the available future labour force. Short-term projections suggest a contraction over much of eastern Lancastria, but a very quick increase in the west and south, especially on Merseyside. Indeed, the latter region will generate about half the total regional increase in employable population to 1981. The above are the reasons for the condition of labour shortage that, paradoxically, has troubled the textile towns. It is not only a factor in the decline of their traditional industries, but it also prejudices their chance of attracting alternative employment. As a consequence, the incidence of unemployment reverses the patterns of sub-regional contrast reviewed so far. During the 1960s, rates varied between 1 per cent and 2 per cent of the insured population in the textile areas (and rarely exceeded the national mean), while on Merseyside the range was between 3 per cent and 4 per cent, with occasionally higher peaks. The recession after 1973, of course, produced higher rates, but the textile areas have not seen the 'crisis' levels suffered on Merseyside, which rose to 11 per cent in 1977. Unemployment rates have traditionally dictated the delimitation of Development and Intermediate Areas, and eligibility for Distribution of

Industry funds. Yet in the North West they are weakly or inversley correlated with most other measures of economic debility. Assisted Area policy, therefore, has added its very powerful influence to strengthening the contrast in economic trends between the two broad divisions of the region. Government intervention has reinforced a 'natural' trend in the North West, the converse of its general influence (and its intent) on the national scale.

Indexes of employment growth sharpen this broad pattern of intra-regional contrast. Total employment, in all sectors, fell in North East Lancashire by 10 per cent over the decade 1953 to 1963, and by slightly lower rates over most of the rest of eastern Lancastria. In the Manchester conurbation it grew by 3 per cent (scarcely half the Merseyside rate of 6.4 per cent), but this increase was wholly confined to the city and its southern industrial outliers. Elsewhere growth ranged from 5 per cent in South Cheshire to 13 per cent in the Fylde. This was the decade of the cotton industry's quickest contraction, and so perhaps was atypical. But data for the period 1961-1966 were even more disturbing. Virtually the whole of the textile zone (including the Manchester sub-region) suffered losses of from 1 per cent to 5 per cent in total employment, compared with growth rates of 4 per cent for Merseyside and 5 per cent for the Fylde. Trends in manufacturing employment repeat these contrasts but with even greater emphasis. The rate of net job losses in the Manchester sub-region was 4.4 per cent for the period 1959-1966, in North East Lancashire it was 3.4 per cent, and in mid-Lancashire it was almost 7 per cent. On the other hand, growth reached almost 8 per cent on Merseyside, and over 13 per cent in the Fylde. It is particularly disturbing that the volume of work for men fell almost throughout the North West during the period 1961-1975, and that the growth early in this period in the Fylde and Merseyside was subsequently reversed. Table 9.1 shows the catastrophic decline in male employment in all those areas with a textile tradition, especially Manchester and North East Lancashire. Yet these are also the areas of the sharpest loss of female work as well, as the textile mills have closed. In the north

Table 9.1 The North West: male employment change, by sub-regions, 1961-1970 and 1971-1975

	1966 (1961 = 100)	1970 (1961 = 100)	1975 (1971 = 100)
Furness	98	96	—
Fylde	102	97	98
Lancaster	95	87	94
Mid-Lancashire	95	91	97
North East Lancashire	99	91	98
Merseyside	104	98	91
South Lancashire	99	92	111
Manchester	97	89	94
South Cheshire and High Peak	96	93	106

Source: North West Economic Planning Council.

The 1961, 1966 and 1970 data refer to the old economic planning sub-regions, the 1971 and 1975 data to roughly comparable journey-to-work areas.

east the female activity rate fell by almost 5 per cent between 1966 and 1971, while it rose nationally by 1.2 per cent. An examination of the more recent data in Table 9.2 leads to gloomy conclusions: every major manufacturing industry in the region has suffered an employment decline; while almost every sub-region is now suffering a loss in male employment. There are both sectoral and areal differences, but between sub-regions the contrast of growth and decline has become, rather, one between levels of economic weakness.

Even within this unhappy context, the textile region of eastern Lancastria has an economy of extraordinary weakness. Almost every indicator (except unemployment) picks out this area as consistently the weakest in the whole of Britain, inside or outside the Assisted Areas. The most obvious cause—too great a dependence on two sharply contracting industries, mining and textiles—is not, by itself, a sufficient explanation. It is possible to assess the influence of an unfavourable structure of industry on the overall trend of employment in an area by applying national rates of growth (or decline) to each of its industries for some period of time. This, in effect, gives a prediction of the change in total employment that the area ought to have experienced, had each industry (or service activity) within it grown or declined strictly in conformity with national trends. It therefore measures a structural component in total employment change, isolating a residual component that reflects the operation of factors peculiar to the areas concerned.

Several studies (Smith, 1969; Secretary of State for Economic Affairs, 1969; Department of the Environment, 1974) made of the effect of economic structure on employment trends in the region have reached complementary but also in part contradictory conclusions. To summarize them, it is plain that an adverse structure with an accent on industries of decline quite largely explains the region's overall poor performance over the period from 1953 to 1964, but even then a strong residual element suggested a weak performance even in those economic sectors that should have grown, in

Table 9.2 The North West: employment change, by sub-regions and major industries, 1953-1973

| | Annual percentage change in total employment in selected manufacturing industries | | | | |
| | The North West | | | The textile areas | Manchester |
	1953-1959	1959-1966	1966-1975	1958-1967	1958-1967
Food, drink, tobacco	+ 2.1	+ 0.1	− 1.8	− 1.4	− 3.8
Chemicals	+ 1.7	− 1.2	− 2.0	+ 0.1	− 1.3
Engineering and electrical	+ 1.1	+ 2.7	− 3.9	+ 0.6	+ 0.1
Vehicles	+ 0.7	+ 2.1	+ 0.6	− 3.5	− 9.5
Textiles	− 3.6	− 3.7	− 4.9	− 4.5	− 5.4
Clothing and footwear	− 2.0	− 0.7	− 3.2	− 2.7	− 4.5
Paper and printing	+ 2.1	+ 1.8	− 1.5	+ 0.9	− 0.4
All industries and services	+ 0.1	+ 0.3	− 1.2	− 0.3	− 0.8

Source: Department of Employment and Lancashire and Merseyside Industrial Development Association.

harmony with national trend. The power of the structural 'excuse' to explain the region's adverse employment trend has diminished with time. By the late 1960s the total employment structure had come much closer to the national average through the decline of the region's weak industries. By then the structural component in overall decline was quite minor, and the blame for continued weakness could be attributed directly to a poor growth record almost throughout the whole spectrum of the regional economy. This non-structural cause of weakness was at its worst precisely in those areas of the North West—in the textile towns and the Manchester conurbation—where, earlier, the structural contribution to economic decline had been greatest. The several analyses agree, broadly, that Merseyside and much of the south and west of the region have experienced a far quicker rate of economic growth than can be explained by their industrial 'mix', while the Manchester city-region has lost employment far more seriously than its relatively favourable industrial structure would have led one to expect. There are many reasons for the unhappy experience of so much of East and South East Lancashire as judged by this yardstick. They are examined in detail later (pp.284-297): they include the rapid conversion of mining and textiles to capital-intensive industries using less labour more productively, the existence of weak sectors like textile and railway engineering in what are, nationally, dynamic growth industries, the slow development of service employment, the effects of physical remoteness, poor communication, and land shortage, and, most powerfully of all, the influence of industrial guidance policies in retarding new growth over almost the whole of the east of the region. This last factor is so crucial that a separate section is devoted to it (pp.270-274). In fact the total area of new industrial floorspace approved by the Board of Trade in the textile districts after 1947 was derisory (except in the short-lived North East Lancashire Development Area), while the south and west, and especially those areas grouped about the Mersey estuary, have benefited significantly. Thus over the twenty years to 1965, coastal Lancashire and South and West Cheshire secured new factories employing a total of about 63,000 workers while the figure for the textile province was 9,000.

Not only in economic vitality but also in the quality of environment are there to be found profound contrasts within the North West. Textile Lancastria contains the great bulk of the region's substandard housing. Official returns (D. of E.: Circular 50/72) show that 74 per cent of the region's 172,000 totally unfit houses were in the textile towns. But these are only the worst slums. In metropolitan Manchester 44 per cent of the housing stock needs some form of treatment to bring it to an acceptable standard; in Preston the figure is 58 per cent and in Blackburn 66 per cent. Non-industrial Cheshire has virtually no slum problem, while in coastal Lancashire is it virtually confined to North Merseyside; here the total number of houses involved is about 50,000. These environmental contrasts have a social dimension. Several East Lancashire towns habitually compete for the unhappy distinction of the highest death rate by bronchitis in Britain. Except for the coastal retirement colonies, they are also among the areas returning the highest gross death rates. That this is not merely a function of their distorted age structures is shown by their high infant mortality experience. On all these counts, except for inner Merseyside, the coastlands and Cheshire have much happier and healthier records.

This dualism of the North West has been explored by aspect; but it is possible to compose a statistical synthesis of all these (and many more) measures of socio-economic health so as to provide a single comprehensive, if more generalized, statement. Smith (1969, pp.171-191) attempted this, in a searching and innovative dissection of sub-regional contrast. He identified two dimensions of economic health, one industrial, the other socio-demographic. For the former, he assembled for each of the ninety-five labour exchange areas data on fourteen criteria of industrial structure and performance. These included measures of change in industrial, service and total employment, data on unemployment and factory building, and indices of industrial specialization and change. A factor analysis was performed on the data-set. Two factors were found to represent the greater part of the total system of variance, as effective proxies for the whole intricate pattern of areal variation in the data. One of these was an industrial change; the other an industrial structure factor. Factor scores plotted on maps very largely repeat the 'textile-areas-versus-the-rest' pattern of contrast noted above. But the structural and change factors are not always in accordance: in central Lancashire and parts of the Manchester sub-region there are areas where scores on the growth factor are low, depite a relatively favourable structure. In a broadly similar way fourteen socio-demographic variables are analysed for the 177 old local authority units—measures of population change and its components; death rate, educational and occupation data, measures of housing quality and car ownership. Again two major synthesizing factors emerge, one reflecting the pattern of population change, the other in essence an index of social structure and personal prosperity. The patterns are more fragmented than those describing the industrial dimension of economic health, but the story follows a similar theme. The heart of the textile zone has almost universally low scores on population growth, and on measures of prosperity it is a sea of relative poverty with but few better-favoured islands within it. Coastal Lancashire and all Cheshire except the north east score high on both growth and affluence, except for a considerable area of relative poverty in inner Merseyside. In brief, the unhappy regional portrait sketched in the first two paragraphs of this section has no general validity: the region has two faces, totally dissimilar in statistical expression.

Although it may seem to be almost an exercise in neodeterminism, these economic and social contrasts within the North West can be put into a physical context. Almost the whole of the area below the 75 metre (250 foot) contour has recorded increases in population and employment during the period since 1945, while the areas enclosed within the 120 metre (400 foot) contour are those of steepest economic and demographic decline. The generalized course of the 875 millimetre (35 inch) isohyet similarly divides the region between its zones of growth and of decline perhaps more neatly than any single economic or social indicator. The major geological boundary separates a Triassic Lancastria of sustained economic progress from a Carboniferous Lancastria of decay, decline and painful industrial readjustment. This is not a search for determinist explanations, but a distinction between two sorts of environment.

The dissected uplands of eastern Lancastria and the low plateau of the coalfield offered every possible attraction to those Victorian industries that were tied, locationally, to specific physical resources: the abundant energy source of upland streams, the superb water supply of deep valleys bathed by the weeping Pennine climate, the cheap coal so readily available from shallow resources. Inevitably, eastern Lancastria dominated the growth of industry and of towns, and largely shaped the evolving pattern of communications, prior to 1914. It clearly has much less to offer to modern industry, little influenced by immediate access to physical resources. In contrast the low, drift-smeared plains of the West Lancashire and Cheshire Trias are crossed by improved communications and especially by the rail and motorway arteries leading into the West

Midlands; they are served not only by the Mersey but also by other specialist ports. They have only a small share of the region's burden of almost 4,500 hectares (10,000 acres) of derelict land. The lowlands of the west and south are now the region of greatest industrial vitality and quickest urban growth. They also remain the areas of highest agricultural productivity from intensive arable and dairy farming, so that a heightening conflict between town and farm must continue to be one of the chief regional policy issues.

Whether the rather neat and simple dualism of the contemporary North West will persist is open to some doubt. The M6 motorway follows, across Lancashire, almost the line of contact between sub-regions of growth and of decline. It must clearly dominate the evolution of a regional planning strategy, and is already seen as the major axis of economic growth. Parts of central Lancashire have already responded to its influence, though much of the new industrial building close to it is for storage and distribution and so generates little employment. The M62 (Lancashire-Yorkshire), M61 (Manchester-Preston) and M56 (North Cheshire) cross or join the M6 axis and the Fylde (M55) motorway runs as a spur from it. This is now a superb system of regional road links, Britain's first example of a complete regional motorway system and the region's chief strength in attracting new enterprises. But it serves the south and west of the region best, and the heart of the textile province, in Rossendale and North East Lancashire, has no place yet on the motorway map—except for a new spur road along the Irwell valley from the south, and trunk road improvement east of Preston.

9.2 Development Area Policy and Industrial Mobility

Through all the many changes in government policies affecting the location of industry during the post-war decades (p.37ff), high and persistent unemployment has been the chief qualification for Assisted Area status. The great paradox of the economic history of the North West since 1945 is that, despite the catastrophic decline of its two staple industries and the marked contraction of several other sectors (for example, engineering and clothing), serious unemployment has been ephemeral and has occurred chiefly outside the textile zone. Only one part of the region, Merseyside, has had the advantage of Assisted Area status throughout the greater part of the period; elsewhere only the fine-weaving towns of North East Lancashire, a part of the South Lancashire coalfield and the Furness district have been scheduled long enough for the status to show any effect on the local structure of industry. When, in 1972, the whole of industrial eastern Lancastria was given Intermediate Area status, this came on the eve of the general recession, and has proved ineffectual. Thus the positive impact of government policy towards the location of industry is confined to a few compact regions; the negative influence of the policy, the restraining of economic growth in areas that failed to qualify for assistance, is much more widely evident through the region. The North West is almost unique among the regions of Britain in that the two aspects of the policy can be studied in closely juxtaposed districts.

9.2.1 Development Areas

In 1946, a section of the South Lancashire coalfield, centred on Wigan and St Helens, was created a Development Area. Here all the classic causes of distress were clearly evident. There was high and prolonged unemployment caused by the contraction of coal mining in a difficult and part-exhausted section of the field; and this was coupled with the long-term decline of a weak manufacturing industry, cotton. Hindsight leads to the conclusion that the scheduling of South Lancashire was neither necessary nor successful. Mining has survived quite strongly near St Helens and the textile industry has suffered a slower contraction here than almost anywhere else in the region. Moreover the continued growth and technological vitality of the St Helens glass industry has helped to balance the loss of male employment following pit closures. This Development Area attracted little interest on the part of mobile industry before it was descheduled in 1960. Although incoming firms made a substantial contribution to the area's modest growth of employment between 1945 and 1965, of a total 14,000 jobs brought in by them, only 4,000 were in firms that had built new factories. The remainder were new enterprises in existing buildings, most of them converted mills. Since moves of this kind at the time derived little or no benefit from Development Area status they would presumably have occurred in any case. In brief, the scheduling of South Lancashire had only a marginal effect on employment growth; the construction across it of the M6 motorway early in the 1960s and, later, the M62, almost certainly had a more powerful impact. Indeed the inflow of new employment accelerated strongly immediately after the descheduling of the area and on the eve of motorway construction (Board of Trade, 1969): between 1971 and 1975 this general area was almost unique in the North West in its strong growth (11 per cent) of male work.

Chronologically, the next part of the North West considered to merit Development Area status was Merseyside, where a considerable area, on both sides of the estuary and reaching eastwards to Widnes, was scheduled in 1949. This region has a long history of male unemployment, rooted historically in the feeble development of manufacturing coupled with the port's declining share in the nation's trade, and nourished since 1945 not only by a relatively high birth rate but also by continuing Irish and—more recently—Commonwealth immigration. In 1932 some 28 per cent of the Merseyside labour force was out of work; after 1945 serious male unemployment returned again and reached 7 per cent within a year. Since then the Merseyside unemployment rate has been persistently between two and three times the national average and reached 11 per cent in 1976. This region is the subject of a separate study (pp.277-284) so that there need be only a very summary treatment here of its fortunes during its period of government assistance. In fact Merseyside has been perhaps the most successful of all Development Areas in the country in attracting mobile industry, particularly those with a dominantly male labour force. Between 1952 and 1966 new industrial enterprises employing 81,000 workers entered Merseyside: this was 70 per cent of all the mobile employment entering the North West during the period, which itself represented one-sixth of the national total of inter-regional movement. With or without any special status, Merseyside would probably remain the region's dominant growth point. Apart from the new and modernized facilities of the port, there are motorways on both sides of the estuary providing links to the M6, and Liverpool is now scarcely more than two and a half hours from central London by rail. By 1970 Merseyside's economic future seemed relatively secure: indeed the Hunt Committee had recommended the descheduling of the area. But the events of the early 1970s showed that the new industrial structure was far from recession-proof. Unemployment rose quickly, and Merseyside was declared a Special Development Area in 1974. It must be remarked that this is an area that has never lacked its political friends in high places.

Although the creation of a Development Area on Merseyside was intended to correct the chronic ailments of an economy that had never developed a satisfactory manufacturing base, the institution in 1953 of the North West's third area with assisted status—in *North East Lancashire*—was a response to a crisis of more immediate origins. The fine-weaving towns aligned along the Burnley-Nelson-Colne axis had been protected by their specialization in high qualities of cloth from the worst of the decline of the cotton industry. In 1952, about 45 per cent of total employment was in the mills, and an economy of Victorian simplicity survived. However, it was brought close to collapse by the first of the post-war textile recessions, in 1952. Unemployment quickly rose to levels reminiscent of the 1930s, and the district was briskly scheduled as a Development Area. In competition with Merseyside and South Lancashire, it had little to offer to mobile industry except an abundant labour supply of high quality, but even this became less certain as the textile trade cycle moved towards its next crest and unemployment disappeared. Remote in its hill-girt valley, separated from the main mass of industrial Lancashire by the Rossendale upland and a little-improved road system, and as far from London as is Carlisle in terms of journey times, this was one of the least promising Development Areas in the country. Yet it did surprisingly well—for a time. It had already acquired a foothold in some branches of industry new to it by wartime dispersal, and a variety of diverse enterprises moved into the area and by 1969 were providing 11,000 jobs. Thus kitchen equipment, vehicle electrical components, electric heaters and tyres are all now produced by flourishing industries in the locality, which today depends for scarcely a quarter of its work on the textile trades.

This better economic balance has been brought about, however, more through the rapid decline of textiles and the overall size of the labour force, than it has by the growth of new employment. The area lost 19,000 jobs in the mills in the decade 1953 to 1963. The number of women in employment dropped by 13 per cent, and of men by 7 per cent; total population fell by 5.3 per cent between 1951 and 1964 but has become more stable since, as is shown by the loss of only 1 per cent between 1961 and 1971. Of the total of new jobs brought to the area since 1952, about a half (5,000) are provided by firms that have arrived since 1960 (when the area was descheduled) and have occupied existing factories, mostly old mills. Thus the net employment gain directly attributable to the area's status as a Development Area represents scarcely more than 4 per cent of its present reduced total in manufacturing, though government intervention provided the first impetus towards the evolution of a more diverse economy. Between 1969 and 1972 North East Lancashire had some advantage in being part of the then-limited Intermediate Area of the North West, but this has been minimized by the extension of this lowest form of assisted status to the entire region. Major trunk road improvements, however, have now made much easier access westwards to the M6 and southwards to the M62. Even during the difficult years 1971-1975, the area suffered only a marginal loss (2 per cent) in its male employment.

Only one other part of the region had had—and still retains—assisted status: the *Furness* peninsula. This is a remote area detached from the rest of Lancashire by the sands of Morecambe Bay. Barrow is as far from Manchester, in terms of journey time, as is London. It remains a remarkably well-preserved example not merely of a one-industry town, but almost of a one-company town, for its fortunes depend largely on the Vickers shipyards and their associated marine engineering works. A new town of the Industrial Revolution, Barrow grew after the beginning of iron smelting in 1859 and of shipbuilding in 1869. Far from the main centres of shipbuilding, the Barrow industry became a remarkably self-contained and vertically integrated system. It survived with little radical change sustained partly by its specialization in naval construction. The yards remained independent until nationalization, having escaped the consequences of the post-Geddes rationalization of the shipbuilding industry (see p.369ff.). But this perfect survival of a Victorian economy is beginning to change. The chief local ironworks has closed and employment in the shipyard complex has fallen progressively, though the engineering plant has diversified away from marine work. In 1963 the area was designated a Development District. Despite its poor landward communications, Barrow and its sub-region managed to attract a number of new firms making, for example, footwear and pharmaceuticals. Most of this movement predated scheduling, however, and was almost certainly a response to the large reserves of non-employed female labour which characterize a metal-working and shipbuilding economy. But there have been other developments that much more directly reflect the influence of the incentives in regional policy on capital-intensive types of industry. Bowater have made a massive investment in paper products manufacture, in a plant with an employment capacity of 1,300. Vickers have recently invested a further £15 million in the yards, and expect to create 1,000 additional jobs. With its new industrial interests of some growth potential and the peculiarly 'protected' character of its staple industry (based on the nuclear submarine programme), this remote community has fared surprisingly well: indeed since 1966 Furness has shown better than national average employment trends, and in terms of male employment it is one of the stronger sub-regions of the North West (Table 9.1).

Furness has only a tenuous attachment, not only in terms of physical connection but also in the sense of economic and industrial linkages, with the remainder of the North West. Its associations are with the discontinuous ribbon of urban and industrial development which follows the coastal coalfield of *West Cumberland*. For regional planning purposes, this area is part of the Northern region (and now within Cumbria). It has enjoyed Development Area status since 1945. The sub-region emerged from the war of 1939-1945 with its traditional economic base shrunken but fundamentally unmodified. Ore mining contracted sharply during the 1930s through a combination of dwindling resources and rising costs. By 1956 output had dropped to 400,000 tons and in 1968 the last of the major deposits, at Hodbarrow, was abandoned. Fortunately the contribution of ore mining to male employment had been relatively small since the 1930s, but the parallel contraction of the coal-mining industry has had far more serious social consequences. This is geologically an unusually complex field, and today the main mass of the reserves is off-shore, with the working faces as much as four miles out to sea. Long underground hauls together with complex faulting make the field a high-cost producer and it has suffered the inevitable consequences. Fourteen pits were at work in 1947; by 1966 there were three and in 1978 only one. Employment dropped from 6,000 in 1954 to 1,100 in 1978. Thus coal mining, too, has reached the relic stage, and has made its contribution to the persistently high male unemployment. The last of the trio of basic industries, metal manufacture, has had a more secure recent history, but it faces equally bleak prospects. Rationalization came early to the Cumberland steel industry; the many small works of the nineteenth century were replaced, in the 1930s, by a single, integrated plant of the United Steel Companies at Workington. Steel making here ceased in 1973, but the plant continues to produce West Cumberland's traditional specialization, railway track, and also rolls special sections.

Despite the prolonged agony of the traditional industries of West Cumberland, the region has grown more quickly in population during the post-1945 years than for several decades previously. The population in the coastal strip rose from 133,000 in 1951 to 150,000 in 1971. Whitehaven increased by almost 11 per cent, much above the national rate. The economy has shown itself able to absorb the greater part of a higher than average rate of natural increase—though with some degree of unemployment. Since 1953 over ninety new industrial projects have been granted industrial development certificates, and these have created about 6,000 new jobs, a little over half of them for men. This new employment is very diverse; it includes the manufacture of food products (Quaker Oats and Rowntrees), paper (Thames Board), carpets, clothing and pharmaceuticals. But three of the new employers have had a dominant influence on the region's prosperity. Marchon Chemicals (at Whitehaven) employs 2,000 chiefly in the manufacture of detergent materials; it is alone among the new industries in depending in part on local physical resources, for it exploits anhydrite in the Trias as a source of sulphur. The Atomic Energy Authority produces plutonium at its Windscale plant; alongside is the first of Britain's atomic power stations, Calder Hall. This complex already employs 4,000, much of it high-grade professional and technical labour. It is likely to be extended in the form of the controversial British Nuclear Fuels development (an investment of some £200 million) which will create an additional 1,000 jobs in the treatment of nuclear waste. A third major development is the B.L. automated bus plant at Workington. The reasons officially given for the choice of location—that the area might expect serious redundancies in the steel industry—have an ominous ring. But, as part of the agreement, the trunk road to Penrith and the M6 has been improved, so that the isolation of the sub-region, its most persistent problem, will be partly corrected. Thus West Cumberland's relative prosperity, after its disastrous experience in the 1930s (when unemployment in Maryport peaked at almost 70 per cent), may be counted a solid achievement of distribution of industry policies: the structure of employment has been transformed. Nevertheless, there are massive physical as well as economic problems to be faced. Much substandard housing survives as part of a Victorian urban environment. And there are over 1,200 hectares (3,000 acres) of derelict land in the areas of once vigorous coal, iron and metal working. Yet beyond the scarred surface of the mineral fields, not 16 kilometres (10 miles) away, is the magnificent backdrop to the sub-region, the western slopes of the Lake District. They offer a reminder that the fastest developing sector in the national economy is the recreation-based group of manufacturing and service industries.

North East Wales (the eastern, industrial areas of the new county of Clwyd) has long had close association with North West England, and especially with Merseyside (Figure 9.2). Chester served, traditionally, as a *de facto* regional capital for much of the north of the Principality, but the future of both the coalfield of North East Wales and the coastal ribbon of industrial, residential and resort development of Deeside must be seen in the context of the future growth of the Merseyside complex (see p.284). In this section we are concerned with the influence of regional policies on North Wales, for the greater part (excluding Deeside and the resort coast) is within the Welsh Development Area.

The coalfield of North East Wales is divided into two parts, not only geologically but also in terms of industrial structure, by an east-west fracture which separated the old Flintshire and Denbighshire sections. In the former the seams were accessible to coastal shipping and were worked early and intensively: mining had become residual by 1939, but a single small pit survives stubbornly at Point of Ayr, working sub-estuarine seams. In this long-relict northern part of the field there are no significant problems of reemploying a redundant mining labour force. Not only a new structure, but also a new alignment of industry has developed along the shore of the estuary, in three major concentrations. At

Hawarden a wartime aircraft factory has survived the rationalization of the industry, though with a reduced labour force. At Shotton an integrated strip-steel plant occupies reclaimed land, while at Flint and Holywell a man-made fibre industry has been developing since 1917 (though the main plant was partly closed in 1977). This estuarine zone has considerable potential for further urban-industrial development. But the area has its problems. The steel plant at Shotton has long been a candidate for closure. It has secured a reprieve only by political intervention, and the B.S.C. has announced a £29 million development for the production of coated steels, to employ 700. But this is little consolation beside the loss, in 1980, of 6,000 jobs in steel-making. In contrast the southern section of the coalfield shows all the classical problems of a declining mining area. Later to develop, as late as 1959, five substantial pits were at work here, with a total employment of 15,000. Three survived, with a labour force reduced, by 1969, to only 2,600. In 1978 a single survivor employed only 600 men. Alternative employment, traditionally, has been available chiefly in an iron industry of vigorous early development, but today represented only by a plant at Brymbo producing electrical steels. But there has been a strong growth of new employment in firms attracted by Development Area status. Much the largest is the Monsanto chemical plant at Ruabon; at Wrexham an old ordnance factory has become the nucleus of a trading estate with a diversity of light industry on it. It is illustrative of the short-range locational shifts that regional policies sometimes cause that Wrexham attracted investment by Courtaulds (whose chief local interests are at Flint). In 1970 the Pilkington group announced plans to invest £8 million in a glass-fibre plant at Wrexham, a development thought likely to be sited in the Merseyside area. On the coalfield as a whole population has grown strongly during the post-war period, by 13 per cent since 1961 to a 1971 total of 225,000, but with greater pace on Deeside than elsewhere. Out-migration has been halted, and even in the Wrexham area the population grew slightly to a total of just over 100,000 for the town and surrounding district combined.

The same distinction between quick coastal population growth and a progressive decline in the hinterland is repeated in *North West Wales:* here the coastal belt grew by 8 per cent between 1961 and 1971, while the population of the interior declined by 8 per cent over the same period. Population increase in the coastlands is related at least as much to the development of the residential-retirement function of the resorts as to the further development of their holiday industries; indeed the latter have attracted little major recent investment except in the proliferation of caravan camps, the form of tourist development that has the slightest impact on the local economy. The North Wales resorts have a serious problem of seasonal unemployment. Population decline in the interior of the sub-region reflects the contraction both of agriculture and primary industry. Slate quarrying at Blaenau-Ffestiniog and in North Caernarvonshire has shrunk almost to extinction; and the primary sector in the economy of North West Wales as a whole lost 30 per cent of its employment between 1959 and 1966. Attempts to revitalize the economy of North West Wales have taken two forms. A number of very large capital investments have been located here; for example, theTrawsfynyth and the more recent Wylfa Head nuclear power stations, the Tanygrisiau pumped storage scheme, the aluminium smelter on Anglesey and the Dinorwic power station. These have created—or will create—large volumes of localized male employment, but chiefly during construction. Secondly, a rather slow flow of manufacturing enterprises, offering more permanent employment, has been attracted through the Assisted Area status of the sub-region; for example,

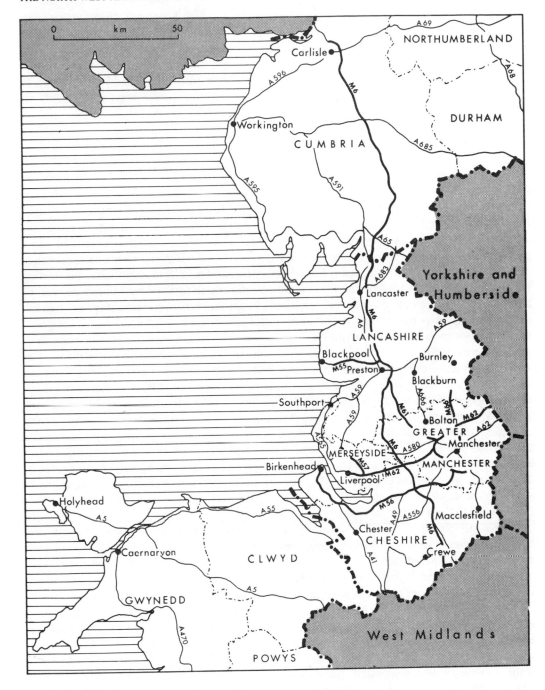

Figure 9.2 The functional North West, including North Wales and Cumbria

Pilkington's have an optical glass plant at St Asaph and Ferodo a friction-materials plant at Caernarvon. Even limited and localized growth of factory employment has a considerable impact in an area in which (in the new county of Gwynedd) only 11 per cent of personal income derives from industry, 18 per cent from agriculture and 15 per cent from tourism. Now with Special Development Area status Gwynedd has funds to establish fourteen advance factory units in an attempt to counteract the effects of remoteness.

9.2.2 Industrial Mobility

The whole purpose of the policies of government intervention in the location of industry which have evolved from the Distribution of Industry Act of 1945 is to persuade or coerce mobile enterprises to move to areas of greatest need for new employment, and from areas in which the further growth of industry would only serve to overheat economic systems growing too quickly for their own good. The acid test of the success of these policies, therefore, lies in an evaluation of the patterns of industrial movement that they have helped to generate and guide, both inter-regionally and intra-regionally. Neglecting for the moment West Cumberland and North Wales, three sorts of movement need to be considered: the entry of new enterprises (whether by total transfer or branch development) into the North West from other regions of Britain; the intra-regional movement of mobile industry from sub-region to sub-region within the North West; and, lastly, the movement of enterprises from the North West to other parts of Britain. The salient facts are quickly stated. Of intra-regional movement into the North West between 1945 and 1967, Merseyside secured much the greatest share, some 70 per cent of the total. In intra-regional shifts within the North West, the Manchester sub-region was by far the greatest 'exporter' of employment, and Merseyside the leading beneficiary; the former provided 15,000 of the 21,000 jobs involved in intra-regional movement, while the latter secured 40 per cent of this total. In the movement of employment out of the North West entirely, Manchester was again the chief sub-region of origin, losing 17,000 of a total of 28,000 jobs to locations elsewhere. This pattern of industrial movement, at its simplest, is a pronounced westwards shift of employment, both in relative and actual terms, from South East to South West Lancashire.

In the movement of mobile industry between regions, the North West has been a very substantial net beneficiary: 108,000 jobs were created by incoming industry between 1945 and 1967, compared with a loss to other regions of only 28,000. Moreover the attractiveness of the North West progressively increased; it secured only 13 per cent of the inter-regional movement of manufacturing between 1952 and 1959, but 25 per cent during the period 1960 to 1965. This is clearly the direct result of Merseyside's success in attracting mobile firms; but other parts of the region shared more modestly in this inflow. South Lancashire and North East Lancashire attracted 14,000 and 11,000 jobs respectively, while the inflow into Furness of 5,000 jobs is the highest share relative to total sub-regional employment (to which it represents a 12 per cent addition). The Manchester area secured a substantial share of employment inflow (9,000), but the outflow was almost four times this size (Board of Trade, 1969).

By the early 1970s the North West was securing a lower share (14 per cent in the five years to 1976) of the national total of new industrial floorspace created, itself reduced by depression. But the broad trends in intra-regional distribution remain much the same

(North West Economic Planning Council, 1975). Between 1966 and 1971, 146 new plants were created by movement from outside the region or by inter-sub-regional movement within it. Of these, sixty-one sought locations on Merseyside and eighteen in South Lancashire. Only thirteen went to Manchester and sixteen to North East Lancashire. They represented an employment increase of almost 12,000 in Merseyside and South Lancashire combined, but only 2,500 in Manchester and 1,500 in the North East. The locations of new investments generated within the region also repeat earlier trends. Manchester generated a hundred new enterprises over the period: sixty-two stayed in the Manchester area, but of the thirty-eight that went elsewhere, Merseyside and South Lancashire secured twenty-one. In contrast, of Merseyside's fifty-seven new enterprises, fifty-two stayed in their own sub-region. The moves form Manchester represent a loss of 4,000 jobs. The evidence is that the 'leakage' of work and investment westwards across the region continues, with Manchester the main origin and Merseyside the chief destination. Whether the extension of the Intermediate Area will change this remains to be seen: North East Lancashire had this status for part of the period reviewed, and did somewhat better in attracting mobile firms than might have been expected otherwise.

Apart from Development Areas policy, a second major influence at work in shaping this pattern of industrial growth is the availability of cheap mill premises for conversion. This not only makes possible the growth of a new enterprise at minimum capital cost, but it also evades the industrial development certificate controls. In all parts of the North West except Merseyside and Furness, a majority of new jobs is attributable to the conversion of existing premises; and in the region as a whole just over half the total of new employment is in converted rather than newly-built accommodation. Even this does not give a full measure of the importance of mill conversion to the changing regional economy, for neither very small firms nor young firms newly born within the region and which have taken up space in old mills are reflected in these figures.

The structure of employment in 'immigrant' industry is significant, for the great bulk is in those growth sectors of which the North West has had an inadequate share. Taking the period 1953 to 1966, some 83 per cent of all new employment entering the region was in the growth sectors, defining these in terms of national trends. The vehicle industry was much the most important, providing 23,000 new jobs within the region, largely concentrated on Merseyside. Electrical products and instruments (7,000), mechanical engineering (7,600) and the food and drink industries were the next most important. All of these, but especially vehicle manufacture, made very great contributions to the overall change in the structure of industry in the North West. Not surprisingly, the greater part (77 per cent) of the mobile employment that left the North West between 1945 and 1967 was also in the growth sectors; by their nature these are inevitably the most mobile sections of the economy. But the loss of industry from the region contains a larger proportion from what are, both nationally and regionally, declining trades—especially textiles and clothing. Progressively the outflow of employment has tended both to decline overall and to become increasingly dominated by the declining sectors: textile and clothing employment accounted for over half of the outflow between 1960 and 1965. Almost exactly the same pattern is true of intra-regional movement. It has shrunk in overall volume in the recent past, and has become more strongly dominated by declining industries, especially textiles and clothing. This might be seen to be no bad thing for those areas of South East Lancashire and North East Cheshire that are the chief areas of 'export' for intra-regional shifts of employment; but in textiles at least the migrating firms are among the more enterprising, for migration is almost inevitably associated with reequipment and the construction of more modern plants.

Only the more salient features of a most complex pattern of industrial movement have been presented here, but a number of conclusions as to the operation of industrial guidance policies in the North West are clear. Only Merseyside has derived major and lasting benefits directly from the 'steering' element in Assisted Area policies. Of the other assisted areas, both Furness and South Lancashire made their fastest acquisition of new employment either before scheduling (the former) or after descheduling (the latter); while in North East Lancashire, despite the 'spearhead' role of guided enterprises, the uncontrolled process of mill conversion has provided the bulk of incoming employment. Mill conversion is in a sense the antithesis of Assisted Area policy. The extraordinarily low cost of space in old mills balances the incentives that Assisted Areas offer, and the re-use of industrial premises avoids the operation of industrial development certificate procedures. The process appears to have brought a greater volume of new employment to the region than the steering powers of government intervention. Without it, the whole of the textile zone, except perhaps North East Lancashire, would have a miserable record of industrial attraction. But even the availability of such cheap premises was unable to prevent South East Lancashire and parts of Cheshire and Derbyshire—in short, the Manchester city-region—from suffering a far greater outflow than inflow of new enterprises. These are the circumstances that led regional interests in South East Lancashire to make such a powerful case in 1968/1969 to the Hunt Committee for 'Intermediate' status in the operation of industrial guidance policies.

To recount the apparent effect of regional policy on sub-regional employment structures, or to summarize the general pattern of employment change, is not, of course, an adequate appraisal of the broader influence of government intervention on the correction of the economic weaknesses of the region. Some of these underlying problems were examined in the preparation of the strategic plan for the region (Department of the Environment, 1974). Is the North West 'inefficient' in terms of overall industrial productivity, unit labour costs and gross profit per employee: are there radical weaknesses that explain its poor performance? Table 9.3 suggests not. The region certainly had a poorer productivity position than the U.K. in 1958, but by 1968 had distinctly out-paced national growth in productivity and was fourth (to the South East, South West and Wales) in the regional table. Unit labour costs in the North West were almost exactly at the national average: gross profit was below national levels in 1958 and 1963, but it is assumed that the rise in productivity would have brought the regional level close to the national by 1968. Dated and incomplete though these figures are, they do not suggest a condition of primary economic failure. Indeed, the North West is distinctly stronger than the East and West Midlands in all these measures of productivity, unit labour costs and gross profit. But there is an obvious intra-regional contrast. On all these measures of competitiveness the Manchester sub-region is far weaker than Merseyside. Plainly the regional average is held back by all those problems of economic debility that have been described for the traditional textile areas of the East. Perhaps, too, the strength of Merseyside's position is one of the subtler successes of the regional policy.

The question is often raised whether there is a radical conflict between the aims of regional policy, to secure a distribution of employment in accordance with social needs, and the aims of national economic planning, to maximize output from the available labour and so raise standards of living by creating wealth through the most efficient use of

Table 9.3 The North West and the U.K.: some economic indicators

		U.K.	North West	Manchester	Merseyside
Average annual	1958	572	540	535	591
wage (£)	1961	717	695	684	746
Productivity:	1958	1,007	963	926	1,115
output per worker,	1963	1,363	1,312	1,243	1,461
manufacturing (£)	1968	1,954	1,996	—	—
Unit Labour costs,	1958	0.57	0.56	0.58	0.53
manufacturing (£)	1963	0.53	0.53	0.55	0.51
Gross profit per	1958	436	423	390	524
employee (£)	1963	646	616	558	715

Source: Department of the Environment (1974)

Table 9.4 The North West: proportion of labour absorbed and proportion of net output generated in manufacturing industries, 1968

	Labour force as % total in manufactures	Net output as % total for manufactures
Food and drink	10	12
Chemicals and allied	9.5	17
Metal	2.7	3
Engineering group	23	21
Shipbuilding	2.3	2
Vehicles	8.9	11
Other metal goods	5	4
Textiles	14.3	10
Leather, etc.	0.7	under 0.5
Clothing and footwear	6.5	3
Bricks, glass, etc.	3.7	4
Timber, etc.	2.7	2
Paper and printing	6.9	7
Other manufactures	4.1	4

Source: Department of the Environment (1974)

resources. This question is explored, for the North West, in Table 9.4. For each industry both the percentage of the total regional labour force it absorbs, and the percentage of the total volume of regional manufactured output it generates, are shown. Discrepancies show that individual industries contribute more or less than their fair share to the total generation of wealth in the region. They also show that the older industries, in the main, absorb far more labour than is justified by their output. This is true of textiles and clothing: unhappily it is also true, more marginally, of the engineering group. In contrast, chemicals (quite dramatically) and vehicles produce more wealth than their labour inputs would indicate. To some extent, of course, this is a contrast between labour-intensive and capital-intensive industries. But this merely restates an objective of regional policy, which ought to be to encourage the growth of the latter at the expense of the former. In the short term this sort of policy objective will not maximize job-creation: in the longer term it will maximize wealth creation and so lead to the highest possible standard of living. Certainly this is the ultimate objective of national economic planning. In general the effect of regional policy has been in this same direction. A comparison of these data with those in Table 9.2 will show a progressive transfer of labour from industries of low per capita generation of wealth to those which contribute much more effectively to the process of wealth generation.

9.2.3 Industrial Decentralization and the Decline of the Inner City*

For at least a quarter of a century the inner areas of the major British conurbations have been passing through a period of quiet and unspectacular decay accompanied by the decomposition of their industrial economies. The general problem is reviewed elsewhere (p.91ff.). In the North West the two major urban masses, Manchester and Merseyside, exhibit this process of industrial decentralization and the economic deterioration of the inner city to an extreme degree. Everywhere, the inner city has become a zone of economic weakness: in a region with a deteriorating economic base this problem is inevitably exacerbated by external causes. However, the general dependence of the regional economy on industries of secular decline is *not* a prime cause of the decay of manufacturing in the inner city. In the case of Manchester, the spectrum of industry within the Victorian core is by no means a reflection of the general regional structure of manufacturing: indeed, some of the weakest sectors regionally (the general textile industries, textile machinery, general engineering) are little represented, while some of the industries most prominent in the inner city (chemicals, rubber, electronic and scientific equipment) are among those with the best employment records, regionally and nationally. In brief, there is no easy structural explanation for the decline of so much inner urban industry. The causes of decline are subtle and complex. Tiny firms dominate the pattern of industry in the urban core: the great majority employ fewer than fifty manual workers and the median size is as low as ten. Most occupy old and converted premises: 37 per cent of the industrial buildings, in Manchester as a whole, are 'poor' or 'obsolete', and the proportion is much higher towards the centre. Such small enterprises often succumb to disturbance. The massive clearance and redevelopment of the greater part of Victorian Manchester over the last fifteen years has caused immense industrial mortality. Where industry is a non-conforming use, it has been dealt with rather ruthlessly: the planned industrial zones provide no suitable substitute environment for the small and struggling firm. Urban renewal is certainly a major cause of the loss of factory employment in the inner city: unlike Birmingham, Manchester made little or no attempt to provide cheap space in 'flatted factories' as a substitute for the rabbit warren of old industrial accommodation that was being cleared. Indeed, the city seems to have identified the size and scale of the problem of job losses in inner urban manufacturing only quite recently.

*This section is based very largely on the series of studies published from the North West Industry Research Unit of the University of Manchester, by P. Dicken & P.E. Lloyd and their associates, to whom full and grateful acknowledgement is made.

A close study of the industrial decline of inner Manchester (Lloyd and Mason, 1978) shows that in an area of 30 square kilometres extending to between 1 and 2 kilometres from the central business district (C.B.D.) there was a net loss of over 30,000 manufacturing jobs between 1966 and 1972: one such job in every three disappeared over this period. Small plants were the most vulnerable: over half the firms that closed employed fewer than ten workers and over 70 per cent fewer than twenty. But in employment terms the problem is most crucial in the middle orders of the plant-size range: about 55 per cent of all the jobs lost by closure was in plants with between 20 and 250 workers. Future urban policy must clearly provide the accommodation needs of plants of this scale, though the 'seed-bed' nature of the mass of even smaller firms is an equally critical one. Away from central Manchester (though only rarely in the city itself) old cotton mills have been converted to supply the space needs of many of those small and middle-sized firms, perhaps a reason why most of the larger textile towns (Bolton and Stockport, for example) have not suffered manufacturing job losses on the scale of inner Manchester.

The contraction of the industrial base of inner Manchester reflects a complex process: at the level of the plant, there are 'exits', 'entries' and changes up or down in the employment levels of plants that remain *in situ*. 'Exits' may mean plant closures, or transfers either outside the study area or to other sites within it. 'Entries' include the births of new plants, transfers from outside the study area or transfers within it. Between 1966 and 1972 'exits' accounted for the loss of 35,400 jobs in inner Manchester: of these, 28,300 were caused by the deaths of plants through closure, while 3,000 jobs were lost through transfer outside the study area and 4,000 jobs were relocated within the inner city. Industrial decentralization in the sense of plant transfers from inner city to suburbs is clearly a very minor cause of employment losses in the urban core. The main cause of the problem is the death of enterprises in what has become an increasingly hostile environment for industry. But a substantial number of firms have moved locations (usually through the disturbance of urban renewal) to new, if temporary, niches that they have found in the inner city. The 'entry' of new plants has created 11,000 inner city manufacturing jobs (3,900 of which can be discounted since they were within-zone transfers). The signs are all too clear that the inner urban environment has almost totally lost its power to attract footloose enterprises. Of the 11,000 jobs in 'entry' plants, 6,500 are the products of new industrial births. Among firms that remained *in situ* during this six-year period, many more declined in employment than grew, so that 6,000 jobs were lost by this cause.

The sad facts are clear enough. Inner Manchester has become a most unhealthy environment for manufacturing. The industrial birth rate versus death rate balance has become strongly adverse: almost 22,000 jobs were lost from this cause alone. A thousand plants died: probably the majority were affected by locational disturbance, though fewer than 10 per cent waited to have compulsory purchase orders served on them. The loss of cheaply convertible premises has depressed the industrial birth rate. Of all the 'exit' cases, only one in twelve found it possible to relocate away from inner Manchester but within the conurbation, so that their employment potential was not lost to the larger labour market area. The most favoured direction of movement was south eastwards towards Stockport. Entries into inner Manchester by transfer from outside were trivial in number and employment. For the plants that remained in their locations over the period, a slow drift to lower employment levels was the general trend. Thus a third of the manufacturing jobs present in the inner city in 1966 were gone by 1972: by 1975 another 9,400 jobs had been lost. Of course, there is something to be offset against this decline. Service employment in Manchester has held up better than industrial (but has declined sharply since 1969). One special case of the generation of replacement employment deserves mention, an example of the rise of the quaternary sector. The Manchester Education Precinct has carved a 3 kilometre long slice from the inner city: scores of small firms occupied small premises in what were rotting slums. Two universities, three other tertiary educational institutions, a major hospital complex and some 'fringe' users like the B.B.C. occupy this redeveloped space. Planned for 25,000 students (and occupied by about 18,000 already), the whole complex must now provide at least 6,000 jobs, with a high technical, white-collar and academic proportion. Alas, this sort of employment opportunity does little to relieve the distress of the multi-racial and underprivileged population living in redeveloped housing close by. In one of these deprived areas male unemployment was 17.5 per cent in 1977, teenage unemployment was over 20 per cent, and the rate among black teenagers is now well above this figure. These are the intolerable social costs of the progressive run-down of the inner urban economy.

The decline of the manufacturing base in the inner areas of Merseyside has taken a somewhat different course, though the consequences are much the same as in Manchester. A parallel study (Lloyd, 1977) defines inner industrial Merseyside rather more broadly than in the case of Manchester, as the pre-1914 urban mass on both sides of the estuary. It is the area in which the bulk of the port-linked manufacturing of the nineteenth century was located (see p.297 below). This is a zone of prolonged and (in the light of employment trends) merciful population decrease, from 725,000 in 1921 to less than 300,000 in 1977. The community left behind is multiply disadvantaged. It has a low level of industrial skill and is inured to casual work and long periods of unemployment: teenagers leave school with little to offer a declining labour market. In some central wards male unemploymnt is as high as 25 per cent. A visibly shrinking economic base can no longer support even this reduced population. For at least twenty years employment growth has been confined to the periphery of the conurbation, but journey-to-work costs have risen to the point at which the net wages of a distant job are scarcely better than welfare payments. This is the background against which the poor industrial relations record of Merseyside has to be seen, and perhaps better understood.

Inner Merseyside lost 18,300 jobs in manufacturing between 1966 and 1975, a decline of 24 per cent: both relatively and absolutely this is a less dramatic decline than in the case of Manchester, where almost 40,000 jobs were lost in a more compact definition of the inner city. The data underline the gravity of Manchester's crisis: measured even by Merseyside standards its inner city employment trend is desperately bad. Moreover, secular changes and structural factors more readily explain the decline of inner urban industry on Merseyside. About 40 per cent of the manufacturing workforce, in 1966, was in shipbuilding and food and drink, both industries of quick recent employment decline (p.280) by about 25 per cent in both cases to 1975. But in fact every industrial group (except two minor ones) suffered serious job losses over the period. There is a further contrast with the case of Manchester: there the massive loss of inner urban employment reflects the deaths of large numbers of the relatively small plants that dominate the zone. But on Merseyside a few large plants account both for a large share of the total employment and the bulk of the losses of work. About a dozen plants, each employing over 1,000 workers, provided 47 per cent of the 1966 employment in the zone, and account for about half the total manufacturing job loss. Plants with fewer than fifty workers provided only 17 per cent of all jobs in 1966 and contributed only about 12 per cent of the employment losses to 1977. The Merseyside problem is not one of smallish firms struggling to retain premises and profitability in the changing environment of the inner city. Rather it reflects the operation of extraneous factors quite outside local influence or control. The fate of the British shipbuilding industry, closure by merger in electrical and telecommunication engineering, rationalization within the food industry (where the fate of a large sugar plant is uncertain) are the underlying causes of Merseyside's inner urban problems. By the same token, the solutions must be largely external: regional policy has brought immense amounts of new work to Merseyside since 1945 (p.281) but to peripheral rather than central locations (Lloyd, 1979).

The mechanics of manufacturing change in inner Merseyside are not known with quite the precise degree of detail that applies to Manchester. 'Exits' from the inner city over the 1966-1975 period affected 766 plants: 108 transferred to other inner city sites and 658 were either closures or transfers outside the study area. Thirty of these latter 'decentralized' to city fringe sites (especially in Speke, Kirkby and Bootle), but the numbers leaving for the more distant periphery (for example, Skelmersdale and Runcorn new towns) are not known, nor is the total of 'deaths'. Most 'exits' from the inner city involved small or medium-sized plants, especially in the 21-50 and 101-250 size ranges. Food-processing and clothing firms were the most vulnerable. 'Exits' accounted for a loss of 15,500 jobs. This was far from balanced by the creation of a net 6,400 jobs by new 'entries' (discounting firms who moved sites within the inner city). These, too, were small firms, none over 250 workers and most with fewer than 50 workers. Many were doubtless new 'births' in the industrial seedbed of the inner city, where cheap premises and low-wage labour attract the entrepreneur. Many such firms have a short life-cycle, and die, move, or change to a new form within five to ten years. Engineering, metal goods and clothing account for most births. But in Liverpool, much more than in Manchester, a large part of the net job loss in inner city industry (about half) reflects *in situ* decline by firms present both in 1966 and 1975. Moreover, this *it situ* shrinkage was not balanced by the level of employment in 'entries' (while in Manchester it was). Despite its appalling net losses in inner city industries, a vigorous plant birth rate persists in Manchester, but this appears less the case on Merseyside. In one respect the two conurbations are similar, in that decentralization by direct movement from inner city to suburban fringe is a very minor cause both of inner city loss and peripheral gain. In Merseyside, especially, the pattern of change is one in which many firms in the inner city (large and small but mostly associated with the traditional port-linked groups) have disappeared or declined, while other enterprises (mostly much bigger and many of them not in port-related groups) have been attracted to the region as a real achievement of regional policy, but have chosen peripheral sites at or beyond the acceptable limits of journey-to-work movement by the underprivileged and increasingly distressed inner urban community. What a comparison of Manchester with Merseyside—an area not 'assisted' until very recently with a development area of thirty years' standing—suggests is that regional policy in its classic form has been very largely irrelevant to the critical problems, both economic and social, of inner urban decay.

9.3 Merseyside: An Economic Miracle?

On any map to show the location of industrial expansion in Britain since 1945, Merseyside is an outstanding node of new growth. By any measure—the volume of new employment created, the total of industrial floorspace built, or size of capital investment

—Merseyside ranks with Teesside, Severnside and the lower Thames as one of those estuarine growth points that have attracted so large a share of the nation's recent heavy industrial development. Yet the Merseyside of 1945 had an economic structure with little capacity for expansion, and much potential for further decline. Indeed, there seemed every prospect in the immediate post-war years that the area would repeat its lamentable inter-war experience. The scheduling of a large part of Merseyside as a Development Area in 1949 saved the region. By 1975, 94,000 new industrial jobs had been created on Merseyside, though not all could be attributed to its special status, nor have all survived. Without the influx of new work that this has brought, factory employment on Merseyside would have fallen substantially and total employment would have been barely stable. The economic transformation of Merseyside is, therefore, one of the undoubted achievements of the Assisted Area concept. It can be argued that the price of success on Merseyside has been too high, for it has meant not only that most mobile industry entering the North West has been steered into Merseyside, but also that there has been a substantial intra-regional transfer of employment to it from the textile towns. In answer to this view, it is plain that with or without the incentives and constraints of industrial guidance policies this great estuary and its port complex must inevitably be, in the long term, the North West's most attractive growth point.

The first half of the twentieth century was an unhappy one for the port of Liverpool. As the century dawned, a newly created port at the end of the 60 kilometre (37 mile) long Manchester Ship Canal was gradually eroding the trade of Liverpool's traditional hinterland. During the 1930s no major British port had so depressed a hinterland; by 1935 the value of exports passing through Liverpool fell to less than half the average of the early 1920s. There had been only a feeble development of manufacturing on Merseyside, and most industry was import-based, so that the bulk of all employment depended directly or indirectly upon the docks and their trade. Thus unemployment rose to a sub-regional rate of 28 per cent in 1932, remained as high as 20 per cent even at the trade cycle crest in 1938, and rose again to a post-war peak of 7 per cent in 1946.

So much attention has centred on Merseyside's industrial progress as a Development Area that it is easy to overlook the revolution that has come, slowly and painfully, to the port itself. There is not one port on the Mersey estuary but several. The Mersey Docks and Harbour Company controls not only the 10 kilometre (6 mile) long line of docks that forms Liverpool's waterfront, but also the dock complex based on Wallasey Pool on the Cheshire shore. Down-river are the private Unilever port at Bromborough on the Cheshire side and the former railway port at Garston on the Lancashire shore, while the terminal facilities at the entrance to the Manchester Ship Canal are, geographically though not technically, part of the Merseyside port system. Of the main mass of the Liverpool-Birkenhead docks it may be said that it entered the second half of the twentieth century admirably equipped to handle the trade of the late nineteenth. Almost 263 hectares (650 acres) of docks provided 60 kilometres (38 miles) of quays—although many of the entrances set serious restrictions of draught and beam—while the great landing stages at the Pierhead provided mass facilities for an overseas passenger trade that has now dwindled to extinction. In short, this was a general cargo and passenger port ill-equipped to handle shipping of increasing size and specialization, and served by an immense, casually employed dock labour force for whose manual skills there was a diminishing demand. The size of the port set its own obvious problems of adaptation, but progress has been made. The obsolete South Dock estate has been closed. There has been general improvement to handling facilities and to dock access, especially at the Canada group, and part of the Gladstone Dock has been converted into a container terminal. Huskisson Dock has been adapted for semi-automatic bulk sugar handling, some of the southern and Birkenhead docks have been further developed for bulk grain discharge, while Birkenhead also had an ore terminal handling over 1.5 million tons annually for the Shotton integrated steel strip mill (now closed). A new drive-on ferry service has strengthened Liverpool's position in competition with specialist ferry ports for the Irish trade, now largely dominated by the container and road-trailer. But much the most ambitious scheme in Liverpool's dockland is the Seaforth extension, at the seaward end of the system: a £33 million investment here has created ten new deep-water berths (three of them for container handling) which will be able to accommodate shipping with a 48 foot draught; the first berths opened in 1972, and a new, automated grain-handling facility, enormously economical of labour by previous standards, is now operating.

Up-river from the main mass of the port, the outlying dock facilities have always been more specialized in function. Bromborough Dock handles bulk cargoes of vegetable oils by a pipeline system, and uses conveyor belts for dry cargo to serve the Unilever food, fat and soap plants. Garston has always specialized in timber, and for both this and chemical raw materials it has advanced equipment. Along its first 8 kilometres (5 miles) from Eastham locks, the Manchester Ship Canal is virtually a linear port; and wood pulp and petroleum are discharged for the Ellesmere Port-Stanlow industrial complex. The development of the oil trade illustrates more clearly than any other the problems that the Mersey ports face. Oil docks to accommodate 16,000 d.w.t. tankers were built at Stanlow in 1922, close to which the Shell refinery was later sited. A realization that tanker sizes would rise led to the development during the mid-1950s of a new oil dock at the canal entrance to handle 30,000 d.w.t. vessels. Initiative then inevitably passed out of the hands of the Manchester Ship Canal company to the then Mersey Dock Board which, in association with Shell, built the Tranmere oil terminal with its twin jetties to take tankers initially in the 60,000-100,000 d.w.t. range, but now able to accept 200,000 d.w.t. vessels. Under development is a new deep-water terminal at Amlwych on Anglesey, linked to Stanlow by pipeline; but Merseyside will still be able to handle short-haul North Sea oil in smaller tankers, as well as the even smaller vessels used to distribute products.

In the development of manufacturing on Merseyside two themes occur; one is the expansion and decline of a range of traditional industries based directly on the trade of the port itself; while the other is the more recent growth of manufactures new to the area and not directly linked to the port. Some traditional trades have had phases of significant growth over the post-war period (Table 9.5) but others have declined. The weakest has been shipbuilding and repairing, with a 36 per cent loss in employment between 1966 and 1975 and considerable uncertainty since then. The major yard (Cammell Laird at Birkenhead) remained independent during the reconstruction of the industry (p.369-371). But by 1970 it was in financial crisis, partly through the loss of nuclear submarine work to Barrow, and was saved by the government taking a 50 per cent equity stake, even before nationalization in 1977. Another of the old port-based industries, the food, drink and tobacco group, showed stability until 1967 but a decline since despite the attraction of new enterprises (for example, frozen foods and chocolate). The engineering and electrical group (once linked to port activities, now largely divorced from them) has shown much the same trend. There was strong growth in the 1960s, stimulated by Assisted Area status, but followed by a sharp decline since. This group has had more than its fair share of

Table 9.5 Merseyside: trends in employment, 1951-1975

	1951	1962	1967	1973	Change (%) 1951-1967	Change (%) 1966-1975
TOTAL	701,000	761,000	779,200	734,200	+ 11	—
Primary sector	14,900	12,000	8,400	7,000	− 44	—
Manufacturing sector	300,000	304,700	323,500	267,600	+ 8	− 14
Food and drink	50,700	53,100	51,100	47,900	+ 1	− 5
Chemicals	47,800	47,800	45,200	32,300	− 5	− 12
Engineering and electrical	73,100	58,600	70,200	63,300	+ 19*	− 23
Ships and repairing		15,200	17,300	24,200	+ 13*	− 36
Vehicles	12,500	9,600	29,500	39,000	+ 136	+ 10
Other metal goods	13,100	14,300	16,100	12,000	+ 22	− 14
Clothing	13,000	12,700	10,500	9,400	− 19	− 14
Bricks, glass	26,300	27,300	26,800	22,800	+ 2	− 20
Paper and printing	14,000	18,700	18,000	16,700	+ 29	+ 1
Service sector	318,400	394,300	385,600	345,300	+ 21	− 14
Transport	105,700	95,900	82,300	71,800	− 22	− 36
Distribution	79,000	101,200	93,700	92,100	+ 19	− 24
Finance	14,300	17,700	18,200	28,400	+ 27	+ 25
Professions	48,100	69,600	83,600	106,500	+ 73	+ 20
Public administration	25,700	29,000	28,600	45,600	+ 12	+ 22

Note: 1951, 1962 and 1967 data are for the Merseyside Development Area.
    1973 data are for the Merseyside group of travel-to-work areas.
    1966-1975 change data are for the Merseyside metropolitan county.
*1962-1967
Source: Department of Employment; North West Economic Planning Council (1975)

misfortunes on Merseyside in the difficult conditions of the 1970s. External factors have caused a number of serious plant closures. English Electric was well represented on Merseyside, and the process of rationalization following the merger with G.E.C. has led to factory closures. Plessey, too, have reduced capacity by closing a plant on Merseyside. A decade ago it was possible to see the engineering group as the spearhead of industrial diversification on Merseyside, but recent losses have wiped out earlier gains, so that 1973 employment was back to the level of 1962.

   Another of the traditional industries of the region, chemicals, has developed very vigorously in a technological sense, has absorbed massive investments, yet has failed to generate significant additions to employment. Investment has often been to reduce labour inputs. The stability in employment total (with a slight decline between 1966 and 1977) masks a major transformation of the industry, a shift from the old alkali-based complex and its modern derivatives in the twin towns of Widnes and Runcorn at the head of the estuary, to petrochemicals based on the Shell oil refinery at Ellesmere Port. The plants here exchange products by pipeline with the Carrington plant 37 kilometres (23 miles) further up the Ship Canal. A recent major expansion more than doubled Shell's chemical production and raised the capacity of the refinery from under 11 million tons to over 19 million tons. This complex is the chemical industry's major growth point in the region. In contrast, the older branches at the head of the estuary have had problems of adaptation and readjustment to face. The old alkali industry at Widnes, based on Lancashire coal,

Cheshire salt and the long-obsolete Leblanc process began to wither a century ago, when the Solvay process was applied on the Northwich saltfield to create what has now become the Winnington-Wallerscotes complex. The alkali industry left Widnes a legacy of miscellaneous chemical manufactures, acids and chlorine compounds, and more recently fertilizers, phosophorous ammonia and potassium products. Runcorn shares in this general chemical industry, but also produces both salt and electrolytic soda from brine piped from the saltfield. One theme common to these diverse industries, and to the soap and detergent manufactures of Warrington, is that technical advances have progressively reduced labour inputs, and at an accelerating rate.

A broad conclusion stems from this selective review of some of the traditional manufacturing industries of Merseyside. None has generated a sustained growth in labour demand over the post-1945 period; all have weak sectors or their problems of adjustment and adaptation. Almost all suffered a marked reduction in employment (or a sharp fall in the rate of growth) during and since the 1960s after a stronger performance during the 1950s. In short, the port-based industries alone were proving themselves entirely incapable of absorbing the very rapid growth in employable population that the region was generating by its high birth rate—this despite their reinforcement by 'mobile' enterprises guided to Merseyside by the distribution of industry legislation, which provided some 12,000 new jobs in the 'old' trades. It was a happy accident (rather than carefully planned timing) that the growth of Merseyside's car industry came as the older industrial base was passing into a period of weak labour demand.

The origins of car assembly in the sub-region lie in the series of bargains struck between the government of the day and the major assembly firms early in the 1960s by which, in effect, their expansion was divided between their traditional locations and the Development Areas (see pp.224-230). Three of the companies affected chose to expand on Merseyside: Ford, Vauxhall and Standard-Triumph, the last now a division of B.L. They doubtless saw good reason, apart from government pressures and the incentive provisions of the 1960 Local Employment Act, to prefer sites there rather than other possible locations. There was the obvious advantage of a major port to an export-orientated industry. There was the further attraction of surplus labour resources (which were continually being replenished by a high birth rate), an existing components industry in industrial Lancashire, and a major steel strip producer at Shotton. Moreover, at the time, progress was advanced both on the building of the M6 motorway and on the electrification of the London-Midland main line, so that communications with the parent plants were in the process of radical improvement.

This was industrial growth on a grand scale, and a remarkable act of faith on the part of the firms concerned. Their total investment by 1969 was of the order of £160 million; their direct employment was over 30,000 workers, and by 1975 the vehicle group provided a total of 39,000 jobs. Yet all three brought quite different approaches to their development on Merseyside. The Ford site at Halewood (closer to Widnes than Liverpool) lies alongside the electrified railway line which provides a high-speed daily shuttle service linking the Halewood and Dagenham production lines. Thus, engines are made by the latter, whilst transmissions are made by the former. Assembly is divided between the two. Vauxhall's original intention was to develop its Ellesmere Port facilities only for components. These were to be transported to Luton for assembly, despite the new factory's poor rail access and indifferent links with the motorway system. In fact, this policy has been reversed. The Ellesmere Port plant has been developed as an almost self-contained unit for small-car production, which it monopolizes, and it also supplies components to the parent plant. Bodies, engines, and transmissions are all produced at Ellesmere Port, which is thus a highly-integrated and automated, low-cost unit. The two Triumph factories at Speke grew from a body and trim plant that sent complete car bodies to Coventry. One plant was later developed for small-car (and later sports-car) production but was closed in 1978 with the loss of 6,000 jobs, the most bitter blow of a bad decade to the morale of Merseyside. The surviving plant continues to make bodies, in much its original role.

The impact of the creation, so quickly, of so much new work in a high-wage industry has been enormous. For a time it more than offset the downward drift of employment in the older industries, so that total factory employment on Merseyside grew by 8 per cent between 1953 and 1966 (though since then it has fallen by 14 per cent). On the other hand, it has not removed (or even reduced) unemployment, which has risen from 3 to 11 per cent; and because of their peripheral sites the benefits of the new firms are by no means confined to central Merseyside. Halewood is easily accessible from the mill and pit towns of Central Lancashire, while Ellesmere Port is much closer to Chester (facing problems of rationalization in the aircraft industry) than to any part of North Merseyside. But the motor vehicle industry cannot, itself, guarantee the region's future. Nationally, it no longer has a growing demand for labour, and (after the Speke disaster) Merseyside's share of future investments will doubtless depend on factors as diverse and unpredictable as the future of regional policy and local experience in labour relations. The strength of the 'multiplier effect', too, is problematical. It was expected that component firms would flood into both Merseyside and the North West generally following the growth of the assembly factories. Certainly, some firms have come into the area—to make, for example, spark plugs and brake assemblies. Others were already established in the region; for example, Dunlop were at Liverpool, A.C.-Delco at Kirkby, and both Lucas and Michelin had plants in North East Lancashire. Others are known to have considered Merseyside sites, and rejected them. In fact, the patterns of subcontracting in vehicle manufacture are so complex, the ease of movement between Lancashire and the West Midlands now so great, and the scale economies and externalities of production in the latter so formidable (pp.224-230), that it would be naive to see the components manufacturers as tied, locationally, to the shirt-tails of the assemblers. Moreover, the survival of components firms depends on the health of the assemblers; thus the Lucas C.A.V. plant closed with the loss of 1,200 jobs (because of the weakness of the heavy vehicle industry) and was one of Merseyside's most serious victims of recession.

Despite these radical changes in the manufacturing sector, Merseyside's economy is still based upon service activities, as it must be a sub-region dominated by a great port, and performing the role of a provincial metropolis. Service employment still represents 62 per cent of the total, and in the pattern of changes since 1945 the dominant trend has been a replacement of the port-based activities by a more general structure of service employment typical of the great city rather than the great port. An accelerating decline (much stronger in the 1960s and 1970s than the 1950s) in transport and communication jobs reflects the reduction of the dock labour force and associated employment in rail and road transport. This sector of service employment had shed 8 per cent of its 1953 labour force of over 90,000 men by 1963; and the fall continued to 72,000 by 1973. Other service sectors have been characterized by relatively slow rates of growth on Merseyside, in most cases distinctly below the national figure. For example, distributive work grew between

1951 and 1967 by only 19 per cent (much below the national average rate), and has since actually declined (by 24 per cent to 1975). But the finance group has recovered from an earlier sluggish growth, with rapid expansion since about 1967, so that 1973 employment was twice that for 1951. As in so many metropolitan cities, the professions and allied services have experienced immense growth: employment expanded by 73 per cent between 1951 and 1967, while by 1973 they gave work to over 106,000 and had become the largest single element in the Merseyside economy.

There is some evidence that, as a centre of office employment in the most general sense, Liverpool is not growing as quickly as other cities in the same size range. Between 1958 and 1961, the gross rateable value of commercial offices increased in Liverpool by only 7 per cent, compared with rises of almost 17 per cent in both Manchester and Birmingham. Later, Liverpool had little share in the boom in speculative office building during the early 1970s, unlike Manchester. Part of the reason for this is to be sought in the fact that the existing level of office development in Liverpool was far greater, whether measured in value or area, than in other cities with a comparable (conurbation or city-region) population. For example, until recently it was twice that in Leeds, and almost the equal of Manchester or Birmingham. This relatively high level of office development reflects the diverse commercial interests of a great port, and it has clearly been affected by the decline of the port's trade and its changing role. Moreover, Liverpool falls in the shadow of Manchester in seeking to attract those types of offices that normally seek a location in the regional capital—and there is little evidence that the relative industrial weakness of South East Lancashire has led to a weakening in Manchester's regional role as the chief focus of tertiary employment. Merseyside has nevertheless derived some benefit from the decentralization of civil service jobs, especially to a major office complex in Bootle. A recent recommendation suggests the transfer of another 3,500 such jobs to the area.

Economic progress on Merseyside since 1945 has been driven along by an exceptionally rapid growth of population. This is an area that has had to run hard, in terms of the creation of new jobs, merely to stand still in terms of activity rates. The rapid population increase of the nineteenth century eased during the 1920s and fell to a minimum of 0.29 per cent per annum in the 1930s. After that, the rate more than doubled, to about 0.65 per cent per annum during the early 1960s. Although this was below the national average, it was low because the area's annual migrational loss remained at about 0.35 per cent. Without migration, the population of Merseyside would have risen at about 1 per cent each year, considerably above the national trend. In fact, migration consistently removed about one-third of the natural increase in the 1950s. With a birth rate that varied between about nineteen and twenty-one per thousand, rising gradually through the 1950s, and always several points above the national average, but with a death rate close to the national value, Merseyside had an exceptionally high rate of natural increase. The primary reasons lay in the high proportion of Roman Catholic families in the total population (at least one-quarter), and the even greater proportion in the lower-income groups. At some point in the decade 1961-1971, however, this dynamic growth in population quite suddenly diminished. The birth rate fell dramatically, converting a rate of natural increase that had peaked at about 1.5 per cent per annum into approximate birth rate/death rate balance by 1974. This suggests a social revolution, a positive control of family size by an increasing proportion among a strongly Roman Catholic population. But was this accentuated by economic recession? Will it persist or will birth rate recover somewhat? If the trend is not reversed then an entirely new set of demographic ground rules apply to the whole problem of regional planning in South West Lancashire. Until very recently all debate on the question of a sub-regional strategy had been based on the assumption of relatively quick population growth.

Until these radical and recent changes in population trend became clear, it seemed likely that any sub-regional plan for Merseyside must be based on the principle of the decentralization of both jobs and people. Had out-migration been corrected as a consequence of the generation of new jobs attracted to Merseyside because of its assisted status, then population would have grown from 1,664,000 in 1963 to 2,026,000 in 1981. The volume of additional employment required would have been 120,000. Had the economic base expanded in this way, Merseyside's land resources could not have met this growth of demand for both industry and housing. Decentralizing forces have been reshaping the urban structure of Merseyside for half a century. In 1921 the four old county boroughs of the core (Liverpool, Bootle, Wallasey and Birkenhead) housed 82 per cent of Merseyside's population, but by 1976 they had little more than half. Short-range dispersal created great seas of municipal housing towards the south east, reaching beyond the Speke industrial complex to the Ford plant at Halewood; Kirkby grew to an overspill community of over 50,000 alongside an industrial estate, while thousands of Liverpool families moved to the Ellesmere Port town expansion project, close to the Vauxhall factory and the industrial zone beside the Manchester Ship Canal. By the mid-1960s, therefore, piecemeal expansion had gone as far as was possible, short of a serious invasion of the belt of arable land of superb quality that encloses the conurbation. The conclusion was reached that population growth possibly envisaged to 1981 could not be accommodated without planning for dispersal over longer ranges, and so there was a search for new town sites.

The new towns growing at Skelmersdale and Runcorn, and the large town expansion projects at Widnes and Winsford, are discussed in the section on the strategy of population dispersal in the North West as a whole (pp.297-307). Their origins lie in the very large estimates, made in the different demographic climate of almost twenty years ago, of the size of the surplus of population that Liverpool would generate, especially if Development Area policy achieved its ultimate aim of eliminating net migration from the area. These calculations showed that between 58,000 families (assuming continued migration) and 95,000 families (assuming migration to be corrected) would need to be relocated as long-range overspill. The recent decline in fertility and the virtual halting of population growth will not, of course, have much effect on new family formation, a net increment to housing demand, in the short term. But what proportion of this estimated overspill need will actually declare itself as housing demand over the next ten or fifteen years? It is only possible to hazard even a guess. It is now unlikely that Merseyside will generate overspill needs beyond the capacity of the first generation of new towns in the region. Other, larger projects like the Central Lancashire New Town and the possible growth of a new city on Deeside must be seen as later and now much more problematical developments (see below p.306).

9.4 The Textile Zone: An Industrial Portrait in Shades of Grey

Location of industry policy in Britain was until recently geographically naive and therefore regionally-insensitive. It contained an implicit assumption that Britain could be neatly and simply divided between regions of growth and of decline, and that high and persistent levels of unemployment are an infallible indicator of economic illhealth and social distress. There has been a growing realization, given its most articulate expression in the report of the Hunt Committee, that there are large areas of Britain that have quite failed to share in the vigorous economic expansion of midland and southern England yet, despite the contraction of their traditional industries, they have never suffered serious unemployment and so have never enjoyed the artificial stimuli of Assisted Area status. The 'Intermediate Areas' are regions of economic stagnation rather than dramatic decline, of persistent out-migration that has balanced falling labour demands within their archaic economic structures, of environmental deterioration and industrial dereliction, and of inadequate levels of investment in the replacement and improvement of their wasting capital assets, in housing, industry and communications. In all these respects the textile zone of eastern Lancastria is archetypal (Smith, 1968).

A general profile of the nature and symptoms of the wasting illness that has reduced the textile areas to so debilitated a condition has been sketched already (pp.260-262). This section is concerned chiefly with their causes and with the possible cures. In varying degrees (for there are considerable sub-regional contrasts) the textile towns are the victims of population loss by age-selective migration so persistent that most are no longer generating any significant and sustained natural increase in population. Local economic structures of Victorian simplicity, based on textiles, mining and their ancillaries, survived late into the twentieth century. Yet the contraction of employment in the cotton industry to less than one-sixth of its peak of over 600,000 workers has left no residual unemployment. The decline was gradual and spread over forty years; out-migration, natural 'wastage' in an elderly working population, and the retirement of women from the labour force as the mills closed down have all contributed to this remarkable situation. Indeed there has been over-correction, for the mill towns became short of labour; for this reason alone, and there are many others, they are unattractive to mobile industry. Assisted Area policy has steered employment away from, rather than into, the greater part of the textile zone, which since 1945 has suffered a net loss of 'mobile' industry (pp.270-274). In the absence of new factory building—except locally and on a limited scale—mill conversion has been the spearhead of economic progress, but this is industrial diversification 'on the cheap' and it is no long-term solution: it prolongs the use of obsolete buildings.

These, then, are the economic measures of 'greyness', but there are the social and physical dimensions to the dilemma too. To take three typical parts of the textile zone (Manchester metropolitan district, Rochdale and Blackburn), their proportion of officially unfit housing in 1972 ranged from 11 to 15 per cent; another 5 to 10 per cent were 'fit but incapable of improvement' and about 20 per cent (but 35 per cent in Blackburn) were substandard but improvable. In total between 35 and 60 per cent of their housing stock has been officially declared to be unacceptable in quality. And this is the housing stock that has survived after twenty years of accelerating slum clearance, which has now removed the worst of the nineteenth-century legacy. Added to the physical obsolescence of much social capital (for example, schools and hospitals), and the limited service provision of all but the largest towns, these factors of environment are at least as important as questions of job security in helping to explain the heavy out-migration from within the 15-44 age band. Nor is this a complete stocktaking of the problems of the area. Its road communications system is largely unimproved (apart from the M62 and Irwell valley spur road), and its railway net is half abandoned. In the textile areas with the strongest mining history, chiefly in central Lancashire, land dereliction is a problem of appalling size. In 1965, Ince-in-Makerfield had almost 40 per cent of its entire area standing derelict. Wigan is encircled by a devastated collar. Leigh stands on the shores of a subsidence lake over a kilometre long. There are areas in South Lancashire incapable of finding sites for the new industry they so desperately need, because of these problems of surface devastation. Of course, there has been progress: 'Operation Eyesore' was launched in 1972 as part of the attack on the problem, and in a single year £17 million were spent, chiefly on visual improvement. By 1975 the reclamation rate had risen to 800 acres a year, but further surveys have shown that the total to be treated (in the region) may be as high as 17,500 acres.

To analyse the industrial problems of eastern Lancastria and to make any appraisal of the region's future involves studies of the fate of the old staple industries, the rise of alternative manufactures, the changing structure of employment, and the factors that are likely both to promote and to restrain its progress towards a new economic stability on a broader base.

9.4.1 The Cotton Industry: The Geography of Rationalization and Reconstruction

One of the greatest changes in the British economy during the last quarter-century has been the collapse and disintegration of the Lancashire cotton manufacture, which at the peak of its fortunes in the early 1920s provided not only almost 40 per cent of all employment in the textile region, but also over a quarter of the total value of the country's exports. This once great manufacture may now be pronounced extinct. From its wreckage there has risen a new industry, a general textiles manufacture, very different both in its materials and products, and increasingly also in its technology and structure, from the old cotton trade. Both in labour force and the volume of output, the new textile industry is much smaller than the old. It is no longer the base of the regional economy but rather an important (but not the largest) element in a much better diversified structure. It now depends as much upon the chemical industry as upon raw cotton imports for its raw materials, and traditional types of fabric are a diminishing proportion of its output. No longer is it divided between a multitude of small firms, many of the 'family' type, but it has now come to be concentrated in the hands of a few large and very powerful companies. By 1966, four combines (since reduced to three) controlled 45 per cent of the spinning, 25 per cent of the weaving and 30 per cent of the finishing capacity. These changes have gone hand in hand with a belated technical modernization. New machinery has been installed, and is worked harder—and over longer periods—than was the old. As a consequence, what was a labour-intensive industry has become much more capital-intensive, with a far lower specific labour demand. Lastly, the old cotton industry was very much Lancashire's monopoly. The new textile manufacture, in contrast, has already shown itself to be locationally much less tied to the mill towns of North West England.

The decline and fall of the cotton industry may be summarized briefly. It employed almost 600,000 before the beginning of contraction in the early 1920s, about 330,000 at the peak of its post-war recovery in the early 1950s, but only 190,000 on the eve of its crisis and reshaping in 1959-1960. By 1975, the mills and finishing works employed scarcely 100,000. The causes of its early contraction are now matters of economic history. Especially important initially was the rise of local cotton industries in countries like India

Table 9.6 The balance of U.K. trade in textiles, 1974

	Imports from	Exports to	Balance
E.E.C.	421	369	− 52
E.F.T.A.	239	237	− 2
Other European	39	38	− 1
Comecon	46	64	+ 18
Other developed	220	261	+ 41
Developing	436	209	− 227

Source: Department of Trade and Industry

and Brazil, which had once been major customers of the Lancashire mills. Later, Japan appeared as a powerful low-cost competitor for the declining volume of world trade in cotton products. During the post-1945 period, however, other factors have been paramount, especially the increasing technical obsolescence of the industry. This was the radical cause of its inability not only to maintain its share of world export markets but also even to prevent imports capturing an increasing share of the British market for cotton textiles.

Imports exceeded exports for the first time in 1958: a decade later they were five times greater in volume, but better balanced in value. Since then the trend in value has been adverse, so that Britain's balance of textile trade (Table 9.6) is in serious and growing deficit. By early 1975, the U.K. output of cotton cloth was running at about 484 million square metres annually, and that of the man-made fibres at 696 million square metres. Imports were exactly half the domestic consumption of the former, and 40 per cent of the latter. Not surprisingly, the industry has cried out for protection from what it sees as intolerable levels of imports, which reduce profitability and thwart investment. From 1960, the chief Commonwealth exporters to Britain—India, Pakistan and Hong Kong— were obliged to accept quota restraints; but the effect was that imports from other areas, for example Portugal, rose to fill the vacuum. By 1971, both tariff and quota protection has been given to the cotton industry, and there were volume restraints on man-made fibre imports. But now Britain stood on the brink of entry to the E.E.C. At first, this was seen as a safe, protected haven by the textile business, after so long a passage on the rough seas of open trade. It has proved anything but that: on entry, U.K. tariffs and quotas were progressively replaced by E.E.C. restraints. These, in turn, are administered from Brussels within the general framework of the G.A.T.T. Multi-Fibre Agreement, which recognizes the special importance of textile exports as currency earners to the developing world. The overall result is that the U.K. system of protection has been replaced by an E.E.C. scheme which gives tariff preference to 'underdeveloped' exporters up to a set of quota ceilings. The effects are rather odd. Hong Kong has lost its privileged position in the U.K. market, but now countries like Korea compete on favourable terms. More significantly, the southern European associates of the E.E.C.—Greece and Turkey especially—have free access to the whole E.E.C. market. In effect, Lancashire has exchanged one set of competitors for another. In particular, the import of yarns is ineffectively controlled, and the spinning branch of the industry has been badly affected.

But what is most serious is that the U.K. has developed an adverse balance of textile trade with the rest of the E.E.C.: yarn and cloth imports from this area grew from £95 million in 1970 to £277 million in 1974. Yet, with the rest of Europe, Lancashire is in very fair trade balance (and there is a very substantial trade surplus on raw fibres). The present agitation in the North West concerns the distribution of textile imports into the E.E.C. The U.K. takes a wholly disproportionate share—70 per cent of all Indian textiles entering Europe, for example. 'Spread the burden' is the present cry. This radically changing commercial environment is the essential backcloth to technical and organizational change in the industry.

There have been immense changes in the structure of the textile industry. By 1959 much of it had reached an enfeebled and moribund condition. Mills had closed in their hundreds, about 550 during the period between 1951 and 1960; over half of the surviving equipment lay idle, much of it almost unbelievably aged and obsolete, and over one-third of the mill labour force had been lost in less than a decade to other more secure employment. The industry was clearly powerless to save itself by its own initiative. A government sponsored rationalization scheme, therefore, was proposed within the Cotton Industry Act of 1960—the first direct intervention by government to secure the reshaping of a major private industry. The Act was limited in its objectives. It sought, first, to reduce the size of the industry to a level more appropriate to its prospects, by offering compensation for the scrapping of machinery. This, it was hoped, would eliminate both the weak firms and the weaker units of stronger firms. In a simple sense, this part of the Act worked. Half the spindles, and 40 per cent of the looms, were offered for scrapping. Much of this machinery, however, had been idle for years, and there was only a slight drop in employment as the direct consequence of the Act. Its other main provision, the offer to subsidize the reequipment of those firms who remained in the industry, was less immediately successful. Uncertainties not only concerning the state of future markets, but also about the future of the labour force, were powerful restraints on expensive schemes to reequip mills, which would then have to recruit labour for two or three shifts to show an acceptable level of return on the capital (Rodgers, 1962).

Paradoxically, the cotton industry has been seriously short of labour during its period of reorganization. Workers have left it faster than the industry has abandoned them. Migration, longer-distance commuting, retirement and the attractions of alternative employment have all contributed to the labour scarcity, while the unpopularity of shift work in a trade which had never known it was also a problem. Shift working has now become more widespread, although full three-shift operation is still less common than it should be, for machine utilization is the key to profitability and to the return on heavy investment. The recruitment of immigrant workers has been indispensable to the spread of shift working, and so has done much to give the industry its best chance of survival. A social side-effect is that the textile zone is now the region of the highest proportions of immigrant to total population, except for limited areas in the cores of the conurbations. Until very recently the Lancashire textile industry lagged behind its international rivals in machine utilization—plant was worked for less than 4,000 hours a year compared with 6,000 in America. But the continued elimination of the less efficient units and progressive investment in the more efficient has slowly improved the position.

Unhappily the 1960 Act also had some less praiseworthy results. In particular, it reduced the size of the industry without radically changing its structure. This has been left to the forces of industrial politics. The changing raw material supply is the key to the process of restructuring. Even between 1962 and 1969 the proportion of cloth made wholly or partly of man-made fibres rose from about 37 per cent to 43 per cent of the total produced in north western mills, while man-made filaments and mixtures now account for more than half the yarn supply. In short, the fate of the industry has increasingly become a matter of crucial concern to those companies with chemical interests who produce the bulk of the man-made fibres. Of this output about one-third consists of cellulosic rayons, while the truly synthetic fibres account for two-thirds (of which half is nylon and the rest shared between terylene and the acrylic group). The production of each of the major man-made fibres is dominated by a single company. Courtaulds supply the great bulk of rayon output (and have smaller nylon and acrylic interests), while Imperial Chemical Industries are the major producers of both nylon and terylene. Almost all the other producers of synthetic fibres (Du Pont, Monsanto, British Enkalon, Beyer) are British branches of overseas companies, and so have a more marginal interest in the Lancashire market. Clearly, therefore, it fell to Courtaulds and I.C.I. to initiate the restructuring of the Lancashire textile trade in order to save it as a major market for their products. These two giants have developed contrasting philosophies in their approaches to the problem.

Courtaulds sought to save the Lancashire textile industry by absorbing large parts of it. I.C.I. have tried to stimulate a restructuring within the industry itself, especially by means of large capital injections designed to make amalgamation and merger possible; their hope was that two or three big groups would emerge. Both policies have had substantial success. Courtaulds absorbed the Lancashire Cotton Corporation, and Fine Spinners and Doublers; these became the basis of the group's Northern Textile Spinning Division, in which at least twenty of the fifty-two mills originally acquired have since been closed. Courtaulds now possess about one-third of Lancashire's spinning capacity, and about 20 per cent of the filament weaving. Meanwhile amalgamation has proceeded within the Lancashire industry in a 'fish eat fish' fashion. To illustrate the process, Tootals merged with English Sewing Cotton, which later amalgamated with Calico Printers Association to form Englich Calico, which then attracted a bid from Courtaulds on which the Monopolies Commission reported adversely. Viyella International and Carrington & Dewhurst, the two remaining giants, both grew with the help of large I.C.I. capital holdings. By 1970 these two companies had merged though I.C.I. retains a large capital holding.

These changes amount to a financial and managerial revolution, the necessary precondition for further technical progress. The giants have together absorbed about 100 other companies since 1960. Not all branches of the trade have been equally affected, however. In 1964, there were 350 weaving firms and 180 finishers, but only 75 spinning firms. Each of the remaining great combines has an identifiable 'personality', and a distinctive range of activities. Carrington & Dewhurst, for example, became Europe's biggest filament weavers; they are highly specialized in this branch and so represent the traditional Lancashire pattern of 'horizontal' specialization carried to its logical extreme by progressive amalgamation. Viyella, on the other hand, was distinctive in having grown 'backwards' from the merchanting branch, and had a balanced vertical structure with about 10 per cent of the industry's total spinning, weaving and warp-knitting capacities. English Calico has its dominant stake in the finishing industry, of which it owns about 40 per cent. Beyond these three (and the Courtauld empire) are many smaller amalgamations and specialist independent firms, particularly in the weaving section.

Any major industrial reconstruction has its locational consequences. Lancashire cotton is no exception. For over forty years the spatial pattern of decline in the industry has exhibited strong areal contrasts. Before and after the depression the coarse cloth producers of the Blackburn area suffered almost twice as sharp a contraction as the fine-cloth weavers of the Burnley district. The Bolton-based fine-spinning industry was long relatively stable, but when its decline ultimately came, in the 1950s, it was catastrophic. In the valley towns of the Rossendale upland, with a strong specialization in heavy industrial textiles and access to a labour supply less eroded by industrial diversification, mill employment has declined more slowly than in almost any other area. But the post-1960 reconstruction of the industry has produced complex locational changes. Along the western border of the textile region, in central Lancashire, the industry has shown great stability; this is associated with the local importance of fabrics made from man-made fibres and the success of Carrington & Dewhurst, a firm historically based in the locality. In South East Lancashire, after the immense number of mill closures during the 1950s, there has been much greater stability; one of the most significant results of the 1959-1960 contraction was to leave a high proportion of the industry's looms in this traditional spinning area. As a result, there is now a better balance of spinning and weaving in the textile towns of the Manchester conurbation, for them a distinct advantage given the trend for the two main branches of the industry—after a century of regional segregation—to become reintegrated geographically, operationally and commercially. Moreover, two of the industry's major combines, and many smaller ones, are Manchester-based. In contrast the old 'weaving area' of the north, from Blackburn to Colne, has suffered a quick decline in its share of both the industry's equipment and employment during the period of reorganization; also the dominant companies are less strongly represented here.

It is too early to deduce firm patterns from these trends. The evidence is mounting, however, that the industry's capacity for survival is greater in West Central and South East Lancashire than elsewhere. Paradoxically, these are areas in which there exists the broadest general diversity of employment, and the greatest apparent potential for economic growth; the weaving towns further north, in contrast, depend more heavily on their shrinking share of textile employment, and have a far slighter potential for attracting replacement industry. But perhaps the most significant locational trend in recent developments is for new textile investments to be made entirely outside the traditional area of concentration in eastern Lancastria. Courtaulds, for example, has increased its share of weaving capacity by building new factories at Carlisle and Skelmersdale. The latter was short-lived and closed in 1977. Indeed, it is generally agreed in the industry that no group building a new plant *ab initio* can afford to ignore the Assisted Area investment help. The 1969 refusal of the government to categorize the whole of East Lancashire as an Intermediate Area, and so to provide greater investment allowances, was a serious blow for the greater part of the region: fortunately the decision was reversed in 1972 when the government included the whole of the North West region (outside the Merseyside Development Area) in an enlarged Intermediate Area. Perhaps Courtaulds' decision to undertake a major new development at its Preston plant reflects this change. If there is a dominant growth region for the British textile industry, it is Ulster. It has attracted huge investments by both British and overseas man-made fibre producers, and since it can offer the full range of locally produced raw materials, plus a surplus labour supply and an enticing package of incentives to migrant firms, it has also attracted investment by a wide variety of fibre-using firms.

9.4.2 The Decline of Coal Mining

Coal mining in the North West is no longer a sufficiently significant industry to merit extended treatment, and only a brief outline of its contraction to its present relic condition is given here. Since nationalizaiton, the great bulk of active mining has been confined to a line of pits from Salford in the east almost to the suburbs of Liverpool in the west. By 1960, ten of these were reconstructed giants, each employing an average of 2,000 men. Together with two new sinkings at Agecroft and Parkside, they employed almost two-thirds of the entire labour force of the field, and were seen as the collieries of the future. Nowhere was this narrow zone of vigorous mining and massive investments in modernization more than 8 kilometres (5 mils) wide, except where it intersected the Wigan-Chorley fault trough, which carried a line of now abandoned pits northwards, through these two towns.

Whatever future the Lancashire coalfield might be thought to have clearly lies in this corridor of active working, where the exposed coal measures dip under Trias in a concealed extension.Many of the older pits here have limited reserves, and a decade ago their future seemed problematical. In 1965 the National Coal Board classified the thirty-eight pits of its then Northwestern Division (which included both North Wales and West Cumberland) on the basis of thier life expectancy. Only fourteen were classified as 'long-life' pits, and another six were thought to have a less assured future. Eighteen were believed to have less than five years' life. On this basis, it seemed that most of the thirteen pits of the South Lancashire field would survive, and that most of the 18,000 jobs they provided were relatively secure. Yet three of the largest and most extensively modernized pits closed within five years, and other minor closures reduced the total of active pits to eight by 1975. Apart from the Agecroft outlier (in Salford) the survivors are grouped into a compact 20 kilometre long band between Leigh and St Helens. Only four pits are of any great size, each producing over 500,000 tons a year. This is the final erosional remnant of a once great coalfield, with a 1978 employment of only 9,000 men.

There is no good reason to assume that, by existing yardsticks of profitability, the field has any long-term potential. Its recent performance has not been entirely unfavourable, alternating between modest operating profits and minor losses; in 1967/1968, despite the burden of loss-making collieries chiefly outside Lancashire, the Northwestern Division made a very small loss of £0.058 per ton, most of it accounted for by two unprofitable pits (Bradford and Mosley Common) which were soon to close. Both in terms of its profit and loss account and in terms of man-shift productivity (1968, 31.5 cwt: U.K. 39 cwt.) the Lancashire field fell into an intermediate category between the profitable Midland and Yorkshire areas and the loss-making Welsh, Scottish and Northern fields. But since 1968, it has become increasingly identified with the latter rather than the former. Productivity has fallen (1970, 36 cwt; 1974, 31 cwt) and now stands 25 per cent below the national average and is worsening in relation to it. Total output has fallen far more quickly than the national trend, from almost 10 million tons in 1966 to only 4 million in 1974. The long decline of mining in the North West has thus come close to its ultimate conclusion: the final elimination of the industry. How soon this may come is impossible to estimate: Agecroft and Parkside have large reserves, and a shortage of male labour is no longer such a threat to the future of the pits as it was in a period of full employment. The total disappearance of so small an industry so compactly located can do little further economic damage on the regional scale. But it is not only largely confined to, but offers a substantial part of the male employment in, two labour market areas, St Helens and Leigh.

9.4.3 The Growth of Alternative Employments

The progressive decay of an archaic economy based on two staple activities—one a low-wage industry and the other a dirty and dangerous occupation—need occasion no regret. Indeed, the ultimate decline of both coal and cotton was alway inevitable. What is much more serious and alarming is that replacement jobs have grown at so inadequate a rate over all but a few parts of the textile zone. Table 9.2 summarizes employment trends in the area since the crises of the textile industries in the late 1950s. Since then, over 170,000 jobs in the mills and pits have disappeared, but the rest of the manufacturing base has been quite unable to generate new employment—either by indigenous growth or by attracting mobile enterprises—to replace this loss. Indeed, several of these alternative industries are themselves declining as quickly as the traditional staples, and what (nationally) are the 'growth industries' have had a lamentable record of expansion in the textile North West. The service trades have experienced modest growth, especially in the larger mill towns, where between 40 per cent and 50 per cent of all work is now provided by service activities, but the record of the service sector in the sub-region is by no means good. Indeed, the increased relative importance of service jobs in the mill towns is the product of the decline of their manufacturing base, rather than any real expansion in the service sector.

There is no great mystery involved in the slow growth (or occasionally the serious decline) in the textile area of industries that are making rapid progress both nationally, and elsewhere in the North West. In eastern Lancastria, many of these broad industrial groups are burdened by weak sectors, declining rapidly both in the region and the country. Within the engineering industry of the mill towns, for instance, there has always been a strong emphasis on textile machinery. This has passed through its own process of contraction, rationalization and modernization in parallel with that in the textile industry itself. A small number of dominant companies has emerged. Stone-Platt Industries unites several of the largest of the formerly independent concerns. Other textile engineers have sought salvation through diversification, and have turned to more general engineering.

Some contraction of textile engineering was to be expected, but the uncertain recent trend of employment in electrical engineering in the textile zone is more alarming. This seemed, until the 1960s, perhaps the most successful of the 'replacement' manufactures. It is an industry of great diversity, ranging from the making of heavy electrical equipment to intricate electronic assemblies. The 'heavy' end of the East Lancashire industry, especially, has been seriously affected by its national reorganization in the 1960s, and the Metropolitan-Vickers plants on the Trafford Park estate at Manchester exemplify the regional impact of this process. These once employed well over 20,000 workers and were the largest single industrial unit in the textile zone. Merged initially into Associated Electrical Industries and subsequently absorbed by the General Electric Company, these plants employ only about 5,000 and are now a relatively minor part of the General Electric Company-English Electric empire. In general, the North West has come rather poorly out of the British electrical industry's reorganization by merger in recent years. This is chiefly the result of the region's concern with the heavier, capital equipment side of the trade, and its rather feeble development of consumer goods production. Thus what was, in the 1950s and 1960s, one of the vital growth industries of the textile towns now faces grave problems of its own.

Of all the alternative industries, the vehicle group has the worst record. Indeed, in Manchester it has declined at a rate far exceeding that of even the textile industry. Again the reasons lie in the detailed composition of the trade. In and near the textile zone, the manufacture of railway locomotives and rolling stock once dominated the vehicle industry. Until a decade ago, there were six large railway engineering plants in the North West, and all but one (the Crewe works) were within the textile sub-region. Four of these plants have closed entirely and the two survivors both have a much reduced labour force. A decade ago it seemed possible that a much newer sector of the vehicle group, aircraft manufacture, might grow to balance this decline. In north east Manchester, at Bolton and Preston, this had grown to a considerable size. Unhappily, not only were the firms concerned caught up in the general rationalization of the British aircraft industry, but they were also victims of changes in national defence strategy. Thus yet another potential replacement industry of the mill towns has itself gone into decline.

During the inter-war and early post-war years, the growth of the clothing industry seemed to offer the prospect of some replacement jobs for those female employments being lost through mill closures. Long established in the Manchester area, this industry was tending to disperse more broadly to the textile towns, where it often took over the premises as well as the labour of the cotton industry; but after reaching its employment peak in the early 1950, the industry has declined at an accelerating pace (by 25 per cent between 1966 and 1976). Its contraction has been quicker in the North West than in the nation and far faster in the textile towns than elsewhere in the region. The causes are complex and obscure. They include increasing imports, changes in fashion, changes in production techniques and the progressive improvement of productivity in what was a labour-intensive trade not outstanding in its efficiency. The effects are simple; the decline of labour demand in the clothing factories now almost rivals mill closures as a cause of the reduction in female employment opportunities in the mill towns.

Very little evidence of industrial growth in the textile zone is presented in Table 9.2. The brightest feature is the modest expansion of engineering, despite the effect of the weak sectors; even so, employment has grown at only about a quarter of the regional and national rates. Chemicals are at least a stable employer, and have escaped the effect of those technological changes that have reduced labour demand in the mid-Cheshire and mid-Mersey regions. Paper-making is still fortunately a relatively healthy industry in parts of the textile zone (for example, at Bury and Darwen), and there has been some change from older activities to new—for example, to wallpaper manufacture. But the food and drink group, a growth industry outside the textile area, is an industry of decline within it. One fact stands out with great clarity from the table. The working populations of textile towns within daily travelling range of Manchester cannot now rely on the more diverse economy of the city for employment as their local economic base contracts: indeed, the city's weakness now exceeds theirs.

The newly formed Greater Manchester Council now administers the greater part of the old textile region of South East Lancashire. Its economic position is dismal in the extreme. From 1959 to 1972, 100,000 jobs were lost in the area (an 8 per cent decline, compared with 1 per cent for the U.K. and 6 per cent for the North West). Work for men shrank even quicker: by 9.4 per cent between 1963 and 1967, and 10.5 per cent between 1967 and 1972. During the 1960s unemployment rarely exceeded the national average, but by 1976 it had reached 5.8 per cent. These values apply to the entire G.M.C. area, but there has been a long-continued decentralization of work and people from the core to the periphery, so that the city itself shows extreme weakness even within this context of decline. In the Manchester group of employment exchange areas, scarcely a single element in either the industrial or service structure has recorded anything except steep decline since the early

1960s. The exceptions are the financial group and the professions. But even Manchester's dominance of office employment in the area seems to be threatened. Between 1966 and 1972 office employment grew by 17 per cent in Bolton and Stockport, and by 24 per cent in Bury: in Manchester it declined by a tenth. More than most British cities, Manchester now exhibits American tendencies, a quick retreat of employment, at first in industry but now in services, too, from centre to periphery. There is tangible evidence of the decline in business activity at the core, and an increasing number of complaints from the retail interests that the heart of the city is dying. Of course, Manchester has had Intermediate Area status, but it is pointed out somewhat sourly that the average spending per capita in assistance to the Intermediate Areas in 1973/1974 was £2.3 compared with £23 in the Assisted Areas. In any case, the whole of the 'growth crescent' round the fringe of the city-region from Bolton-Wigan in the north and west to Stockport and Hyde in the south east has the same assisted status. Neither regional policy nor the somewhat tentative and vacillating urban aid programmes have so far brought much comfort to a city which disputes with Glasgow the dubious honour of being, in the economic sense, the most moribund in Britain.

During all the changes of fortune that have affected the non-textile manufactures of the North West since the late 1940s there has been one major factor only making for growth and diversity in employment, the conversion of textile mills for other types of industrial use. This is no new trend. Some of the largest firms in the region's most important growth industries grew from infancy in this way—for example the Avro Aircraft Company and Ferranti, the electrical engineers. But the massive contraction of the textile industry freed cheap space for new enterprises on a very great scale indeed. Of the thousand or more mills and finishing factories that have closed their gates since 1945 many are so old and ruinous, or so poorly sited in deep valleys or beside silting canals, that they can interest no one save the demolition contractor or the industrial archaeologist. Others, in the congested factory zones that enveloped the centres of Victorian cotton towns, have been demolished as part of clearance schemes to improve central areas and their traffic flows. Yet at least 400 old mills have been reoccupied, wholly or partly, by new enterprises which now provide a total of rather more than 120,000 jobs. Indeed, at least two-thirds of the jobs lost in cotton since 1953 have been replaced by the reoccupation of textile factories. Some have been turned into flatted factories to accommodate many small firms. In this they play a most important role as industrial nurseries, sheltering the immature firm with a low rent until it can look for better premises elsewhere.

It is impossible to generalize about the types of industry that have come into old mills. Almost every order in the standard industrial classification is represented, although engineering in a wide variety of forms, clothing, plastics and plastic foam, surgical dressings, food and tobacco products and paper manufacture are among the most important. Many of the new firms are not manufacturers at all, but rather wholesalers or distributors; mail-order houses, for example, are common users of converted mills. In general, this type of accommodation has proved most adaptable to labour-intensive enterprises without the need for complex and heavy plant. This is fortunate in that the ratio of operatives to site area almost rivals that in many textile mills, and is indeed often higher than in a modern mill with automated machinery. The advantages of converted mills are two-fold. First, space in them can be bought or rented at an exceedingly low cost, so that they probably represent the cheapest industrial floorspace in the country. Second, they avoid the need to secure an industrial development certificate and so they provide a considerable loophole in industrial guidance policies. For both these reasons, the converted mill permitted the textile region to compete on more equal terms with the development areas and the attractive package of financial incentives that is available there, and it has been quite vital to the economic progress of many mill towns. This is, however, industrial diversification on the cheap. It may bring a sort of first-aid relief to alleviate the sufferings of the stagnant textile economy, but it is clearly no long-term solution. Mill conversion perpetuates a problem of physical obsolescence. A sample of 290 firms—not chosen because they were in converted premises—was surveyed in 1971. Thirty-five per cent of them were in pre-1914 premises; 49 per cent of the firms in the total sample thought that the age of their buildings affected their productivity. In this sort of context mill conversion makes sense only in the very short term. The general results of this inquiry are disturbing in the extreme in their implications for the efficiency of industry in the North West within the wider European market.

9.4.4 Employment Diversification in the Textile Towns

The industrial revolution produced, during the nineteenth century, almost a 'standard' economy among the mill towns of eastern Lancastria, in which textiles absorbed between half and two-thirds of the available labour, and mining or engineering the bulk of the remainder. Service employment was of stunted size, but here and there other local manufacturing specialisms (paper making near Bury and Darwen, railway engineering at Horwich) gave some variety. For almost half a century there has been slow, often uncertain and spatially varying progress towards a better balance of employment. Several general principles can be discerned in this progression from almost total specialization in textiles towards diverse economies. The larger towns have made faster progress towards a better economic balance than the textile villages: they have acquired not only a diverse manufacturing base, but also a stronger element of service employment. Indeed rank in the urban hierarchy is a reasonably accurate proxy for employment diversity. But also, accessibility has stimulated diversification. Towns remotely located in the Rossendale upland or in North East Lancashire have tended to retain simpler economies, still strongly based on mill employment, whatever their size; while even the smaller settlements closer to Manchester and the major axes of communication have progressed towards diversity.

Among towns with a strong textile tradition Stockport and Preston have undergone the most complete economic transformation. In the former the mills employ (1975) only 3 per cent of the total workforce and clothing 4 per cent. Engineering is the largest manufacturing employer (13 per cent) but there is now a very broad spectrum of industrial opportunity, enriched by the transfer of firms from inner Manchester. Services provide almost 50 per cent of total employment, a reflection of substantial town centre redevelopment and some growth of office investment. Stockport can no longer be described as a textile town: a tradition begun 250 years ago with the development of a silk-throwing industry is virtually dead. Preston, the county administrative centre, is almost Stockport's economic twin. Services provide well over half the employment (with a strong white-collar and professional component), while the role of textiles is as a provider of jobs for women. The engineering and vehicles group supplies about a fifth of total employment. Today Preston is much more concerned with the success and the policies of British Aerospace and the truck and bus division of B.L. than with trends in the textile trades. Most of the major towns in the old 'spinning belt' of South East Lancashire have economic structures in which textiles continue to supply 10 per cent to 15 per cent of total employment (but up to a third of work for women) but with a diverse range of engineering, electrical and electronic work that accounts for 20 per cent to 25 per cent of labour demand. There are variations: Bolton and Bury have relatively slighter interests in engineering and a greater survival of textile employment than Ashton or Oldham. Mill conversion has greatly increased employment diversity in all these towns of the Greater Manchester County.

Further north, the old economy survives with slighter change. In Nelson and Colne, as late as 1975, the mills continued to provide almost 30 per cent of all the work available, but this was a reduction from 41 per cent and 38 per cent, respectively, in 1967. To this day, in these areas, the typical working woman (especially in middle age) is a mill hand. But the larger towns of North East Lancashire have broadened their employment structures. In both Blackburn and Burnley the mills occupy about 10 per cent of the labour force and engineering about 20 per cent. Both have totally reconstructed city centres and have tried to attract office as well as retail development so that the service sector provides about 40 per cent of the work available.

It is in the smaller towns and industrial villages that the old textile-based economy survives in its simplest form, despite all the vicissitudes that the mills have had to face over the last thirty years. In the Rochdale area in general, and in the smaller communities within it in particular, the textile industry survives not only strongly, but also very competitively: Littleborough has 30 per cent of its employment in the mills. The valley towns of Rossendale retain an even greater dependence on textiles: 40 per cent of Ramsbottom's work is in the mills, while Bacup has retreated further from one weak industry into another: 16 per cent of its employment is in textiles and 34 per cent in clothing and footwear, both threatened by low-cost imports. Further south, Golbourne can claim to be almost the last classical representative of the old 'mill and pit' economy, once so typical of the Lancashire coalfield, with 17 per cent of its work in mining and 18 per cent in textiles. Its larger neighbour, Leigh, has become a middle-rank service centre with strong electrical engineering interests: these, together, provide two-thirds of its work with the mills and pits contributing little more than 10 per cent each.

The old, simple structures of employment—variations on a theme in which textiles were dominant and mining, engineering and the services local modulations—have dissolved into an intricate mosaic of economic contrast. There are few parts of the North West that could be damaged by any further contraction in textile employment (which in any case has moved towards greater stability at a much lower level), but there are many that depend directly or indirectly on the international success of the British engineering industry and the major electrical, electronics, aerospace and vehicle groups. In any case, the measurement of differences in employment structures at the level of employment exchange areas is increasingly irrelevant. Greater mobility has enlarged labour-market areas and made journey-to-work systems more extensive and complex. The threat of unemployment is no longer localized; nor is it especially serious over most of the textile province of East Lancashire. In mid-1976 the total unemployment rate (as an unweighted average) of the traditional 'spinning' towns of the south east was 5.3 per cent compared with a rate of 5.7 per cent for Manchester city. The journey-to-work areas that make up the textile districts of Rossendale and North East Lancashire had a mean unemployment rate of only 4.5 per cent (and as low as 2-3 per cent in some cases). Set against a Merseyside county rate of 13.5 per cent at the same date, these data give some evidence not only of the greater resilience of the balanced economies that have replaced textile specialisms, but also of the better stability of the new, smaller, more efficient textile industry.

9.5 A Regional Strategy for the North West

Planners' perceptions of the central problems in devising appropriate frameworks, on the broadest scale, for the region's future have changed dramatically over the post-war period. In the 1950s and 1960s the major preoccupation was with accommodating the industrial growth that the hoped-for transformation of the region's economy would bring, and with housing the population increases that a sounder economic structure would ensure. Twenty years ago the primary strategic target was the encouragement of 'replacement' manufactures and of the service sector to balance the inevitable contraction of the staple trades of the Victorian era. As a more secure economic base was found, so migration from the North West would slow and population growth would quicken. But already the cities and major towns were over-swollen. Housing conditions were inadequate and congestion extreme. Success in the economic sphere would therefore add to an already intolerable problem of urban deterioration and overcrowding. The cities must change their structures. Massive clearance of their Victorian cores would add enormously to the growth pressures at their margins. To avoid unconstrained physical expansion, much of it into land of high agricultural quality, an orderly dispersal of population must take place to new communities in the form of new towns, expanded towns and smaller-scale overspill schemes. These would be the growth points to which much of the new industry of the economic transformation would be attracted. So, until about 1970, a 'regional strategy' meant, essentially, a blueprint for dispersal planning which would both solve the environmental problems of the conurbations and accelerate the transformation of the economy away from its obsolete nineteenth-century structure.

Much has changed since then. The old industries are now reduced almost to vestigial size. The concern of the late 1970s is for the stability of those new manufactures—electrical and electronic work, aircraft, motor vehicles, chemicals—on which hopes for the future were pinned. In the deep recession of this period the extent of the economic decay of the inner areas of the conurbations has been revealed with cruel clarity (pp.274-277). Physical reconstruction of the conurbation cores, whatever its environmental achievements, has accentuated if not precipitated a crisis of loss of employment. Nationally as well as regionally, the condition of the inner city—so long neglected by the policy makers and weakened by the dispersal process—has been brought firmly to the top of the planners' agenda. In any case, population trends have moved to the zero-growth condition, so that the need for overspill must be radically recalculated; and the slackening of industrial investment has put at great risk the dispersal schemes currently in operation. In brief, the regional planning debate has now shifted to preoccupations very different from those of a decade ago.

In fact enormous progress has been made towards urban reconstruction. Between 1951 and 1972, 232,000 slum houses were cleared in the North West, an immense achievement which represents one-quarter of all the slum clearance in England and Wales over the period. There is little doubt that in the future the emphasis will shift distinctly from clearance to the improvement of ageing houses and the betterment of the environment of which they are part. One can discern a radical change in the social philosophy of housing policy, in a direction in which the land requirement for housing may be very significantly reduced: combined with much reduced estimates of population growth this clearly changes the whole background to the regional planning debate.

Even so, Manchester has over 90,000 unfit houses still, and Merseyside 55,000; adding an estimate of present housing shortage, there is an existing need for perhaps 215,000 new and replacement homes in the two major urban concentrations. To this must be added an estimate of 25,000 houses to 1981 to cover net new family formation, which will continue—at least on Merseyside—despite the recent down-turn in population growth. These are large totals, but much smaller than the estimates of a few years ago, and it seems likely that a much higher proportion can be accommodated in the two metropolitan counties than seemed possible earlier. As recently as 1968 the total housing need from all causes, to be generated by the conurbations by 1981, was being put at around 500,000. It was thought that about 80,000 of these would represent an overspill beyond the capacity of the dispersal sites (in the form of new and expanding towns) then in operation. This led to a phase of grandiose but unrealistic paper planning in which a plethora of new development proposals were pencilled in on the regional map. In short, the strategic planning debate of the 1960s was conducted from what now seems to be, quite clearly, a false statitistical foundation. This must be borne in mind in reading the following account.

Table 9.7 shows how radically both regional population forecasts and the estimates of conurbation overspill have been revised since 1951. In 1966 it was believed that the total population of the North West would rise to 7.4 million by 1981. On present trends it will

Table 9.7 The North West: projections of population growth and overspill

---

A. PROJECTIONS OF TOTAL REGIONAL POPULATION ('000s)

Date of calculation	To 1981	To 2001
1966	7,401	—
1968	7,115	—
1972	6,824	7,241
1975	6,468	6,470

B. ASSESSMENTS OF OVERSPILL FROM THE CONURBATIONS ('000s)

			Merseyside		Manchester
County assessments					
1951-1952	(to 1971)	(people)	172-179		317-344
N.W. Study 1965	(to 1981)	(dwellings)	45.1 / 2.7	.... (No migration) .... / ...... (Migration continues)	65.9 / 29.3
N.W.R.P.C. 1968	(to 1981)	"	23 / 8	.... (No migration) .... / ...... (Migration continues)	42 / n.a.
J.S. Millar		"	320	.... (Including private sector)	341
Structure Plans 1975		"	15		3,400 (acres of land requirement)

---

be only 6.5 million (below today's figure) and remain stable to the end of the century. The enormous calculations of overspill from the two major urban clusters were always tentative and confused. They were tentative because it was never possible to know whether out-migration (to the rest of the region and beyond) would continue at prevailing rates. It has, and so the lower ranges of values have, in fact, applied. The estimates were confused because they never effectively separated two elements in the out-migration, the 'genuine' shift of population away from the conurbations associated with a change of job, and a local shift between housing sectors, from public to private. Thus, in effect, the 1965 and 1968 estimates in the table refer essentially to public sector housing demand. J.S. Millar, in his calculations, added this private sector element in demand to the total demand for sites—of course, quite correctly—and showed that the overspill pressures that would be generated by the conurbations were very large (but his estimates apply to 2001 and are based on the then far too high and optimistic official estimates of population growth). A present appraisal of the position, in the G.M.C. and Merseyside structure plans, suggests that, given the much greater land resources of the metropolitan counties, the bulk of the housing demand can be met within them, whether it expresses itself in the public or private sectors.

9.5.1 Anti-planning and Overspill, 1945-1961

In a timorous fashion, planning for some degree of dispersal began early in the 1950s. It was entirely in the form of short-range movements, chiefly of small bodies of population, and arranged by *ad hoc* agreements between the cities and some of their smaller neighbours. The largest scheme of the period was the 'export' of Liverpool families literally only 2 or 3 kilometres beyond the city boundary to Kirkby. Then a mere rural parish, Kirkby has become an urban district of almost 50,000 people, a close packed, 'one class' community with a flourishing industrial estate developed from the nucleus of a wartime factory. It scarcely represents the planner's art in its highest form. Other pieces of peripheral enlargement to the conurbations were simultaneously in progress. Salford had begun the export of about 16,000 people to overspill estates clustered around the mining town of Walkden to the west; this was a scheme which, whatever its lack of visual amenity, at least took no good farmland and reclaimed a semi-derelict landscape.

Manchester had by now exhausted the potential of its huge Wythenshawe complex of estates in the far south—a salient thrust deep into the countryside of North Cheshire, which quickly consumed a district of intensive market gardening—and was looking for alternative sites. Manchester's experience is typical of the frustration of the early post-war period. As early as 1946 the city attempted to secure a site for new town development. Mobberley, some 24 kilometres (15 miles) south of the city centre, and with a rail link to it, was its first choice. The quality of the first-class grassland that formed the site, and its supposed potential liability to brine-pumping subsidence, led to the abandonment of the project. The small town of Lymm, 27 kilometres (17 miles) to the south west, was the subject of the next proposal. At a ministry inquiry in 1958 the project failed, again largely because of the weight of agricultural opposition. In the interim, there had been desultory discussions concerning the possibility of overspill on a new town scale at Congleton, more than 32 kilometres (20 miles) to the south.

Sensing that expansion into Cheshire, its traditional direction of suburban growth, would continue to be checked by a combination of agricultural and political opposition, the city turned to Lancashire. In the early 1960s it wooed the little mining town of Westhoughton: here was a site of almost no agricultural value, and much was semi-derelict. The proposals failed, largely through local political opposition. Meanwhile a site at Risley, a little east of Warrington, had been examined; part consisted of derelict wartime installations and part of reclaimed peat under intensive arable farming. From the Risley scheme grew the concept of developing Warrington itself under new town procedures to take Manchester overspill. It may seem odd that proposals to create new towns deep in pastoral Cheshire should ultimately fructify with the designation of Warrington—a very old town indeed, and a large one of over 75,000 inhabitants—as a new town. But such has been the achievement of regional planning in the North West.

During its twenty-year-long search for a major reception site capable of development on new town principles. Manchester was forced to the expedient of short-range piecemeal population dispersal. It is almost literally true to say that it 'got rid of' surplus population, in consignments of a few hundred or a few thousand families, to any local authority in or near the conurbation that would take them. Some nine agreements were made with Cheshire authorities (all on the southern fringe of the conurbation), five with Lancashire authorities (all of them small textile towns within the northern zone of the conurbation), and one with a Derbyshire authority, Glossop. In short, this was a process of infilling, and minor peripheral expansion of the conurbation. By 1959, some 37,000 people had been moved from the city to overspill estates within the conurbation. The major new project of the 1960s—the Hattersley scheme to the east of Hyde—was another peripheral addition. It can, of course, be argued that the very fact that the rest of the conurbation could house the Manchester population surplus is the best demonstration possible that no long-range movement to a new town was necessary.

Dispersal planning for Merseyside has pursued a far more rational course, after the emergency rehousing operation of the mushroom growth of Kirkby. While Manchester's overspill has gone either to suburbs without industry or textile towns with declining economies, Liverpool's overspill has gone to major industrial growth points, though chiefly at the edge of the conurbation rather than beyond. For example, overspill development at Halewood accompanied the growth of the Ford enterprise there; the transfer of several thousands of Liverpool families to Ellesmere Port helped to provide a local labour force for the Vauxhall factories. Such a planned transfer of population to sites on the margin of the conurbation was inevitable given the strong tendency for the dispersal of employment on Merseyside—though any expansion of industry or population at the margins of the urban mass almost inevitably meant the loss of farmland of high quality. It was on Merseyside that the first stage of population dispersal in the North West—piecemeal, short-range overspill—came to an end; this was with the designation of Skelmersdale and Runcorn, in 1961 and 1964 respectively, as new towns.

9.5.2 Towards a Regional Strategy

In the shaping of a regional strategy to guide growth into the twenty-first century, three alternative principles at once suggest themselves, and all have received serious consideration in the current debate about the region's future. In brief, the main mass of population growth might be accommodated by the further expansion of the two major conurbations, by development athwart the east-west axis between the two conurbations (along the line of the Ship Canal and the Manchester-Merseyside motorways), or by the selection of growth nodes along the north-south axis of the M6 between Lancaster and Crewe. These alternatives are clearly not mutually exclusive. The recent pattern of change contains a little of all three, and the debate about their relative merits is essentially a discussion of emphasis.

For twenty years after 1945 it was accepted almost as dogma that the major conurbations were already too large and that their outward growth must be restrained. This view was held to be as self-evidently true of the conurbations of feeble growth, for example Manchester, as it was of London itself. This gigantic assumption, and the green belt policy that gives it physical form and legal force, has since been challenged. Certainly a prima facie case exists—on the physical grounds of land use and land availability—for the Manchester conurbation to contain a large part of its (slackening) housing demand. It is, especially in the north and east, an open textured conurbation of cellular structure. Already the open enclaves have absorbed some tens of thousands of families both by planned intraconurbation rehousing and by the usual processes of speculative housing development. Their capacity is by no means exhausted. There are other cogent arguments for encouraging the conurbation to 'solidify' and expand peripherally in this way. All the major towns of the outer girdle have attracted considerable investment in central area redevelopment, and they are much better equipped than a decade ago to meet the service needs of new populations brought into their hinterlands. The M62 motorway traverses these half-developed areas, and ought to stimulate the quicker reconstruction of the declining economic base of the spinning towns.

There are, of course, counter-arguments to the thesis that a combination of infilling and limited peripheral growth could largely solve the problem of population surplus in the Manchester region. Expansion to the north and east would quickly meet the physical barrier (expressed in slope rather than altitude) of the Pennine flanks. Advance to the south would meet the equally difficult problem of high-grade farmland in the North Cheshire arable/dairy zone. There is little open land left here that is not earmarked for green belt. On the other hand, the conurbation has an open flank, to the west and north west, against the abandoned coalfield. There, the major physical problem limiting expansion is the extent of derelict land, and it is clearly capable of solution (at a cost). The most powerful argument against the proposal that the conurbation should retain all or most of its population growth is the economic one—the area's general industrial weakness, and the overall decline in employment. Even if population growth were to be contained physically, it might not be capable of being supported in the economic sense. Even with South East Lancashire now scheduled as an Intermediate Area, hope of quick industrial progress through the offer of direct incentives must be tempered with the knowledge that employment in manufacturing industry has ceased to grow in the U.K., and that the Development Areas still can offer more substantial inducements to footloose enterprises.

The Merseyside conurbation, far more strongly mono-focal than Manchester, has a different framework of urban growth. On the Lancashire shore, development around the core is compact and continuous, without any open enclaves which could be used for expansion. Beyond, however, well-developed salients reach out some distance, their tips defining the urban region. Suburban settlement follows the electric railways discontinuously to Southport along the coast, and to Ormskirk inland and to the north. A continuous ribbon of urban uses joins Liverpool to St Helens, while to the south east the Speke-Halewood expansion with its massive industrial development now virtually joins

Liverpool to Widnes. On the Cheshire shore, a similar ribbon of estuarine settlement extends continuously to Ellesmere Port.

The crucial policy decisions for Merseyside have in fact already been taken piecemeal. Runcorn has been scheduled as a new town, to grow to 90,000 by migration from Merseyside. With limited dock facilities along the Ship Canal, and with connection to the M6 via the North Cheshire motorway, it ought to be able to secure the new industry it needs to reduce its almost total dependence on the salt and chemical group. Its first major industrial acquisitions are partly chemicals-linked. Across the narrows of the estuary, joined by a new, high-level bridge, Widnes is also growing quickly under the Town Development Act. It, too, desperately needs non-chemical employment to diversify its economic base and provide female work. In effect these decisions mean that the estuary will be almost continuously enveloped in urban-industrial development, virtually to Warrington. But estuarine development from a Liverpool core can be seen in a much broader context. The recently completed second Mersey tunnel, an improvement to trans-Wirral road links, and a Dee barrage across sand-spreads that are rapidly reclaiming themselves by salt-marsh colonization, would bring the whole of the Welsh shore of the Dee estuary, and the resorts beyond, much more firmly into contact with Merseyside. As recently as 1970 there were serious investigations into the feasibility of a Dee barrage carrying a motorway, linked to the concept of a new city on Deeside to grow to a population of 280,000 by the year 2000. It is now clear that such a development could not look to Merseyside for its population growth, at least on present trends and during the present century. The question is, rather, whether there will be a sufficient surplus to sustain the programmed growth of the existing reception areas, Runcorn and Skelmersdale, Widnes and Winsford.

The planning philosophy expressed in the view 'let the conurbations grow' has its attractions. However, in effect, the guided peripheral expansion of the conurbations would quickly lead to the second general principle for which a planning strategy could be developed. This is the deliberate merging of the Manchester and Liverpool city-regions into a single continuous city system, of at least 5 million in its developed form, reaching from the Pennines to the Wirral coast. This model of regional development has an almost mystical appeal to some of its proponents. Here, it has been argued, is the only prospect for the creation of an urban unit large enough almost to rival London. Here is that northern equipoise to the overweening growth of the metropolis that, alone, can restore some balance of urban and economic power in Britain. This is plainly a false prophesy. The two dominant cities would clearly continue their independent existence, and their regional rivalry. No new, central and dominant focus within the entire urban mass could replace them, and so develop service and social facilities appropriate to the total population of the entire city system, except in the distant future. Thus no real challenge to London's hegemony could develop.

The basis of any 'east-west' development strategy in the region lies in the excellence of communications between Manchester and Liverpool. The Ship Canal, an ocean waterway, and in some senses a linear port, the South Lancashire and North Cheshire motorways, and main railway lines with high-density services, all provide for an enormous mass movement of people and commodities along this axis. Two airports, Speke and Ringway, in addition afford the zone easy European and inter-continental contact; the latter is the leading international airport outside the London region. Moreover, the Manchester-Merseyside axis is already largely committed to an urban future. Discontinuous urban growth, accompanied by considerable industrial development, now links South West Manchester with Warrington. The latter is already a town of almost 130,000 population, including its suburban extensions; designated a new town, it will take at least 13,000 families from South East Lancashire, chiefly on open areas to the east and bordering the peatland of Risley moss. Warrington's growth towards the 200,000 mark is thus already accepted. In every sense—in terms of physical urbanization, social affiliation and industrial linkages—Warrington is the bond between South East and South West Lancashire. Its soap-detergent-chemical group of industries are part of the chemical complex of the mid-Mersey region, and so look westwards; metal working and engineering have closer links eastwards, at one time particularly with the small (formerly integrated) Irlam steel plant on the Ship Canal 11 kilometres (7 miles) away.

The Ship Canal has had a diminishing impact on industrial location, after its early success. The growth of the great Trafford Park industrial estate (at its peak employing over 50,000 workers but now scarcely 30,000) near the terminal docks began at the turn of the century, and was virtually complete by 1950. The Irlam steelworks, using the canal for ore transport, was a development of the early 1930s, but has now been reduced to a small finishing facility. The growth of oil refining and petrochemicals at Stanlow and Carrington reflected the increasing importance of the canal as an oil port in the 1950s; in this case, however, continuous expansion is assured. It is clear that the impetus of canalside industrial growth has slackened. Though there is apparently a lot of space still undeveloped beside the waterway, not all of it is likely to be available for urban and industrial use. There is a dredging problem that makes necessary the retention of land for spoil discharge. And much canalside land is first-class quality farmland. The east-west motorways, too, cross dairy and arable areas of high productivity. In short, there are powerful constraints upon the implementation of an east-west strategy pinned to the Ship Canal and adjacent motorways and, unless present green belt policy is much modified, Manchester and Warrington will remain separated by a broad gap in urban development (see Figure 9.1).

The third possible alternative in shaping the region's future—the alignment of growth-nodes along the north-south corridor of movement traversed by the M6—was for long the most fashionable, and part of the declared policy of the Regional Economic Planning Council. Across Lancashire, the M6 and the railway to Glasgow (now electrified) are rarely more than 2 or 3 kilometres apart. Long before any attempt at coherent regional planning began, this zone had attracted interest as a location for urban investment. About ten new town and major town expansion projects (active, proposed or abortive) are threaded along it like beads on a string. Two major developments within about 8 kilometres (5 miles) of the motorway have made progress (at Skelmersdale and Winsford), two others (at Warrington and in the Preston-Leyland-Chorley area) are in the earlier stages.

The new town under construction near the old mining village of Skelmersdale, 24 kilometres (15 miles) north east of Liverpool, is to absorb at least 14,000 Merseyside families, chiefly on land of low fertility left half-derelict by a long-dead mining industry, and has a population target of 80,000. Winsford, 45 kilometres (almost 30 miles) south east of Liverpool, is planned to grow under the procedures of the Town Development Act, but virtually on a new town scale, from 12,000 to at least 60,000—though its future is threatened by Liverpool's reappraisal of overspill needs. This was a salt town with an almost moribund economy, largely dependent on the employment offered by the Northwich chemical complex. Almost every possible factor favours the industrial expansion of both towns. They can offer an ample and quickly-growing labour supply, excellent communications southwards and (since they are linked by overspill agreements with a Development Area) major investment incentives too (at Winsford, now reduced to 'Intermediate Area' status). Both have already attracted a broad range of firms, some from Manchester and Merseyside, but most from outside the region and so a net gain to the North West. Skelmersdale, especially, was at first outstandingly attractive to industry. By mid-1968, it had 240,000 square metres (2.5 million square feet) of factory space built or under construction, and almost 4,000 jobs in an indescribably diverse range of manufactures; but some of the industrial growth at Skelmersdale has been short-lived. Courtaulds placed one of their large and semi-automated weaving factories here (at the nearest point to the textile zone, with its experienced labour, at which Development Area incentives applied). The plant closed in 1977: the weakness of the market for cloth, but also the low productivity record of a factory with recurrent labour relations problems, were given as the reasons. At almost the same time the Thorn television-tube plant closed, a victim of reduced demand and import competition. Skelmersdale was by 1977 a depressed community with an unemployment rate (11 per cent) that rivalled that of inner Merseyside.

There are two further growth points on the M6 that were planned to take overspill population chiefly from South-East Lancashire. One of these, the expansion of Warrington, has been discussed above: the other is the Central Lancashire New Town. In fact, the latter is a project of new city scale, designed to receive a population of about 150,000, and so to create an urban unit, based on Preston, with a total population of about half a million. This is a development that has been debated for almost twenty years. The immense commercial success of Leyland motors in its old form as a truck-bus group created a complex of factories in the Leyland-Chorley area with a labour demand that far outstrips local resources. As early as 1951, it was suggested that this area could absorb a substantial overspill from South-East Lancashire. With the completion of the M6 and the belief at the time that inadequate provision had been made to accommodate the regional growth of population, what had been seen as a modest overspill scheme became a new city project. No longer was it confined to Leyland-Chorley; instead it was recentred upon Preston. This is, however, an area of quite serious economic weakness. Apart from the troubles of its textile industry, it has seen the contraction of what was once its chief growth sector, the aircraft industry. Certainly the Leyland Company has had continued success, at least in this area. But as a national and international rather than a regional enterprise there is no longer any guarantee that its expansion will be chiefly within Lancashire. Indeed, for its most recent project, the firm has turned to the Development Areas, and specifically to West Cumberland. In brief, the Central Lancashire New Town cannot look to any certain expansion of its own economic base to provide for its growth of employment. Moreover, even with its Intermediate Area status, the town may find itself in unequal competition with Liverpool-linked rivals for mobile industry. No major new town scheme has had such an inauspicious start. The conurbations no longer need any part of its capacity to absorb their population surpluses, certainly not during this century and maybe not even early in the next. The down-turn in the general regional population growth rates suggests that the sorts of development pressures that the scheme was set up to help relieve are now unlikely to materialize. Plainly if the Central Lancashire

New Town did not exist, few would now see the slightest reason to invent it. Nevertheless, it survived a critical ministerial review in 1977. It now looks to private sector housing growth and sees both environmental improvement and social provision as among its major objectives.

9.5.3 A Strategic Plan for the North West

By about 1970 all the executive decisions that would shape the region's future growth at least to the year 2000 had been taken, more or less irreversibly and in the piecemeal form described above. Indeed the combined development potential of the four new towns, the three major town expansion schemes and the many minor overspill arrangements far exceeded the demands that were likely to be generated in a region that was no longer one of population growth. At this perhaps untimely juncture, nevertheless, a planning team was established to compose a regional strategic plan, *A Strategic Plan for the North West* (Department of the Environment, 1974). Fortunately and sensibly the planning team did not confine their efforts to the task of designing a spatial blueprint to guide the region's growth to and into the twenty-first century. Clearly their power to 'steer' development was largely eroded by the decisions already taken. In fact, the study places great emphasis—much more than its counterparts in other regions—on the problem of environmental pollution and its cure, on the need to improve the setting and general quality of life in the region, and on the opportunities to improve the general housing stock and so to conserve the social vitality of the inner residential areas of the great cities and the older districts of the textile towns. The towns of North East Lancashire have led the way in this direction. Blackburn in particular has made very great efforts to establish General Improvement Areas as an alternative to the sociologically insensitive policy of total clearance. But the conurbation authorities, with the exception of Rochdale, have been slow to use this instrument of environmental repair. The report addresses itself, also, to the fundamental problem of the costs of upgrading both the general physical environment and the urban environment, in relation to the very limited financial resources of the local authorities of the region. In some senses the sheer size of the programme of repair and rehabilitation that must be undertaken is at the heart of the region's problems, and in the past it has had inadequate help from outside. Indeed, the equation between what the region contributes to the exchequer and what it draws in return suggests that there is a net outflow of public funds from the region. Its index of public spending on capital acount was the lowest in the nation in 1964 (75, compared with 133 for Wales and 121 for Scotland), and on current account the index was the third lowest (82, compared with 140 for the South East). The region has limited local resources with which to attack its environmental problems and appears to receive little support from the outside, if these data for a single year are significant.

These problems of environmental rehabilitation, just like the problems of population shift in the course of redevelopment, are strongly concentrated spatially. The North West is dominated by an urban axis from the Pennines to the Mersey estuary which contains 4.5 million of the total populaiton of 6.7 million. In this zone, now administered almost in its entirety by the Manchester and Merseyside metropolitan counties, the great weight of the problem of repair, renewal and rehabilitation falls. The bulk of the population occupies the most deteriorated environment. Almost the whole of it is classified as a 'black area' in terms of air quality with smoke and SO_2 levels still over twice the acceptable standard.

This is despite controls that have produced a tangible climatic improvement—fog incidence has been reduced by 40 per cent and winter sunshine increased by 50 per cent within a decade. Metropolitan Manchester, alone, has inherited 45 per cent of the region's derelict land. There is scarcely a stretch of river within the entire east-west axis of urbanization that is not classified as 'grossly polluted' or of poor quality. The significance of this outline of the environmental problems of the 'Mersey Belt' is that this is the zone that the Strategic Plan team ultimately recommends as the key to the development of the region.

The Strategic Plan team investigated six alternative 'shapes' for the broad pattern of development in the North West. These were a policy of peripheral enlargement of the two conurbations; a 'Mersey Belt' solution which combines short-range dispersal to the conurbation margins with infilling between them; and, thirdly, a series of strategies, each keyed to a major development proposal made in the past. A 'Central Lancashire New Town' strategy postulates massive growth on the Chorley-Preston axis and in the Fylde, while a 'Deeside' strategy assumes growth in Flint, following the completion of a barrage. Two other variants pursue kites flown in the past by the counties and the North West Regional Planning Council; a 'Weaver City' strategy with massive urban growth in mid-Cheshire, and a rather forlorn proposal for a major growth point in the Lancaster area. In fact this range of options reflects the three basic alternatives discussed above—the enlargement of the conurbations, their virtual coalescence by development between them, and, lastly, a north-south M6-based dispersal of growth. A somewhat complex process of evaluation was applied to all these alternative futures for the region. In essence twenty-three policy objectives were listed—social, environmental and economic—and the success of each strategy in meeting these objectives was measured. Almost at once 'Deeside' and 'Lancaster' dropped out. The rest were reexamined in a second cycle of evaluation, against such yardsticks as regional industrial policy, land resources, urban social provision and questions of access. From this the 'Mersey Belt' alternative emerged triumphant. It is at least an expedient solution. It legitimizes all existing new town and major town expansion projects, while deferring the hopes of the Central Lancashire New Town until late this century, or perhaps early next. It fits the now virtually complete regional motorway net, and it does not offend against present regional industrial policy. It also channels development into what is perhaps the most deteriorated and polluted environment in Britain. But at least the strategy would focus upon the one area eligible for the substantial investment funds available from two of the deeper pockets in the public purse, housing finance and the funds available under the various environmental repair and improvement programmes.

Events since the publication of the plan make it much more likely that this favoured zone could accommodate the bulk of the pressure that will fall upon it, since emigration from the region continues and population growth diminishes. The plan has no statutory force, and those at whom it is aimed have given it a somewhat mixed reception. But if its chief proposals take a physical form, on the ground, then they will produce a new cohesive urban region which was first envisaged half a century ago when it was suggested that a city of enormous size—it was dubbed 'Lancaston'—would grow through the mergence of the Manchester and Merseyside urban clusters.

Is it right to see the future 'shape' of the North West keyed in this way to a massive (but bi-focal) linear city? In a sense the proposals give a spatial form to what already exists, as a system of contact, interaction and even interdependence. People and products move in enormous volumes along this east-west axis, by Ship Canal, high-frequency rail services, motorway and pipeline. The two urban cores are no more than 45 minutes apart, either by rail or motorway. Journey-to-work systems interlock and overlap throughout the entire corridor. Manchester's airport increasingly serves the whole of the zone, as Speke's status declines. Certainly any deflection of development and investment to distant sites in North Lancashire or Central Cheshire would scarcely be helpful to the economic prospects of the deteriorated inner cities at either end of the axis. The relative scarcity of land within the corridor, however, is at least an encouragement to developers to look seriously at possible within-city sites. But would a tight planning discipline (if any agency existed to impose it) that compressed development into this east-west corridor polarize social groups? Public sector housing might well be confined to the near vicinity of employment within the corridor, but the middle-income commuters would doubtless escape to the pleasanter environments to the north and south, especially in North Cheshire. Plainly the 'Mersey Belt' strategy could only work in a slow-growth or a no-growth sutiation: there are not the land resources to absorb massive development. But given a negative-growth assumption, a progressive reduction in regional population coupled with an even greater decline in employment as effective work-sharing by early retirement and shorter weeks redresses unemployment, would a Mersey strategy have any relevance? This may be the position towards the end of the century. Given this possibility, any regional strategy becomes almost redundant, and planning becomes much more a matter of the tactics of environmental improvement, of community development, of quality of life, within a spatial frame little different from that of the present.

REFERENCES

Board of Trade (1969), *The Movement of Manufacturing Industry in the United Kingdom: Study of Movement Affecting the North West Region,* B.O.T., Regional Office, Manchester.
Campbell, M. (1975), A spatial and typological disaggregation of unemployment as a guide to regional policy, *Regional Studies,* 9, 157-168.
County of Greater Manchester (1975), *Structure Plan: Report of Survey,* Greater Manchester Council, Manchester.
Department of Economic Affairs (1965a), *The North West: A Regional Study,* H.M.S.O., London
Department of Economic Affairs (1965b), *Problems of Merseyside,* H.M.S.O. London.
Department of the Environment (1974), *A Strategic Plan for the North West,* H.M.S.O., London.
Dicken, P., and Lloyd, P.E. (1978), Inner metropolitan industrial change enterprise structures and policy issues: case studies of Manchester and Merseyside, *Regional Studies,* 12, 181-198.
Freeman, T.W., Rodgers, H.B., and Kinvig, R.H. (1966), *Lancashire, Cheshire and the Isle of Man,* Nelson, Edinburgh.
Kantorowich, R.H., and others (1964), *Regional Shopping Centres in North West England,* University of Manchester Department of Town and Country Planning, Manchester.
Lancashire and Merseyside Industrial Development Association (1967a), *Closure and Re-occupation of Cotton Mills,* L.A.M.I.D.A., Manchester.
Lancashire and Merseyside Industrial Development Association (1967b), *Decline of the Cotton and Coal Mining Industries of Lancashire,* L.A.M.I.D.A., Manchester.
Law, C.M. (1970), Employment growth and regional policy in North West England, *Regional Sutdies,* 4, 359-366.
Lawton, R., and Cunningham, C.M. (Eds) (1970), *Merseyside: Social and Economic Studies,* Longmans, London.

Lloyd, P.E. (1964), Industrial changes in the Merseyside Development Area, 1949-1959. *Town Planning Review,* **35,** 285-299.

Lloyd, P.E. (1977), *Manufacturing Industry in the Inner City; a Case Study of Merseyside,* University of Manchester School of Geography, Manchester.

Lloyd, P.E. (1979), The components of industrial change for Merseyside inner area 1966-75, *Urban Studies,* 16, 45-60.

Lloyd, P.E., and Mason, C.M. (1978). Manufacturing industry in the inner city: a case study of Greater Manchester, *Transactions and Papers, Institute of British Geographers,* N.S., **3,** 66-91.

Merseyside County Council (1975), *Structure Plan, Stage 1, Report,* Merseyside County Council, Liverpool.

Miles, C. (1968). *Lancashire Textiles; A Case Study of Industrial Change,* Cambridge University Press.

Ministry of Housing and Local Government (1966). *Expansion of Warrington,* H.M.S.O., London.

Ministry of Housing and Local Government (1967a). *Central Lancashire: A Study for a City,* H.M.S.O., London.

Ministry of Housing and Local Government (1967b). *Dee Crossing Study, Part 1,* H.M.S.O., London.

Ministry of Housing and Local Government (1967c). *Expansion of Winsford,* H.M.S.O., London.

Ministry of Housing and Local Government (1968), *Central Lancashire New Town Proposal: Impact on North East Lancashire,* H.M.S.O., London.

Ministry of Housing and Local Government (1970), *Dee Crossing Study, Part 2,* H.M.S.O., London.

North West Economic Planning Council (1975).

Robson, R. (1957), *The Cotton Industry in Britain,* Macmillan, London.

Rodgers, H.B. (1962), The changing geography of the Lancashire cotton industry, *Economic Geography,* **38,** 299-314.

Rodgers, H.B. (1964), *Overspill in Winsford,* Winsford U.D.C.

Salt, J. (1967), The impact of the Ford and Vauxhall plants on the employment situation of Merseyside, 1962-1965. *Tijdschrift voor Economische en Sociale Geografie,* **58,** 255-264.

Secretary of State for Economic Affairs (1969), *The Intermediate Areas* (Chairman, Sir Joseph Hunt) (Cmnd. 3998), H.M.S.O., London.

Smith, D.M. (1968), Identifying the grey areas: A multivariate approach, *Regional Studies,* **2,** 183-193.

Smith, D.M. (1969), *Industrial Britain: The North West,* David & Charles, Newton Abbot.

Wallwork, K.L. (1956). Subsidence in the mid-Cheshire industrial area. *Geographical Journal,* **122,** 40-53.

Warnes, A.M. (1975). Commuting towards city centres: A study of population and employment density gradients in Liverpool and Manchester. *Transactions and Papers, Institute of British Geographers,* **64,** 77-97.

Williams, G. (1975). *Metropolitan Manchester: A Social Atlas,* privately published, Manchester.

CHAPTER 10

Yorkshire and Humberside

Kenneth Warren

10.1 Introduction

A composite Yorkshire and Humberside region gained recognition only in the mid-1960s, and was the product of a belated introduction of forward-looking regional economic planning in which at least some emphasis was given to prospective functional relationships. It was, arguably, a somewhat premature creation—a view supported by the subsequent changes in its boundaries. On the southern edge of the region, for example, where Sheffield overspill was already flowing across into the East Midlands, as early as 1967 parts of Derbyshire were transferred to the county borough and to Yorkshire and Humberside; again, in 1974, with local government reorganization, more substantial changes were made, the most important being the acquisition from the Northern region of parts of the (old) North Riding of Yorkshire, and the loss of a large area of South Lindsey in the south to the East Midlands. Internally, the region has two key components, a basic division which is indicated by its title: on the one hand, there are the older industrial and urban complexes of the west, now substantially administered by the West and South Yorkshire councils, and, on the other hand, there is the estuarine and more rapidly changing county of Humberside on the east. These two components are characterized by very different patterns of activity and economic orientation, and there is a consequential conflict of interest and planning priorities between them—as is illustrated by the clash of development interests in steel between Sheffield and Scunthorpe over many decades, the conflict between coal and oil development, and the different attitudes towards the priorities in road and motorway development within the region.

Yorkshire and Humberside shares characteristics with planning regions both to the north and south, yet in economic structure, prosperity and prospects it differs greatly from both. Yorkshire and Humberside is a basic industrial region. Indeed in many respects it is the primary heavy industrial region of Britain, producing one-third of the nation's steel in 1977, one-quarter of its coal and a great deal of its thermal electricity. Like the East Midlands, it contains a low-cost coalfield and an even bigger mine labour force. Its steel industry, centred in Scunthorpe and Sheffield, in 1977 produced more than twice the output of the works in the North East, and the emphasis on quality steel in the Sheffield area renders the value of its output a number of times greater still. (However, if the British Steel Corporation's development strategy is finally carried through, the North East will eventually have a greater tonnage.) As in the East Midlands, textiles are a major interest, with emphasis on spinning, weaving and finishing of woollens and on clothing, as opposed to hosiery and knitwear. The East Midlands' growth prospects are clearly centred in the west, near to existing foci of population or along the new motorways; in the North East, the favoured zone is definitely coastal. Like the Northern region, Yorkshire and

309

Humberside potentially has a major estuarine growth focus; but, as in the East Midlands, the existing population concentrations and new motorways are western. The centres of existing population both to the north and south of the Yorkshire and Humberside region generally lie in favoured areas; in Yorkshire and Humberside itself, by contrast, population, established industry and political influence alike are concentrated in the west, but some of the region's best growth prospects lie on or near the estuary in the east. Essentially, as in many other areas of Britain, there is a dilemma concerning how much of the nineteenth-century pattern of economic activity and population can or should be refurbished, and how much investment should conversely be given to new foci of economic growth.

There are, of course, traditional links between the West Riding and Humberside, and these are being matched by newer ones. Hull has long handled much of the import traffic for West Riding textile mills and the foreign coal sales of Yorkshire pits. Scunthorpe from its beginnings as a metal centre 100 years ago has had close links with the Yorkshire coalfield and with the Sheffield steelworks—in raw material and finished product flows and in organization. On the other hand, West Yorkshire also has made major use of Merseyside ports, Hull has served the East and West Midlands, and two of the three Scunthorpe steelworks through most of the twentieth century were closely linked with South Wales rather than with South Yorkshire. The eastward shift of coal mining, the construction of big new coal-fired generating stations at Drax and Eggborough, and more recently the development of the Selby coalfield are closing the gap of rural land between West Yorkshire industry and the Humber. A decisive new factor involves the construction of motorway standard roads to link with the conurbations of the west. In the patterns of economic growth in the last quarter of the twentieth century it is certain that the estuary will be more important than in the past; but it is much more debatable whether it will receive in full measure the development which an objective assessment of its assets and prospects suggests.

The economic planning region shows all the signs of an Intermediate Area, as spelled out in detail in the Hunt Report of 1969. Economic growth generally, and increases in per capita income, have been at rates intermediate between those of the more prosperous regions and those of the Development Areas. Some of the post-war growth industries are noticeably absent—in 1972, for instance, the region had fewer than 16,000 employees in the motor industry, only 3.2 per cent of the British total. The downward drift in the region's share of national population is long-established and has, in fact, been greater than in the Northern region. Out-migration has been considerable, so that slow economic growth is in this area combined with low unemployment rates (at least until the 1970s when the latter crept slowly upwards). The region has severe environmental problems, notably a very large acreage of derelict land, and in the 1960s there was a worsening of river pollution whilst national standards improved. Not only does the image and therefore the attractiveness of the region for new investment and employment suffer from this, but industrial efficiency is imperilled as well. And there is a great deal of poor housing in the region, particularly in its western portions.

These conditions were, however, slow to attract government assistance. The first break was made with Yorkshire and Humberside's previously unassisted status in 1969, when Intermediate Area designation was given to the coalfield and to North Humberside. In 1972, the whole planning region was made an Intermediate Area. In 1974, with local government reorganization, that part of the Northern region transferred to Yorkshire and

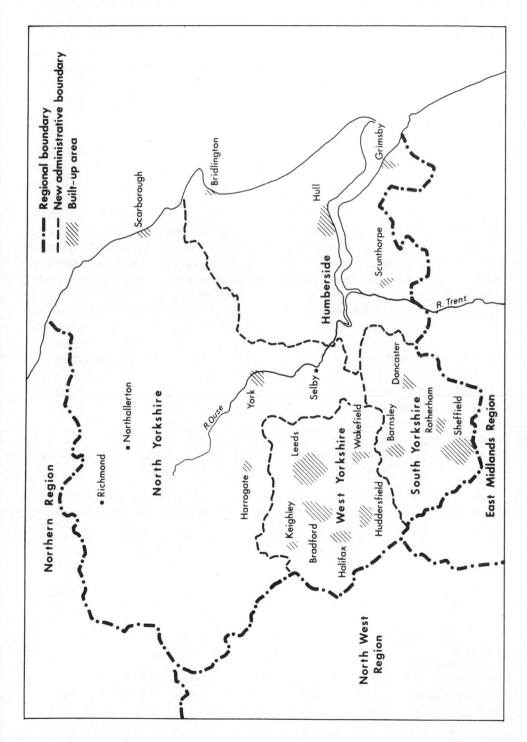

Figure 10.1 Yorkshire and Humberside: administrative divisions, 1979

Humberside retained its Development Area status. In 1977, with problems in the fishing industry and by-elections pending, Hull and Grimsby obtained Development Area status. A year later, the whole of North Yorkshire was made into merely an Intermediate Area. Then in 1979 most of Yorkshire lost all assisted status (Figure 2.7). It is within these shifting central government priorities for investment that local economic development and planning preferences have evolved.

10.2 West Yorkshire

The old West Riding dominates the whole planning region. It had 79 per cent of the population in 1965. Its two successors, West Yorkshire and South Yorkshire, slightly modified in the details of their boundaries, had respectively 42.3 per cent and 26.9 per cent of the 1976 population (Table 10.1). West Yorkshire contains an urban core within the irregular line joining Leeds-Keighley-Halifax-Huddersfield-Wakefield. Eastwards the county includes parts of the active coalfield from Garforth southwards, and north of this (up to Wetherby) the good agricultural lands of parts of the Vale of York. Its northern fringe in the Wharfe valley contains the largely commuting centres of Ilkley and Otley. In south Kirklees and west Calderdale it contains much sparsely populated Pennine upland.

The West Yorkshire conurbation remains extraordinarily dependent upon textile employment. By 1965, only 3.3 per cent of the country's workers were employed in the industry; but in the 'textile zone' of West Yorkshire at that time the proportion was 20.4 per cent, and in some parts the share was a good deal higher—at Morley, Shipley and Keighley it was between 31 and 35 per cent, and at Elland the figure was a remarkable 54.1 per cent of the workforce. The woollens and worsted industry made up over 80 per cent of the textile employment throughout most of the industrial region, but on the fringes (notably at Todmorden and Skipton) cotton was more important. However, this distinction is increasingly artificial as by 1970 half the fibre used in British textile production was man-made and was used in both cotton and wool fabrics. Between 1953 and the late 1960s some 200,000 jobs were lost in Lancashire textiles. During the same

Table 10.1 Yorkshire and Humberside: population and employment by country, 1975/1976

	Humberside	North Yorkshire	South Yorkshire	West Yorkshire	Yorkshire and Humberside
POPULATION					
Mid-1976 ('000s)	849	653	1,318	2,072	4,892
Share of regional total (%)	17.3	13.3	26.9	42.3	
EMPLOYMENT STRUCTURE					
Mid-1975. % of total: Engineering and allied industries	15.8	5.6	26.3	15.3	17.4
Other manufacturing	18.9	18.1	11.8	24.9	19.5
Mining, etc.	1.6	2.3	11.4	5.0	5.9
Services	52.7	61.1	44.3	49.6	49.9

Source: C.S.O., *Regional Statistics,* 12, 1977.

period the decline in Yorkshire was much smaller, though still substantial: in December 1960 there were almost 153,000 production workers in wool textiles, but by the end of 1970 there were only 94,000. This steady decline appeared likely to continue. In a study of the national industry—some 73 per cent of whose workforce was in the West Riding—W.S. Atkins suggested to the Economic Development Committee for the Wool Textile Industry (1969) that employment ought to drop to 121,000 by the mid-1970s. However, no large displacement of workers was expected since natural wastage would account for most of the reduction, and with female activity rates in the wool and textile zone relatively high, unemployment low, and unfilled vacancies usually at a high level, these traditional sub-regional economic indicators were often interpreted as signifying reasonably healthy conditions. By 1970/1971, however, many firms were closing, unemployment rates were creeping up and the situation in the textile communities was seen to be far from satisfactory. In fact, rationalization has been much quicker than was expected. It was speeded by government assistance under the Industry Act of 1972 which was used to provide funds for the modernization of the textile industry. Between 1970 and 1976 the workforce fell by 40 per cent to 62,000. During the same period there was a substantial though smaller decline in the workforce of the associated clothing industry from 56,000 to 43,000.

The economic structure of both these West Yorkshire industries is weak. Many of the firms are small, and most are in family ownership. By the mid-1960s, for instance, the twenty largest public companies were still operating only about one-fifth of the 750-800 textile mills in Yorkshire. At that time, the average number of production workers per mill was well under 200. Many of the buildings were over 100 years old and contained much old machinery. The industry thus found itself unable to make a return upon its capital sufficient to finance desirable reorganization and reequipment. With such levels of investment beyond the resources of most firms, operations remained labour-intensive, hence the relatively low level of output per worker. This low productivity in turn made it difficult for the industry to pay wages competitive enough to retain many employees, especially the more skilled of its workforce—and many drifted away from textiles and even left the region. All this made increased mechanization, which the industry could not afford, still more desirable.

One response to this situation in the 1950s and 1960s was for the textile and clothing industries to employ increasing numbers of Commonwealth immigrant workers who were prepared to work under relatively difficult conditions for low wages. The Industry Act scheme for textiles also helped to break through some of the difficulties. Between 1973 and 1978 about 60 per cent of the industry's assets are said to have been modernized at a cost of £86 million (of which £16 million was government money). In this period, some ninety mills were closed. The desired change from 'a craft-based, labour intensive industry to a scientific, technological, capital-based industry' was long ago recognized as desirable, and is clearly now under way. Shift working, a necessary accompaniment to mechanization, has increased and there have been some outstanding instances of productivity improvements.

Labour shortages have also been singularly important in changing the economic geography of these two industries. First, they caused the textile and clothing industries to look beyond West Yorkshire in order to tap the under-utilized female workforce on the coalfield; in the 1960s up to 6,000 women were travelling daily from the mining communities to the mills in West Yorkshire. This movement reached its peak in the early 1960s and subsequently declined. In addition, branch factories were built on the coalfield to tap the available supplies of labour on the spot. Meanwhile a number of textile and clothing firms elected to move further afield and especially into the Development Areas, where labour supplies were easier and government financial assistance was available long before Yorkshire became an Intermediate Area.

Engineering in West Yorkshire was originally closely linked with the textile trade, but this has declined and some firms have turned to continental machines in the reequipment of their mills. At a later stage the engineering industries became increasingly concerned with railway equipment, and then with a host of diversifying lines of activity. The emphasis of activities within the sub-region, however, is still on heavier lines for which demand has generally grown more slowly than for lighter products. As a result the post-1945 growth in engineering employment was at only a little more than half the national rate until the end of the 1960s. Within the sub-region there were widely varying experiences in this and related trades. In the mid-1950s, for example, Bradford lost its role as a car-manufacturing centre, as the long-established firm of Jowetts felt the effects of remoteness from Midland components and from assured supplies of car bodies. In Leeds, some of the industry on the south side was physically so crowded that it was described as a manufacturing ghetto. In Huddersfield, textile engineering has declined, but there was a counterbalancing growth in both electrical engineering and in the tractor production of the David Brown organization.

Other new industries came into the West Yorkshire sub-region, but not on a scale to match the area's past industrial importance, or to compensate fully for the decline in the old, staple trades. In manufacturing, the sub-region has in certain respects fared much worse than other parts of the Yorkshire and Humberside region. However, in the last decade there has been an important growth of service industries. Office rentals and labour costs within West Yorkshire are generally amongst the more competitive in Britain, but most of the growth in office jobs has been in Leeds which has become one of the major provincial locations for commercial and administrative activities. Together with new educational, health and retail services, their growth has permitted a substantial reconstruction of the conurbation core. Elsewhere, however, modernization and redevelopment have proceeded at a slower pace.

In the 1970s, the economy of West Yorkshire overall has done better than was expected at the beginning of the decade. Long-term growth prospects are still, however, highly uncertain—in 1977 a forecast of employment changes within the sub-region to 1986 pointed to a possible increase of 25,000 jobs if circumstances were favourable; but an alternative projection, making less favourable assumptions, was for a massive loss of 83,000 jobs.

10.3 The Coalfield Zone

Developing several decades after the West Yorkshire conurbation, the economy of the Yorkshire coalfield to the south east has remained much more dependent upon primary activity. Here there was no preexisting textile industry to provide a market for engineering goods, and there were no major iron ore resources in the coal measures to stimulate a metallurgical industry. In any case, the large mines required by the deeper coal measures around Pontefract and Doncaster provided ample employment for all the available male labour, and excellent railway communications enabled their output to be delivered to distant markets. In 1959, the primary industries employed the extraordinarily high proportion of 40.5 per cent of the labour force in the sub-region. Mining, almost all of it for coal, had 117,000 out of a total insured workforce of 301,000. However, between 1959 and 1965 the industry began to contract and to displace labour even quicker, so that the number of men engaged in mining fell dramatically by 20,000. There was compensating growth of female employment in the service and manufacturing sectors, but overall there was only a 1.3 per cent increase in insured employees on the coalfield (compared with 2.6 per cent in the West Riding, 4.3 per cent in Yorkshire and Humberside and 7.0 per cent nationally). Late in 1967, the N.C.B. employed 88,500 workers in Yorkshire. At that time, its own estimates, regarded by many as optimistic in the light of an increasingly competitive energy market in Britain, suggested that this workforce would decline to 78,000 by 1971, to 42,000 by 1975 and to 18,500 by 1980. In fact, as a consequence first of government assistance and then the transformed general energy situation, the decline of jobs in coal mining has been much slower, so that in 1976 there were still 66,000 workers employed by the N.C.B. in Yorkshire and Humberside.

The Yorkshire coal industry has a considerable output (29 million tons in 1976/1977, or 27 per cent of the national total), relatively high productivity, and a largely local market in the power stations of the C.E.G.B. and in the steel industry's coke ovens at Scunthorpe and Corby and in the Sheffield district. Conditions in the different parts of the coalfield, however, vary widely. In West Yorkshire the industry has declined rapidly and the Wakefield economy, for instance, has suffered as a result. Elsewhere, rationalization in order to lower costs still further is clearly essential, and in the process more men are likely to be displaced. The concentration of the industry in larger pits is proceeding steadily—sixteen smaller units were closed between 1969 and 1976—and other mines are being reconstructed with impressive productivity increases. Kellingley, the only new pit to be opened since the war (in 1965), was designed for an initial output of 1 million tons a year, 2.2 million tons later. The very big development at Selby which will produce its first coal in the 1980s will eventually have an annual production of 9 million tons—but it will employ only 4,000 men. These will be mostly redeployed from other pits on the coalfield, but their output will mean more displacement elsewhere. In the old coal zone diversification is clearly essential, for in some communities as much as three-quarters of male jobs are in coal mining.

Unemployment on the coalfield generally remained at a relatively low level into the late 1950s. It then began to rise. Commuting to jobs in the bigger neighbouring urban centres afforded a partial solution. This apart, however, the rationalization of the coal industry meant either out-migration, intolerable levels of unemployment, or the steering of new jobs onto the coalfield. To ease the last solution, the West Riding County Council, in its submission to the Hunt Committee, suggested that the coalfield should be given full Development Area status. The Committee 'found no other problem which was comparable in scale, given the size and the speed of the rundown and the key position of the [coal] industry in the area'. They did not, however, recommend special action other than the Intermediate Area status they suggested for the whole of the economic planning region. The government, however, in 1969 designated the coalfield as the only Intermediate Area in the West Riding and offered it not only the benefits of building grants and the construction of advanced factories at public expense, but also additional spending on roads and housing. As noted above, the whole of Yorkshire and Humberside was given Intermediate Area status in 1972, to reduce this relative advantage afforded briefly to the coalfield.

The most obvious attraction for new industry in the coalfield zone is the large male workforce that is likely to become available as pits close, plus a good deal of untapped female labour. The major disincentives are the drabness of the settlements and the unsightliness of a landscape often dominated by huge pits and waste heaps; large areas have also been made unattractive by the steam and gas emissions from coke ovens, and by extensive subsidence. Considerable net additions to the area of waste land accrue each year as a result of mine closures, which leave pit-head gear, railway sidings and general waste littering large areas of the sub-region. These problems were highlighted by a study of migration which was made by the Standing Conference of West Yorkshire Local Planning Authorities in 1968 and 1969: in 80,000 replies to its questionnaire, 'environment' accounted for only 7 per cent of the moves through the whole study area, but for 18 per cent of the moves that were made from the central areas of the coalfield (defined as a narrow strip of urban districts lying between Doncaster, Sheffield, the Five Towns and Wakefield). In this area, 71 per cent of the moves that were attributed to environmental factors were said to be due to visual matters and pollution (whereas 66 per cent of the moves from the Halifax area that were attributed to environmental causes were related to concerns about housing standards).

In the south east of the coalfield lies Doncaster, the largest urban centre in the sub-region. It exemplifies the considerable possibilities and the problems of the zone as it tries to diversify away from coal. Doncaster became an important railway engineering town after 1853 when the Great Northern Railway moved its workshops from Boston; nevertheless in 1901 (with a population of 36,000) it was still much smaller than Barnsley. In 1907 the exploitation of the local deep coal began, and the population of the town and neighbourhood surged upwards. The so-called Doncaster Study Area (Yorkshire and Humberside Economic Planning Council, 1970) contained 48,000 people in 1901, but by 1931 its population was 178,000. In the 1930s new diversifying industry arrived, and there was further industrial expansion in the late 1940s and 1950s. The main industries of the post-1945 expansion, however, have been substantially male-employing—British Ropes, I.C.I. Fibres and International Harvester especially—with the result that the traditionally low ratio of female to male jobs persisted. The railway workshops remain important, as indeed does the coal industry. In 1967 some 28 per cent of all the male employment in the Doncaster Study Area was in coal. Only in the 1970s, when male employment in the district fell slightly, has female employment begun to grow with the further diversification of the manufacturing base, with the arrival of some office jobs (including some of the N.C.B. jobs transferred from central London) and, helped by the new motorway nodality of the town, with the development of Doncaster as a major sub-regional focus. By the late 1970s, the city-region had a population of some 250,000.

10.4 South Yorkshire

To the south west of the coalfield is South Yorkshire. In 1965 the former South Yorkshire planning sub-region contained some 350,000 insured employees—compared with 305,000 in the coalfield and 833,000 in the West Yorkshire sub-region. Less than 3 per cent of its workers were in coal mining and only a small proportion in textiles. In 1965 three orders of the Standard Industrial Classification (S.I.C.)—iron and steel, metal goods, and engineering and electrical goods—had 43 per cent of the total insured employees (a much higher proportion than textile and clothing employment in West Yorkshire), and for some time employment in these industries had been stable. In the 1970s there was a slight decline but, in the case of steel especially, it was accompanied by substantial investment to ensure the industry's future.

In South Yorkshire the steel and the engineering industries are impressively diverse. The former produces not only common carbon grades, but also a whole range of more specialized products through to the finest alloy steels using electric arc furnaces. Engineering output extends from the manufacture of large chemical plant and oil refinery pressure vessels, through marine engineering, to the fine and delicate products of the cutlery trade. The two activities, steel making and engineering, are often closely interwoven, but geographically there is still a clear division of activities between 'Sheffield on the Sheaf' and 'Sheffield on the Don', the first concerned with light products, the other with heavy lines. Both sections face serious planning problems.

'Sheffield on the Sheaf' covers much of the west and centre of Sheffield. Industry there is conducted in what are often highly congested premises, operating on slopes of inconvenient steepness with difficulties of access. In the 1970s its surviving cutlery businesses were badly hit by low-cost imports. This blow has affected an industry already in decline since the early 1950s. The cutlery industry still employed some 6,000 in Sheffield by 1977, but it was fragmented into many small concerns, had too little modern machinery, and was often operating in totally unsuitable tenement premises. The heavy industrial section of Sheffield's activities stretches eastward from near the centre of the city out towards Rotherham and beyond. It focuses on the valley of the Don, which in parts is almost filled to capacity with heavy industry. It is a splendidly impressive sight from the train or from the Tinsley Viaduct of the M1, but it represents an essentially haphazard growth, affording little room for well laid out expansion. Road access is also inadequate; the local housing stock is of low quality and is intermixed with manufacturing; and environmental problems are intensified by industrial and power station effluent—steam, smoke, gases and heavily polluted water.

From the congested parts of the Don valley, and from the centre of Sheffield, a certain amount of out-movement has long been and is still taking place. In the 1960s the English Steel Corporation built a major new works at Tinsley; later, Osborn Steel concentrated the activities of its several Sheffield plants (plus those of the Low Moor works, Bradford) at Ecclesfield; and in the mid-1970s the British Steel Corporation built its new and highly efficient Thrybergh Bar mill. Further out still, Chapeltown-Thorncliffe has lost its old iron trade, but retains important engineering and chemicals activities, while Stocksbridge, in a narrow tributary valley of the upper Don, remains heavily dependent upon an important anomalously located steel plant. Sheffield is the headquarters for the British Steel Corporation's Special Steels Division and the centre also of a good deal of the private steel industry. Both have been rationalizing their activities, though output has held up well in the acute steel depression of the mid-1970s. By 1977 the British Steel Corporation employed 20,000 in Sheffield and district, whilst the private industry employed 9,000.

In all directions except the north east, the built-up area of the city of Sheffield has been extended considerably since 1945. With rebuilding taking place at lower densities than are found in the small houses at the centre of the urban area, or the dreary Victorian industrial rows of Attercliffe and Brightside, the city's population fell from a peak of 512,000 to some 489,000 by 1965. However, with the inclusion of parts of the West Riding and later parts of Derbyshire, centred on Mosbrough, Sheffield's population has increased again to make it the largest city in Yorkshire. Mosbrough has been designated by Sheffield as its major growth focus and will eventually house 90,000 people. Sheffield's programme of pollution controls and urban reconstruction must be reckoned one of the most successful in Britain's big cities. The city centre has already been impressively redeveloped and, with new motorway accessibility, has become an attractive regional shopping centre. At the same time, office growth has occurred on a substantial scale. Central area office accommodation in Sheffield was 140,000 square metres (1.5 million square feet) in 1945, 220,000 square metres in 1971, and nearly 400,000 square metres (4.3 million square feet) in 1978. The Midland Bank has moved over 1,000 of its London head-quarters staff to Sheffield, and by 1980 the Manpower Services Commission will employ still more there.

In short, there have been no shifts in the economic structure of South Yorkshire as disturbing as those experienced in the other sub-regions of industrial Yorkshire, and at its core the city of Sheffield affords a reassuring example of an old industrial centre that is successfully diversifying its economy and renewing its built environment.

10.5   The Future of Industrial Yorkshire

The changing pattern of transport facilities, and above all the emerging motorway network, is a major new element in the economic geography of West and South Yorkshire. It is widely believed that this will improve the region's economic standing within Britain; more certainly, it will alter the economic prospects of the component parts of the region. The Doncaster (motorway) bypass has been open since the early 1960s. In 1968 the M1 was completed to Leeds, and the M18 was opened from the M1 east of Sheffield to the A1(M) west of Doncaster. The M62 now runs from Stratford and Worsley (west of Greater Manchester) to Lofthouse on the M1 south of Leeds and on towards Humberside (Figure 10.2). It is clear that initially the motorways have had a permissive rather than an automatic economic impact. They have allowed for the first time into Yorkshire goods and services which can be more efficiently produced in the Midlands and South, and provided a challenge that requires a positive response from local industry. Certainly they are not a magnet which will automatically ensure the growth of the region.

Within Yorkshire, motorway access has nevertheless been regarded as a prize worth fighting for. Local agitation secured more access points than were originally planned on the M62 in the west of the region. In the east it was originally believed by central government planners that it was impracticable to route the M1 through the old mining and industrial areas between Sheffield, Barnsley and Leeds. An alternative alignment was planned curving eastwards towards the A1 and then back to Leeds. Together, however, the local authorities pressed the Ministry of Transport to think again, and at a considerable cost the present route was chosen, running to the west of Barnsley and snaking northwards through the outskirts of Leeds. Foci of growth at motorway interchanges were widely expected, and they have in fact begun to emerge. The Halifax and upper Calder valley study identified Brighouse and Elland as most likely to benefit from the M62, and Slough Estates Ltd, fifty years ago the pioneers of industrial estate development in Britain and well noted for their perceptive location policies, opened a new factory and warehouse estate on the edge of Wakefield, at the M1/M62 interchange. West Riding planners also responded to opportunities of good motorway access in their proposals for new population and development foci to relieve the problems of the coalfield.

In 1966 the Yorkshire and Humberside Economic Planning Council estimated that natural increase and prospective net out-migration would give a 1981 population of 5.2

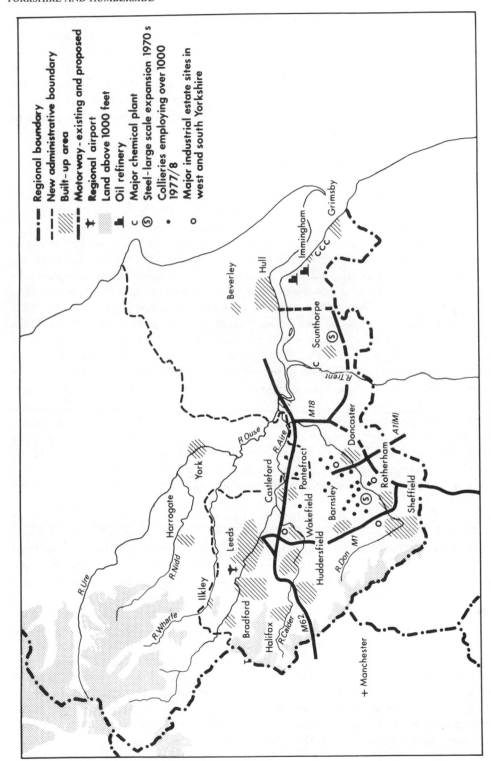

Figure 10.2 Industrial Yorkshire and Humberside

million, an annual increase of 30,000. In the light of these estimates six growth points were chosen on the coalfield—three being designated as 'primary' and three as 'major'. By 1976, however, revised projections of the Registrar General led the E.P.C. to expect an annual rate of population increase less than one-sixth of that which had been forecast in the mid-1960s, and the view has been expressed within the region that the growth points should feel the full impact of these reductions, leaving growth and reconstruction in the conurbation little affected. It is a moot point whether industrial Yorkshire can afford to forego some of the benefits that the motorways might bring.

10.6   The Rural North and Middle

North of and between industrial Yorkshire and Humberside are extensive rural districts. North Yorkshire, the new county created in 1974 from the North Riding (excluding Teesside) and the northern parts of both the old West and East Ridings is in a number of senses a hybrid. Those parts transferred from the Northern region kept their Development Area status until April 1978 when, like the rest, they became Intermediate Areas (and it was soon being said that this change was causing some companies to abandon intended expansion plans there). North Yorkshire contains the high millstone grit country north of mid-Wharfdale, where pastoral farming is confined to narrow valley bottoms, the population is sparse, and the road access is poor, and the limestone uplands of the North Yorkshire moors, another area of rough pasture. Both upland areas have an important recreational role these days. Between them is the rich northern end of the Vale of York. The drained glacial drift and improved outwashed gravels of the vale support a varied and generally prosperous farm economy. To the south and south east this area is replaced by the Fens and Warplands of Thorne, Axholme and Ancholme. The rolling landscapes of the Lincolnshire Wolds support a grain (largely barley) and sheep economy. Accessibility varies greatly, from a proximity to main routeways in the Vale of York to the remoteness of many wold villages. Apart from the processing of farm produce and the servicing of agricultural machinery, the towns in this varied area have very little industry. Towards the fringes, however, many are mushrooming as commuter centres for the bigger industrial centres.

The city of York dominates the northern part of this agricultural zone. As a route focus and industrial centre, as well as a fine historic city with major tourist and cultural activities, its traffic and physical planning problems pose a real challenge. Employment prospects in the city's large food and drink industries seem good, though there have been problems in the transport and communication sector. History and location at first sight make York an extremely attractive location for a regional capital standing apart from the partisanship of either West and South Yorkshire or of Humberside. In a minority report to the Maud Commission on Local Government in England, it was suggested that it might become the capital of an even bigger province extending from the Humber to the Tweed. Today, however, there seems no prospect whatsoever of this wider destiny being achieved. West of the vale, Harrogate is not only a noted tourist centre, but also today a place of retirement, for office activities and for conferences. It has grown briskly in the 1970s, commuter and residential growth being accompanied by an expansion of science-based industry and the development of research establishments. In the old East Riding and only 13 kilometres (8 miles) from central Hull, Beverley has grown chiefly as a commuter centre.

In the south of the rural zone there are no urban foci, although the former parishes of Lincolnshire have been increasing steadily in population recently as a result of developments at Scunthorpe and along the Humber bank. More impressive, however, have been the gains recorded in the centre of the zone. Between Gainsborough and Goole, industrial Yorkshire and Humberside are separated by a belt of low-lying, mainly rural and sparsely populated land. Between 1951 and 1971, however, its increase in population was 15.4 per cent as compared with 11.0 per cent for England and Wales and it is an area of enormous growth prospects. Motorways and other major road improvements now give it good access to both the banks of the Humber, to West and South Yorkshire, and so to the M1 and Lancashire. The area is also an important rail focus. Taking into account the facts of existing and prospective accessibility to considerable concentrations of populations, consultants have even advised the development of an international airport in the area. Thorne Waste, the suggested site, will almost certainly not be developed for such a purpose, but it could well become the centre of a major new urban and industrial complex by the end of the century.

10.7 Humberside

Humberside was created as a separate county and administrative unit only in 1974. In some ways it might be regarded as a premature creation—the integrating effect of a Humber bridge being logically a prerequisite rather than an addition to its facilities. Although Humberside is widely acknowledged to have great development prospects, and the sobriquet 'Britain's Europort' has been frequently applied to it, short-term problems have recently been as much a preoccupation as its longer-term potential. It was immediate difficulties in the fishing industry, for example, which caused the designation of Hull and Grimsby in 1977 as Development Areas. Moreover, there has to date been a lack of resolution concerning ways in which the area's development potential can best be handled. The broad Humber estuary divides the region into two parts. South Humberside has a number of economic foci; activity on the north bank of the Humber, on the other hand, is concentrated at one centre, Kingston-upon-Hull, which has a conurbation population of over 350,000.

Hull is served by docks stretching more than 11 kilometres (7 miles) along the estuary. The approach channel so far has been deep enough for vessels carrying its main primary imports of grain, timber, wool and oil. The early docks along the river Hull are now redundant. The city, and more recently the British Transport Docks Board, have spent liberally on new facilities, with the King George Dock to the east as the centre of modernization work. New container berth facilities have been developed there, and at Alexandra Dock. Looking ahead, there exists a scheme for new deep-water facilities yet further down the estuary between Spurn Head and Hawkins Point. With E.E.C. trade growing rapidly, Hull has inceasingly supplemented its old predominantly import business with a bigger export component. Yet in the early 1960s and late 1970s, as a result of a switch to container handling methods, port employment was cut by about half. Modern dock development always involves new patterns of urban expansion and improvements in land transport. The physical setting of Hull has meant these changes have created serious planning problems. There were no major variations in rock-type or topography on the lowlands of the river Hull, and there were no important agricultural villages to provide nuclei for suburban development as very rapid economic growth occurred in Hull towards the end of the nineteenth century; as a consequence, the urban area spilled out across the lowlands. Within the expanding conurbation, only a little above sea-level, railway construction involved the proliferation of level crossings. Today, with the subsequent growth of road transport, these have become a serious cause of traffic congestion, and the problem has been compounded by the development of new port facilities to the east of Hull that involve (in the absence of a major bypass) increasing the movement of port traffic through the central parts of the city.

Hull failed to become a major industrial centre. Compared with the five county boroughs in the country nearest in population, it has the lowest proportion of its rate income provided by industry, or even by commerce and industry together. It has, of course, a complement of port industries though some of these have been in difficulties in recent years. Shipbuilding and ship-repairing activities, for instance, were adversely affected by the lack of Development Area status until 1977, a status which it was reckoned in the early 1970s would have reduced labour costs in shipbuilding by about 12 per cent. The Drypool Group, the town's biggest shipbuilding concern and with yards also in Selby and Beverley, was in receivership by 1975. There is some metallurgical activity on north Humberside such as the Rio Tinto tin refinery in North Ferriby (west of the conurbation), but even here there has had to be a certain amount of retrenchment in the mid-1970s. Engineering is a prominent activity, and at Brough an aircraft industry employing some 4,000 was built up after 1945 as an overspill from Leeds enterprise; in the 1970s, however, as part of the Hawker Siddeley Group, it has suffered decline. In 1925, in a development stemming from a traditional port activity, the Distillers' Company acquired a plant at Salt End (to the east of Hull) to make industrial alcohol from molasses; this has become an important, diverse and expanding chemical operation, with an improved tanker terminal. There are large tracts of land suitable for further industrial development—for example, some 260 hectares (660 acres) in the Salt End area, and the former pit wood storage land on the dock estate. In seeking to attract further industrial investment, however, it is clear that the relative remoteness, and still more the perceived remoteness, of Hull will have to be broken down.

The old main road along the north bank of the Humber estuary to West Yorkshire was once described as an 'archaic disgrace', and the tortuousness of rail links with the Midlands has long been a problem. At the end of the 1950s a Hull planning report unconsciously betrayed the psychological remoteness which these conditions then engendered: there were, it maintained, commercial connections with the North Midlands and the West Riding, 'but these links with distant centres of population are commercial only. There are no large towns near enough for Hull to have close social contact, and much of the day-to-day life of the city is bound up with the predominantly rural East Riding' (Kingston-upon-Hull, c.1959). Even after the Department of Economic Affairs linked Hull with the West Riding for regional planning purposes, the city seems to have been very careful from the start to guard its own interests. There can be little doubt, however that in future its interconnections must and will be seen in a wider context than hitherto, and that the new road infrastructure of Humberside will reduce—indeed is already reducing—its isolation. The new motorway links with Doncaster and West Yorkshire, and improvements of the road to York, are bringing Hull into easier contact with a wider hinterland, and the decision to build a Humber bridge—suggested for over 100 years—opened still greater if somewhat speculative horizons. This investment will bind the future of Hull much more closely than ever before to the people and places south of the Humber estuary.

During the past twenty to twenty-five years, population and employment have grown much more rapidly on south Humberside than to the north of the estuary, and there seems every sign that this difference will continue. There was substantial industrial growth on both sides in the 1960s but, although half of the industrial development certificates approved for the whole of Humberside between 1956 and 1967 were for projects in Greater Hull, the yield in additional employment there was considerably less than half the total for Humberside as a whole. Overall from 1967 to 1978 north Humberside lost about 10,000 jobs whilst south Humberside gained about the same number. In its review of the period 1975 to 1985, the E.P.C. anticipated continuing high unemployment and out-migration from the north bank. The opening of the Humber bridge in 1981 should ease the attainment of a better balance between northern unemployment and south-side opportunities in industrial jobs, possibly with a counterbalance in the journey to work from south to north for women workers. As this implies, south Humberside has increasingly come to be preoccupied with larger schemes of heavy industry, in contrast to the increasing prominence of service employment in Hull.

One hundred years ago Hull already had a population of 120,000. Grimsby was then only one-sixth as large, and there was no other important centre throughout the whole of Humberside. In the late nineteenth century Grimsby became a great fishing port, and in 1912 the port of Immingham was opened nearby in order to handle big vessels exporting coal from the Yorkshire fields. Grimsby, of course, retained its fishing trade, its port activities and a small amount of ship construction and repairing (mainly of fishing craft); until World War II its manufacturing activity was largely confined to biscuit and jam making. Since then, however, this part of Humberside has become an outstanding growth area for heavy industry.

The prosperity of south Humberside in heavy industrial development has been founded on the close proximity of a deep-water channel (suitable for further dredging), an abundance of low-lying, flat land available for bulk-reducing industries, and the perceptiveness of the local authorities which recognized the existence of this potential over thirty years ago. Immediately before World War II, Grimsby Rural District began to acquire land specifically for industrial development, and the Borough of Grimsby soon followed suit. British Titan Products (which already had big Teesside operations), and Fisons with a nitrogen fertilizer plant, pioneered post-war development in the Grimsby-Immingham belt. Later other major chemical firms came to the area—for instance, Laporte Industries, C.I.B.A., Courtaulds operating a major acrylic fibre plant, and I.C.I. with an ammonia installation. East of Immingham is an area that is well favoured for the future growth of space-extensive industry, and near Killingholme there are already large electricity-generating and petrochemical developments—partly associated with the fact that this is a landfall for natural gas from the North Sea. Two oil refineries have been built in this locality since 1966, and are served by a terminal capable of handling (partly-laden) 250,000 d.w.t. tankers. In addition to its suitable site, Humberside offers other locational attractions to the oil companies: it is close to the Yorkshire and Midlands markets, and it provides interesting possibilities of linked developments with Continental refinery operations.

The small up-swing in coal exports by the National Coal Board, especially following devaluation in the late-1960s, is largely through the Humber ports. This traffic has been concentrated at Immingham, to which all former shipments through Hull have been diverted. At the end of 1970 a new deep-water terminal at South Killingholme came into operation, designed initially to handle coastal and foreign coal shipments of up to 6 million tons a year. The National Coal Board at an early stage expressed a hope that the British Steel Corporation might make joint use of this facility for its iron ore imports, taking advantage also of empty wagons returning through Scunthorpe to the South Yorkshire pits. (By 1969, the Steel Corporation had decided not to locate any steel-making capacity on a green-field site at Immigham—for reasons which, though logical and economic in the short term, appear highly questionable as part of a long-term development strategy—but rather to concentrate its investments on an existing site inland at Scunthorpe.) A year later B.S.C. agreed to join with the N.C.B. and the British Transport Docks Board to extend the existing terminal to make it capable of handling 70,000 d.w.t. bulk-carriers, and 9 million tons of import and export traffic each year.

Humberside has for generations been the leading fishing focus in Europe. In recent years the trade has been severely hit by rising costs and by international disputes which have led to British fishing vessels being shut out of many distant waters. Hull and Grimsby remain the country's major fishing ports, but their share of the national landings has dwindled alarmingly. In 1978, 20,000 people were still dependent on fishing for their living. Yet more rationalization, possibly involving some focusing of activity on Hull and a run-down in Grimsby, seems desirable—but Grimsby depends much more heavily on fishing-related employment than does Hull.

There are other, though smaller, foci of industry along the Humber. Barton-upon-Humber, for example, was already important before Albright & Wilson opened a new fertilizer plant there in 1969 to supply the considerable markets of the region. In the Flixborough-Keadby area, where the Trent is still navigable for vessels of some 2,000 d.w.t., the ammonia plant of Nitrogen Fertilizers was linked through raw material and product flows with the joint Fison/Dutch/National Coal Board caprolactin plant nearby, which has been reconstructed on the same site following the disaster there in the mid-1970s. Goole is now recognized as having good growth prospects for industry and for distribution activities reflecting its accessibility to the motorway network and its upper estuarine port location. Eastwards is the very different but equally dynamic economy of Scunthorpe, land-based and until recent years dependent in the main on local resources.

Scunthorpe, Brigg and the nearby rural areas—an area which in 1966 the Leeds School of Planning defined as the Scunthorpe Study Area—doubled in population between 1900 and 1961 to 112,000. Growth at the heart of this area had been very much more impressive. Scunthorpe itself increased by just under 15,000 between 1951 and 1966, a 22.8 per cent increase. This expansion was overwhelmingly dependent upon three steelworks. Indeed the degree of specialization in metal manufacturing at Scunthorpe, as indicated by a 'coefficient of town specialization', is greater than in any of the seventy British towns outside the conurbations and with a population of over 50,000. Diversification of jobs is clearly highly necessary, although the steel industry in the town has benefited from major new developments.

Scunthorpe's share of national steel output went up from 10 per cent in 1952 to 11.8 per cent by 1968; by the late-1970s its share of national capacity had increased to about 17 per cent. In the mid-1960s it was decided by the private companies then controlling the industry, and notably by United Steel Companies, that major new capacity should be provided in North Lincolnshire; and after some hesitation it was decided that this should be at the existing works in Scunthorpe rather than at a green-field, Humberside site. At the same time it was decided to switch to a much higher proportion of foreign ore in the blast furnaces of the district in order to reduce the use of Frodingham stone which is so lean that it has even been called ferruginous limestone! The subsequent common ownership of the three plants, under nationalization, gave the B.S.C. the opportunity of considerable cost reductions through rationalization, though the Normanby Park works is still operated separately from the other and very much larger agglomeration of iron- and steel-making plant. The corporation also elected in 1969 to make Scunthorpe one of its major sites under its corporate planning proposals for the early 1970s. Its investment programme there has not only replaced the old open hearth and rotary furnaces with three basic oxygen converters, but has also provided a new, continuous-casting plant and an impressive increase in rolling mill capacity. Its steel-making capability there has been raised to well over 5 million tons, although it now appears that this is backed by inadequate iron-making plant. As output expands so will the steel industry's workforce be reduced, and it is difficult to identify any major industries which appear likely to generate new job opportunities there in the next few years. However, it has been argued that the Humber bridge and improved road communications will sweep Scunthorpe into a new growth spiral.

Prospects of major growth for the whole of Humberside have been widely anticipated, but rarely have they been closely analysed. There can be few doubts about the area's assets. In the mid-1960s, for example, the sharp increase in the level of assistance given to industry in Development Areas showed no sign of checking growth on Humberside. Its greater proximity to national markets than the Development Areas was a substantial countervailing asset for the heavy trades—for instance, for the cost of operating the estimated 1,800 or so road tankers which served the Humber refineries in the early 1970s. Even more than on Teesside, there remains an abundance of land to accommodate development on almost any conceivable future scale, and there are equally good conditions for the disposal of effluent or the dispersal of atmospheric pollution. And the provision of adequately deep water is unlikely to present insuperable difficulties in the foreseeable future. On the other hand, supplies of fresh water are potentially a serious problem and one which in the past has served to frustrate major metallurgical plans for Immingham. Remedy may be found in the use of Trent water, but this will involve a huge investment and a comprehensive basin-wide improvement programme (which would involve pollution control as far away as the Black Country and even the Potteries). Another difficulty may be a shortage of labour, although most of the traditional activities need relatively small workforces. A final uncertainty is the effect, and particularly the geographical effect, of the Humber bridge.

The Humber estuary has been an important barrier to movement in the past. By 1961 there were only 500 daily journeys to work across the estuary. Believing that better access to the south will improve its economic prospects, Hull has actively promoted the idea of a bridge across the Humber for over forty years. South bank communities, by contrast, have been much less enthusiastic. Grimsby promised its support for a bridge in 1964, but did not back it with any financial commitments. Many argued that better road links to the national motorway network should be given priority. Then, in the mid-1960s, the Minister of Housing and Local Government proposed a new city of three-quarters of a million on the south bank of the Humber (involving a timetable which would postpone construction into the 1980s). At about the same time, the Central Unit for Environmental Planning began work on the feasibility of major urban development on Humberside, and a little later there were suggestions of a 'million city' there, probably on the low-lying land between Selby and Goole, and thus north of the new Thorne motorway. These schemes, giving the impression of ever-escalating dreams, were shelved when slower population growth was forecast and straitened economic circumstances came to dominate planning thinking in the 1970s. It was at this time, too, that government decided against a Maritime Industrial Development Area (M.I.D.A.) on Humberside. However, at the same time as these grandiose plans were set aside, the decision to build the Humber bridge was confirmed and construction was undertaken.

The bridge was originally expected to be completed by 1976 at an overall cost (including the approach roads) of some £23 million. By 1978, however, construction was three years behind schedule, it was costing more than three times as much as originally estimated, and forecasted traffic in the early 1980s was only one-quarter the level anticipated in 1970. This decline was in part due to the high tolls planned, and in part due to a lack of motorway access southwards from the river so that motorway-oriented traffic would still use the north bank from Hull to the M1. The Humber bridge, unlike the Severn or Forth bridges, is not a vital part of a national motorway system. However, the completion of the bridge is expected greatly to extend Hull's function as a regional metropolis. The total spending power in the catchment area of the north bank in 1978 was estimated to be of the order of £360 million; but, with its extension onto the south bank via the bridge, the total catchment area of Hull could well have a spending power of £560 million. Some of this, of course, could well gravitate away towards the larger conurbation of West Yorkshire via the M62 to the north and via the M180 and M18 from the south bank.

10.8   Continuing Dilemmas

From the postponement of the ambitious plans for population growth and economic development on Humberside stems a weakness of current Yorkshire and Humberside planning strategy. Whereas the Humber bridge and the related motorway developments on Humberside should have been considered, judged, programmed and undertaken hand in hand with population and land use planning, they appear in fact to have been examined and carried through quite separatcly. Major road infrastructure investment, therefore, is now proceeding without any deliberately planned urban and industrial development, and in consequence the fuller economic benefits which might hae been derived from this investment will not be forthcoming. The same point applies, though with rather less force, to the land use planning in industrial Yorkshire, where once again some of the benefits of motorway construction could well be substantially forgone in favour of conurbation renewal.

Related to this is a larger-scale question of development priorities between planning areas. There remains an unresolved dichotomy of interest between industrial Yorkshire in the west and Humberside in the east. Alone amongst the country's great conurbations, those of West and South Yorkshire have never shown any desire for planned overspill or for new town construction. Partly, no doubt, this reflects their already dispersed pattern and their distinctive physical frameworks. In addition it is a response to their economic status which is intermediate between the dynamism of the London, West Midland and even the South East Lancashire conurbations on the one hand, and the more depressed but overcrowded ones in the Development Areas on the other. It is also a product of deliberate policy. The E.P.C. has consistently preferred to give redevelopment in the west precedence over new developments on Humberside. Indeed, their attitude provoked a mild rebuke from the Hunt Committee ten years ago when it observed that 'any deliberate designation of regional growth points ought preferably to be made in a wider context [than industrial Yorkshire]' (Secretary of State for Economic Affairs, 1969, p.61). In 1970 the authors of the only major geographical study of Humberside described the sub-region as 'a nascent industrial area', and argued that 'bold decisions are needed by industrialists or government to invest the capital necessary to transform [it] from an almost rural backwater to a central position in the industrial Britain of the next century' (Lewis and Jones, 1970, p.11). It has been clear for some time, therefore, that opportunities were going to be forgone in a sub-region where development costs were likely to be amongst the lowest in Britain, and where the benefits could be exceptionally large.

The intra-regional problems of Yorkshire and Humberside elegantly pose—but leave unanswered—the question of how much maintenance and repair in the west should be balanced against the possibilities of new growth in the east. In many ways it is an object lesson in the dilemmas of a mature industrial economy facing slow population and economic growth, and unwilling to go fully for long-term economic gain for fear of short-term economic loss and social disruption.

REFERENCES

Central Unit for Environmental Planning (1969). *Humberside: A Feasibility Study,* H.M.S.O., London

Commission of the European Communities (1975). *A Study of the Evolution of Concentration in the United Kingdom Textile Industry,* E.E.C., Luxembourg.

Economic Development Committee for the Wool Textile Industry (1969). *The Strategic Future of the Wool Textile Industry,* H.M.S.O., London.

Kingston-upon-Hull (*c.*1959). *Planning in Action,* City Council, Kingston-upon-Hull.

Lewis, P. and Jones, P.N. (1970). *Industrial Britain: The Humberside Region,* David & Charles, Newton Abbot.

Secretary of State for Economic Affairs (1969). *The Intermediate Areas* (Chairman: Sir Joseph Hunt) (Cmnd.3998), H.M.S.O., London.

Yorkshire and Humberside Economic Planning Council (1966). *A Review of Yorkshire and Humberside,* H.M.S.O., London.

Yorkshire and Humberside Economic Planning Council (1968). *Halifax and Calder Valley. An Area Study,* H.M.S.O., London.

Yorkshire and Humberside Economic Planning Council (1969). *Huddersfield and Colne Valley,* H.M.S.O., London.

Yorkshire and Humberside Economic Planning Council (1970). *Doncaster: An Area Study,* H.M.S.O., London.

Yorkshire and Humberside Economic Planning Council (1976). *Regional Strategy Review, 1975. The Next Ten Years,* Y.H.E.P.C., Leeds.

CHAPTER 11

The South West Region

KENNETH WARREN

11.1 Introduction

South West England is a problem region, but of a very different nature from that of other major peripheral areas. In places, and above all on its eastern edges, its difficulties are associated with rapid growth. Sometimes the challenge is from unbalanced urban expansion or employment crises, as with Torbay and Plymouth respectively. Elsewhere there are problems associated with old extractive and industrial districts and tracts of difficult upland farming country in which population decline continues.

On the map, the South West is a fairly clear-cut entity; but in terms of either formal regional criteria or functional relationships it is clearly not a region but an amalgam of regions. The economic planning region, analysed here, extends for 320 kilometres (200 miles) from Swindon to Land's End. Its length and tapering character, and its division by embayments of the sea and by upland masses, reduce its economic cohesion so that there is neither an undoubted core area nor a regional metropolis. The eastern third of the region contains the scarp and vale country of the English lowlands; from central Devon and Somerset westwards lies older, generally higher country of what Unstead termed the Devonian Peninsula; and between the two there are the red sandstones and marls of Central Somerset and East Devon. Differences in position and in physical endowment, compounded by the inheritance of different responses over centuries to the opportunities which they present, have made it difficult to plan overall for the South West. As a result, the Economic Planning Council (E.P.C.) has concluded in recent years that 'the interrelationships between the main areas of the region are few, and, in consequence, the economic development options on a regional scale are limited. Our work has shown that the strategic planning problems now existing in the South West are primarily sub-regional or local, and that the nature of the problems vary' (South West Economic Planning Council, 1974, p.1). In some ways this may be seen to represent a denial by the council of the very rationale of economic planning. There are other difficulties too.

A three-fold division of the South West, based on geology and relief, does scant justice to the region's diversity, and particularly to its variations in economic activity and potential. In 1945 the economist, Fogarty, though dealing with only part of the region, considered six sub-regions. Caesar in 1949, in an analysis which was followed by some remarkably progressive recommendations, examined eleven sub-regions in Wiltshire, Gloucestershire and Somerset and six more in Devon and Cornwall. The new South West Economic Planning Council in its first major planning document—the optimistic *A Region with a Future* (1967)—analysed nine areas within the then six constituent counties. (Since 1974, with the creation of Avon, there have been seven counties.) It grouped them

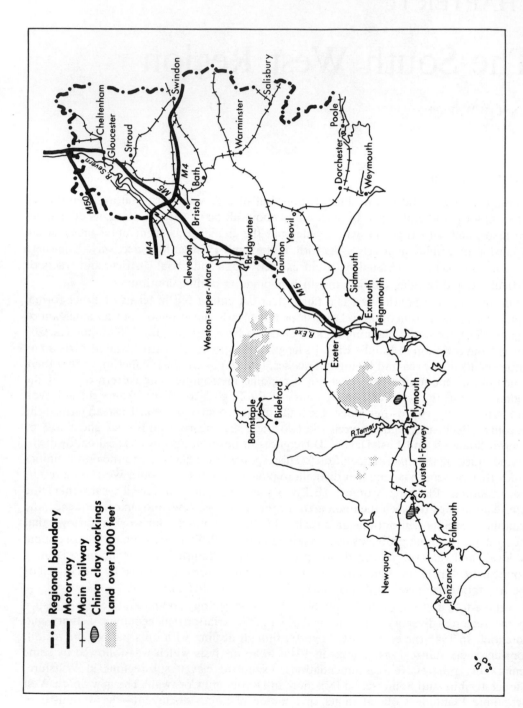

Figure 11.1 The South West region

into the four major sub-regions which form the main divisions for discussion below—the Northern (broadly speaking Severnside), Central (South Somerset and the south eastern part of the region), Southern (South Devon with its three main urban foci at Exeter, Torbay and Plymouth), and Western (part of Exmoor, North Devon and West Cornwall). Seven years later, in an analysis of population and settlement, the council broke up its earlier four sub-regions into twenty economic planning areas which it claimed to be 'broadly homogenous economically and environmentally'.

Over a long period the region has been of declining national significance in terms of population numbers, Wiltshire sharing with Merioneth and Radnor the distinction of being the first counties of England and Wales to register a decline in population (at the 1851 Census). The region gained relatively little nineteenth-century industry and its share of the population of England and Wales fell from 15.3 per cent in 1801 to a low of 7 per cent during the 1930s. Since World War II, however, the trend has been upwards to 7.9 per cent at the 1971 Census, and 1974 forecasts were for 9.1 per cent of the national total by 2001. Between 1954 and 1971, 60 per cent of the South West's gain in population resulted from net immigration, a characteristic in remarkable contrast with other peripheral areas of either the 'old industry' or 'problem rural' type.

The overall growth of population in fact hides considerable sub-regional variations. There are within the South West large areas of population decline, particularly in North Devon, and in the east and north east of Cornwall. It is these characteristics which have led, in part, to the designation of half the region as either a Development or Intermediate Area. In upper Severnside, on the other hand, the region has one of the nation's most rapidly growing employment nodes. But throughout the whole region a large proportion of population growth has been as a result of the inward movement of older people for retirement, a characteristic that has skewed the South West's age distribution and left a low ratio of employed to total population by national standards. Despite the burden that this component of the population imposes on the social services, however, recent research suggests that a large number of the immigrant retired contribute more to the annual per capita expenditure in the region than do their indigenous counterparts.

Although it has several major urban foci, the region is still much more rural than most English planning regions. In 1971, some 56 per cent of the population of England and Wales lived in settlements of over 100,000; but in the South West the figure was only one-quarter, and indeed 28 per cent of the regional population lived in communities smaller than 2,000 (South West Economic Planning Council, 1974, p.7). This pattern reflects the fact that agriculture in the South West remains proportionately much more important than in Britain as a whole, which in turn accounts for the low level of average wages in the region—they stood at almost 7 per cent below the national average in 1972. This rural character, together with the region's extensive sea coast, provide the backdrop for the South West's tourist trade which, despite the problems that it poses through its seasonal variations in employment, is a second mainstay of the regional economy. Notwithstanding its rural character, and still more its rural and tourist image, the South West also has important industrial activities. In addition to its very important aerospace industry, manufacturing is very diverse, often technologically advanced and widely spread through the region's towns (Table 11.1). The latter are so well scattered as to have made the absorption of the workers displaced by the modernization of agriculture remarkably easy.

The population and employment characteristics of the South West pose many planning questions. From its beginnings the South West E.P.C. planned for growth. In 1967, in a

Table 11.1 The South West: some components of the regional economy, by county, 1976

	Avon	Cornwall	Devon	Dorset	Glouces-tershire	Somerset	Wiltshire	South West
Population mid-1976 ('000s)	920.2	407.1	942.1	575.8	491.5	404.4	512.8	4,253.9
Employment distribution by major category, June 1975 (% of total):								
Agriculture, forestry & fisheries	1.1	6.9	3.7	3.3	3.2	5.0	3.5	3.3
Engineering & allied industries	14.0	9.5	12.4	13.9	22.2	12.8	18.1	14.8
Other manufacturing	15.8	8.2	9.4	9.8	12.9	21.9	14.8	13.2
Services	60.8	61.3	64.0	65.7	53.0	51.5	56.5	59.7

Source: C.S.O., *Regional Statistics, 13,* 1977.

setting of expansive national projections, it anticipated a population increase to the end of the century of 40 per cent, as compared with 37 per cent for Great Britain. Even as late as 1974, with national projections slipping down towards stability, the South West E.P.C. was still forecasting a growth of up to one-third in regional population to 2000, as compared with 13.5 per cent for England and Wales. Undoubtedly, this will prove to have been too large a figure; but there will be considerable expansion nevertheless. The council's ability to help shape the geography of this growth is constrained considerably by the regional inheritance and considerations of amenity, for there is some form of planning restraint over almost half the region in the form of National Parks, Areas of Outstanding Natural Beauty, Areas of Great Landscape Value and green belts. Moreover, there is a range of difficult strategic planning choices within the assumption that economic growth prospects are good. Should policy aim to spread growth widely throughout the region, or to focus it? If the latter is chosen, with its inevitable implications for major Severnside growth, how can such policy be integrated with planning in South Wales? Appropriate responses have perhaps been made unnecessarily difficult by the South West E.P.C.'s notably passive, almost defeatist, attitude towards really purposeful intervention in the process of growth, an attitude which is summed up in its opinion that 'the scope for influencing the balance of population distribution within the region which is implicit in present trends is no more than marginal' (South West E.P.C., 1974, p.8). Beyond these strategic issues, South West planners face serious seasonal problems—of winter unemployment, and of congested holiday towns and roads in summer. The transport problems within the region and the continuing complaints of remoteness from national markets, however, have been eased by the completion (in 1975) of the M5 to Exeter and of improved dual carriageway access on to Plymouth, although some areas have gained from this improvement at the expense of other parts of the South West away from the motorways which have become, relatively speaking, still more remote.

A large number of country towns are scattered through the region; each has its own sphere of influence and helps to form a pattern of functional sub-regions. A few bigger

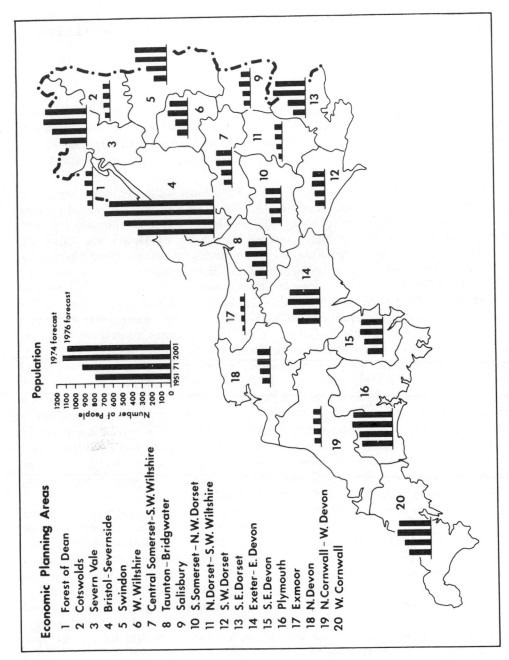

Figure 11.2 The South West: population trends by planning division, 1951-2000

nuclei provide a higher level of spatial articulation: Exeter, Plymouth and Torbay perform this function in the centre of the region, while Poole-Bournemouth, Swindon and the Severnside cities act in more dynamic fashion along the north eastern and eastern edge. The latter are the centres destined to generate the future growth of the regional economy, but the following review of the component parts of the South West begins with the more rural areas.

11.2 The Western Sub-region

West of the Mendips and Cranborne Chase, almost half of the area of the peninsula is included within the planning council's Western region, extending from Land's End and Fowey across the northern half of the peninsula and as far north as Bridgwater Bay. It contains only two centres with a population of 25,000 or over—Camborne-Redruth with 42,000 and St Austell-Fowey with 32,000.

Historically, the Western sub-region had important local resources—minerals, favoured (but limited) agricultural areas and fish. Its mineral endowment was in the past singled out as the reason for the relatively high population density in Cornwall (in 1891, Cornwall had 41.4 per cent of the combined population of Devon and Cornwall, compared with less than 30 per cent today). Two tin-mining operations (Geevor and South Crofty) survived the long decline in metal mining and the last great spate of closures in the 1920s. In the 1970s there has been a modest revival with new mines—Wheal Jane near Truro, Mount Wellington and Pendarves near Camborne—but even so, by the mid-1970s mining employed only 1,500. In spring 1978, the closure of both Mount Wellington and Wheal Jane threatened almost half those jobs. There remains uncertainty over the government's long-term policy in relation to British mining. Nevertheless, it is clear that metal mining in the South West will never again support a major economic and social structure. China clay working continues to expand, mainly in the St Austell area, though with some small operations in south west Dartmoor. The associated export trade is a valuable source of foreign exchange, but the amenity cost is high. Nineteenth-century mining bequeathed to modern planners several urban areas needing adjustment to a more modest role as service and minor industrial centres. Camborne-Redruth and the several small ports which once shipped tin, copper, slate, stone and imported Welsh coal—such as Hayle, St Agnes and Port Isaac—are in this category. As mining has shrunk, Cornwall's standing in the South West region has declined.

In the last century, early vegetables and dairy produce became major regional exports of the western half of the peninsula. Agriculture and horticulture have continued to expand, but their overall growth hides the severe problem of the hillfarms with poor soils, a difficult climate, poor communications, and inferior social provision. In the future, competition from E.E.C. producers may adversely affect the horticultural and the dairying base of the economy. Thus, the opening of the Roscoff-Plymouth ferry service, a boon both to holidaymakers and industry, may prove disadvantageous to those already facing market garden competition from Brittany. Fishing for pilchards and mackerel was at one time very important in Cornwall and Devon, but it has since declined until it is now significant only at Newlyn and Brixham.

Manufacturing has traditionally been of little importance in the Western sub-region—in 1965 it accounted for only 13 per cent of the workforce as compared with 22 per cent in the Southern, 26 per cent in the Central and 38 per cent in the Northern sub-regions of the

South West. There are long-established mining equipment operations at Camborne, ship repairing at Falmouth and shipbuilding at Appledore where, following failure in 1963 and subsequent reconstruction, operations remained successful. There is also a scatter of light industries throughout the sub-region. In 1970 the Cornwall County Council's *West Cornwall Study* advocated an expansion of manufacturing industry in the area west of Truro, in the hope that this would encourage both immigration and higher wages. Four years later the E.P.C.'s Settlement Strategy singled out Camborne-Redruth as one of its major growth areas. In fact there are difficulties in an industrialization policy. Unemployment rates may be high and wages may look attractively low; but the numbers of unemployed are so small, and in many parts of the sub-region so scattered, that it is often difficult to meet the workforce requirements of a factory of even modest size. Falmouth to Camborne-Redruth is and will remain the axis of Cornish industrialization.

The problems of remoteness in the far south west are even greater for the small Scillies community of some 2,000. There, tourism provides 60 per cent of income and early flowers much of the rest. Against the obvious environmental and amenity attractions must be set the need for a high degree of self-sufficiency, a narrow range of employment and the high costs of living including freight charges to the mainland.

11.3 The Southern Sub-region

The Southern sub-region contains both the high, barren mass of Dartmoor and the main urban centres within the South West apart from those in its northern subdivision. There is a rich agriculture, both in the Exe valley and in the South Hams district of Devon, but such areas have done little more than hold their populations.

Exeter is the smallest of the three urban nodes of the sub-region. It has administrative, educational and service functions and has made good progress with new industries, trends which the 1975 completion of the M5 seems certain to encourage. Its expansion has been slower than that of Torbay where the high growth rate of 1.24 per cent per year in the 1960s, largely of immigrant retired people, threw a heavy burden on the social services. Retirement has nevertheless brought an increase of wealth as well as numbers, and it has created many ancillary jobs. A 1975 South West E.P.C. study showed that in 1971 some 138,000 retired immigrants lived in the South West, and that their arrival had created 44,000 jobs and provided £54 million annual income; the latter was only just less than one-half of the annual tourist income to the region.

In contrast, Plymouth, though the sub-region's biggest city, has had an uncertain economy. For too long it depended on the Devonport dockyard. It diversified in the early 1960s, when it was a Development District, and more recently after being given Intermediate Area status. Meanwhile, however, run-down at the dockyard went on. In the mid-1960s it employed 18,500, but by 1975 only about 12,000. There were other big cutbacks in local firms in the mid-1970s—Rank, the largest private employer with 2,000 workers, lost heavily in the three years 1975-1978 at its two Plymouth and its Redruth factories—so that by late 1975 the local unemployment rate was 7 per cent. There is now, however, good access to the national maket via the M5 motorway. Along with Plymouth's size, this accessibility justifies its choice as one of the South West's six major growth areas, and there has been discussion of the possibility of exploiting this new access to the Midlands by developing container facilities to compete with those of Southampton; however, Plymouth's plans lag years behind in this, the port lacks adequate water frontage, and by the early 1970s there were also container port plans for Falmouth, to say nothing of Royal Portbury. Intermediate Area status was extended from Plymouth to the Tavistock Rural District in 1971 (and at the same time into the neighbouring parts of the Western sub-region to include Okehampton Rural District), and there can be little doubt that localities in the shadow of the Assisted Areas suffer somewhat. Newton Abbot, a town which otherwise has good manufacturing growth prospects, is a good example.

Apart from the uncertainty of the effects of the M5 link, there are exciting possibilities—but even less concrete prospects—associated with Celtic Sea oil. In mid-1976 licences were issued for the exploration of the sea bed from the Lizard to the Scilly Islands. There is much vague hope and also some deep fears. 'We could lose much of the charm, dignity and manners which mark Cornwall apart from the great cosmopolitan centres', remarked a report of the Cornwall Conservation Forum. If large-scale oil development does get under way, supply bases will be needed. Fowey and Plymouth have both entertained hopes that they might be chosen though, as with its container port ambitions, Plymouth suffers from a lack of room. Falmouth in the Western sub-region seems a more likely prospect, since its dock (employing 1,400) is well equipped and has spare capacity in ship repairing which could be extended into oil-related work. Moreover, there is room for expansion there, 28 hectares (70 acres) between the docks and Pendennis Head being reclaimable for the industry. Falmouth's need for jobs is great as is shown in its high unemployment levels (9.9 per cent in autumn 1975). However, the impact of possible Celtic Sea oil development must be put into perspective. Most of the rigs and much of the labour could be drawn from the North Sea. Altogether, the South West Economic Planning Board has concluded that oil and gas exploration in the Celtic Sea will not have a major economic, social or environmental impact in the region (South West Economic Planning Council, 1975). If within a decade large-scale production supersedes exploration, the effect may be very different.

In both the Southern and the Western sub-regions tourism is of great importance. At peak times half the people in Cornwall are holidaymakers; and the arrival of the M5 to replace or supplement the A38 to the Midlands, and the A303 to the South East, has dramatically increased the catchment area. Before the motorway the population within a three and a half hour road journey of the South Devon resorts was estimated at 5 million; after its completion the number is 18 million. The obvious amenity dangers have been anticipated. By 1972, Devon County Council had identified two holiday expansion areas—the 'Devon Riviera' from Exmouth to Brixham, and the North Devon coast between Ilfracombe and Westward Ho. The latter area will be served by an improved road connection to the M5, pressed for by the South West E.P.C., which designated the Barnstaple area as one of its six major growth areas in 1974. Recognizing the 'wilderness' needs of many holidaymakers, Devon County Council has scheduled other 'Areas of Restraint', including the Exmoor coast, the Hartland area and the coast of South Hams.

11.4 The Central Sub-region

This section of the South West lacks any major centre of population and looks in different directions for its higher-order services—to Bristol-Bath, Southampton-Bournemouth or Exeter. The area south of the Marlborough Downs has natural drainage to the heart of the Hampshire basin and routeways and traffic flows over the centuries have come to conform to this physical pattern; it therefore looks to the coast of

Hampshire as its focus. Salisbury and Poole (another of the council's six major growth areas and one which has gained from a great surge of office employment by virtue of its position just outside the controls of the South East region) are included in the South West economic planning region only by the accident of the old county boundaries. They are not considered further here.

The Central sub-region contains a number of country towns, important alike for marketing and manufacturing. Their service functions are large considering their size, a reflection in part of their remoteness from major service centres. Taunton is the biggest town (38,000), Bridgwater and Yeovil (each of some 25,000) come next, while both Frome and Glastonbury-Street have 11,000 inhabitants. Between 1951 and 1971 the populations of all the towns in the sub-region except Yeovil and Taunton grew at rates in excess of the South West regional average of 15.9 per cent. Taunton is an administrative, major market and service centre as well as a significant manufacturing centre with especial interests in clothing. The others are to a greater extent manufacturing towns, sometimes almost dominated by a single firm or trade as with helicopter production at Yeovil and leather goods at Glastonbury-Street. The sub-region is much more important for manufacturing industry than either its Southern or Western counterparts.

In 1967 the South West E.P.C. anticipated no great change in the relative standing of the Central sub-region, its forecast share of the region's population being projected to change from 21.1 per cent in 1964 to 21.5 per cent in 1981 and probably 20.0 per cent by 2001. However, in its Settlement Strategy in 1974, the council put the 2001 share at 23.6 per cent. Much the biggest growth was anticipated for the Poole district; but good expansion prospects were also recognized for towns in the centre of the region like Yeovil, Chard, Ilminster and Crewkerne, and for others such as Taunton and Bridgwater aligned along the M5. Whether the impact of the motorway will be as relatively undifferentiated as the council's forecasts suggest may be doubted, but there is little evidence to suggest that the even tenure of market town life there will be disrupted. The same steadiness cannot be anticipated for the Northern sub-region.

11.5 The Northern Sub-region

The Northern sub-region extends from the Mendips and the Wye valley to the upper Thames basin. Its 1971 population was 1.7 million, out of the South West regional total of 3.8 million. In the next thirty years it is anticipated to gain 0.5 million of the region's 1.2 million increase.

The sub-region has some areas of old extractive industry. The Norton-Radstock area, for instance, has for some time been without its coal industry (which employed 1,800 in five mines as late as 1960), but it has attracted alternative footloose manufacturing industries instead, notably in printing and publishing, and has even registered a higher than average regional population growth. The high-cost Forest of Dean coalfield, with 1,150 men in two collieries in 1960, has also ceased production. Amenity needs are now seen to require some limitation on new employment growth there, and Lydney has been singled out by the South West E.P.C. as the location for the limited amount of growth which should be permitted.

There is a considerable number of old market towns and manufacturing centres in the Northern sub-region. Some are small, but of great architectural or historical interest such as Tewkesbury, Malmesbury and Winchcombe which, now little more than a village, was once the capital of Mercia. Most are long established—for example, Cirencester, Chippenham, Marlborough and Devizes. Several, such as Stroud, have had to make major adjustments to changing economic opportunities over the last two generations. And a handful are modern growth points: a spectacular example is Melksham where, from local tyre manufacture established in the 1880s, Avon Rubber have expanded to employ 3,300 in a town of only 10,000, and have extended their plant and their growth impetus to other towns nearby such as Bradford.

The present economy and the economic growth prospects of the sub-region are, however, dominated by the three largest centres of population—Thamesdown, Gloucester-Cheltenham and the urban core of the new county of Avon centred on Bristol. The main foci of the Northern sub-region benefit from a long-established but recently much increased nodality within the national transport system. Bristol has had a long history as a great coordinating centre for the activities and the trade of its hinterland, activities which once embraced medieval merchants of Welsh origin on the one hand and the Cotswold and West Country wool trade on the other. In the eighteenth century it played a key role in the Welsh cattle trade and in the nineteenth it was important in coal and iron development there. Trade via the Severn extended its hinterland to the West Midlands. The significance of the Bath Road and of the main line of the Great Western Railway system accentuated these advantages of location. In the 1960s and 1970s a new motorway network provided a further nodality while modifying in detail its locational impact. The opening of the Severn bridge in 1966 emphasized the direct South Wales-Bristol link at the expense of that via Gloucester. Now the whole region occupies a position of remarkable centrality between the major urban-industrial regions of the South East, West Midlands and South Wales, and with the completion of the M5 to Exeter in 1975/1976 it is reaching out to dominate more of the South West in terms of higher-order services. At the same time as the sphere of influence of the main centres at the core of the transport network is increased, so growth is fastest at the access points, and by the mid-1970s the M4 had already had a profound effect in raising property prices in the area through which it passed.

The new borough of Thamesdown was created in 1974 from the boom town of Swindon and the whole of North East Wiltshire between the Marlborough Downs and the Thames. Its population is one-quarter, and its rateable value one-third, that of its county. Chosen in 1834 as the main workshop town of the Great Western Railway, Swindon was dominated by railway engineering until after World War II. At their peak the railway workshops employed 12,000. Its locational attractions within the G.W.R. system have been mirrored in the new space relationships of a motorway age, with the M4 being aligned north of the old Bath Road to serve both Swindon and Bristol and to reach an obvious bridging point across the Severn to Wales. Swindon serves as an overspill centre for the South East, and has both a record of solid achievements and good growth prospects for industry, distribution and offices. Manufacturing employment has in fact moved to Swindon from both east and west. An early example was a branch of the Bristol tobacco firm of Wills in 1915. After World War II, Pressed Steel (now B.L.), unable to extend at Cowley, built at Swindon and has since used the site and railway access facilities of part of the old G.W.R. works; the car body works now employs 5,000 and the railway workshops only about 3,000. There are many other new industries, largely of an estate type such as clothing, chemicals, containers. Because it is a focal point, Thamesdown has also been recognized as a good warehousing centre; both Woolworth and W.H. Smith have major depots there. Office employment too has moved there—examples being the international headquarters of Burmah Oil, the headquarters of Nationwide Building Society, Vickers Engineering division and Hambro Life Assurance. The Science Research Council and the National Environment Research Council have also moved their headquarters there. By the mid-1970s the old industrial image was so outmoded that 50 per cent of Swindon's employment was in service industries.

A 1966 consultant's report suggested a population growth of 125,000 for the Swindon area by 1981 and a town population of perhaps 400,000 (nearly three times the present population) by 2000. The government refused to accept what it regarded as too ambitious a growth target, and proposed instead a 75,000 increase to 1981. In spite of the decline in the projected national rate of population increase, the South West Economic Planning Council in 1974 raised the expected population of the town and hinterland from 210,000 in 1971 to 330,000 in 2001.

Gloucester-Cheltenham grew rapidly after 1945, the former preeminently in industry and the latter in commercial and cultural employment. Between 1951 and 1971 the population of the two cities, their respective rural districts and the urban district of Charlton Kings (next door to Cheltenham) went up from 195,000 to 248,000. The aircraft industry has long been important in a local economy which has proved buoyant, though by no means without its crises. In the early 1960s the closure of the Gloster Aircraft factory and the run-down in railway carriage work threatened Gloucester's future, but firms such as I.C.I. Fibres and Walls were attracted in and there was steady expansion at the major aviation equipment firm of Dowty. In 1964 the old Gloster Aircraft site was laid out as the Gloucester Trading Estate and, although eight years later only one-eighth of the site had been occupied, 2,000 came to be employed there. Engineering and the lighter, rapid growth engineering trades are typical of Gloucester.

Physical planning in this area is complicated by the existence of two distinct urban nuclei less than 16 kilometres (10 miles) apart and by the lack of room between the Cotswold scarp and the Severn. The Severnside Study of 1971, working on a forecast growth of population for Great Britain of 20 million between 1966 and 2001, looked to growth in this North Gloucestershire area within the range of 200,000 to as much as 400,000. By 1974 the South West Economic Planning Council had reduced this to 120,000 and simultaneously decided to give up the idea for two new towns west of the Severn (Table 11.2).

Bristol-Severnside has one-quarter of the whole population of the South West planning region, and provides its best growth prospect. The dynamism of the whole sub-region, in fact, is the outgrowth of that of Bristol. Historically Bristol grew to a prominent position in Britain's population and wealth on the basis of waterborne trade with the western coasts of Europe and then in the wider Atlantic basin. In the middle decades of the nineteenth century, with the focusing of national growth on the emerging coalfield conurbations, and the growing inconvenience of a shallow-channelled Avon, Bristol stagnated. It revived with the development of Portishead (opened 1879) and still more with the development of Avonmouth from the mid-1860s. More bulk-processing industries were soon established there to supplement the largely import-related food, drink and tobacco industries of Bristol itself. The aircraft industry was first established on an important scale in 1910 and between the wars provided a major boost to the area. Filton, one of the major inter-war growth areas near the city, and Patchway, a little further north, are major centres of the aircraft trade which dominates north Bristol, just

Table 11.2 North Gloucestershire and Bristol-Severnside: projected populations to 2001 ('000s)

Area and source of projection	1964 (actual)	1971 (actual)	1981	1991	2001
NORTH GLOUCESTERSHIRE	437	465			
South West Planning Strategy, 1967			542		
Severnside Study, 1971 A			550	600	650
B			550	700	850
South West Settlement Study, 1974					585
Working Paper Study, 1976					575
BRISTOL-SEVERNSIDE	870	930			
South West Planning Strategy, 1967			1,021		
Severnside Study, 1971 A			1,000	1,100	1,200
B			1,000	1,200	1,350
South West Settlement Study, 1974					1,140
Working Paper Study, 1976					1,090

Note: Severnside A and B distinguishes between a projection based on previous trends and one assuming accelerated growth.

Table 11.3 Bristol: employment in Bristol group of employment exchanges, 1971 and 1975*

	1971	1975
Primary	1,574	1,440
Manufacturing of which:	94,780	85,330
Aerospace	(26,000)	(25,000)
Food, drink and tobacco	(19,000)	(17,000)
Paper, printing, publishing	(16,000)	(14,000)
Engineering	(9,000)	(7,000)
Construction	15,460	15,140
Services	162,500	177,840
TOTAL	274,315	279,750

*Note: comparable figures are not available for later dates.
Source: Bristol Council Research Department.

as tobacco is prominent in the south of the city. The very success of this industry makes the idea of its future rationalization and run-down an outstanding threat to the continuing prosperity of Bristol. By 1970 the aerospace industries employed 25,000 of whom 10,000 were working at Filton and Patchway on Concorde alone. By this time many of the old Bristol port processing industries were still important—tobacco, cocoa and chocolate prominent among them—but others such as sugar refining or soap making had died out (Table 11.3).

In the period 1950 to 1970, employment in the Bristol (built-up) area increased by 40,000. Aircraft was the major growth sector in the 1950s and generated secondary developments in other engineering trades and in service employment. In the 1960s, however, office employment was the major growth sector. This expansion paralleled the major changes in the city's nationwide access by road. Between 1971 and 1975, while total employment in the Bristol group of employment exchanges rose slightly, there was a significant change of emphasis; the manufacturing categories fell from 34.5 to 30.5 per cent of the total while the service sector increased from 58.9 to 63.6 per cent (Table 11.3).

Planning approvals for office accommodation in central Bristol rose from an annual average of about 9,300 square metres (100,000 square feet) in the late 1950s to 46,500 square metres (500,000 square feet) in 1963. By the mid-1970s there were 0.65 million square metres (7 million square feet) of offices there, and in newly-erected floorspace Bristol ranked among the major provincial centres, attracting many large firms, either in whole or in part, from London. By mid-1974, centrally-heated and air-conditioned offices which would cost a rental of as much as £161 per square metre (£15 a square foot) in central London, were available in central Bristol for about £32 per square metre (£3 per square foot). Two years later, it was noted that, with lower labour costs as well as lower rents, a secretary/shorthand typist with the rent and rates attributable to her in a prime air-conditioned office in Bristol cost £1,999 a year as compared with £4,797 in London (*Financial Times*, 1976). The spectacular success in office expansion was associated with population growth, city affluence, the increasing regional primacy of Bristol offices (with the consolidation and rationalization of local offices), but perhaps above all with Severnside's new centrality within national economic space as a result of motorway construction. The Severn bridge opened up the South Wales area and the gradual extension of the M4 westwards within the Principality has been extending Bristol's influence further there ever since. The M5 link to the Midlands and the M4 link to London (including Heathrow) have now been supplemented by the M5 extension south westwards. Bristol has responded to the opportunities which this new road centrality has presented by planning for seven road links from the city system to the motorways. A significant indication of sub-regional as well as national centrality is the fact that by mid-1974 there had been seven applications for planning permission to develop hypermarkets at Cribbs Causeway on the northern side of the city, where there is excellent M5 and M4 access to markets eastwards, northwards, south westwards and into Wales.

New road accessibility brings increments of tertiary and quaternary employment; along with improvements of port facilities it can also bring further prospects of growth in secondary industry. Bristol has an important complex of docks. The city docks now have an amenity rather than a commercial potential. All the others, at the mouth of the Avon and along the Severn, have an overwhelming import role; in the mid-1970s, at 5.5 million tons, imports were ten times the volume of exports. Portishead handles timber and chemicals, and also oil and coal for the C.E.G.B. The Avonmouth dock is concerned with milling and compounding, and a certain amount of general cargo. Between 1902 and 1908 Bristol Corporation built the Royal Edward Docks at Avonmouth, then said to be able to admit the largest passenger liners yet built. By the mid-1970s this dock was specially equipped to unload oil, grain, chemicals and refrigerated bulk imports and had roll-on/roll-off facilities. However, a decade earlier it had become clear that Bristol was falling behind other British ports. In 1964, when it was the sixth port in Britain, it planned a £30 million new dock at Portbury, east of Portishead docks, a scheme which it was hoped would raise it to third position. The government, concerned for the first time with an attempt to coordinate port development, rejected both this scheme and a £14 million scheme for a West Dock just west of the Avon. By 1970 Bristol had dropped to the tenth port in Britain. However, by 1970 it had also received permission to go ahead with a revived Portbury Dock, and this was brought into operation in 1978 providing facilities

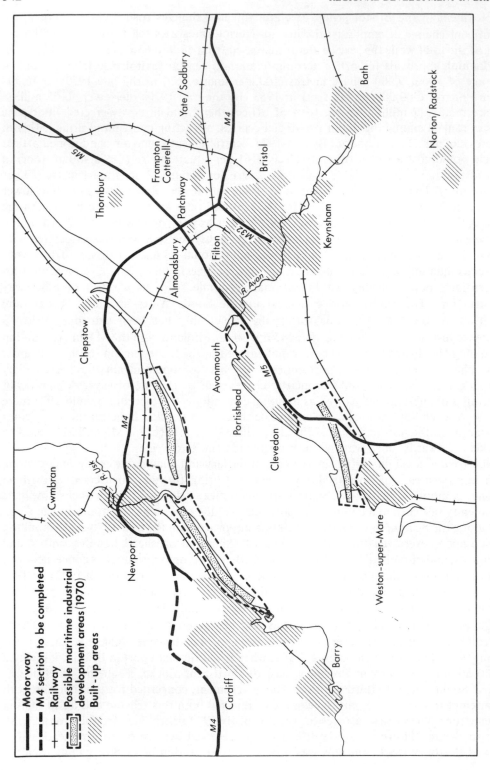

Figure 11.3 Bristol and upper Severnside

able to handle up to 70,000 d.w.t. ships, vessels some three times as big as those using the other Avonmouth docks.

Royal Portbury brings great advantages. Although, as Britain's largest tidal dock, it lacks really deep water for low-grade raw material imports such as ores or oil, there is adjacent to the dock ample flat land—nearly 700 hectares (1,700 acres)—for warehousing and industry. Many thousands of hectares for further industrialization are also available from the Avon northwards to the Severn bridge, though much is already occupied by smelting (for instance R.T.Z. in zinc) and chemicals (notably I.C.I.'s Severnside complex). Both east and west of the Avon there is excellent access to local transport, rail, road and now motorway facilities.

With new economic activities, and the groundwork laid on the Severnside lowlands for a further extension of the traditional heavier trades, there seems every prospect of the realization of the 1967 forecast made by the South West E.P.C. that the Bristol-Bath subdivision has 'exciting prospects for economic growth'. In the even more ambitious expansion plans of the 1971 Severnside Study these growth prospects were seen as an integral part of a greater, estuary-wide development in which a new open-structured regional metropolis seemed to be taking shape: to this Manners (1966) gave the evocative name 'Randstad Severn'. Within this distinctive system of cities, 'Newport has an emphasis on heavy industry; Cardiff on an administrative and political role; Gloucester has lighter engineering industries; Bristol manufacturing and commerce; and Bath a new educational role' (Manners, 1972, p.264). To accommodate the growth which the Severnside Study expected over thirty years, major new developments were planned in the urban fabric, including two new towns west of the Severn in Gloucestershire and a 150,000 increase in the Cwmbran-Pontypool area. Additionally, a 300,000 population new city was projected at Frampton Cotterell, as yet only a small village 12 kilometres (7½ miles) north east of central Bristol, but excellently located for access to the M4, beyond the Bristol green belt and attractively placed near to the Cotswolds' edge. The 1974 South West Settlement Strategy, however, anticipated a growth in Bristol-Severnside to the end of the century of only 210,000, or half the forecast made only three years earlier by the Severnside Study; it still planned for large expansion at Frampton Cotterell. A number of facts suggest that perhaps even the 1974 forecast of growth will prove excessive.

One is the continuing reduction of the birth rate so that 'no growth' conditions now prevail nationally. Another problem concerns the difficulty of financing the spiralling costs of major projects. The other major factor involves intra-regional and inter-regional opposition to further Bristol-Severnside growth. A number of years ago the Shipping Correspondent of *The Times* remarked how difficult it was to see the justice of refusing the Portbury scheme, while allowing Merseyside's similar but even more ambitious Seaforth scheme to go ahead—a latter-day example of the centuries-old rivalry between the two main west coast English ports. The main opposition has, however, come from nearer at hand. Interests in the Western and Southern sub-regions of the South West have opposed the north eastern growth point emphasis of their planning council. The Welsh office, much less forward-looking than the South West E.P.C. (as *Wales, the Way Ahead*, compared with *A Region with a Future,* showed), has been consistently opposed to integrated Severnside development; it even showed an antipathy to a study of the prospects, and has consistently opposed (and with the strong help of leading South Wales M.P.s did much to frustrate) the Portbury scheme. Further opposition has come from the

West Midlands E.P.C. which recognized that major Severnside growth would involve a continuing attraction of industries and people from their region.

In spite of these difficulties there seems to be no reason to doubt that the upper Severnside section of the South West region will remain disproportionately prosperous and expansive. The improvement of access to the centre and south west of the region suggests that its growth will continue to be in part at the expense of those areas. New national accessibility, however, points to a wider tributary area beyond the South West regional boundary. Despite changing national circumstances, the South West can still be described in the optimistic tone of the planning council's 1967 Draft Strategy as a 'Region with a Future'; and within it upper Severnside must be reckoned the most favoured of its subdivisions.

REFERENCES

Caesar, A.A.L. (1949). Gloucester, Wiltshire and Somerset. In G.H.J. Daysh, *Studies in Regional Planning,* Geo. Philip, London.
Central Unit for Environmental Planning (1971). *Severnside: A Feasibility Study,* H.M.S.O., London.
Financial Times (1976). Survey of property in the South West, 23 April.
Fogarty, M.P. (1945). *Prospects of the Industrial Areas of Great Britain,* Methuen, London.
Jervis, W.W. (1928). The lower Severn basin and the plain of Somerset, In A.G. Ogilvie, *Great Britain: Essays in Regional Geography,* Cambridge University Press.
Manners, G. (1966). *The Severn Bridge and the Future,* T.W.W., Cardiff.
Manners, G. (1972). The South West and South Wales, *Regional Development in Britain* (1st ed.), Wiley, London.
South West Economic Planning Board (1975). *The Implications of Off-Shore Oil and Gas for the South West,* South West Economic Planning Council, Bristol.
South West Economic Planning Council (1967). *A Region with a Future: A Draft Strategy for the South West,* H.M.S.O., London.
South West Economic Planning Council (1974). *A Strategic Settlement Pattern for the South West,* H.M.S.O., London.
South West Economic Planning Council (1975). *Retirement to the South West,* H.M.S.O., London.

CHAPTER 12

South Wales

KENNETH WARREN

12.1 Introduction

By almost all criteria, the whole of Wales is one of Britain's less prosperous regions. Income and activity rates are low; unemployment and dependence on various forms of assistance high. In recent years there have been major structural changes in and to the benefits of its economy, but even so it still lags behind the national economy. Between 1960 and 1972 some 250,000 new jobs were needed in Wales to replace jobs lost and to bring activity levels up to the United Kingdom average—but the number actually created was 80,000. All these changes are summed up in Wales' share of the national population. In 1921, at its peak, its proportion was 5.91 per cent of that of Great Britain; in 1971, 5.04 per cent. North and Central Wales have many problems (see pp.240ff.; 267ff.), but the Welsh difficulties are above all concentrated in industrial South Wales. Here, the four new counties of Gwent and Mid, South and West Glamorgan contained 1,743,000 people in 1975—63.0 per cent of the population of Wales in 17.4 per cent of its area (Table 12.1). The full extent of industrial South Wales reaches westwards into the old Carmarthenshire section of the new county of Dyfed; and around Milford Haven it has an important outlier, small in both area and population, but economically much more important.

12.2 Industrial South Wales

With a smaller population and in a considerably smaller area than industrial mid-Scotland, and with a smaller population though larger area than the industrial core of the North East, South Wales historically had a less diversified economy than did either of its traditional rivals in heavy industrial production. Coal, iron and steel, sheet steel and tinplate were its chief specialisms, with no important diversifying employments such as shipbuilding, chemicals or various engineering activities provided in the others. Its inter-war crisis was even more severe than theirs. Yet after 1945 South Wales for long seemed to be much more successful in achieving economic reconstruction, and has diversified spectacularly away from its old coal and primary metal emphasis. Even so, with coal and steel still its two main basic trades, probably no part of Britain so nearly approaches the state of the nationalized regional economy. Another leading theme in its economic development is an acute clash, far stronger and more fully articulate than in Scotland or the North East, between the interests and planning of the older foci of the regional economy and those of the newer growth areas; that is, between the valleys and the coastlands.

South Wales is physically much nearer to the West Midlands and to the South East than either of its major peripheral area rivals. It has, therefore, been able to attract overflow or

345

Table 12.1 Britain and industrial South Wales: rates of growth of population, 1891-1976

	1891-1921	1921-1951	1951-1976
Britain	29.5	14.2	11.3
Mid Glamorgan	95.4	−17.9	1.9
West Glamorgan	69.9	3.2	4.5
South Glamorgan	71.7	15.5	10.8
Gwent	71.8	−4.9	8.6

Based on *Digest of Welsh Statistics*.

diverted industry with relative ease. The opening of the Severn bridge in 1966 and the links via the M5 and M4 have helped to convert it even more emphatically into an industrial supply region or the branch plant appendix of these more sophisticated industrial regions of Britain. It has benefited considerably in terms of employment from this relationship. In the twenty-eight years to 1973, the movement of manufacturing establishments from the South East and from the West Midlands provided two-thirds of the 120,000 jobs directly generated by moves from outside South Wales (see Tables 12.2 and 12.3). Contrary to popular belief, recent research suggests that employment in British branch plants, whether in the Assisted Areas or not, is more secure than in employment in main plants (Atkins, 1973). Foreign investment in South Wales has also been important. In 1945 there were only four foreign manufacturing concerns in Wales; as late as 1964 there were no more than forty-three; but by 1976/1977 about 138 foreign-owned firms existed in the Principality and employed 53,000 workers. Nine-tenths of the investment, employment and sales were from North American firms (Davies, 1977). Significantly, overseas firms have been especially important in the growth sectors of the economy. By 1974 they employed 16 per cent of the Welsh manufacturing workforce, but 38 per cent in chemicals, some 30 per cent in electrical and instrument engineering and 29 per cent in vehicles and components. In addition to the feature of considerable external control in the private sector, South Wales also has a very large proportion of its industry controlled by national corporations. Both for private and nationalized industry, the English market and English capital are much more important than is the case in Scotland, for example. This means that many of the higher control functions of Welsh industry and commerce are located outside the region, though important divisional control may exist within the Principality, as for instance in the headquarters of the British Steel Corporation's Strip Mills Division (later, Welsh Division). High-level decision taking and the higher orders of business administration, therefore, tend to be lost to Wales.

Topography dominates the patterns of communication, population and journeys to work in South Wales to a greater extent than anywhere else in Britain. In the traditional industrial geography of the region, an array of separate railway lines was built to link the coalfield valleys with the national rail system and the ports for export. As many as six main ports were in fact established to handle coastwise and overseas shipments of coal. In turn, these encouraged the emergence of three nodes of coastal population, which stand in contrast to the two much bigger nodes that developed in the North East and in mid-Scotland. There is, therefore, in South Wales an absence of an undoubted regional capital. Cardiff, Swansea and Newport are all relatively small cities, quite overshadowed by Bristol. (In the two other peripheral industrial areas, the urban foci are not only bigger but are further from major rival centres.) In more recent years also, the topography of

Table 12.2   Wales: employment in incoming manufacturing plants, by origin, 1945-1971*
('000s)

	1945-1951	1952-1959	1960-1965	1966-1971
All origins	69.5	8.5	16.0	28.0
of which,				
South East	35.0	2.0	6.0	15.5
West Midlands	12.0	0.5	6.0	4.0
Foreign	6.5	2.0	0.5	1.5

*Employment figures are for end of 1966 for all moves to that time, and for 1973 for all openings after 1966.
Source: Welsh Office, *Welsh Economic Trends,* **3**, 1976.

Table 12.3   Wales: ownership of private industry, 1969-1971

	Firms employing over 25	Firms employing over 500
Total number of firms	2909	143
Wholly Welsh	38.2%	16.1%
Branch or subsidiary of non-Welsh U.K. company	51.6%	65.7%
Subsidiary of foreign company	5.4%	14.7%
Branch or subsidiary of U.K. company itself a subsidiary of a foreign company	3.6%	—

Source: Tomkins and Lovering, (1973).

South Wales, and its coastal centres of population, have been important influences in the location of the new enterprises attracted there to replace lost jobs and to diversify the industrial structure. Within the region there has been a major shift of activity from the coalfield southwards. Major routeways and junctions, the bigger nodes of population, and environmentally attractive areas near the coast now provide the magnets of employment which in the past concentrated on material resource locations. The process of change, however, has been restrained in South Wales by the longstanding desire to preserve the culture and the society of the coalfield and by the persistent attempts by central and local government to locate a good deal of new employment there to this end.

12.3 The Valleys

Between the Swansea valley and the plain of Gwent, a distance of 56 kilometres (35 miles), sixteen main river valleys are cut deeply into the Pennant Sandstone moors which occupy the high ground of South Wales. East of the Rhondda the valleys trend N.N.W. to S.S.E.; west of it they trend southwards, and then, further on, N.E. to S.W. These differences of alignment have been important in the past in the shipment patterns of iron and steel and, above all, of coal. Today, they are of great importance in shaping the pattern of journeys to work and movement for services.

By the second quarter of the nineteenth century there was a string of ironworks along the northern outcrop of the South Wales coalfield from Blaenavon to Brynamman, with their associated coal mines and mushrooming growth towns. From this time onwards the sparsely populated valleys of the coalfields were peopled by a great influx of working men whose principal source of employment was in the collieries. In the late Victorian age most of the old ironworks closed and no more than half a dozen were converted into steel plants; the last of these, Dowlais, closed in 1930. Eight years later a reconstructed works at Ebbw Vale was the sole important steel operation on the coalfield. In the inter-war years, coal mining employment also fell—in bituminous coal mining from 213,000 in 1923 to 108,000 in 1937. Nationalization of coal mines, the change in the competitive position of coal, alterations in national fuel policy and N.C.B. rationalization programmes further reduced the number of jobs to some 30,000 by 1977/1978. By the mid-1970s it was confidently expected by some that the run-down of coal mine employment had run its course; others believed a further decline was inevitable.

In 1947 the N.C.B. took over almost 300 mines in South Wales. Many of them were insignificant in scale and were abandoned quickly without displacing much labour. South Wales has the advantage of good quality coals, including effectively the whole of the nation's anthracite and some 70 per cent of its resources of coking coal. But costs are high due to low productivity, which reflects the age of the field and geological problems—such as faults and soft floors and roofs—which make mechanization difficult. Output per man-shift in 1970 was 1.52 tonnes and it was then said that it would need to be 2.03 tonnes by the mid-1970s to maintain a competitive industry. By 1976/1977 the O.M.S. had fallen away to 1.23 tonnes and in 1977/1978 six South Wales pits lost a combined total of £27 million. Given these circumstances, the run-down of the industry over the last thirty years is understandable. In 1954 the South Wales mines produced 20.9 million tonnes of coal, in 1976/1977, 7.5 million tonnes. The number of pits fell from 164 to 41 between 1950 and 1977. In some parts of the field the decline has been even more complete. The Rhondda at vesting day had twenty-five pits, and as late as 1949/1950 nearly 20,000 coal miners were registered at its four employment exchanges—a figure only just short of half of the total for all categories of both male and female employment. Yet by 1977 Maerdy and Fernhill were the only two mines left in the Rhondda, and their combined employment was less than 2,500.

The outlook for the South Wales coal industry certainly does not involve any large-scale expansion. In its 1975 study *Medium Term Guidelines for Coal 1975-1985,* the E.E.C. Commission excluded South Wales from the list of British fields considered suitable for major further development. However, even before the 1973 energy crisis the closure of pits in South Wales was slowing down and in recent years investments and new developments have been increasing. In the three years to early 1977, over £40 million was invested by the N.C.B. in South Wales, and in 1975/1976 the board were prospecting for suspected large reserves of coal south of Maesteg and Ogmore Vale. By 1978, in fact, there were plans for a major new coking coal mine at Margam, and in that year the new ½ million tonnes per year Bettws anthracite mine came into production with a labour productivity expected to be four times the South Wales average. Other anthracite mines are being reorganized. Future uncertainties centre on the extent to which the production and employment effects of these new investments will be exceeded by the inevitable closure of older high cost mines. At best, and though stabilizing, South Wales coal is unlikely ever again to be a significant growth sector either in terms of output or employment.

New employment has not found the coal valleys attractive. The physical environment is harsh (all the coalfields have over 1,270 millimetres (50 inches) of annual rainfall, and some parts over 2,280 millimetres (90 inches)). There are few level sites for new industry or for spacious housing layout, and the man-made environment is unpleasant. Population has therefore continued to decline. Between 1951 and 1971 the population of the neighbouring urban districts of Abertillery and Pontypool shrank from 70,300 to 58,100, and the Municipal Borough of Rhondda from 111,400 to 88,900. Those who remain live in conditions that are poor by Welsh averages and still lower by British standards. The new Rhondda district of Mid Glamorgan had a 1971 male activity rate of 75.5 per cent and a female rate of 34.0 per cent, as compared with 78.7 per cent and 41.3 per cent, respectively, for Cardiff. Only 49.3 per cent of its households had exclusive use of basic amenities (hot water, bath or shower, inside w.c.) as compared with 79.5 per cent in Swansea or 82.4 per cent in Newport. In the twenty years to 1971, of twenty-two local authorities in the central and eastern valleys, only two gained population. At the same time as the attractions of the valleys have declined, however, so have those of the head of the valleys, and still more of the Vale of Glamorgan and of the coast, increased.

The modern Head of the Valleys road (A465) bypasses a string of old iron towns on the North Crop of the coalfield—but their fair-sized populations, the new ease of east-west movement, and the relatively open sites in this broad zone between the coalfield upland and the Brecon Beacons make this a relatively more attractive place for new industry and employment than the valleys to the south. In the late 1930s, Merthyr-Dowlais became a pioneer focus of industrial diversification, though on a very limited scale. After the war growth snowballed there, particularly with the arrival of Hoover, and other growth foci were also established; the Hirwaun industrial estate and the expansion of the Ebbw Vale steelworks are two examples. At the same time journeys to work at the more favoured locations became easier. There has been considerable turnover of premises on many of the North Crop industrial estates, but major foci have continued to grow. Merthyr in 1971 had daily employment for 21,800 of whom 4,100 came from outside the large local authority. On the other hand Tredegar, with 4,600 jobs, only provided 3,400 of its own workers with employment and sent an equal number out daily to find work elsewhere (Welsh Development Agency, 1977). Apart from Merthyr, the largest North Crop focus of employment has long been Ebbw Vale; changes in the British steel industry, however, imply an immediate and sustained threat to employment prospects there.

In 1971 there were fourteen travel-to-work areas in Britain where the B.S.C. provided directly more than 10 per cent of male employment. In Ebbw Vale the proportion was 38 per cent (Fisk and Jones, 1971). The Welsh iron and steel industry has been shifting coastwards for over a century, after local ore production almost ceased and a dependence on ore imported through the Bristol Channel ports became paramount. After the 1930s only Ebbw Vale survived as an inland integrated steelworks, and by the 1960s South Wales had three other integrated works, at Port Talbot, Cardiff and Newport. The first of these was singled out by the B.S.C. as a major growth point, and by 1970 it had been provided with an ore terminal for vessels of up to 150,000 d.w.t. The corporation's Development Strategy of 1972 provided for a large-scale expansion of Port Talbot and smaller extensions at Newport. (Not until 1977, however, was a delayed approval given to £835 million worth of extensions at Port Talbot designed to double its output to 6 million tons over a period of ten years, and to raise its output per man-year from approximately 230 tons to 500 tons partly through cutting its workforce from 13,000 to 12,000.

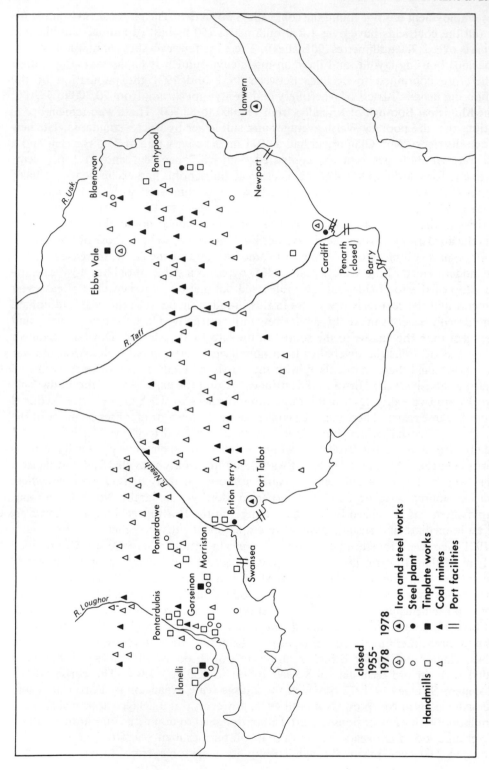

Figure 12.1 South Wales: changes in the location of coal and steel production

Subsequently, as the depression of the industry deepened, even this was deferred.) The B.S.C. Development Strategy also specified the closure of the Cardiff works with the loss of 4,500 jobs, and the loss of half of the 9,000 jobs at Ebbw Vale. There the plan specified the ending of iron and steel making and (by 1978/1979) of hot strip rolling; it did, however, make provision for major extensions of tinplate capacity. Adverse trading conditions eventually speeded the closures. In 1978 the Cardiff works was closed, and at Ebbw Vale only the tinplate and galvanized steel departments survived the closures of May 1978; the workforce fell from almost 6,000 to no more than 4,200. The local impact through loss of associated jobs will be even greater, for one steel job is reckoned to support one and a half other jobs in the locality. The B.S.C. has shown an active social concern in trying to attract new jobs to Ebbw Vale, but the general recession brought unemployment in that area to 10.6 per cent by March 1978. The Welsh Council, among others, was predictably cautious in its reaction to the steel industry's rationalization programme: 'in welcoming expansion at Port Talbot, the Council does not accept that it must inevitably follow that plants everywhere in Wales must close' (Welsh Council, 1974b, p.2). Such an attitude, however, does not recognize that the failure to close some works may make the expansion of others unviable. New centres of employment, to help reduce the loss of Ebbw Vale works, are being developed near the Head of the Valleys road: for instance, a new, privately owned tube mill at Tafarnaubach and, on an even bigger scale, a major new industrial estate at Rassa.

12.4 The Coastlands

Decline in coal, and rationalization and closure in steel, from the 1930s onwards, marked a new emphasis on the areas on the periphery of, or away from, the coalfield. Government help to diversify the economy, though on a modest scale, initially focused on growth points which were on the periphery. Most notable was the pioneer South Wales industrial estate at Treforest in the broad Taff valley below Pontypridd, and major industrial investments at Merthyr or Dowlais. The immediate post-war developments confirmed this feature. Several new employers were attracted to the Merthyr valley; Cwmbran new town was designated beyond the eastern edge of the field; and new industrial estates were located either at the head or the foot of the valleys, as at Hirwaun, Bridgend and Forest Fach on the western edge of Swansea. Rail closures in the valleys and the building of new roads and motorways helped to polarize development away from the coalfield, and especially to the south. Most recently, the improvement of links to the M5, the opening of the Severn bridge, and the piecemeal western extension of the M4 to join the three main coastal nuclei, and therefore to integrate the whole of the coastal economy, have accentuated this trend. The growing importance of the tertiary sector confirm this process of focusing development in and around the bigger coastal nodes.

The traffic through the string of ports along the Bristol Channel—Newport, Cardiff, Penarth, Barry, Port Talbot, Swansea—reached a peak of 47 million tons in 1913. It is now about 20 million tons. As coal shipments shrank, oil, oil products, and ores have become partial replacements, but still leave much under-used capacity. In 1974 coal constituted only 5.1 per cent of the total tonnage handled at all Welsh ports, but oil made up 75.2 per cent. With difficulty they all, and particularly Cardiff, have built up a general cargo trade which an earlier preoccupation with coal had caused them to neglect (Welsh Council, 1974a). Newport, which handled 2.9 million tons of iron ore in 1973, imported none from 1976 onwards following the transfer of all Welsh ore imports to the Port Talbot terminal.

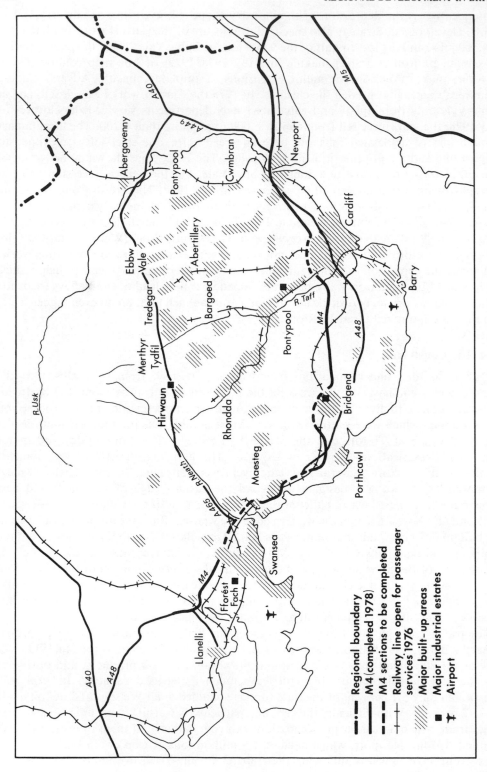

Figure 12.2   Industrial South Wales

As the three biggest coastal centres have become the most attractive places for new development, they have also become major foci of journeys to work. Indeed, in the planning for growth in South Wales, one of the oversights seems to have been an underestimation of the much-increased daily mobility of workers, especially when in the South Wales physical setting this mobility is uniquely channelled. Had this been recognized in the 1930s, then the first hot strip mill could well have been located in the Severnside lowlands where Llanwern was built twenty-five years later, and could still have employed daily labour from the valleys. Diesel trains in the mid-1950s, and increased private car ownership later, have extended personal mobility more. The travel-to-work area of Port Talbot, for example, now extends as far as Ystradgynlais at the northern end of the Swansea valley. Such long journeys to work, however, do decline in importance when nearer jobs become available.

12.4.1 *The Tidewater Nuclei*

Swansea Bay City, as it has been described by Humphrys (1972), is marginally the largest of the three coastal agglomerations, both in population and in extent (Table 12.4). It stretches from the commuting zone of Gower to that of Porthcawl, focusing on the industrial and other employments of Swansea, Port Talbot and Neath. Until after World War II several parts of this area were physically and to a considerable degree functionally separate. But new bridges, a developing road network, new industry and the pattern of housing development have begun to integrate and link the whole area into a conglomerate mix of old and new. Industrially, there are impressive modern investments such as, and preeminently, the B.S.C. Port Talbot works, the B.P. Llandarcy Refinery and from the early 1960s the associated Baglan Bay petrochemical complex, new motor component plants of Ford at Jersey Marine (Swansea) and of Borg Warner at Cornelly, and many new industrial estate or advance factories, some of them on the sites of old works. Over many years a variety of metal trades have come to be located in the sub-region, such as nickel at Clydach and titanium in Swansea. Aluminium is prominent with Alcoa recently completing a £40 million plant extension at its Waunarlwydd rolling mill. Elements of the old industrial structure still survive, such as the unintegrated and small Briton Ferry Steelworks (soon to be closed by its West Midland owners), and some old steel and tinplate works taken over and converted to other steel-finishing or processing activities. Many of the old metal works have disappeared altogether and nothing has taken their place locally—the site of the Gowerton steelworks, completely bare and stretching out towards the Loughor estuary, is strikingly impressive in this respect. Necessarily, local journey-to-work patterns have had to change, sometimes more than once. The small Swansea valley community of Morriston illustrates this very well (Seaborne, 1977). In 1954, Morriston had six steel and tinplate works employing over 4,200, or nearly half of the town's insured workforce. By 1961 all except one of the plants had closed; but by accepting a longer journey to work half of the town's employees were still in the metal trades. By the mid-1970s, however, less than one-third of Morriston labour was in metals, with new local employments having substantially reduced the amount of daily journeying to Port Talbot in particular.

Swansea has not only grown as an industrial centre but also as a service focus for the western part of industrial South Wales. More recently it has received many new government office employments, notably in the Vehicle Taxation Office and the Land

Registry. The M4 and the new high-speed British Rail services to London have lessened the penalty of its relative remoteness from British markets. Physically the growth of the city itself is constrained, on the west by the amenity land of Gower and on the east by the great trench of the Swansea valley. In spite of the major reclamation work of the Lower Swansea Valley Project, the latter still contains much dereliction—wrecked buildings, old rows of houses, waste heaps covered with scrubby vegetation and the occasional contorted heap of metal slag—dating from the time when this locality was the centre of world copper smelting.

Although Swansea Bay City may hold a few more thousand people, it is made up of more diffuse parts, and has lower-order central place functions, than Cardiff. Cardiff became officially the capital of Wales in 1948; in 1964 it became the headquarters of the Welsh Office; and twelve years later, as active planning for devolution was under way, the converted Coal Exchange Building in the docklands was singled out as the seat of any future Welsh assembly. It is, however, a location for a capital which can only with difficulty serve the middle and north of the Principality, and it is an inconvenient centre even for South West Wales. Cardiff is also a growing office and service centre. The Inland Revenue has already established substantial offices there, and the Ministry of Defence is to move in and provide some thousands of new jobs. By the mid-1970s a new central office was being established there to put under one roof over 1,000 Welsh Office staff until then scattered throughout the city, and its generally greater office function than that of Swansea is indicated by the larger number of modern concrete, aluminium and glass structures which now shoot upwards from its Victorian terraces.

Cardiff has naturally attracted new industry, such as the Rover works at Pengam. It also has major continuing trades, such as the rolling mills of G.K.N., a company which invested over £50 million in the 1970s in new electric arc furnaces and a rod mill to replace its dependence on steel bought from the British Steel Corporation. This, however, only provided 400-500 new jobs while some 3,000 were lost with the closure of the B.S.C. East Moors works in 1978. When cleared, the steelworks site will be developed for new industry.

Though it is as yet the smallest, the Newport-Chepstow urban region would seem to be the most favoured in terms of growth potential. There is more room; it offers an attractive, generally less scarred, environment; and superb conditions of wider access exist, north eastwards to the Ross Spur motorway and M5, across the Severn bridge to the M4 and the south western extensions of the M5, and westwards via the Welsh portions of the M4. On the other hand, the Newport area has suffered in competition with the rest of South Wales in seeking to attract new industry—first because for long it received no development assistance; more recently because, while Cardiff is now within the Welsh Development Area, the coastlands of Gwent are only classified as of Intermediate Area Status. In spite of this, an expansion of employment greater than that in the other two urban regions occurred in the 1960s, though much of that growth was associated directly with the Llanwern steelworks opened in 1962.

Nothing better sums up the continuing 'export' dependence of the Welsh regional economy than Llanwern, for the steel making which supports a few thousand jobs in Monmouthshire (and in 1971 B.S.C. provided in all its Newport plants 25 per cent of all the male jobs in that travel-to-work area) generates many times that number in the metal-fabricating trades of the Midlands and the South East. A longer-term, more ambitious development policy than one which made this into an Intermediate Area only as late as

Table 12.4 Industrial South Wales: population by selected subdivisions*, 1951, 1961 and 1971
('000s)

	1951	1961	1971
Industrial South Wales, Total	1,590.2	1,618.3	1,645.5
Newport-Chepstow city-region	139.3	147.8	162.2
Cardiff city-region	339.6	369.4	377.2
Swansea Bay City	358.7	369.9	379.3
Vale of Glamorgan	153.3	164.3	200.3
Central & eastern coalfield valleys	599.3	566.9	526.5

Source: *Based on journey to work patterns.

Table 12.5 Industrial South Wales: population of the new counties, 1951-1991

	1951	1961	1971	1976	1991 (projected)
Industrial South Wales* ('000s)	1,642	1,690	1,736	1,741	1,769
	(%)	(%)	(%)	(%)	(%)
Gwent	24.7	25.1	25.4	25.3	24.6
Mid Glamorgan	32.3	30.8	30.6	31.0	31.9
South Glamorgan	21.4	22.5	22.5	22.3	22.6
West Glamorgan	21.7	21.6	21.5	21.4	20.9

*Excluding that portion of industrial South Wales around Llanelli and therefore within Dyfed.
Based on *Digest of Welsh Statistics*.

1971 might have brought in a wider range of metal-using trades, and might at least have begun to build up a steel and steel-using complex. It is noteworthy that thirty years ago, when the Ebbw Vale strip mill was in full work, and the Port Talbot mill was being built, the flats between Cardiff and Newport (the Wentlooge levels) were remarked upon as an ideal location for a motor industry with direct export prospects. Some fifteen years later, with a decisive sub-regional promotion policy still lacking, the city of Cardiff itself had to take the initiative in providing a site and access route to induce Rover to locate there. In 1976 a report submitted to Gwent County Council proposed major development on the Caldicot levels to the east of Newport, and revived ideas for a deep-water dock at Uskmouth. Yet there is no reason to suppose that traditional Welsh opposition to this sort of development—in defence of the valleys—will decline.

Newport, as an urban focus not only for the Severnside lowlands but also for the rapidly increasing population of the western plain of Gwent, is struggling to improve its urban fabric. The new bridge over the Usk has reduced the bottleneck within the town and the M4 now provides an important northern bypass. Six miles to the north is another, smaller but rapidly growing nucleus, Cwmbran-Pontypool. This area had old coal, steel and tinplate trades, but as early as the 1930s a number of new firms arrived and began to provide a great upward thrust to the local economy. Some of those early arrivals have gone on to spread development elsewhere in Gwent, as with the car component firm of Girling which has since built at Pontypool and plans to expand at Ebbw Vale. In 1949

Cwmbran new town was designated and work began on it in 1951. Cwmbran was designed to act as a dormitory, service centre and new employment focus for a problem area. But it has become first an important manufacturing growth point, and then a retail centre estimated to serve a population of as much as 100,000. In absolute terms, the population growth for Pontypool Rural District and Cwmbran Urban District between 1951 and 1971 has been exceeded only by Cardiff and the Vale of Glamorgan—in relative growth it has been quite unrivalled in industrial South Wales.

There has been a slight fall in the population of the westernmost coastal section of industrial South Wales between the Loughor River and Kidwelly. The old metal centre of Llanelli has retained some of its old firms, such as Llanelly Steel whose works (now owned by Duport of the Black Country) are being reequipped with electric furnaces in place of their open-hearth operations. Llanelli has also attracted important new industries in the post-war period, most notably the B.S.C. Trostre cold reduction and tinplate mill, and B.L. which by 1978 employed 4,500 in two plants. Even so, the town's population fell by 8,000 or almost one-quarter, from 1951 to 1971, and the increase in the population in Llanelli Rural District was smaller than the decline in Llanelli town population. Burry Port, a much smaller outlying tinplate town, has also shrunk following the closure of its local works.

12.4.2 *The Vale of Glamorgan*

In spite of the growth of the three urban centres on the coast, even bigger increases in population have been registered in the Vale of Glamorgan, especially in the 1960s (Table 12.4). In 1961 the population of the vale was only 164,000 as opposed to 887,000 in the three city-regions. Between 1961 and 1971 the city-regions added 32,000, the vale 36,000. Undoubtedly much of this growth reflects an even wider radius of commuting to the coastal centres; but there has also been much growth of employment within the vale itself. The steady, if piecemeal, completion of the M4 and the movement of people from the valleys to jobs and often homes in the easier physical environment of the vale, have been important factors in the growth of Bridgend, Cowbridge and, more recently, Llantrisant to which the Royal Mint has been moved from London. In 1969 the consultant Colin Buchanan recommended that an already designated new town there should become a major centre of employment and should grow over a period of thirty years from 12,000 to 145,000 people. Llantrisant, like the upper Severnside lowlands, focused the continuing planning conflict between preservation and bold new departures; opposition from valley communities and lower population forecasts subsequently led to the abandonment of the idea of a new town there.

In 1977 the vale received a major new economic boost with the announcement of an £180 million Ford engine plant to serve that company's West European operations and to be built at Bridgend. Bridgend had already built up industrial estate employment of over 6,600 though mostly in units employing a small workforce. The completion in the late 1970s of the M4 in this section of the vale gave a particular attraction to the location. Good labour relations and productivity in Ford gearbox and axle operations set up in Swansea in 1965, and sparking-plug ceramics at Treforest, made South Wales generally attractive; and as a Development Area location, £35 million will be provided by government grants. When in full production in 1980, the Bridgend engine plant should employ 2,500. It may poach skilled workers from other employers. On the other hand, it will provide a larger number of construction jobs in the meantime, some important multiplier employment, and valuable help in cutting local unemployment. Perhaps even more important is its psychological impact, helping as it does to transform the traditional image of industrial South Wales still more.

12.5 Development Strategy for South Wales

New industries, alterations in the internal pattern of circulation, shifting national space relationships, changes in energy supply, and many other developments, all demand new thinking about the physical form of economic development in South Wales. Far-sighted policies should obviously stress the long-term development of favoured areas, ease adjustment in areas of difficulty, and abandon the worst prospects. To some extent this has been done, but less emphatically in Wales than in other problem regions of Britain. Above all, there has been a woeful lack of a spatially explicit policy of development in the region, and at both ends of the policy spectrum more radical initiatives are needed.

On the positive side there are undoubtedly superb growth prospects in the Cardiff-Chepstow lowland belt. Opportunities exist not only for industries requiring deep water—and as Llanwern planning showed in the mid-1960s, this could be provided by a jetty built into the middle of the Severn estuary—but also for activities requiring extensive and flat sites, benefiting from agglomeration economies, and oriented via good transport facilities to major national markets and other centres of manufacturing activity. Yet the enormous and long-term development potential of this upper Severnside sub-region has not been adequately recognized in Wales; and, certainly, it has not been translated into an articulate long-term programme for action. Indeed, official policies have all too often seemed to restrain its growth in order to preserve older industrial communities elsewhere in South Wales.

To some extent this was the outcome of nationally agreed policies. In 1966 most of Wales (the exceptions were the south eastern and north eastern coastlands) was made into a Development Area. In the following year, at a time of accelerated run-down in coal, the Special Development Areas were created to give increased assistance to areas especially hurt by this policy. This gave money and priorities to replacement industry for the coalfield. In the same year the Secretary of State for Wales published *Wales: The Way Ahead,* and deliberately argued in favour of the revival of older industrial areas rather than the development of new areas. The 'primary objective' of development planning should, it suggested, be to divert new employment to areas 'where it is most needed'. Even when the Welsh Development Area was extended to include Cardiff in 1971, the older spatial bias was preserved with the Severnside zone to its east only being accorded Intermediate Area status. At a lower level of planning activity, also, the same bias exists. Monmouthshire County Council, for instance, actively pursued a policy which aimed to divert new industry onto the coalfield.

In 1974 the new Welsh counties were established. In the next few years, they sought to produce their structure plans even though the fundamental issue of whether redevelopment in the valleys should be encouraged at the expense of development on the coastlands had in no way been settled. Indeed, the division of Glamorgan into three planning authorities made the scope for unintegrated planning greater than ever. The Welsh Development Agency (W.D.A.) was established in 1976. In its first important document, *A Statement of Policies and Programmes* (1977), it could only make proposals to identify the sectors and localities in which growth should be encouraged. There still does not exist, therefore, a strategic plan for South Wales. The result has been a continuation of the 'destructive squabbling of Welsh local authorities as they clutch and grab for the few crumbs of industrial investment left on the table' (*Western Mail*, March 1977), and the loss of unquantified investments in its most favoured zone.

ı Such a policy is not without its articulate defenders. Plaid Cymru, the Welsh Nationalist Party, has argued for the preservation of the old pattern of population in South Wales. In a parliamentary debate in 1976/1977 its spokesman deplored the 'unitarist, centralist, metropolis-dominated state' within which such a growth zone as upper Severnside might be expected to have great prospects of success. The government was criticized for 'not creating an industrial infrastructure for Wales which includes a road, rail and air communications system ... which would make possible the development of a balanced Welsh economy' (Evans, 1976). The latter included a strong preference for a road improvement priority which would more effectively bind together North and South Wales rather than placing the emphasis on completing the M4—which serves not only to improve internal South Wales links, but also to tie the region more closely into English Severnside and South East England. Four years earlier, to the Commission on the Constitution, Plaid Cymru had listed Westminster policies or decisions which it considered 'irrelevant or unsuitable to the economic and social needs of Wales': these included 'the priority given to the Severn Bridge rather than the Cardiff-Merthyr dual carriageway; the priority given to the feasibility studies of the Dee barrage rather than similar studies of the Dyfi, Mawddach or Conway barrages; [and] the uncoordinated rundown of the Welsh railway system' (King, 1973, p.70). The priorities of Plaid Cymru assume a much greater unity of interest between the different parts of Wales than now exists. Moreover, they ignore the liabilities of many coalfield locations for modern industrial and commercial investment, and undervalue the assets of the coastlands.

The provision of local industries in the coalfield valleys of South Wales may be socially desirable. Yet economically it would represent a dissipation of scarce funds which might be better used to provide the attractions of the growth foci. Already on the coast, at the valley heads and mouths, at the inland centre of Merthyr, and at the four major peripheral industrial estates now operated by W.D.A. (at Treforest, Hirwaun, Bridgend and Swansea) new growth has been firmly established on the fringes of the coalfield and beyond. No surviving community on the coalfield is beyond a reasonable journey-to-work distance from a growth focus. In consequence, the reconstruction of the region's urban fabric, so obviously needed in all old Welsh industrial towns, need not take place in all the smaller coalfield centres. Their population should be allowed to shrink still more and, for the smallest, a policy like the Durham 'D' village scheme is probably long overdue.

There can be no doubt that the South Wales economy remains subservient to that of the English axial belt. Its relatively small size, and therefore its dependence on English markets, emphatically implies that the devolution of political power can never be carried through into meaningful economic independence. Moreover, if separatism became a really active issue it seems likely that South Wales would lose its present attraction as an overflow area for industry from England and, nearer to hand, from Bristol in particular. The decline in projected population growth levels over the last four years suggests also that there will be fewer people in South Wales in the last years of the century than were planned for in *Wales: The Way Ahead*. The need to make a decision betwen the stabilization of the population of the valleys and the growth of Severnside is, therefore, becoming even more urgent. The development of Severnside as a large and diverse industrial agglomeration gives the best hope of reducing a colonial-type dependence on England, and instead becoming a true growth pole of the British economy. Moreover, there is a need, in a time of national economic difficulties but of increasing personal mobility, to stress the development of optimum locations *within* the problem regions. South Wales is fortunate in having sub-regions with splendid growth prospects. It is important that this fact should be more formally recognized by the planning agencies and in the plans of the Principality.

REFERENCES

Atkins, D. (1973). *Trade and Industry,* 30 August, 437-439.
Council for Wales and Monmouth (1955). *Report on South Wales Ports* (Cmnd. 9359), H.M.S.O., Cardiff.
Davies, R. (1977). *The Times,* 15 March, quoting G. Davies and I. Thomas, *Overseas Investment in Wales,* 1977.
Evans, G. (1976). Speech by the M.P. for Carmarthen in a House of Commons debate on Welsh Affairs, reported in the *Guardian,* 6 February 1977.
Fisk, T.A., and Jones, T.K. (1971). Regional planning from the point of view of a major employer. Paper presented to a Regional Studies Association Conference, Cardiff, September.
Humphrys, G. (1972). *Industrial Britain: South Wales,* David & Charles, Newton Abbot.
King, D.N. (1973). Financial and economic aspects of regionalism and separatism. *Commission on the Constitution, Research Paper 10,* H.M.S.O., London.
Manners, G. (ed.) (1964). *South Wales in the Sixties,* Pergamon, Oxford.
Seaborne, A. (1977). Unpublished Ph.D. thesis, University College of Swansea.
Tomkins, C., and Lovering, J. (1973). *Location, Size, Ownership and Control Tables for Welsh Industry,* Welsh Council, Cardiff.
Welsh Council (1974a). *The Welsh Ports,* H.M.S.O., Cardiff.
Welsh Council (1974b). *The Steel Industry in Wales,* H.M.S.O., Cardiff.
Welsh Development Agency (1977). *Labour Market Study,* W.D.A., Cardiff.
Welsh Office (annually). *Welsh Economic Trends,* H.M.S.O., Cardiff.

CHAPTER 13

North East England

KENNETH WARREN

13.1 Introduction

The North East of England is comparable in many ways with mid-Scotland and South Wales—in its economic history and industrial structure, in its peripheral location within the British economy, and in its shared indices of relative deprivation or slow growth. Such comparisons, however, hide contrasts. Though a member of a class of problem British regions, like the others the North East has its marked individuality. Coal, iron and steel were common bases to the economies of all three major industrial peripheral regions in their hey-day. In addition the North East shared with Scotland a major involvement in shipbuilding and marine engineering. Mechanical engineering was also once of great importance there, and early in the twentieth century Tyneside acquired a large share of the new heavy electrical engineering industry. Later, in the 1920s, as crisis hit most of the other basic trades, a heavy chemical industry grew rapidly on Teesside. In the 1930s, however, the whole region was chronically depressed. In 1938, when the national economy turned down for the last time before World War II, monthly average unemployment in Northumberland and Durham was 14.5 and 20.5 per cent respectively as compared with 12.7 per cent for Britain as a whole.

A generation later the problem remained, although in the meantime huge sums of public money had been spent supporting the staple trades and seeking to encourage a new economic base to take root there. In recent years especially, the region has been the biggest beneficiary of regional development grants; over the five years to March 1977, for example, it received £356 million, one third of the national total, well over twice as much as Wales, and 17 per cent more than Scotland. Yet by April 1978 the seasonally adjusted unemployment rate for the South East was 4.1 per cent and for the West Midlands 5.2 per cent, but in the Northern region (that is, Cumbria combined with the North East) it was 8.2 per cent. Of the eleven regions of the nation only Northern Ireland had a higher rate.

Unemployment has, of course, come to be regarded as an inadequate index of regional problems. In other respects, too, the North East is clearly a disadvantaged region. The Northern region had 5.9 per cent of the country's employment in 1975, but it suffered 7.8 per cent of the nation's redundancies in that year, 12.7 per cent in 1976 and 14.9 per cent in 1977 (T.U.C., 1978). Research and development activity in industry is relatively unimportant, even though the region now has a slightly higher percentage of its workforce in manufactures than the United Kingdom as a whole. Average wages may be approximate to those at the national level, but activity rates for men and particularly for women are low, and family income and Gross Domestic Product (G.D.P.) per head are well below the national norms. In 1976 per capita G.D.P. was only 84.1 per cent of the U.K. average and lower than in any other region in Britain. Of the dwellings existing in the Northern region in 1973, 33.1 per cent had been built before 1917. The number of pupils staying on at school beyond the statutory leaving age or going on to full-time further education lags well behind national levels. Regional health services are overloaded. Housing conditions, car ownership, and the availability of certain domestic appliances and conveniences—though not now central heating—are below national averages. Similarly, the area ranks very high in the incidence of derelict land, having 22 per cent of the English total in 1974. Nevertheless, spectacular success has been achieved in some areas with tip reclamation and land restoration schemes.

The causes of the undoubted difficulties of the North Eastern economy, and of some aspects of its socio-economic structure, are to be found in the changing value of its resource endowment, its employment structure, its location within Britain, and the perception of these conditions and of development prospects by people both within and outside the region. Yet broad regional characteristics, though important, are a compound of sub-regional trends which are often widely at variance. Economic and physical planning require a consideration of the sub-regions as well as of the North East as a whole.

13.2 A Changing Resource Base

In the nineteenth century and into the twentieth century, the North East seemed a richly endowed area, particularly with respect to minerals. Its coal basin was not only large but well-favoured in the wide range of its coals—from the finest British coking coals in West Durham to gas, steam and industrial coals. Just before World War I the North East produced 56 million tons of coal annually, and in 1913 some 20 million tons were exported from the Tyne. Then, there were 266 collieries, mostly in a triangular area whose base extended from Hartlepool to Barnard Castle and whose apex was on the south shore of Druridge Bay in Northumberland. Employment in the coal industry was then widely scattered through the coalfield. By 1978, the North East produced under 16 million tons of coal annually (2.3 million tons from open cast sites), only thirty-two pits were still at work and employment was no more than 35,000. Much of the decline of the industry was concentrated in the fifteen years from 1958 when demand shrank rapidly in the face of competition from oil; between 1960 and 1973 alone employment in mining and quarrying in the Northern region fell by 102,000, and its share in total regional employment dropped from 12.01 to 4.4 per cent. This had important sub-regional implications.

The surviving collieries are mostly east of the A1 and predominantly near the coast, where by the mid-1970s major reconstructions were underway at Horden-Blackhall, Easington, Dawdon-Vane Tempest and Lynemouth-Ellington, in part to supply the coking coal needs of Redcar. In consequence, large areas of West Durham or South East Northumberland, and many individual communities throughout the coalfield, have lost their local source of employment. In spite of the various new industries introduced into the region substantially as a result of government policies, the old coalfield areas still suffer from high unemployment. In July 1976 the unemployment rate in the Northern region was 8.7 per cent; in South West Durham the figure was 9.3 per cent and in North West Durham 10.8 per cent. Despite its persistent contraction and its bad image, however, in 1975/1976 the coal industry alone injected £120 million into the region's economy, £50 million more than I.C.I. with its large chemical complex on Teesside. Moreover, by this time it was widely believed that most of its adjustments had been completed. 'Unlike the situation at any time in the postwar period, the future development of coal mining does not pose any major issues of significance for the region' was the comforting conclusion of the Third Interim Report of the Northern Region Strategy Team in 1976. Given the large scale, modernized character and important regional outlets of the collieries which remain, this seems a reasonable contention, at least in the short to medium term.

The second great mineral resource of the North East, Cleveland iron ore, is no longer worked. Despite considerable government subsidy over its last years, production ceased in 1964. In this case the problems of a much more sparsely populated mining area have been largely solved by the growth of commuting over the relatively short distances to Teesside. Indeed, in the 1960s, the urban districts which covered a very large part of the old ore field—Guisborough, Skelton and Brotton, and Saltburn and Marske-by-the-Sea—all increased their population by a substantially greater proportion than the Teesside county borough; only one, Loftus Urban District, declined. The development of potash mining on the south east edge of Cleveland and towards Whitby in North Yorkshire has provided only a small amount of direct and ancillary employment locally, but a great deal of continuing dispute about amenity.

Teesside salt and anhydrite, once so important in shaping its pattern of chemical development, are now of negligible significance; both the local minerals and coal (up to 1 million tons a year was used in the late 1950s) have now been superseded as the industry's material base by oil and natural gas. Crude oil is brought to the Phillips north Teesside terminal from the Ekofisk field by pipeline and to the Shell Teesport terminal by tanker from the North Sea and other fields.

The other raw material resources of the North East are found in the uplands of the west. Lead mining, once so important in shaping the economy there, has been dead for generations, but its influence is still seen in the pattern of settlement and communications. Without its historical influence, Alston and Allendale Town, for instance, would be much less prominent members of the lower urban hierarchy. The carboniferous limestone of Weardale and Teesdale (and the Magnesian Limestone of the great East Durham escarpment) are both still important minerals for the Teesside steel and chemical plants. Pennine fluorspar found in the early 1970s a new regional market in the needs of Alcan's Lynemouth aluminium smelter. Barytes and witherite are less important Pennine mineral products.

The needs of North East industry and, more recently, wider national needs have given a new value to the region's water resources. It is almost ninety years since parliamentary approval was secured for Catcleugh reservoir at the head of Redesdale and a few kilometres south of Carter Bar. Major and highly controversial modern construction in the rural periphery of the North East began with the Cow Green scheme for upper Teesdale in the mid-1960s, and now provides a medium-term solution to Teesside water problems. By the mid-1970s the new Northumbrian Water Authority, whose sphere of operation extends beyond the North East region, had embarked on the equally controversial Kielder reservoir in the North Tyne valley; its cost was estimated in 1973 at £40 million, and in addition it involves substantial social, economic and scenic disruption in its locality. On completion, it will increase the daily water supply for the region from 1,100 million to 2,050 million litres (250 million to 450 million gallons), and by guaranteeing water supplies to A.D. 2000 it will provide a long-term asset for industry in the region.

The North East has three other important non-urban/industrial resources—agriculture, forestry and tourism. Generally speaking, the quality of North East agriculture is high, particularly in the efficiently farmed high-yield area of lowland eastern Northumberland.

Upland grazing, notably for sheep, surrounds the lower agricultural area from the Cleveland Hills, through the Pennines to the Cheviot mass. A scatter of market towns serves this rural fringe. Forestry, now so prominent in the landscape, is largely the outcome of the work of the Forestry Commission. It has been aesthetically controversial, though new planting policies and better public relations, including the establishment of forest parks, nature trails and so on, have made it more acceptable. Kielder and Byrness are forest villages but their impact on employment and settlement has been marginal. Although there has been a good deal of discussion about further processing activities, these have not developed on any considerable scale, and those which do exist are along the Tyne and at Sunderland. Scope for further afforestation seems small. Natural beauty, a rich historical heritage, an uncrowded environment, and, away from the major conurbations, a marvellous clarity of air, all make the North East an area of outstanding tourist potential. Tourism has in fact grown locally, as for instance along the Roman Wall and in the city of Durham; but overall the region remains undeveloped in this respect.

In summary, the North East has suffered an impressive decline in the value of some of its traditional resources. Concern for this obvious characteristic of its economic geography tends to obscure the fact that in other respects is still possesses an impressive range of assets. Today, it is not resource poor; rather its resource base has changed. Even so, its growth foci have shifted from a resource orientation to one based upon its major urban agglomerations.

13.3 Changing Economic Structure and Geography

Although some diversification of industry in the North East occurred in the late 1930s, and still more during World War II, by the early post-war years the employment structure of the region was still very specialized. However, in the 1950s to some extent, but still more in the 1960s and early 1970s, the Northern region's employment in the traditional heavy industries declined rapidly. The number employed in mining and quarrying, metals, shipbuilding and marine engineering fell in the fifteen years to 1975 from 281,000 to 144,000. New employment did not quite keep pace with the loss of old jobs, so that between 1966 and the end of 1975 the total number of employees at work in the region fell from 1,255,000 to 1,248,000. The decline in male employment was greater—between 1966 and 1973 from 807,000 to 768,000—but this was partly cancelled out by an increase in female workers from 448,000 to 477,000. Spatially, as well as in terms of male/female employment levels, the loss of old jobs and the creation of new ones did not coincide. Coal mining provides merely the most spectacular example of this. Notwithstanding the impact of Special Development Area incentives which were initially confined to the declining areas of the coalfield, the spread of new factory employment has not matched the distribution of old colliery towns and villages; and clearly from the viewpoint of future economic efficiency it would be very undesirable if it had done so. Metal manufacture was traditionally highly localized, especially in the steel towns of Consett, Hartlepool and South Teesside; and shipbuilding was concentrated in the main estuaries and at Blyth. Yet even in steel and shipbuilding localities there have been problems in providing enough replacement jobs, particularly in Hartlepool, Blyth and in some of the specialized Tyne shipbuilding towns such as Wallsend.

The new employment has been strongly attracted to the major urban centres. Population concentrations with good intra-regional and external communications have

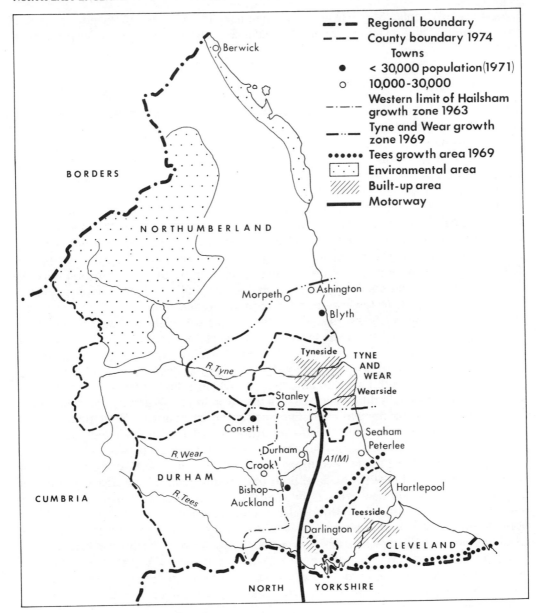

Figure 13.1 North East England: elements in the economic structure

become vital factors in shaping the new patterns of economic activity which must replace the resource-oriented old ones. Yet there is no clear-cut and simple divide between the distribution of old industry and the distribution of the new. Existing patterns of population, local and wider political pressures and a higher immediate cost of making a break with old distributions have ensured that a compromise has been struck between the traditional and what is intrinsically the most desirable new economic geography of the North East. The wisdom of regional planners must be judged by the way in which, negotiating this admittedly difficult strait, they none the less steer the region towards a better economic and social geography. On balance in the North East the auspices seem good.

13.4 The Coalfield

The western part of the Durham coalfield is located in dissected upland with large areas over 150 metres (500 feet). Mining has declined almost to extinction as the high-quality coking coals have been worked out. Bishop Auckland, Stanley and Consett are the only major foci of population, and together they declined by 13,000, or almost 11 per cent, between 1951 and 1971. Away from the splendidly scenic A68, communications are poor in the whole zone west of the A1. The 'D' villages of County Durham—communities in which the planning authority regards further public investment as unjustified, and which will be gradually run down, if possible to extinction—are heavily concentrated in this part of the county. Although there are important centres of new factory employment, particularly at the larger urban centres, or on the eastern margins of the region (such as Team Valley, Spennymoor or Aycliffe), the long-term future of this sub-region must be one of widespread and continuing decline, as the distribution of population gradually conforms more closely to the geography of economic opportunity.

The East Durham and South East Northumberland parts of the coalfield are in a very different situation. They lie in the lower, environmentally more favoured areas of the coalfield where colliery employment is still quite widely important and locally dominant. Certainly there are problems here—in July 1976, for instance, with an unemployment rate of 11.6 per cent, the South East Durham group of exchanges had a higher rate than any of the other eleven groups in the North East with the exception of Wearside. There have been areas of steady post-war population decline, such as the urban district of Hetton or that of Seaham. Others, however, like Easington Rural District with its major pits, have continued to expand. These areas lie near to—and in Durham between—the region's major conurbations and are crossed by good communications, both road and rail. New industrial estates and new towns have been built within them to act as redevelopment points, and to provide new centres for coalfield services and growth points for new industry. The new towns of Aycliffe, Peterlee and Washington in 1951 had a combined population of 21,500, but by 1971 it was 67,300. To the north of the Tyne, the Cramlington and Killingworth new towns sponsored by the Northumberland County Council have become other major growth foci. The opening of the Tyne Tunnel in 1967, and the subsequent road links to the dual carriageway A1 north of the conurbation and to the Durham motorway south of it, have made these two centres and Washington increasingly attractive.

The White Paper on *The North East* in 1963 designated the area southwards from Cramlington and Ponteland to Teesside and the middle valley of the Tees as a 'growth zone'. West Durham, Blyth, East Cleveland and the eastern part of the North York Moors were designated, euphemistically perhaps, 'other development districts'. By the mid-1960s there was discussion about a new 'corridor city' strung out along the A1 from the Tyne to Darlington. The new government of 1964 quickly abandoned the notion of overt growth zone or corridor planning, but the Northern Economic Council later recognized the realities of planning in a difficult region when it selected growth nodes centred on Tyne-Wear and Teesside. There were attempts to spread growth psychology through a hierarchy of other centres (relay towns and holding points); but the reality of growth prospects was clearly focused.

The persistent question remains: has the spatial redevelopment strategy been too cautious in the North East? Should planning have much more boldly capitalized on the best opportunities in the region and abandoned as hopeless much more of the inherited nineteenth-century fabric? Given the geographical realities of employment and unemployment, and given also the political pressures and limits of planning in a democratic society, it seems probable that the regional planners have done as much—and have moved as quickly—as they could. Certainly the County Durham 'D' village programme represents a much bolder move than is to be found in other problem regions of Britain. However, it may well be that despite the industrial estates that are strung along it, the development potential of the A1-Durham motorway corridor has been underestimated, and that in view of the mobility of the workforce in the 1970s less investment in the areas to the west could have been possible. Significantly, the report of the Northern Region Strategy Team (April 1977) reemphasized the attractions of a central Durham growth corridor. Within such a strategy, the growth prospects of the Darlington-Aycliffe sub-region are especially noteworthy. This area has a 'gateway' role in the region, located as it is towards the southern end of the Durham motorway and with fast access to Teesside. Between 1951 and 1971 the population of Darlington County Borough and Darlington Rural District grew by 21,000 or 21 per cent, while the population of the North East as a whole increased only by 5 per cent. The Darlington area, with a wide range of engineering trades and with other estate-type industries, has great potential—but a relatively small population. Although the 'growth zone' of 1963 officially ceased to exist within two years of its designation, in practice it is very much alive. In terms of population, political power, current problems and specialized potential, however, this belt is overshadowed by the great estuarine conurbations at its northern and southern ends.

13.5 The Estuaries

In the local government boundary reorganization of April 1974, the six-year-old County Borough of Teesside was merged with the County Borough of Hartlepool (and small portions of the former counties of Durham and the North Riding along or immediately tributary to the Tees) to form the new county of Cleveland. At the same time a much larger unit, Tyne and Wear, penetrating in parts down almost into mid-Durham, became the dominant authority in the region. Cleveland's population is 0.57 million; Tyne and Wear's is 1.2 million (just twice that of the county of Durham). Before examining the principal attributes of their economic geography, however, the three major manufacturing activities of the estuaries should be placed in their national context.

13.5.1 *The Iron and Steel Industry in a National Context*

The iron and steel industry is the archetypal heavy or basic industry, not only in the sense of the conventional divisions of manufacturing, but because it provides the foundation for a metal-using industrial superstructure which, though ever more elaborate, is still dependent upon bulk metal supply. The industry has a massive inherited investment in old plant; replacement costs are, however, vastly greater still; as a result only relatively slow change occurs in the number and location of its operations. This applies especially to the bulk-producing, fully integrated works, but rather less to re-rolling operations or to mini-mills (usually rolling mills backed up by relatively small capacity electric furnaces). Both at individual plant and national levels, work forces in the industry have fallen sharply in recent years—from 428,000 in 1955 to some 290,000 twenty years later—and it is clear that there will have to be yet further contraction in the foreseeable future.

For historic reasons Britain has more distinct steel-producing districts than most advanced industrial nations, yet steel making is unevenly spread through the country. There is negligible activity in the South East (though probably great potential, to which the new Sheerness coal metal works is no more than a small-scale pointer). The West Midlands has a major industry, though it is one divided into a large number of units, none of which was integrated by 1978; few are large steel makers; and a large number operate only rolling mills and are designated re-rollers. Sheffield is a major focus of quality steel making and of re-rolling. There are two important nodes on Humberside and in the East Midlands at Scunthorpe and at Corby. Of the rest, almost all is located in the Development Areas—indeed, the Northern, Welsh and Scottish Development Areas accounted for 53.3 per cent of national crude steel output in 1977.

Though scattered through many districts, the industry has marked regional specialisms such as wire in South Lancashire, tubes in the West Midlands, central Scotland and at Corby (and more recently on Teesside), tinplate wholly in South Wales, sheet steel in Wales and Lanarkshire, and plate in Scotland, the North East and at Scunthorpe. Partly because of differential growth of these regional specialisms, partly because of their intrinsic suitability for modern bulk steel making, and partly also because of policy (either company or government inspired), the districts have grown at different rates. As a consequence, output has increased very much more rapidly in recent decades in South Wales than in Scotland, and other once important districts in terms of crude steel output like South Lancashire have now ceased to be of any importance. At the sub-regional or local level, steel making may dominate the economy and society, a situation which makes rationalization difficult to secure in a socially conscious age. Thus, important towns such as Workington, Corby, Hartlepool, Consett, Ebbw Vale or Motherwell have been almost wholly dependent on a single steel firm, whilst the fortunes of such districts as Teesside, Sheffield-Rotherham and the Black Country are to varying degrees closely involved with the industry.

On the map of British iron and steel making, the influence of old sources of materials is still clearly visible as, for instance, in the existence of the Black Country, Ebbw Vale, Consett or the Lanarkshire works, which indicate the importance of old coal and (coal measure) ore production. Other locations were established when home ore was of vital importance, either in the form of haematite (Workington) or bedded carbonate ore, as in the Jurassic belt. Others were market locations, often concentrating initially on overseas outlets, which later grew to use imported material and often to serve predominantly home markets, as with Shotton or Port Talbot. Yet others, such as Cardiff or Newport, were built from the start to be integrated and depend on imported ore. The Teesside works, originally raw material oriented to the local Cleveland ore, proved ideally situated to switch to imported ore. Indeed, over the last fifteen years or so there has been a major shift by the whole industry from home ore supplies to the richer and purer ores from overseas. From 1962 to 1977 home ore production fell by some three-quarters, whereas in the same period the tonnage of imported ore went up by 40 per cent. Yet, from almost twenty ore ports in the early 1960s, ore handling has been concentrated at four major terminals—Port Talbot, Redcar, Immingham and, completed in 1979, Hunterston. Britain still satisfies most of its own coking coal requirements, though some coals of better quality have been imported since 1970.

From 1967 the bigger works producing bulk products were nationalized as the British Steel Corporation (B.S.C.). A large number of smaller works, though none of them integrated, remained in private hands. The B.S.C. inherited too many plants, including twenty-one integrated works. Realizing the need to concentrate its output in fewer facilities to gain the scale economies from new equipment in locations more directly linked with very large capacity terminals handling imported ore, the corporation attempted in its *Ten Year Development Strategy,* 1972, to concentrate integrated steel making in only five locations by the mid-1980s. These were necessarily a compromise with existing distributions of plant. The locations chosen were Port Talbot, Llanwern (Newport), Scunthorpe, Lackenby-Redcar (south Teesside) and Ravenscraig (Motherwell). Shrinking home demand and growing B.S.C. financial problems in a setting of chronic world depression, spiralling development costs, and long delays resulting from opposition to plant closure, had so jepardized the rationalization scheme by 1978 that the corporation was settling for a compromise plan. Although this is less disturbing in the short run, it is for that very reason likely to be highly unsatisfactory in the longer term. By the end of 1977, B.S.C. had reduced its number of integrated works to twelve. By early 1980 the number was to fall to seven—the Consett and Normanby Park works (Scunthorpe) surviving as well as the five sites of the 1972 strategy. In a world of giant plants, producing common grades of steel, this is still too large a number of works for an internationally viable industry, particularly since the B.S.C. has now reduced its target production level for the early 1980s to no more than 30 million tons.

British steel producers, mainly serving a mature domestic economy, are in a slow growth industry. In 1977 crude steel output at 20.5 million tons was 17.4 per cent less than in 1966, and only 93.2 per cent higher than in 1938. In comparison, world output in 1977 was 433 per cent greater than the 1938 level, and, in spite of world recession, 42 per cent greater than in 1966. In the world depression conditions of 1977 and 1978, the E.E.C. Commission was actively trying to restrict competition between members by securing restrictions upon Community output.

13.5.2 *The Shipbuilding Industry in a National Context*

Although it is now quite eclipsed in national standing by the automobile industry, shipbuilding is the typical assembly trade. It therefore provides a large market for a range of supply trades, and above all is associated with marine engineering and with portions of the heavy steel industry (notably the plate and angle mills). Partly because of the high level of organization, partly because of the size of product, both firms and plant in the industry are fairly large. Between 1966 and 1972 the number of important firms in British shipbuilding fell from twenty-seven to eleven, and by 1977 all were included within British Shipbuilders. The number of yards has not declined as much, though increases in the size of ships point strongly to the need for further concentration.

To a very large extent British shipbuilding is concentrated in the peripheral areas of the country, notably on the three estuaries of the North East, on the Clyde, on the Lagan, at Barrow and at Birkenhead. Though ship repairing exists there, shipbuilding has never been of great importance in South Wales. Within these main centres there has been much pruning of work forces, the closure of many yards and sometimes the elimination of shipbuilding altogether from once important locations such as Hartlepool and Blyth. Elsewhere shipbuilders and repairers have suffered not only from remoteness from their component and steel suppliers, but also by lack of Development Area assistance, so that Hull, for instance, (a secondary shipbuilding centre) has been severely hit, as has Bristol (a ship repairer).

Within the Assisted Areas, shipbuilding often has a status which is now out of all proportion to its relative economic importance; notably is this so on the Clyde. Yet, in the Northern region (which includes Vickers at Barrow, as well as the north eastern yards) shipbuilding and marine engineering still employ as many as chemicals or metal manufacture (48,300, 50,900 and 48,900 respectively in 1974). Moreover, the industry makes a further regional impact through the supply trades—a wide range of engineering activities, electrical and instrument equipment manufacture, and steel (at least half a million tons of steel a year), to mention only a few.

The need for rationalization in British shipbuilding has long been recognized. In the 1930s draconian measures were adopted to try to reduce the over-capacity. The Geddes Report of 1966 stressed the need for mergers into regional groups and economies to be derived from concentration of production and from specialization. In 1967 the Shipbuilding Industry Board was set up to make loans and grants to assist the rationalization process. Although no new yards were built—indeed no new major shipyard has been built in Britain for fifty-five years, in which time scale the types of ship required and method of building have been largely revolutionized—some big investments have been made in new facilities, notably steel yards and fabricating facilities. Despite these investments, productivity remains low by international standards. Apart from during the two world wars, during which United States capacity was greatly extended, the United Kingdom was the world's leading shipbuilder until the mid-1950s. In 1913 her yards launched 57.9 per cent of the world's tonnage, and in 1936 to 1938 they managed 36 per cent of a smaller world figure. In 1950 the United Kingdom share was still 38 per cent and in 1955 almost 27 per cent. But in the following year Japan established a lead which it has never lost. By 1971 Britain launched only 5.1 per cent of the world total, ranking her fourth. In short, in no other major industry has Britain's relative decline been so great. Perhaps even more startling, as opposed to most other British industries, and even such a crisis-ridden one as steel, output in shipbuilding is less than it was sixty years ago.

By 1977, when British Shipbuilders was formed, estimates of the proportion of the British industry that would survive the next few years varied from as little as 30 per cent to as much as 70 per cent. Because of the cyclical nature of the demand for new shipping, it is difficult to plan for rational closure, and the incidence of depression falls unevenly—between 1972 and 1976, for instance, out of seven major companies, three increased their employment and four slimmed down their workforce. E.E.C. rationalization programmes and attempts at agreeing a world policy—in part frustrated not only by established builders but also by new Third World entrants to the trade—complicate national efforts to shape a more efficient industry. A final indication of the industry's changing status (and one with major and obvious regional implications) is that, whereas in the early 1920s shipbuilding and ship repairing employed over 250,000 while employment in motor vehicles, cycles and aircraft together was under 200,000, by the mid-1970s employment in the motor industry alone was in the range 400,000-450,000 but British Shipbuilders found work for no more than 82,000 men.

13.5.3 *The Chemical Industry in a National Context*

Among British basic, bulk-reducing industries, the chemical sector has been a notable exception in being a major growth activity over the last decade. As opposed to steel making or shipbuilding, or even the automobile industries, chemical manufacture is notoriously difficult to define, its products ranging from bulk acid or alkali to plastic and yarns, metal products, pharmaceuticals, pesticides and paints. At its heavy end, capital outlay is large and firms tend to be very big. Not surprisingly, therefore, the industry contains some of the largest businesses in Britain, such as I.C.I., Shell and B.P. A multitude of small firms exist in the myriad lines at the lighter end of the trade, though many of the biggest concerns spread over the whole range. With rapid product innovation, entry into the lighter, less capital-intensive, more research-oriented end is easy, but new firms cannot easily make their way into heavy chemicals. In soda ash, for instance, no new company has made a long-term, successful independent entry since the modern processes were introduced into Britain in the 1870s.

A large range of lighter or fine chemicals and of those directly supplied to the public at large depend on a limited range of mass produced chemicals basic to the whole structure—'building blocks' as they have been called. Such products are sulphuric acid, soda ash, caustic soda, ammonia and ethylene. These in turn are the products of the bulk reduction of minerals, many of them imported (such as crude oil, sulphur, phosphate and potash), while others are derived from home mineral fields (as with salt, now almost wholly derived from Cheshire, gypsum, limestone, fluorspar and, with the beginning of mining in Cleveland, potash). Coal chemicals are much less important than a decade or so ago, though N.C.B. and B.S.C. coke ovens do still provide them. Heavy chemicals, the base of the ever-increasing pyramid of the industry, are raw material or break-of-bulk point oriented, though this locational principle is modified by the inheritance of past patterns. This, for instance, helps explain why Merseyside is such a major centre of the industry, even though the original basis for its importance, the Leblanc alkali process, began to be superseded there 100 years ago and was entirely given up well before 1930. Diversity of feed stock, as well as the existence of a number of distinct companies, also complicates the locational picture.

Overall the chemical industry is widely distributed through Britain. Lighter chemicals are well represented in the London area, in Lancashire and in mid-Scotland. But the leading two centres of British heavy chemical manufacture are Teesside and the Mersey basin. Added to this pattern over the last twenty years has been a growth of a major petrochemical industry, naphtha becoming the common base for a range of what were formerly distinguished as inorganic and organic chemicals. Usually the petrochemical plants are near to the oil refineries, as at Fawley, south Humberside, Heysham or Belfast. By reason of remoteness from markets and site difficulties, however, three of the four refineries at Milford Haven have no locally associated petrochemical production, while, conversely, Avonmouth's important concentration of petrochemicals has no local refinery, though it has pipeline links to Fawley and Merseyside refineries. On Teesside the oil-refining industry is at least in part derived from the established chemical trades.

As opposed to many basic industries, there seems no reason to doubt the future buoyancy of the chemical industry. Even so, its growth rate in Britain is low by world standards. Thus, 1966-1975, world sulphuric acid output increased by over a third but British output remained virtually unchanged. Over a similar period world output of nitrogen fertilizer almost trebled but in Britain the increase was well under 100 per cent. Productivity in British chemicals is low—in 1978 I.C.I. was reckoned to have an annual sales value per employee of £23,000, as compared with £30,000 to £35,000 for main continental competitors, and £35,000 to £45,000 in the United States. On the other hand, wages in Britain are also low—less than half those of German chemical workers. Over recent years British leading chemical firms have invested heavily in plants overseas, notably in the E.E.C. and the United States. Greater international trading, and world over-capacity which seems likely to last into the early 1980s (particularly that within the E.E.C.), suggest that part of the British chemical consumption may be met in the future from overseas; certainly overseas markets for products made by British companies in home plants may fall. Even so, to the benefit of Britain's problem regions, the chemical industry is likely to remain a growth sector, though the ever-increasing capital/employment ratio indicates that the benefits in terms of new jobs may be small—indeed a dynamic chemical industry is all too often associated with a shrinking workforce. This certainly is the case on Teesside, to which attention is now turned.

13.5.4 *Cleveland*

Cleveland was traditionally an extremely narrow-based economy. Until the inter-war years, iron and steel was dominant with a little associated but very subsidiary shipbuilding and engineering. Since the 1920s, the chemical industries have grown to become a second and equally important industrial base alongside steel, and by the mid-1970s almost one-third of the workforce of the new county was employed either by the British Steel Corporation or by Imperial Chemical Industries. Both are involved in major additional investments and extensions to their capacity; in terms of employment, however, a slimming down rather than growth is the leading theme.

Teesside has the largest share of the steel industry of the North East, Consett being the only producer of any significance away from the estuary. The most distinctive products of Teesside have long been plate and heavy structural steels. Throughout the century, and notably after major investments were made there in the early 1960s (first with a completely new integrated works, and then with major pipe capacity), Hartlepool has been an important centre of the trade. However, the B.S.C. early took the view that activity should be concentrated increasingly on south Teesside, where Lackenby already had major capacity; and later they planned major investments in the whole production sequence there, based on iron making near to the new Redcar ore terminal with its ability to handle vessels of 150,000 d.w.t. In 1973 the steel-making tonnage projected for Teesside was put at 12.5 million tons. Plans have been delayed and revised downwards since then, but Teesside is still prospectively the largest national focus of integrated steel-making capacity, with one-third of the British total. Hartlepool (and Consett also) are to retain some finishing operations. By early 1978, half of the Hartlepool workforce of 3,000 had been made redundant with the closure of iron and steel making and primary rolling. B.S.C. has plans to replace Hartlepool's plate mill with a 2 million ton mill at Redcar, but recession caused first a scaling down of this project and then its postponement, so that for

Table 13.1 Northern region: employment by major divisions, 1975
(% of total employment)

	Cleveland	Durham	Northumberland	Tyne and Wear	(Cumbria)	Northern region
Engineering and allied industries	22.6	19.8	9.7	20.5	(15.8)	19.4
Other manufacturing	19.7	14.9	15.6	13.7	(22.7)	16.4
Mining, quarrying and gas, electricity and water	1.4	' 10.1	13.8	5.2	(2.8)	5.5
Services	46.3	45.8	48.6	53.3	(49.3)	49.7

Source: C.S.O., *Regional Statistics*, **13**, 1977.

some time the Hartlepool plate mill will continue to operate on slabs brought from Lackenby. This has naturally been a relief to heavily afflicted Hartlepool, though at the same time a blow to the heavy plant equipment makers a few kilometres away in Stockton. Because of current B.S.C. difficulties, the depressed state of the world markets, and E.E.C. wishes to exercise a stricter control over capacity, the extension of south Teesside from 5 million tons of steel per year up to even 10 million tons seems likely to be delayed for a number of years. Yet in spite of all the current difficulties, any reasonable assessment of future steel making there must conclude that it has site, assembly and marketing conditions (particularly for European sales) which could enable it to be of world rank in size and competitiveness.

The heavy chemical industry is also expanding its production capacity on Teesside, as indeed it has done consistently for thirty years; but its workforce continues to fall. Northern region chemicals employment declined between 1970 and 1975 from 59,000 to 50,000. By 1978 a handful of chemical companies were investing a total of some £1 billion in developments on Teesside, but there will be very small gain in jobs. On Seal Sands, for example, Monsanto was spending £180 million on a new plant that would provide no more than 4,200 permanent jobs. I.C.I. in 1976 employed some 25,000 in the North East—about 5,000 less than at one time—and its £250 million investment programme was expected to provide 5,000 construction jobs in the Cleveland area over the years 1976-1978; but there were fears in some quarters that the same investment programme could reduce the company's permanent northern workforce by as much as 25 per cent over five years (T.U.C., 1978). The two main foci of heavy chemicals production on Teesside are Billingham, established fifty-five years ago, and Wilton, built immediately after World War II. The two works are linked by a complex of pipes which provide for the interchange of large tonnages of intermediate products. In tonnage terms the main inputs are natural gas and oil, but others of importance are sulphur, phosphates and potash. Both plants have a complex output, but Billingham is above all distinguished by its production of ammonia and fertilizers, whilst Wilton is the biggest unit in Britain for ethylene and derivative chemical products including plastics. The Teesside plants exchange semi-products with other regions—notably the great chemical focus of Merseyside, and more recently Grangemouth which receives ethylene from a new joint I.C.I./B.P. facility. From the viewpoint of regional economic growth, however, the further processing within the area of the bulk chemicals which Teesside produces in such large quantities is highly desirable. The needs of the petrochemical industry, as well as the wider energy needs of a major industrial region and the obvious assets of its estuary, have made Teesside into an important centre of oil refining, with operations by both Shell and Phillips: in 1976 the Northern region refineries dealt with 10 million tons of the national total of 146 million tons of crude oil. By the late 1970s Teesside will handle up to 40 million tons of Ekofisk crude oil annually, but will ship much of it out for refining elsewhere.

A shipbuilding industry, although one that now is active at only one yard, also exists on Teesside. Flat land, deep water, steel, engineering and shipbuilding expertise made the area suitable for oil rig and platform construction. Steel and chemical plant manufacture also characterize the conurbation. Thus Cleveland has built up and is maintaining a notable tradition as a major national focus of heavy industry. This has meant the persistence of a very one-sided employment structure, notably a lack of jobs for women. Light industries have moved in in recent years, largely to industrial estates located widely throughout the county. This type of development has been helped by an impressive if long overdue improvement in its roads, both within the conurbation and outside. A traditional deficiency in service industries has also been in part made good so that by the mid-1970s about 52 per cent of the Cleveland workforce was in services. Office employment, particularly deficient in the past, is now making headway. Barclaycard have a regional centre in Cleveland, and in a bigger development the government's Property Services Agency will bring in some 3,500 jobs over the next few years. By 1978, to boost the office side of its diversification campaign, Cleveland county was pressing for Special Development Area status for service employment only. The county has a twenty-year plan to create 750 new jobs a year, mainly in the light manufacturing and service sector. But even if this programme is successful, Teesside will remain above all a heavy industrial area.

The urban fabric of Cleveland bears strong evidence of its industrial history. There is much drabness still, and much interweaving of housing, often of poor quality, with unsightly industry or industrial relics. There has, however, been much progress in recent years. Massive new housing estates and new bypasses—for instance, at Eston—combined with new plant construction had helped by 1978 to reclaim about one-tenth of the land area within the county that was identified as in need of clearance as recently as 1974. Because of its growth around a large number of major industrial plants, there are many distinct nodes of population, but none of them has been big enough or dominant enough in the past to develop the metropolitan role so clearly as in the case of Newcastle. In size and location, Middlesbrough is clearly the focal point of the urban region, but significant central area redevelopment there did not begin until 1970 and has still far to go. Older, originally market town foci like Stockton, with its excellent shopping facilities, and (much lower down the scale) Guisborough compete successfully with Middlesbrough; and many other places have been more enterprising in the early development of new shopping centres, like Billingham and Thornaby.

Hartlepool is physically separate from the rest of Cleveland, though industrial developments begun in the 1960s and 1970s have been rapidly filling up the area between. In 1968 it remained outside the new Teesside county borough; but in 1974 it was included in Cleveland county. It has suffered very severely from industrial contraction—in shipbuilding, paper, engineering and more recently in steel. Some smaller new employers of labour—for instance, packaging and refrigerator production—have been attracted onto former steel sites with help from B.S.C. Industry, the corporation's industrial diversification subsidiary. Hartlepool has also built up some eminence as a timber port. Even so, unemployment rates in the town are invariably high by Cleveland and by North Eastern standards generally; in spring 1978 the unemployment rate for men in Hartlepool was 17 per cent.

13.5.5 *Wearside*

Though it is quite different in economic structure, the recent economic and employment history of Wearside has in some ways been similar to that of Hartlepool. Both have unemployment rates higher than those of the bigger population agglomerations nearby; both have lost firms and employment in their basic trades; both suffer from the effects of public perceptions which caricature them as old industrial areas, lying away from the main foci of development in the North East region.

Wearside has a difficult site. Housing, offices, civic buildings and industry (still including some coal mining within the old Sunderland county borough boundary) are closely intermingled, and crowd the narrow and entrenched estuary of the river Wear. The most distinctive trade is still shipbuilding. Site conditions are extremely difficult; yet, surprisingly, the two firms which survived to be nationalized in 1977 have had a high degree of commercial success. Since the early 1970s the yards at the mouth of the river have specialized in the serial production of small general purpose vessels, particularly the famous SD14. Well before the formation of British Shipbuilders, the old Doxford and Sunderland group levelled completely and rebuilt their main yard on the south bank. Clearly such a development was desirable to the extent that it cut costs and preserved both direct employment and ancillary work. Whether it has contributed to the long-term health and survival of British shipbuilding is perhaps more doubtful. Forty-five kilometres (28 miles) away on the north side of the Tees estuary—within commuting distance—are ideal sites for assembly-line type layout leading to deep-water berthage, an arrangement which is so wanting in British shipbuilding (and which elsewhere in the troubled world of shipbuilding has proved to be a means of attaining the highest efficiency); yet the opportunity to relocate the industry was missed.

Since the late 1930s, Wearside has attracted new industries to diversify its old shipping, shipbuilding and engineering activities and image. By 1970 industrial estates at Pallion, Southwick and Hendon employed over one-quarter of the manufacturing workforce on Wearside. In the course of the 1970s, however, some of its well-known firms, such as Rolls-Royce and Plessey, have had to cut down their workforces, making the diversification attained less impressive than it seemed a few years earlier. In consequence, too, unemployment rates remained high. In March 1978, when male unemployment in Newcastle was 7 per cent, it was almost 15 per cent in Sunderland.

Sunderland is a relatively important shopping centre, substantially serving the borough's population of 217,000. Although there has been some attractive development, there is much that is drab, road access in a constricting physical setting is often difficult, and a Victorian legacy is still prominent in the city centre. The service sector is small. Today, as throughout its modern industrial and urban development, Wearside is overshadowed by its near neighbour, Tyneside.

13.5.6 *Tyneside*

Whilst the older staple trades are conspicuously dominant on the Tees, and shipbuilding and even coal mining are still obtrusive on Wearside, Tyneside's old staples like coal, steel and heavy chemicals are either completely or almost completely gone. Shipbuilding, the most prominent member of the group to survive, is found only well down the river. With a 1971 conurbation population of 804,000, Tyneside's economy and social structure is altogether bigger and more diverse than that of the other estuarine conurbations of the North East.

The largest single category of employment is in the very broad class of 'engineering and electrical engineering'; it employed a little over twice as many as shipbuilding and marine engineering in the late 1960s. Much of the engineering is in a multitude of small firms, but some of the bigger ones have suffered severe setbacks in recent years. A spectacular example is the former great armament and heavy engineering complex of Vickers-Armstrong, strung out between the Tyne above the bridges and the Scotswood Road. This plant is now a mere shadow of its old glory and importance as a source of employment for that section of the conurbation. Electrical engineering has also taken severe blows. With the crisis of over-capacity in British heavy electrical engineering, Reyrolle at Hebburn, Parsons at Heaton and Clarke Chapman at Gateshead (and on Teesside Whessoe and Head Wrightson) have all suffered from shrinking orders. They have had to cut their workforces accordingly. At their peak in the 1960s, both Reyrolle and Parsons employed 10,000; but by the crisis conditions of 1976/1977 Parsons was cutting back from a 6,000 job level. In 1977 a 'defensive' merger of Reyrolle (transformers and switchgear), Parsons (turbine generators) and Clarke Chapman (boiler making—but also much else including locomotives, cranes and marine equipment) was agreed. Orders for the Drax 'B' power station—on government insistence placed in advance of demand in order to boost jobs in the plant equipment industry—maintained employment prospects at Parsons, but at the expense of jobs lost at G.E.C.'s Trafford Park (Manchester) works. For a long-term, internationally viable turbine generator industry, however, there is wide agreement that a merger between G.E.C. and Parsons is essential. Inevitably this will be followed by rationalization, and by further redundancy at Heaton.

Tyneside shipbuilding was rationalized in the second half of the 1960s, with the merger of all yards into the control of Swan Hunter and the concentration of central services at the main yard of Wallsend. The smaller yards at Walker, Hebburn and South Shields still built specialized vessels as opposed to Wallsend's concentration on oil tankers; and, in addition to shipbuilding and its associated activities, there are major ship repair yards at North Shields, Hebburn and Wallsend. Conditions for the construction of very large vessels are not good on the Tyne. But the upheaval which a transfer of this activity elsewhere would entail suggests that, though there will be some slimming down and even further closures under British Shipbuilders, there will not be a wholesale transfer of shipbuilding away from the district. On the other hand, world recession and difficult labour relations have hit it severely. In the winter of 1977/1978 inter-union difficulties caused Swan Hunter to lose a large, British-subsidized shipbuilding order for Poland. The almost immediate result was redundancy for one-eighth of the firm's 9,000 workforce. British Shipbuilders have established their national headquarters in Newcastle, though the region's claim for it was long disputed with Merseyside.

The Port of Tyne has been of declining importance for many years, and each fall in its

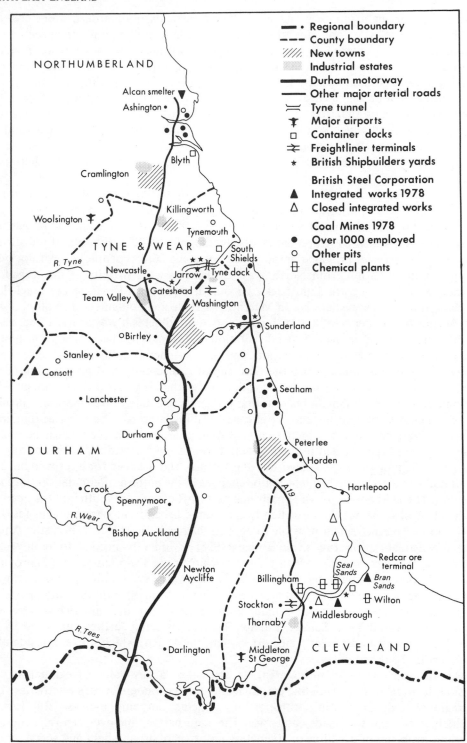

Figure 13.2 North East England: the economic core

traffic makes the maintenance of its services and particularly of a deep-water channel more difficult. The once dominant coal trade survives now only in a nominal sense; and oil handling, which replaced it, has fallen away as rail bulk shipments from Teesside refineries have increased. Tyne Dock (South Shields) was one of the chief iron ore importing docks in Britain into the 1970s, but the transfer of ore handling to Redcar, even for the supply of Consett, has caused the loss of that trade and its revenue. A plan for a direct reduction iron plant on reclaimed land at Jarrow Slake, sponsored by a group of private firms, and which would have needed 0.8 million tons of ore a year (and so have kept the Tyne Dock terminal operational), was shelved in 1977 as a result of the world recession in steel. The decline in the status of the Tyne as a port, therefore, goes on.

The economy of Tyneside is, however, diversified by a wide range of manufacturing. There are a number of important industrial estates, particularly around the fringes of the conurbation. Of these the oldest and largest is Team Valley (Gateshead), the pioneering trading estate for British Development Areas. By the mid-1970s, a diversity of industries, warehouses and services provided employment for some 20,000 people, drawn not only from the conurbation but from North West Durham as well. In spite of the spread of these new and often growth industries, the outlying parts of Tyneside are much less prosperous than its Newcastle core. In March 1978, male unemployment in Wallsend and North Shields was 12 per cent, and in Jarrow and South Shields it was nearly 15 per cent.

Another new element in the industrial evolution of Tyneside has been the establishment of new towns beyond the conurbation and its peripheral industrial estates. Two, Killingworth and Cramlington, are the outcome of city, county and private enterprise; the other, Washington new town, is a creation under the New Towns Act, though with many new concepts of design and layout that reflect its late date of designation. The new towns provide overspill housing and are already fulfilling impressive new service functions for their sub-regions, notably in the case of Washington. With their construction, a further stage has been reached in the evolving form of the Tyneside conurbation.

The changing pattern of workplace and of residence, and the need for improved links to the national economy, have brought major changes in the pattern of circulation since the mid-1960s. The Durham motorway link brings fast traffic from the south into the heart of Gateshead. Across the river, an excellently engineered urban road system makes fast but largely unobtrusive movement possible to beyond the northern edge of Newcastle. A new bridge downstream from the Tyne Bridge (1928) is urgently needed to remove the bottleneck at the river crossing. Much further downriver the Tyne Tunnel (1967) provides the first link, other than by water, between the Durham and Northumberland shores, with fast connecting roads to the Durham motorway and the A1 in Northumberland providing a bypass around the conurbation's main built-up areas. By the mid-1970s there was pressure for a second Tyne Tunnel. Finally, Tyneside is being further integrated by an impressive new urban passenger transport system, the Metro, which makes considerable use of existing British Rail track.

Newcastle and its neighbouring districts also have a key role in regional service provision, in warehousing, in public employment and in commercial office activities. The new regional and conurbation transport investments can only increase still further Tyneside's attractions to outside enterprise. The conurbation, and even central Tyneside, has serious problems of declining or stagnating industry, of urban blight and social service provision; but its primacy within the region, and the viability if not the buoyancy of its economy, can never be in doubt.

13.6 Regional Subservience, Rationalization and Political Influences

In the nineteenth century the North East, like Scotland (Wales provides a much less positive case), was a major generator of its own sustained economic growth, through local innovation, finance and entrepreneurship. The control functions—the headquarters—of the new enterprises were in the region. Even into the twentieth century, when regional growth slowed, most amalgamations of formerly independent firms left control in the region (though there were exceptions as with the formation of I.C.I. and of Vickers-Armstrong). In the last twenty years or so, in contrast, economic reconstruction has largely been associated with the arrival of firms from elsewhere, and their headquarters have usually remained outside the North East. At the same time, with the nationalization of the ownership of basic industries, other control functions have been moved away from the region. Despite the N.C.B.'s regional offices in Team Valley, therefore, major decisions about coal mining, once taken by regional companies at their Newcastle headquarters, are now handed down from Hobart House in London. British Steel has its headquarters next door to the N.C.B. in Grosvenor Place. With British Shipbuilders, Tyneside has been fortunate to gain a nationalized industry's headquarters. Generally speaking, however, major decision taking about the North East has been moved from it. Not only has this left civic leaders in the region with a sense of having lost control of their future, but to some degree it has impoverished the social structure and hence the quality of social life there.

Regional regeneration is faced with another and associated problem. The rationalization of industry now increasingly takes place within a national framework, and in many respects this is a highly desirable development. Unfortunately, it can also expose a region's employment situation to political pressures which may have somewhat perverse effects. The North East provides many examples of these. In 1977, it was announced that the Central Electricity Generating Board would build the £600 million Drax 'B' power station. After political pressure from the North East, Parsons of Heaton were given the £125 million order for the station's turbines. This benefited Parson's Heaton labour force, already seriously depleted in recent years, but only at a very high public cost. A direct employment cost was in jobs lost at the rival G.E.C. plant at Trafford Park. Another cost, more widely spread throughout the nation, will be in the extra charges to electricity consumers to compensate the C.E.G.B. for building the new capacity at least two years before it is needed. Yet another collateral effect will be the earlier closure of older generating plants which effectively represents a transfer of unemployment from the plant making industry to the electricity supply industry. Perhaps even more serious is the fear that, as a result of the decision, an essential rationalization of the turbine generator business in Britain has been postponed for several more years. Thus were Parsons' stability and employment in the North East dearly bought. At the same time, 1977, inter-regional and inter-union rivalries were operating decisively against the North East. Negotiations with north eastern interests had led Hitachi to decide on Washington as the location for a new plant to produce colour television sets. Unions elsewhere in Britain, however, opposed this Japanese invasion. They secured the opposition of firms such as Mullard which would lose trade and jobs; they caused political uncertainty in Whitehall; and eventually Hitachi decided not to go ahead.

There is a further dimension of political disquiet, if not weakness, about the North East. This is its position compared with Wales and Scotland, both of which have been afforded a voice in Cabinet plus a variety of development instruments that are denied to the English region. As a result, there have been expressions in recent years of a wish for a greater degree of regional autonomy, and particularly for a Northern Development Agency, a body which would probably serve the North West and Yorkshire and Humberside as well as the North East. Alternatively, it has been suggested that the National Enterprise Board might become a more effective catalyst for development in these English regions. Over the years the North East has benefited considerably from national intervention in employment location and regional economic growth and welfare. Even so, many now believe that a greater devolution of economic power and initiative might serve the region's interests more effectively.

13.7 Regional Prospects

The North East has two clear-cut growth foci—Teesside for heavy, capital-intensive industry, with scope for the planned diversification of a narrow range of traditional activities; and Tyneside as a much bigger metropolitan core. Darlington, with good road links to both, and poised as the 'gateway' between the 'Durham growth corridor' and the midland and southern economy of Britain, is a third yet smaller growth node. Other concentrations of population such as Hartlepool or Wearside seem likely to grow less impressively or may stagnate; in any case they will present continuing problems to regional economic planners and local authority development officers. Surrounding these nodes, some parts of the coalfield will retain population or even grow, mainly because of commuting to the nodes, but also because of stabilizing colliery employment and (in the East Durham growth zone) the area's intrinsic attractions for manufacturing investment stemming from a new road-based accessibility. In the rest of the coalfield, more remote from the nodes and away from the main lines of movement, employment and population will continue to drift downwards, a decline eased here and there by a new advance factory or another industrial estate. Yet further afield lies the rural North East, sparsely populated, ignored in the perceptions of a wider world in their image of 'the North', but for those who know it providing aesthetic compensation for all the difficulties and all the scars of the rest. Clearly, however, this can be little consolation to those in distressed West Durham or Wearside communities.

The North East must continue to struggle with the disadvantage of its small-sized and narrowly-based economy. However, it has the asset of a good position on the North Sea front of Britain, having particularly well-established links with Scandinavia, and (compared with other Development Areas) an advantageous sea access to the countries of the E.E.C. As yet there is little sign in any of the indices of regional health that it has made or is approaching a breakthrough into calmer economic circumstances. But neither can anyone surveying the major new industrial developments, the large-scale urban renewal and the new transport facilities continue to think of the region as merely a 'depressed area'.

REFERENCES

Durham County Council (1951). *Development Plan,* and subsequent revisions, D.C.C., Durham.
House, J.W. (1969). *The Industrial North East,* David & Charles, Newton Abbot.
Northern Economic Development Council Annual Report and occasional reports.
Northern Economic Planning Council (1966). *Challenge of the Changing North,* H.M.S.O., London.

Northern Economic Planning Council (1969). *Outline Strategy for the North,* H.M.S.O., London.
Northern Region Strategy Team Reports (1977). Newcastle.
Teesside Survey and Plan (1969). *Teesplan,* H.M.S.O., London.
T.U.C. (1978). Report prepared by the Northern Regional Council of the T.U.C.

CHAPTER 14

Scotland

KENNETH WARREN

14.1 Introduction

Scotland covers more than one-third of the land area of Britain, but its population is only 9.4 per cent of the national total. Because of its size, remoteness, and distinctive political history, Scotland combines more economic and political autonomy than any of the other older industrial areas. Nevertheless, its economy is small by the standards of the city-regions of southern England and has always been heavily dependent upon English and overseas demands. Moreover, it is an economy that has become increasingly internationalized. By the late 1960s, of 618 privately owned firms in Scotland employing over 200 people, 47 per cent had their headquarters in Scotland, 47 per cent in England and 12 per cent overseas. The exploitation of North Sea oil may have given Scotland a new economic self-confidence, but it has been at the cost of a further increase in the already substantial foreign control of its economy. Another result of North Sea oil has been the growing danger of over-ambition, of unrealistic hopes for the economic future of the nation.

As with other Development Areas, the most obvious source of weakness of the Scottish economy has been its traditional industrial structure, and its continuing overdependence on old basic trades which have been contracting in their output, their geography and their employment. Persistent attempts have been made to deal with these problems over the last forty years. Even so, into the mid-1970s unemployment rates remained high by national standards, activity rates and wages were low, and net out-migration persisted on a considerable scale. In more recent years, however, there has been growing evidence of a relative improvement in the standing of Scotland within the British economy. In the mid-1960s the rate of Scottish unemployment was commonly twice that of the national average; by 1978, however, with oil developments well under way, the proportion was much reduced with the Scottish unemployment rate only 36 per cent higher than that of Britain as a whole. Similarly, in 1965 the wages of manual workers in Scotland stood at 74.2 per cent of the United Kingdom average; by 1977 they were above the national average at 100.9 per cent.

Some three-quarters of Scotland's population and 80 per cent of its industry are located in less than 9 per cent of its area, the central industrial belt. At its most extreme this extends some 145 kilometres (90 miles) from Kilmarnock to Dundee; at its mid-Clyde to Musselburgh core, it is less than 100 kilometres (60 miles) long. Its width is no more than 50 kilometres at any point. In the midst of this belt, between Scotland's largest centres of population, is the old nineteenth-century heart of the Scottish manufacturing economy, the coal-iron-engineering complex which spreads from the Forth to the mid-Clyde. Much of the nation's modern economic development may be seen as an attempt not only to diversify and replace this old industry, but, looked at spatially, as an attempt to move the centre of activity from the interior to the coast, against a long and not unsuccessful rearguard action from Lanarkshire. One aspect of North Sea oil exploitation has been to take the growth focus of Scotland outside this region altogether for the first time.

14.2 The Traditional Industrial Base of Central Scotland

Of the old, basic trades, coal has declined rapidly and shifted greatly in location; steel is being rationalized but, though its locations are being reduced in number, the old sub-regional concentration is being reaffirmed; and shipbuilding, already largely reconstructed, has moved down the Clyde. New industries have been an inadequate replacement for these staple trades.

14.2.1 Coal

Changes in output and the national standing of the Scottish coal industry have been marked. There has been a steady decline since 1913, the year of peak production. In the crisis years following 1958, output of Scottish coal declined more than that of Britain as a whole. As late as 1945 Scottish pits produced about 22 million tons of coal annually, or 11.7 per cent of the national output; in 1976/1977 its 9 million tons was only 8.4 per cent of the N.C.B. total. Employment at the latter date was only 23,000. Financial losses per ton of coal mined were, in the mid-1970s, some three times those of the national average. Not only has production declined, but it has undergone very substantial changes of distribution (Figure 14.1). In 1910, Lanarkshire produced 58.5 per cent of the output, but as early as 1967 only 18 per cent. In 1960 there were thirty-six active collieries in the central area (between Glasgow and Bathgate and from Kilsyth south to Stonehouse); by 1978 only three of these remained. Over this period, in this section of the Scottish coalfields particularly, employment fell disastrously. Output in the outlying fields of Ayrshire, the Lothians and Alloa-Fife, on the other hand, has held up better.

Compared with British standards overall, Scottish geological conditions for mining are not good, and mechanization has lagged behind that achieved in English fields. The Longannet and Seafield pits by the Forth, Bilston Glen (a sinking of the 1960s some 6 miles south of Edinburgh) and Killoch in central Ayrshire, were by the early 1970s the only pits employing over 2,000 men. About 80 per cent of Scottish coal goes to power stations. The Kincardine and Longannet stations are well placed to use Fife and Alloa coal, and Cockenzie draws on the Midlothian pits. The second biggest market is in coke ovens, and it has long been one of the problems of Scottish heavy industry that the only areas of coking coal are in the expensive central field, notably around its north western and south eastern edges. In 1960, eleven pits produced coking coal as one of their grades; by 1978 only three were left. The N.C.B. itself has little coking capacity in Scotland, most of the coal going to British Steel Corporation ovens at Rutherglen and Ravenscraig.

14.2.2 Steel

By international standards, or even those of South Wales, the North East or Yorkshire and Humberside, the Scottish steel industry is small, and in spite of much modernization

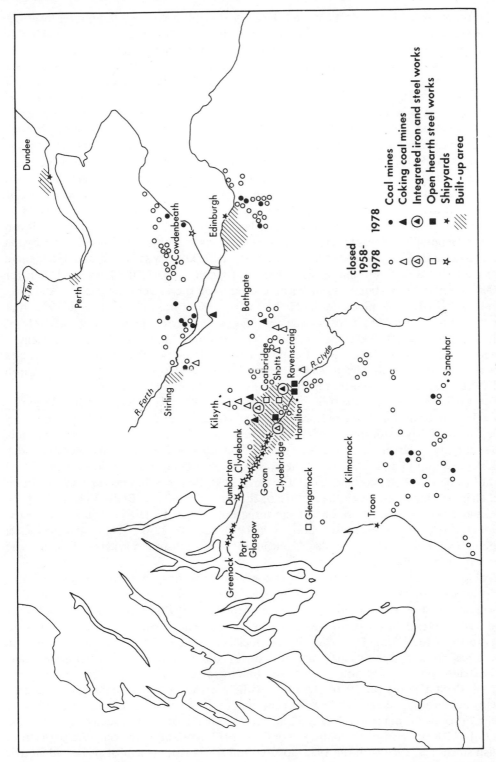

Figure 14.1 Central Scotland: changes in the location of coal, steel and shipbuilding

its plants are probably less efficient, and certainly of smaller capacity and poorer location, than those in other major districts. In fact, Scottish steel making has for long been highly anomalous. Until just before World War II, it was wholly unintegrated; and its antiquated iron industry was owned and operated separately from a much divided but more modern steel industry, which used cold metal, largely scrap. In a series of development decisions made since the 1920s the industry has compromised on its modernization. A greater degree of technical integration has been attained, many plants have been closed, but the old concentration on the East Glasgow-Coatbridge-Motherwell area has been preserved. Beginning in the late 1930s with Clyde Ironworks-Clydebridge Steelworks, and after the mid-1950s with Ravenscraig, two nuclei of integrated operations were belatedly established. There remained also a significant and high-cost cold metal operation at Glengarnock in one of the main corridors of movement between Clydeside and the central Ayrshire coast but B.S.C. closed this at the end of the '70s (Figure 14.1).

For many years Scottish steel making has been wholly dependent upon imported iron ore. The General Terminus Quay, Glasgow, which was the major ore import point by the late 1950s, cannot handle ore carriers in excess of 21,000 d.w.t. In the mid-1960s there were plans for a new terminal at Clydebank, originally for 45,000 d.w.t. and then for 65,000 d.w.t. vessels, but it soon became clear that these were too small. Attention therefore shifted to the middle of the Firth of Clyde, but it was only by the mid-1970s that work was under way there to provide the biggest ore terminal in Britain, capable of handling vessels of 300,000 d.w.t. and over. The persistent failure until this investment to develop good facilities for handling imported ore cost the Scottish industry dearly, and even though this has now been made good the desirable relocation on tidewater of iron and steel making itself appears highly unlikely in the foreseeable future.

The final weakness of Scottish steel making concerns its product mix in relation to demand. The traditional tube business does well, with demand for oil and gas pipes now added to its fairly traditional outlets. Structural steel is another long-established line. Plate, originally largely destined for shipbuilding, or for structural engineering, today suffers as shipbuilding declines, and the now much more important outlets for plate steel are not to be found in Scotland. Since the early 1960s Scotland has become an important steel strip producer, and with the closure of the hot strip mills at Ebbw Vale and (by the 1980s) at Shotton it will have one of the three hot strip mills left in Britain. However, although the local motor industry in the mid-1970s took 27-30 per cent of the steel sheet made in Scotland, much of the plant's output must go to distant markets in England and bear a high transport charge.

Problems in material assembly, processing and marketing, therefore, together imply that the Scottish steel industry is a high-cost sector of a national industry that is by international standards a costly producer. In 1976/1977, although Scotland only produced one-tenth of the crude steel made by B.S.C., it accounted for more than half the corporation's total loss. By 1978, Glengarnock was said to be losing £6 on every ton produced. Not surprisingly, the share of British production made in Scotland has fallen fairly steadily. In its traditional, scattered, unintegrated form the industry made 23 per cent of Britain's steel in 1920. By 1951, with integration and rationalization in part already achieved, its share was 13.5 per cent; and by 1968, the first full year of the British Steel Corporation, output at 3.07 million tons, though 45 per cent greater than in 1951, was only 11.8 per cent of the national total. In 1977 Scotland made only 9.5 per cent of British steel. Yet, even with the 1978 closures and the postponement of projected electric arc capacity at Ravenscraig and at Hunterston, the extension of the oxygen steel plant at the former will give Scotland 14.0 per cent of British capacity in the 1980s. The danger of continuing low operating rates is obvious and serious.

The future of Scottish steel making is, therefore, in doubt. In 1954, Colvilles, the only major Scottish steel-making firm, turned its back on the prospect of a new integrated operation at tidewater and began to build the Ravenscraig works. In 1958 it was decided to add a Scottish strip mill to this plant; and in 1972, the B.S.C. announced that Ravenscraig would be developed as one of its five major integrated operations by the early 1980s, even though its indifferent location had been recognized by some senior executives in the industry (Select Committee on Nationalised Industries, Sub-committee B, 1976, p.50). Some Scottish development planners, and even former Colville executives, have urged the claims of major steelwork expansion next to the new Hunterston ore dock, and the B.S.C. has made vague promises of a major works there in the 1990s. In the meantime only direct reduction plants for making high iron content pellets are being built at Hunterston, while steel making and steel expansion remain firmly inland. Clearly, important social and physical planning considerations constrain the wholesale relocation of Scottish steel making; and every additional investment at Ravenscraig has made such a change economically less attractive in the short term. On the other hand, there can be no doubt whatsoever that the ideal location for modern Scottish steel making is at tidewater. In addition to the possibility of low, even world-ranking, costs of integrated steel making there, the bonus of green-field site development on the Firth of Clyde might generate a completely new scale of thinking, and new internationally competitive standards of associated shipbuilding as well. It might, in other words, not only have a cost-saving impact, but also provide a new vision for the Scottish economy. By 1978 there seemed no prospect of such a development.

14.2.3 *Shipbuilding*

'Whichever type of measurement is used, the performance of Scottish shipbuilding has been little short of disastrous since the mid-1950s.' This assessment of what, from many points of view, has been regarded as the most distinctive Scottish industry was made in 1971 (Johnston, Buxton and Mair, 1971, p.118). In spite of depression, closure and rationalization in the 1930s, twenty-three shipyards, capable of building 0.6 million tons annually, were still at work on the Clyde just after World War II. In the ten years to the end of the 1960s her proportion of national output declined; whereas United Kingdom ship production fell by 30 per cent, in Scotland the decrease was 40 per cent. By the early 1970s most of the yards had closed and annual output was less than 300,000 tons. Yet Scotland's share of the national employment in shipbuilding and marine engineering has remained about 20-21 per cent. From 79,000 in 1950 shipbuilding and related employment fell to 69,000 by 1960 and 42,000 by 1975. Pessimistic projections of employment for 1985 and the year 2000 offer a total of only 25,000 and 15,000 shipbuilding and related jobs, respectively (Mackay, 1977, p. 166).

Attempts to tackle the shipbuilding industry's problems have so far had only limited success. By 1967 the Clyde's seven yards were clearly divisible into two groups—those of the lower estuary centred on Scotts (Greenock) and Lithgows (Port Glasgow) and able in the 1960s to construct vessels of up to 100,000 d.w.t.; and the upper yards, at least 20 kilometres (12 miles) up-river, some of them in the heart of the conurbation (Partick and

Scotstoun, for example). The latter were unable to build big vessels and were mostly unprofitable (except for Yarrow's, preoccupied with naval work). Lithgows and Scotts merged in 1967; and a year later Stephens, Connells, Yarrow, Fairfields and John Brown formed Upper Clyde Shipbuilders (U.C.S.). Labour difficulties, low levels of productivity and inadequate coordination soon brought this group to the verge of failure, and in 1971 it collapsed with liabilities of £21 million. In 1971 Yarrow left U.C.S.; the John Brown yard was sold for oil rig construction to the American firm Marathon; and the three other firms were reconstructed as Govan Shipbuilders. In the ten years to 1977, the government had invested £100 million in the preservation of shipbuilding on the upper Clyde, where by the end of the period there were only some 5,500 jobs left in the industry. Though short of orders, by 1977 Govan Shipbuilders had two potentially efficient, reconstructed yards at Govan and Scotstoun.

On the lower Clyde, Scott Lithgows, after several years of success, was in difficulties by the mid-1970s, in part due to the collapse of a major purchaser in 1976, but also to increasing competition in a stagnant world shipbuilding market. By the end of 1976, in consequence, men were being laid off on the Clyde once again. Social as well as economic factors now dominated discussion and decision making as they had done with U.C.S. The outcome was a reluctance to contemplate further rationalization.

Clearly the problems of Scottish shipbuilding have by no means been solved. Marathon at Clydebank, for example, rescued with £12 million of government money in the 1970s, was by late 1976 wanting up to £10 million more. Moreover, it was buying many of its components overseas, so that the multiplier effect on Clydeside and mid-Scottish engineering was reduced. Govan Shipbuilders, where production is being concentrated on runs of smallish ships (26,000 d.w.t. bulk carriers and 23,000 d.w.t. general cargo vessels), have found it very difficult despite modernization to reach the targets of steel-handling productivity which were set in the early 1970s. By spring 1976, £60 million of public money had been committed to Govan Shipbuilders, but the newly-formed British Shipbuilders was faced with the likelihood of early redundancy for as much as one-fifth of the Govan workforce. With some 6,000 jobs in Clydeside shipbuilding and engineering reckoned to be at risk early in 1977, the snowball effects, and perhaps still more the psychological impact of any closure, is daunting. In these circumstances the possibilities of radical restructuring, perhaps with a completely new Firth of Clyde yard, are understandably regarded as visionary. Yet there can be little doubt that the vested interests of both the former private companies and the workers, a natural desire to avoid social disturbance, a preoccupation with short-term rather than long-term economies, and (more recently on the part of the nationalized industry) a heightened sense of social responsibility, have contributed to a failure to recognize—or to act on the recognition—of the high contemporary costs of certain locations for shipbuilding. Yet, as with steel, such a radical reshaping may provide the only way in the longer term to avoid an almost complete elimination of the industry from the Scottish, and more particularly the Strathclyde, economy. It is clear enough now that the old order cannot be maintained; the critical point is whether anything will take its place.

14.2.4 Other Basic Trades

Scotland's share in national *mechanical engineering* has also historically been large, though there have been some major contractions since the early 1960s. Between 1961 and

1971 alone, Scottish employment in mechanical engineering fell from 123,000 to 102,000 (in railway equipment manufacture, an important traditional line, the fall was from 15,000 to 4,000). Even so, in 1972, when Scotland had 8.3 per cent of the net output of all British industries, it still retained 9.1 per cent of the output of British mechanical engineering. *Textiles*, another traditional trade, has also shrunk, employment declining from 103,000 in 1961 to 76,000 ten years later. The impact in this case has been widely scattered—jute in the Dundee area, tweed and knitwear in the Borders, and Harris Tweed in the Outer Isles.

14.3 Industrial Diversification

Scotland's planning problems, even before oil exploitation compounded them, largely focused on the scale of the adjustments which had to be made in the old industries, and the fact that the growth industries to a large extent were located in other parts of the country, notably in the eastern section of the industrial belt. These foci are perhaps only 25-30 kilometres from the old industrial areas, but too far for mass daily movement to work.

14.3.1 *Electronics*

Industrial diversification began in central Scotland, as in the other Special Areas, with industrial estates built at the end of the 1930s. After the war a number of nationally known firms were persuaded to build branch plants in the Greater Glasgow area—Rolls-Royce at Hillington, Hoover at Cambuslang and Pressed Steel at Linwood (though the latter had wished to expand at Cowley). There were also some foreign branch plants in the early post-war years, but the major influx of American firms came after 1950. In this flow electronic equipment became a major new growth industry. Much has been written of the Scottish electronics industry. Its development is not an unqualified success story; indeed it highlights the strengths and weaknesses of Scotland as a host for new and technologically advanced industries, and also perhaps the limited degree to which such activities can be an answer to a country's problems. Even so, between 1961 and 1971, while employment in such traditional lines as shipbuilding and marine and mechanical engineering fell from 186,000 to 147,000, the workforce in instrument and electrical engineering went up from 42,000 to 69,000. The electronics industry is 'footloose' in the conventional sense; components and products are all valuable in relation to weight and bulk so that the costs of transport are low relative to overall costs and prices, and in consequence, so long as deliveries are reliable, locational choice is fairly free. However, agglomerative forces in the industry are strong. There are linkages between firms in the industry; local reserves of skilled labour are valuable; common training facilities are often provided; and the reputations of districts become established. (Deglomerative forces can also operate, of course—established districts can become areas of labour shortage and possibly of disturbed labour conditions.) These characteristics imply that the industry might well have been strongly attracted to Lanarkshire or Clydeside. In fact, it was East Scotland that became the important centre (Figure 14.2).

Ferranti, having developed in Edinburgh in wartime with the help of the Scottish Council, thereafter acted as an important seeder unit in the growth of the Scottish electronics industry. Later, American enterprise became of central importance, with

Honeywell and I.B.M. major employers. Labour was relatively cheap and adaptable. The pioneers provided an attraction for others and growth snowballed. This agglomerative force became a much more important factor than the early and relatively small regional incentives available in Lanarkshire. In 1949, Scottish electronics employed about 2,000 persons; by 1960, 9,000; during the 1960s growth was at twice the national rate and by early 1974 electronics employed 43,000 in Scotland. Five of the six biggest computer firms in the western world had Scottish plants by this time. However, only in exceptional cases—as at Cowdenbeath—has the new employment replaced the older shrinking trades *in situ*. Further, the jobs gained are fewer than the number lost, and over half of the workers in Scottish electronics are women.

Much of the multiplier effect of electronics development—component supply, for example—has been felt south of the border or overseas, for many of the firms were initially only assembly operations. Moreover, until recent years the industry has been preoccupied with routine production and has had a very low R & D element. By late 1971, for instance, Ferranti employed over 5,000 in Scotland but only 370 of those were graduate engineers, scientists or technologists. At the same time, fewer than ten of more than 100 electronic concerns in Scotland had R & D there, and new innovations usually took a number of years to filter through from the companies' main plants elsewhere. By the mid-1970s, however, there seems to have been a marked increase in the indigenous R & D work, and the Department of Electrical Engineering in Edinburgh University has become a major academic research focus for the industry.

Meanwhile, in line with other electronic districts of the world, there was a tendency for the industry to move into country towns—for instance, to the Borders—where there was an ample female workforce, and industrial strife was much less noticeable than in the older industrial centres. The agglomerating forces which brought the industry to Scotland still remained; but the links were becoming looser. To American firms, in this as in other trades, Scotland continued to offer the attractions of a European foothold, an English-speaking workforce, and one which is now cheap by West European standards. By 1977, 16.1 per cent of all Scottish manufacturing workers were employed by North American companies. Their share of Scottish exports has also been steadily mounting. Electronics exports are commonly 75 per cent of production, and in some plants may be over 90 per cent.

14.3.2 *The Automobile Industry*

Into the late 1920s, Scotland had an important automobile industry centred in Glasgow and Dumfries. The McKenna duties of 1916, however, cut off foreign component supplies; and remoteness from alternative West Midland sources, plus (in the mid-1920s) the introduction by English firms of mass production, almost killed the Scottish industry, except for the heavy commercial vehicle firm, Albion Motors of Scotstoun. In 1960 the government took the opportunity of an expansion phase in the British motor industry to steer important elements to Central Scotland once again, in part to provide a market for the Colville strip mill, then being built. It was also hoped that automobile production would provide a 'propulsive industry' as in Midland England and that a multiplier growth of metal and metal-fabricating activities might be built onto an initially illogical decision about the steel strip mill. Production of a new Rootes light car began at Linwood, Renfrewshire, in 1963, after the company had been reluctantly diverted from plans to

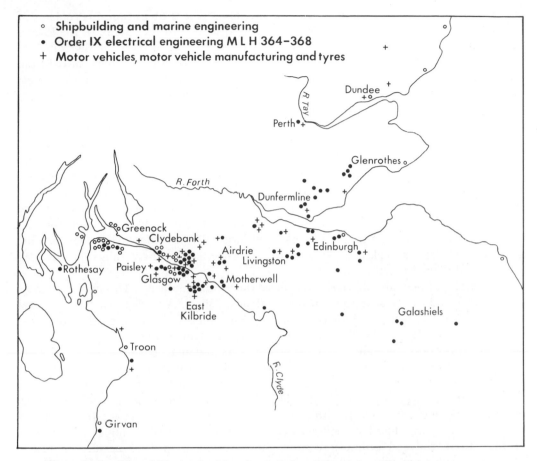

○ Shipbuilding and marine engineering
● Order IX electrical engineering M L H 364–368
+ Motor vehicles, motor vehicle manufacturing and tyres

Figure 14.2 Central Scotland: old and new industrial complexes

extend its existing plant at Ryton, Coventry. At a neighbouring Linwood works, Pressed Steel (then making railway wagon and car pressings for export) expanded to meet Rootes's needs for body pressings. Later, this works passed into Rootes's ownership. Simultaneously, in 1961, B.M.C. opened a plant at Bathgate, West Lothian, capable of assembling 50,000 commercial vehicles and 35,000 tractors annually.

The new Scottish automobile industry was variously hailed as 'an important symbol of industrial regeneration', and 'the beginning of a new era'. Yet before the end of the 1960s the industry was in distress; and in the mid-1970s was only saved by emergency government action. In 1975, the Ryder Report on British Leyland observed that 'although some progress has been made since the merger towards a more logical arrangement of manufacturing operations in the different locations, there is still too much movement of manufactured parts and sub-assemblies between plants'. Against this analysis, and in view of its remoteness, Bathgate posed real problems: in 1971 the plant's operating rate was no more than 45 per cent. At the same time, Linwood was operating at only 50 per cent of capacity and within a few years it was even more clearly at risk than Bathgate.

For both Scottish motor plants, there were problems which had little (directly) to do with location. In order to get British government approval for their takeover of Rootes,

Chrysler had to guarantee the maintenance and development of Linwood. Problems of low utilization rates there seemed initially to be largely due to the failure of the Rootes Imp car to command a mass market. In the case of trucks, progress at Bathgate was hindered by the fact that the plant was initially equipped with old machinery moved from the Midlands, and its product, too, did not readily gain consumer acceptance. Other problems were, however, related to location, either through the ingrained qualities of the Scottish business environment, or because of distance from the Midland centres of the motor trade. Labour difficulties have also been considerable. Scotland has had only limited experience with mass production activities that involve the regular discipline of the assembly line, and the training of assembly workers took longer than had been expected. Moreover, the Scottish unions proved restless after their initial acceptance of lower wage scales than those of the Midland car workers. It is significant that Albion Motors, long-established, has had a satisfactory labour record, whilst Bathgate has suffered from the fact that its largely ex-mining workforce was unused to non-stop production routine. Linwood, which had recruited its workforce largely from redeployed dock labour, averaged one strike a week in 1970, and five years later strikes there almost precipitated the death of Chrysler U.K.

Small scales of operation have also penalized the Scottish industry. This applies to most components and to car assembly. In the Midlands, fuller market knowledge, a central location, scale economies and the economies which can be derived from using 'off-cuts' (the waste products of others' operations) give component makers lower costs than in Scotland. Linwood, though in the mass car assembly market, suffered from early technical problems with its Imp car, from low capacity and from low-operating rates. By the mid-1970s it was being said that the optimum size of a British assembly plant was about 270,000 units per annum; Chrysler U.K., on the other hand, had a record output of only 281,000 units from two British assembly plants (Ryton and Linwood). Ryton was modern, well equipped and suitably located in the Midland supply complex. Yet in spite of this, for social and political reasons, the government in 1975 decided to rescue Linwood, resulting in only small redundancies there but very large ones in the Midlands. (The Central Policy Review Staff report of 1975, *The Future of the British Car Industry,* suggests a consequence of this decision will be continuing chronic under-utilization in the British motor industry as a whole.) With the government decision to put £162 million into Chrysler, it was expected that the Linwood labour force would be cut by 3,000 (from 6,900 in November 1975), but in the event the decline was only 1,350. By autumn 1977 the reconstructed Linwood operations were still only operating at about half capacity.

Locational difficulties were also associated with the need to bring components from, and to market vehicles in, southern Britain, the very conditions which led to the elimination of the pioneer Scottish motor industry. By 1970 or so, some 80 per cent of the home market for Bathgate commercial vehicles was said to be south of Birmingham, but 75 per cent of the materials for their manufacture came from the Midlands, the castings from Wellingborough and most of the rest from the West Midlands. By 1972 the extra assembly costs and shipping expenses on trucks for southern England increased Bathgate unit costs by about £58, or 3-4 per cent of the selling price (Keeble, 1976, p.191). By the late 1970s, therefore, Leyland were working to reduce this handicap—Bathgate's assembly facilities being expanded and the Albion plant, short of room for assembly, gradually becoming a major component supplier to the Bathgate works 50 kilometres away by road. Chrysler U.K. bought components from some 8,000 companies. It tried to give Linwood the benefits of bulk production by making components there for the Midlands, and by 1970 Linwood produced 95 per cent of the body pressings for all British Chrysler cars (turning out 1,800 a week for Scottish assembled units and 3,500 Avenger bodies for Coventry, delivered by rail). By the mid-1970s it also sent out gearboxes, rear axles, front suspension units and steering arms for the Avenger. But at the same time it received from the Midlands engines, gearboxes and many other components. These arrangements still embodied a cost disadvantage. Over the period 1963 to 1970, government grants, loans and premiums for Linwood totalled £5.8 million, and the additional costs of that location as compared with a Midland one were reckoned to be some £12 million. By the mid-1970s, the extra costs as compared with the English Midlands were estimated to run at £1-2 million each year. The rationalization achieved by the agreement between Chrysler U.K. and the British government in 1975/1976 gave Linwood further bulk production at the expense of worsening transport balance. The assembly of Avenger cars was moved to Linwood which meant that the flow of parts became essentially one-way; although they were balanced by the return shipment of completed cars, the latter required a different style of rolling stock. Set against these experiences, it is not at all clear how the Chrysler Corporation could agree with the British government both 'to continue operations at the [corporation's] five main sites, [and] make Chrysler UK increasingly competitive in the world market and improve its opportunities for growth and increased employment' (Varley, 1976). Along with all its other European operations, Chrysler sold its British operations to Peugeot in 1978.

Even looking optimistically at past costs and operating figures, neither Scottish motor plant can be regarded as a 'good' development economically speaking. They represent perhaps the clearest evidence of the marginality of the Scottish location in any activity which involves very large levels of output, close integration with English operations, and the supply of mass markets which are necessarily concentrated in southern Britain. Moreover, the progressive internationalization of the British motor industry (p.224ff.), especially the growing linkages between different Western European assembly plants and component sources, potentially makes Scottish operations even less competitive than they have been within a purely British setting.

14.4 Strathclyde

As the traditional industries of Scotland have declined and new ones have grown up to replace them, the geography of the country's employment has progressively changed. Simultaneously, urban and other infrastructural investments, variations in population growth and the overall impact of economic and physcial planning have all helped to shape new regional geographies within the industrial belt of Central Scotland. The largest of these is the Strathclyde region, centred upon Glasgow.

By the mid-1970s Strathclyde had over 1 million of the 2.5 million employees in Scotland, and was the core of the nation, economically and socially. It also posed Scotland's outstanding planning problem. In 1976 Strathclyde had 49 per cent of Scotland's employment and 56 per cent of that in manufacturing. Its net annual average loss by migration in the six years to 1977 was 22,000, yet by April 1978 its unemployment rate was 9.8 per cent as compared with 8.2 per cent for Scotland as a whole. Many of its industries are not only old but have low productivity. And Scotland's worst housing problem is localized in this region.

Growth, and still more growth prospects, have been moving westwards from the nineteenth-century core of the Lanarkshire coalfield, and the early twentieth-century dominance of Glasgow and the upper Clyde, to new and attractive late-twentieth-century locations on the Firth of Clyde—and eastwards to the Forth. In the nine years to 1970, Scotland's population increased by 0.4 per cent, that of Midlothian and West Lothian by 5.2 per cent, and of Stirlingshire by 10.1 per cent; but in the same period Lanarkshire's population fell by 6.1 per cent and that of the city of Glasgow by 14.1 per cent. In 1975, of 375,000 manufacturing jobs in Strathclyde almost half were in sectors with doubtful long-term ability to hold onto their workforces—heavy engineering (118,000), steel (32,000) and shipbuilding and marine engineering (30,000).

Mid-Lanarkshire has long been an area of contracting activity, notably in coal and steel. There is much industrial dereliction, and acute problems of urban renewal. However, it lies between Glasgow and Edinburgh and has therefore been greatly affected by the interaction between them, an interaction which has been made easier by the substantial development of motorways and improved arterial roads. Remote areas like the Slamannon plateau or the Shotts-Wilsontown area have declined; but the main nineteenth-century growth points have held their population. In this respect Coatbridge and Motherwell contrast markedly with Merthyr Tydfil or the Rhondda. Important new industrial growth foci at Larkhall, Newhouse, Blantyre or Hamilton are all well located in relation to motorway access points. Hamilton grew noticeably in the 1960s in comparison with Motherwell and Coatbridge.

14.4.1 Glasgow

Nineteenth-century industrialization and urbanization made Glasgow a grossly overcrowded city. By 1931, at its peak, it had a population of almost 1.1 million in an area within which only about one-third of that number would be permitted under modern standards. Even by 1945 its population density was two and a half times that of Birmingham. In the Gorbals, its most renowned slum, densities were up to 180 persons per hectare (450 persons per acre). The serious social and urban planning problems were compounded by changes in and the decline of its industrial structure. In east Glasgow, for instance, the important steel industry at Blochairn and at Beardmore's Parkhead works, heavy engineering at Springburn and much of the shipbuilding on the upper Clyde, all have gone or substantially reduced their workforces. Glasgow is usually at or near the top of the national list in terms of big city unemployment. Old-style industries are still strongly represented. New industries have only partly replaced the jobs lost. And the new trades have often provided jobs mostly for women. Between 1958 and 1968, for example, in central Clydeside, 55,000 manufacturing jobs were lost and only 33,000 created; 42,000 of the lost jobs were male; more than one-third of the new jobs were for women (*Financial Times,* 12 November 1972). A deeply entrenched fear of the dole queue has bred political and trade union militancy, and the Glasgow Trade Council has suggested that it may take two or three generations for the legacies of past economic distress and continuing difficulties to work themselves out.

Employment changes have been matched in scale by alterations in Glasgow's fabric. By 1960, with its population still well over a million, housing and traffic problems had reached crisis proportions—some 100,000 houses were classified below acceptable standards, and city centre traffic was reduced to a crawl. The city therefore decided on a

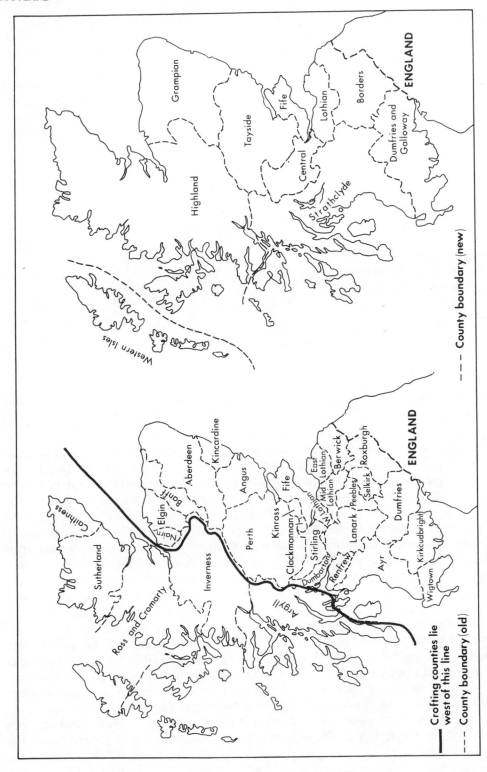

Figure 14.3 Scotland: administrative divisions before and after 1976

twenty-year programme of urban redevelopment involving very large-scale demolition and rehousing, and 20,000 families being moved beyond the boundary. By 1971 about 70,000 houses had been demolished, and 50,000 new units built, many of them in high-rise blocks (of up to thirty storeys) with all their attendant social problems. By 1973, also, 200,000 people had been rehoused outside the city. Further housing needs between 1972 and 1982 have been put at 100,000 units, of which no more than 23,000 can be built in the city. Along with rehousing has gone a revolution in circulation, with new bridges, the Clyde Tunnel, motorway and dual-carriageway access to the city centre and important bypass routes, including the opening of the Erskine Bridge across the Clyde. Yet Glasgow remains a problem city (Table 14.1).

Table 14.1   Glagow and the three largest English provincial cities: social indices, 1970-1971

	Giagow	Birmingham	Liverpool	Manchester
Dependency ratio*	683	552	563	570
Housing: % of population living at over 1.5 persons per room	11.8	5.6	5.3	4.5
Households lacking:				
hot water tap (%)	23.8	17.5	20.2	13.0
bath (%)	32.7	18.6	25.6	19.5
Economic group, % of total males:				
professional, managerial, etc.	8.7	10.2	9.3	10.7
semi-skilled and unskilled	48.0	44.2	52.1	46.7

*Dependency ratio indicates number under 15 or over 65, per 1,000 population.

Population and industry alike have been growing much more rapidly beyond Glasgow in the overspill and new towns. East Kilbride new town, established in 1947 around an old village only 15 kilometres from central Glasgow, had a population of 65,000 by 1970/1971, 70 per cent of its people originating in the city. Over its thirty years' history, factory employment has grown to 19,000, and by late 1973, out of an estimated 136 overseas firms operating in Scotland, thirty-one were in East Kilbride. Cumbernauld, started nine years later and further away from Glasgow, has a similar proportion of its population from that city and an even higher share of its employment in overseas firms. Livingston, Irvine and Glenrothes new towns have progressively decreasing proportions of Glaswegians (29, 18 and 11 per cent respectively in 1973). The advantages of centrality in the Edinburgh-Glasgow zone of movement are emphasized by the fact that East Kilbride and Cumbernauld have been the most successful of the Scottish new towns. Between 1960 and 1970 the former alone accounted for 65 per cent of all industrial growth in Lanarkshire, and by the mid-1970s, with a population of 73,500 it was only just smaller than Motherwell, had good labour relations, an unemployment rate (in mid-1974) of only just over 2 per cent when Lanarkshire's rate was 8 per cent, and a new shopping centre that had doubled its retail space and made it a major regional focus.

By the 1970s their success in industrial growth made new town building seem progressively less attractive to Glasgow as a means of solving that city's problems. The situation came to a head with the plan for a new town at Stonehouse. In 1970 the Secretary of State for Scotland accepted the recommendation of a Joint Working Party on the Glasgow housing programme, which suggested that 65,000 more houses might be needed beyond the boundary by 1981. Stonehouse new town was designated in 1973 to help with this problem. It was then anticipated that by 1981 its population of 7,000 would have grown to 21,000, and its intended functions were to provide for Glasgow overspill, to support physical and social revival in a neglected area of former small mining villages, and to provide relief for burgeoning East Kilbride with which it shared a Development Corporation. Eventually it was envisaged that Stonehouse might grow to 70,000. However in the mid-1970s opposition to the new town began to grow. The Strathclyde Regional Council claimed that it was diverting funds, new jobs and the most enterprising firms not only from Glasgow but also from other old industrial towns in the region. In 1977, therefore, the Secretary of State for Scotland, almost in anticipation of the development of national inner area policies, decided to cancel the Stonehouse new town plan, and the Strathclyde council sought to divert the funds that would have been spent on the town to the renewal of existing urban areas in the region. After this success, Strathclyde also hoped to slow the growth of other new towns within its boundaries, and the Scottish Development Agency committed itself to a £120 million redevelopment of the east end of Glasgow. Compared with the Scottish Registrar General's population forecast of 742,000 for Glasgow in 1981, the Strathclyde council has adopted a figure of 828,000. Given the decline in the rate of national and regional population growth and the worsening economic situation, this change of policy is understandable. But it is questionable whether the potential employment which the new town would have attracted will come to Glasgow instead. Central Scotland as a whole may well be the poorer. The new towns have all been spectacular successes. Policies for the redevelopment of Glasgow will take longer to yield returns. A defensive policy has superseded an offensive one. A critical question is whether this will also affect the growth potential of the Clyde estuary and of the Firth of Clyde.

14.4.2 *The Clyde*

In the eighteenth century Port Glasgow and Greenock boomed as a result of poor navigation above them. Later improvement of the Clyde, and the development of the central coalfields and their superstructure of iron and steel and engineering, took growth up-river into mid-Lanarkshire. The estuary of the Clyde thus came to be industrialized from Glasgow to Duntocher on the north bank; on the south development was less extensive, reaching to Renfrew and Paisley, and with Greenock and Port Glasgow as outliers. Prospectively, the declining importance of coal, the need for bigger sites and deeper water for shipbuilding, and the growing significance of major tidewater processing industries could be expected to encourage growth further out from Glasgow, on the Firth of Clyde. There, deep water, sheltered anchorages, and wide turning spaces make the area, from the point of view of seaward facilities at any rate, without rival in north western Europe. In several regional planning studies the development opportunities have been acknowledged. The Scottish Council (1971), for example, put forward its 'Oceanspan' scheme which sought to exploit the European potential of the Firth of Clyde by using its ability to handle very large vessels, by encouraging the processing of imported materials in central Scotland, and by developing the export of the semi-products for finishing or consumption from the Firth of Forth across the North Sea. An enthusiastic reviewer envisaged the result as a great crescent of development from mid-Lanarkshire, through Glasgow and out along the estuary and Firth to Ayr, and as 'a masterpiece of strategic planning by any standards' (*Financial Times*, 19 November 1973).

Achievement has, however, fallen far behind these ambitions. Since 1967 there have been a number of specific schemes for development on the Firth of Clyde. One was for an integrated steelworks ranging in capacity from 3 million to 12 million tons, another involved an oil terminal at Wemyss Bay and a refinery at Portencross; and there was an Italian scheme for an oil refinery and steel and engineering plants at Hunterston. There were also plans for petrochemical developments at Irvine and Stewarton. By the late 1970s, however, only the B.S.C. major ore terminal to handle 350,000 d.w.t. vessels was completed and almost all the other schemes had ceased to be discussed. The reasons for this hiatus were several. In the first place it has to be recognized that the Firth of Clyde in reality poses certain difficulties in the way of development, not least being the lack of extensive flat areas of land near to its deep water. There is a small site at Wemyss Bay and scope for a much bigger one around Ardmore Point, but this would involve reclamation and is some distance from really deep water. At Hunterston over 500 hectares (1,300 acres) are suitable for industrial development and there is scope for the reclamation of another 350 hectares; yet these are small sites compared with Europoort or the land available alongside some British estuaries such as the Tees, upper Severn or Humber. There is also an important amenity issue. The Firth has some magnificent landscapes, valued both by tourists and a growing body of commuters, and in the late 1960s the North Ayrshire Coast Development Committee suggested a development strategy for this area based on recreation. Certainly when industry has shown a desire to move into the area its ambitions have frequently been frustrated by local and central government planners very conscious of amenity considerations. Moreover, major developments on the Firth of Clyde would strike directly at jobs and therefore at urban areas elsewhere in Scotland. In 1973, for instance, B.P. made it known that if the Italian project went ahead it would not consider an early expansion of its Grangemouth refinery. Major steel expansion at Hunterston would have been to the detriment of jobs at Motherwell. A final problem concerns the costs of job creation there. Eight groups considering development in 1973, for example, might have involved the government in an expenditure of £230 million to create some 3,000 jobs, an outlay of over £70,000 per job created.

The continuing global and national recession of the late 1970s, the eastward lure of available investment funds with the development of North Sea oil, and the new Glasgow-oriented policies of the Strathclyde regional council cast new doubts upon the timing of any further exploitation of the Firth of Clyde's potential—although the new Strathclyde Development Plan (1977) still provides for a number of possible industrial developments there, including a major petrochemical complex in the beauty spot, Glen Fruin, north of Clydeside. Even with a revival of national economic fortunes and more forward-looking planning policies, however, there still remains a serious conflict between British and merely Scottish development strategies. Firth of Clyde development is obviously attractive from the viewpoint of Scottish basic industries; but, within the United Kingdom context, scarce development funds might be better spent elsewhere—perhaps at Maplin, perhaps on Humberside, or Severnside. This national framework of decision taking is unfortunately all too often lost in the debates on Clydeside's future.

14.5 The East Central Area

So economically dominant has the western part of the central lowlands been that it is
salutary to recall that some of the critical earlier steps in Scotland's industrial revolution
were taken on or near the shores of the Firth of Forth, at places such as Prestonpans and
Carron. Since World War II the eastward shift of Scottish coal mining, the emergence of
Grangemouth as a major refining and petrochemical location, developments in electricity
generation and the concentration in the region of a large proportion of Scotland's growth
industries have made this area—now administered by three regional authorities (Central,
Fife and Lothian)—much more comparable in standing with Clydeside, though still very
much smaller in terms of population. While Clydeside was still losing heavily, between
1971 and 1977 the Lothian region had a net annual in-migration of 1,000 per year.

The Firth of Forth has become a major new focus of power generation. Up to the
mid-1950s the only important tidewater power station was at Portobello on the eastern
outskirts of Edinburgh. Subsequently, however, major new stations were built at
Kincardine Bridge, Cockenzie and Longannet. Longannet alone was planned to take 5
million tons of coal a year, or half the total current Scottish output. Even though no more
coal-based developments seem justified, nuclear power and the availability of North Sea
gas suggest the possibility of further power station development in this area. Already the
South of Scotland Generating Board has been given government permission to proceed
with an advanced gas-cooled reactor at Torness Point near Dunbar, and there have been
proposals for a gas or oil-fired station at Carriden (Bo'ness) on the Firth.

Other changes in this area involve transport facilities. Road connections with England
remain poorer than those of Glasgow, though the M8 gives good access through to
Carlisle. However, the opening of the Forth Road Bridge in 1964 and the construction of
the M90 through Central Fife have given that area a completely new nodality in the routes
to Perth and to the Highlands; and the Tay Road Bridge has opened new growth
prospects for east central Fife. Early in 1968 the Forth Ports Authority was created to
operate six ports in the region. Granton and Kirkaldy are small. Burntisland and Methil,
once primarily export points for coal, have become significant import facilities for bauxite
and paper-making materials respectively, the first for the long-established British
Aluminium plants and the latter for the important papers mills of Fife. Leith, primarily a
bulk raw material import point from northern Europe, has been equipped with a new
entrance lock to enable it to handle up to 30,000 d.w.t. vessels where previously 12,000
d.w.t. had been its maximum. Grangemouth, with its important trade in refinery
products, is primarily an export port. An excellent rail service southwards, and Turnhouse
Airport (west of Edinburgh), complete an impressive array of transport facilities.

Many years ago the Cairncross Report (1952) and the Toothill Report (1961) advocated
a long-term positive growth strategy for this part of central Scotland. Accepting this
point, the *Central Scotland* White Paper of 1963 designated growth areas within the
region, notably at Livingston and at Falkirk-Grangemouth. But the areas involved were
too small and the growth forecasts were unrealistic. In 1963/1964 greater Livingston was
anticipated to grow from 85,000 to 185,000 by the 1980s and eventually to reach 250,000,
and the Falkirk-Grangemouth area was planned to double from 110,000 to 230,000—both
during a period when Scotland's population was expected to increase by 600,000 before
1981. In fact, between 1951 and 1971 Scotland's population increased by only 125,000,
and since then there has been a sharp decline in the rate of increase. Clearly there is very

little hope for development on the scale previously anticipated, quite apart from the claims of other areas, such as Irvine, the Moray Firth or Aberdeen-Peterhead. Changing political priorities, in fact, ensured that the strategy was shortlived. The plan of 1966, *The Scottish Economy 1965-1970,* made no mention of growth areas in the central belt of Scotland, and the target for Livingston new town has now been reduced to a more modest 70,000 in the 1980s.

Arguably, an even better focus for growth would have been Edinburgh itself, which for many years was denied Assisted Area status and had experienced a somewhat inconsistent development history. By the end of the 1960s, some 57,000, or roughly one-quarter of Edinburgh's insured workers, were in manufacturing—16,000 in food and drink, 11,000 plus in mechanical and electrical engineering, and there were 10,000 in printing and publishing. Science industries, which seemed to be attracted to the city in the mid-1960s, however, were subsequently attracted elsewhere by the availability of government grants, and a number of the existing firms wishing to expand chose to build at Dalkeith to the south east, or in Broxburn, Newbridge or Livingston to the west. Edinburgh, therefore, has increasingly become concerned with tertiary and quaternary functions. Its status as a financial centre, for instance, has increased rapidly in recent years and further devolution could increase greatly its already important governmental functions. Meanwhile, in 1970 Leith was made an Intermediate Area; Edinburgh and Portobello (the only two remaining unassisted areas in Scotland) became Intermediate Areas in the following year: and in 1974 Edinburgh achieved full Development Area status.

The East Central area in consequence has been subject to a series of short-term and piecemeal physical planning strategies—the growth points of 1963, the Special Development Areas of 1967 and their subsequent extensions, the vacillating attitudes towards the development of the Edinburgh area, new town construction and port development programmes. Each may have led to local successes, but in total there is a sense of dissipated effort and an opportunity missed to implement a coherent growth-oriented plan. The same charge might equally well be applied to the planning of the whole of industrial central Scotland in recent decades; and the creation of new, much more powerful, local government units in 1975 seems likely to make agreement on a desirable overall development strategy for the whole of the central lowlands even more difficult to secure.

14.6 Tayside

Tayside is another of the Scottish regions where many factors seem more favourable than in the past, but where soaring ambitions have recently become rather clouded. The old nodality of Perth and the new centrality given to Dundee by the Tay Bridge, and the region's location between the oil development areas of the North East and the industrial heart of Central Scotland, all seem favourable factors. The old trades such as jute and jam production have declined over a long period. In 1949 the former alone employed 38,000 in Dundee and neighbouring towns, but by 1970 only 13,000. Much more worrying is the fact that recently a number of the area's post-war growth industries have themselves encountered crises. Tayside was fortunate in attracting an early post-war generation of foreign, mainly American, firms. National Cash Register (N.C.R.) came in 1946 and Timex with mass produced watch manufacture a little later. In the late 1960s N.C.R. employed over 6,000 in nine factories, and in the mid-1970s Timex provided almost as many jobs. Yet from the early 1970s progress in electronics hit the market for N.C.R.'s mechanical accounting machines and caused a sharp reduction in its workforce. By 1978 it was cutting back to an employment of no more than 1,000. At the same time Timex has been threatened by the rapid growth of the digital watch market. A certain amount of oil platform fabrication, and the servicing of B.P. and Conoco rigs, provided some new employment. Yet the overall situation is worrying. By late 1976 the rate of male unemployment in Dundee was over 11 per cent.

In 1971 the region had a population of 451,000. At that time planners were thinking of possible increases up to 200,000 by the year 2000. Such growth forecasts now seem totally unrealistic.

14.7 The Southern Uplands

Traditionally, the Southern Uplands have been a zone of passage between the heartlands of the Scottish economy and the coastal routes to England. They retain this function still, and as a result the transport facilities of Dumfries and Galloway and of the Borders regions do not articulate their own internal economy. Into the 1960s five main railway lines penetrated the region. Three, which pass fairly directly through the region to link with the main Scottish cities, survive—the East Coast, Annandale and Nithsdale lines—but the two railways which did most for internal integration of the region have closed, including the famous 'Waverley Line' from Edinburgh to Carlisle via Hawick and Melrose. Meanwhile, symbolic of the 'bridge' function of the region, the A75 road from Stranraer to Gretna has become part of the Ireland to Europe road/water route, the number of commercial vehicles using it increasing four-fold between 1968 and 1975. The Glasgow to Carlisle dual carriageway through Annandale remains, however, the only good, high-quality road passing through the Southern Uplands.

In the period 1951 to 1971, the population of the two regions of southern Scotland fell from 265,000 to 252,000. In both of them traditional primary activity and industries have been declining, the retail and service sector has stagnated and there have been few new job opportunities. As a result the able and the young have moved away. Dumfries and Galloway are still mainly concerned with rural activities. With the exception of Dumfries itself—the only town over 10,000—the area is extremely deficient in industrial employment. The ideas of a Solway barrage, and major associated port and manufacturing development, which were widely canvassed only a little more than a decade ago, now seem wildly visionary. However, the Scottish Development Department in its *Strategy for South West Scotland* (1970) looked to a revitalization of the area through agriculture and forestry, and through a diversification into manufacturing and services, including tourist development. The Regional Council hopes to check the drift from rural areas and to encourage industrial growth by providing advanced factories in such towns as Dumfries, Stranraer, Dalbeattie and Gretna. It has also been suggested that the deep-water harbour of Stranraer could become a major service point for a Celtic Sea oil industry—if such an industry were ever to materialize.

The population of the Border counties has also drifted away. At the beginning of the century, Peebles, Selkirk, Roxburgh and Berwick had 118,000 people; by 1970 there were only 97,000. Berwickshire, the most accessible and with excellent farming land, has none the less declined the fastest over this period. Unemployment is low, but the area's economy remains small and narrowly based. Farming and fishing are important. High-quality knitwear employs some 20,000 and is the only significant manufacturing activity. A few new firms have been brought in, notably in light engineering and electronics and these have replaced jobs in wool and textile factories; the small and scattered population makes such industries well suited to the region's needs. The service sector is small, with shopping and transport facilities inferior and difficult to organize in a region where 40 per cent of the population is in communities of less than 1,500.

The White Paper on the Scottish Economy (1966) suggested the need for an influx of about 25,000 people into the Border region by the 1980s if the damage caused to the population structure and economic well-being by continuing emigration was to be remedied. This was confirmed by the *Central Borders' Report* of 1968. There was much dispute within the region about the location of these infusions. Eventually the Central Borders Plan for significant development at St Boswells-Newtown was scaled down, and it was agreed that expansion should be on a bigger scale at both Galashiels and Hawick (the only two centres already with over 10,000 people) and a much smaller development at Jedburgh. However, given the lower rate of growth of the United Kingdom population that is now in prospect, and the new growth foci in Scotland occasioned by the exploitation of North Sea oil, development is unlikely to reach the levels anticipated in the Central Borders Plan. Although there is some evidence of the population in the region stabilizing in recent years, in part through limited in-migration, the Scottish Development Agency has suggested that a continuing though much slower decline of population will occur in the Border region into the 1990s. In 1951 the South West and the Border region together had 5.2 per cent of Scotland's population; in 1970 it was 4.8 per cent; by 1990 4.4 per cent is expected.

14.8 The Highlands and Islands

North of the central lowlands are two major and very different areas of Scotland. Much the larger area is the Highlands and Islands which comprises the crofting counties of Caithness, Sutherland, Ross and Cromarty, Inverness and Argyll, and all the islands in the wide arc from the Kintyre peninsula to Shetland. Administratively, however, Argyll is now anomalously included within the Strathclyde region, the Hebrides and the Orkney and Shetland Islands are under separate local authorities, and the region excludes large areas presenting similar problems, such as the Cairngorms and Rannoch. The seven counties cover over one-fifth of the land area of Britain and 47 per cent of that of Scotland. They reached their highest populations during the middle of the nineteenth century when (at the 1861 Census) the area had 396,000 people, 15.1 per cent of the population of Scotland. There followed an increasing rate of decline until the 1930s, and a slower rate of contraction after that; by 1970 their population of 276,000 was a mere 5.3 per cent of the Scottish total. This long-term, large-scale fall in numbers has resulted above all from a selective out-migration of people and enterprise. As a result the rate of natural increase itself has been low by national standards (in 1961-1970, 2.9 per cent compared with the Scottish average of 6.1 per cent). In five of the seven counties intercensal decline continued into the 1970s, but it is noteworthy that in two it has been reversed—Inverness's population began a modest increase after the 1931 Census (though reversed slightly at the 1961 Census), whilst Caithness's numbers began to grow again in the 1950s. The general shrinkage and the localized growth are alike the outcome of important changes in the area's economy. Generally these changes have been a piecemeal response to market forces; but periodically in the past and increasingly in recent decades they have represented a purposeful intervention by government.

Until the break-up of the clan system, a dispersed population had been supported by widespread grazing and fishing, and cultivation in the valleys and coastlands. Later sheep replaced cattle and in the last decades of the nineteenth century 'clearances' were undertaken to create more deer forests. People moved to increasingly over-populated crofts on the west coast, migrated to lowland or English factories, or emigrated. From the last quarter of the nineteenth century the Highlands were acknowledged to constitute a national problem. Unfortunately, remedial action was usually based on social factors rather than concentrated at suitable growth points. The Crofters' Acts of 1886 and 1892 ossified the farming system of the western fringe of the Highlands by giving the peasants security of tenure; in consequence the farming structure was sheltered from those economic forces which would have secured amalgamation of units and so provided those who remained with a more satisfactory income. The social bias of policy took a long time to die. As late as 1954 the Taylor Committee on Crofting recorded its unanimous conviction that 'in the national interest the maintenance of these communities is desirable because they embody a free and independent way of life which, in a civilisation predominantly urban and industrial in character, is worth preserving for its own intrinsic quality'. By the 1960s, however, there was a strong reaction in favour of applying economic criteria to Highland assistance and a new emphasis on commercially viable enterprises. This was reflected in the policies of the Scottish Office, and was accepted by the Highlands and Islands Development Board (H.I.D.B.) formed in 1965.

Today the consolidation of crofts to form viable farm units and a further development of roads to increase farm accessibility is regarded as desirable; at the same time, and for the Islands, water transport to the mainland must continue to be subsidized. Many of the crofters obtain a portion of their income from fishing, and the H.I.D.B. has encouraged the improvement of this industry by making grants for new boats and by the development of fish-processing plants. The impact of these policies on crofting and fishing has fortunately benefited above all the west coast of northern Scotland which in other respects has suffered most in recent years. Away from the crofting coastlands, cattle and sheep rearing, farming and tourism are the staples. In farming the H.I.D.B. has begun to make important departures. It has provided financial assistance for improvements—£0.8 million in 1976—and output on assisted farms has gone up over a period of years at twice the rate for the region as a whole. While farm jobs generally in the Highlands have fallen by 2 per cent, on assisted farms there has been a 10 per cent increase. More recently the H.I.D.B. has proposed stronger powers of compulsory purchase to ensure that land is more fully utilized. Indeed, good land use management has come to be as much emphasized as the provision of manufacturing employment. Tourism has been extended, and the H.I.D.B. early embarked on the provision of large modern hotels at a limited number of points on the west coast, which until then was quite inadequately provided. The large-scale development of tourism at the Aviemore centre dates from the 1960s. Forestry and hydro-electric power are other modern developments of which a great deal has been expected in twentieth-century Highland rehabilitation. Both, however, have been unreasonably promoted as solutions.

Hydro-electric power in the Highlands began in 1896 with the Foyers plant of British Aluminium, though there was no more than a handful of stations before the creation of the North of Scotland Hydro-Electric Board (N.S.H.E.B.) in 1943. The N.S.H.E.B. was commissioned not only to produce electricity but also to attract industry, to improve standards of living (in part by exporting power to the Lowlands as a means of subsidizing connection and supplies to scattered Highland communities), and thereby to help check the outward drift of population. Its social obligations added to the difficult generating conditions—resulting from variable rainfall, small catchment areas and the consequent need for many small dams or for expensive linking tunnels—and they have burdened it throughout its career. The work of the board has undoubtedly improved the region's standards of living; its presence has provided employment in construction work and in electricity supply; and it has given the region a valuable morale boost. However, from the early years its operations have been recognized as, strictly speaking, uneconomic, and more recently—notwithstanding its social responsibilities—the N.S.H.E.B. has decided not to provide electricity connections to some of the remoter parts of the Highlands and Islands, such as Colonsay and North Ronaldsay, because of excessive costs. Moreover, as hydro-electricity development costs have risen relative to those of thermal power the pace of new hydro construction has been slowed. By the early 1970s fifty hydro and pumped storage stations made up 80 per cent of the N.S.H.E.B.'s capacity; but the new Peterhead oil- and gas-fired station, to be in operation by 1980, will alone provide over one-third of the enlarged capacity in the area. The N.S.H.E.B. does, however, have plans for some new capacity based on pump storage at Craigroyston on Loch Lomond, as well as a possible nuclear plant at Stake Ness just north west of Banff.

With forestry, by contrast, the rate of development has increased. On the other hand, the regional impact has not kept pace. The Forestry Commission area in Scotland doubled between 1951 and 1961, and by 1977 had almost doubled again. As late as 1969 the H.I.D.B. characterized forestry as 'one of the three great hopes for a more secure Highland economy' (Select Committee on Scottish Affairs, 1969/1970). In the 1966 White Paper on the Scottish economy the government announced its intention to increase annual planting after 1969 to 8,000 hectares (20,000 acres), and a year later the government announced agreement that the planting would in fact be two and a half times this level by 1976. By the early 1970s Scotland had about 40 per cent of the woodland acreage in Britain and approximately 75 per cent of the planting. Of the Scottish forests some 35 per cent of the acreage is in the Highlands, 15 per cent in the North East, while Tayside and the South West each have about 11 per cent. The Scottish National Party advocates an increase in the present forested and woodland area to 2.4 million hectares (6 million acres) soon after the year 2000, and claims that this can be done without damage to agricultural interests. However, the Forestry Commission is committed to more modest targets, and the H.I.D.B., while recognizing that further prospects exist in the north and north west, agrees that afforestation has already adversely affected sheep production in Argyll where it has taken much improvable land out of agricultural use. At the same time, the employment effects of forestry are clearly more limited than was once thought. By 1972/1973 no more than 5,000 persons were employed directly by forestry in Scotland and this number was the result of a slight fall over the previous decade as work was mechanized and rationalized, even as the acreage planted increased. More of the work is now being done by contract, migrating labour than by workers fixed in small forest villages. Although in Scotland as a whole some 85,000 jobs are said to be 'wood dependent', many of these are concerned with imported timber. While the contribution to the Highland economy's employment prospects of major extensions to the forestry programme is clearly limited, their commercial viability looked at from the national perspective has also been questioned—though in the difficult economic circumstances of the 1970s the future substantial foreign exchange savings seemed an attractive proposition.

14.8.1 *Industry in the Highlands*

A few years after it was set up, the Highlands and Islands Development Board argued that 'manufacturing industry is an activity which ... can do most to stem the drift of young people from the Region as a whole' (Select Committee on Scottish Affairs 1969/1970, p.4). By 1976/1977 the proportion of employees in manufacturing was still only half the national average, though it had increased from 12 per cent in 1971 to 17 per cent by 1975. The hydro-electric programme and afforestation laid foundations for a manufacturing programme. A pioneer was British Aluminium which was operating three small smelters at Foyers, Kinlochleven and Lochaber by the 1930s. With the N.S.H.E.B. went early hopes and disappointments for a Highland electro-chemical industry. The new forests encouraged wood processing in some lines of which, though not in all, the scale of entry could be quite small. Scale is indeed a vital issue in connection with Highland industrialization. In many Highland and Island townships provision of a dozen jobs may make all the difference between the continuing viability of a community, with a reasonable age structure and able to support essential services, and long-term decline. Small-scale, widely spread industry is therefore vital to the regional economy. On the other hand, large-scale industry, able to absorb high transport costs and to capitalize on local resources or the exceptional asset of deep water which the Highland shores provide, should clearly not be ruled out—though the very scale which makes it commercially viable may render it environmentally suspect and, given the small widely scattered population, unable to find adequate workforce or services.

The H.I.D.B. are imaginatively tackling these problems with a three-level approach: the encouragement of any industry wherever a developer wishes to locate; the establishment of a few major growth points for industrial development; and a methodical programme of helping manufacturers in small centres, as they put it, 'in scale with the possibilities of the West and Islands'. If it is designed to provide a wide spread of small anchor points for the Highland economy and society, the small-firm policy is logical. The growth point policy is more difficult to implement. Only one town in the Highlands contains over 10,000 inhabitants—indeed Inverness (with 34,000 in 1971) is almost four times the size of Thurso, its nearest rival. Transport facilities, nodality, flat land and recent developments all alike point to three groupings of mainland population which by Highland standards stand well above the rest—Thurso-Wick, the much smaller Lochaber-Fort William area, and the Moray Firth towns. Oban and Campbelton are possible additions, but the first is preoccupied with tourism, and the latter is eccentrically placed in relation to the Highlands. Even before the creation of the H.I.D.B. the three main nodes of growth had been chosen for important development projects. In the Thurso-Wick area, for example, the early decision of the Atomic Energy Authority (A.E.A.) to build an experimental reactor at Dounreay (7 miles west of Thurso), and then in 1966 to locate a prototype fast-breeder reactor there, attracted a younger, well-educated and socially active population to the area. This has brought new growth not only to Thurso-Wick but also to Caithness, although it is clear that further injections of new activity are needed to maintain the momentum which the A.E.A. gave.

At Fort William recent growth began with a project to install major pulp and paper plant. As early as 1949 the Scottish Council (Development and Industry) undertook to assess whether Scotland had sufficient timber supplies to support such a home processing industry. It was 1962, however, before Wiggins Teape decided to build a mill at Corpach with the government providing half of the £20 million investment. Three years later, Corpach was able to handle 260,000 tons of Scottish soft woods and 110,000 tons of imported hard woods annually and by the early 1970s it was taking 200,000 tons of Forestry Commission wood each year and a similar tonnage from Scottish private estates. However, early operational experience was disappointing for the plant proved to be too small to meet the prices of overseas rivals. Even so, the beneficial multiplier effects within the Highland economy suggests that a˙commercially questionable project may be worthwhile in a wider development sense—a plant uneconomic in its own right being highly desirable as part of a wider economic complex. Forty per cent of the equipment for the Wiggins Teape mill was bought from Scottish firms, £1 million was spent on road improvements, new piers were put up to handle imported timber, and the threatened West Highland railway line was saved to carry in supplies. Construction employed 1,500 men; the mill's initial workforce was 700, and rose to 1,300 by 1970. Two thousand more jobs were supported in the forests, on the railway lines or at the piers. Fort William began to grow rapidly, its population increasing 52 per cent between 1961 and 1971, and there was the unquantifiable boost of new confidence and expansionist thinking. Similar attributes characterize the larger-scale developments and the plans for growth on the Moray Firth.

In population and existing economic activity the lowlands of the Moray, Cromarty and Dornoch firths from east of Inverness, through Dingwall to beyond Invergordon are the prime new centre for Highlands industry. For almost thirty years consultants have recognized this area as an ideal growth focus. The 1966 White Paper on the *Scottish Economy 1969-1970* suggested more than doubling its current 75,000 population; and in 1968 the Jack Holmes Planning Group outlined a scheme for expansion to 250,000 or even 300,000, a bold scheme even at a time of prevailing expansionist projections of population. By the mid-1960s there were plans for a small oil refinery and associated petrochemical plants on the Moray Firth. At the end of that decade the proposal was revived in a bigger form by American interests under the name Grampian Chemicals; planning approval was given in spite of vigorous environmental opposition; but in 1970 the project was indefinitely postponed. However, local planners and the H.I.D.B. were by then determined to promote the development of what was seen as a uniquely endowed zone where sheltered deep water, ample fresh water for processing and suitable areas of flat land were available. The cost penalty of remoteness from the national market was not explored publicly. In its second report the H.I.D.B. stressed that it hoped that the Moray Firth growth area would create for the Highlands a major centre of 'modern job opportunity', offer a full range of commercial, social, cultural and other activities, provide a local market of reasonable size for regional products such as food, justify further improvements of infrastructure, and lead to a more balanced economic and social structure. The next step involved the winning of a major new investment.

By 1967 the British government had decided to assist in the development of a substantial primary aluminium industry, and inter-regional politics if nothing else ensured that Scotland would benefit from the investment. Sites in Fife and on the Firth of Clyde were considered before Invergordon was chosen as the best location in Scotland; and

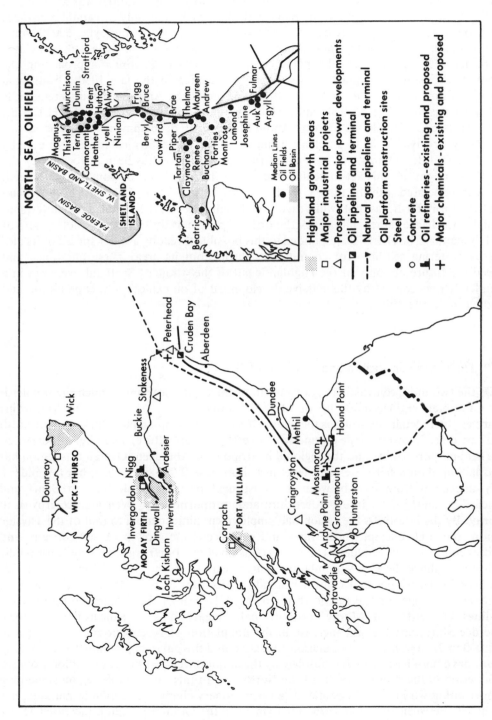

Figure 14.4 North Scotland: Highland and North Sea oil-related developments

(after a dispute between rival firms plus the defeat of local opposition) it was decided that British Aluminium should build the plant with the benefit not only of capital assistance but also low tariffs for power. By 1971 Invergordon was at work employing 600 persons. Six years later its 100,000 ton annual output provided jobs for 850. Even with associated multiplier effects, however, the plant could not support anything approaching the population expansion planned for the Moray Firth area in the late 1960s. Additional major investments have not yet been forthcoming, however. And wider doubts remain. Is such an investment out of scale and, whatever the rationale offered by the H.I.D.B., inappropriate to a Highlands context? And if Moray Firth development were to be carried further by a revival of the Grampian Chemicals oil and petrochemical project, or even by the successful development of light industrial parks such as has been advocated by the H.I.D.B., might not this act to denude the rest of the Highlands of population? Indeed, one fear associated with the three growth areas of Thurso-Wick, Lochaber-Fort William and the Moray Firth was that, while their growth might revive their immediate hinterland, it might accelerate rather than check the drift of people away from the remoter parts of the Highlands. The H.I.D.B. responded to this possible threat by a wider spread of its aid, and by fostering self-help for communities throughout its area. These questions, and indeed the future not only of the Highlands but of the whole of Scotland, were put in a completely new context by the massive development of oil exploration, exploitation and production in the 1970s.

14.9 The Grampian Region and North Sea Oil

Of the two quite contrasting regions north of the central lowlands, much the smaller is the Grampian region, made up of the old Moray, Banff, Aberdeen and Kincardine counties. Included in the south is the main mass of the Grampian plateau; but to the north and east there is lower, fertile ground with an efficient agriculture, a number of important market and port towns, and the regional metropolis of Aberdeen. Overall this region has held its population fairly well at a level just short of 450,000 since 1931; but this hides a very uneven performance between its constituent parts, with declines in Banff and Kincardine and growth in Aberdeenshire and, proportionally, even greater growth in Moray. By the late 1960s the region had employment almost equal to that of the Tayside region, but high unemployment rates and slow economic growth caused concern, and studies conducted by Aberdeen University (Gaskin *et al.*, 1969) argued the need for public action to stablize the area's population. Three years later, the Central Planning Unit of the Scottish Development Department made projections of population which suggested no overall change for the region through to 1991, though this was made up of small declines in Banff and Moray, proportionally bigger falls in Kincardine and rural Aberdeenshire, and a slight increase in the population of Aberdeen and district (from 218,000 to 227,000). These population forecasts, and the physical planning to accompany them, have both been rendered obsolete by the major developments of oil exploration and production in the Scottish sector of the North Sea. In this fairly stable region something almost unknown in modern Scotland, a revolutionary change in economic standing, has occurred. Between 1971 and 1976 employment in the Grampian region increased 15 per cent and net annual in-migration averaged 2,500 over the same period.

14.9.1 *North Sea Oil*

From the mid-1920s Scotland had an important centre of oil refining at Grangemouth, which after World War II was connected by pipeline to a new deep-water terminal on the west coast at Finnart on Loch Long. In the late 1960s three other important oil-refining projects for the estuary and the Firth of Clyde and for Cromarty Firth were refused planning permission or (in the latter instance) pigeon-holed; all would have used imported oil. Yet within a decade, Scotland was to gain access to its own substantial oil province.

The discovery of the Groningen gas field in 1959 encouraged interest in the prospects of development in the North Sea and, after political agreement between seaboard countries, the exploration and development of gas fields in the southern North Sea took place in the mid-1960s. By 1967 the search for oil and gas began to shift northwards, though many senior executives and geologists in the oil companies were still doubtful. The first success was the Phillips discovery of oil in the Ekofisk field of the Norwegian sector in 1969; at the end of the same year the Montrose field was proved in the British sector, and a year later B.P.'s Forties field was the first in the British sector to be declared a commercial proposition. By 1971 the search had shifted further north still, to areas east and north east of Shetland, and there the Brent field was proved in July 1971. At an early stage it was realized that the impact on the Scottish economy, on the relative prospects of its regions, and on its landscapes and society would be both substantial and rapid.

Four phases are involved in oil development. Geophysical exploration involves little on-shore impact. By contrast, exploratory drilling requires considerable provision of service bases. These were being developed by 1972 at Aberdeen, Montrose, Dundee, Peterhead and Lerwick, and new bases were announced for Wick and for Kirkwall. At the next stage yet more extensive facilities are required—especially construction sites for drilling rigs, production platforms and pipeline preparation. The final stage involves the facilities for moving, processing and using the oil—pipelines and tanker terminals, refineries, chemical plants and power stations.

It soon became clear that the early stages of impact would be focused particularly on Aberdeen, which as an urbanized area of some 200,000 could offer many of the essential services required. In 1970 the city of Aberdeen and the counties of Aberdeen, Banff, Kincardine, Moray and Nairn set up the North East Scotland Development Authority (N.E.S.D.A.). Its 1975 list of 276 firms in the region that were involved in the oil industry as a principal activity contained 238 located in Aberdeen; Peterhead, the next most important centre, had only thirty. Before the exploitation of oil, Aberdeen had a static population and a declining hinterland. At the end of 1973, by contrast, unemployment there was a low as 1.8 per cent, house building was reckoned to be only one-third the level necessary to meet a booming demand, and prices for housing had risen more than anywhere in Britain except in central London. In April 1978 the Aberdeen employment exchange area with 60 per cent of the region's Grampian population was down-graded from a Development Area to an Intermediate Area, and as the Aberdeen economy became over-heated Peterhead began to grow more rapidly to provide complementary facilities; with Peterhead remaining within the Development Area, it may benefit still more in the future.

As exploratory drilling passed into development and production, the need for rig and platform construction sites became important. Steel platforms require extensive sites for their assembly since the legs and other parts of the platform are built separately; but they do not require particularly deep water offshore. Concrete platforms, on the other hand, are built complete, and though smaller sites can be used they require much deeper water than the steel ones. By early 1973 two steel yards were at work, at Methil and at Nigg Bay. Three years later there were two other east coast steel platform yards at Ardesier on the Moray Firth and at Graythorpe on Teesside. A switch to concrete then led to the establishment of four yards on the west coast, three of them on the Firth of Clyde or its branches, the other on Loch Kishorn. Eager not to slow down development of the North Sea fields, the government introduced special legislation to speed the planning approval process. It was quickly realized, however, that in a fluctuating market too many construction sites had in fact been developed. By 1977 it was also clear that still newer trends in platform design would favour the steel construction yards on the east coast as opposed to the concrete construction yards on the west coast. In consequence, the government was expected to endorse the closure of two concrete platform sites, Hunterston on the Firth of Clyde and Portavadie on Loch Fyne. These yards had cost more than £20 million of government capital and involved annual maintenance costs of £400,000, but they had never had a single order. In 1978 Lewis Off-shore, a platform subcontracting operation built near Stornoway four years earlier, was closed. The loss of 300 jobs pushed unemployment in the very small Western Isles economy to about 20 per cent. If, after launching its only platform, the Kishorn yard closes, not only will local employment and that from a wider area of Wester Ross and Skye suffer, but the single track West Highland Railway Line from Inverness to Kyle of Lochalsh will again be at risk. Rig and platform construction is not an unmixed blessing.

Along with site and general service activity has gone the provision of oil handling and processing facilities. Sullom Voe in the Shetlands, and a site in the southern Orkneys, have become pipeline and tanker terminals; the village of St Fergus north of Peterhead has been provided with a major gas terminal from which a pipeline feeds into a national gas grid; oil also comes ashore at Cruden Bay south of Peterhead, and is pumped south to Grangemouth where the associated gas is extracted. The B.P. refinery at Grangemouth is being substantially extended and modified to deal with both light Forties crude and heavy imported crude still brought in through Finnart. A new terminal for 250,000 d.w.t. tankers at Hound Point just down-river from the Forth Bridge is now used to export the rest of the Forties crude, as well as products. At Nigg Point a £280 million oil terminal and refinery for Cromarty Petroleum was approved in June 1977 by the Development Committee of the Highland Regional Council. This will ship out 10 million tons of North Sea crude and refine another 10 million tons. In chemicals there will be major extensions at the existing Grangemouth complex and a new ammonia plant near Peterhead.

The development of North Sea oil has been on a world-ranking scale, and the investment far in excess of any previous development in the Scottish economy. The original estimated cost of developing the Forties field, for example, was put at £700 million, but if it had been begun under the cost conditions of 1975 the total would have been £1,200 million. The multiplier effects and the psychological impact have both been great—a mixture of the same nature as, but on an incomparably greater scale than, Highland power or forestry—and generally speaking the effects have been beneficial. However, on the deficit side must be set certain losses of skilled workers from older activities to oil-related concerns willing and able to pay higher wages, and some damage to the environment. The latter is a particularly sensitive issue when, as is often the case with oil, the number of permanent jobs created is limited. For instance, by mid-1977

Shell-Esso were seeking approval against much local opposition for a marine terminal, a gas liquification plant and an ethylene development (which they had initially planned for the gas pipeline terminal of St Fergus) at Mossmorran on the coast of Fife, down-river from the Forth Road Bridge. The opposition claimed that the environmental impact was undesirable and the returns few. The scheme would cost £400 million, would provide only eighty jobs in the gas plant, and at best only 300 permanent jobs. The cost to the taxpayer was put at £288 million plus infrastructure spending. Similarly, on the west coast the development of oil platform construction at Loch Kishorn, formerly a notable beauty spot, has aroused continuing opposition and much distress among environmentalists.

Table 14.2 Scotland: oil employment and unemployment rates, by region, July 1976

Region	Employment by main firms wholly or partly in oil	Oil employment as proportion of total employment (%)	Unemployment rates (%)
Strathclyde	11,400	1.1	9.0
Fife	2,250	1.9	7.6
Tayside	1,350	0.9	7.0
Grampian	12,650	7.3	3.9
Highland			6.5
Western Isles	7,950	9.3	15.5
Orkney			5.6
Shetland			3.9
Lothian	1,900		6.4
Central	400		7.3
Borders	minimal	0.5	3.8
Dumfries and Galloway	minimal		8.2

Sources: *Scottish Abstract of Statistics,* 1976; *Scottish Economic Bulletin, 11,* Winter 1977.

It has also to be recognized that the economic benefits of oil development have been geographically uneven (Table 14.2). Naturally the early impact was concentrated on the coast of the North East region. By March 1973, this region had over 34 per cent and Inverness and Easter Ross 45 per cent of the 4,100 directly employed in the industry. Already, however, the indirect effect was wider. Clyde shipyards, like those of Aberdeen, Dundee and Leith, were involved with the rig work, and from 1972 onwards the whole future of the old Clydebank yard was tied to rig construction. For the Scottish economy as a whole, it became clear that direct and indirect employment in oil-related developments would go some way to make up for the continuing run-down of such older staples as coal, steel, shipbuilding and engineering. Another important test of oil's benefits was its ability to impart a new growth momentum to the West Central region. A considerable amount of oil-related employment came, in fact, to the Clydeside region, so that by the middle of 1976 it ranked second only to the Grampian region in its share of the (estimated) 38,000 employed by the main firms engaged wholly or partly in oil activities. Such numbers are, however, small in relation to overall employment problems on Clydeside where by 1976 oil-related jobs represented only a little over 1 per cent of total employment: there is, therefore, no evidence whatsoever to suggest that oil promises a breakthrough into a new era of prosperity there. Elsewhere, however, oil is giving Scotland a chance to extend or to build rather than merely to counteract the decline in its old economy and society. Particularly is this the case with transport infrastructure; for example, oil exploitation has justified major spending on both road and rail links from Perth to Inverness, and on further bridge building over the inlets of the Moray Firth.

Where the local economic gains are large, there is posed an equivalent and wider threat. Zetland County Council has been impressively enterprising in securing legislation which will give it a considerable income from oil, but in many respects oil seems in danger of overwhelming these Islands. In Orkney and Shetland, for example, agriculture (the predominant traditional source of employment) provides jobs for some 5,000; yet in 1978 the constructional workforce on the Sullom Voe oil tanker terminal (costing £670 million and to handle tankers of up to 300,000 d.w.t.) alone was 4,000. The economic and social impact of such an activity is not only great but upsets traditional value systems. Indeed the authors of a notable survey of oil development in Scotland, when considering the Western Isles, sounded a warning which might well be applied to the whole of the country: 'Having suffered from unemployment and emigration for generations they are faced today with the prospect of welcoming a development which might meet their material needs but which could completely change their way of life' (Hutcheson and Hogg, 1975). In spite of all its difficulties Scotland today has so many assets that such a development would indeed have been dearly bought.

14.10 Conclusion

In the late 1970s, Scotland has new resources and fresh planning objectives. Robertson (1974) referred to her 'cluster of new natural advantages—deep water, oil, fresh water, unspoilt environment'; Aberdeen has become a boom city; and Highland and Island depopulation has been checked and locally reversed. On the other hand, the adjustments of the basic industries of mid-Scotland have not yet been completed; and many judge Glasgow and the West Central region to pose the biggest challenge in industrial and urban conversion and modernization throughout the whole of the E.E.C. Whilst there are strong grounds for hope and even optimism, the problems of Scottish planning will not yield to speedy or inexpensive solutions.

REFERENCES

Cairncross, A.K. (ed.) (1954). *The Scottish Economy*, Cambridge University Press.
Central Policy Review Staff (1975). *The Future of the British Car Industry*, H.M.S.O., London.
Crofers Commission. *Annual Report*, H.M.S.O., Edinburgh.
Forsyth, D.J.C. (1972). *United States Investment in Scotland*, Praeger, New York.
Gaskin, A. (1971). *Freight Rates and Prices in the Islands* (a report for the H.I.D.B.), Inverness.
Gaskin, M., and others (1969). *North East Scotland: A Survey of its Developmental Potential*, H.M.S.O. for Scottish Office, Edinburgh.
Geddes, A., and Spaven, F.D.N. (1949). The Highlands and Islands. In G.H.J. Daysh (ed.), *Studies in Regional Planning*, George Philip, London.
Highlands and Islands Development Board. *Annual Report*, H.I.D.B., Inverness.
Hutcheson, A.M., and Hogg, A. (1975). *Scotland and Oil*, Oliver & Boyd, Edinburgh.
Johnston, T.L., Buxton, N.K., and Mair, D. (1971). *Growth and Structure of the Scottish Economy*, Collins, London.
Keeble, D. (1976). *Industrial Location and Planning in the United Kingdom*, Methuen, London.

McCrone, G. (1969). *Scotland's Future. The Economics of Nationalism,* Blackwell, Oxford.

McGill, J. (ed.) (1975). *Investing in Scotland.* The Fifth International Forum of the Scottish Council (Development and Industry), Collins, Glasgow.

Mackay, D. (ed.) (1977). *Scotland 1980. The Economics of Self Government,* Q Press, Edinburgh.

McNicoll, I.H. (1976). *The Shetland Economy,* Glasgow.

Robertson, W.S. (1974). *Scotland Today—Economic Developments* (the Betts Brown Memorial Lecture), Herriot Watt University, Edinburgh.

Scottish Council (1971). *Oceanspan I: A Maritime-Based Strategy for a European Scotland, 1970-2000,* Edinburgh.

Scottish Council (Development and Industry) (1973). *A Future for Scotland* (the Nicoll Report), Edinburgh.

Scottish Development Department (1970). *Strategy for South West Scotland,* H.M.S.O., Edinburgh.

Scottish Office (quarterly). *Scottish Economic Bulletin,* H.M.S.O., Edinburgh.

Select Committee on Nationalised Industries, Sub-committee B (1976). *Minutes of Evidence.* H.C., London.

Select Committee on Scottish Affairs (1969/1970). *Minutes of Evidence,* 14 January 1970, H.C., London. 267-1.

Toothill (1961). *Report of the Committee of Inquiry on the Scottish Economy,* Scottish Council, Edinburgh.

Turnock, D.C. (1974). *Scotland's Highlands and Islands,* Oxford University Press.

Varley, E. (1976). *Minutes of Evidence and Report from the Expenditure Committee* (1975/1976), H.C. 596-1 (on Scottish motor industry).

Wolfe, J.N. (ed.) (1969). *Government and Nationalism in Scotland,* Edinburgh University Press, Edinburgh.

Location Index

415

Subject Index